# PUBLICATIONS
## OF THE
## NATIONAL BUREAU OF ECONOMIC RESEARCH, Inc.
### 51 MADISON AVENUE, NEW YORK

*1. INCOME IN THE UNITED STATES
  By Wesley C. Mitchell, Willford I. King, Frederick R. Macaulay and Oswald W. Knauth
  Volume I (1921) Summary                                    152 pp.
*2. Volume II (1922) Details                                 440 pp.
3. DISTRIBUTION OF INCOME BY STATES IN 1919 (1922)
  By Oswald W. Knauth                               30 pp., $1.30
4. BUSINESS CYCLES AND UNEMPLOYMENT (1923)
  By the National Bureau Staff and 16 Collaborators   405 pp., $4.10
*5. EMPLOYMENT, HOURS AND EARNINGS IN PROSPERITY AND DEPRESSION, UNITED STATES, 1920-22 (1923)
  By Willford I. King                                        147 pp.
6. THE GROWTH OF AMERICAN TRADE UNIONS, 1880-1923 (1924)
  By Leo Wolman                                      170 pp., $2.50
7. INCOME IN THE VARIOUS STATES: ITS SOURCES AND DISTRIBUTION, 1919, 1920 AND 1921 (1925)
  By Maurice Leven                                   306 pp., $3.50
8. BUSINESS ANNALS (1926)
  By Willard L. Thorp, with an introductory chapter, "Business Cycles as Revealed by Business Annals," by Wesley C. Mitchell     380 pp., $2.50
9. MIGRATION AND BUSINESS CYCLES (1926)
  By Harry Jerome                                    256 pp., $2.50
10. BUSINESS CYCLES: THE PROBLEM AND ITS SETTING (1927)
  By Wesley C. Mitchell                              489 pp., $5.00
*11. THE BEHAVIOR OF PRICES (1927)
  By Frederick C. Mills                                      598 pp.
12. TRENDS IN PHILANTHROPY (1928)
  By Willford I. King                                 78 pp., $1.00
13. RECENT ECONOMIC CHANGES (1929)
  By the National Bureau Staff and 15 Collaborators
                                            2 vol., 950 pp., per set, $7.50
14. INTERNATIONAL MIGRATIONS
  Volume I, Statistics (1929), compiled by Imre Ferenczi of the International Labour Office and edited by Walter F. Willcox  1,112 pp., $7.00
18. Volume II, Interpretations (1931) edited by Walter F. Willcox  715 pp., $5.00
*15. THE NATIONAL INCOME AND ITS PURCHASING POWER (1930)
  By Willford I. King                                        394 pp.
16. CORPORATION CONTRIBUTIONS TO ORGANIZED COMMUNITY WELFARE SERVICES (1930)
  By Pierce Williams and Frederick E. Croxton        347 pp., $2.00
17. PLANNING AND CONTROL OF PUBLIC WORKS (1930)
  By Leo Wolman                                      260 pp., $2.50
19. THE SMOOTHING OF TIME SERIES (1931)
  By Frederick R. Macaulay                           172 pp., $2.00
20. THE PURCHASE OF MEDICAL CARE THROUGH FIXED PERIODIC PAYMENT (1932)
  By Pierce Williams                                 308 pp., $3.00
21. ECONOMIC TENDENCIES IN THE UNITED STATES: ASPECTS OF PRE-WAR AND POST-WAR CHANGES (1932)
  By Frederick C. Mills                              639 pp., $5.00
22. SEASONAL VARIATIONS IN INDUSTRY AND TRADE (1932)
  By Simon Kuznets                                   475 pp., $4.00

\* *Out of print.*

PUBLICATIONS OF THE

NATIONAL BUREAU OF ECONOMIC RESEARCH, INCORPORATED

NUMBER 21

ECONOMIC TENDENCIES

IN THE UNITED STATES

# NATIONAL BUREAU OF ECONOMIC RESEARCH, Inc.

The National Bureau of Economic Research was organized in 1920 in response to a growing demand for scientific determination and impartial interpretation of facts bearing upon economic, social and industrial problems. Freedom from bias is sought by the constitution of its Board of Directors in which entire control is vested and without whose approval no report may be published. Rigid provisions guard the National Bureau from becoming a source of profit to its members, directors or officers, or from becoming an agency for propaganda.

### OFFICERS

H. W. LAIDLER . . . . . . . Chairman of the Board
OSWALD W. KNAUTH . . . . . . . . . . President
JOSEPH H. WILLITS . . . . . . . . . Vice-President
GEORGE E. ROBERTS . . . . . . . . . . Treasurer

### DIRECTORS AT LARGE

OSWALD W. KNAUTH  ELWOOD MEAD
H. W. LAIDLER  SHEPARD MORGAN
L. C. MARSHALL  GEORGE SOULE
GEORGE O. MAY  N. I. STONE
MATTHEW WOLL

### DIRECTORS BY UNIVERSITY APPOINTMENT

THOMAS S. ADAMS, Yale University
EDWIN F. GAY, Harvard University
HARRY JEROME, University of Wisconsin
HARRY ALVIN MILLIS, University of Chicago
WESLEY C. MITCHELL, Columbia University
JOSEPH H. WILLITS, University of Pennsylvania

### DIRECTORS APPOINTED BY OTHER ORGANIZATIONS

HUGH FRAYNE, American Federation of Labor
DAVID FRIDAY, American Economic Association
LEE GALLOWAY, American Management Association
GEORGE E. ROBERTS, American Bankers Association
M. C. RORTY, American Statistical Association
A. W. SHAW, National Publishers' Association
ROBERT B. WOLF, American Engineering Council

### RESEARCH STAFF

EDWIN F. GAY  WESLEY C. MITCHELL
*Directors of Research*

SIMON KUZNETS  FREDERICK C. MILLS
FREDERICK R. MACAULAY  WILLARD L. THORP
LEO WOLMAN

# ECONOMIC TENDENCIES

## IN THE UNITED STATES

*Aspects of Pre-War and Post-War Changes*

*by*

FREDERICK C. MILLS

*With an Introduction by*
THE COMMITTEE ON
RECENT ECONOMIC CHANGES

*A Publication of*
THE NATIONAL BUREAU OF ECONOMIC RESEARCH, INC.
*in Coöperation with*
THE COMMITTEE ON RECENT ECONOMIC CHANGES
1932

COPYRIGHT, 1932, BY
NATIONAL BUREAU OF ECONOMIC RESEARCH, INC.
51 MADISON AVE., NEW YORK, N. Y.

*All rights reserved*

PRINTED IN THE UNITED STATES OF AMERICA
BY J. J. LITTLE & IVES COMPANY, NEW YORK

# RELATION OF THE BOARD OF DIRECTORS TO THE WORK OF THE NATIONAL BUREAU OF ECONOMIC RESEARCH

1—The object of the Bureau is to ascertain and to present to the public important economic facts and the interpretation thereof in a scientific and impartial manner, free from bias and propaganda. The Board of Directors is charged with the responsibility of ensuring and guaranteeing to the public that the work of the Bureau is carried out in strict conformity with this object.

2—The Directors shall appoint one or more directors of research chosen upon considerations of integrity, ability, character, and freedom from prejudice, who shall undertake to conduct economic researches in conformity with the principles of the Bureau.

3—The director or directors of research shall submit to the members of the Board, or to its executive committee when such is constituted and to which authority has been delegated by the Board, proposals in respect to researches to be instituted; and no research shall be instituted without the approval of the Board, or of its executive committee.

4—Following approval by the Board, or its executive committee, of a research proposed, the director or directors of research shall as soon as possible submit to the members of the Board, by written communication, a statement of the principles to be pursued in the study of the problem and the methods to be employed; and the director or directors of research shall not proceed to investigate, study, and report in detail, until the plan so outlined has been approved by the Board or the executive committee thereof.

5—Before the publication of the results of any inquiry the director or directors of research shall submit to the Board a synopsis of such results, drawing attention to the main conclusions reached, the major problems encountered, and the solutions adopted, the nature of the sources from which the basic facts have been derived, and such other information as in their opinion shall have a material bearing on the validity of the conclusions and their suitability for publication in accordance with the principles of the Bureau.

6—A copy of any manuscript proposed to be published shall also be submitted to each member of the Board, and every member shall be entitled, if publication be approved, to have published also a memorandum of any dissent or reservation he may express, together with a brief statement of his reasons therefore, should he so desire. The publication of a volume does not, however, imply that each member of the Board of Directors has read the manuscript and passed upon its validity in every detail.

7—The results of any inquiry shall not be published except with the approval of at least a majority of the entire Board and a two-thirds majority of all those members of the Board who shall have voted on the proposal within the time fixed for the receipt of votes on the publication proposed; such limit shall be 45 days from the date of the submission of the synopsis and manuscript of the proposed publication, except that the Board may extend the limit in its absolute discretion, and shall upon the request of any member extend the limit for a period not exceeding 30 days.

8—A copy of this memorandum shall, unless otherwise determined by the Board, be printed in each copy of every work published by the Bureau.

*Resolution Adopted October 25, 1926.*

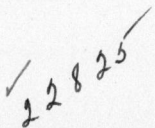

# COMMITTEE ON RECENT ECONOMIC CHANGES
## OF THE PRESIDENT'S CONFERENCE ON UNEMPLOYMENT

ARCH W. SHAW, *Chairman*

RENICK W. DUNLAP, Assistant Secretary of Agriculture

WILLIAM GREEN, President, American Federation of Labor

JULIUS KLEIN, Assistant Secretary of Commerce

JOHN S. LAWRENCE, Merchant

MAX MASON, President, Rockefeller Foundation

ADOLPH C. MILLER, Member, Federal Reserve Board

LEWIS E. PIERSON, Chairman of the Board, Irving Trust Company

JOHN J. RASKOB, Member of Finance Committee, General Motors Corporation

SAMUEL W. REYBURN, President, Associated Dry Goods Corporation of New York

LOUIS J. TABER, Master, The National Grange

DANIEL WILLARD, President, Baltimore & Ohio Railroad

CLARENCE M. WOOLLEY, Chairman of the Board, American Radiator and Standard Sanitary Corporation

OWEN D. YOUNG, Chairman of the Board, General Electric Company

EDWARD EYRE HUNT, *Secretary*

# Introduction by the Committee on Recent Economic Changes

This volume is devoted, primarily, to a survey of economic tendencies which developed and prevailed during the period preceding the current economic depression. In order the better to bring out the character of these tendencies, they are reviewed in comparison with the tendencies prevailing during the period preceding the World War.

As a survey this study is important in its own right because of the economic importance of the period 1922-1929. It presents an extremely valuable segment of the continuing study of the phenomena of economic activity, which is being carried forward by the Committee on Recent Economic Changes in conjunction with the National Bureau of Economic Research.

For the scientific competency of this study—the gathering of the material brought together in the present volume, its interpretation, and the conclusions drawn therefrom—the National Bureau of Economic Research is solely responsible; but the Committee on Recent Economic Changes is happy to join with the Bureau in the publication of a study throwing such a flood of light upon the nature of recent economic movements in the United States, and the features and forces marking their essential character. It is most timely as a study of recent economic history and as such will be welcomed. But its importance goes beyond its timeliness. Because of its intelligent application of the methods of scientific analysis, assembly, and organization to the understanding of a body of actual economic phenomena, its importance as a contribution to realistic thinking and procedure, in the economic field, deserves appreciative recognition.

In the Committee's opinion, while this volume is important currently as a background study of our economic processes, its greatest value will be realized when the time comes that the depression itself can be analyzed. In the meantime the evidence it presents may profitably be studied, checked and challenged, so that when the full record of the depression shall be ready for analysis, it may be studied and interpreted against a background of fact and conclusion made sound and useful by the processes of deliberation, verification and assimilation. The present volume and others shortly to follow may, therefore, be considered interim reports, bridging the span between the previous study, *Recent Economic Changes in the United States,* published by the Committee on Recent Economic Changes early in 1929, and the report this Committee anticipates publishing at that future date when the present economic cycle shall have run its course.

"If ultimately," says Dr. Mills in his conclusion, "we are able properly to interpret this complex experience, we may hope to determine whether anything approaching true economic equilibrium was achieved within the era bounded by the two great post-war recessions. We may hope, too, to determine more precisely the conditions that conduce to stable economic processes, and to define more accurately than is now possible the limits of tolerance of the existing order, in relation to the stresses and strains to which it is exposed."

This well expresses the underlying hope of the Committee on Recent Economic Changes, and the motive which has prompted the Rockefeller Foundation, the Carnegie Corporation, the Economic Club of Chicago, and various socially-minded groups and individuals who have so generously supported and encouraged the Committee in its continuing study of recent economic experience.

ARCH W. SHAW, *Chairman*    LEWIS E. PIERSON
RENICK W. DUNLAP    JOHN J. RASKOB
WILLIAM GREEN    SAMUEL W. REYBURN
JULIUS KLEIN    LOUIS J. TABER
JOHN S. LAWRENCE    DANIEL WILLARD
MAX MASON    CLARENCE M. WOOLLEY
ADOLPH C. MILLER    OWEN D. YOUNG
EDWARD EYRE HUNT, *Secretary*

*October, 1932*

# Contents

|  | PAGE |
|---|---|
| FOREWORD | xvii |

### CHAPTER I

**PRE-WAR CHANGES IN THE VOLUME AND CHARACTER OF PRODUCTION IN THE UNITED STATES** . . . . . . . . . . . . . . . 1

CHANGES IN THE VOLUME OF PRODUCTION, 1901-1913 . . . 2

    Production of raw materials and of manufactured goods . . 4
    § On the stability of productive processes, 1901-1913 . . . 10
    Physical output of products of American farms and of all other products . . . . . . . . . . . . 13
    Production of foods and of non-foods . . . . . . . 17
    Production of consumption goods and of capital equipment . 20
    Production of non-durable, semi-durable and durable goods . 23

PHYSICAL OUTPUT AND PRODUCTIVITY OF MANUFACTURING INDUSTRIES, 1899-1914 . . . . . . . . . . . . . 25

    Growth of manufacturing production and number of wage-earners employed . . . . . . . . . . . . 25
    § Changes in physical volume of production and in output per wage-earner, individual industries . . . . . . . 29
    Manufacturing establishments and volume of manufacturing production . . . . . . . . . . . . . . 36
    § A revision of the index numbers of manufacturing production . . . . . . . . . . . . . . . . 39

SUMMARY: PRODUCTION TENDENCIES IN THE UNITED STATES, PRE-WAR . . . . . . . . . . . . . . . . 43

    § On methods of measuring economic movements . . . . 46

## CHAPTER II

### PRE-WAR CHANGES IN COMMODITY PRICES .. 50

GENERAL MEASUREMENTS . . . . . . . . . . . . . 51
    Comparison of movements of wholesale prices and production, all commodities . . . . . . . . . . . 55

PRICE MOVEMENTS, MAJOR COMMODITY GROUPS . . . . . 57
    Raw materials and manufactured goods . . . . . . 57
    Products of American farms and other products . . . . 65
    Farm crops, animal products, mineral products and forest products . . . . . . . . . . . . . . . . . 69
    Foods and non-foods . . . . . . . . . . . . 75
    Producers' goods and consumers' goods . . . . . . 76

SUMMARY: PRE-WAR MOVEMENTS OF COMMODITY PRICES . . 81

## CHAPTER III

### PRICE AND COST CHANGES IN MANUFACTURING INDUSTRIES OF THE UNITED STATES, 1899-1914    88

CHANGES IN PHYSICAL OUTPUT AND IN AGGREGATE VALUES AND COSTS, MANUFACTURING INDUSTRIES . . . . . . . . 88

CHANGES IN THE SELLING PRICES OF MANUFACTURED GOODS . 94
    § On changes in the apparent physical contributions of different agents of manufacturing production . . . . . . 94
    § Selling prices, individual industries . . . . . . . 99

CHANGES IN MATERIAL COSTS AND IN FABRICATION COSTS, MANUFACTURING INDUSTRIES . . . . . . . . . . 101
    § Material costs and fabrication costs, individual industries . 105

CHANGES IN LABOR COSTS AND IN OTHER FABRICATION COSTS, MANUFACTURING INDUSTRIES . . . . . . . . . . 109
    § Labor costs and other fabrication costs, individual industries . . . . . . . . . . . . . . . . . . 111

ON THE RELATIVE IMPORTANCE OF DIFFERENT ELEMENTS OF COST AS FACTORS IN PRICE CHANGES, 1899-1914 . . . 115
    The activity ratio . . . . . . . . . . . . . 117

SUMMARY: PRICE AND COST MOVEMENTS IN MANUFACTURING INDUSTRIES, 1899-1914 . . . . . . . . . . . . 121

## CHAPTER IV

## OTHER ECONOMIC CHANGES, 1901-1913 . . . . 124

A SURVEY OF MAJOR TENDENCIES . . . . . . . . . 126
CHANGES IN DISTRIBUTIVE SHARES . . . . . . . . . 132
    Wage trends . . . . . . . . . . . . . 132
    § Changes in earnings, by occupational groups . . . . 134
    Cash receipts and capital gains of stockholders . . . . 138
        Industrial and public utility stocks . . . . . . 144
        § Returns to industrial stockholders, other records . . 146
        Railroad stocks . . . . . . . . . . . . 148
        § Returns to railroad stockholders, other records . . 150
    Investment experience of bondholders . . . . . . . 152
    Summary of changes in distributive shares . . . . . 153
    Comparison of changes in distributive shares, in dollars of constant purchasing power . . . . . . . . . 158
    § On changes in the purchasing power of the capital assets of stockholders and bondholders . . . . . . . 160
FOREIGN TRADE AND THE BALANCE OF INTERNATIONAL PAYMENTS . . . . . . . . . . . . . . . . 161
    Changes in the foreign trade of the United States . . . 161
    The balance of international payments . . . . . . 165
CHANGES IN THE AGGREGATE REWARDS OF ECONOMIC CLASSES . 166
    § A further view of factors affecting the aggregate purchasing power of agents of fabrication . . . . . . . 171
CHANGES IN THE AGGREGATE PHYSICAL CONTRIBUTIONS OF ECONOMIC CLASSES, IN RELATION TO THEIR AGGREGATE PHYSICAL REWARDS . . . . . . . . . . . . . . . 173
    § Contributions and rewards of agents of fabrication . . . 179
DIVERSITY OF PRE-WAR ECONOMIC MOVEMENTS . . . . . 184

## CHAPTER V

## INTERREGNUM

PRODUCTION, PRICE AND COST CHANGES, 1913-1923 . . . . . . . . . . . . . . . . . 186
THE END OF AN ERA . . . . . . . . . . . . . 186
PRODUCTION AND CONSTRUCTION . . . . . . . . . 188

## CONTENTS

| | PAGE |
|---|---|
| Construction | 191 |
| Volume of manufacturing production | 192 |
| § Changes in physical volume of production and in output per wage-earner, individual industries | 193 |
| § Volume of manufacturing production, revised measurements | 198 |
| CHANGES IN COMMODITY PRICES, 1913-1922 | 201 |
| § The influence of price changes on the value stream, 1913-1922 | 203 |
| Price movements of raw materials and of manufactured goods | 205 |
| Price movements of products of American farms and of other products | 208 |
| § Prices and purchasing power of agricultural products at the farm | 209 |
| Price movements of farm crops, animal products, mineral products and forest products | 211 |
| Price movements of foods and non-foods | 213 |
| Price movements of producers' goods and consumers' goods | 214 |
| CHANGES IN PRICES AND COSTS IN MANUFACTURING INDUSTRIES, 1914-1923 | 220 |
| § On changes in the apparent physical contributions of different agents of manufacturing production, 1914-1923 | 221 |
| § Selling prices, individual industries | 223 |
| § Material costs and fabrication costs, individual industries | 227 |
| § Labor costs and other fabrication costs, individual industries | 234 |
| SUMMARY OF PRICE CHANGES, 1913-1922 | 238 |

### CHAPTER VI

### CHANGES IN THE VOLUME AND CHARACTER OF PRODUCTION IN THE UNITED STATES, 1922-1929 — 241

| | |
|---|---|
| CHANGES IN THE VOLUME OF PRODUCTION, 1922-1929. GENERAL MEASUREMENTS | 243 |
| § On the stability of productive processes, 1922-1929 | 246 |
| CHANGES IN THE CHARACTER OF PHYSICAL PRODUCTION, 1922-1929 | 248 |

# CONTENTS

|  | PAGE |
|---|---|
| Production of raw materials and of manufactured goods | 249 |
| § Unrevised index numbers of physical production | 251 |
| Physical output of products of American farms and of all other products | 258 |
| § Comparison of identical commodities, pre-war and post-war | 260 |
| The value and volume of construction | 263 |
| § Construction volume | 266 |

PHYSICAL OUTPUT OF FINISHED PRODUCTS, 1922-1929. CONSUMPTION GOODS AND CAPITAL EQUIPMENT . . . . . 269

| Non-durable consumption goods | 270 |
|---|---|
| Semi-durable consumption goods | 272 |
| Durable consumption goods | 273 |
| Elements of capital equipment | 276 |
| Capital equipment, consumption goods and all finished goods | 279 |
| Durable and non-durable goods | 282 |
| § On changes in the relative importance of certain types of commodities | 286 |

PHYSICAL OUTPUT AND PRODUCTIVITY OF MANUFACTURING INDUSTRIES, 1923-1929 . . . . . . . . . . . 289

| § Changes in physical volume of production and in output per wage-earner, individual industries | 292 |
|---|---|
| Manufacturing establishments and volume of manufacturing production | 299 |
| § Changes in output per establishment, individual industries | 301 |
| § On the diversification of manufacturing production: A revision of index numbers of output | 307 |

SUMMARY: PRODUCTION TENDENCIES IN THE UNITED STATES, POST-WAR . . . . . . . . . . . . . 310

## CHAPTER VII

# PRICE MOVEMENTS, 1922-1929 . . . . . . . 315

MOVEMENTS OF THE LEVEL OF WHOLESALE PRICES. PRICE TRENDS AND CYCLES . . . . . . . . . . . 316

| § World movements of wholesale prices | 317 |
|---|---|
| The influence of price changes on aggregate values, 1922-1929 | 321 |

PRICE STABILITY AND ECONOMIC FLEXIBILITY . . . . . 323

|                                                                                   | PAGE |
| --------------------------------------------------------------------------------- | ---- |
| PRICE MOVEMENTS, MAJOR COMMODITY GROUPS                                           | 332  |
| Raw materials and manufactured goods                                              | 332  |
| § Price variability of raw and processed goods                                    | 338  |
| Products of American farms and other products                                     | 340  |
| § Price variability of farm and other products                                    | 345  |
| Changes in farm prices                                                            | 346  |
| Farm crops, animal products, mineral products and forest products                 | 349  |
| Foods and non-foods                                                               | 353  |
| Producers' goods and consumers' goods                                             | 357  |
| Goods entering into capital equipment and articles of human consumption           | 363  |
| On the levels of operating and capital costs, 1922-1929                           | 370  |
| § Other commodity groups                                                          | 371  |
| SUMMARY: POST-WAR MOVEMENTS OF COMMODITY PRICES                                   | 372  |

CHAPTER VIII

# PRICE AND COST CHANGES IN MANUFACTURING INDUSTRIES OF THE UNITED STATES, 1923-1929 — 375

|                                                                                   |     |
| --------------------------------------------------------------------------------- | --- |
| CHANGES IN PHYSICAL OUTPUT AND IN AGGREGATE VALUES AND COSTS, MANUFACTURING INDUSTRIES | 375 |
| CHANGES IN THE SELLING PRICES OF MANUFACTURED GOODS                               | 378 |
| § Selling prices, individual industries                                           | 380 |
| CHANGES IN MATERIAL COSTS AND IN FABRICATION COSTS, MANUFACTURING INDUSTRIES       | 384 |
| § Material costs and fabrication costs, individual industries                     | 387 |
| CHANGES IN LABOR COSTS AND IN OTHER FABRICATION COSTS, MANUFACTURING INDUSTRIES    | 393 |
| A comparison of sales and profits, manufacturing corporations                     | 397 |
| § Labor costs and other fabrication costs, individual industries                  | 404 |
| ON THE RELATIVE IMPORTANCE OF DIFFERENT ELEMENTS OF COST AS FACTORS IN PRICE CHANGES, 1923-1929 | 409 |
| SUMMARY: PRICE AND COST MOVEMENTS IN MANUFACTURING INDUSTRIES                     | 412 |

CHAPTER IX

OTHER ECONOMIC CHANGES, 1922-1929 . . . . 416

POPULATION CHANGES AND INDUSTRIAL DISPLACEMENT . . . 416
    § On the extent of industrial displacement, 1899-1929 . . 419
AVAILABILITY OF CAPITAL AND CREDIT . . . . . . . . 423
    Supply of capital . . . . . . . . . . . . . 424
        Annual increments to capital funds: new issues . . . 426
        Annual increments to capital funds: corporate savings . 428
        Savings deposits . . . . . . . . . . . . 429
        Reserves of life insurance companies . . . . . . 431
        Assets of building and loan associations . . . . . 431
        Corporate savings . . . . . . . . . . . 431
        § On the method of estimating the volume and rate of increase of corporate savings . . . . . . . . 432
        An estimate of the growth of aggregate corporate capital 436
    Supply of credit . . . . . . . . . . . . . 442
        Primary funds . . . . . . . . . . . . 443
        Secondary funds . . . . . . . . . . . 448
        Increase in mortgage indebtedness . . . . . . . 452
    Cost of capital and credit . . . . . . . . . . 454
    Summary: Capital and credit . . . . . . . . . 459
INTERNATIONAL MOVEMENTS OF GOODS AND OF CAPITAL . . . 461
    Changes in the foreign trade of the United States . . . . 461
    § On the proportion of American manufactured products entering into foreign trade . . . . . . . . . . 467
    The balance of international payments . . . . . . . 470
CHANGES IN DISTRIBUTIVE SHARES . . . . . . . . . 476
    Wages . . . . . . . . . . . . . . . . 476
    § Changes in earnings, industrial groups . . . . . . 479
    Profits . . . . . . . . . . . . . . . . 482
        The growth of profits, manufacturing corporations . . 485
        Dividend payments . . . . . . . . . . . 488
        Cash receipts and capital gains of stockholders . . . 491
        § Returns to stockholders, various corporate groups . 496
    Investment experience of bondholders . . . . . . . 500
    Summary of changes in distributive shares . . . . . 501

|    | Page |
|---|---|
| Changes in the Aggregate Purchasing Power of Different Economic Classes | 505 |
| § Comparison of pre-war and post-war tendencies among producers of economic goods | 509 |
| Changes in the Aggregate Physical Contributions of Economic Classes in Relation to Changes in their Aggregate Physical Rewards | 513 |
| § Contributions and rewards of agents of fabrication | 520 |
| A comparison of the fortunes of different producing groups, pre-war and post-war | 525 |

CHAPTER X

## A SUMMARY: SOME ATTRIBUTES OF THE POST-WAR DECADE . . . . . . . . . . . 529

| | |
|---|---|
| Retardation of Population Growth | 529 |
| Productive Processes | 530 |
| Trade Movements and the Balance of International Payments | 536 |
| The Growth of Capital and Credit | 538 |
| Movements of Prices and Costs | 541 |
| Changes in the Aggregate Purchasing Power of Producing Groups | 549 |
| Aggregate Contributions in Relation to Aggregate Rewards of Economic Classes | 552 |
| Changes in Distributive Shares | 555 |

## APPENDICES . . . . . . . . . . . . . 559

| | |
|---|---|
| I. Section 1. The Construction of Index Numbers of Physical Volume of Production, 1901-1913 | 560 |
| Section 2. The Construction of Index Numbers of Physical Volume of Production, 1922-1929 | 569 |
| II. Classifications of Commodities Entering into the Index Numbers of Wholesale Prices Constructed by the National Bureau of Economic Research | 572 |

|     |     | PAGE |
| --- | --- | --- |
| III. | Index Numbers of Wholesale Prices by Groups, 1891-1901, 1901-1913, 1913-1931 | 584 |
| IV. | Section 1. List of Commodities Included in Index Numbers of Physical Volume of Manufacturing Production, 1899-1914 | 591 |
|     | Section 2. List of Commodities Included in Index Numbers of Physical Volume of Manufacturing Production, 1914-1929 | 594 |
| V.  | Descriptions and Sources of Annual Production Series | 602 |

LIST OF TABLES . . . . . . . . . . . 609

LIST OF CHARTS . . . . . . . . . . . 623

INDEX . . . . . . . . . . . . . . . 631

# Foreword

Certain of the attributes of two economic eras are summarized in the following figures:

|  | Average annual rate of change, | |
|---|---|---|
|  | 1901-1913 (per cent) | 1922-1929 (per cent) |
| Population of the United States | + 2.0 | + 1.4 |
| Physical volume of production | + 3.1 | + 3.8 |
| Volume of production, per capita of the population | + 1.1 | + 2.4 |
| Prices, wholesale | + 1.8 | − 0.5 |
| Volume of employment, manufacturing industries | + 2.7 | + 1.0 |
| Per capita real earnings, manufacturing workers | − 0.1 | + 1.4 |
| Prices of industrial common stocks | + 2.8 | + 19.4 |

There are notable differences between these two periods. The physical volume of production expanded at a more rapid rate in the recent period, while population grew less rapidly. Wholesale prices rose in the earlier period, declined in the later. The volume of employment in manufacturing plants expanded considerably during the pre-war era and increased but slightly during post-war years. The real earnings of manufacturing workers declined slightly in the first period, increased substantially during the second. The prices of industrial common stocks rose in the earlier period at a rate but slightly in excess of that prevailing among wholesale prices; the more recent period was marked by a rapid climb in stock prices, at a rate sevenfold that of the pre-war era.

These figures have been given for the purpose of presenting a problem. In themselves they indicate certain resemblances and emphasize certain major differences between the two eras, but the questions they raise are more significant than is the information they give. Why do we find such pronounced differences among the changes in the real earnings of labor, in the volume of manufacturing employment, in the prices of common stocks? Over such periods of time as these, what relations prevail among the various economic processes represented in the above table? More generally, upon what does the productivity of an economy depend? What conditions conduce to stability in the working of an economy? to instability? How should one define stability and instability in the working of an economy? Conceiving of an economy as a closely-knit system of elements moving forward in time through a related series of changes, it is desirable to know what elements play an active part in these changes and what elements are on the whole passive. One would like to differentiate between flexible and inflexible elements, between elements which adapt themselves promptly to changes in other factors, and in the general economic situation, and elements which are relatively rigid in the face of changing conditions. Finally, in any study of the parts played by different elements in economic operations, some effort should be made to distinguish between those elements upon which the finger of conscious control may be placed and those elements which are not subject to direct control.

These questions will be in the backs of our minds in surveying the tendencies which prevailed during the period preceding the World War and that which followed it. Complete answers are not sought, for the present task is primarily descriptive. The descriptive work must, of course, be carried on within the framework of certain working hypotheses, must be based on certain assumptions concerning the ground plan of the economic structure. But the full interpretation of the complex changes which occur in an economy in operation, the complete tracing of the relations of cause and effect, of antecedence and consequence, among the elements of such an economy, lies beyond the present objective, and, indeed, beyond the limits of existing knowledge. This task of interpretation is an urgent one, if we are to secure a clearer understanding of economic processes than we now have. The present experimental study may contribute to a solution of the larger problem.

This investigation is, at once, a continuation of the general price studies begun by the National Bureau some time ago,[1] and an extension of certain work done for the Committee on Recent

---

[1] See *The Behavior of Prices,* National Bureau of Economic Research, New York, 1927.

Economic Changes.[1] The examination of price changes and of related industrial movements, which was one phase of the general study of economic changes, extended only to 1928 and dealt almost exclusively with post-war events. In order that the rate and character of the industrial advance of the 1920's might be more exactly defined, a broadening of that study was required. Furthermore, it seemed desirable to define in great detail differences between the movements of recent years and those which occurred from the turn of the century to the outbreak of the World War. These considerations were strengthened when the recession which began in 1929 set a terminus to the post-war expansion. The era from 1922 to 1929 constitutes a clearly-defined epoch, which lends itself to study as a unit. It is proper that the tendencies characteristic of post-war conditions in the United States be studied within this eight-year period.

The present study does not aim at an explanation of the recession of 1929, nor of the depression which ensued. It deals with tendencies prevailing in certain economic fields during the years preceding the crisis of 1929. These tendencies had a bearing, of course, on that crisis, but they do not necessarily account for the economic collapse. That is a problem which calls for a wider survey than is here attempted.

This account of economic tendencies runs in terms of measured events—of changes in the number of units of goods produced, in per-unit prices and production costs, in wages, in dividend payments, in trade and capital movements. These measurements cover a wide range, with respect to both subject matter and accuracy. Figures compiled and published by various agencies have been utilized. Many of the measurements cited have been derived in connection with the present study, and are here published for the first time. These have been given as high a degree of accuracy as the original data permit. This is believed to be reasonably high, as regards new index numbers of production and prices, and new measurements of changes in costs, derived from census compilations. In some other cases estimates of economic changes have been based upon less exact data. These rougher estimates are put forward without apology, for approximations are preferable to complete absence of knowledge, but with full recognition of the margins

[1] *Recent Economic Changes,* National Bureau of Economic Research, New York, 1929, Chapter IX.

of error involved in their use. They will have served a useful purpose if they stimulate further work aimed at more exact determination of the magnitudes involved.

The facts assembled in such an account as this do not fit into a nicely articulated structure. "It isn't a constructed tale I have to tell," says Ponderevo, in *Tono-Bungay,* "but unmanageable realities." It is difficult to give order and coherence to the refractory data of economic reality. Instead, then, of looking for perfect unity in this survey of tendencies, I have sought significant methods of handling and organizing the relevant data, suggestive ways of viewing them, possible modes of combining them, to the end that some light might be thrown on the processes of a going economic system during two eras of expansion. The resulting measurements, as presented in the following pages, lack the nice coherence which they might have if they were fitted into a constructed tale. But the telling of such a tale, and the precise fitting of observed facts into it, has not been one of the objectives of the present study. A new cosmology is not a necessary accompaniment of every new set of observations.

The task of giving a reasonably comprehensive factual basis to an account of economic movements is, of necessity, laborious. I have had the assistance, at different stages of this work, of Charles Bliss, Vladimir Kolesnikoff, Solomon Fabricant, Maude Remey, Mildred Uhrbrock and Gertrude Reaske. My debt to these co-workers for help in the tasks of compilation and calculation, for searching criticism and for fruitful suggestion, is a heavy one. I am indebted, in addition, to Mr. LeVerne Beales, of the Bureau of the Census, for his generous compliance with numerous troublesome requests. Finally, I wish to express my appreciation of the action of the President and Trustees of Columbia University in granting me a leave of absence from my University duties for the prosecution of part of this investigation.

F. C. M.

# ECONOMIC TENDENCIES
IN THE UNITED STATES

## CHAPTER I

## Pre-War Changes in the Volume and Character of Production in the United States

IN describing productive processes during a given period two matters are of immediate interest. These are the degree of change in the total physical volume of production in an economy, and the regularity or stability of this change. The flow of real income and the stability of economic processes in general rest upon these fundamental conditions of production. But even more valuable information may be gained by a study of the working of the productive mechanism in detail. The rates of exploitation and the stability of growth (or decline) among the various extractive industries, agricultural and non-agricultural, are of obvious concern. The relations between extraction and fabrication help to reveal the direction in which an economy is moving. Again, the relation between the output of goods destined for human consumption and of goods destined for use as capital equipment serves as an index of the manner in which human effort is being expended—toward the direct satisfaction of wants, or toward that indirect satisfaction of wants which involves the construction of ever more elaborate equipment for the roundabout production of consumable goods. For other purposes a classification of output by industries is significant. Measurements of changes in these various categories, measurements based upon accurate and comprehensive production statistics, record the story of a nation's development and trace the persistent tendencies of an era.

The statistical record of the physical volume of production in the United States during the years preceding the World War is not as complete as is the corresponding post-war record. In constructing the present series of index numbers of productive activity use has been made of available annual data, supplemented by census statistics of manufacturing production. Technical details are given in Appendix I.

## Changes in the Volume of Production, 1901-1913

The increase in aggregate physical production in the United States between 1901 and 1913 is defined by the index numbers in the following table. These, with corresponding population figures, are plotted in Figure 1.

TABLE 1

Growth of Physical Volume of Production in the United States, 1901-1913

| Year | Volume of production | Year-to-year change in volume of production (per cent) |
|---|---|---|
| 1901 | 100 | .... |
| 1902 | 116 | +16 |
| 1903 | 115 | − 1 |
| 1904 | 118 | + 3 |
| 1905 | 129 | + 9 |
| 1906 | 137 | + 6 |
| 1907 | 134 | − 2 |
| 1908 | 126 | − 6 |
| 1909 | 136 | + 8 |
| 1910 | 142 | + 4 |
| 1911 | 139 | − 2 |
| 1912 | 158 | +14 |
| 1913 | 156 | − 1 |
| Average annual rate of change (per cent)[a] | +3.1 | |
| Index of instability of growth[a] | 3.7 | |

[a] The method of deriving these measurements is explained in a note at the end of this chapter.

During the period covered by these measurements the volume of production in the United States increased at a rate of approximately 3.1 per cent a year. Over the same period the population of the United States increased at an average annual rate of 2.0 per cent a year. Per capita of the total population, the stream of goods increased at an average rate approximating 1.1 per cent a year. There was here the material basis, clearly, of a notable gain in national wealth and well-being, an advance which, if sustained, would result in a doubling of aggregate physical income in some 23 years, of per capita physical income in about 63 years.

Perhaps of equal importance with the rates of growth of these series is the degree of steadiness of the advance. Between 1901 and 1913 the average annual deviation from constancy of growth in aggregate production amounted to approximately 3.7 per cent.[1] These rather wide changes occurring from year to year in the growth of the physical volume of goods are in pronounced contrast to the relatively smooth and regular growth of population.

FIGURE 1

GROWTH OF POPULATION AND OF PHYSICAL VOLUME OF PRODUCTION IN THE UNITED STATES, 1901-1913*

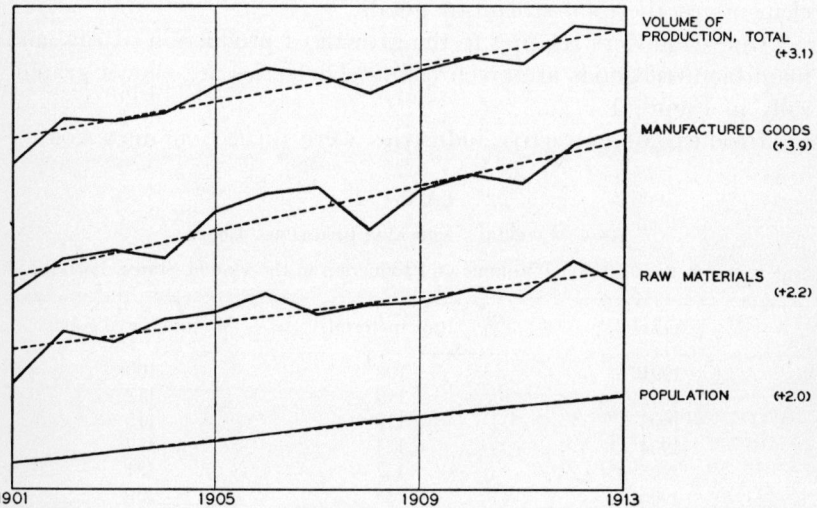

* This is a ratio chart, as are all following charts of the same general type. The solid lines trace the actual movements of the several series. Trends, or tendencies, between 1901 and 1913 are shown by the broken lines. Numbers in parentheses define average annual rates of change (in percentage form).

Instability of population change, as determined from rough annual population estimates, averaged 0.3 per cent.[2] During these years a

---

[1] This means that the average yearly departure from the values which would have been recorded had the growth of production been perfectly regular, at a constant rate of 3.1 per cent a year, amounted to 3.7 per cent. Not variations from year to year, nor deviations from a constant figure, but departures from regularity of growth (or decline) are measured by this index of instability. This measurement conforms to the concept of stability of growth as a desirable objective in a dynamic economy.

[2] This measurement has been derived from estimates of the growth of population made by W. I. King from available information on births, deaths and migra-

population subject to but slight undulations in its growth produced and supported itself by a stream of goods with annual fluctuations many times as wide.

## Production of Raw Materials and of Manufactured Goods

The story of production in terms of aggregates is incomplete. What was the rate of change in the output of important types of goods? What were the variable elements of the aggregate output? To appreciate the economic significance of the figures we have cited, we must know more about the behavior of the constituent elements of the total stream of goods.

Index numbers relating to the growth of production of raw and manufactured goods are given below. The series are shown graphically in Figure 1.

Products of extractive industries were turned out in a volume

TABLE 2

RAW MATERIALS AND MANUFACTURED GOODS

Index Numbers of Physical Volume of Production in the United States, 1901-1913 [a]

| Year | Raw materials | Manufactured goods |
|---|---|---|
| 1901 | 100 | 100 |
| 1902 | 119 | 112 |
| 1903 | 115 | 115 |
| 1904 | 124 | 112 |
| 1905 | 127 | 131 |
| 1906 | 135 | 139 |
| 1907 | 126 | 142 |
| 1908 | 130 | 123 |
| 1909 | 131 | 141 |
| 1910 | 137 | 148 |
| 1911 | 134 | 144 |
| 1912 | 151 | 164 |
| 1913 | 139 | 173 |
| Average annual rate of change (per cent) | +2.2 | +3.9 |
| Index of instability of growth | 3.8 | 4.7 |

[a] A description of these index numbers is given in Appendix I.

tion. Deficiencies in the statistical records of this period prevent the attainment of any high degree of accuracy in the measurement of the year-to-year variations in population growth.

which increased at a rate of 2.2 per cent a year between 1901 and 1913. The output of manufacturing industries rose during the same period at a rate of 3.9 per cent a year. The margin of almost two per cent which represents the more rapid advance in the output of industries engaged in fabrication is the resultant of several forces. Within the group of raw materials, as we shall see, those entering in considerable degree into manufacturing processes were increasing more rapidly in volume of output than were those subject to but slight processing, or consumed in a raw state. On the manufacturing side fundamental changes were occurring. The factory was performing new functions, taking over tasks formerly performed in the home. Again, the degree of fabrication through which materials passed was tending in many lines to increase. This has been one of the outstanding features of modern economic development. The intermediary processes of fabrication, particularly fabrication outside the home, become increasingly important in an industrial civilization.

The changes in our foreign trade during this period also affected the course and character of production. We were exporting smaller quantities of crude foodstuffs, and importing more, while exports of semi-manufactured and finished goods were increasing at very rapid rates.[1] These developments contributed to the growth of domestic manufactures.

Such index numbers, defining movements of output by broad classes, do not permit a full comparison of the processes of production within the groups distinguished. Analysis of the individual production series, which are plotted in Figure 2, reveals wide differences in growth tendencies during this period. In the group of raw materials 28 series were studied in detail. These show rates of change between 1901 and 1913 varying from —3.0 per cent a year for flaxseed to +13.8 per cent a year for cement.[2] Among 31 series

[1] Average annual rates of change between 1901 and 1913 in the major export groups were as follows:

| | |
|---|---|
| Crude foodstuffs | — 2.4 per cent |
| Manufactured foodstuffs | — 0.7 " " |
| Crude materials | + 5.9 " " |
| Semi-manufactures | + 8.7 " " |
| Finished manufactures | + 7.6 " " |

[2] Cement production has been included in the classification of raw materials (as well as among manufactured goods) as representative of changes in the output of materials utilized in cement manufacture. Use has been made of 58 independent production series. Because of the double use of the cement statistics, the sum of the series in the two major groups is 59.

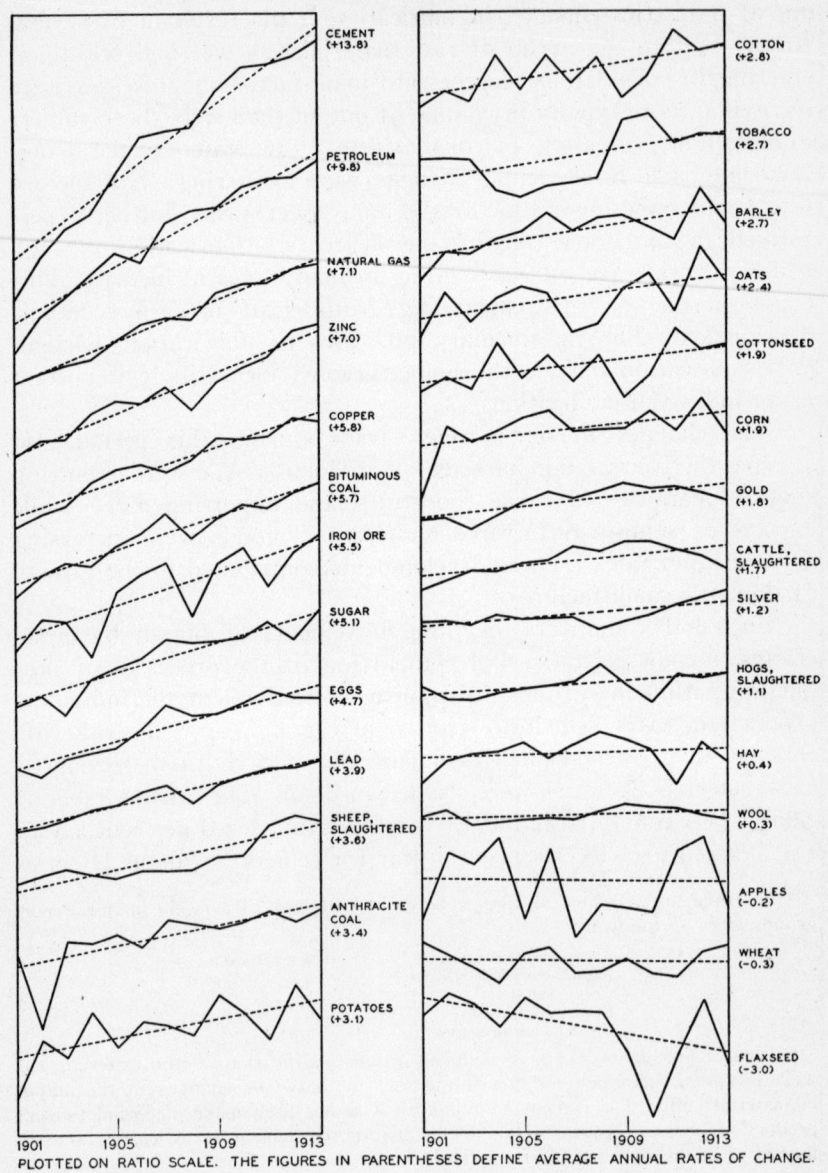

# PRODUCTION CHANGES, PRE-WAR

## FIGURE 2 (CONT.)
### CHANGES IN PHYSICAL VOLUME OF PRODUCTION IN THE UNITED STATES, 1901–1913
#### B- PROCESSED GOODS

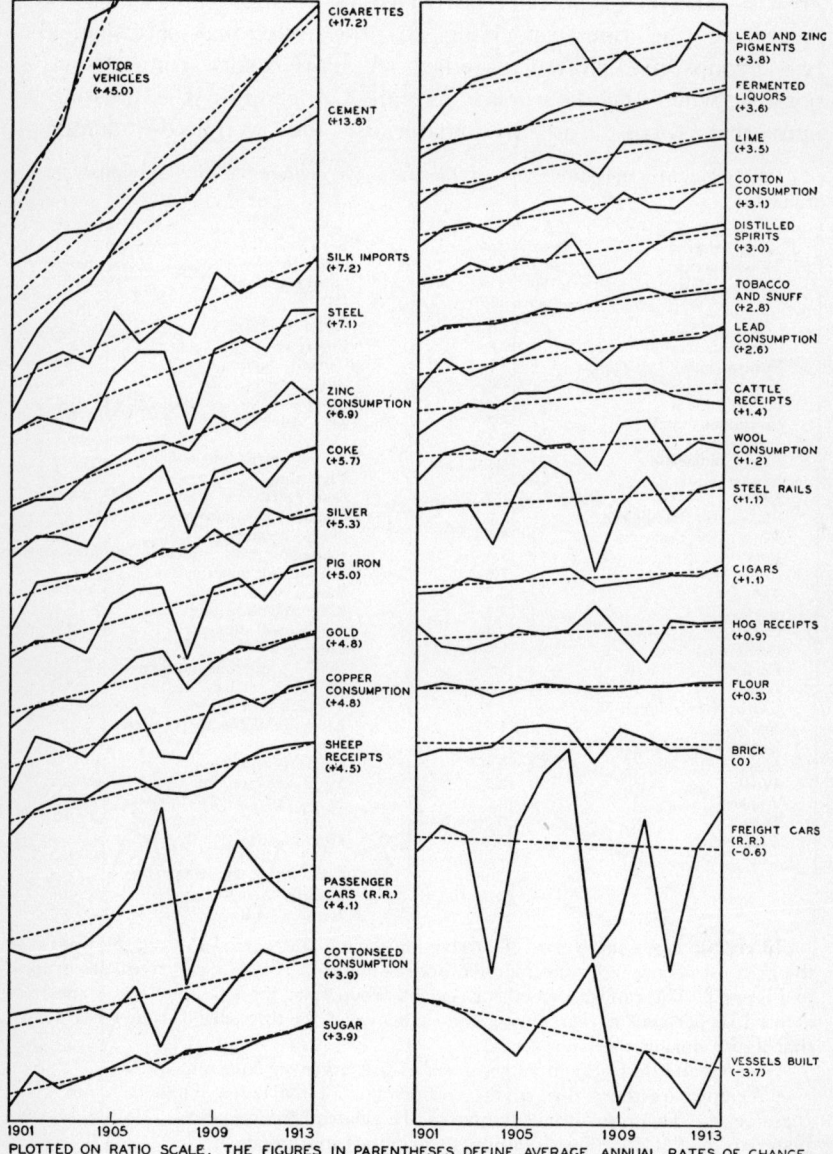

PLOTTED ON RATIO SCALE. THE FIGURES IN PARENTHESES DEFINE AVERAGE ANNUAL RATES OF CHANGE.

relating to processes of fabrication the rates of change varied from —3.7 per cent a year for vessels built, to +45.0 per cent a year for the production of motor vehicles.[1] The degree of variation among commodities within these groups in respect of growth rates is graphically portrayed in Figure 3, in which lines measuring the rates of change of the individual series in the two groups are plotted together. A more exact comparison is possible when the divergence of rates of change is expressed in numerical form. For raw materials, the weighted [2] standard

[1] Following are measurements of the rates of change in the individual series studied:

| Series relating to production of materials | Average annual rate of change 1901-1913 (per cent) | Series relating to processes of fabrication | Average annual rate of change 1901-1913 (per cent) |
|---|---|---|---|
| Cement, total | + 13.8 | Motor vehicles | + 45.0 |
| Petroleum, crude | + 9.8 | Cigarettes | + 17.2 |
| Natural gas | + 7.1 | Cement, total | + 13.8 |
| Zinc | + 7.0 | Silk imports, raw | + 7.2 |
| Copper | + 5.8 | Steel | + 7.1 |
| Bituminous coal | + 5.7 | Zinc consumption | + 6.9 |
| Iron ore | + 5.5 | Coke, total | + 5.7 |
| Sugar, domestic | + 5.1 | Silver (mfr. and arts) | + 5.3 |
| Egg receipts | + 4.7 | Pig iron | + 5.0 |
| Lead | + 3.9 | Gold (mfr. and arts) | + 4.8 |
| Sheep, total slaughter | + 3.6 | Copper consumption | + 4.8 |
| Anthracite coal | + 3.4 | Sheep receipts | + 4.5 |
| Potatoes | + 3.1 | Passenger cars, railroad | + 4.1 |
| Cotton | + 2.8 | Cottonseed consumption | + 3.9 |
| Tobacco | + 2.7 | Sugar, total supply | + 3.9 |
| Barley | + 2.7 | Zinc and lead pigments | + 3.8 |
| Oats | + 2.4 | Fermented liquors | + 3.6 |
| Cottonseed | + 1.9 | Lime | + 3.5 |
| Corn | + 1.9 | Cotton, mill consumption | + 3.1 |
| Gold | + 1.8 | Distilled spirits | + 3.0 |
| Cattle, total slaughter | + 1.7 | Tobacco and snuff | + 2.8 |
| Silver | + 1.2 | Lead, available for consumption | + 2.6 |
| Swine, total slaughter | + 1.1 | Cattle receipts | + 1.4 |
| Hay | + 0.4 | Wool consumption | + 1.2 |
| Wool | + 0.3 | Steel rails | + 1.1 |
| Apples | — 0.2 | Cigars | + 1.1 |
| Wheat | — 0.3 | Hog receipts | + 0.9 |
| Flaxseed | — 3.0 | Flour, wheat | + 0.3 |
| | | Common brick sold | 0.0 |
| | | Freight cars | — 0.6 |
| | | Vessels built | — 3.7 |

In certain cases the trends of production during this period are not defined with the greatest accuracy by the function here employed. This is clear from the graphs in Figure 2. The rate of growth of cement production, for example, was somewhat above 13.8 per cent a year during the earlier years of this period, somewhat below that figure during the later years.

Sources and descriptions of these series are given in Appendix V.

[2] Weights are those used in the construction of the index numbers based upon these series. The standard deviation of the unweighted measures relating to raw materials is 3.3; for those relating to manufactured goods it is 8.2.

## FIGURE 3
### ILLUSTRATING THE DIVERGENCE OF PRODUCTION TRENDS IN THE UNITED STATES, 1901-1913*

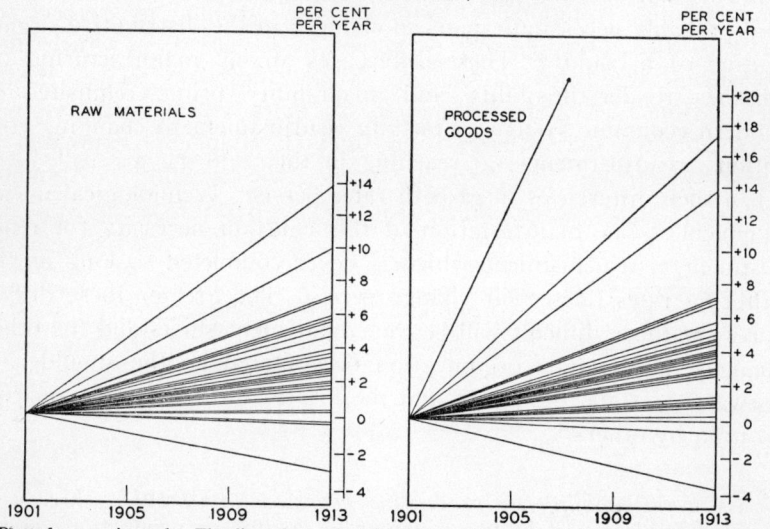

* Plotted on ratio scale. The lines here plotted relate to the commodities listed in footnote, p. 8, in the order of that listing.

deviation [1] of the 28 measurements of rates of change is 2.1; for the 31 fabricated goods it is 5.7.

These several comparisons point clearly to the same conclusion. Not only was the rate of increase in the physical volume of production of fabricated goods distinctly higher than the rate of increase in the output of raw materials during the period 1901-1913, but within the manufacturing group the divergences among the rates of change for different commodities were much greater. This is probably to be expected. In the manufacturing field we are accustomed to find new industries coming into favor, pushing ahead at exceptional rates, only in time to be supplanted by others. The automobile, the radio and artificial refrigeration devices are recent examples of commodities produced under such conditions. Extreme differences among the rates of exploitation of raw materials are more rare.

[1] The standard deviation is a measure of the dispersion of numerical items about their average. It is expressed in terms of the unit of measurement used for the original observations. When a distance equal to the standard deviation is laid off on each side of the arithmetic average, about two-thirds of all the items will be included.

Differences among long-time rates of growth (or decline) constitute a highly important feature of modern industrial systems. They involve shifting capital investments and a mobile labor supply, and probably necessitate material changes in the distributive organization of a country. These differences among manufacturing industries render flexibility and adaptability prime requisites of modern economic systems. Constant readjustment to changing conditions, readjustments far-reaching in their effects, are called for when such differences in growth rates persist. Technological unemployment is one manifestation of this constant necessity for readjustment, a readjustment which is never completed so long as the differing rates of secular change persist. The greater these differences the more difficult will be the employment shifts and the other changes in economic organization necessitated by the shouldering forward of some industries and the loss of absolute or of relative position by others.[1]

§ *On the stability of productive processes, 1901-1913.*—Measurements defining the stability of change in volume of production appear in certain of the preceding tables. Total production, we have seen, gained in volume somewhat irregularly, showing annual variations averaging 3.7 per cent of the aggregate volume. For the index numbers relating to extractive and fabricating industries measurements of instability are, respectively, 3.8 and 4.7. These probably reflect with reasonable accuracy the relative stability of change in the output of these two industrial groups.[2]

---

[1] It is a plausible hypothesis that the amplitude and, perhaps, the duration of business cycles are functions of the degree of difference among rates of change in important industries. The greater the differences the more economically painful and difficult the readjustments. These readjustments are probably closely related to the fluctuations commonly identified as cyclical. Under certain circumstances the readjustments of capital and labor and the changes in economic organization necessitated by differing rates of secular change may be made without major breakdowns. Under other conditions these readjustments may involve rather widespread disturbances. The conditions which conduce to economic flexibility and adaptability, and which engender ability to make readjustments readily, are undoubtedly complex and difficult to classify. Yet this type of flexibility in an operating economy is so important today that the conditions essential to it (conditions of interchangeability and mobility of labor, liquidity of capital, flexibility of transportation and distributive organizations) are worthy of detailed study.

[2] The annual values of the index of production of manufactured goods are not derived directly from statistics of quantities produced. For inter-censal years this

The aggregate production of raw materials is more stable, in its year-to-year change, than is the total output of manufactured goods. There are unstable elements in the first group, but many of these instabilities are of independent origin, and hence their fluctuations may be of an offsetting character. A good year for wheat may be a poor year for iron ore. Such offsettings tend to reduce the variations of the aggregate. More closely linked, on the whole, are the fluctuations in output of manufacturing industries. Here business considerations, rather than the vagaries of weather, dominate production, and these considerations tend toward reënforcing rather than offsetting variations of output.

Figures not affected by such offsettings are secured by averaging the instability measurements relating to the various individual production series. In doing this we are not dealing with irregularities in the aggregate output, but with the irregularity of flow of the individual streams making up the aggregate. As regards the fortunes of individual producers and the stability of employment in particular industries, the measurements of the instability of production of individual commodities are more important than are those relating to the aggregate volume of production, an aggregate which has social rather than individual significance. For all production series the weighted arithmetic average of the measures of instability of output is 8.2. This means that among the individual elements of the total stream of production the annual deviations from constant rates of change averaged 8.2 per cent of the normal volume of production. This figure, which is distinctly greater than the index of 3.7 defining variations in the growth of aggregate production, is perhaps the most significant available measure of the irregularity of production growth in the United States between 1901 and 1913. If stability of growth be a desirable condition, average annual departures of eight per cent from such stability represent a rather erratic course of economic development.

For raw materials and for manufactured goods, respectively, the weighted averages of instability measurements are 8.3 and 8.0.

One further measurement is of interest. The degree of difference among the instability indexes for raw materials is indicated by a weighted standard deviation of 2.8, among manufactured commodities by a weighted standard deviation of 4.8. The latter is substantially larger, suggesting differences among the commodities in that group, in respect of stability of production, rather greater than those found among raw materials. That is, certain manufactured goods are highly stable in their output, from year to year, while certain others are highly

---

index is secured by interpolation, in which account is taken of the fact that the total volume of manufacture is more stable than is the output of those goods for which statistics of production are readily available. This same comment applies to variations in total output, as measured by the index numbers given in Table 1 above.

unstable. It is the latter series which give manufactured goods as a class the high measure of instability we have secured.[1]

In summary: Between 1901 and 1913 the output of manufactured goods in the United States advanced at a rate of approximately 3.9 per cent a year; the volume of raw materials produced increased at an average rate of 2.2 per cent a year. The increasing proportion of fabricated goods consumed with rising living standards, the steady advance in fabrication outside the home and changes in the character of our foreign trade help to account for these differences. Rates of growth in different industries were markedly uneven, the differences being most pronounced among manufacturing industries. Such differences, which are doubtless necessary accompaniments of economic progress, involve readjustment and adaptation not always effected without friction.

The advance of this pre-war period was not a smooth and regular movement; economic progress was jerky and uneven.

[1] Following are the indexes of instability for the individual series studied:

| Series relating to production of materials | Index of instability of growth | Series relating to processes of fabrication | Index of instability of growth |
|---|---|---|---|
| Lead | 2.7 | Flour, wheat | 1.7 |
| Natural gas | 2.7 | Tobacco and snuff | 2.6 |
| Wool | 3.4 | Fermented liquors | 3.1 |
| Silver | 3.6 | Cigars | 3.6 |
| Swine, total slaughter | 4.0 | Sugar, total supply | 3.8 |
| Bituminous coal | 4.4 | Lead, available for consumption | 4.5 |
| Egg receipts | 4.7 | Lime | 4.7 |
| Copper | 4.8 | Cotton, mill consumption | 5.4 |
| Gold | 4.8 | Sheep receipts | 5.8 |
| Sugar | 5.0 | Zinc consumption | 6.0 |
| Zinc | 5.4 | Distilled spirits | 6.0 |
| Cattle, total slaughter | 5.4 | Gold (mfr. and arts) | 6.1 |
| Sheep, total slaughter | 6.6 | Cattle receipts | 6.4 |
| Petroleum, crude | 6.6 | Silver (mfr. and arts) | 6.4 |
| Hay | 7.5 | Hog receipts | 6.4 |
| Wheat | 7.7 | Common brick sold | 7.5 |
| Barley | 7.9 | Wool consumption | 8.2 |
| Anthracite coal | 8.0 | Cottonseed consumption | 8.9 |
| Cottonseed | 9.3 | Silk imports, raw | 9.0 |
| Cement, total | 9.3 | Cement, total | 9.3 |
| Corn | 9.4 | Cigarettes | 9.4 |
| Cotton | 9.5 | Coke, total | 10.2 |
| Potatoes | 11.4 | Pig iron | 10.2 |
| Iron ore | 11.5 | Copper consumption | 10.5 |
| Oats | 11.7 | Steel | 10.8 |
| Tobacco | 12.9 | Zinc and lead pigments | 10.9 |
| Flaxseed | 13.6 | Steel rails | 12.4 |
| Apples | 22.2 | Motor vehicles | 12.6 |
| | | Vessels built | 16.5 |
| | | Passenger cars, railroad | 22.4 |
| | | Freight cars | 33.6 |

The index of instability for cement is somewhat greater than it would be if the line of average growth defined the secular movement more accurately.

Yearly variations in the growth of aggregate production averaged 3.7 per cent of normal output. Fluctuations among the 58 constituent elements of the total averaged 8.2 per cent a year. These departures from constant rates of growth appear to have been about the same among manufacturing and among extractive industries, considered individually, though the aggregate output of manufactured goods was somewhat less stable than the aggregate output of raw materials.

## Physical Output of Products of American Farms and of All Other Products

In any general survey of productive processes particular interest attaches to the distinction between products of cultivation and other products. The latter are, in considerable part, products of exploitation, materials definitely withdrawn from the natural resources of the earth. There can be, of course, predatory exploitation of the soil, precisely similar in results to the depletion of mineral resources or the destruction of forests. Under modern conditions in this country, however, farm crops and animal products probably represent no such depletion of the soil, and the distinction between cultivated and non-cultivated products is a significant one. The measurements given in Table 3 relate to this classification. They are plotted in Figure 4.

The growth of production in the years preceding the World War was attributable in large degree to the development of our mineral resources and to the increasing volume of fabricated goods into which raw mineral products enter. There was a steady increase in the volume of agricultural production, at a rate about equal to that at which population increased, but the greatest advance occurred in the output of non-cultivated products. With regard both to the character of the resources and the nature of the wants to be satisfied, rapid expansion in the output of agricultural products is probably not to be expected. The rapid exploitation and utilization of mineral resources, on the other hand, gives to the present age its distinctive industrial tone.

There is a notable difference between these groups in respect to degree of divergence of the rates of change of the constituent elements. Among American farm products, raw and processed, the standard deviation of the rates of change (weighted) is 1.5; for

## TABLE 3

PRODUCTS OF AMERICAN FARMS AND ALL OTHER PRODUCTS [a]

Index Numbers of Physical Volume of Production in the United States, 1901-1913

| Year | Products of American farms (raw and processed) | All other products (raw and processed) |
|---|---|---|
| 1901 | 100 | 100 |
| 1902 | 118 | 115 |
| 1903 | 114 | 116 |
| 1904 | 121 | 111 |
| 1905 | 125 | 134 |
| 1906 | 132 | 145 |
| 1907 | 124 | 149 |
| 1908 | 128 | 121 |
| 1909 | 130 | 143 |
| 1910 | 133 | 155 |
| 1911 | 131 | 149 |
| 1912 | 146 | 173 |
| 1913 | 136 | 184 |
| Average annual rate of change (per cent) | +2.1 | +4.3 |
| Index of instability of growth | 3.4 | 6.1 |

[a] The individual series included in these two commodity groups are given in Appendix I.

products not originating on American farms it is 6.7. Although products of cultivation differ somewhat among themselves in their rates of change, they constitute a quite uniform group in comparison with commodities not originating on American farms. Agricultural products meet certain basic needs for food and clothing, and here there is not the room for variety and rapid expansion of wants that exists for non-agricultural products.

Irregularity of growth in the aggregate volume of production of American farm products and of non-farm products is measured by indexes of instability of growth of 3.4 and 6.1, respectively. The aggregate output of non-farm products is distinctly more variable than is that of farm products. When measurements relating to the individual series in two groups are combined, we obtain 7.7 as the average index of instability of growth for 30 series relating to the output of farm products, raw and processed, and 9.8 as the average for 31 series relating to products other than those of

## FIGURE 4
### GROWTH OF PHYSICAL VOLUME OF PRODUCTION IN THE UNITED STATES, 1901-1913
#### PRODUCTS OF AMERICAN FARMS AND ALL OTHER PRODUCTS

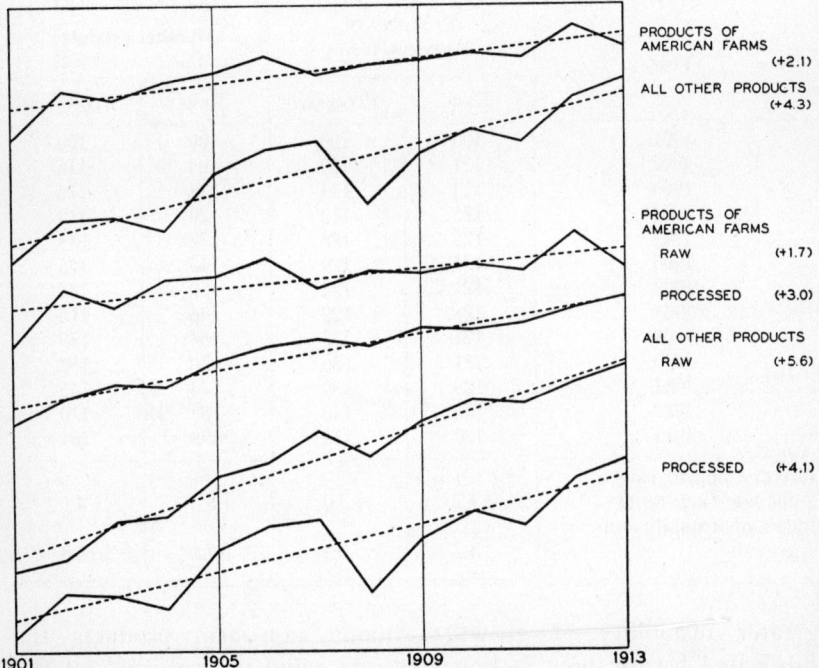

Plotted on ratio scale. The figures in parentheses define average annual rates of change (in percentage form).

American farms.[1] These figures confirm the result secured in the comparison of aggregates, though the difference is less pronounced.

Subdividing products of American farms and all other products into raw and processed forms, we have the measurements in Table 4, which are shown graphically in Figure 4.

These figures indicate that the output of manufactured farm products increased at a higher rate over this period than did the output of raw farm products. The latter were marked by much

[1] Two series relating to manufacturing production (wool consumption and sugar, total supply) have been included in the averages for both commodity groups. The weight in each case has been divided on the basis of the relative importance of imports and domestic production in the supply of raw materials utilized in the manufacturing process.

## TABLE 4

Products of American Farms and All Other Products, Raw and Processed
Index Numbers of Physical Volume of Production in the United States, 1901-1913

| (1) Year | (2) (3) Products of American farms | | (4) (5) All other products | |
|---|---|---|---|---|
| | Raw | Processed | Raw | Processed |
| 1901 | 100 | 100 | 100 | 100 |
| 1902 | 121 | 109 | 104 | 116 |
| 1903 | 114 | 114 | 118 | 115 |
| 1904 | 125 | 113 | 120 | 110 |
| 1905 | 126 | 123 | 137 | 134 |
| 1906 | 134 | 129 | 143 | 145 |
| 1907 | 121 | 132 | 159 | 148 |
| 1908 | 128 | 129 | 146 | 116 |
| 1909 | 127 | 137 | 164 | 139 |
| 1910 | 131 | 136 | 176 | 152 |
| 1911 | 128 | 139 | 174 | 145 |
| 1912 | 146 | 146 | 187 | 170 |
| 1913 | 130 | 152 | 198 | 181 |
| Average annual rate of change (per cent) | +1.7 | +3.0 | +5.6 | +4.1 |
| Index of instability of growth | 4.7 | 2.3 | 3.8 | 6.8 |

greater instability of growth. Among non-farm products the fabricated forms show a somewhat less rapid increase and, at the same time, a much higher degree of variability than do the raw materials.[1]

This general comparison reveals one of the most important features of the table just presented. The aggregate output of fabricated products not originating on American farms was distinctly less stable than the output of any other of the four groups shown. Raw farm products come next in order, well below the manufactured non-farm products, while raw non-farm and fabricated farm products stand at the bottom of the list. This evidence suggests that the irregularities in the growth of the productive stream are found in the initial stages of cultivation and in the final stages of the fabrication of non-farm products. (In this latter group, how-

---

[1] The importance among raw non-farm products of coal and natural gas, which advanced with but slight fluctuations over this period, helps to account for the relative stability of this group.

ever, are many quite stable series. Instability in the production of a few highly important commodities appears to be responsible for most of the variation in this class of goods.)

We must look in quite different directions for explanations of the variability here observed. Variability in the output of raw products of cultivation is doubtless attributable in considerable part to the vagaries of the weather. Fluctuations in the output of manufacturing industries working on non-agricultural materials are due, presumably, to changes in wants and in purchasing power, and to fluctuations of business. The weather at one end, the erratic processes of business at the other—these are suspect as contributing to economic instability.

## Production of Foods and of Non-foods

The fortunes of food producing and non-food producing industries during pre-war years may now be traced. The index numbers given in the next table are plotted in Figure 5.

### TABLE 5

Foods and Non-foods

Index Numbers of Physical Volume of Production in the United States, 1901-1913

| Year | Foods (raw and processed) | Non-foods (raw and processed) |
|---|---|---|
| 1901 | 100 | 100 |
| 1902 | 120 | 113 |
| 1903 | 114 | 116 |
| 1904 | 119 | 117 |
| 1905 | 125 | 132 |
| 1906 | 132 | 142 |
| 1907 | 123 | 144 |
| 1908 | 126 | 126 |
| 1909 | 130 | 140 |
| 1910 | 134 | 149 |
| 1911 | 128 | 146 |
| 1912 | 147 | 166 |
| 1913 | 132 | 175 |
| Average annual rate of change (per cent) | +1.9 | +3.9 |
| Index of instability of growth | 4.0 | 4.7 |

## FIGURE 5
### GROWTH OF PHYSICAL VOLUME OF PRODUCTION IN THE UNITED STATES, 1901-1913
#### FOODS AND NON-FOODS

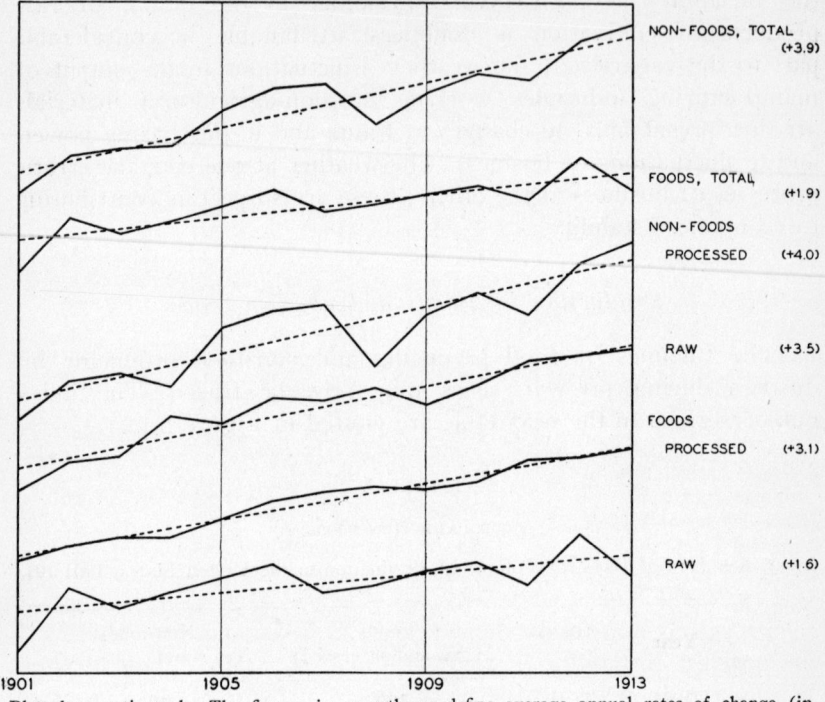

Plotted on ratio scale. The figures in parentheses define average annual rates of change (in percentage form).

The output of foods increased between 1901 and 1913 at a rate of 1.9 per cent a year, a figure approximately equal to the rate at which population grew. For non-foods the rate of growth averaged 3.9 per cent a year. Some such difference as this is to be expected. The expansibility of human wants for food is limited, once the standard of normal requirements is attained, but in the satisfaction of other wants and the building up of capital equipment there is no such necessary limit. In respect of instability, the index is slightly greater for the non-food than for the food products group.

Subdivision of each classification according to degree of fabrication gives the following index numbers.

## TABLE 6
### Foods and Non-foods, Raw and Processed
Index Numbers of Physical Volume of Production in the United States, 1901-1913

| (1) Year | (2) Foods Raw | (3) Foods Processed | (4) Non-foods Raw | (5) Non-foods Processed |
|---|---|---|---|---|
| 1901 | 100 | 100 | 100 | 100 |
| 1902 | 124 | 105 | 110 | 114 |
| 1903 | 116 | 108 | 112 | 117 |
| 1904 | 122 | 108 | 128 | 112 |
| 1905 | 128 | 115 | 125 | 136 |
| 1906 | 134 | 122 | 136 | 144 |
| 1907 | 122 | 126 | 135 | 147 |
| 1908 | 125 | 128 | 141 | 120 |
| 1909 | 131 | 127 | 133 | 142 |
| 1910 | 135 | 130 | 142 | 153 |
| 1911 | 125 | 140 | 154 | 142 |
| 1912 | 148 | 141 | 157 | 169 |
| 1913 | 129 | 145 | 160 | 181 |
| Average annual rate of change (per cent) | +1.6 | +3.1 | +3.5 | +4.0 |
| Index of instability of growth | 5.1 | 1.6 | 3.4 | 6.3 |

Processed non-foods show the greatest advance in output and the greatest instability of growth found in any of these groups. Within the food group the high rate of growth of the output of manufactured foodstuffs, as contrasted with that of unprocessed foods, is notable. Particularly striking is the high degree of instability in the production of raw foodstuffs and the marked stability of the finished products.[1]

[1] These measurements are substantiated by the averages (weighted) of the indexes of instability for the individual series. In two cases the same series is included in two different groups. The classification of the 58 independent series is given in Appendix I.

| Group | Number of series | Average of indexes of instability, individual series | Group | Number of series | Average of indexes of instability, individual series |
|---|---|---|---|---|---|
| Foods | | | Non-foods | | |
| Raw | 14 | 8.8 | Raw | 15 | 7.3 |
| Processed | 11 | 4.4 | Processed | 20 | 9.5 |
| Total | 25 | 7.8 | Total | 35 | 8.9 |

## Production of Consumption Goods and of Capital Equipment

Significant from another point of view is the distinction between articles intended for direct human consumption (and use) and articles destined for use as capital equipment.[1] During the period of fairly rapid economic advance which fell between the beginning of the century and the outbreak of the war, was the emphasis in production placed on the output of goods for direct consumption, such as food, clothing, passenger automobiles, or on the swelling of our supply of machines, tools and implements intended for use in further production? The following measurements, which are shown graphically in Figure 6, throw light on this question.

It should be understood that the index numbers of capital equipment (and also of consumption goods) refer to annual production, not to the total existing stock. If we could measure changes in the total stock of capital equipment in the country the picture would be quite different. But data for such a series of index numbers are not available. What we do measure are annual increments to the existing stock, increments which include replacements as well as net additions to that stock. Such index numbers are properly comparable with measurements of changes in the annual output of goods intended for human consumption.

We can not define with precision the proportion of the total annual production consisting of goods intended for use as capital equipment. If we restrict ourselves to physical, movable goods (i.e., excluding services, and all products of the construction industries) we may estimate that approximately 20 per cent of the total production of the year 1909, by value, consisted of goods intended for use as capital equipment, while 80 per cent consisted of goods intended for human consumption. These rough figures,

[1] This classification differs, of course, from one which would distinguish consumers' goods and producers' goods. Among articles of human consumption and use there are here included raw and semi-finished goods which will ultimately become consumers' goods proper. Capital equipment includes only those articles, raw and processed, which are intended for ultimate use as instruments of production. In general the classification has been based upon the chief use made of the product, although in some instances it has been necessary to include the same series in both groups, apportioning the weight in accordance with the use made of the commodity represented. This method fails to take into account relative changes in the use made of the products in question, but in the absence of adequate data it is the only procedure available. The actual classification of the series used in the preliminary annual index numbers is indicated in Appendix I.

## TABLE 7
### ARTICLES OF HUMAN CONSUMPTION AND ARTICLES ENTERING INTO CAPITAL EQUIPMENT
Index Numbers of Physical Volume of Production in the United States, 1901-1913

| Year | Goods destined for human consumption (raw and processed) | Goods destined for capital equipment (raw and processed) |
| --- | --- | --- |
| 1901 | 100 | 100 |
| 1902 | 116 | 115 |
| 1903 | 115 | 114 |
| 1904 | 120 | 106 |
| 1905 | 126 | 140 |
| 1906 | 132 | 158 |
| 1907 | 128 | 162 |
| 1908 | 128 | 117 |
| 1909 | 134 | 145 |
| 1910 | 137 | 167 |
| 1911 | 136 | 155 |
| 1912 | 150 | 189 |
| 1913 | 146 | 197 |
| Average annual rate of change (per cent) | +2.6 | +5.0 |
| Index of instability of growth | 2.8 | 8.8 |

based on the value of raw materials produced, and on 'value added', indicate the relative importance of the two categories under review.

The output of articles of human consumption increased between 1901 and 1913 at a rate of 2.6 per cent a year, a rate comfortably in excess of the rate of growth of population (2.0 per cent a year). The margin of approximately 0.6 per cent a year represents the increase in volume of consumption goods available, per capita of the population, for raising the standard of living. (Changes in the character of imports and exports are not here considered, since their effect on the figure cited would be negligible.) The growth of production of this type was relatively stable, fluctuations averaging but 2.8 per cent a year.

The output of additions to the total supply of capital equipment increased by 5.0 per cent a year.[1] The much more rapid rate of

[1] There are very definite indications that the rate of obsolescence of machine equipment is increasing from year to year. This tends to increase the gross figures for additions to capital goods. Figures for physical production that add, to the production of consumption goods, the *tools* consumed in such production may tend to be deceptive.—M. C. Rorty.

### FIGURE 6
#### GROWTH OF PHYSICAL VOLUME OF PRODUCTION IN THE UNITED STATES, 1901-1913
##### ARTICLES OF HUMAN CONSUMPTION AND ARTICLES ENTERING INTO CAPITAL EQUIPMENT

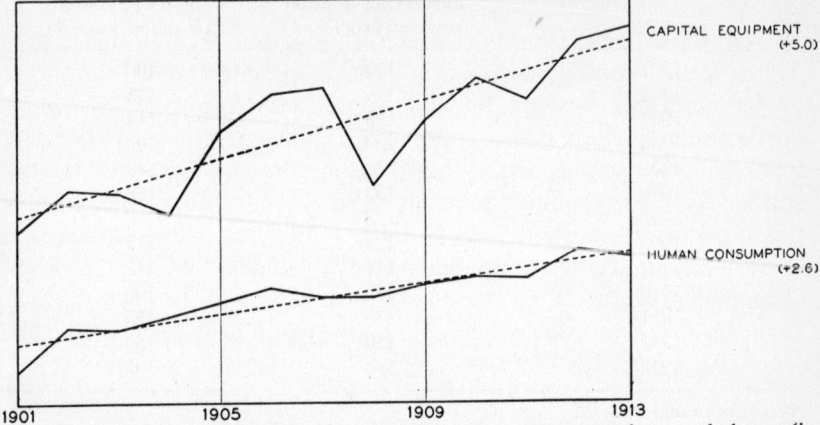

Plotted on ratio scale. The figures in parentheses define average annual rates of change (in percentage form).

advance of this series indicates that the proportion of our annually available productive resources which was devoted to the output of articles of capital equipment was increasing during this period. Per capita of the population, the annual increments to the country's stock of capital equipment (including replacements) were increasing at a rate close to 3.0 per cent a year. Current well-being, as affected by the output of consumption goods, was being steadily enhanced during this period. More rapid, however, was the flow of new goods (and replacements) into the fund of capital. The margin between the two rates of advance is wide. Lacking figures for other times and other places we cannot say whether this margin represents an abnormally rapid rate of accumulation of capital equipment. As a standard of reference the figure will be useful in later chapters, in appraising the post-war record.

The growth in the output of capital equipment during this period was not steady. The advance recorded occurred as a result of three remarkable spurts, one beginning in 1904 and culminating in 1907, one beginning in 1908 and culminating in 1910, the third extending from 1911 to 1913. This irregularity of growth is evidenced by an index of instability of 8.8 per cent, a figure notably higher than the corresponding measure of 2.8 for consumption goods. Wide variations in the output of capital goods are, of course, a customary feature of cycles in industrial activity.

## Production of Non-durable, Semi-durable and Durable Goods

An economic system in which the output of durable goods bulked large would possess characteristics quite different from those of an economic system devoted to the production of perishable goods for immediate consumption. The output of goods of the latter type must always be a major economic concern, but with the increased use of capital equipment and the growing diversity of consumer wants durable goods increase in relative importance, and corresponding changes take place in the behavior of the economic system as a whole. If we divide all movable goods into non-durable, semi-durable [1] and durable goods, as in Table 8, we may trace cer-

TABLE 8

Non-durable, Semi-durable and Durable Goods

Index Numbers of Physical Volume of Production in the United States, 1901-1913

| Year | Non-durable goods (raw and processed) | Semi-durable goods (raw and processed) | Durable goods (raw and processed) |
|---|---|---|---|
| 1901 | 100 | 100 | 100 |
| 1902 | 116 | 116 | 115 |
| 1903 | 114 | 117 | 114 |
| 1904 | 118 | 127 | 109 |
| 1905 | 126 | 127 | 134 |
| 1906 | 131 | 136 | 152 |
| 1907 | 128 | 129 | 154 |
| 1908 | 129 | 129 | 114 |
| 1909 | 134 | 132 | 141 |
| 1910 | 138 | 134 | 158 |
| 1911 | 134 | 146 | 145 |
| 1912 | 151 | 147 | 181 |
| 1913 | 141 | 154 | 191 |
| Average annual rate of change (per cent) | +2.5 | +2.6 | +4.6 |
| Index of instability of growth | 3.0 | 3.4 | 8.1 |

[1] Semi-durable goods include, for the most part, textile and leather products.

tain changes in the direction in which productive energies were being expended during the years preceding the war.

These index numbers are plotted in Figure 7.

### FIGURE 7
### GROWTH OF PHYSICAL VOLUME OF PRODUCTION IN THE UNITED STATES, 1901-1913
#### DURABLE, SEMI-DURABLE AND NON-DURABLE GOODS

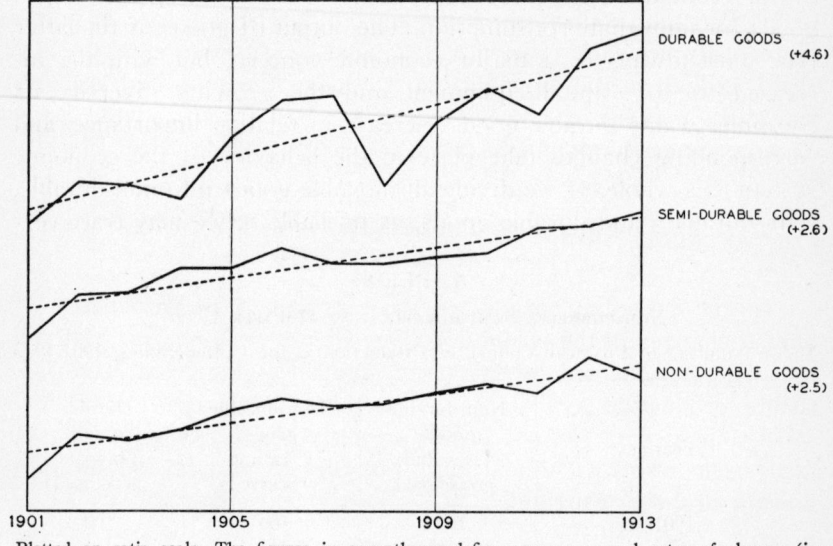

Plotted on ratio scale. The figures in parentheses define average annual rates of change (in percentage form).

Non-durable goods (which in 1909 made up approximately 55 per cent, by value, of all movable goods produced in the United States) increased in volume of output between 1901 and 1913 at a rate of 2.5 per cent a year. The growth was regular, even the years of recession bringing only minor checks to the steady advance. Slightly more rapid and slightly less regular was the increase in output of semi-durable goods. Most rapid and most erratic was the gain in the volume of production of durable goods. Over the thirteen-year period the annual output of such goods increased 91 per cent, at an average annual rate of 4.6 per cent.

It is a leading attribute of durable goods, whether intended for capital equipment or for consumption, that demand for new supplies is subject to rapid expansion and sharp curtailment. These constitute the highly variable elements in the aggregate annual production of economic goods. Perishable goods, which are consumed as purchased, are subject to no such sharp fluctuations in demand. Users of durable goods are able to withdraw from the market if business prospects darken, or if incomes decline, to a degree not possible in the case of goods which are consumed over a short period of time. For this reason exceptionally rapid exploitation of the markets for durable goods might be expected to pave the way for exceptionally severe declines. The sharp drop from 1907 to 1908 in the production of goods of this type is a case in point. Here again we lack criteria as to what constitutes 'exceptionally rapid' growth in the output of such goods. The record of the pre-war years may serve, however, as a standard for use in the study of more recent developments.

## Physical Output and Productivity of Manufacturing Industries, 1899-1914

In the preceding pages we have presented measurements of annual changes in the physical volume of production. This material may be supplemented by the more detailed statistics of manufacturing production available for the years 1899, 1904, 1909 and 1914. These data do not cover precisely the period selected for analysis in terms of annual data, but the census statistics are significant in their own right.[1]

### Growth of Manufacturing Production and Number of Wage-earners Employed

Changes in physical volume of manufacturing production, and in certain related elements, are defined by the index numbers in

[1] In the interpretation of census data we should recall that the year 1899 was one of marked prosperity in the United States, with a particularly pronounced boom in the iron and steel trades. In 1914 a general state of depression prevailed. The existence of these conditions during the terminal years would tend to dampen apparent rates of growth, and to accelerate apparent rates of decline, in industries materially affected by cyclical fluctuations of business.

The index numbers of manufacturing production and of productivity employed in this section differ somewhat from index numbers constructed from census data by other investigators. This is due, in part, to differences in methods of construction, in part, to differences in the industries represented. A detailed explanation of procedure is given in Chapter III, which deals with the general problem of deriving index numbers of production, prices and costs from census data.

the following table.[1] These measurements are shown graphically in Figure 8.

### TABLE 9
Growth of Manufacturing Production in the United States, 1899-1914
Index Numbers of Physical Volume of Production, Number of Wage-earners and per Capita Output [a]

| Year | Physical volume of production | Number of wage-earners | Output per wage-earner |
|---|---|---|---|
| 1899 | 100.0 | 100.0 | 100.0 |
| 1904 | 120.2 | 108.1 | 111.2 |
| 1909 | 154.5 | 130.0 | 118.9 |
| 1914 | 176.3 | 136.1 | 129.6 |
| Average annual rate of change [b] (per cent) | +3.9 | +2.2 | +1.7 |

[a] These index numbers are based upon direct data of physical production. Modifications designed to correct for the omission of output not measured in physical units are made at a later point.

In the derivation of these index numbers a variation of the 'ideal' formula was employed. The form used is

$$I_q = \sqrt{\frac{\Sigma \frac{q_1}{q_0} w_0}{\Sigma w_0} \cdot \frac{\Sigma w_1}{\Sigma \frac{q_0}{q_1} w_1}}$$

where
$q_0$ = quantity produced in base year
$q_1$ = quantity produced in given year
$w_0$ = weight in base year
$w_1$ = weight in given year

As is explained more fully in Chapter III, the weights used depend on the purpose to which the index is to be put. Value of product, 'value added', cost of materials, or another value may provide appropriate weights for a particular purpose. In the above table, 'value added' has been used. (For a full discussion of the 'ideal' formula see Irving Fisher, *The Making of Index Numbers*, Houghton Mifflin Co., Boston, 1927.)

In constructing index numbers for the pre-war period, 1914 has been employed as the base year in all calculations. For convenience of presentation the base has been shifted to 1899 in the exposition of results.

[b] The average rate of growth over the three quinquennial census periods, reduced to an annual basis. Because of the greater length of the period covered, differences in general business conditions in the four census years and the character of some of the omitted years, comparison of these rates of change with those based upon annual data must be made with care.

[1] The industries represented by these index numbers do not include all those covered in the Census of Manufactures, for data relating to physical output are not available in all cases. The proportion of the total value of product of all manufacturing industries included in this sample at different dates is shown below:

| Year | Percentage of total value of manufactures included in index |
|---|---|
| 1899 | 40.9 |
| 1904 | 38.9 |
| 1909 | 38.1 |
| 1914 | 39.2 |

In general, in the construction of these index numbers, weights are based upon 'value added' in the particular industries included. Imputed weights (i.e., weights

## FIGURE 8
### GROWTH OF MANUFACTURING PRODUCTION IN THE UNITED STATES, 1899-1914
PRODUCTION, NUMBER OF WAGE-EARNERS AND OUTPUT PER WAGE-EARNER

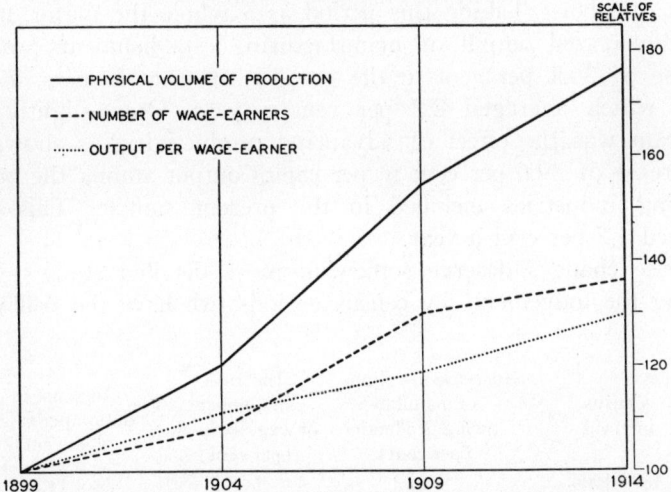

During this fifteen-year period there was an increase of 76.3 per cent in the physical volume of production of manufacturing

---

derived from larger industrial groups which the industries actually included are supposed to represent) have not been employed. For three of the industries included (industries producing motor vehicles, lumber products at the sawmill stage, and petroleum products) weights have been reduced, in order that they might not exercise excessive influence upon the results. These industries have been given the weights they would have if the sample included all census industries.

There is two-fold justification for this. Each of these three industries is in many respects distinctive, subject to special influences which did not affect manufacturing industries in general. Total and per capita output increased far more rapidly between 1899 and 1914 in the automotive and petroleum refining industries than in manufacturing industries in general, while the reverse was true of the lumber and timber industry. These industries should not, therefore, be over-weighted in index numbers of output and of productivity. Yet over-weighting results from the use of weights based upon actual values added in these industries, for practically all their products are included among the commodities for which statistics of quantities produced are available. There is almost complete coverage for automotive products, for example, whereas the textile products included represent only a portion of all textile products. In view of the rather exceptional character of the changes occurring in these three industries and the high degree of coverage of the quantity statistics available for them, it has seemed proper to reduce their weights to approximately the proportion that would prevail if there were complete coverage of all industrial groups.

plants. The average annual rate of increase was 3.9 per cent. We may view this increase as the resultant of two factors—number of wage-earners employed and the combination of elements (human, mechanical, organizational) which affect the per capita output of labor.[1] Taking this period as a whole the major factor in the increased output of manufacturing establishments was an increase of 36.1 per cent in the number of wage-earners, an increase which averaged 2.2 per cent a year. Only slightly less important was the effect of advancing productivity, as shown by an increase of 29.6 per cent in per capita output among the manufacturing industries included in the present sample. This gain averaged 1.7 per cent a year.

These changes deserve somewhat more detailed study. Considering the movements by census periods, we have the following record:

| Census interval | Increase in volume of manufacturing production (per cent) | Increase in number of wage-earners (per cent) | Increase in output per capita (per cent) |
| --- | --- | --- | --- |
| 1899-1904 | +20.2 | + 8.1 | +11.2 |
| 1904-1909 | +28.5 | +20.2 | + 6.9 |
| 1909-1914 | +14.1 | + 4.7 | + 9.0 |

The first of these intervals bridges a gap between a year of prosperity and a year marked by a minor business depression. Yet the increase in volume of production was substantial. Among the industries here included the gain in output per wage-earner slightly exceeded the increase in number of wage-earners. The next five-year period opens in a year of slight depression and ends in a year of mild prosperity. The increase in physical volume of production amounted to no less than 28.5 per cent. By far the most important factor in this advance was an increase of 20.2 per cent in number

[1] In interpreting the index of per capita output it is to be borne in mind that index numbers of per capita output do not measure changes in the specific productivity of labor. Per capita productivity may increase because of improvements in equipment or in industrial organization, increased skill on the part of personnel or enhanced productive capacity due to changes in any of the factors of production. Indexes of per capita productivity may be accepted as measures of changes in the productive efficiency of industrial organizations viewed as functioning units, but not as measures of the net contribution of any one factor to these changes.

The index of per capita output here employed is based upon the number of wage-earners in manufacturing plants. No account is taken of salaried workers, nor of changes in hours of employment of wage-earners.

of wage-earners employed. This was a period of unrestricted immigration, and reviving industry called upon an elastic labor market for the instruments of expansion. Output per capita increased 6.9 per cent between 1904 and 1909.

During the next period there was another shift in the relative position of these two factors. In spite of the fact that 1914 was a year of depression, the volume of production exceeded that of 1909 by 14.1 per cent. The chief factor in this advance was an increase of 9.0 per cent in output per worker employed. (This increase reflected, in part, the increasing importance of certain industries in which production per capita was relatively large, and was expanding.) Number of workers increased by but 4.7 per cent between 1909 and 1914.

Among the 35 industries represented by these index numbers the main factor in the increase of production between 1899 and 1914 was an expanding working force. The survey by periods shows, however, that the only notable gain in number of workers occurred during the expansion from 1904 to 1909. From 1899 to 1904 and from 1909 to 1914 the main agencies of increased production were those elements of skill, mechanism and management which affect per capita output. Twice thereafter, during the exigencies of the war years and in the sharp recovery from 1921 to 1923, the chief factor in expanding production was a rapidly swelling labor force, but after 1923, as we shall see, there was again a remarkable shift from the worker to mechanical and organizational factors as the readiest instruments of expanding production.

§ *Changes in physical volume of production and in output per wage-earner, individual industries.*—When individual observations differ widely, the representative value of an average is seriously impaired. This is particularly true in the present case. Difficulties due to pronounced variation among industries are enhanced by perplexing problems of weighting. There is no clear justification for an elaborate system of imputed weights, for we can not assume that changes in production, productivity, prices and costs in the various individual industries included in the sample paralleled those occurring among selected excluded industries. Nor may we assume that weights based on the relative importance of the included industries will yield results representative of all manufacturing industries. Some industries fully represented in the sample would by this procedure be obviously over-weighted, as regards manufacturing industries in general. The method of weighting actually employed is a compromise, being of the second type (i.e., with weights based on the relative importance of individual industries among

## TABLE 10
CHANGES IN PHYSICAL VOLUME OF MANUFACTURING PRODUCTION IN THE UNITED STATES, 1899-1914

Index Numbers for 35 Industries, with Average Annual Rates of Change

| Industry | Index numbers of physical volume of production | | | | Average annual rate of change 1899-1914 (per cent) |
|---|---|---|---|---|---|
| | 1899 | 1904 | 1909 | 1914 | |
| Automobiles, including bodies and parts | 100.0 | 609.7 | 3758.1 | 16129.0 | +36.8 |
| Sugar, beet | 100.0 | 309.9 | 621.5 | 934.6 | +13.6 |
| Ice, manufactured | 100.0 | 171.8 | 306.7 | 450.9 | +10.4 |
| Gas, manufactured, illuminating and heating | 100.0 | 174.1 | 250.5 | 349.9 | + 8.2 |
| Petroleum, refining | 100.0 | 123.5 | 188.6 | 296.5 | + 8.0 |
| Fertilizers | 100.0 | 131.0 | 199.1 | 296.4 | + 7.8 |
| Explosives | 100.0 | 190.6 | 302.5 | 337.4 | + 7.6 |
| Salt | 100.0 | 112.3 | 198.9 | 228.3 | + 6.2 |
| Canning and preserving: fruits and vegetables; pickles, preserves, and sauces | 100.0 | 138.6 | 163.9 | 239.2 | + 5.8 |
| Paper and wood pulp | 100.0 | 147.3 | 186.3 | 230.8 | + 5.4 |
| Silk goods | 100.0 | 135.5 | 184.1 | 219.6 | + 5.3 |
| Hosiery and knit goods | 100.0 | 131.9 | 182.3 | 215.3 | + 5.3 |
| Coke, not including gas-house coke | 100.0 | 129.8 | 213.7 | 205.3 | + 5.1 |
| Rice, cleaning and polishing | 100.0 | 255.2 | 257.2 | 273.1 | + 4.9 |
| Butter, cheese, and condensed milk | 100.0 | 121.6 | 147.9 | 199.2 | + 4.7 |
| Paint and varnish | 100.0 | 124.6 | 175.1 | 187.3 | + 4.4 |
| Iron and steel: steel works and rolling mills | 100.0 | 122.8 | 181.2 | 178.6 | + 4.2 |
| Wood distillation, not including turpentine and rosin | 100.0 | 139.2 | 175.2 | 180.5 | + 3.8 |
| Iron and steel: blast furnaces | 100.0 | 116.3 | 178.9 | 163.3 | + 3.7 |
| Musical instruments: pianos | 100.0 | 132.4 | 184.7 | 166.8 | + 3.6 |
| Cotton goods | 100.0 | 112.4 | 140.2 | 153.9 | + 3.1 |
| Woolen and worsted goods | 100.0 | 118.6 | 146.6 | 145.4 | + 2.6 |
| Slaughtering and meat packing | 100.0 | 113.1 | 127.8 | 127.1 | + 1.7 |
| Carpets and rugs, other than rag | 100.0 | 114.0 | 132.8 | 121.3 | + 1.4 |
| Hats, fur-felt | 100.0 | 131.9 | 158.2 | 113.9 | + 1.1 |
| Flour-mill and gristmill products | 100.0 | 103.8 | 109.0 | 114.1 | + 0.9 |
| Gloves and mittens, leather | 100.0 | 114.1 | 115.7 | 107.2 | + 0.4 |
| Lumber and timber products | 100.0 | 91.1 | 98.2 | 102.2 | + 0.3 |
| Musical instruments: organs | 100.0 | 103.9 | 81.4 | 111.5 | + 0.2 |
| Motorcycles, bicycles, and parts | 100.0 | 21.4 | 47.8 | 92.6 | + 0.1 |
| Turpentine and rosin | 100.0 | 80.5 | 75.9 | 69.2 | − 2.4 |
| Hats, wool-felt | 100.0 | 51.3 | 75.4 | 45.5 | − 4.1 |
| Boots and shoes, other than rubber | 100.0 | 110.4 | — | 131.4 | — |
| Cordage and twine | 100.0 | — | 121.8 | 144.4 | — |
| Jute and linen goods | 100.0 | — | 159.5 | 187.5 | — |
| Average [a] | 100.0 | 118.5 | 164.3 | 165.6 | + 3.6 |

[a] An arithmetic average of the central items of a weighted frequency distribution, with weights based on 'value added', averaged for the base year and the given year. The central one-fifth of the items, by weight, were included in computing the average.

those actually included in the sample) but with reduced weights for three large industries which would otherwise dominate the sample.

In the face of these differences and complexities no set of averages may be taken to measure with precision changes occurring in manufac-

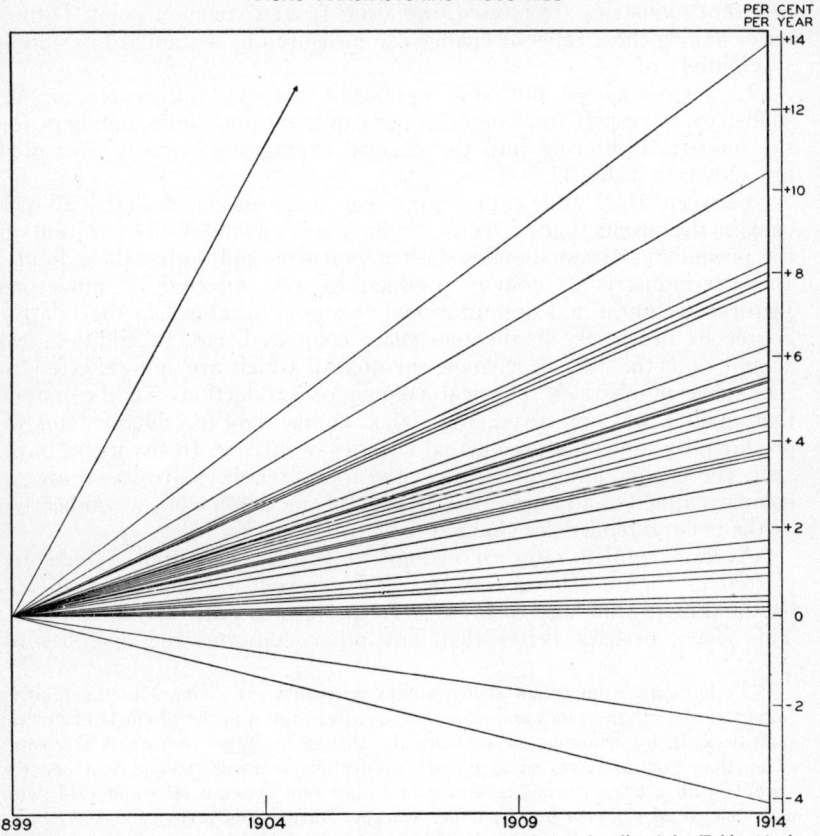

FIGURE 9

GROWTH OF MANUFACTURING PRODUCTION
IN THE UNITED STATES, 1899-1914*

ILLUSTRATING THE DIVERGENCE OF PRODUCTION TRENDS
AMONG MANUFACTURING INDUSTRIES

* Plotted on ratio scale. The lines here plotted relate to the industries listed in Table 10, in the order of that listing.

turing industries at large. For a more accurate though less simple picture it is well to go beyond the averages to the records of individual industries. Index numbers measuring the changes in volume of production between 1899 and 1914 in 35 industries are given in Table 10. Their trends are graphically pictured in the above figure.

Averages such as those previously given lead us to think of manufacturing industries as a whole, reacting uniformly to certain general influences in respect of productivity, mass output, etc. The index numbers for separate industries show how divergent, in fact, are the fortunes of different manufacturing industries. Between 1899 and 1914 the production of wool-felt hats declined 55 per cent; over the same period the output of automobiles increased over 16,000 per cent. These are extreme cases, of course, but even when these are excluded the variations are of extraordinary amplitude. The divergence is vividly portrayed in Figure 9, in which the rates of change of production in the different industries are plotted, radiating from a common point. Differences among these rates of change are measured by a standard deviation (weighted) of 5.7.

Less pronounced but still significant are the differences among industries in respect to changes in per capita output. Index numbers for the industries entering into the general averages previously presented are shown in Table 11.

Between 1899 and 1914 output per wage-earner declined 23 per cent in the production of wool-felt hats and advanced 184 per cent in the production of automobiles. Other industries fall within these limits. In each industry, of course, productivity was affected by numerous factors—technical and organizational changes, variations in the relative degree of prosperity in the two years compared, etc. In addition, we should note the fact of changes in quality which are not reflected in the index numbers of physical volume of production. To the extent that quality was improved, the index numbers of production and of productivity understate the actual changes occurring. In the main, however, the commodities upon which the index numbers are based are of standard quality, and we may accept the measurements as indicative of the general tendencies characteristic of the period.[1]

Average annual rates of change in per capita output, which are plotted in Figure 10, vary from —1.5 per cent a year, for wool-felt hats and turpentine and rosin, to +7.8 per cent a year, for automobiles. This chart, perhaps better than any other, indicates the diversity of

[1] Perhaps more important than changes in quality are changes in the relative importance of cheap grades and of more expensive grades in the products of certain industries. If, for example, we measure the change in output of carpets and rugs, other than rag, in terms of aggregate production in yards, adding together the output of all grades, we find a decline of 16 per cent between 1899 and 1914, with a decline of 24 per cent in output per worker. During this period, however, there was a marked increase in the relative importance of high grade rugs in the total output, and a decline in the relative importance of cheap rugs. If the rugs of different grade be treated as separate commodities, and an index be constructed on this basis, we find an increase of 21 per cent in total output between 1899 and 1914, and a gain of 10 per cent in output per worker. The latter measurements are, of course, the proper ones to employ. Index numbers of this type have been constructed wherever possible in the present study, in place of indexes based upon aggregate quantities, summed without regard to differences of quality.

# TABLE 11
## Changes in Output per Wage-earner in Manufacturing Industries of the United States, 1899-1914
### Index Numbers for 35 Industries, with Average Annual Rates of Change

| Industry | Index numbers of physical volume of production per wage-earner | | | | Average annual rate of change 1899-1914 (per cent) |
|---|---|---|---|---|---|
| | 1899 | 1904 | 1909 | 1914 | |
| Automobiles, including bodies and parts | 100.0 | 113.2 | 111.0 | 283.8 | +7.8 |
| Motorcycles, bicycles, and parts | 100.0 | 112.9 | 188.9 | 243.0 | +6.7 |
| Explosives | 100.0 | 147.9 | 217.1 | 240.8 | +5.9 |
| Salt | 100.0 | 114.9 | 192.4 | 214.2 | +5.7 |
| Iron and steel: blast furnaces | 100.0 | 130.1 | 182.7 | 218.3 | +5.4 |
| Sugar, beet | 100.0 | 154.0 | 169.9 | 230.2 | +5.2 |
| Wood distillation, not including turpentine and rosin | 100.0 | 145.6 | 174.7 | 200.4 | +4.4 |
| Gas, manufactured, illuminating and heating | 100.0 | 127.9 | 151.2 | 179.5 | +3.9 |
| Canning and preserving: fruits and vegetables; pickles, preserves, and sauces | 100.0 | 126.9 | 145.4 | 168.9 | +3.4 |
| Petroleum, refining | 100.0 | 89.8 | 165.2 | 142.6 | +3.3 |
| Coke, not including gas-house coke | 100.0 | 116.3 | 124.1 | 165.3 | +3.3 |
| Fertilizers | 100.0 | 107.0 | 125.9 | 150.4 | +2.9 |
| Rice, cleaning and polishing | 100.0 | 111.3 | 135.2 | 141.9 | +2.5 |
| Iron and steel: steel works and rolling mills | 100.0 | 108.4 | 138.3 | 131.6 | +2.1 |
| Ice, manufactured | 100.0 | 117.0 | 131.0 | 134.8 | +2.0 |
| Silk goods | 100.0 | 111.4 | 121.6 | 132.8 | +1.9 |
| Gloves and mittens, leather | 100.0 | 153.7 | 146.2 | 144.1 | +1.9 |
| Paper and wood pulp | 100.0 | 110.9 | 121.7 | 129.5 | +1.7 |
| Musical instruments: organs | 100.0 | 98.5 | 117.3 | 125.1 | +1.7 |
| Musical instruments: pianos | 100.0 | 113.0 | 129.8 | 125.2 | +1.6 |
| Hosiery and knit goods | 100.0 | 106.1 | 118.0 | 119.7 | +1.3 |
| Cotton goods | 100.0 | 107.9 | 112.5 | 120.8 | +1.2 |
| Paint and varnish | 100.0 | 103.8 | 119.3 | 112.9 | +1.0 |
| Woolen and worsted goods | 100.0 | 105.2 | 113.1 | 115.4 | +1.0 |
| Carpets and rugs, other than rag | 100.0 | 97.5 | 113.3 | 110.1 | +0.9 |
| Butter, cheese, and condensed milk | 100.0 | 100.0 | 102.7 | 110.6 | +0.7 |
| Hats, fur-felt | 100.0 | 113.0 | 119.1 | 100.8 | +0.2 |
| Flour-mill and gristmill products | 100.0 | 85.5 | 89.1 | 92.6 | —0.4 |
| Slaughtering and meat packing | 100.0 | 104.3 | 99.6 | 88.0 | —0.8 |
| Lumber and timber products | 100.0 | 93.1 | 74.2 | 88.0 | —1.2 |
| Hats, wool-felt | 100.0 | 72.0 | 80.1 | 76.8 | —1.5 |
| Turpentine and rosin | 100.0 | 101.0 | 80.4 | 83.2 | —1.5 |
| Boots and shoes, other than rubber | 100.0 | 104.4 | — | 97.3 | — |
| Cordage and twine | 100.0 | — | 109.2 | 120.0 | — |
| Jute and linen goods | 100.0 | — | 121.3 | 126.4 | — |
| Average [a] | 100.0 | 107.4 | 117.7 | 119.9 | +1.3 |

[a] An arithmetic average of the central items of a weighted frequency distribution, with weights based on 'value added', averaged for the base year and the given year. The central one-fifth of the items, by weight, were included in computing the average.

## FIGURE 10
### GROWTH OF MANUFACTURING PRODUCTION IN THE UNITED STATES, 1899-1914*
ILLUSTRATING THE DIVERGENCE OF TRENDS IN PRODUCTION PER WAGE-EARNER IN MANUFACTURING INDUSTRIES

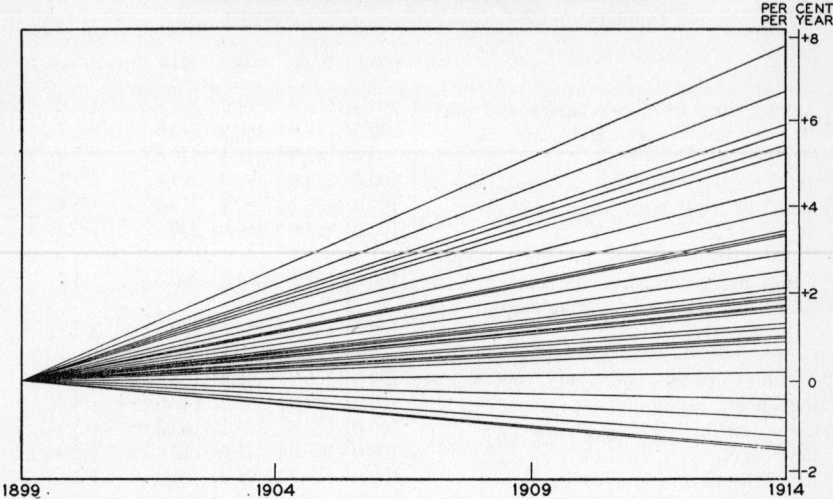

* Plotted on ratio scale. The lines here plotted relate to the industries listed in Table 11, in the order of that listing.

the factors affecting manufacturing industries, and the resulting divergence of tendencies. Here, as units in the same industrial structure, are industries in which output per worker had more than doubled in fifteen years, and industries in which output per worker had declined from 7 to 23 per cent. In making use of index numbers defining general tendencies amid this diversity of movement, we must do so with the clear recognition that any measure secured will be a statistical average, standing for values which, in fact, are marked by wide variation.

The degree of variation in the rates of change of index numbers of per capita output is defined by a standard deviation (weighted) of 2.0. This is materially smaller than the standard deviation of 5.7, which measures divergence of rates of change in volume of production.

The index numbers of physical volume of production and of output per wage-earner among manufacturing establishments given in Table 9 were derived by means of the 'ideal' formula, a procedure which has the virtue of insuring consistent results among index numbers of aggregate output, output per worker and number of workers. There are certain objections to its use when some industries are growing much more rapidly than others, both in output per capita and in aggregate output. It may be desirable to allow these rapidly growing industries to influence the averages, but for some purposes one may wish to follow the course of manufacturing industries in general, without allowing changes in a few industries to exert too strong an influence upon the index numbers which are taken to be representative. Tables 10 and 11 show the behavior of the constituent elements of the sample of manufacturing industries we have employed. These are the basic figures to which one must turn in securing a true conception of the tendencies prevailing in American industry. At the foot of each of these tables there appears a series of index numbers, secured by averaging the central one-fifth of the items in the sample, by weight. These averages have not the mathematical elegance of the 'ideal' index, but they are in some respects better representatives of typical conditions in manufacturing industries in the several census years. Exceptional changes occurring in outlying industries will not be reflected in these averages, which define the movements among the central items. These two sets of index numbers are brought together in the next table.

TABLE 12

Growth of Manufacturing Production in the United States, 1899-1914

Averages of Aggregate Production and of per Capita Output
(Derived from the central items of frequency distributions)

| Year | Physical volume of production | Output per wage-earner |
|---|---|---|
| 1899 | 100.0 | 100.0 |
| 1904 | 118.5 | 107.4 |
| 1909 | 164.3 | 117.7 |
| 1914 | 165.6 | 119.9 |
| Average annual rate of change (per cent) | +3.6 | +1.3 |

These measurements show smaller gains in aggregate output and in output per wage-earner than do the 'ideal' index numbers derived from the same data. The latter are materially affected by the rapidly growing industries in which the force of secular advance outweighs the cyclical recessions which are more apparent in the figures for industries at large. The present representative values show a greater gain in aggregate output between 1904 and 1909, a much smaller gain between 1909 and 1914. With respect to output per worker, the chief difference is found in the record for the period 1909-1914. Only a slight gain is indicated by the averages derived from central values in the frequency distribution, while a substantial advance is recorded by the 'ideal' index. This latter figure reflects the shouldering forward of the automotive industries, of petroleum refining, and of other new industries which were marked by relatively large increases in output per capita, and which were gaining rapidly in relative importance. Typical manufacturing industries, if we may so view those which lie close to the center of the general array, were not marked by such a rapid growth during this five-year period. But for the entire pre-war period a substantial advance in productivity, a total gain of 20 per cent and an annual increase of 1.3 per cent, is shown by the averages which reflect tendencies among representative American industries.

## Manufacturing Establishments and Volume of Manufacturing Production

Certain of the tendencies prevailing in manufacturing industries are revealed when the establishment is viewed as the unit of production.[1] The records in the following table define these movements.

TABLE 13

GROWTH OF MANUFACTURING PRODUCTION IN THE UNITED STATES, 1899-1914

Index Numbers of Physical Volume of Production, Number of Establishments and Output per Establishment

| Year | Physical volume of production | Number of establishments | Output per establishment |
|---|---|---|---|
| 1899 | 100.0 | 100.0 | 100.0 |
| 1904 | 120.2 | 98.1 | 122.6 |
| 1909 | 154.5 | 118.4 | 130.5 |
| 1914 | 176.3 | 113.0 | 156.0 |
| Average annual rate of change (per cent) | +3.9 | +1.1 [a] | +2.8 |

[a] Measurements of average annual rates of change are based upon data for intermediate as well as for terminal years. In this case, the low value for 1904 and the high value for 1909 serve to give the measurement of average growth a higher value than it would have if data for terminal years alone were employed.

[1] The Bureau of the Census publishes the following explanation of its use of the term 'establishment'.

"As a rule the term 'establishment' signifies a single plant or factory. In some cases, however, it refers to two or more plants operated under a common ownership

Between 1899 and 1914 there was a net increase of but 13.0 per cent in the number of manufacturing establishments in the 35 industries included in the sample. The physical volume of manufacturing production was increased primarily by greater output per establishment. But here again the story is one of uneven and irregular growth, with the factors varying in importance from period to period.

During the first of the five-year periods covered by the table there occurred a moderate increase in volume of production, accompanied by a decline of some 2 per cent in number of establishments, and by an advance of 23 per cent in output per establishment. The first of these years (1899) was relatively prosperous, the last (1904) slightly depressed. The change between 1909 and 1914, which also marks a transition from prosperity to recession, was marked by a similar, but greater, decline in number of establishments and by another pronounced increase in production per establishment. Production was maintained, and increased, during these periods by a greater flow of goods from individual plants, though the number of plants actually declined under the competitive stresses of liquidation and depression. In sharp contrast is the story of the change from 1904 to 1909, an advance from depression to a state of relative prosperity. During this period (more exactly, between the terminal years of this period) output per establishment advanced but 6 per cent. The chief factor in the substantial increase in physical volume of production was an advance of over 20 per cent in the number of establishments in operation.[1]

---

and located in the same city, or in the same State, but in different municipalities or unincorporated places having fewer than 10,000 inhabitants. On the other hand, separate reports are occasionally obtained for different industries carried on in the same plant, in which event a single plant is counted as two or more establishments." *Biennial Census of Manufactures, 1927,* U. S. Department of Commerce, Washington, 1930, p. 7.

Essentially the same definition of the term has appeared in all reports of the Census Bureau. The establishment is not as clearly defined a unit as is a wage-earner. Variations in the interpretation of the term and variations between census dates in the accounting records of given enterprises would tend to cloud the statistics of number of establishments and of output per establishment. There is no reason to believe, however, that such variations have been of sufficient magnitude materially to affect the general tendencies shown by the census statistics.

[1] It is probable that changes during specific census periods are not as accurately measured as are changes over longer periods. Manufacturing census compilations which were made in connection with the general decennial censuses (relating to production in 1899 and 1909) are somewhat broader in their coverage than are those made in intervening years (1904, 1914). The difference in coverage is not great enough materially to affect any of the derived measurements given in this

One more step may be taken in tracing the factors that affect production. The increase in production per establishment may be due to an increasing number of workers per establishment, or to increasing output per worker. The chief factor in enhancing output per worker has probably been improved material equipment. The present contrast, therefore, is primarily one between an increased number of workers and improved tools, equipment and working facilities generally. The relative importance of changes in these two factors is indicated in the next table.

TABLE 14

Growth of Manufacturing Production in the United States, 1899-1914

Factors Affecting Output per Establishment

| Year | Output per establishment | Number of workers per establishment | Output per worker |
|---|---|---|---|
| 1899 | 100.0 | 100.0 | 100.0 |
| 1904 | 122.6 | 110.3 | 111.2 |
| 1909 | 130.5 | 109.8 | 118.9 |
| 1914 | 156.0 | 120.4 | 129.6 |
| Average annual rate of change (per cent) | +2.8 | +1.1 | +1.7 |

For the period as a whole the chief factor in increasing output per establishment was the combination of improved material instruments and enhanced skill which leads to increasing output per worker. If the story be followed by census intervals shifts in emphasis are found, but because of the greater coverage of the 1909 Census, as regards number of establishments included, too much significance should not be attached to these inter-censal changes.

The record of the fifteen years from 1899 to 1914 indicates that the factors responsible for the great advance in production of

---

study except those relating to output per establishment and to number of workers per establishment. The decennial censuses include proportionally more small establishments, establishments making only slight contributions, in the aggregate, to total volume of production and to number of wage-earners employed. (Cf. *Thirteenth Census of the United State, Vol. VIII, Manufactures,* 1910, p. 20.)

In the analysis of changes in manufacturing production after 1914, only those establishments producing goods of an aggregate annual value of $5,000 or more were included. (For the years 1899 to 1914 the lower limit was $500.) This raising of the limit probably served to reduce discrepancies due to varying coverage of decennial and other censuses.

manufactured goods were an increasing number of workers, larger and better equipped establishments, and steadily rising output per worker employed. (The growth of demand was, of course, essential to the realization of the advantages of large-scale production.) The stream of manufactured goods produced in 1914, a stream greater by 76 per cent in volume than that of 1899, was turned out by a working force (of wage-earners) only 36 per cent greater, and by a number of establishments only 13 per cent greater. There are clear signs here of the growing emphasis upon technical efficiency and enhanced productivity per unit as factors of increased production, an emphasis which has been even more pronounced in recent years.

§ *A revision of the index numbers of manufacturing production.*— Index numbers of the physical volume of production of the type employed in the immediately preceding pages are subject to two limitations. In the first place they are restricted to commodities for which adequate quantity statistics are available. This means, in general, that they are restricted to commodities of standardized types, with units of output which are uniform and easily enumerated. Complex machines, more highly fabricated articles of all sorts, are usually excluded from such index numbers. Secondly, they are generally restricted to commodities for which statistics are available over the entire period covered in a given study. Thus, with a few exceptions, new products developed after 1899 are not included in the index of production of manufactures given above. But new products, properly weighted, should be included in a comprehensive index of volume of production. If this is not done, the rate of increase of production in an economy marked by increasing diversification is understated.

The significance of these limitations, with reference to the measurement of output of manufacturing industries in the United States, is indicated by the figures in Table 15, on the following page.

The 'value added' by all census industries increased 104.5 per cent between 1899 and 1914. For the industries included in the present sample the increase amounted to 92.2 per cent; for industries not included in the sample the increase in value added by manufacture amounted to 110.5 per cent. This difference between the gains shown for included and for excluded industries calls for investigation. The more rapid advance in 'value added' in industries for which quantity statistics are not available may be due to a more rapid growth of physical output among the excluded industries, or to a more rapid advance in the cost of fabrication, per unit of product, among these industries. It does not seem likely that this latter condition prevailed. The survey of census industries in detail has revealed far greater uniformity in respect to changes in fabricating costs than in respect to changes in volume of output, and it is reasonable to assume that this

## TABLE 15
### Changes in Value Added by Manufacture, 1899-1914

| (1) | (2) | (3) | (4) | (5) | (6) | (7) |
|---|---|---|---|---|---|---|
| | 'Value added', all census industries | | 'Value added', industries included in sample [a] | | 'Value added', industries not included in sample [a] | |
| Year | In millions of dollars | In relatives | In millions of dollars | In relatives | In millions of dollars | In relatives |
| 1899 | 4,831 | 100.0 | 1,583 | 100.0 | 3,248 | 100.0 |
| 1904 | 6,294 | 130.3 | 1,906 | 121.3 | 4,388 | 134.6 |
| 1909 | 8,529 | 176.5 | 2,546 | 171.6 | 5,983 | 179.2 |
| 1914 | 9,878 | 204.5 | 3,042* | 192.2 | 6,836* | 210.5 |
| 1914 | 9,878 | | 3,019** | | 6,859** | |
| 1914 | 9,878 | | 2,851*** | | 7,027*** | |

[a] The values for 1914 marked with a single asterisk (*) are comparable with the data for 1899, those marked with two asterisks (**) are comparable with 1904, and those marked with three asterisks (***) are comparable with 1909. Relatives were first computed on 1914 as base and then shifted to 1899.

is true of all manufacturing industries. As between the two alternatives, it is far more probable that the excluded industries showed more rapid gains in volume of physical production.[1] The index of physical output derived from 35 industries probably understates the true gain in output registered by all manufacturing industries between 1899 and 1914.

The data available permit us to approximate the rate of increase of production among all industries, taking account of new products as well as of the possibly more rapid growth of output of commodities for which quantity statistics are not available. This may be done by two partially independent operations, to permit checking of results. We may assume, first, that output per capita for all census industries increased at the rate found to prevail, on the average, among the 35 industries studied. Multiplying the index of per capita output by an index of the total number of wage-earners employed, we secure the desired index of physical production. Again, we may assume that the cost of fabrication, per unit of product, changed at the same rate among all census industries as among the sample industries studied.[2] Having

[1] It is impossible to say to what extent more rapid growth in the production of excluded industries is due to the appearance of new products among these industries, to what extent to the increasing output of old commodities. Though the Bureau of the Census publishes statistics showing the quantities and values of new classes of products, when practicable, it is generally impossible to set up separate industrial classifications for new products. In many cases, indeed, the manufacture of both old and new products is reported by the same establishment.

[2] This method permits certain changes in the quality of manufactured goods to be measured, when such changes occur in greater degree among the excluded than

figures as to aggregate cost of fabrication (i.e. aggregate 'value added') in all census industries, an index of physical production may be readily derived. The procedure followed is illustrated in Table 16.

**TABLE 16**

Illustrating the Derivation of Index Numbers of the Physical Volume of Manufacturing Production, 1899-1914

All Census Industries

| (1) | (2) | (3) | (4) | (5) | (6) | (7) | (8) | (9) |
|---|---|---|---|---|---|---|---|---|
| | Derivation of index numbers based on 'value added' | | | | Derivation of index numbers based on number of wage-earners employed | | | |
| Year | Total 'value added', all census industries | | 'Value added' per unit of product, industries included in sample | Derived index of physical volume of production | Number of wage-earners, all census industries | | Index of per capita production, industries included in sample | Derived index of physical volume of production |
| | In millions of dollars | In relatives | | | In thousands | In relatives | | |
| 1899 | 4,831 | 100.0 | 100.0 | 100.0 | 4,713 | 100.0 | 100.0 | 100.0 |
| 1904 | 6,294 | 130.3 | 98.5 | 132.2 | 5,468 | 116.0 | 111.2 | 129.0 |
| 1909 | 8,529 | 176.5 | 108.2 | 163.2 | 6,615 | 140.4 | 118.9 | 166.8 |
| 1914 | 9,878 | 204.5 | 104.6 | 195.4 | 7,036 | 149.3 | 129.6 | 193.4 |

The results secured by the two methods appear in columns (5) and (9). Their close agreement tends to confirm their substantial accuracy as indexes of the actual change in volume of manufacturing production between 1899 and 1914. Averages of the index numbers derived from fabrication costs and from number of wage-earners employed may be taken to represent the best approximations to the changes we seek to measure. This average shows an increase of 94.4 per cent in volume of output over this period, an average annual increase of about 4.5 per cent. These figures are appreciably higher than those derived from the sample of 35 industries, which indicated a gain of about 76 per cent during this period. The rate of increase in these industries averaged 3.9 per cent per year.

If it be true that the output of industries for which quantity data

---

the included industries. This would be the case if the more rapid increase in 'value added' among the excluded industries was due to a more rapid increase in degree of fabrication (assuming the cost of a given degree of fabrication to change at the same rate among excluded and included industries). The measurement of changes in fabrication costs, per unit of product, is explained in Chapter III.

are not available increased at a higher rate than did the output of industries for which production is readily measured, indexes of production based on annual data probably understate the true rate of growth in physical output. We may estimate the degree of understatement by comparing index numbers of manufacturing output based on annual data (before adjustment to the census averages) with corresponding index numbers derived from census data.

TABLE 17

COMPARISON OF INDEX NUMBERS OF PHYSICAL VOLUME OF MANUFACTURING PRODUCTION IN THE UNITED STATES, 1899-1914

| Year | Census index numbers of volume of fabrication | | Unadjusted annual index numbers of manufacturing output |
|---|---|---|---|
| | Based on 35 industries | Derived from 'value added' and number of employees for all industries | |
| 1899 | 100 | 100 | 100 |
| 1904 | 120 | 131 | 120 |
| 1909 | 154 | 165 | 158 |
| 1914 | 176 | 194 | 176 |

The two series of index numbers based on directly measurable output are almost identical, both being substantially lower than the corrected census index which includes elements of physical production not capable of direct enumeration.

The general index of physical volume of production shown in Table 1, which represents our best estimate of the true course of aggregate production between 1901 and 1913, was derived from a combination of index numbers of raw material production and revised index numbers of manufacturing production based on census data. In deriving corrected annual indexes of manufacturing production, interpolation for inter-censal years was based upon independently constructed annual index numbers of manufacturing output. In this interpolation account was taken of the fact that the volume of all manufacturing production is more stable than is the volume of production among the selected industries represented by the annual data.

It is clear that the correction of census index numbers in order to approximate the course of manufacturing production at large, and the subsequent interpolation to secure index numbers for inter-censal years, involve a departure from numerical accuracy based upon direct measurement of quantities produced. The formal accuracy which is possible when such direct methods are employed does not necessarily yield the best approximation to the true course of production. The present index numbers are frankly estimates, based in the first instance upon direct measurement of physical output in a wide range of industries, but adjusted, by methods which have been described, in order to overcome the obvious limitations of such enumeration.

## Summary: Production Tendencies in the United States, Pre-war

During the thirteen years preceding the World War the physical volume of production in the United States increased at a rate approximating 3.1 per cent a year; population increased at a rate of 2.0 per cent. Oscillations in the growth of aggregate production averaged about 3.7 per cent a year, being many times as wide as the fluctuations in population growth. The meaning, for the country at large, of unstable processes is suggested by the difference between the amplitude of the variations in population growth (variations probably not exceeding an average of 0.3 per cent) and the deviations from stability of growth in the volume of goods which support that population.

During the pre-war period the rate of increase in the production of manufactured goods exceeded that of raw materials. Changes in our foreign trade, diversification of domestic demand, the taking over by organized industry of operations formerly performed in the home—all those processes which accompanied the increased industrialization of American life—contributed to the more rapid development of manufacturing. In the mass, the output of raw materials was more stable than was the output of manufactured goods, but the production of certain classes of manufactured goods was marked by notable instability.

Far greater than the difference between the rates of increase in the output of raw and manufactured goods was the margin between the output of farm and non-farm products. A population growing at the rate of 2.0 per cent a year was increasing the exploitation of its raw mineral resources [1] at a rate of 5.6 per cent a year, between 1901 and 1913. The rapid exploitation of mineral resources is a characteristic of the age in which we live. The output of raw American farm products, on the other hand, increased by but 1.7 per cent a year, a rate of advance less than the rate of increase in population.

The trend toward industrialization characteristic of this period

[1] The commodities included among raw materials other than products of American farms are all minerals.

is even more clearly revealed by the contrast between the output of goods intended for use in capital equipment and of goods intended for direct human consumption. Capital equipment, though making up a minor part of the total productive stream, set the pace of the industrial advance between 1901 and 1913. The production of such goods was increasing at a cumulative rate of 5 per cent a year, as compared with a rate of 2.6 per cent for goods intended for consumption. It was an irregular growth, this increase in the annual output of capital equipment, reflecting in intensified form the ebbs and flows of industrial activity, but it was none the less persistent. Each interruption was followed by an elastic rise to new heights.

Another distinctive attribute of the movement toward a more complex economic life is found in the relatively rapid growth of durable goods. While the production of non-durable and semi-durable goods increased between 1901 and 1913 at rates approximating 2.5 per cent a year, the output of relatively long-lived goods increased at a rate of 4.6 per cent a year. Such goods, we have noted, are characterized by relatively high elasticity of demand and instability of production. The problem of maintaining equilibrium in an economic system may be expected to become more difficult as more of its productive energies are devoted to the output of capital equipment, and of durable goods generally.

In discussing the growth of manufacturing production attention has been directed to certain of the factors affecting volume of production. Viewing the two factors of production as number of wage-earners employed, and the technical, mechanical, educational and organizational elements which affect the per capita output of labor, we observe that these varied in importance during the different inter-censal periods falling between 1899 and 1914. In the first and third of these five-year period (periods which opened in prosperity and closed in depression) technical and organizational elements were the more potent as factors tending to increase production. Between 1904 and 1909, on the other hand, an increase in the number of wage-earners was the chief factor in expanding production.

It is a suggestive fact that in two of the three pre-war inter-censal periods under review, technical skill and improved equipment were of greater importance than an increase in the number of working units, in stimulating the growth of manufacturing production.

The great increase in number of workers between 1904 and 1909 tends to obscure the other tendencies which were affecting manufacturing industries before the war. There were periods later, notably during the war, when numbers again played a dominant part, but in retrospect these appear to have been interludes. The tendency to subordinate numbers to mechanical and organizational factors, a tendency which has attracted so much attention in recent years, was clearly in evidence during these pre-war years.

Manufacturing output is seen in a different light if the establishment be viewed as the unit of production. Production may expand through an increase in number of establishments, or through increased output per establishment. An index of output per establishment is an index of the growth of large-scale production. A survey of these elements during the years 1899 to 1914 reveals a clear tendency toward large-scale production, with a declining number of establishments, except between 1904 and 1909.[1]

A final analysis was made of the factors affecting output per establishment. Here again we may set in opposition the human factor, as measured by an index of number of workers per establishment, and the complex of technical, mechanical and organizational factors reflected in output per worker. The evidence indicates that during the early years of the century the movement toward large scale production was promoted by putting more men into a smaller number of establishments and by means of technical and mechanical improvements which permitted increased output per worker. From 1904 to 1909 the movement toward more workers per establishment appears to have been checked, though conclusions are clouded by the fact of variation in coverage. After 1909 both elements of large scale production were again called into play. The number of employees per establishment increased sharply, and further play was given to the elements of technique and equipment which stimulate output per worker. During the war years, as we shall see, the factor of technical efficiency was subordinated to the cruder instrument of numbers, but it again became the dominant

[1] It is worth noting that the combination movement in American industry, so active after 1899, was checked in 1904 by the decision in the Northern Securities case. The growth of new establishments between 1904 and 1909 may have been in part a result of this check to integration. Probably more important, however, was the fact that the degree of coverage was somewhat higher in the Census of 1909 than in the Census of 1904. Variation in coverage was not significant except as regards number of establishments.

agent of advance when the war-time boom had passed. It is this factor, of course, which has placed its impress on recent economic changes.

A detailed picture of the course of production in the United States between the turn of the century and the outbreak of the World War reveals a host of productive elements changing at rapidly diverging rates. Virile young industries were moving forward rapidly; others were keeping comfortable pace with the growth of population; still others were dropping behind, many with volume of output declining. These differing rates of change present in concrete form one of the pressing problems of an industrial civilization, the problem of securing that flexibility and adaptability which will permit prompt readjustment to changing industrial demands. The persistence of differing rates of secular advance makes these demands—demands for a mobile and adaptable labor force, for a liquid supply of capital, for flexible transportation and distributive organizations, and demands for social machinery which will lighten the human burdens arising from rapid technical changes and from shifting tides of employment.[1]

§ *On methods of measuring economic movements.*—The measurements used in this and the following chapters require brief explanation. The prevailing tendency of a statistical series during a period is given by the average annual rate of change, as defined by the value of $r$ in the equation to an exponential curve fitted to the data in question.[2] This is the slope of a line which is straight on ratio paper. Measure-

---

[1] It has not been possible in this chapter to go into a number of questions which might properly be treated in connection with the measurement of volume of production. For discussions of various technical matters relating to the measurement of changes in physical volume see:

Edmund E. Day, "An Index of the Physical Volume of Production", *Review of Economic Statistics,* September, October and November, 1920;

Walter W. Stewart, "An Index Number of Production", *American Economic Review,* Vol. XI, No. 1, March, 1921, pp. 57-70;

Woodlief Thomas, "The Economic Significance of the Increased Efficiency of American Industry", *Supplement, American Economic Review,* Vol. XVIII, No. 1, March, 1928, pp. 122-138;

E. E. Day and W. Thomas, *The Growth of Manufactures, 1899 to 1923.* Census Monograph, No. VIII, Bureau of the Census, Washington, D. C., 1928;

A. W. Flux, "Indices of Industrial Productive Activity", *Journal of the Royal Statistical Society,* Vol. XC, Part II, 1927, pp. 225-271;

J. W. F. Rowe, "An Index of the Physical Volume of Production", *The Economic Journal,* Vol. XXXVII, No. 146, June, 1927, pp. 173-187;

Carl Snyder, *Business Cycles and Business Measurements,* Macmillan, New York, 1927, pp. 44-51.

[2] More precisely, the value we have used is that of $(r-1) \times 100$, $r$ being taken from the equation $y = ar^x$. The curve is fitted to the data by the use of

ments of this type, which were employed in the opening section of this chapter, possess the advantages of simplicity and ease of calculation. They lend themselves readily, moreover, to comparison and combination, since they are expressed in percentage form.[1]

There is one obvious objection to the employment of a single curve type to represent the secular changes found in a wide variety of economic series. It may be said that the type of curve employed to measure secular tendency in each case should be adapted to the particular series being studied, that no single type can be thus generally employed. There is merit in this objection, if we are thinking of these tendencies as secular trends in the usual sense. The first answer must be that we are not concerned with the measurement of secular trends in the abstract; our interest is in persistent tendencies during definite periods of time. Each of these periods is assumed to be a reasonably homogeneous economic era, an era during which the direction of the general economic development of a nation was not altered by catastrophic events. During such periods, it is here suggested, the single function proposed for the measurement of secular tendencies gives an adequate and satisfactory representation of these movements for a very large percentage of all economic series. This claim cannot be supported by *a priori* argument; the proof is to be found in a study of the data. The series employed in the present study are presented graphically, and the reader may judge for himself as to the accuracy of each measure em-

---

Glover's mean value table (cf. James W. Glover, *Tables of Applied Mathematics*, George Wahr, Ann Arbor, Michigan, 1923, pp. 468 ff.)

Rates of change derived from census data have been reduced to an annual basis by taking the fifth root of the rate of change for a five-year period, as determined by fitting a line to data for the years 1899, 1904, 1909, and 1914.

[1] A further technical virtue of this method, which has important practical consequences, may be pointed out. When the values of $a$ and of $r$ (in the equation $y = ar^x$) have been secured for two annual series, which we may designate series A and series B, it is possible to determine quite readily the values of $a$ and of $r$ for a third series C, secured by dividing the annual values of series A by the corresponding annual values of series B. Under these conditions, we have

$$a_C = \frac{a_A}{a_B}$$

$$r_C = \frac{r_A}{r_B}$$

This relationship prevails when lines have been fitted to the logarithms of the data by the method of least squares. It is not a necessary relationship when the fitting has been effected by the use of Glover's table, but the margin of error involved in the application of the method is slight.

This procedure is extremely useful in securing the rate of change in the purchasing power of a commodity, or of wages, when the rates of change in the original price or wage series, and in indexes suitable for reducing prices or wages to a purchasing power basis, have been computed. It may also be employed in deriving rates of change in per capita earnings of factory labor, when total payroll and employment figures are given, as in the publications of the U. S. Bureau of Labor Statistics.

ployed. A detailed inspection of the series used indicates that, during the periods here studied, economic series have tended to increase (or decrease) by fairly constant percentage increments (or decrements), year by year. During an era marked by no sudden breaks in the general economic development of a country, sharp interruptions in the rates of change of individual series are the exception, not the rule. In the body of the present study special reference is made to the few cases in which such sharp breaks have been observed.

There is a final justification for the employment of the procedure here described. This method yields, for each series, a single measurement which summarizes the direction and degree of change of that series during a stated period and which is directly comparable with similar measures derived from other series, regardless of the units of measurement in which the various series may have been expressed and of the magnitude of the figures in the various series. Unrestricted comparison and combination of measures relating to this aspect of economic change are possible only if a function of the general type here suggested be employed. This last consideration would have no weight, of course, if the particular function did not provide an accurate measurement of the economic change in question. This, fortunately, it does in the great majority of cases.

The second measurement descriptive of the behavior of individual series, the mean percentage deviation about the line measuring average rate of change, is an index of instability of growth. This measurement, being in percentage form, is suitable for comparison and combination with similar measurements for other series, regardless of the magnitudes of the items in the other series and of the nature of the original units. It is a statistically simple measure, but adequate to the present purpose. The more stable and regular the growth or decline of a given series, the smaller will this measure be.[1]

The characteristic measured by such an index is instability of growth (or decline), not the variability of given economic series. Various statistical devices are available for the measurement of variability, devices adapted to the measurement of seasonal or cyclical variability, or of

[1] This method of measuring stability of economic growth (or decline) during a stated period ensures comparability, in so far as the observations included in the original series are comparable. When the original data are annual aggregates or monthly averages of simple economic series the measures of instability are fully comparable. But the annual data of certain economic series are not aggregate or averages of monthly items; they relate to specific dates. A series of this type might be expected to show somewhat less regularity in its secular change than would a corresponding series of aggregates or monthly averages. Difficulties of another sort arise in handling series relating to annual increments to an existing total. Fluctuations in such increments are not comparable with fluctuations in aggregates. Again, indexes or averages representing combinations of several series tend to be somewhat more stable than items representing the movements of individual economic series. But such difficulties are due to differences in the structure of the original series, not to the method of measurement employed. They must be borne in mind in making comparisons among different series.

week-to-week, month-to-month or year-to-year changes. If variability is to be measured the significant fluctuations are the actual changes, not deviations from hypothetical or 'normal' values. But if *stability of growth* is in question the measures which possess significance are those defining departures from values which would have been recorded if a given rate of change had prevailed with absolute regularity. (Stable growth might be defined, of course, by a function involving changing rates of growth. The simpler function furnishes the present standard.) The magnitude of these departures, in relation to the expected values, is defined by the index of instability.

## CHAPTER II

## *Pre-War Changes in Commodity Prices*

THE flow of physical goods must for many purposes be viewed as a stream of pecuniary values. In this form it is amenable to the operations of business, for only as a pecuniary flow can the stream be divided, apportioned and regulated as the interests of business require. But this value stream is not an exact counterpart of the stream of physical quantities. It has variations, sinkings and risings of its own. Changes in the fortunes of producers and consumers cannot be understood without a knowledge of the movements of both streams—of commodities and of values. Prices are the link between goods and values, and shifting prices may constitute elements of economic change as important as are alterations in physical volume.

In tracing price movements over a period those general changes which reflect alterations in the purchasing power of monetary units are of obvious interest. But the story of price movements should go beyond these. Perhaps of greater immediate importance are the inequalities of price movements which alter the terms of exchange among different industrial groups. The general dispersion of prices resulting from such unequal changes may be studied as a problem in itself. In more concrete form, these shifts may be examined with reference to the fortunes of specific economic groups. A pronounced rise in the prices of one class of commodities, such as manufactured goods or agricultural products, a rise not shared by other groups, will materially affect economic processes. Such an alteration in the terms of exchange among economic groups may occur as a result of a sharp price movement or as a result of persistent secular tendencies. In either case the effect may endure for years. These shifting relations, measured in the abstract by index numbers of dispersion and manifest in concrete form in the varying movements of commodity prices in different groups, are matters of concern in a survey of price movements during a given economic era.

The fortunes of certain groups are of particular interest in such a survey. Are products of cultivation rising in value, in relation to other commodities? Are raw materials becoming higher priced, relatively, while the prices of products of manufacture decline? Are goods destined for human consumption rising or falling in price, in relation to goods entering into the capital equipment of the economy? What industries are marked by the falling prices of their products, and what by rising prices? If persistent and differing tendencies in the price movements of major commodity groups are discernible, light will be thrown on important aspects of our economic development.

These price movements must be studied with reference to the production tendencies discussed in the preceding chapter. It is of interest to know whether, over a period of years, there is a consistent relation between price trends and production trends. Again, questions of stability must concern us in this study. In what industrial groups are prices most stable? least stable? To what extent are unstable prices associated with unstable production? Finally, there are questions of cost to be considered. Our information concerning costs of production falls short of what might be desired, but it has been possible to measure movements of certain important cost elements for products of manufacture. Trends in general fabrication costs, in labor costs and in overhead costs plus profits may be traced, in connection with price and production changes.

## General Measurements

In summarizing the movements of prices during the pre-war period we deal first with changes in the general level of wholesale prices and in the general price structure. Certain of these changes are defined by the measurements in the next table, which are shown graphically in Figure 11, on page 55.

During this pre-war era the rate of advance in wholesale prices averaged 1.8 per cent a year. The degree of instability in the level of wholesale prices, that is, the degree of departure from a uniform rate of increase, is measured by an index of 2.2. This figure (which is to be judged with reference to similar measurements relating to production and to other series) is relatively low, indicating fairly regular changes from year to year in the general price level.

The general price index does not tell the whole story of the

## TABLE 18
### Changes in the Level of Wholesale Prices in the United States, 1901-1913

| Year | Index numbers of wholesale prices [a] | Year-to-year change in wholesale prices (per cent) |
|---|---|---|
| 1901 | 100.0 | .... |
| 1902 | 106.5 | +6.5 |
| 1903 | 107.8 | +1.2 |
| 1904 | 108.0 | +0.2 |
| 1905 | 108.7 | +0.6 |
| 1906 | 111.8 | +2.9 |
| 1907 | 117.9 | +5.5 |
| 1908 | 113.7 | —3.6 |
| 1909 | 122.2 | +7.5 |
| 1910 | 127.3 | +4.2 |
| 1911 | 117.4 | —7.8 |
| 1912 | 125.0 | +6.5 |
| 1913 | 126.2 | +1.0 |

[a] The index numbers are those of the U. S. Bureau of Labor Statistics, with base shifted to 1901

major price changes of this period. Such an index measures the intensity of the force, or combination of forces, which is affecting the purchasing power of the dollar in wholesale markets. There are many specific price-making forces which affect, primarily, the prices of individual commodities. These forces operate to change individual commodity prices unequally, and to prevent the prices of individual commodities from accommodating themselves promptly to changes in the purchasing power of the dollar. The influence of these disruptive forces is reflected in the dispersion of prices. The less direct the incidence of the forces acting upon the price level, and the greater the relative importance of specific price-making factors, the more widely dispersed will prices be. These disruptive forces possess considerable economic significance, for every inequality of movement affects the buying and selling relations upon which the movement of goods depends.

Index numbers designed to measure the year-to-year dispersion of prices, for the period 1901-1913 are given in Table 19, together with geometric means of annual link relatives. For comparison there is given an average of index numbers of dispersion computed from annual link relatives covering the ten years 1891-1900.[1]

[1] The index of dispersion is the antilogarithm of a fractional part (.6745) of the logarithmic standard deviation. It defines, in percentage form, the approximate

## TABLE 19

#### Index Numbers of Annual Price Changes and of Price Dispersion in the United States, 1901-1913

Geometric Means and Measures of Dispersion Computed from Weighted Link Relatives of Wholesale Prices, 1901-1913, with an Average Measure of Dispersion for the Period 1891-1900 [a]

| Year (or period) | Number of price series | Geometric mean of link relatives | Index of year-to-year dispersion |
|---|---|---|---|
| 1891-1900 | 195 | .... | 9.0 |
| 1901 | 195 | 99.2 | 7.9 |
| 1902 | 195 | 107.3 | 8.6 |
| 1903 | 205 | 100.8 | 9.2 |
| 1904 | 205 | 99.6 | 10.2 |
| 1905 | 205 | 100.6 | 7.4 |
| 1906 | 205 | 103.6 | 7.7 |
| 1907 | 205 | 106.4 | 5.7 |
| 1908 | 205 | 96.0 | 8.7 |
| 1909 | 205 | 106.1 | 7.6 |
| 1910 | 205 | 102.9 | 7.9 |
| 1911 | 205 | 94.5 | 8.7 |
| 1912 | 205 | 106.8 | 7.3 |
| 1913 | 205 | 101.1 | 8.4 |

[a] The commodities employed are those for which wholesale price quotations are published by the U. S. Bureau of Labor Statistics. The weights are based upon the approximate values of the quantities marketed during the period 1920-1923.

It is significant that only twice during the years from 1901 to 1913 did the index of dispersion exceed the average value for the ten years preceding. The decade of the 'nineties was marked by a relatively high degree of dispersion, that is, by relatively severe disturbances in price relations. Greater stability characterized the years from the turn of the century to the outbreak of the war.

We investigate another characteristic of pre-war price behavior by measuring the variability of the prices of individual commodities, that is, the degree of price change occurring within a stated period of time. Such variability may not be registered at all in changes in the price level. Though price-level changes and the variability of individual prices are not unrelated, the one furnishes no accurate index of the other. For each of more than 200 com-

limits of the zone within which would fall 50 per cent of the price relatives at a given date, and on a given base. Thus a value of 10 for a given date means that, on that date, approximately half the price relatives deviated from the geometric mean of all the relatives by less than 10 per cent. For a full description of this measure, see *The Behavior of Prices,* National Bureau of Economic Research, New York, 1929, pp. 256-262.

modities we have a measure of the variability of prices within each of the years studied.[1] The averages of these annual measurements are given in Table 20, for the period 1901-1913, together with an average for the ten years 1891-1900.

The points noted in connection with the dispersion of prices appear to be true of these measurements. The decade of the 'nineties was marked by high price variability. Not once between 1901 and 1913 was the mean measure of variability as great as the average for the years 1891-1900. The lowest value for the period is found in 1913, the last year covered.

The measurements of dispersion and price variability define the degree of sub-surface disturbance occurring in the price system, disturbance resulting from month-to-month variations and from inequalities in the year-to-year movements of the prices of individual commodities. Conditions of high price variability and marked disturbance of established price relations offer opportunities to business men for those conjunctural profits (or losses) which re-

TABLE 20
Monthly Variability of Wholesale Prices

Averages Computed from Measures of Price Variability for Individual Commodities, 1901-1913, with an Average Measure of Monthly Variability for the Period 1891-1900

| Year (or period) | Number of price series | Arithmetic mean of measures of price variability |
|---|---|---|
| 1891-1900 | 206 | 5.0 |
| 1901 | 205 | 4.3 |
| 1902 | 214 | 4.7 |
| 1903 | 214 | 4.8 |
| 1904 | 214 | 4.1 |
| 1905 | 214 | 4.5 |
| 1906 | 214 | 3.5 |
| 1907 | 214 | 4.5 |
| 1908 | 214 | 4.7 |
| 1909 | 214 | 4.6 |
| 1910 | 214 | 4.3 |
| 1911 | 214 | 4.3 |
| 1912 | 214 | 4.6 |
| 1913 | 213 | 3.7 |

[1] This measure is the average deviation of monthly prices from the mean price for the year. Each average deviation is expressed as a percentage of the mean annual price. See *The Behavior of Prices,* pp. 39-49.

sult from faulty economic adjustments and temporary dislocations. Uncertainty is introduced into business dealings by the existence of such conditions, and the speculative element in business is intensified. It is a notable fact that the degree of such disturbance, which was high during the decade of the 'nineties, appears to have been relatively low during the years immediately preceding the war. At a later point we shall revert to this apparent gain in stability, in relation to a possible corresponding loss in flexibility.[1]

## Comparison of Movements of Wholesale Prices and Production, All Commodities

Strictly comparable index numbers of prices and production are lacking. Such annual index numbers as we have differ in respect to commodities included, weights employed and technical methods used in averaging the observations. However, for the sake of getting a

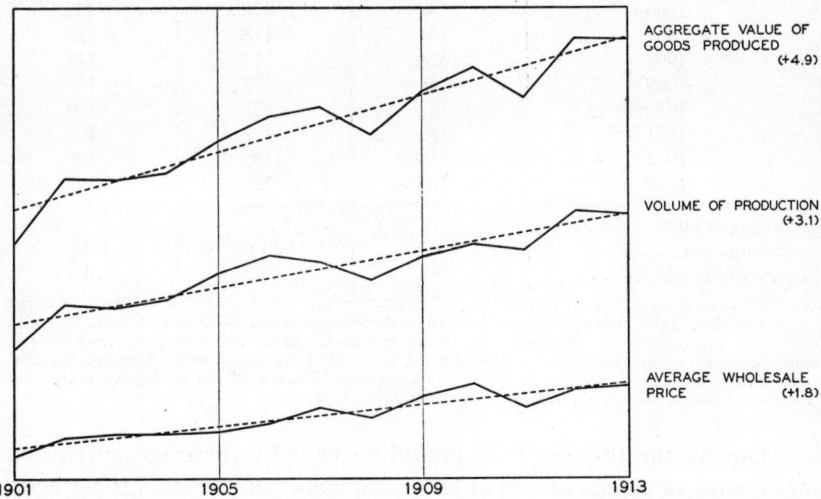

FIGURE 11

CHANGES IN VOLUME OF PRODUCTION, AVERAGE PRICE AND AGGREGATE VALUE OF GOODS PRODUCED IN THE UNITED STATES, 1901-1913

Plotted on ratio scale. The figures in parentheses define average annual rates of change (in percentage form).

[1] The two tables immediately preceding, and the accompanying discussion, are adapted from the chapter on "Price Movements and Related Industrial Changes" in *Recent Economic Changes,* Vol. II, pp. 610-613.

general picture of the relative movements which have occurred in these two fields of interest, and of approximating the changes in aggregate values between 1901 and 1913, we may accept the price index of the Bureau of Labor Statistics as representative of general price changes at wholesale and the index of aggregate production cited in the preceding chapter as representative of production changes. Making these assumptions, we secure index numbers of changes in the total value of goods produced in the United States between 1901 and 1913. These, with corresponding price and production index numbers, are given in the next table, and are plotted in Figure 11.

TABLE 21

INDEX NUMBERS OF PHYSICAL VOLUME, PRICES AND AGGREGATE VALUES OF GOODS PRODUCED IN THE UNITED STATES, 1901-1913

| Year | Physical volume of production | Wholesale prices | Aggregate values [a] |
|---|---|---|---|
| 1901 | 100 | 100 | 100 |
| 1902 | 116 | 107 | 124 |
| 1903 | 115 | 108 | 124 |
| 1904 | 118 | 108 | 127 |
| 1905 | 129 | 109 | 141 |
| 1906 | 137 | 112 | 153 |
| 1907 | 134 | 118 | 158 |
| 1908 | 126 | 114 | 144 |
| 1909 | 136 | 122 | 166 |
| 1910 | 142 | 127 | 180 |
| 1911 | 139 | 117 | 163 |
| 1912 | 158 | 125 | 198 |
| 1913 | 156 | 126 | 197 |
| Average annual rate of change (per cent) | +3.1 | +1.8 | +4.9 |
| Index of instability | 3.7 | 2.2 | 4.9 |

[a] The above price index measures changes in the average wholesale prices of units of goods, both raw and processed; the production index measures change in output of units of raw and processed goods. The value series, derived by multiplying these index numbers together, measures changes in the aggregate value of transactions involved in the productive process. It does not relate to the total value of finished products alone.

During the thirteen-year period covered by these measurements aggregate values increased at an average annual rate of 4.9 per cent. The flow of physical goods increased at a rate of 3.1 per cent a year, while prices, rising at a rate of 1.8 per cent a year, accounted for the additional increment in total values. The index of aggregate values shows annual deviations from constancy of growth averag-

ing almost 5 per cent a year. Prices, as we have already noted, were the more stable of the two elements of total value.
We turn now to certain of the details of the picture.

## PRICE MOVEMENTS, MAJOR COMMODITY GROUPS

### Raw Materials and Manufactured Goods

In the following table are given index numbers of the prices, at wholesale, of raw materials and of manufactured goods, together with measurements of changes in the prices of identical commodities in the raw state and in manufactured form.[1]

TABLE 22

RAW MATERIALS AND MANUFACTURED GOODS

Index Numbers of Wholesale Prices in the United States, 1901-1913 [a]

| (1) | (2) | (3) | (4) | (5) |
|---|---|---|---|---|
| | | | Prices of identical commodities | |
| Year | Prices of raw materials | Prices of manufactured goods | In raw state | In manufactured form |
| 1901 | 100.0 | 100.0 | 100.0 | 100.0 |
| 1902 | 108.2 | 102.9 | 106.8 | 106.6 |
| 1903 | 108.5 | 103.6 | 106.0 | 105.4 |
| 1904 | 106.9 | 102.9 | 109.6 | 105.8 |
| 1905 | 109.1 | 105.8 | 108.3 | 108.6 |
| 1906 | 112.7 | 111.9 | 112.6 | 107.4 |
| 1907 | 119.5 | 117.5 | 119.9 | 115.6 |
| 1908 | 110.0 | 110.0 | 115.9 | 113.9 |
| 1909 | 116.7 | 111.4 | 126.2 | 120.0 |
| 1910 | 119.6 | 116.3 | 132.1 | 124.4 |
| 1911 | 120.2 | 111.4 | 119.5 | 114.0 |
| 1912 | 128.5 | 114.1 | 131.7 | 122.3 |
| 1913 | 121.2 | 116.2 | 138.5 | 122.7 |

[a] The index numbers of wholesale prices of raw materials given in column (2) are based upon 49 price series, those in column (4) upon 27 price series. The index numbers of prices of manufactured goods given in column (3) are based upon 178 price series (168 in 1901-02); those in column (5) upon 70 price series.

[1] The general index numbers of the prices of raw and of manufactured goods are unweighted geometric means of price relatives, computed by the National Bureau of Economic Research. The index numbers of prices of identical commodities in raw and manufactured state have been derived by the U. S. Bureau of Labor Statistics from weighted aggregates of actual prices. See pp. 28-34 of *Bulletin No. 440* (1926), Wholesale Price Series, U. S. Bureau of Labor Statistics.

The reader should note that the group index numbers of the National Bureau

These index numbers are plotted, with their respective lines of trend, in Figure 12. Measurements summarizing the behavior of these series during the period 1901-1913 are given below.

TABLE 23

WHOLESALE PRICES OF RAW AND MANUFACTURED GOODS

Summary of Rates of Change and Measurements of Instability, 1901-1913

| Commodity group | Average annual rate of change, 1901-1913 | | Index of instability, 1901-1913 |
|---|---|---|---|
| | In current dollars (per cent) | In purchasing power [a] (per cent) | |
| Raw materials (general index) | +1.6 | +0.3 | 2.3 |
| Manufactured goods (general index) | +1.2 | —0.1 | 2.1 |
| Index numbers, identical commodities: | | | |
| In raw state | +2.5 | +0.3 | 2.5 |
| In manufactured form | +1.6 | —0.5 | 2.1 |

[a] Measurements of changes in purchasing power relate to the annual index numbers of prices of the several commodity groups divided ('deflated') by an index number of wholesale prices. These deflated measurements may be taken to define changes in the values of goods in the several commodity groups, measured in terms of commodities in general, at wholesale. The index numbers relating to identical commodities in raw and processed form have been deflated by an index of the prices of commodities in the two groups, in combination.

In each case the rate of change of the deflated series has been secured by dividing the rate of change of the undeflated value by the rate of change of the all commodities index. (For this purpose rates of change must be expressed in full, e.g., as 1.03, rather than as +3 per cent.) See note at end of Chapter I for a discussion of this procedure.

The measurements relating to the two sets of index numbers cannot be expected to agree in detail, but they show the same general relations between the price movements of raw materials and of manufactured goods. Raw materials were rising in price, the gain in real value per unit approximating 0.3 per cent a year, while

---

of Economic Research are not necessarily consistent with the general price index of the U. S. Bureau of Labor Statistics, which was cited in earlier sections. The general index of wholesale prices constructed by the National Bureau of Economic Research shows a rate of change of +1.3 per cent a year, between 1901 and 1913, as compared with a rate of +1.8 per cent for the index of the U. S. Bureau of Labor Statistics. The rates of change of the commodity sub-groups of the National Bureau of Economic Research are consistent with the first of these figures.

In the discussion, comparability of group measurements derived from different sources is secured by reducing rates of change to purchasing power form. This is done by dividing the rate of change of actual prices for each group by the rate of change of the general index to which it is subordinate.

manufactured goods were being progressively cheapened. The divergence of trends is pronounced in the case of the index numbers derived from identical commodities in raw and processed form. With respect to long-term movements during this period, price tendencies were the reverse of production tendencies. The volume of

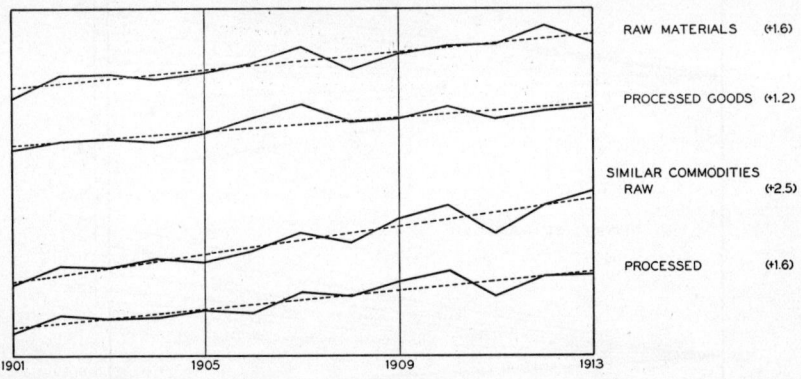

FIGURE 12

MOVEMENTS OF WHOLESALE PRICES IN THE UNITED STATES, 1901–1913

RAW MATERIALS AND PROCESSED GOODS

Plotted on ratio scale. The figures in parentheses define average annual rates of change (in percentage form).

manufacture was increasing between 1901 and 1913 at a rate materially higher than that at which the volume of production of raw materials was increasing. This was accompanied by a gradual cheapening of manufactured goods (prices being expressed in dollars of constant purchasing power), and a sustained advance in the real prices of raw materials.

As in the case of the production measurements cited in the last chapter, each of these averages conceals a host of divergent movements. This is brought out graphically in Figure 13, which portrays the price trends of 20 raw materials and 16 processed goods.[1] Considering first the entire group of 36 price series, the degree of divergence is indicated by a standard deviation (unweighted) of

---

[1] The actual prices of these commodities are plotted in Figure 14. These are but samples of the commodities included in the index numbers; as regards degree of divergence the samples are undoubtedly representative of the groups from which they come. The data here plotted, with descriptions of the price quotations employed, may be found in the bulletins on *Wholesale Prices,* published by the U. S. Bureau of Labor Statistics.

## FIGURE 13

### MOVEMENTS OF WHOLESALE PRICES IN THE UNITED STATES, 1901-1913*

PRICE TRENDS OF TWENTY RAW MATERIALS AND SIXTEEN PROCESSED GOODS

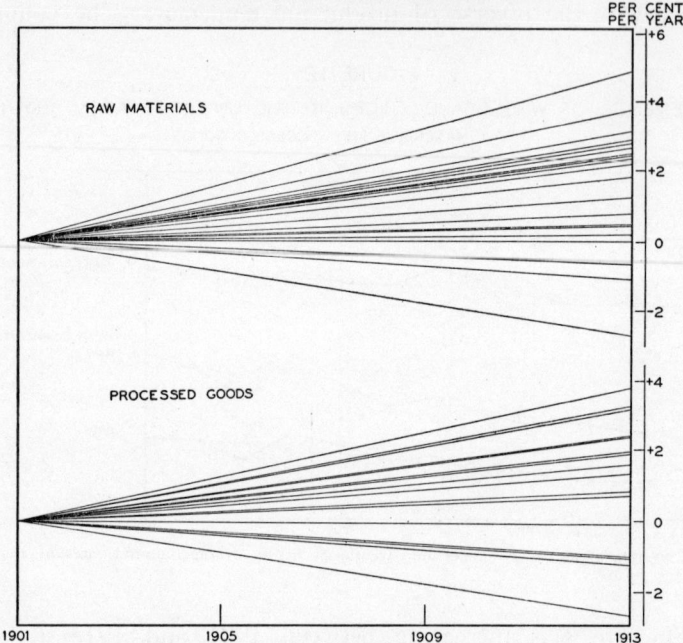

* Plotted on ratio scale. The lines here plotted relate to the commodities in the order in which they appear in Figure 14.

1.8. Among production series relating to the same 36 commodities the standard deviation of the rates of change was 3.1. There were notable differences of trend among the price series, but the differences among production tendencies were even more pronounced.

Breaking the price series into two groups, relating to raw and processed commodities, no significant difference between standard deviations of rates of change is revealed. For raw materials this measurement is 1.8; for processed goods it is 1.6. Here again the price materials differ from those measuring the production of the same commodities. Among processed goods included in the present sample production advanced or declined, between 1901 and 1913, at rates which varied widely, as is shown by a standard deviation of 3.6. This is more than twice as great as the divergence among the prices of the same commodities. The standard deviation of rates of

# FIGURE 14
## MOVEMENTS OF WHOLESALE PRICES IN THE UNITED STATES, 1901-1913

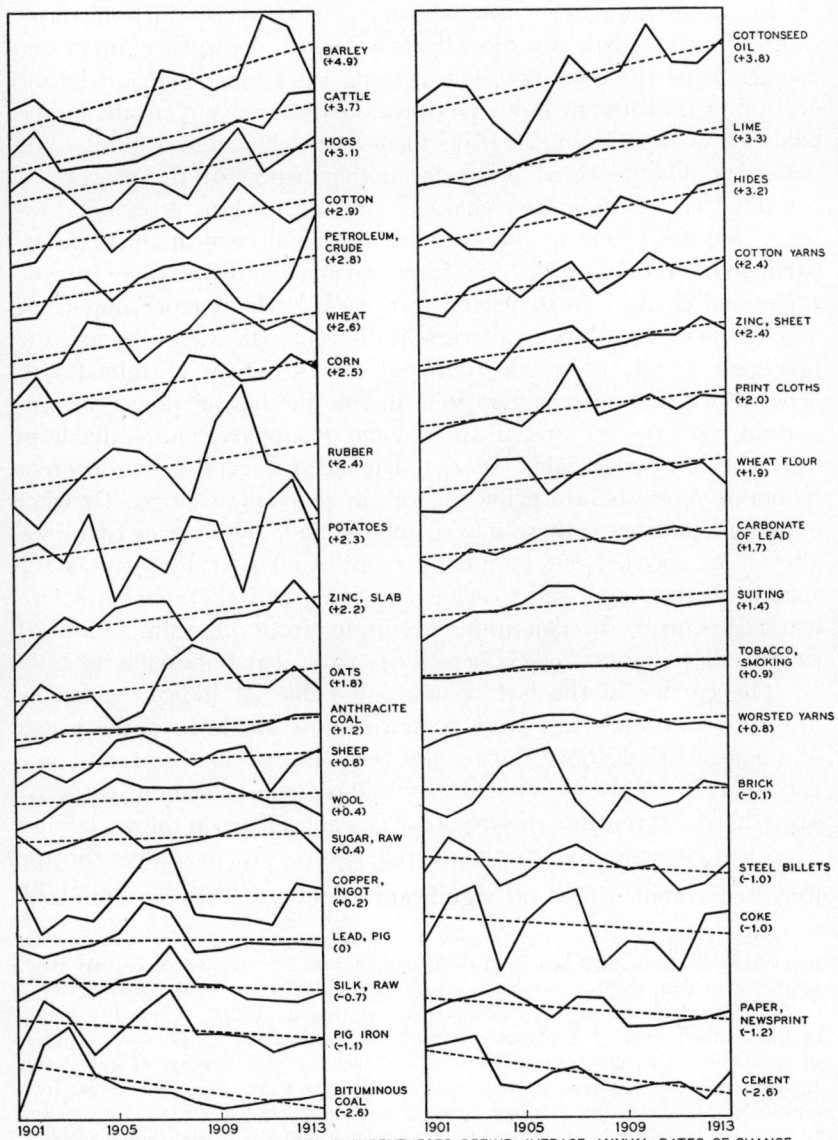

PLOTTED ON RATIO SCALE. THE FIGURES IN PARENTHESES DEFINE AVERAGE ANNUAL RATES OF CHANGE.

change relating to the production of individual raw materials is 2.5, appreciably higher than the corresponding measure for prices, but much lower than the measure of divergence in the production of processed goods.

In discussing the continuing divergence of production series reference was made to the effects of such divergence upon the operations of the economy. The varying rates of growth or decline prevailing in different industries necessarily involve constant industrial shifts, continuing readjustments of labor and capital. The persistent divergence of prices is another aspect of the process of continual change which is characteristic of modern economic systems. We are prone to think of seasonal and cyclical fluctuations, particularly the latter, as the forces primarily responsible for the shifts and changes in industrial processes. Perhaps more important as elements of enduring alterations in economic relations are the divergent trends of production and prices. These sustained tendencies, which involve alterations in the purchasing power of important economic groups, in the volume of employment available in different industrial fields, in the demand for capital by different economic interests, are prime factors in economic change. To what extent adaptation to these movements is made by a series of minor alterations, carried out month by month and year by year as the secular shifts occur, and to what extent by periodic and more violent adjustments to conditions resulting from the cumulation of such secular changes over a period of years, it is impossible to say.[1]

The entries in the last column of Table 23 indicate that the prices of raw materials were somewhat less stable than the prices of manufactured goods during the years preceding the war. These entries relate only to annual deviations from constant rates of growth. Measurements of two other types, bearing on the variability of prices of raw and manufactured goods, are available for the period 1898-1913. (This includes three years, 1898, 1899 and 1900,

[1] The existence of diverging trends among production and price series is not necessarily evidence of a condition of 'maladjustment'. Such divergence may itself be the form that adaptation takes, as when a rapid increase in the demand for a new product leads to a sharp advance in the output of that commodity and a decline in the output of displaced commodities. Yet, whether cause or consequence of economic shifts, divergent tendencies are evidence of a process of cumulative change, change which must include economic readjustment over wide areas. It is reasonable to assume that the more pronounced the divergencies the more pressing is the need for adaptability in the economic system and for flexibility and mobility among the elements of that system.

which did not fall in the period first studied.) One defines the average magnitude of the variations of monthly prices about annual average prices, while the other measures the frequency of price changes.[1] The latter is a coefficient which ranges in value between 0 and 1, a value of 0 indicating no price changes whatever during the period in question, while a value of 1 indicates a change in price during every month of the period covered.

TABLE 24

RAW MATERIALS AND MANUFACTURED GOODS

Measurements of Variability of Wholesale Prices, 1898-1913

| Commodity group | Number of price series | Measurement of monthly variability of prices | Measurement of frequency of price change |
|---|---|---|---|
| Raw materials ....... | 49 | 8.2 | .82 |
| Manufactured goods .. | 158 | 3.6 | .34 |

These measurements show that during the period in question the prices of raw materials were decidedly more variable and were subject to much more frequent changes than were prices of manufactured goods. Raw materials changed in price, on the average, during 82 per cent of the months covered, while manufactured goods changed in price during only 34 per cent of these months. The average magnitude of the fluctuations of monthly prices was over twice as great for raw materials as for manufactured goods.

§ The index numbers of production and of prices of raw and processed goods are not directly comparable, as regards composition. Instability measurements for these groups are suggestive of the relations between production and price movements, though their evidence is by no means conclusive.

| | Measurement of instability | |
|---|---|---|
| Commodity group | Index of production | Index of wholesale prices |
| Raw materials ..................... | 3.8 | 2.3 |
| Manufactured goods ............... | 4.7 | 2.1 |

For each group production was less stable than price; the margin of difference was much greater for processed goods. More important,

[1] See *The Behavior of Prices,* pp. 39-49, 56-60, for explanations of these measurements.

perhaps, is the indication that the process of manufacture brings reduced stability of production, increased stability of price.

Measurements relating to the production and prices of identical individual commodities may be compared with more confidence.

| Commodity group | Number of commodities | Averages of measurements of instability | |
|---|---|---|---|
| | | Production | Wholesale prices |
| Raw materials | 20 | 7.1 | 10.0 |
| Manufactured goods | 16 | 7.5 | 7.6 |

These averages, which are not subject to the offsetting which occurs in the construction of general index numbers, indicate that the prices of raw materials were distinctly more variable than was their volume of production. For the somewhat smaller sample of manufactured goods the difference was not marked. Control of production and consequent adaptation to fluctuating conditions of demand is more readily achieved in manufacturing industries than in those producing raw materials. This power to control and vary production has been used in some manufacturing industries to secure relative stability of prices. Among many classes of raw materials the erratic swings of production are not readily adapted to changing demand, and high price variability results. These characteristics are not unfamiliar, but it is useful to have precise measurements of the varying modes of price behavior.

FIGURE 15

MOVEMENTS OF WHOLESALE PRICES IN THE UNITED STATES, 1901-1913

PRODUCTS OF AMERICAN FARMS AND ALL OTHER PRODUCTS

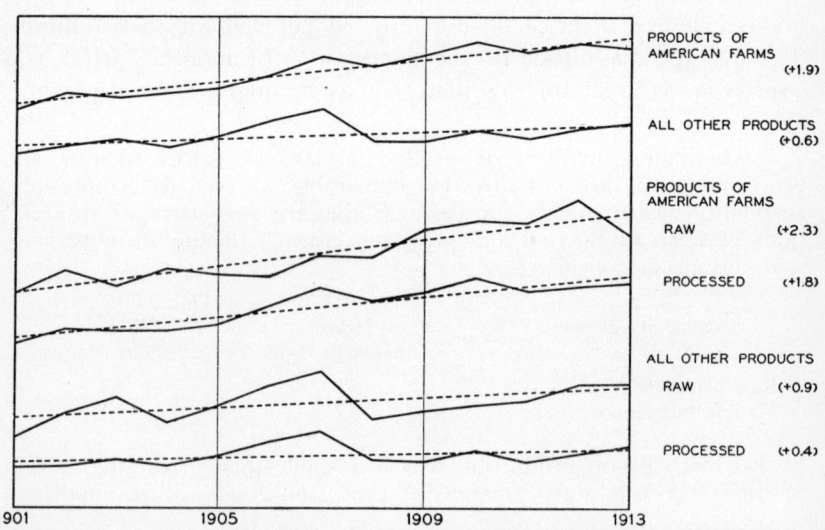

Plotted on ratio scale. The figures in parentheses define average annual rates of change (in percentage form).

## Products of American Farms and Other Products

What alterations were occurring between 1901 and 1913 in the terms of exchange between agricultural producers and other producers? How stable were price conditions for these two groups of producers? What relations prevailed between the trends of production and the trends of prices for these two groups? The index numbers following, shown graphically in Figure 15, have a bearing upon these questions.

TABLE 25

PRODUCTS OF AMERICAN FARMS AND ALL OTHER PRODUCTS

Index Numbers of Wholesale Prices in the United States, 1901-1913 [a]

| (1) | (2) | (3) | (4) | (5) | (6) | (7) |
|---|---|---|---|---|---|---|
| | Products of American farms | | All other products | | All products of American farms | All other products |
| Year | Raw | Processed | Raw | Processed | | |
| 1901 | 100.0 | 100.0 | 100.0 | 100.0 | 100.0 | 100.0 |
| 1902 | 108.0 | 104.8 | 108.3 | 100.8 | 105.6 | 102.5 |
| 1903 | 102.4 | 104.3 | 114.5 | 102.8 | 104.0 | 105.3 |
| 1904 | 108.6 | 104.7 | 105.3 | 100.8 | 105.7 | 101.7 |
| 1905 | 106.6 | 107.1 | 111.5 | 104.4 | 107.0 | 105.9 |
| 1906 | 105.8 | 113.9 | 119.5 | 109.8 | 112.5 | 111.9 |
| 1907 | 113.6 | 121.0 | 125.4 | 113.7 | 119.5 | 116.3 |
| 1908 | 113.0 | 115.9 | 107.0 | 103.6 | 115.4 | 104.4 |
| 1909 | 124.0 | 119.7 | 110.0 | 102.8 | 120.7 | 104.4 |
| 1910 | 127.4 | 125.4 | 112.4 | 107.0 | 125.9 | 108.2 |
| 1911 | 126.9 | 119.9 | 114.1 | 102.7 | 121.5 | 105.2 |
| 1912 | 137.4 | 122.1 | 120.4 | 105.9 | 125.2 | 109.0 |
| 1913 | 121.8 | 123.4 | 120.6 | 108.6 | 123.2 | 111.2 |

[a] Unweighted geometric averages constructed by the National Bureau of Economic Research from data compiled by the U. S. Bureau of Labor Statistics. The number of price series in each group is given below:

    All products of American farms
        Raw      24
        Processed      94 (87 in 1901-02)
        Total      118 (111 in 1901-02)
    All other products
        Raw      25
        Processed      84 (81 in 1901-02)
        Total      109 (106 in 1901-02)

Measurements which summarize the behavior of these series are given in the following table.

## TABLE 26
### Wholesale Prices of American Farm Products and of All Other Products
Summary of Rates of Change and Measurements of Instability, 1901-1913

| Commodity group | Average annual rate of change, 1901-1913 | | Index of instability, 1901-1913 |
| --- | --- | --- | --- |
| | In current dollars (per cent) | In purchasing power (per cent) | |
| All products of American farms | | | |
| Raw .................. | +2.3 | +1.0 | 3.4 |
| Processed ............ | +1.8 | +0.6 | 2.3 |
| Total ................ | +1.9 | +0.7 | 2.0 |
| All other products | | | |
| Raw .................. | +0.9 | −0.4 | 4.1 |
| Processed ............ | +0.4 | −0.8 | 2.4 |
| Total ................ | +0.6 | −0.7 | 2.6 |

Between 1901 and 1913 farm products were increasing in price at an average rate more than three times that prevailing among non-farm products. In terms of purchasing power per unit farm products were gaining at a rate of 0.7 per cent a year, while non-farm products were losing at the same rate. Within each of the major groups the rates of advance of raw material prices exceeded those of fabricated goods.

The respective indexes of instability (which measure the average degree of departure from constant rates of growth) show that between 1901 and 1913 products of American farms were more stable in price, on the average, than were non-farm products. Within each group raw products were less stable than processed goods. The difference is pronounced among the prices of non-farm products, the measurements of instability being 4.1 for raw materials and 2.4 for processed goods.

§ A comparison of instability measurements relating to index numbers of prices for these groups with corresponding measurements relating to production index numbers is illuminating.

Farm products, at their raw stage, are marked by instability of both production and prices, with fluctuations in production more pronounced. Variability of both price and production is reduced in the processed stage. Relatively high variability of prices and production characterizes raw non-farm products. Processing reduces the price variability, but serves to increase substantially the variations of production. Relatively stable prices and unstable production were found among processed non-farm products between 1901 and 1913.[1]

Relevant measurements for these groups are summarized below.

| Commodity group | Index of instability | |
|---|---|---|
| | Price | Production |
| Products of American farms | | |
| Raw | 3.4 | 4.7 |
| Processed | 2.3 | 2.3 |
| All other products | | |
| Raw | 4.1 | 3.8 |
| Processed | 2.4 | 6.8 |

These indexes of price instability may be supplemented by measurements of the month-to-month variability and of the frequency of the price change of the prices of individual commodities falling in the general classes distinguished above.

TABLE 27

PRODUCTS OF AMERICAN FARMS AND ALL OTHER PRODUCTS
Measurements of Variability of Wholesale Prices, 1898-1913

| Commodity group | Number of price series | Measurement of monthly variability | Measurement of frequency of price change |
|---|---|---|---|
| Products of American farms | | | |
| Raw | 24 | 9.0 | .92 |
| Processed | 83 | 3.7 | .42 |
| Total | 107 | 4.9 | .53 |
| All other products | | | |
| Raw | 25 | 5.4 | .74 |
| Processed | 75 | 3.4 | .26 |
| Total | 100 | 3.9 | .38 |

The prices of farm products were somewhat more variable than those of non-farm products. In each group the price variability of

[1] The sample of production series upon which these conclusions rest is not as large or as representative as the sample of price series. Instability of production has been characteristic of certain important industries, but by no means of all manufacturing industries. Moreover, non-farm products in the raw stage include such commodities as bituminous coal and natural gas which are not subject to further processing, and which are marked by relatively high productive stability.

raw materials was distinctly greater than that of processed goods.[1]

Summarizing, and contrasting price and production movements, we have seen that the period immediately preceding the World War was marked by an increase in the volume of agricultural production (in raw and processed form) at a rate approximately equal to the rate of growth of population. The output of non-agricultural industries was growing at a much more rapid rate. Among prices these tendencies were reversed. The terms of exchange between agricultural and non-agricultural industries were being altered to the distinct advantage of the former. The average real price per unit of agricultural products (that is, the purchasing power of such products in terms of all commodities at wholesale) was increasing at a rate of 0.7 per cent a year. Their purchasing power in terms of non-agricultural products was increasing at a rate of 1.3 per cent a year. This change was accompanied by corresponding declines in the purchasing power of the products of non-agricultural industries. These tendencies contributed to a definite improvement in the status of the farmer.

As regards stability of production there were differences of some importance among the groups under review. The output of raw farm products appears to have been less stable than the output of processed agricultural products. Explanations of this difference are found, in part, in the prompt reaction of export trade in raw agricultural products to variations in domestic production; exceptional variations in crop production were partially absorbed by foreign markets. In addition, domestic fabrication processes introduced elements of productive stability. Presumably a reservoir in the form of stocks of cotton, wheat, etc., was used to offset the natural fluctuations in agricultural production, so that the stream of products, as it reached the consumer, was steadier than it was at the source. On the other hand, non-farm products which had undergone some degree of fabrication seem to have been more variable than raw products of the same general class.

No significant difference appears between farm and non-farm products, as major classes, in the matter of price instability. Within each of the groups, however, there was an appreciable difference

---

[1] It is noteworthy that the measurement defining the month-to-month price variability of processed non-farm products declined from 4.0 for the period 1898–1905 to 2.9 for the period 1906–1913. The tendency toward greater price stability which prevailed before the war has already been mentioned.

between the prices of raw and manufactured goods, with raw materials distinctly more variable in each case. The production and marketing of raw farm products were characterized by instability of output and by variability of prices; production became more stable and prices became less variable as the degree of fabrication increased. Among raw non-agricultural products we find somewhat steadier productive processes and prices which, while relatively variable, were less so than those of farm products. In general, prices became more stable as the degree of fabrication of non-agricultural products increased, but in certain important industries production became less stable with increasing fabrication. Manufacturers of these goods appear to have secured stability of price in spite of (or, more likely, by means of) highly unstable processes of production.

### Farm Crops, Animal Products, Mineral Products and Forest Products

In classifying commodities into farm crops and animal, mineral and forest products, we define groups marked by characteristic conditions of production and marketing. The effects of these conditions may be expected to appear in the measurements descriptive of production and price behavior. Index numbers of the prices of commodities in these several groups are given in the following table. They are plotted in Figure 16.

FIGURE 16
MOVEMENTS OF WHOLESALE PRICES IN THE UNITED STATES, 1901-1913
FOREST PRODUCTS, ANIMAL PRODUCTS, FARM CROPS AND MINERAL PRODUCTS

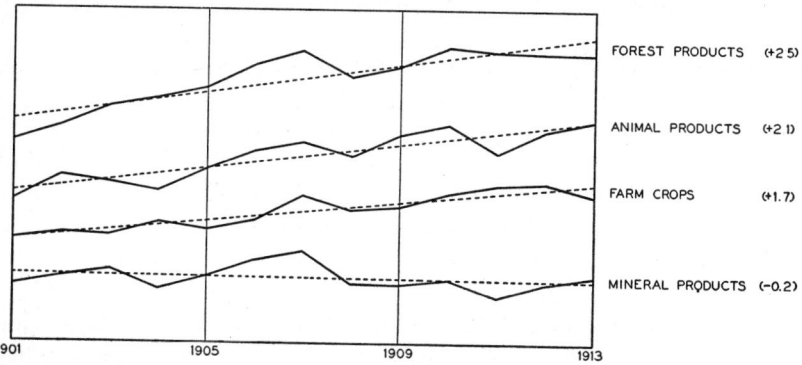

Plotted on ratio scale. The figures in parentheses define average annual rates of change (in percentage form).

## TABLE 28

FOREST PRODUCTS, ANIMAL PRODUCTS, FARM CROPS AND MINERAL PRODUCTS

Index Numbers of Wholesale Prices in the United States, 1901-1913 [a]

| (1) Year | (2) Forest products (raw and processed) | (3) Animal products (raw and processed) | (4) Farm crops (raw and processed) | (5) Mineral products (raw and processed) |
|---|---|---|---|---|
| 1901 | 100.0 | 100.0 | 100.0 | 100.0 |
| 1902 | 105.6 | 108.9 | 102.4 | 103.0 |
| 1903 | 112.7 | 106.5 | 101.3 | 104.9 |
| 1904 | 116.1 | 103.4 | 105.8 | 98.4 |
| 1905 | 120.4 | 111.3 | 103.3 | 102.9 |
| 1906 | 130.3 | 118.8 | 106.9 | 108.8 |
| 1907 | 137.3 | 122.4 | 116.3 | 112.3 |
| 1908 | 125.7 | 116.9 | 110.6 | 100.4 |
| 1909 | 129.8 | 126.1 | 112.2 | 100.2 |
| 1910 | 139.3 | 130.5 | 117.5 | 102.1 |
| 1911 | 136.9 | 118.1 | 120.9 | 96.0 |
| 1912 | 136.5 | 127.7 | 121.9 | 100.3 |
| 1913 | 136.1 | 132.4 | 116.5 | 102.9 |

[a] Unweighted geometric averages constructed by the National Bureau of Economic Research from data compiled by the U. S. Bureau of Labor Statistics. The number of price series in each group is given below:

| | |
|---|---|
| Forest products | 22 |
| Animal products | 52 (47 in 1901-02) |
| Farm crops | 74 (72 in 1901-02) |
| Mineral products | 70 (67 in 1901-02) |

Nine price series included in the all commodities index have been omitted from these averages because of the difficulty of proper classification.

Measurements derived from the above index numbers appear in the next table.

With reference to the change in relative position of the several groups here shown, the figures in column (3) of Table 29 are probably most significant. Mineral products (both raw and processed) were falling in purchasing power per unit at a rate of 1.4 per cent a year—a notable decline, indeed. Products of all other types were gaining in purchasing power, the advance in prices of forest products being most pronounced.

A record of comparative stability is furnished by the indexes appearing in column (4) of Table 29. But these do not provide unequivocal measurements of the average degree of price instability of the individual commodities falling in the several groups. Off-

## TABLE 29

Wholesale Prices of Forest Products, Animal Products, Farm Crops and Mineral Products

Summary of Rates of Change and Measurements of Instability, 1901-1913

| (1) | (2) | | (3) | (4) |
|---|---|---|---|---|
| | Average annual rate of change, 1901-1913 | | | Index of instability, 1901-1913 |
| Commodity group (raw and processed) | In current dollars (per cent) | | In purchasing power [a] (per cent) | |
| Forest products | +2.5 | | +1.2 | —[b] |
| Animal products | +2.1 | | +0.8 | 3.2 |
| Farm crops | +1.7 | | +0.4 | 2.1 |
| Mineral products | —0.2 | | —1.4 | 2.9 |

[a] Purchasing power measured in terms of general commodities at wholesale.
[b] The measurement for forest products is omitted. Because of a change in the rate of increase in the prices of forest products after 1907 the fit of the trend line is poor.

setting fluctuations in the prices of different commodities in the same group may give the index numbers a quite misleading appearance of stability. The following averages, derived from measurements of the magnitude of monthly fluctuations and of the frequency of changes (from month to month) during the period 1898-1913 in the prices of individual commodities, are not subject to such offsetting.

## TABLE 30

Forest Products, Animal Products, Farm Crops and Mineral Products

Measurements of Variability of Wholesale Prices, 1898-1913

| Commodity group (raw and processed) | Number of price series | Measurement of monthly variability of prices | Measurement of frequency of price change |
|---|---|---|---|
| Animal products | 46 | 5.1 | .59 |
| Farm crops | 69 | 4.9 | .52 |
| Forest products | 20 | 3.9 | .32 |
| Mineral products | 63 | 3.7 | .36 |

This record shows animal products to have been the most variable in price, and to have been subject to the most frequent price changes, with farm crops and their derived products a close second. Forest and mineral products stand close together, both considerably less variable in their monthly price movements than the two classes of farm products.

TABLE 31

WHOLESALE PRICES OF FOREST PRODUCTS, ANIMAL PRODUCTS, FARM CROPS AND MINERAL PRODUCTS, IN RAW AND PROCESSED FORM

Summary of Rates of Change and Measurements of Instability, Pre-war

| (1) | (2) | (3) | (4) | (5) | (6) |
|---|---|---|---|---|---|
| | Average annual rate of change, 1901-1913 | | Index of instability of price index 1901-1913 | Measurement of monthly variability of prices 1898-1913 | Measurement of frequency of price change 1898-1913 |
| Commodity group [a] | In current dollars (per cent) | In purchasing power [b] (per cent) | | | |
| Forest products [c] Processed ..... | +2.5 | +1.2 | — | 3.7 | .28 |
| Animal products Raw .......... | +1.8 | +0.5 | 3.9 | 8.0 | .88 |
| Processed ..... | +2.2 | +0.9 | 3.1 | 3.9 | .48 |
| Farm crops Raw .......... | +2.8 | +1.5 | 5.6 | 8.5 | .91 |
| Processed ..... | +1.3 | 0 | 1.8 | 3.8 | .39 |
| Mineral products Raw .......... | +0.3 | —0.9 | 4.7 | 5.2 | .69 |
| Processed ..... | —0.4 | —1.6 | 2.7 | 3.1 | .23 |

[a] The numbers of price series upon which these measurements are based are given below:

| Commodity group | Number of price series relating to entries in | |
|---|---|---|
| | Columns (2)-(4) | Columns (5)-(6) |
| Forest products Processed | 21 | 19 |
| Animal products Raw | 13 | 13 |
| Processed | 39 (34 in 1901-02) | 33 |
| Farm crops Raw | 17 | 17 |
| Processed | 57 (55 in 1901-02) | 52 |
| Mineral products Raw | 18 | 18 |
| Processed | 52 (49 in 1901-02) | 45 |

[b] Purchasing power is measured in terms of the commodities in the wholesale price index of the National Bureau of Economic Research.

[c] All forest products included in the sample with the single exception of crude rubber, have been classified as processed goods. No measurement of instability is given for this group because of the inadequacy of the fitted trend line.

The story of price changes in these groups during the pre-war era may be continued with reference to the measurements in Table 31 relating to raw and processed commodities under each head. Corresponding price index numbers are given in Appendix III.

The necessity of distinguishing raw from processed commodities in a given group is clear from a survey of these figures. Farm crops in raw form were increasing in purchasing power at a rate of 1.5 per cent a year, while processed farm crops showed no net change in purchasing power. Animal products in processed form were gaining in purchasing power somewhat more rapidly than were raw products. Processed mineral products were declining in real value, per unit, at a rate substantially greater than that measuring the drop in the values of raw minerals. Of the three groups for which comparison is possible (forest products being excluded) two showed a relative cheapening of processed goods, with reference to raw materials. Among animal products this tendency was reversed.

Without exception, the various measurements of instability and of price variability show raw materials to be materially less stable in price than processed goods. Raw farm crops appear to have been least stable, whether judged with reference to their annual deviations from trend, to their monthly price variations or to the frequency of price changes. Most stable, with reference to annual movements, were processed farm crops, while processed mineral products were most stable in their monthly changes. The superior stability of processed mineral products is most clearly manifest in the figures showing frequency of price change. In less than one month out of four (23 per cent) did the prices of such products vary from the prices prevailing during the preceding month. For processed animal products the ratio is close to one out of two (48 per cent), while for raw farm crops it approaches unity (91 per cent).

The constancy shown by the prices of manufactured mineral products may represent a desirable freedom from untoward fluctuations, or it may represent failure to conform to changes in market conditions due to the exercise of price control. That such price stability does not necessarily represent stability of the corresponding industrial processes is shown by the relatively high indexes of instability relating to the production of processed minerals. Instability in the stream of mineral manufactures is higher than that recorded for any other production group, while the averages of instability measurements for the production of individual commodities are highest for processed non-farm products (primarily mineral). Price stability and productive instability appear to have been characteristic of industries fabricating mineral products.

Comparison of rates of change in prices and production is possible for certain of the above groups. Between 1901 and 1913 the volume of crop production (as measured by the index of mass of crop production compiled by the United States Department of Agriculture) advanced at a rate of 1.5 per cent a year; the per-unit purchasing power of raw farm crops was increasing at the same rate during this period. The volume of production of raw mineral products expanded at a rate of 5.6 per cent a year, while the per-unit purchasing power of such products declined by 0.9 per cent a year. This cheapening of mineral products and the advancing real price of farm crops were natural accompaniments [1] of the sharply differing rates of change in production volume.

FIGURE 17

MOVEMENTS OF WHOLESALE PRICES IN THE UNITED STATES, 1901-1913

FOODS AND NON-FOODS

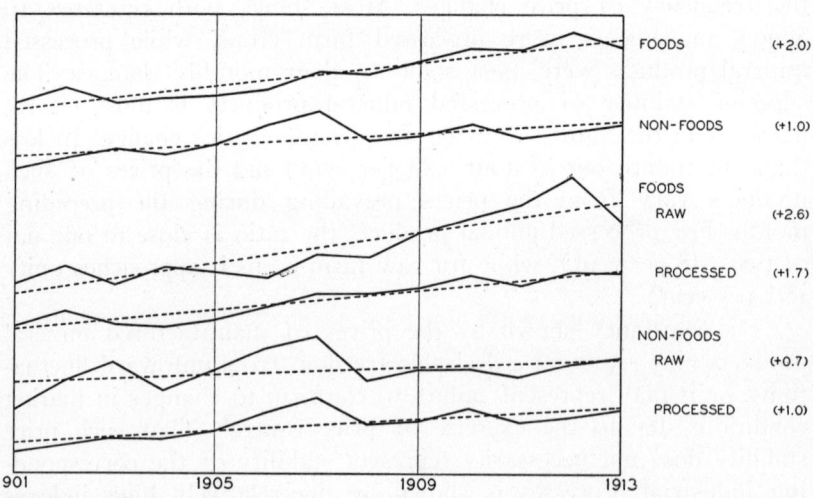

Plotted on ratio scale. The figures in parentheses define average annual rates of change (in percentage form).

[1] Neglecting possible effects of foreign trade movements.

## Foods and Non-foods

Pre-war price changes in two other major categories, and in their raw and processed subdivisions, are traced in the next table. These index numbers are plotted in Figure 17.

TABLE 32

Foods and Non-foods

Index Numbers of Wholesale Prices in the United States, 1901-1913 [a]

| (1) | (2) | (3) | (4) | (5) | (6) | (7) |
|---|---|---|---|---|---|---|
| | Foods | | Non-foods | | All foods | All non-foods |
| Year | Raw | Processed | Raw | Processed | | |
| 1901 | 100.0 | 100.0 | 100.0 | 100.0 | 100.0 | 100.0 |
| 1902 | 106.3 | 104.9 | 109.9 | 102.1 | 105.4 | 103.5 |
| 1903 | 99.7 | 100.4 | 116.9 | 104.5 | 100.2 | 106.6 |
| 1904 | 106.0 | 99.6 | 107.8 | 103.9 | 101.7 | 104.7 |
| 1905 | 104.0 | 102.0 | 113.8 | 106.9 | 102.6 | 108.2 |
| 1906 | 101.9 | 106.3 | 123.0 | 113.8 | 104.7 | 115.4 |
| 1907 | 110.5 | 111.2 | 127.9 | 119.4 | 111.1 | 120.9 |
| 1908 | 109.1 | 111.2 | 110.5 | 109.4 | 110.4 | 109.7 |
| 1909 | 118.7 | 113.4 | 114.8 | 110.6 | 115.2 | 111.5 |
| 1910 | 124.7 | 118.0 | 115.1 | 115.7 | 120.2 | 115.7 |
| 1911 | 130.1 | 114.5 | 112.0 | 110.4 | 119.6 | 110.9 |
| 1912 | 142.8 | 119.6 | 116.9 | 112.3 | 127.1 | 113.1 |
| 1913 | 123.0 | 119.4 | 119.6 | 115.0 | 120.7 | 115.9 |

[a] The index numbers are unweighted geometric averages of relative prices, computed by the National Bureau of Economic Research from price quotations compiled by the U. S. Bureau of Labor Statistics. The number of price series in each group is given below:

| Foods | | Non-foods | |
|---|---|---|---|
| Raw | 23 | Raw | 26 |
| Processed | 44 (43 in 1901-02) | Processed | 134 (125 in 1901-02) |
| Total | 67 (66 in 1901-02) | Total | 160 (151 in 1901-02) |

Measurements of the price behavior of commodities in these groups are summarized in Table 33, on the next page.

The general picture is one of food products rising in purchasing power per unit, with non-food products becoming relatively cheaper. This was, of course, a period of rapid expansion in the output of non-foods, with consequent possibilities of mass production at lower costs. The output of non-foods increased at an average annual rate of 3.9 per cent, between 1901 and 1913, while the production of foods increased at a rate of 1.9 per cent a year.

In the matter of instability the picture is much like that presented by other classifications. The raw materials are distinctly

## TABLE 33

### Wholesale Prices of Foods and of Non-foods
Summary of Rates of Change and Measurements of Instability, Pre-war

| (1) | (2) | (3) | (4) | (5) | (6) |
|---|---|---|---|---|---|
| | Average annual rate of change, 1901-1913 | | Index of instability of price index 1901-1913 | Measurement of monthly variability of prices 1898-1913 | Measurement of frequency of price change 1898-1913 |
| Commodity group [a] | In current dollars (per cent) | In purchasing power [b] (per cent) | | | |
| Foods | | | | | |
| Raw ....... | +2.6 | +1.3 | 4.3 | 9.2 | .95 |
| Processed .. | +1.7 | +0.4 | 1.9 | 5.1 | .57 |
| Total ....... | +2.0 | +0.7 | 2.4 | 6.5 | .70 |
| Non-foods | | | | | |
| Raw ....... | +0.7 | −0.6 | 4.0 | 5.3 | .72 |
| Processed .. | +1.0 | −0.2 | 2.6 | 3.0 | .26 |
| Total ....... | +1.0 | −0.3 | 2.7 | 3.4 | .34 |

[a] The numbers of price series for the entries in columns (2) to (4) are given in the footnote to the preceding table; for the entries in columns (5) and (6) they are given below.

| Foods | | Non-foods | |
|---|---|---|---|
| Raw | 23 | Raw | 26 |
| Processed | 43 | Processed | 115 |
| Total | 66 | Total | 141 |

[b] Purchasing power is measured in terms of the commodities in the wholesale price index of the National Bureau of Economic Research.

more variable in price than are the processed goods. Foods in both raw and processed forms are less stable in price, in their month-to-month movements, than are the corresponding classifications of non-foods. The annual deviations of the group index numbers from constant rates of growth, as measured by the index of instability, were slightly greater for non-foods than for foods.

### Producers' Goods and Consumers' Goods

Particular interest attaches to the changes occurring in the prices of goods in shape for final consumption (consumers' goods) and of goods destined for use as capital equipment, or not yet in shape for use by the final consumer (producers' goods). Relevant index numbers are given in the following table, and are shown graphically in Figure 18.

## TABLE 34
### Producers' Goods and Consumers' Goods
Index Numbers of Wholesale Prices in the United States, 1901-1913 [a]

| (1) | (2) | (3) | (4) | (5) | (6) | (7) |
|---|---|---|---|---|---|---|
| | Producers' goods | | Consumers' goods | | All producers' goods | All consumers' goods |
| Year | Raw | Processed | Raw | Processed | | |
| 1901 | 100.0 | 100.0 | 100.0 | 100.0 | 100.0 | 100.0 |
| 1902 | 110.0 | 102.7 | 101.9 | 103.0 | 105.2 | 102.9 |
| 1903 | 109.4 | 103.6 | 105.4 | 103.4 | 105.7 | 103.6 |
| 1904 | 105.7 | 100.6 | 111.0 | 104.5 | 102.4 | 105.1 |
| 1905 | 110.0 | 105.1 | 105.8 | 106.1 | 106.9 | 106.1 |
| 1906 | 114.2 | 112.4 | 107.1 | 111.5 | 113.3 | 111.1 |
| 1907 | 124.4 | 116.9 | 103.9 | 117.7 | 119.7 | 116.3 |
| 1908 | 110.9 | 106.1 | 106.3 | 112.9 | 107.9 | 112.2 |
| 1909 | 119.0 | 107.7 | 108.6 | 114.2 | 111.6 | 113.7 |
| 1910 | 123.2 | 113.7 | 107.3 | 118.2 | 116.9 | 117.1 |
| 1911 | 120.9 | 107.1 | 117.6 | 114.8 | 111.7 | 115.1 |
| 1912 | 127.6 | 109.3 | 130.9 | 117.9 | 115.3 | 119.1 |
| 1913 | 122.9 | 111.6 | 115.3 | 119.6 | 115.5 | 119.2 |

[a] The index numbers are unweighted geometric averages of relative prices, computed by the National Bureau of Economic Research. The commodities employed are those for which prices are compiled by the U. S. Bureau of Labor Statistics. The number of price series in each group is given below:

Producers' goods
  Raw        38
  Processed  77 ( 73 in 1901-02)
  Total     115 (111 in 1901-02)

Consumers' goods
  Raw        11
  Processed  101 ( 95 in 1901-02)
  Total     112 (106 in 1901-02)

### FIGURE 18
MOVEMENTS OF WHOLESALE PRICES IN THE UNITED STATES, 1901-1913
PRODUCERS' GOODS AND CONSUMERS' GOODS

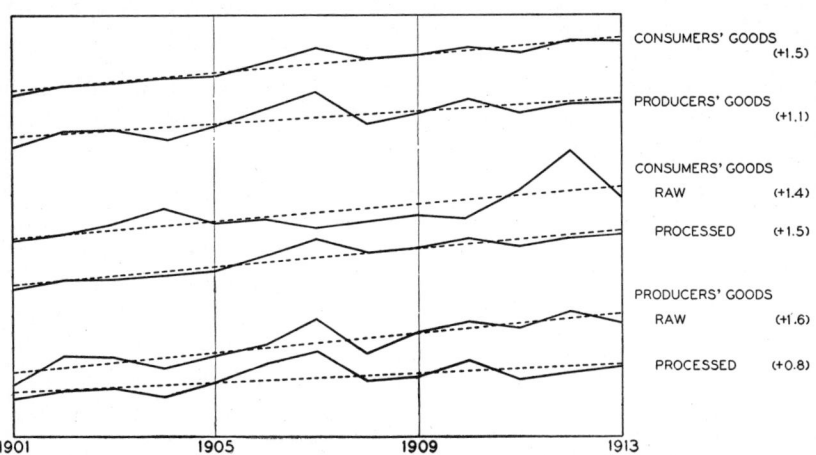

Measurements relating to the movements of these index numbers, and to certain other aspects of the behavior of the prices of producers' and consumers' goods, are summarized in the next table.

TABLE 35

WHOLESALE PRICES OF PRODUCERS' GOODS AND OF CONSUMERS' GOODS
Summary of Rates of Change and Measurements of Instability, Pre-war

| (1) | (2) | (3) | (4) | (5) | (6) |
|---|---|---|---|---|---|
| | Average annual rate of change, 1901-1913 | | Index of instability of price index 1901-1913 | Measurement of monthly variability of prices 1898-1913 | Measurement of frequency of price change 1898-1913 |
| Commodity group [a] | In current dollars (per cent) | In purchasing power [b] (per cent) | | | |
| Producers' goods | | | | | |
| Raw .......... | +1.6 | +0.4 | 2.9 | 6.5 | .80 |
| Processed ..... | +0.8 | −0.5 | 2.7 | 3.6 | .32 |
| Total ......... | +1.1 | −0.2 | 2.6 | 4.6 | .49 |
| Consumers' goods | | | | | |
| Raw .......... | +1.4 | +0.1 | 3.4 | 9.3 | .90 |
| Processed ..... | +1.5 | +0.2 | 1.6 | 3.6 | .36 |
| Total ......... | +1.5 | +0.2 | 1.2 | 4.2 | .42 |

[a] The numbers of price series relating to the entries in columns (2) to (4) are given in the footnote to the preceding table; for the entries in columns (5) and (6) they are as follows:

| Producers' goods | | Consumers' goods | |
|---|---|---|---|
| Raw | 38 | Raw | 11 |
| Processed | 71 | Processed | 87 |
| Total | 109 | Total | 98 |

[b] Purchasing power is measured in terms of general commodities at wholesale, as these enter into the index of the National Bureau of Economic Research.

Between 1901 and 1913 goods ready to be purchased by the consumer for immediate and personal use were increasing in real value (i.e., in per-unit purchasing power) at a rate of 0.2 per cent a year, a very slight annual change. Producers' goods were declining each year in real value per unit at the same rate. Such a slight margin is negligible, of course, over a short period, but as an element to be compounded it becomes substantial in time. An inspection of the annual records in Table 34 reveals an interesting reversal of the relative movements of these index numbers after 1907. During the prosperous period which preceded the break in October, 1907, producers' goods remained higher in price, in relation to the 1901 base, than consumers' goods. (Only in 1904, a year of depression, was this not true.) In 1908, also a time of depression, these positions were reversed. Producers' goods fell sharply in price, and consumers' goods were left with higher real values. This situation continued without a break through 1913. Even the relatively good times of 1909 and 1912 failed to restore the parity of 1901.

If we separate the raw and processed goods falling in each of these broad classes we secure a clearer view of certain tendencies of this era. The sample of raw consumers' goods [1] is so small (including only 11 price series) that no general conclusions may be drawn from the movements of this index number. The trend of prices of these commodities between 1901 and 1913 was substantially the same as that of all consumers' goods. Much sharper is the divergence between the trends of producers' goods in raw and processed forms. Raw materials advanced in price and in purchasing power, with temporary checks during the recessions of 1904, 1908 and 1913. Processed producers' goods (fabricated goods intended for use in the construction of capital equipment, or for human consumption after further processing) were affected most immediately by the increased productivity of labor and by economies of large scale production during this period. Such goods were progressively cheapened during this period, in relation to other goods. In 1913 their real value, per unit, was 5 per cent lower than in 1901.

With respect to stability, the several measurements cited in Table 35 indicate that the prices of consumers' goods were more stable than the prices of producers' goods, a conclusion supported by various other types of evidence. Raw consumers' goods, a small and highly erratic group, were the least stable of the sub-groups, with raw producers' goods standing next in order.

The group of producers' goods includes two quite distinct classes of commodities, goods intended for use in the construction of capital equipment (e.g., structural steel) and goods intended for human consumption, after further fabrication. Measurements de-

[1] The division of consumers' goods into raw and processed classes calls for a word of comment. In all cases consumers' goods are in shape for final consumption; the classification into raw and processed forms is a mutually exclusive one. The two classes do not, as in the case of certain other divisions, represent the same goods in different stages of fabrication. Goods that may be consumed either in raw or processed form constitute the only exceptions to this rule.

fining changes in the prices of goods in these classes are given in the following table.

TABLE 36

PRODUCERS' GOODS DESTINED FOR USE IN CAPITAL EQUIPMENT AND FOR HUMAN CONSUMPTION

Index Numbers of Wholesale Prices in the United States, 1901-1913 [a]

| Year | Producers' goods destined for use in capital equipment | Producers' goods destined for human consumption |
|---|---|---|
| 1901 | 100.0 | 100.0 |
| 1902 | 105.2 | 105.2 |
| 1903 | 106.8 | 103.8 |
| 1904 | 100.4 | 105.3 |
| 1905 | 108.0 | 105.3 |
| 1906 | 118.0 | 106.6 |
| 1907 | 123.3 | 114.3 |
| 1908 | 107.0 | 108.8 |
| 1909 | 107.9 | 116.7 |
| 1910 | 114.0 | 121.0 |
| 1911 | 108.3 | 116.3 |
| 1912 | 111.5 | 120.6 |
| 1913 | 113.6 | 117.9 |
| Average annual rate of change in wholesale prices (per cent)..... | +0.7 | +1.5 |
| Average annual rate of change in purchasing power (per cent)... | −0.5 | +0.3 |

[a] The number of price series in each commodity group is given below:
    Producers' goods destined for use as capital equipment    67 ( 64 in 1901-02)
    Producers' goods destined for human consumption    48 ( 47 in 1901-02)

It is clear that the figures in the general index conceal two differing trends. The net change over the period was in the direction of distinctly lower purchasing power, per unit, for goods intended for use in the construction of capital equipment; the average annual rate of decline was 0.5 per cent. Goods intended for ultimate human consumption showed a net advance in purchasing power, per unit, at an average rate of 0.3 per cent each year. (The predominance of mineral products among articles of capital equipment has a bearing on these movements, of course.) Here again we find a notable reversal of trend occurring about the middle of the period. The boom times which culminated in 1906 and 1907 placed articles of capital equipment at somewhat of a premium (these were worth in 1906 5.2 per cent more, per unit, than in 1901), and lowered the real worth of goods intended for ultimate consumption (these were worth in 1906 5.0 per cent less, per unit, than in 1901). Thereafter, goods for use in capital equipment declined steadily in value, while goods for human consumption advanced. Even in the comparatively good years of 1909 and 1912 there was no advance in the worth of goods intended for capital equipment, a condition in sharp contrast to that prevailing in 1903, 1906 and 1907. The nine years preceding 1908 had been marked by only brief lapses from prosperity; the prosperous years following that date were interludes in a period of subnormal business activity.

During this pre-war period the output of goods intended for use in capital equipment increased at a more rapid rate (5.0 per cent a year) than did consumption goods in general (2.6 per cent a year). It is a notable fact that there was no such relative decline in the output of capital equipment after 1907 as occurred in the per-unit worth of goods intended for use in capital equipment. The index numbers cited in the preceding chapter show that between 1908 and 1913 the production of capital equipment continued the advance which had prevailed between 1901 and 1907. Relatively high production of capital equipment co-existed with low prices during the years immediately preceding the war.

## Summary: Pre-war Movements of Commodity Prices

The threads of economic change during an epoch are interlaced in subtle ways. The movements of a dynamic economy are not amenable to simple description or to ready explanation. This is as true of variations in prices and costs as it is of any other phase of economic change. Certain general features of changing price levels and fluctuating relations among major commodity groups are readily established, but the interpretation of these changes and their linking with other economic movements are problems of a different order. To these problems the present discussion is merely an introduction.

The rising tendency of the price level during the years prior to the outbreak of the World War placed a distinctive impress upon the economic life of that era, affecting buying and selling practices, altering the relations of debtors and creditors, shaping the character of business cycles. This price advance caused aggregate commodity values to increase more rapidly than the volume of physical goods, injecting into the economic situation values not based on new services or additional commodity units. We may not trace with any high degree of accuracy the effects of this slow, secular inflation upon the values of goods and services of different types, for these effects are interwoven with the results of numerous other economic changes. The introduction of novel production methods, the fluctuations of consumption habits and those broader movements that mark the passing of economic power from one group to another all influence the course of prices. Our present concern is with the combined effects of all these forces upon the purchasing power of the commodities marketed by different groups of producers.

Conspicuous among the economic changes occurring in the United States between the opening of the twentieth century and the outbreak of the World War were the advancing real worth of raw materials and the declining real worth (per unit) of manufactured goods. Here, it is probable, the secular change in the value of money, technical improvements in processes of fabrication and the widening of markets characteristic of this era all worked in the same direction, to cheapen products of manufacture in relation to their raw ingredients. Experience indicates that the effects of changes in the value of money are felt, in general, in raw material markets before they are felt in the markets for finished goods. Certain elements of manufacturing cost are particularly slow to react to changes in monetary values, a condition which tends to hold the prices of manufactured goods to a pre-existing level when general prices move either upward or downward. During any period of rising prices we thus have forces at work in the direction of higher real values of materials, lower real values of manufactures. These tendencies were reënforced between 1901 and 1913 by improved industrial technique, and by the repercussions upon costs and prices of widening markets and of increasing emphasis upon mass production in manufacturing industries.

Among raw materials the gains in real worth, per unit of product, were greatest for farm crops; the purchasing power of these commodities increased at the notable rate of 1.5 per cent a year. Raw animal products gained at a lower rate. Producers of raw minerals suffered a decline in purchasing power per unit of product, a decline which was associated with a remarkable increase in the volume of production of these materials. In the group of manufactured goods, processed forest and animal products actually gained in purchasing power per unit, while processed farm crops remained practically constant. The full effects of the forces acting in the direction of lower real values were felt among fabricated mineral products, a group of major importance in an industrial civilization. These declined in exchange value per unit at a cumulative rate of 1.6 per cent a year during the years before the war.

If we separate products of American farms from all other commodities, we find clear-cut differences in price behavior. The real value of farm products, per unit, was being steadily enhanced during pre-war years; the per-unit value of other commodities was steadily declining. The terms of exchange between agricultural and non-agricultural producers were being modified, on a per-unit basis, to the advantage of agricultural interests. Every unit of farm produce was commanding, year by year, an increasing quantity of other goods. This steady gain contributed to the rising scale of well-being of American farmers which was one of the outstanding economic characteristics of this period.

The shift in the terms of exchange between farm and non-farm elements of the population during these years was due, in considerable part, to differences in productive conditions. The volume of agricultural production was increasing at a rate slightly below that at which population was growing; the volume of production of non-agricultural commodities (in which mineral products are the most important element) was increasing at a rate approximately two and one-half times as high as the rate of population increase. It is true, of course, that wants were expanding more rapidly in the latter field, but not with sufficient rapidity to enable this swelling mass of goods to be marketed without material reductions in the amounts asked in return for each unit of product. Such reductions were possible partly because of the advantages conferred by mass production, partly because the reduction of real manufacturing costs which a rising price level permits [1] worked to the particular advantage of the industries which were able to expand production at a rapid rate. These were, notably, industries fabricating non-agricultural products.

If we consider the change of values during this pre-war era with reference to consumers' budgets, interest attaches to the distinction between foods and non-foods. Foods satisfy certain wants

[1] Because of the lag of labor costs and various elements of overhead costs.

which are not capable of great expansion, but which stand first in order of necessity. Less urgent, but capable of wide expansion and great diversity, are other wants of human kind. During the years under review food values advanced, in relation to other commodities, while non-foods were progressively cheapened. It was in the latter field, again, that volume of output was advancing most rapidly. Mass production permitted lower prices, and lower prices stimulated demand for a wider variety and for greater quantities of goods. The characteristic features of industrial advance during the years before the war were found in their clearest form in the production and marketing of non-food products. The nature of food products and the conditions circumscribing both supply and demand in this field did not permit the full flowering of the new technology.

Another classification has to do with the relative price trends during pre-war years of consumers' goods and producers' goods— of goods in shape to serve or to be consumed by the final consumer, and of all other goods. Here we have a classification of obvious economic significance, since it separates goods which are only one degree removed from ultimate consumption (one degree removed because the prices here employed, even for consumers' goods, are wholesale prices) from goods which are still several stages removed from ultimate use. Purely business considerations, considerations of profit and loss, dominate in the markets for producers' goods. These considerations still are of weight in the wholesale markets for consumers' goods but do not have full sway. The stabilizing effect on prices of the relative inertia of mass demand is felt; considerations of utility and of ready marketability are more immediate and pressing in the markets for consumers' goods. As a result we should expect consumers' goods to be more stable in price and, in particular, to be less sensitive to changes in the purchasing power of money. We should expect producers' goods to react more promptly to the monetary factors which affect all prices, with consumers' goods lagging during both rising and falling prices. This would lead us to look for a cheapening of consumers' goods during the pre-war era of rising prices.

The actual figures, however, do not bear out our expectations. The two groups moved with but a slight margin between them during the years 1901-1913, producers' goods being cheapened slightly, consumers' goods gaining slightly in real value. If we are right in assuming that consumers' goods are less sensitive to changes in the value of money than producers' goods, some other factor must have been in operation, serving to cheapen producers' goods and to offset the tendency of such goods to react promptly to changing values of the monetary unit. If we break producers' goods into two groups, raw and processed, the nature of this offsetting factor is suggested. Raw producers' goods advanced in real value between 1901 and 1913, at a rate exceeding the advance of raw and of processed consumers' goods. Processed producers' goods (a class including 77 commodities during the pre-war years) declined in real value, at a rate of 0.5 per cent a year. Processed producers' goods are heavily weighted by fabricated mineral products, destined for use in the construction of capital equipment. This class of goods felt most immediately the effects of improved manufacturing technique, of falling production costs, of mass production, all of which were characteristic of this era. The actual movement of the prices of producers' goods during the pre-war era thus reflected the resultant of two conflicting tendencies, a tendency to rise because of a characteristic sensitivity to changing monetary values, and a tendency to decline because of falling production costs and widening markets.

Similarly, it may be hazarded, the prices of consumers' goods moved in response to conflicting forces pulling in opposite directions—toward lower real value per unit, because of a tendency to lag behind general prices, toward higher real worth because of the heavy weight given to farm products among consumers' goods. The net movement of per-unit purchasing power was slightly upward.

This discussion of the movement of prices among producers' and consumers' goods during the pre-war era is suggestive, apart from its historical interest, because of its bearing on more recent tendencies. The close concordance of pre-war price movements among these two groups of goods, and the failure of a marked secular divergence to emerge, was perhaps due to an offsetting of conflicting tendencies within each group. Under different conditions the tendencies prevailing among commodity prices in each of these groups might reënforce one another, and a pronounced divergence of trends might result. If sustained by the influence of continuing secular movements, divergence of this sort would present novel economic and business problems. This subject will be considered further in the treatment of more recent tendencies.

A significant feature of the price movements of the pre-war

period is found in the cheapening of commodities destined for use in capital equipment, a cheapening which was in evidence, however, only after the crisis of 1907. During the sustained business advance of the years preceding that recession goods for use in capital equipment were bid up in price, selling at substantial premiums in 1906 and 1907. Thereafter they declined in exchange value, either because of diminished demand during the lean years between 1908 and 1913 or because of large supply. In respect to prices of materials, these latter years were particularly favorable for capital expansion.

Divergent price trends of the type dealt with in the preceding paragraphs have a clear bearing upon the fortunes and status of different groups of producers. For such divergent trends reflect the play of forces which are altering the real worth of goods of various kinds, changing their command, in exchange, over other goods. Price changes of another type are matters of concern to producers and dealers. These are fluctuations over short periods, and departures from the regular movements suggested by the annual rates of change which have been cited in discussing long-term tendencies. These short-period movements are indications of price variability. They may reflect necessary and orderly adaptations to changing conditions of supply and of demand, they may reflect ill-ordered production or marketing programs, or they may be due to faults and excesses of other sorts in the working of the competitive system. Whatever the cause, each fluctuation represents some degree of uncertainty to the producers and dealers concerned, an injection of a speculative element into the engineering task of combining productive elements for a specific technical purpose. In this sense, then, price variability represents economic instability, though the factors of instability may lie far below the monetary surface.

There was evidence of a considerable degree of price instability in the United States at the opening of the century. There was further evidence, however, of a tendency toward greater stability during the years preceding the war, with signs of a distinct lessening of the speculative element in business transactions. In brief summary of the survey of price variations:

> Raw materials were less stable in price than manufactured goods. The difference was not great, as regards deviations of annual averages from long-term trends, but the superior stabil-

ity of manufactured goods was much more pronounced with reference to the degree and frequency of monthly price fluctuations.

In stability of secular price movements farm products, both raw and processed, ranked slightly higher than non-farm products. In their monthly movements, however, prices of farm products were considerably less stable than the prices of non-farm products. Most violent in their monthly price changes were raw farm products. Among such products crops were more variable in price than animal products, though both were highly unstable. After fabrication, however, crop products became more stable in price than animal products. Mineral products in processed form showed a relatively high degree of price stability, a condition which stands in interesting contrast to the marked instability of production characteristic of such goods.

Non-foods were less stable than foods, in respect to deviations of annual averages from constant rates of growth, but in their month-to-month price movements foods were distinctly less stable.

Consumers' goods were more stable in price than producers' goods, a condition to be expected. Among consumers' goods, however, a small group of raw materials were marked by a very high degree of price instability.

Finally, we have emphasized the general significance of the divergence of secular trends among commodity prices. Such divergence represents a constant shift of purchasing power from group to group, and a constant readjustment among the elements of the price system. The notable feature of this aspect of economic change is that it is continual and cumulative, that the margins between commodity prices expand or contract year after year. The degree to which these expanding margins represent adaptations to other economic changes, the degree to which they necessitate readjustment among other elements, cannot be stated. Nor may we say whether the adjustment of other economic elements to these divergent movements is secured through continual adaptation, or whether the periodic disturbances which constitute one phase of business cycles represent (in part) more painful adaptations to secular price divergence. We know only that such mutual adjustment there must be; we do not understand its precise mechanism.

CHAPTER III

# Price and Cost Changes in Manufacturing Industries of the United States, 1899-1914

IT is a commonplace that in a modern industrial society the pursuit of material satisfactions centers about the making and spending of money. Economic desires and activities alike are defined in terms of money and measured on a scale of prices and costs. In view of the wide scope of the activities which are thus measured, it is surprising that the price record is so scanty. Only for a limited number of goods, and these of restricted types, do we have adequate statistics of changing market values. The record is particularly meager for highly fabricated goods, and for the various services which enter as costs in the making of such goods.

There is no prospect of filling this great gap in our economic records by means of a direct attack. The statistics which would permit us to trace changes in labor costs, in overhead costs, and in the selling prices of complicated products of manufacture simply do not exist. In default of such materials we may attempt by indirect means to secure these highly important records for certain leading industries. To this end we turn to data compiled by the Bureau of the Census on manufacturing industries of the United States.[1] These include statistics relating to value of products, to certain elements of cost, and to the physical volume of production. Census records for the pre-war period are restricted to the four years, 1899, 1904, 1909 and 1914.

### Changes in Physical Output and in Aggregate Values and Costs, Manufacturing Industries

In Table 37 are summarized certain statistics of manufacturing production which are to be utilized. The figures in this table do not

---

[1] I am indebted to LeVerne Beales, Chief Statistician for Manufactures, Bureau of the Census, for numerous courtesies in connection with the compilation of materials for use in this chapter and in Chapter VIII, and for a critical review of the procedure employed.

## TABLE 37

### Statistics of Selected Manufacturing Industries of the United States, 1899-1914 [a]

(All value figures in thousands of dollars)

| (1) | (2) | (3) | (4) | (5) | (6) | (7) | (8) |
|---|---|---|---|---|---|---|---|
| Year | Total value of products [b] | Cost of materials [c] | Cost of fabrication, plus profits [d] | Total wages paid [e] | Overhead expenses, plus profits [f] | Actual value of products entering into index of physical volume of production | Ratio of col. (7) to col. (2) |
| | Statistics relating to all products of industries represented in index of physical volume of production | | | | | | |
| 1899 | 4,669,569 | 3,086,322 | 1,583,247 | 696,369 | 886,878 | 4,203,180 | .900 |
| 1904 | 5,757,111 | 3,850,977 | 1,906,134 | 838,759 | 1,067,375 | 5,267,314 | .915 |
| 1909 | 7,883,874 | 5,337,880 | 2,545,994 | 1,056,923 | 1,489,071 | 7,268,558 | .922 |
| 1914 * | 9,513,844 | 6,471,723 | 3,042,121 | 1,353,262 | 1,688,859 | 8,655,465 | .910 |
| 1914 ** | 9,430,609 | 6,411,249 | 3,019,360 | 1,341,820 | 1,677,540 | 8,586,887 | .911 |
| 1914 *** | 9,012,084 | 6,161,366 | 2,850,718 | 1,247,567 | 1,603,151 | 8,187,655 | .909 |

\* The statistics for 1914 which appear on this line are comparable with the data for 1899.
\*\* The statistics for 1914 which appear on this line are comparable with the data for 1904.
\*\*\* The statistics for 1914 which appear on this line are comparable with the data for 1909.

[a] For the years here covered the census enumerations included all establishments having products of an annual value of $500 or more.

[b] The item 'value of products', as reported by manufacturing establishments, represents the selling value, at the factory, of all products manufactured during the year, whether sold or not. In estimating 'selling value', account is taken of the increase or decrease in the stock of manufactured goods (or of stocks in process of manufacture) on hand at the end of the year as compared with the beginning of the year. When possible, freight and delivery charges and discounts from list prices are deducted. Establishments working under contract or doing repair work report the amounts received for such services rather than the value of the products.

For those establishments which make partly finished products, such as pig iron, destined to be used by other establishments under the same ownership, the value of the product must be estimated. Estimates of such 'transfer values' (made by the manufacturer) are based sometimes on market prices, sometimes on cost of manufacture.

[c] Cost of materials represents the cost, delivered at the factory, of "all materials and mill supplies of every description, whether raw or partly manufactured, or whether entering into the product, used as containers, or consumed in the process of manufacture; and all fuel, whether used for heat or power or in process of manufacture, as in making coke, gas, or pig iron, . . . actually *used* during the year covered by the report." (*Abstract of the Census of Manufactures, 1914*, p. 12.) The cost of those materials produced in the plant itself and used by it for further manufacture is not included.

[d] 'Cost of fabrication, plus profits', or 'value added to materials by manufacture', is the difference between the value of products and the cost of materials. Cost of fabrication does not include the cost of fuel, payments for rented power, or cost of mill supplies. These are included under cost of materials.

[e] The item 'total wages paid' represents the total amount paid to wage-earners (including piece-workers) during the year. It includes board or rent furnished as part compensation.

[f] 'Overhead expenses plus profits', being secured by deducting wages paid from 'value added by manufacture', includes salary payments, rent, interest, depreciation, repairs, insurance, advertising costs and taxes, as well as profits.

relate to all manufacturing industries. Selection has been necessary to ensure the comparability of the statistics relating to physical volume and to other aspects of production. (In general, the volume figures are not as comprehensive as the other manufacturing statistics, and are not in all respects comparable with them.) In column (7) is given the value of the products actually employed each year in constructing the index numbers of physical volume of manufacturing production which were presented in Chapter I. The ratio of this value to the value listed in column (2) is given in column (8). Such a ratio was computed for each of the smallest industrial groups for which statistics relating to volume of production, value of products, cost of materials, etc., are given. This ratio serves as a measure of the adequacy of the index of physical volume, or as a measure of the degree of comparability of the volume figures and the other statistics. For example, in 1899, for all commodities, the products entering into the index of physical volume had a value of 4,203,180 thousands of dollars [column (7)]. The entries in columns (2) to (6) for the same year relate to the production of manufactured goods having a value of 4,669,569 thousands of dollars [column (2)]. The ratio of the first of these figures to the second is .900. In other years covered by Table 37 this ratio varies from .909 to .922. The two sets of statistics have nearly identical coverage.

In the present study use has been made only of statistics relating to those industries for which the 'adequacy ratio' exceeded .60. Industries for which no quantity figures, or only inadequate figures, were available have been excluded.[1]

It is possible to break up the total value of products of manu-

[1] The relative importance of the industries covered is indicated by the following summary, giving the percentage relation of the value of products included in the index of physical volume of production to the total value of manufactured products reported by the Bureau of the Census.

| Year | Total value of products reported in Census of Manufactures (thousands of dollars) | Value of products in industries represented by index numbers of physical volume (thousands of dollars) | Percentage of total value of manufactured products represented in index numbers |
|---|---|---|---|
| 1899 | 11,406,927 | 4,669,569 | 40.9 |
| 1904 | 14,793,903 | 5,757,111 | 38.9 |
| 1909 | 20,672,052 | 7,883,874 | 38.1 |
| 1914 * | 24,246,435 | 9,513,844 | 39.2 |
| 1914 ** | 24,246,435 | 9,430,609 | 38.9 |
| 1914 *** | 24,246,435 | 9,012,084 | 37.2 |

\* The statistics for 1914 which appear on this line are comparable with the data for 1899.
\*\* The statistics for 1914 which appear on this line are comparable with the data for 1904.
\*\*\* The statistics for 1914 which appear on this line are comparable with the data for 1909.

facture into three elements, measuring the costs of the contributions of sellers of materials, of wage-earners, and of a composite group of owners, creditors, managers and other salaried employees. These are distinct and significant classes, though rather far removed from the classical economic categories of land, labor, capital and business enterprise. Measurements relating to the elements noted are to be interpreted with an understanding of their precise significance. Thus, the materials of manufacture are in many cases semi-processed before they reach a given manufacturing plant. Moreover, the cost of transportation to the manufacturing plant is included with material costs, as are, also, costs of fuel, power and containers. Again, the second item in the list includes only wages paid, not salaries. Finally, the third element, which we have called 'overhead expenses plus profits', includes such items as interest charges, depreciation, taxes, rent and salaries, as well as profits.[1]

Since our interest is not in the absolute figures but in changes occurring in these various elements, we present them in relative form in Table 38, together with an index of the physical volume of manufacturing production between 1899 and 1914.

The index numbers of physical volume given in this table have been constructed by means of the 'ideal' formula, weights being based upon 'value added' (i.e., upon cost of fabrication, plus profits).[2] In this process each of the years, 1899, 1904 and 1909, has been paired, in turn, with 1914, the base being shifted later to 1899. The only novel feature of the procedure lies in the correction of the original quantity data to offset the variations from year

[1] Data on salaries are available, but it has not seemed desirable to treat them separately, or in combination with wages. Salary payments relate to a wide range of services. In some cases the distinction between profits and salaries may not be clearly drawn. Wages, as a separate item in manufacturing costs, constitute a far more clearly-defined and homogeneous element than would wages and salaries in combination.

Colonel M. C. Rorty comments: "Special care must be taken in interpreting the results secured when salaries are combined with returns to capital. It is my opinion that a tendency prevailed, over the period here covered, to place more and more of productive labor on a salaried basis."

[2] In averaging data relating to different industries weights have been based upon the materials actually included in the index. In general, no attempt has been made to employ imputed weights, by means of which given commodities might be made to represent related commodities for which no data are available. However, industries producing automobiles, forest products and petroleum products have been given reduced weights, proportionate to their relative importance among all industries covered by the Census of Manufactures. For an explanation of this reduction see footnote, pp. 26-27.

## TABLE 38
RELATIVE NUMBERS DEFINING CHANGES IN IMPORTANT ELEMENTS OF MANUFACTURING PRODUCTION IN THE UNITED STATES, 1899-1914 [a]

| (1) Year | (2) Physical volume of production (fabrication) | (3) Value of products | (4) Cost of materials | (5) Cost of fabrication, plus profits | (6) Total wages paid | (7) Overhead expenses plus profits |
|---|---|---|---|---|---|---|
| 1899 | 100.0 | 100.0 | 100.0 | 100.0 | 100.0 | 100.0 |
| 1904 | 120.2 | 125.1 | 128.2 | 118.5 | 119.5 | 117.7 |
| 1909 | 154.5 | 178.2 | 183.5 | 167.2 | 158.7 | 173.5 |
| 1914 | 176.3 | 199.5 | 206.7 | 184.4 | 186.6 | 182.7 |

[a] The entries in columns (3) to (7) define changes in aggregates; they do not measure changes per unit of product. As is explained elsewhere, three industries were given reduced weights in securing relative numbers from the data given in Table 37.

to year in the adequacy ratio. This is a matter requiring some further explanation.

As will be clear from the subsequent uses to which the measurements in Table 38 are to be put, the highest possible degree of comparability between the index numbers of physical volume and the other index numbers in the table is desirable. If, for a given industry, the adequacy ratio were .90 in one year and .80 in a later year, direct comparison of changes in volume of output and, let us say, in number of workers employed, would be invalid. Either because the coverage of the quantity statistics was less complete in the second year, or because the industry in question devoted more of its resources to the production of secondary products, the quantity index would show a decline in production which did not actually occur, or would understate the advance which did occur. If we are interested in variations in the aggregate output of that industry some correction must be made for the variation in the degree of coverage of the quantity statistics. If this is not done quite misleading conclusions as to the degree of change in productivity per worker (and in other respects) will be drawn.[1]

---

[1] If the adequacy ratio declines because, in a given industry, a secondary product for which quantity statistics are not compiled is being produced in greater quantities, it may be justifiable, for certain purposes, to make no correction. This would be proper if sole interest attached to the variations in production of the major product, let us say automobiles. But in this case it would not be valid to compute index numbers of per capita production, and similar measurements, with-

In the present study correction for a changing adequacy ratio has been made, for each industry, by increasing the number of physical units reported for each census year to a standard corresponding to an adequacy ratio of 1.00. The index numbers of physical output thus secured for individual industries measure changes in the aggregate output of those industries, not changes in the output of specific commodities. The problem of correcting for changes in adequacy does not then arise when the group index numbers are combined in an index number of volume of production for all manufacturing industries. The ratios in Table 37 have been included because of their bearing on the representativeness of the data employed.

The construction of index numbers of the physical volume of manufacturing production which are comparable with other census statistics opens the way for further exploitation of the detailed statistics of manufacture. In such exploitation, however, certain of the difficulties involved in the construction of quantity index numbers must be recognized. The chief of these difficulties is that, from time to time, changes occur in the *quality* of manufactured goods. Thus, an automobile in the year 1932 is many degrees removed in quality from the automobile of 1920, and still further removed from the automobile of 1900. For a large number of standard commodities such quality changes do not occur, or are of minor importance. But for manufactured commodities as a whole they cannot be ignored. A thoroughly accurate index of the physical volume of production should perhaps measure the production of units of service and use, rather than the production of harvesting machines, automobiles, sides of bacon, loaves of bread, pairs of shoes. It is, of course, impossible to construct such an index, and we must restrict ourselves to measurements of changes in the number of physical units produced.[1]

This fundamental difficulty which arises out of quality changes is involved in all attempts to measure changes in the volume of production or in the prices of manufactured goods. In the construc-

---

out adjusting either the production index or the index measuring changes in the number of employed workers.

[1] In some cases it has been possible to take account of changing quality in the output of a given industry, by using detailed statistics of output in which goods of different grades, or quality, are distinguished. If this had not been done, an increased output of goods of high quality would have been submerged in an aggregate dominated by cheaper products.

tion of index numbers of prices we must content ourselves with measuring changes in the prices of what are designated shoes, tractors, automobiles, even though we know or suspect that the purchaser of these commodities may, at a given time, be getting more or less in the way of serviceability and utility than at a previous date. There appears to be no solution of the problem beyond that of dealing with the actual physical units and interpreting our results with the realization that these units may have undergone quality changes. In this interpretation, therefore, we shall attach greater weight to comparisons over short periods of time, during which quality changes would ordinarily be slight, than to comparisons covering longer periods.[1]

## Changes in the Selling Prices of Manufactured Goods

Having comparable measurements of the volume of physical production and of the aggregate value of product between 1899 and 1914, it is possible to derive index numbers defining changes in the average selling price per unit of manufactured products during this period. An index of changes in aggregate value, divided by a properly weighted index of changes in volume of production, yields a properly weighted index of changes in average price.[2]

§ *On changes in the apparent physical contributions of different agents of manufacturing production.*—The method of weighting em-

[1] This same problem arises in attempting to measure changes in the purchasing power of the dollar, or of other monetary units. For this purpose it would appear to be proper to employ only standard commodities not subject to quality changes from time to time. Yet this is not a perfect solution. Standard commodities which do not change in quality are in all probability subject, as a group, to particular price-determining forces. Their price movements, therefore, measure not only changes in the purchasing power of money, but also alterations in the terms of exchange between this group and all other commodities, alterations not necessarily proportionate to quality changes in these other commodities.

[2] The operation is the reverse of the 'factor reversal test' suggested by Professor Irving Fisher (*The Making of Index Numbers,* Houghton Mifflin Co., Boston, 1927, pp. 72-82) and used extensively by him in testing different types of index numbers. That is, a properly weighted price index number multiplied by a properly weighted volume index number yields a series of relatives defining accurately changes in aggregate value. In reversing the process, as is done in the present case, it is essential that the index numbers employed satisfy the factor reversal test. It is for this reason, in part, that the 'ideal' formula has been used in constructing the present volume index numbers. The same argument applies, of course, to the process of deriving the index numbers of per capita output and of per establishment output which were presented in Chapter I.

ployed must be appropriate to the purpose in mind. Thus in deriving an index number of selling price per unit of product of manufacture, the weights employed in constructing the index of physical volume should be based upon value of product. The volume index number, that is, should measure changes in the aggregate output of manufacturing establishments, not changes in the specific contribution of agents of fabrication. In deriving an index of per capita production, on the other hand, the weights used in constructing the index of physical volume should be based upon value added in manufacture, for it is the contribution of fabricating agents which is here in question. In deriving measurements of changes in various elements of cost, as is done hereafter, weights should be based upon the corresponding elements of total value of product (e.g., upon wages paid, if labor cost per unit is being measured). Index numbers of physical volume in which these several weighting factors have been used are given below.

TABLE 39

Index Numbers Measuring Changes in the Apparent Physical Contributions of Different Agents of Manufacturing Production, 1899-1914

| (1) Year | (2) Aggregate output (weights based on value of product) | (3) Volume of materials (weights based on cost of materials) | (4) Volume of fabrication (weights based on 'value added') | (5) Apparent contribution of labor (weights based on wages paid) | (6) Apparent contribution of ownership and management [a] (weights based on overhead expenses plus profits) |
|---|---|---|---|---|---|
| 1899 | 100.0 | 100.0 | 100.0 | 100.0 | 100.0 |
| 1904 | 118.8 | 118.0 | 120.2 | 118.3 | 120.8 |
| 1909 | 148.5 | 145.8 | 154.5 | 151.6 | 155.6 |
| 1914 | 163.3 | 157.8 | 176.3 | 169.4 | 180.4 |
| Average annual rate of change 1899-1914 (per cent) ........ | +3.4 | +3.2 | +3.9 | +3.7 | +4.1 |

[a] The phrase 'ownership and management' is used for convenience to include owners, managers and salaried employees, as well as the agents represented by such items of overhead expense as rent and interest payments. Where this composite element—the difference between 'value added' and wages—bulks large, it means, presumably, that the contribution of ownership and management in the form of equipment and organization is relatively important. To the extent that monopoly and windfall profits swell this item, the assumption of a corresponding 'contribution' is not justified. It should be made clear, moreover, that the use of the term 'con-

For each individual industry there is, of course, but one index of changes in physical volume of production. If the volume of output increases in a certain proportion we are forced (in default of exact knowledge) to assume that the contributions of those providing materials and of those providing labor and management have all increased in that proportion. But when averages relating to the production of a number of industries are secured we may take some account of the varying contributions of these different factors. Index numbers of volume of output secured by the use of different weighting factors will differ, and should differ, when there are differences in the rates of growth of industries in which cost of materials bulk large and of industries in which fabrication costs are relatively large. If the latter industries are growing more rapidly, the aggregate physical contribution of agents of fabrication is increasing more rapidly than is the aggregate physical contribution of those providing materials.

That this was the case between 1899 and 1914 is apparent from the measurements in Table 39. The increased importance of fabrication in manufacturing processes is shown by the sharper advance of the index weighted by 'value added'. Most rapid was the gain in the index which purports to measure changes in the physical contribution of ownership and management. The increasing importance of overhead with the growth of industrial equipment is indicated by this series.

This method of measuring changes in the prices of manufactured products differs materially, of course, from that ordinarily employed in constructing price index numbers. The normal procedure is to collect price quotations in representative markets and, by appropriate technical methods, to secure weighted averages of these quoted prices, the weights being based, ordinarily, upon quantities marketed. In the present case we start with a series of figures measuring the actual values of the products of manufacture of all, or nearly all, the establishments in the United States producing commodities of the type included. We have, that is, a practically all-inclusive record of the values of the commodities in question. Paralleling this, we have a series of index numbers defining changes in the aggregate physical output of the establishments to which the value figure relate. A simple process of division gives us, then, a series of relatives measuring changes in the average selling price, per unit of product.

The wide coverage of the data employed in deriving price index numbers by this method is notable. Instead of basing estimates of

---

tribution' does not imply that the specific productivity of different agents is being measured. There are here measured only those apparent changes in the physical contributions of different agents which result from the varying rates of growth of industries with widely different combinations of the factors of production.

price movements upon occasional quotations in a restricted list of markets, it is possible to employ data relating to about 90 per cent of the total sales of manufacturing establishments producing the commodities in question. The securing of separate price quotations as comprehensive in scope as the census value and quantity figures would be quite impossible. For the commodities and industries actually included in the present study the main problem encountered in the use of price index numbers, that of the representativeness of the quotations, does not arise, for the quantity, value and price figures relate to practically the entire universe of inquiry, and not to a selected sample. (If we wish to go beyond this group of industries the usual questions of representativeness must of course be faced.)

Price index numbers derived from census statistics of manufacture have another distinct advantage, in their homogeneity as regards the markets to which the prices relate. Such index numbers measure changes in the prices received by manufacturers. The term 'wholesale price' has come to be a very vague term. Most wholesale price index numbers are based upon quotations drawn from many markets, at different distributive stages, and relating to transactions of the most diverse sorts. An index of prices received by manufacturers has a clear and unequivocal meaning.

Index numbers of value of product, of physical volume of production and of average price per unit appear in Table 40, below. These and the other index numbers cited in this chapter are derived from statistics relating to approximately 40 per cent of the total product, by value, of all manufacturing industries in the United States. The industries directly covered by the compilations are enumerated in the next section, while a list of the commodities included is given in Appendix IV. These index numbers are shown graphically in Figure 19.

Between 1899 and 1914 the stream of values derived from manufacturing operations increased 100 per cent, at an average rate of 4.9 per cent a year. This gain was due to an increase of approximately 63 per cent in physical volume of production and of 22 per cent in average selling price per unit. On a yearly basis the average rate of increase was 3.4 per cent in volume, 1.5 per cent in price per unit. The gain in volume, as we have seen, was most rapid during the census interval 1904-1909. This was also

## TABLE 40

INDEX NUMBERS OF AGGREGATE VALUE, PRODUCTION AND PRICE, 1899-1914 [a]
Manufacturing Industries of the United States

| Year | Aggregate value of manufactured products | Physical volume of output [b] | Average selling price per unit, products of manufacture |
|---|---|---|---|
| 1899 | 100.0 | 100.0 | 100.0 |
| 1904 | 125.1 | 118.8 | 105.3 |
| 1909 | 178.2 | 148.5 | 120.0 |
| 1914 | 199.5 | 163.3 | 122.2 |
| Average annual rate of change 1899-1914 (per cent).. | +4.9 | +3.4 | +1.5 |

[a] The volume, price and per-unit cost index numbers given in this and later tables are all derived from 'ideal' indexes, on the 1914 base. The comparison of each year with 1914 is accurate, but the cross-comparison of other years introduces a slight element of error.
[b] The components of this index are weighted according to value of product. These weights give the correct quantity index to use in deriving an index of changes in average selling price per unit from an index of changes in aggregate value.

### FIGURE 19

CHANGES IN AGGREGATE VALUE, VOLUME OF PRODUCTION AND AVERAGE PRICE OF PRODUCTS

MANUFACTURING INDUSTRIES OF THE UNITED STATES, 1899-1914

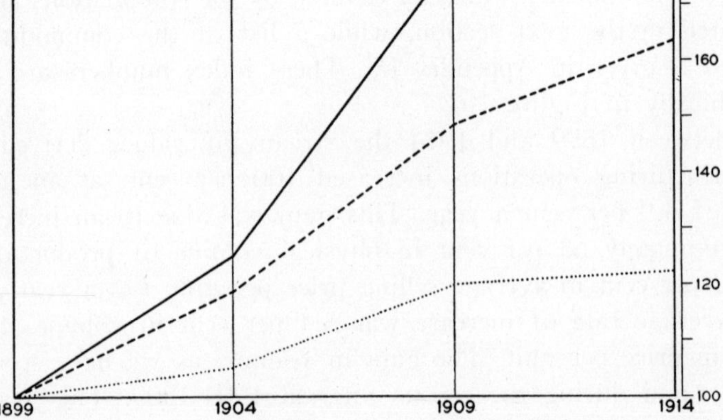

the period of most rapid rise in the prices of manufactured goods.[1]

§ *Selling prices, individual industries.*—A truer picture of changes in the selling prices of manufactured goods is secured when we view these movements in detail. The interpretation of such detailed measurements is not clouded by the problems of weighting and of representativeness that must be faced in dealing with averages. Index numbers for separate manufacturing industries, as given in the following table, reveal the great diversity of the changes that lie behind the general averages. The rates of change of the selling prices of manufactured products are shown graphically in Figure 20.

The variations in selling price changes between 1899 and 1914 are fairly wide, from industry to industry. Explosives, at one extreme, declined at an average annual rate of 2.3 per cent, while products of slaughtering and meat packing industries, at the other, advanced at a rate of 3.7 per cent per year. The degree of variation among these rates is measured by a standard deviation of 1.7.[2] This figure is significantly lower than the corresponding value of 5.7, measuring the standard deviation of the rates of change in quantities produced by the same industries. There is far more coherence among the price changes than among the quantity changes. There is a suggestion here that the prices at which the products of a given industry are sold are more subject to the influence of economic forces at large, are less free to diverge radically from the general trend, than is the physical production of that industry. It is the price nexus which binds industries together, and unequal price changes are probably more disturbing to a given economic equilibrium than are unequal changes in quantities marketed.

[1] It is of interest to compare these index numbers of the prices of manufactured goods with a series derived directly from the price quotations compiled by the U. S. Bureau of Labor Statistics. Such index numbers, constructed as unweighted geometric averages of 178 series of price quotations (168 in 1899), appear in column (3) below:

| (1) | (2) | (3) |
| --- | --- | --- |
| Year | Index of average selling price per unit of manufactured goods, derived from census data | Unweighted geometric average of price relatives, manufactured goods |
| 1899 | 100.0 | 100.0 |
| 1904 | 105.3 | 109.5 |
| 1909 | 120.0 | 118.6 |
| 1914 | 122.2 | 120.9 |

There is no reason to expect very close agreement between those two independently derived series. The degree of resemblance actually existing must be in part accidental, but it justifies belief in the substantial accuracy of the two sets of measurements.

[2] Weights drawn from the terminal years, 1899 and 1914, have been used throughout in the computation of standard deviations of rates of change for census data.

## TABLE 41
### Changes in the Selling Prices of Products of Manufacturing Industries of the United States, 1899-1914
Index Numbers for 35 Industries, with Average Annual Rates of Change

| Industry | Index numbers of selling price, per unit of product | | | | Average annual rate of change 1899-1914 (per cent) |
|---|---|---|---|---|---|
| | 1899 | 1904 | 1909 | 1914 | |
| Slaughtering and meat packing....... | 100.0 | 103.1 | 135.3 | 165.8 | +3.7 |
| Flour-mill and gristmill products...... | 100.0 | 137.0 | 161.6 | 153.4 | +2.7 |
| Butter, cheese, and condensed milk.... | 100.0 | 105.8 | 141.9 | 139.8 | +2.6 |
| Turpentine and rosin................. | 100.0 | 146.1 | 163.9 | 149.0 | +2.4 |
| Coke, not including gas-house coke.... | 100.0 | 112.0 | 125.9 | 135.9 | +2.1 |
| Cotton goods ........................ | 100.0 | 118.3 | 131.9 | 132.1 | +1.8 |
| Lumber and timber products.......... | 100.0 | 114.6 | 138.2 | 126.2 | +1.7 |
| Gloves and mittens, leather........... | 100.0 | 91.9 | 120.7 | 119.1 | +1.6 |
| Hosiery and knit goods............... | 100.0 | 108.4 | 114.6 | 125.5 | +1.5 |
| Hats, wool-felt ...................... | 100.0 | 133.3 | 161.7 | 119.1 | +1.3 |
| Fertilizers .......................... | 100.0 | 96.6 | 116.9 | 115.7 | +1.3 |
| Hats, fur-felt ....................... | 100.0 | 99.8 | 108.8 | 118.0 | +1.2 |
| Carpets and rugs, other than rag...... | 100.0 | 112.1 | 111.3 | 118.2 | +1.0 |
| Paper and wood pulp................. | 100.0 | 100.6 | 112.8 | 113.0 | +1.0 |
| Woolen and worsted goods........... | 100.0 | 108.8 | 119.9 | 109.3 | +0.7 |
| Silk goods .......................... | 100.0 | 91.7 | 99.8 | 107.8 | +0.6 |
| Paint and varnish.................... | 100.0 | 104.8 | 102.5 | 111.7 | +0.6 |
| Canning and preserving: fruits and vegetables; pickles, preserves, and sauces | 100.0 | 97.4 | 98.3 | 109.9 | +0.6 |
| Musical instruments: pianos.......... | 100.0 | 100.0 | 101.7 | 106.2 | +0.4 |
| Rice, cleaning and polishing.......... | 100.0 | 73.2 | 99.7 | 96.7 | +0.4 |
| Petroleum, refining ................. | 100.0 | 114.3 | 101.4 | 107.9 | +0.2 |
| Musical instruments: organs.......... | 100.0 | 102.1 | 102.5 | 99.2 | 0.0 |
| Ice, manufactured ................... | 100.0 | 100.5 | 101.6 | 97.2 | −0.1 |
| Iron and steel: blast furnaces......... | 100.0 | 96.4 | 105.8 | 94.1 | −0.2 |
| Sugar, beet ......................... | 100.0 | 107.4 | 105.7 | 91.4 | −0.5 |
| Iron and steel: steel works and rolling mills ............................. | 100.0 | 91.9 | 91.1 | 86.1 | −0.9 |
| Gas, manufactured, illuminating and heating ........................... | 100.0 | 94.9 | 88.0 | 83.1 | −1.3 |
| Wood distillation, not including turpentine and rosin ..................... | 100.0 | 91.7 | 84.8 | 79.8 | −1.5 |
| Automobiles, including bodies and parts | 100.0 | 92.3 | 109.0 | 66.0 | −1.8 |
| Motorcycles, bicycles, and parts....... | 100.0 | 75.5 | 70.1 | 75.2 | −2.0 |
| Salt ................................ | 100.0 | 105.5 | 71.5 | 77.4 | −2.3 |
| Explosives ......................... | 100.0 | 90.7 | 77.5 | 71.7 | −2.3 |
| Boots and shoes, other than rubber.... | 100.0 | 112.0 | — | 147.4 | — |
| Cordage and twine................... | 100.0 | — | 91.0 | 109.4 | — |
| Jute and linen goods................. | 100.0 | — | 110.5 | 128.4 | — |
| Average [a] ......................... | 100.0 | 104.6 | 124.6 | 127.4 | +1.8 |

[a] The average for each year is the arithmetic mean of the central items of a weighted frequency distribution, with weights based on value of product, averaged for the base year and the given year. The central one-fifth of the items, by weight, were included in computing the average.

## FIGURE 20
### ILLUSTRATING THE DIVERGENCE OF PRICE TRENDS AMONG 32 MANUFACTURING INDUSTRIES OF THE UNITED STATES, 1899-1914*
AVERAGE RATES OF CHANGE IN SELLING PRICE PER UNIT OF PRODUCT

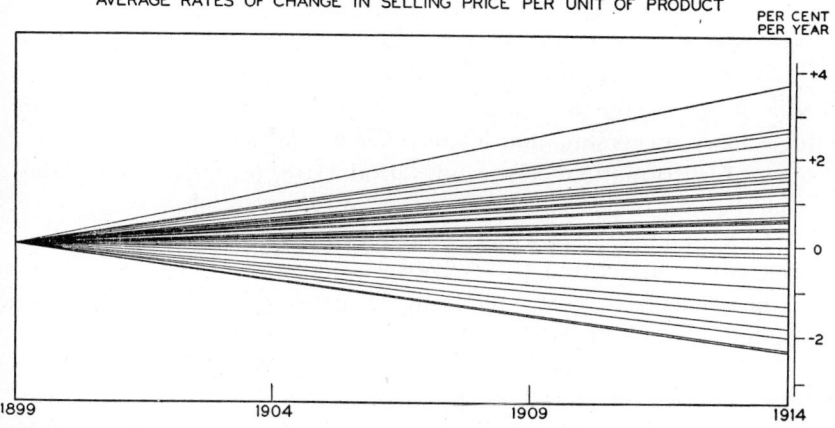

* Plotted on ratio scale. The lines here plotted relate to the industries listed in Table 41, in the order of that listing.

The averages of selling price changes among manufactured goods, as derived from the records for individual industries, differ somewhat from the 'ideal' indexes previously cited. The averages given in Table 41 are derived from the central values of frequency distributions, and are designed to represent *typical* situations among manufacturing industries (weighted, of course, by value of products). These averages of selling prices are slightly higher for 1909 and 1914 than are the 'ideal' index numbers.

### Changes in Material Costs and in Fabrication Costs, Manufacturing Industries

The compilations of the Census of Manufactures yield not only data on the total value stream; they permit that value stream to be divided in various ways, as was shown in Table 37. Thus we have the total cost of materials and the total value of the services of agents of fabrication ('value added'). Each of these may in turn be compared with the index of physical volume, and from the comparison may be derived index numbers of cost of materials and of cost of fabrication, per unit of manufactured product. The total value of the services of fabricating agents may again be subdivided into two streams, total wages paid and total overhead expenses plus profits, and from these, in relation to the stream of physical volume, we may derive index numbers of labor costs and of overhead costs plus profits, per unit of manufactured product.[1] In addition, then, to the measurement of changes in the average selling price of products of manufacture, we may measure changes in the prices, per unit of manufactured product, of the services of various agents of production—of those who provide materials, on the one hand, and of fabricating agents, including labor, ownership and management, on the other. Here is a type of information concerning productive processes and industrial changes impossible to secure by direct methods.

Index numbers showing changes in the average per-unit selling price of manufactured goods between 1899 and 1914, and in two major elements of cost, appear in the next table. These are shown graphically in Figure 21.

Between 1899 and 1914 material costs per unit of manufactured product increased 31 per cent, while fabrication costs rose only 4.6 per cent. Material costs (the most heavily weighted factor) were primarily responsible for the increase of 22 per cent

[1] In connection with this procedure a question of some general significance may be raised. Are we justified in assuming, as we do throughout the study, that changes in the constituent elements of value of products indicate changes in the costs of the contributions of the several factors, rather than changes in the amounts of their physical contributions? If changes in the relative physical contributions of the different factors occur (for example, if a given quantity of raw materials is subject to a greater degree of fabrication in turning out a final product which remains the same in name) and if, at the same time, changes in the costs of the different factors occur, it is clear that there is no way of separating the two and measuring each in isolation. To the extent that changes in the physical contributions of the different factors have occurred, the indexes of costs to be presented hereafter are, in fact, measures of changing costs and of changing physical contributions combined in unknown proportions.

This is another aspect of the problem of changes in quality. As in the general case, it is probably safe to assume that over short periods indexes of changing costs measure, primarily, true alterations in costs, and that the relative physical contributions of the different factors are not altered. Over longer periods, and for certain classes of commodities (of which automobiles may be cited as an example), changes in the relative physical contributions of the different factors undoubtedly occur, and indexes of cost are to be interpreted with this fact in mind.

In so far as changes in the contributions of the several productive agents to the product of industry at large are due to the changing importance of individual industries (which differ among themselves with respect to the relative importance of material costs, labor costs and overhead costs) these changing contributions may be measured by constructing different index numbers of physical volume of production. This has been done in the present survey. But changes in the relative physical contributions of different agents within individual industries are not measurable.

## TABLE 42

**Changes in Selling Price, Cost of Materials and Fabrication Costs, plus Profits, 1899-1914**

Manufacturing Industries of the United States
(All measurements relate to changes per unit of product)

| (1) | (2) | (3) | (4) | (5) | (6) | (7) |
|---|---|---|---|---|---|---|
| | In current dollars | | | In dollars of constant purchasing power | | |
| Year | Selling price | Cost of materials | Fabrication costs, plus profits | Selling price | Cost of materials | Fabrication costs, plus profits |
| 1899 | 100.0 | 100.0 | 100.0 | 100.0 | 100.0 | 100.0 |
| 1904 | 105.3 | 108.6 | 98.5 | 92.1 | 94.9 | 86.2 |
| 1909 | 120.0 | 125.9 | 108.2 | 92.6 | 97.2 | 83.5 |
| 1914 | 122.2 | 131.0 | 104.6 | 93.6 | 100.4 | 80.2 |
| Average annual rate of change 1899-1914 (per cent) ......... | +1.5 | +1.9 | +0.5 | —0.3 | +0.1 | —1.3 |

in the average selling price of manufactured products. [The elements represented by the index numbers in columns (3) and (4) are, of course, components of selling price. The index of changes in the latter is, in effect, a weighted average of the two index numbers of per-unit cost.]

These movements are registered in terms of dollars which were declining in real value, for the level of wholesale prices advanced some 30 per cent between 1899 and 1914. If the true significance of changes in selling prices and costs is to be appreciated these should be expressed in dollars of constant purchasing power, as is done in columns (5), (6) and (7) of the above table. The transition from current dollars to dollars of constant purchasing power is made by dividing the price and cost index numbers, as first computed, by the index of wholesale prices of the United States Bureau of Labor Statistics. This is equivalent to evaluating the products of manufacture, the cost of materials and the services of the several agents of fabrication in terms of physical commodities, as they exchange at wholesale, rather than in terms of a monetary unit of changing value.

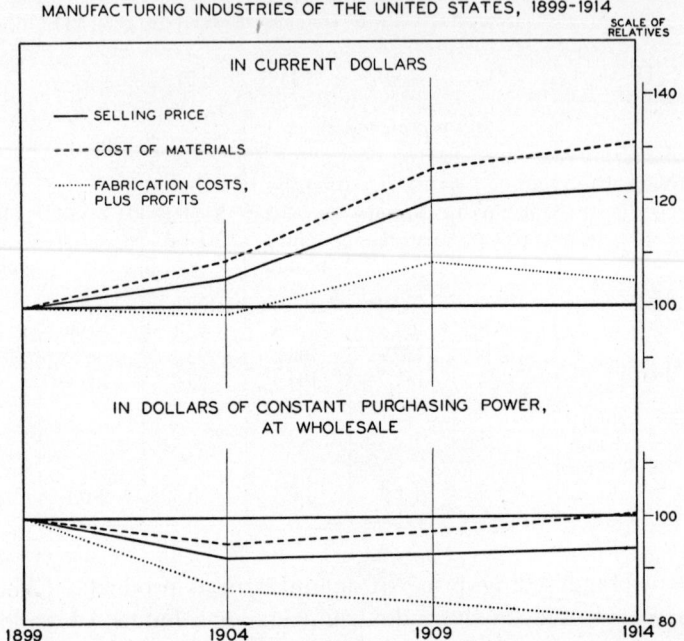

### FIGURE 21

**CHANGES IN AVERAGE SELLING PRICE, COST OF MATERIALS AND FABRICATION COSTS, PLUS PROFITS, PER UNIT OF PRODUCT**

MANUFACTURING INDUSTRIES OF THE UNITED STATES, 1899-1914

When the effect of fluctuating dollar values is thus removed, and changes in the prices and production costs of manufactured goods are measured against constant commodity values, a truer picture of the developments of this era is obtained.[1] As we have noted, manufactured goods were being steadily cheapened during the years preceding the war. The present figures indicate a fall in real value per unit amounting to about 6 per cent between 1899 and 1914, and averaging 0.3 per cent a year. Material costs, per unit of final product, remained practically constant,[2] when mea-

[1] Deflation by the wholesale price index of the Bureau of Labor Statistics only serves as an approximation, of course, to a full correction for fluctuating dollar values. This general index is used in default of more appropriate specific deflators for the particular value series cited.

[2] Material costs, it must be remembered, include the cost of fuel, power, containers and supplies, and semi-processed materials, as well as the cost of raw materials proper. In so far as the materials employed in one manufacturing plant are products of other manufacturing industries, the general decline in fabricating

sured in dollars of constant purchasing power, while fabrication costs declined about 20 per cent during these fifteen years. The notable decline in fabrication costs reflects, in part, the increasing technical efficiency and advancing productivity which were characteristic of this period. In part this decline is due to the lagging adjustment of wages, and of some elements of overhead costs, to the secular decline in the purchasing power of the dollar.

§ *Material costs and fabrication costs, individual industries.*—Turning now to the changes occurring among individual industries, we have the records summarized in Tables 43 and 44. Average annual rates of change are shown graphically in Figures 22 and 23.

### FIGURE 22
ILLUSTRATING THE DIVERGENCE OF COST TRENDS AMONG 32 MANUFACTURING INDUSTRIES OF THE UNITED STATES, 1899-1914*
AVERAGE RATES OF CHANGE IN MATERIAL COSTS PER UNIT OF PRODUCT

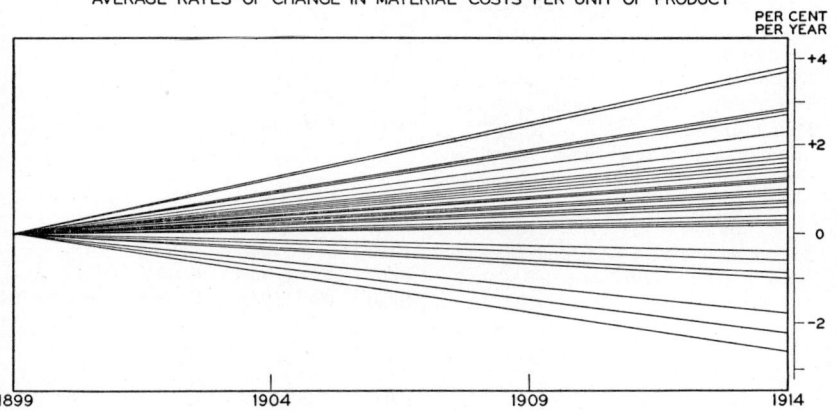

* Plotted on ratio scale. The lines here plotted relate to the industries listed in Table 43, in the order of that listing.

costs would be reflected in their prices. A large proportion of the materials of manufacture are non-fabricated goods, which rose in real value between 1899 and 1914.

The following figures, taken from the *Census of Manufactures, 1905,* indicate the relative importance of the various items entering into material costs during the census year 1904:

| | | |
|---|---:|---|
| Total cost of materials | 100.0 | per cent |
| Raw | 37.0 | " " |
| Partially manufactured | 57.8 | " " |
| Fuel | 3.6 | " " |
| Mill supplies, oil, waste, etc. | 0.7 | " " |
| Freight | 0.7 | " " |
| Rent of power and heat | 0.2 | " " |

## TABLE 43
### Changes in Material Costs, Manufacturing Industries of the United States, 1899-1914
Index Numbers for 35 Industries, with Average Annual Rates of Change

| Industry | Index numbers of cost of materials, per unit of product | | | | Average annual rate of change 1899-1914 (per cent) |
|---|---|---|---|---|---|
| | 1899 | 1904 | 1909 | 1914 | |
| Coke, not including gas-house coke.... | 100.0 | 117.1 | 152.4 | 171.3 | +3.8 |
| Slaughtering and meat packing....... | 100.0 | 104.5 | 136.6 | 166.3 | +3.7 |
| Butter, cheese, and condensed milk.... | 100.0 | 108.0 | 146.3 | 145.3 | +2.8 |
| Cotton goods ....................... | 100.0 | 144.6 | 149.7 | 161.7 | +2.8 |
| Flour-mill and gristmill products...... | 100.0 | 139.5 | 164.5 | 153.9 | +2.7 |
| Turpentine and rosin................. | 100.0 | 75.8 | 104.6 | 129.3 | +2.3 |
| Paper and wood pulp................. | 100.0 | 107.1 | 125.9 | 131.0 | +2.0 |
| Hosiery and knit goods .............. | 100.0 | 113.7 | 118.1 | 133.1 | +1.8 |
| Fertilizers ......................... | 100.0 | 103.5 | 120.6 | 125.8 | +1.7 |
| Gloves and mittens, leather........... | 100.0 | 92.5 | 120.4 | 119.7 | +1.6 |
| Iron and steel: blast furnaces......... | 100.0 | 117.0 | 136.3 | 123.2 | +1.5 |
| Lumber and timber products.......... | 100.0 | 83.1 | 111.4 | 113.8 | +1.4 |
| Carpets and rugs, other than rag...... | 100.0 | 122.3 | 109.4 | 128.0 | +1.2 |
| Musical instruments: pianos.......... | 100.0 | 97.5 | 117.0 | 114.9 | +1.2 |
| Ice, manufactured ................... | 100.0 | 105.7 | 111.4 | 118.9 | +1.2 |
| Woolen and worsted goods........... | 100.0 | 112.4 | 125.9 | 114.5 | +1.0 |
| Hats, fur-felt ....................... | 100.0 | 89.6 | 103.4 | 110.1 | +0.9 |
| Canning and preserving: fruits and vegetables; pickles, preserves, and sauces ............................ | 100.0 | 96.0 | 100.4 | 113.3 | +0.9 |
| Hats, wool-felt ..................... | 100.0 | 130.8 | 160.5 | 105.4 | +0.7 |
| Rice, cleaning and polishing.......... | 100.0 | 68.9 | 100.1 | 99.7 | +0.7 |
| Musical instruments: organs.......... | 100.0 | 89.7 | 95.4 | 107.4 | +0.6 |
| Silk goods ......................... | 100.0 | 89.7 | 93.8 | 105.4 | +0.4 |
| Gas, manufactured, illuminating and heating ............................ | 100.0 | 103.6 | 101.6 | 106.5 | +0.3 |
| Petroleum, refining .................. | 100.0 | 109.8 | 102.7 | 106.7 | +0.2 |
| Paint and varnish.................... | 100.0 | 107.4 | 100.8 | 105.6 | +0.2 |
| Wood distillation, not including turpentine and rosin ..................... | 100.0 | 102.2 | 93.5 | 96.6 | −0.4 |
| Sugar, beet ......................... | 100.0 | 97.3 | 91.4 | 92.2 | −0.6 |
| Automobiles, including bodies and parts | 100.0 | 88.4 | 112.0 | 77.5 | −0.9 |
| Iron and steel: steel works and rolling mills ............................. | 100.0 | 92.0 | 92.8 | 84.6 | −1.0 |
| Salt ............................... | 100.0 | 111.2 | 78.4 | 82.4 | −1.8 |
| Explosives ......................... | 100.0 | 87.3 | 73.0 | 73.5 | −2.2 |
| Motorcycles, bicycles, and parts....... | 100.0 | 73.2 | 63.3 | 70.3 | −2.6 |
| Cordage and twine .................. | 100.0 | — | 90.4 | 113.4 | — |
| Jute and linen goods................. | 100.0 | — | 115.1 | 161.6 | — |
| Boots and shoes, other than rubber.... | 100.0 | 106.0 | — | 140.0 | — |
| Average [a] ........................ | 100.0 | 106.0 | 136.0 | 143.9 | +2.7 |

[a] The average for each year is the arithmetic mean of the central items of a weighted frequency distribution, with weights based on cost of materials, averaged for the base year and the given year. The central one-fifth of the items, by weight, were included in computing the average.

## TABLE 44

CHANGES IN FABRICATION COSTS, MANUFACTURING INDUSTRIES OF THE
UNITED STATES, 1899-1914

Index Numbers for 35 Industries, with Average Annual Rates of Change

| Industry | Index numbers of cost of fabrication, plus profits, per unit of product | | | | Average annual rate of change 1899-1914 (per cent) |
|---|---|---|---|---|---|
| | 1899 | 1904 | 1909 | 1914 | |
| Slaughtering and meat packing....... | 100.0 | 94.0 | 126.2 | 162.7 | +3.8 |
| Flour-mill and gristmill products...... | 100.0 | 122.3 | 145.2 | 149.9 | +2.7 |
| Turpentine and rosin................. | 100.0 | 176.8 | 189.8 | 157.7 | +2.4 |
| Hats, wool-felt ..................... | 100.0 | 136.7 | 163.4 | 137.0 | +2.1 |
| Lumber and timber products.......... | 100.0 | 139.1 | 159.0 | 135.8 | +1.9 |
| Gloves and mittens, leather.......... | 100.0 | 91.2 | 121.0 | 118.4 | +1.6 |
| Hats, fur-felt ....................... | 100.0 | 109.5 | 113.9 | 125.3 | +1.4 |
| Paint and varnish.................... | 100.0 | 100.3 | 105.5 | 122.9 | +1.4 |
| Butter, cheese, and condensed milk.... | 100.0 | 94.7 | 120.2 | 112.7 | +1.2 |
| Hosiery and knit goods............... | 100.0 | 102.4 | 110.5 | 116.7 | +1.1 |
| Silk goods .......................... | 100.0 | 94.5 | 108.0 | 111.2 | +0.9 |
| Carpets and rugs, other than rag...... | 100.0 | 98.9 | 113.6 | 105.5 | +0.6 |
| Cotton goods ....................... | 100.0 | 89.5 | 112.5 | 99.9 | +0.5 |
| Fertilizers .......................... | 100.0 | 83.9 | 110.2 | 97.2 | +0.4 |
| Woolen and worsted goods........... | 100.0 | 102.7 | 110.1 | 100.9 | +0.2 |
| Canning and preserving: fruits and vegetables; pickles, preserves, and sauces ............................ | 100.0 | 99.8 | 94.6 | 103.8 | +0.1 |
| Petroleum, refining ................. | 100.0 | 136.9 | 94.9 | 113.8 | 0.0 |
| Musical instruments: pianos.......... | 100.0 | 102.0 | 90.3 | 99.7 | —0.3 |
| Sugar, beet ......................... | 100.0 | 126.9 | 133.2 | 90.1 | —0.4 |
| Musical instruments: organs.......... | 100.0 | 110.1 | 107.0 | 93.9 | —0.4 |
| Paper and wood pulp................. | 100.0 | 92.6 | 96.6 | 90.8 | —0.5 |
| Ice, manufactured ................... | 100.0 | 98.8 | 98.5 | 90.3 | —0.6 |
| Coke, not including gas-house coke.... | 100.0 | 105.7 | 93.1 | 92.2 | —0.7 |
| Iron and steel: steel works and rolling mills ........................ | 100.0 | 91.9 | 87.8 | 89.0 | —0.8 |
| Motorcycles, bicycles, and parts....... | 100.0 | 78.1 | 77.6 | 80.7 | —1.4 |
| Rice, cleaning and polishing ......... | 100.0 | 101.8 | 97.2 | 77.3 | —1.5 |
| Gas, manufactured, illuminating and heating .......................... | 100.0 | 91.7 | 82.8 | 74.4 | —2.0 |
| Explosives ......................... | 100.0 | 95.8 | 84.4 | 69.0 | —2.4 |
| Automobiles, including bodies and parts | 100.0 | 94.4 | 106.7 | 58.5 | —2.5 |
| Salt ................................ | 100.0 | 101.4 | 66.5 | 73.8 | —2.6 |
| Wood distillation, not including turpentine and rosin ..................... | 100.0 | 79.3 | 74.7 | 60.2 | —3.1 |
| Iron and steel: blast furnaces......... | 100.0 | 60.4 | 52.6 | 43.2 | —5.5 |
| Boots and shoes, other than rubber.... | 100.0 | 123.1 | — | 161.2 | — |
| Cordage and twine................... | 100.0 | — | 92.4 | 99.8 | — |
| Jute and linen goods................. | 100.0 | — | 104.2 | 84.1 | — |
| Average [a] ......................... | 100.0 | 95.3 | 108.9 | 102.0 | +0.4 |

[a] The average for each year is the arithmetic mean of the central items of a weighted frequency distribution, with weights based on 'value added', averaged for the base year and the given year. The central one-fifth of the items, by weight, were included in computing the average.

Material costs advanced most rapidly in the production of coke. Next in order were four industries utilizing agricultural products. Automotive and steel products, salt and explosives registered the greatest declines in the cost of materials. The degree of variation from industry to industry in the rates of change in material costs is measured by a standard deviation of 1.7, equal to that for index numbers of selling prices.

The averages secured from the central items of weighted frequency distributions, averages designed to represent typical situations among manufacturing industries, show substantial advances in material costs after 1904. Industries fabricating farm products, which were marked by advancing material costs during this period, exert a strong influence upon these averages.

Changes in fabrication costs in 35 individual industries are shown in Table 44, while the trends in such costs are depicted below.

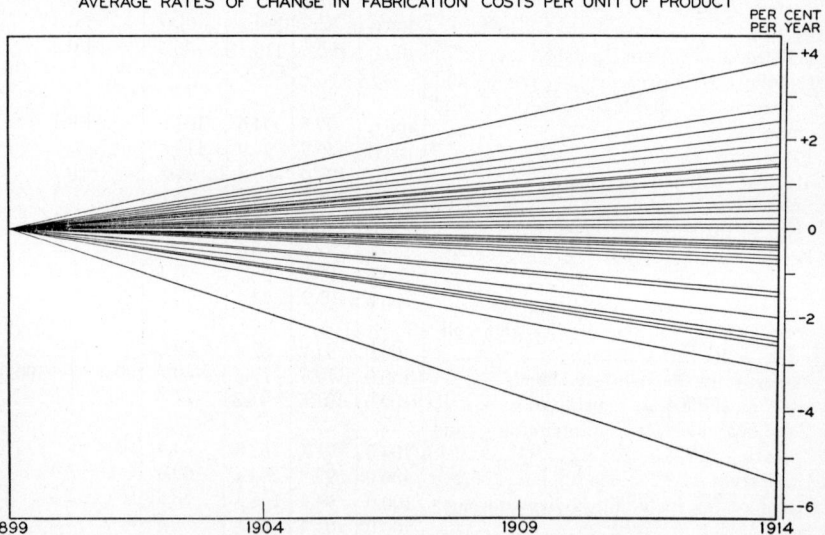

FIGURE 23

ILLUSTRATING THE DIVERGENCE OF COST TRENDS AMONG 32 MANUFACTURING INDUSTRIES OF THE UNITED STATES, 1899-1914*

AVERAGE RATES OF CHANGE IN FABRICATION COSTS PER UNIT OF PRODUCT

* Plotted on ratio scale. The lines here plotted relate to the industries listed in Table 44, in the order of that listing.

Between 1899 and 1914 the cost of fabricating a ton of pig iron declined 57 per cent,[1] while among slaughtering and meat packing indus-

[1] Profits are lumped with fabrication costs in the returns we are utilizing. The great decline in this element between 1899 and 1914 for blast furnaces is due in considerable part to exceptional conditions prevailing in the steel industry in 1899.

tries fabrication costs per unit of product increased 63 per cent. For 19 of the 35 industries studied, fabrication costs in current dollars actually declined. The concurrence of such declines with a steady advance in the general level of prices was, of course, a conspicuous feature of the pre-war period.

The standard deviation of the rates of change of index numbers of fabrication costs is 1.9, indicating slightly greater variation among industries than was found in dealing with changes in material costs.

### Changes in Labor Costs and in Other Fabrication Costs, Manufacturing Industries

We now consider separately the two major elements of fabrication costs—labor costs and the composite of overhead costs, salaries and profits. Changes in these elements are shown graphically in Figure 24.

TABLE 45

Changes in Total Fabrication Costs, Labor Costs and Overhead Costs plus Profits, 1899-1914

Manufacturing Industries of the United States

(All measurements relate to changes per unit of product)

| (1) | (2) | (3) | (4) | (5) | (6) | (7) |
|---|---|---|---|---|---|---|
| | In current dollars | | | In dollars of constant purchasing power | | |
| Year | Fabrication costs, plus profits | Labor costs | Overhead costs plus profits | Fabrication costs, plus profits | Labor costs | Overhead costs plus profits |
| 1899 | 100.0 | 100.0 | 100.0 | 100.0 | 100.0 | 100.0 |
| 1904 | 98.5 | 100.9 | 97.5 | 86.2 | 88.3 | 85.2 |
| 1909 | 108.2 | 104.6 | 111.5 | 83.5 | 80.8 | 86.1 |
| 1914 | 104.6 | 110.2 | 101.3 | 80.2 | 84.4 | 77.7 |
| Average annual rate of change 1899-1914 (per cent) | +0.5 | +0.7 | +0.3 | −1.3 | −1.1 | −1.4 |

Output was large, prices were exceptionally high, and profits were large. The year 1914 was one of depression, with low profits. While fabrication costs proper undoubtedly declined in the steel industry during this period, the degree of decline was probably much smaller than is shown by this index.

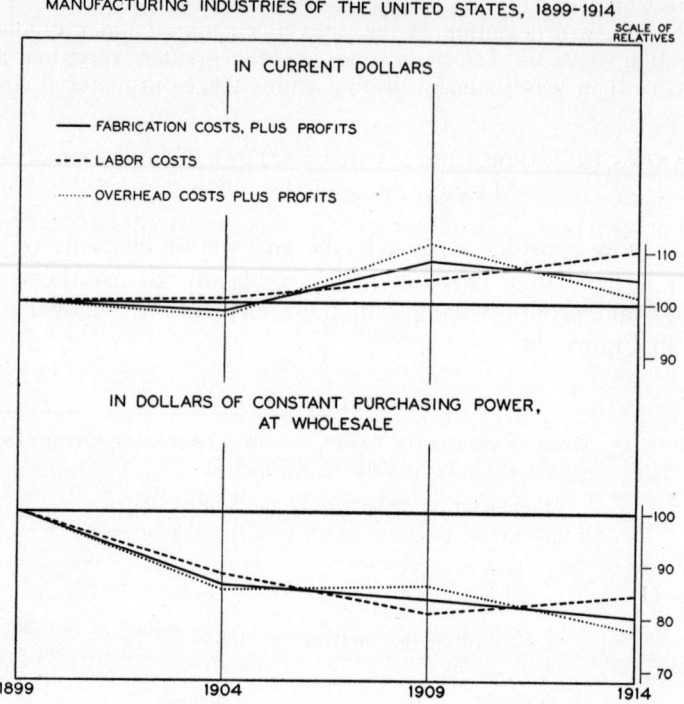

**FIGURE 24**

CHANGES IN AVERAGE FABRICATION COSTS, LABOR COSTS AND OVERHEAD COSTS PLUS PROFITS, PER UNIT OF PRODUCT

MANUFACTURING INDUSTRIES OF THE UNITED STATES, 1899-1914

During the fifteen years before the war the two elements of fabrication costs moved forward at average rates which did not differ materially ($+0.7$ and $+0.3$ per cent a year), but they were not at all in step with each other. The comparative prosperity of 1909 increased overhead costs plus profits to a level over 11 per cent above that of 1899, while labor costs advanced less than 5 per cent. Depression in 1914 reduced overhead costs plus profits to a level close to that of 1899, and carried labor costs over 10 per cent above that standard.

Measuring changes in these elements of cost in terms of constant commodity values (at wholesale), we find a notable cheapening in both series. The real cost of the contribution of labor to each unit of manufactured goods was in 1914 some 16 per cent lower than in 1899, while the real cost of the contribution of ownership and management [using that term to cover the heterogeneous items represented by the index numbers in column (7)] was, in 1914, 22 per cent lower than in 1899.[1]

§ *Labor costs and other fabrication costs, individual industries.*—The record of changing labor costs in 35 industries is contained in Table 46, on the following page. Trends in labor costs, by industries, are plotted in Figure 25.

The divergent changes revealed by this table emphasize the fact that the index numbers in Table 45 define average movements only, and ignore striking differences among industries. In the production of lumber products (at the sawmill stage) labor costs advanced 59 per cent, per unit of product, between 1899 and 1914; at the other extreme are motor vehicles, for which labor costs per unit of product declined 52 per cent over this fifteen-year period. Into the reasons for these differences we do not at present inquire, except to note that costs dropped most sharply in industries marked by the greatest increases in volume of production and in output per capita.

Considerable as were the differences which developed in labor costs, the degree of divergence among industries was less than for any of the other factors studied. The standard deviation of the rates of change is 1.4. Pre-war tendencies in labor costs were more uniform, from industry to industry, than were the tendencies prevailing among any other element of selling price.

The composite item which we have called 'overhead costs plus

[1] In the main, these declines in real costs of fabrication are the results of persistent trends, but the difference between business conditions in the two terminal years has undoubtedly affected the index numbers of costs for these years. In 1899 a general state of prosperity prevailed, while 1914 was a year of rather severe depression.

It is possible to trace changes in certain of the component items of 'overhead costs plus profits'. Expressing these components as percentages of the total, we have the following record of changes. (The data for 1899 are incomplete.) These figures, taken from the *Census of Manufactures,* relate to all manufacturing industries in the United States.

| Item of cost | Percentage of total overhead costs plus profits | | | |
| --- | --- | --- | --- | --- |
|  | 1899 | 1904 | 1909 | 1914 |
| Rent .................................... |  | 2.0 | 2.1 | 2.4 |
| Taxes ................................... |  | 7.9 | 6.9 | 7.6 |
| Salaries ................................. | 13.5 | 15.6 | 18.4 | 22.0 |
| Payments for contract work.............. |  | 3.9 | 3.5 | 3.4 |
| Other elements of overhead plus profits.... |  | 70.6 | 69.1 | 64.6 |
| Overhead costs plus profits, total........... |  | 100.0 | 100.0 | 100.0 |

The relative importance of rent increased slightly over this period, while taxes declined slightly. Salaries, which constituted but 13.5 per cent of the total in 1899, made up 22 per cent of all overhead costs (plus profits) in 1914. There is probably a reflection here of the expansion of corporate activities, as well as of the growing importance of 'organization' in the conduct of manufacturing operations.

## TABLE 46
### Changes in Labor Costs, Manufacturing Industries of the United States, 1899-1914
Index Numbers for 35 Industries, with Average Annual Rates of Change

| Industry | Index numbers of labor costs, per unit of product | | | | Average annual rate of change 1899-1914 (per cent) |
|---|---|---|---|---|---|
| | 1899 | 1904 | 1909 | 1914 | |
| Lumber and timber products.......... | 100.0 | 135.7 | 164.4 | 158.8 | +3.0 |
| Turpentine and rosin ................ | 100.0 | 124.0 | 147.0 | 147.7 | +2.6 |
| Slaughtering and meat packing....... | 100.0 | 106.8 | 118.1 | 146.3 | +2.6 |
| Hats, wool-felt ...................... | 100.0 | 128.6 | 139.7 | 140.7 | +2.1 |
| Flour-mill and gristmill products..... | 100.0 | 111.3 | 120.9 | 132.3 | +1.9 |
| Butter, cheese, and condensed milk.... | 100.0 | 112.6 | 121.9 | 129.4 | +1.7 |
| Hats, fur-felt ........................ | 100.0 | 93.8 | 98.6 | 116.3 | +1.1 |
| Woolen and worsted goods........... | 100.0 | 103.6 | 106.0 | 116.5 | +1.0 |
| Cotton goods ....................... | 100.0 | 98.6 | 108.8 | 111.6 | +0.9 |
| Hosiery and knit goods............... | 100.0 | 98.1 | 100.5 | 113.6 | +0.8 |
| Paper and wood pulp................. | 100.0 | 104.8 | 105.6 | 111.2 | +0.7 |
| Paint and varnish.................... | 100.0 | 102.1 | 95.9 | 110.3 | +0.5 |
| Gloves and mittens, leather........... | 100.0 | 80.5 | 98.4 | 101.7 | +0.5 |
| Carpets and rugs, other than rag...... | 100.0 | 108.3 | 105.2 | 109.1 | +0.5 |
| Silk goods .......................... | 100.0 | 94.2 | 99.9 | 102.2 | +0.2 |
| Musical instruments: organs.......... | 100.0 | 113.8 | 102.0 | 103.8 | 0.0 |
| Iron and steel: steel works and rolling mills ............................. | 100.0 | 97.5 | 88.0 | 103.0 | 0.0 |
| Coke, not including gas-house coke... | 100.0 | 101.1 | 102.1 | 98.2 | −0.1 |
| Ice, manufactured ................... | 100.0 | 94.9 | 93.7 | 96.7 | −0.2 |
| Musical instruments: pianos.......... | 100.0 | 93.3 | 86.5 | 95.6 | −0.4 |
| Canning and preserving: fruits and vegetables; pickles, preserves, and sauces | 100.0 | 92.9 | 90.3 | 92.0 | −0.6 |
| Rice, cleaning and polishing .......... | 100.0 | 94.4 | 82.4 | 88.9 | −1.0 |
| Petroleum, refining .................. | 100.0 | 120.4 | 77.6 | 97.4 | −1.0 |
| Fertilizers .......................... | 100.0 | 93.5 | 89.7 | 84.9 | −1.1 |
| Wood distillation, not including turpentine and rosin...................... | 100.0 | 89.5 | 86.6 | 80.6 | −1.4 |
| Iron and steel: blast furnaces......... | 100.0 | 88.1 | 74.4 | 75.5 | −2.0 |
| Sugar, beet ......................... | 100.0 | 73.5 | 70.8 | 64.7 | −2.8 |
| Salt ................................ | 100.0 | 96.3 | 66.6 | 69.7 | −2.9 |
| Gas, manufactured, illuminating and heating ........................... | 100.0 | 78.8 | 67.2 | 61.6 | −3.3 |
| Motorcycles, bicycles, and parts....... | 100.0 | 112.6 | 74.3 | 62.5 | −3.4 |
| Automobiles, including bodies and parts | 100.0 | 88.6 | 97.8 | 47.7 | −3.5 |
| Explosives .......................... | 100.0 | 72.8 | 59.7 | 55.8 | −4.0 |
| Boots and shoes, other than rubber... | 100.0 | 107.1 | ——— | 137.6 | ——— |
| Cordage and twine................... | 100.0 | ——— | 105.9 | 117.8 | ——— |
| Jute and linen goods................. | 100.0 | ——— | 100.0 | 106.8 | ——— |
| Average [a] ......................... | 100.0 | 100.0 | 103.4 | 111.6 | +0.7 |

[a] The average for each year is the arithmetic mean of the central items of a weighted frequency distribution, with weights based on aggregate wages paid, averaged for the base year and the given year. The central one-fifth of the items, by weight, were included in computing the average.

## FIGURE 25

### ILLUSTRATING THE DIVERGENCE OF COST TRENDS AMONG 32 MANUFACTURING INDUSTRIES OF THE UNITED STATES, 1899-1914*

AVERAGE RATES OF CHANGE IN LABOR COSTS PER UNIT OF PRODUCT

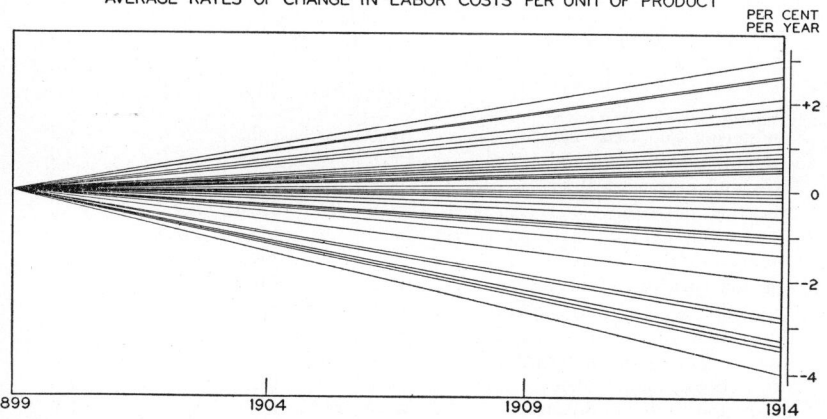

* Plotted on ratio scale. The lines here plotted relate to the industries listed in Table 46, in the order of that listing.

profits' includes all fabrication charges other than the cost of labor. It measures what is paid by the buyers of manufactured goods for the services of owners and managers, in the broadest sense. Index numbers defining changes in this element between 1899 and 1914 in 35 manufacturing industries are given in Table 47, on the next page. Average annual rates of change in overhead costs plus profits are shown graphically in Figure 26.

The measurements in this table reflect more closely than do other elements of selling price the ups and downs of business fortunes with the expansion and contraction of trade. We start with 1899, a good year, when profits were relatively high. The year 1904 was one of mild depression, and we find a drop in overhead costs plus profits in those industries which are most immediately affected by trade fluctuations. For blast furnaces the drop amounted to 49 per cent, for plants producing cotton goods, 21 per cent. Variations in profits, of course, are reflected in such fluctuations as these. In 1909, a year of prosperity, the general average was distinctly higher, while the depression of 1914 brought lower values again. Changes over the entire fifteen-year period varied from a drop of some 67 per cent, for blast furnaces, to an advance of more than 100 per cent for boots and shoes.

The degree of variation among the tendencies prevailing in different industries is measured by a standard deviation (of rates of change) of 2.4, a figure materially higher than that found among other elements of selling price. Manufacturing industries showed greatest uniformity in labor cost tendencies, least uniformity in respect of changes in overhead costs plus profits. Labor costs, it would appear, are most affected

## TABLE 47

CHANGES IN OVERHEAD COSTS PLUS PROFITS, MANUFACTURING INDUSTRIES OF THE UNITED STATES, 1899-1914

Index Numbers for 35 Industries, with Average Annual Rates of Change

| Industry | Index numbers of overhead costs plus profits, per unit of product | | | | Average annual rate of change 1899-1914 (per cent) |
|---|---|---|---|---|---|
| | 1899 | 1904 | 1909 | 1914 | |
| Slaughtering and meat packing....... | 100.0 | 87.7 | 130.2 | 170.6 | +4.3 |
| Flour-mill and gristmill products..... | 100.0 | 125.5 | 152.2 | 155.0 | +2.9 |
| Gloves and mittens, leather........... | 100.0 | 104.9 | 150.0 | 139.8 | +2.7 |
| Turpentine and rosin................. | 100.0 | 253.7 | 252.0 | 172.2 | +2.2 |
| Hats, fur-felt ....................... | 100.0 | 137.2 | 140.8 | 141.3 | +2.0 |
| Hats, wool-felt ...................... | 100.0 | 149.0 | 199.7 | 131.5 | +1.9 |
| Paint and varnish.................... | 100.0 | 99.8 | 107.9 | 126.0 | +1.6 |
| Silk goods .......................... | 100.0 | 94.8 | 115.1 | 119.2 | +1.5 |
| Hosiery and knit goods............... | 100.0 | 107.6 | 122.6 | 120.6 | +1.4 |
| Motorcycles, bicycles, and parts....... | 100.0 | 37.4 | 81.7 | 102.2 | +1.3 |
| Butter, cheese, and condensed milk.... | 100.0 | 87.7 | 119.5 | 106.2 | +1.0 |
| Lumber and timber products.......... | 100.0 | 142.2 | 154.1 | 115.1 | +0.9 |
| Fertilizers ......................... | 100.0 | 80.4 | 117.6 | 101.7 | +0.9 |
| Carpets and rugs, other than rag...... | 100.0 | 88.4 | 123.1 | 101.6 | +0.8 |
| Sugar, beet ......................... | 100.0 | 167.7 | 180.8 | 109.4 | +0.6 |
| Canning and preserving: fruits and vegetables; pickles, preserves, and sauces | 100.0 | 103.8 | 97.2 | 110.6 | +0.5 |
| Petroleum, refining ................. | 100.0 | 144.6 | 103.1 | 121.5 | +0.4 |
| Cotton goods ....................... | 100.0 | 79.1 | 116.7 | 86.5 | −0.1 |
| Musical instruments: pianos.......... | 100.0 | 110.2 | 93.8 | 103.7 | −0.1 |
| Woolen and worsted goods........... | 100.0 | 101.9 | 114.0 | 85.6 | −0.6 |
| Ice, manufactured .................. | 100.0 | 100.7 | 100.8 | 87.2 | −0.8 |
| Musical instruments: organs.......... | 100.0 | 106.5 | 111.9 | 84.2 | −0.8 |
| Coke, not including gas-house coke.... | 100.0 | 109.4 | 85.9 | 87.4 | −1.3 |
| Paper and wood pulp................ | 100.0 | 85.6 | 91.4 | 79.0 | −1.3 |
| Gas, manufactured, illuminating and heating ........................... | 100.0 | 95.5 | 87.4 | 78.1 | −1.6 |
| Iron and steel: steel works and rolling mills ........................ | 100.0 | 86.4 | 87.6 | 75.2 | −1.7 |
| Rice, polishing and cleaning.......... | 100.0 | 104.0 | 101.6 | 73.8 | −1.7 |
| Explosives ......................... | 100.0 | 108.2 | 97.7 | 76.1 | −1.7 |
| Automobiles, including bodies and parts | 100.0 | 98.2 | 112.8 | 66.7 | −1.8 |
| Salt ................................ | 100.0 | 105.0 | 66.4 | 76.6 | −2.5 |
| Wood distillation, not including turpentine and rosin...................... | 100.0 | 73.9 | 68.4 | 49.4 | −4.3 |
| Iron and steel: blast furnaces......... | 100.0 | 51.4 | 45.5 | 32.7 | −7.3 |
| Boots and shoes, other than rubber.... | 100.0 | 152.5 | — | 204.5 | — |
| Cordage and twine.................. | 100.0 | — | 84.6 | 89.3 | — |
| Jute and linen goods................. | 100.0 | — | 109.0 | 58.5 | — |
| Average [a] ........................ | 100.0 | 94.3 | 113.5 | 98.6 | +0.3 |

[a] The average for each year is the arithmetic mean of the central items of a weighted frequency distribution, with weights based on overhead costs plus profits, averaged for the base year and the given year. The central one-fifth of the items, by weight, were included in computing the average.

## FIGURE 26

ILLUSTRATING THE DIVERGENCE OF COST TRENDS AMONG
32 MANUFACTURING INDUSTRIES OF THE UNITED STATES, 1899-1914*
AVERAGE RATES OF CHANGE IN OVERHEAD COSTS PLUS PROFITS PER UNIT OF PRODUCT

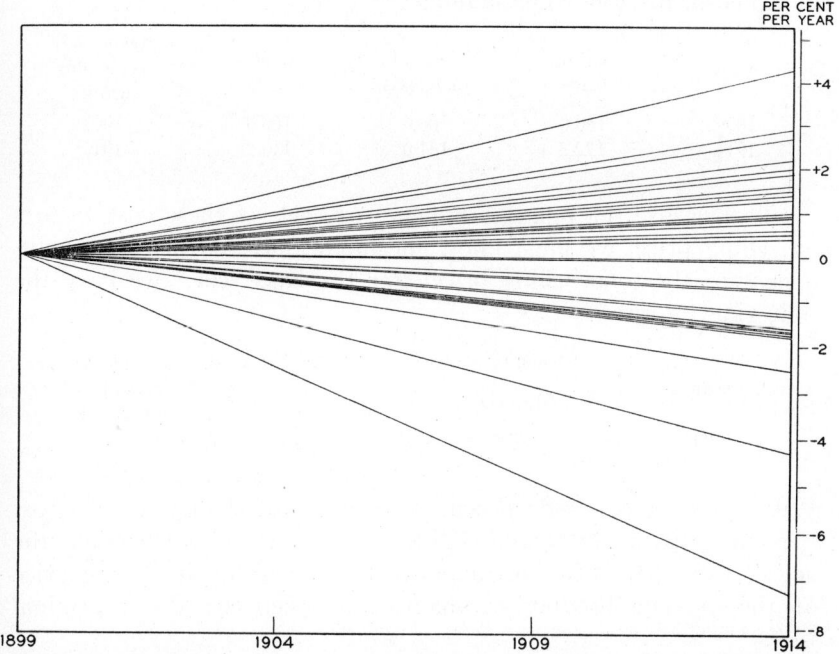

* Plotted on ratio scale. The lines here plotted relate to the industries listed in Table 47, in the order of that listing.

by factors common to all industries, while overhead costs plus profits are least affected by such factors. These varying degrees of divergence are clearly portrayed in Figures 25 and 26, and in similar charts previously presented.

### On the Relative Importance of Different Elements of Cost as Factors in Price Changes, 1899-1914

The above index numbers reveal the changes occurring in the different elements of cost of manufacture, but they do not indicate the degree of importance of these elements, as factors in changing selling prices. We know that the average selling price per unit of manufactured goods increased 22.2 per cent between 1899 and 1914. In precisely what degree is this due to rising material costs, in what degree to rising labor costs, and in what degree to increasing costs of overhead and management?[1]

The change in each of these elements, per unit of product, is indicated in the following summary:

| Year | Selling price | Cost of materials | Labor costs | Overhead costs plus profits |
|---|---|---|---|---|
| 1899 | 100.0 | 100.0 | 100.0 | 100.0 |
| 1914 | 122.2 | 131.0 | 110.2 | 101.3 |

To measure the relative influence of each of these cost factors on selling price, we must know the importance of each as a component of the total selling price. For the base year,[2] we have the following figures:

| Year | Elements of cost as decimal fractions of value of product: | | |
|---|---|---|---|
| | Materials | Labor | Overhead costs plus profits |
| 1899 | .678 | .140 | .182 |

With these figures, and knowing the degree of change in each cost element between 1899 and 1914, we may readily determine the degree to which each contributed to the change in the selling price of the average product of manufacture between these terminal years.[3]

We may summarize the results:

92.6 per cent of the gross change in the selling price per unit of manufactured goods between 1899 and 1914 is attributable to rising material costs.

---

[1] Profits, it has been explained, are included with overhead expenses in this last item, as the data available do not permit the separation of these two elements. Objection might be made to the above terminology on the ground that profits are not part of the costs of production, and should not be assumed to play an active part in price changes. In many cases, of course, the stimulus to changing prices is first felt in the markets for the final product, and the elements of selling price reflect in varying degrees the changes in the market price of the product. Terms which imply that changes in selling prices always originate in changing costs (profits being included in costs) are used for reasons of convenience, and for the sake of brevity of expression.

[2] Base year weights are used for convenience, though this usage involves the incorrect assumption that the relative physical contributions of the different productive agents did not change during the period. The error resulting from this assumption is small.

[3] The advance of 22.2 per cent in the selling price of the product is the result

6.3 per cent of the gross change is attributable to rising labor costs.
1.1 per cent of the gross change is attributable to rising overhead costs (including profits).

Each of these figures should be compared with the corresponding item in the summary immediately above. Thus materials constituted 67.8 per cent of the total selling price, but accounted for 92.6 per cent of the change in price; labor costs made up 14.0 per cent of the total selling price, but accounted for only 6.3 per cent of the change; costs of ownership and management (overhead expenses plus profits) made up 18.2 per cent of the total selling price, and accounted for but 1.1 per cent of the price change.

## The Activity Ratio

This last comparison may be facilitated by the use of what we may call an *activity ratio,* a ratio which serves as an index of the degree of activity of each element of cost, measured with reference to a standard of normal activity.[1] This is the ratio of the mea-

---

of an advance of 30.96 per cent in material costs, with weight of .678, an advance of 10.17 per cent in labor costs, with weight of .140, and an advance of 1.32 per cent in overhead costs plus profits, with weight of .182.

The detailed computations, upon which the measurements in the text are based, are given below.

Computation of influence of cost factors upon price change per unit of product, 1899-1914

| Element of cost | Degree of change in cost (per cent) | | Weight | | Contribution to change in selling price | Percentage distribution of elements of gross change in selling price |
|---|---|---|---|---|---|---|
| Materials | + 30.96 | × | .678 | = | + 20.99 | 92.6 |
| Labor | + 10.17 | × | .140 | = | + 1.42 | 6.3 |
| Overhead costs plus profits | + 1.32 | × | .182 | = | + 0.24 | 1.1 |
| Total | | | | | 22.65 | 100.0 |

The discrepancy between 22.65 and 22.2 is due to the presence of minor errors in the weights used and to the dropping of fractional values.

[1] The word 'activity' is here used without any implication as to the direction in which price-determining and cost-determining influences run. It is difficult to avoid a terminology which suggests that causal influences run from changes in costs to changes in selling prices. The present analysis does not bear on that problem, and such terminology is used for convenience only. If the cause and effect chain is assumed to run in the other direction, with changes in costs reflecting changes in selling prices, the above ratio may be thought of as a *sensitivity ratio,* an index of the sensitivity of elements of cost to changes in selling price. As regards certain of the elements in the item of 'overhead costs plus profits' this is certainly the proper view.

surement defining the actual importance of a given cost element in a given price change to the figure defining the importance of that element as a component of the total selling price. Thus, for the cost of materials, the *activity ratio* for the period 1899-1914 would be 92.6/67.8 or 1.37. (This measurement relates, it should be noted, to the terminal years of the period, since no use is here made of intervening values.) In this case the ratio exceeds unity, indicating that changes in material costs exerted a greater influence upon changes in the selling prices of manufactured goods between 1899 and 1914 than was to have been expected in view of the proportionate importance of that factor in total costs.

Such a ratio offers a very convenient summary of the information defining the rôle of each cost element in selling price changes. The ratio is particularly useful in comparing data relating to different cost elements and different industries. It may be usefully interpreted in percentage form, as a measure of the proportion of the expected or 'normal' influence actually exerted by a given cost element upon a particular change in the selling price of the product.

Using the figures given in a preceding paragraph, we have the following ratios, relating to net changes in current dollars between the terminal years of the period 1899-1914:

| Element of manufacturing cost | Activity ratio (current dollars) |
|---|---|
| Materials | 92.6/67.8 = 1.37 |
| Labor | 6.3/14.0 = .45 |
| Overhead costs plus profits | 1.1/18.2 = .06 |

The contribution of overhead costs plus profits to the gross change in the average selling price of manufactured goods between 1899 and 1914 (or the degree to which that element reflected the change) amounted only to 6 per cent of what might have been expected, in view of the place occupied by that element in the total selling price. The influence of labor costs amounted to 45 per cent of expectancy. The influence of changes in material costs was 37 per cent greater than 'normal', as above defined.

In tracing the course of prices and costs among manufacturing industries we found it desirable to measure changes in terms of dollars of constant purchasing power, as well as in current dollars. We may now determine the relative importance of the different elements of manufacturing costs as factors in changes in the *real values* of manufactured goods. The problem may be put in this form: Between 1899 and 1914 the average price of manufactured goods, per unit, in terms of dollars of constant purchasing power, declined 6.4 per cent. To what cost factors was this notable cheapening of manufactured goods due? This is an entirely different problem from that faced in the preceding section. There we sought to measure the influence of various cost factors in causing the prices of manufactured goods to depart from the level prevailing in 1899. We found that the costs of materials had played a leading part in this change. Now we seek to measure the influence of various cost factors in causing the prices of manufactured goods to deviate from the average of general prices, during the period 1899 to 1914. For it is such deviations from the general average which cause changes in purchasing power, or in real value.

Changes between 1899 and 1914 in selling price and in the chief elements of cost, per unit of manufactured goods, expressed in dollars of constant purchasing power, were as follows:

| Year | Selling price | Cost of materials | Labor costs | Cost of management |
|---|---|---|---|---|
| 1899 | 100.0 | 100.0 | 100.0 | 100.0 |
| 1914 | 93.6 | 100.4 | 84.4 | 77.7 |

Proceeding as before, we secure the following results:

4.0 per cent of the gross change in the per-unit purchasing power of manufactured goods between 1899 and 1914 is attributable to rising material costs (costs being expressed in dollars of constant purchasing power).[1]
33.5 per cent of the gross change is attributable to declining labor costs.
62.5 per cent of the gross change is attributable to declining costs of management and overhead plus profits.

This is quite a different story from that which related to current dollars. Changes in material costs, which were responsible for 92.6 per cent of the change in actual prices of manufactured goods

[1] The influence of this element was positive, while that of the other two factors was negative. The base of the percentage figures which define the degree of influence of the several cost elements upon selling price is, of necessity, the numerical sum of the changes in the several elements (each factor properly weighted), this sum being taken without regard to sign. It is the *algebraic sum* of these changes which defines the actual movement of the price of the product, or the *net change*. The numerical sum measures the aggregate price-affecting changes among the several elements of cost, without reference to possible offsetting when the changes are in opposite directions. It is this aggregate, here

between 1899 and 1914, accounted for but 4.0 per cent of the change in purchasing power of manufactured goods, per unit. (The influence of material costs in this latter case was upward, moreover, while the other factors contributed to a decline in the real value of manufactured goods.) The explanation is found, of course, in the fact that material costs, which had departed farther than any other element of manufacturing costs from the absolute price level of 1899, deviated less than any other cost element from the 1914 level of wholesale prices. (If material costs had changed by exactly the same amount as had the general price level, no part of the change in the purchasing power of manufactured goods could be attributed to this factor.) Changes in costs of fabrication, including labor and overhead costs plus profits, were more potent in their effect on the real values of manufactured goods than upon current prices. These fabrication costs, making up but 32 per cent of total selling price, accounted for 96 per cent of the gross change and for all the reduction in the real per-unit value of the products of manufacture, as these are represented in our sample.

We summarize these figures in the form of *activity ratios:*

| Element of manufacturing cost | Activity ratio (dollars of constant purchasing power) |
|---|---|
| Materials | 4.0/67.8 = .06 |
| Labor | 33.5/14.0 = 2.39 |
| Overhead costs plus profits | 62.5/18.2 = 3.43 |

called the *gross change,* which is significant for the present purpose, and it is to this aggregate that the percentages and ratios relate.

The computations upon which the above results rest may make this point clearer.

Computation of influence of cost factors upon price change per unit of product, 1899-1914

| Element of cost | Degree of change in cost (per cent) | Weight | | Contribution to change in selling price | Percentage distribution of elements of gross change in selling price |
|---|---|---|---|---|---|
| Materials | + 0.38 | × .678 | = | + 0.26 | 4.0 |
| Labor | − 15.55 | × .140 | = | − 2.18 | 33.5 |
| Overhead costs plus profits | − 22.34 | × .182 | = | − 4.07 | 62.5 |
| Gross change (sum of items disregarding signs) | | | | 6.51 | 100.0 |
| Net change (algebraic sum) | | | | − 5.99 | |

The discrepancy between −5.99 and −6.4, the actual net change in selling price per unit, in dollars of constant purchasing power, is due to the presence of minor errors in the weights used and to the dropping of fractional values.

The reason for the reversal in the positions of these elements has been suggested. As a factor in changing real values material costs were relatively inactive, while labor and the residual element making up overhead costs and profits each exerted an influence out of proportion to its relative importance.[1]

## SUMMARY: PRICE AND COST MOVEMENTS IN MANUFACTURING INDUSTRIES, 1899-1914

The materials just reviewed have served, in the first place, to support the general findings of Chapter II concerning the relative cheapening of manufactured goods during the decade and more preceding the World War. Using measurements derived quite independently of those based upon direct price quotations, we have found clear evidence of a reduction in the real per-unit value of manufactured goods between 1899 and 1914.

Beyond this confirmation of previous results, we have employed measurements which permit some of the forces lying back of price changes to be examined, and their relative importance appraised. Changes in selling prices of manufactured goods have first been studied as the resultant of changes in material costs and in fabrication costs. Expressing changing values in terms of a constant monetary standard (i.e., in terms of dollars of constant purchasing power in wholesale markets) we have found that the per-unit worth of manufactured products declined, from 1899 to 1914, by 6.4 per cent. This was the net result of an advance of 0.4 per cent in the real cost of the materials entering into the average unit of finished product, and a decline of 19.8 per cent in the real cost of fabrication, per unit of product. In 1914, in other words, the services of the agents of fabrication in producing a unit of manufactured goods commanded 19.8 per cent less in terms of commodities in general than in 1899. The most conspicuous result of the improvements of manufacturing technique and of other changes

[1] The reason for this is found, in part, in the characteristics of the U. S. Bureau of Labor Statistics' index of wholesale prices which was used in deflating the various price series. This index, in common with all other indexes of wholesale prices for this period, is heavily weighted with raw and semi-manufactured goods. (This is partly due to the difficulty of securing representative quotations on highly fabricated goods.) As a result, its movements accord most closely with those of the raw and partially fabricated goods which are used as materials of manufacture.

affecting manufacturing operations during the fifteen years preceding the war was this notable decline in fabrication costs.

We distinguish two elements of fabrication costs—payment for the services of wage-earners and a residual element representing overhead expenses, salaries and profits. Labor costs (still in terms of a commodity standard of value) declined approximately 16 per cent per unit of product between 1899 and 1914, while overhead costs plus profits declined 22 per cent. In some degree the substantial decline in labor costs reflects improved equipment, superior skill, better organization. In addition, however, the lagging adjustment of wages to the changes in values resulting from an advancing price level was a notable factor in this decline. Laborers in manufacturing plants barely maintained their standard of living during these years of rapid industrial expansion. A drop in real labor costs was a natural accompaniment of this movement.

The decline in overhead costs plus profits is doubtless due, in part, to the use of improved equipment and to the development of methods of mass production. Here, also, a lagging adjustment of certain fixed elements of cost to changing values of the dollar helped to reduce production costs. It is probably true, in addition, that profits per unit of product were substantially lower in 1914, a year of depression, than they were in 1899, when prosperity prevailed.

Taking account of the relative importance of each of the three cost elements in the aggregate of manufacturing costs, we have expressed in percentage terms the actual contribution of each of these elements to the gross change in the real per-unit value of manufactured goods between 1899 and 1914. Approximately 96 per cent of the gross change (the change being measured in terms of a commodity standard of value) was attributable to declining fabrication costs, plus profits, while only 4 per cent was attributable to changing material costs. (The influence of the change in fabrication costs was downward, while that of the change in material costs was upward. The former, of course, predominated.) Breaking the cost of fabrication into its two components, it appears that about 33 per cent of the gross change in selling price was attributable to declining labor costs, while 63 per cent was attributable to declining costs of management and overhead plus profits.[1]

---

[1] The use of the phrase 'attributable to' must be qualified, since it does not follow that selling prices merely reflect, in a passive fashion, changes occurring in the elements cited. The causal sequence may run in the other direction.

The significance of these changes may be more accurately appraised when we have before us materials relating to other periods. Here, however, is a standard of reference, in the record of changes occurring in the various component elements of the selling prices of manufactured goods during the decade and a half of fairly stable growth that preceded the World War. These years saw no such violent changes as the next two decades were to bring. American economic powers pursued their 'manifest destiny' in comparative tranquillity. No cataclysmic price movements distorted business relations overnight. Slowly-acting secular forces dominated the course of events. It is for this reason, as much as any other, that later comparison with more disturbed epochs will engage our interest.

## CHAPTER IV

## Other Economic Changes, 1901-1913

A NOTABLE period of economic expansion was under way in the United States at the opening of the twentieth century. The rising trend of commodity prices, following some three decades of almost unbroken decline, had generated a spirit of optimism in business. Rising prices helped, too, to improve the state of mind and the economic condition of the farmer, who had labored under debt burdens steadily enhanced by the increasing value of the monetary unit during the preceding decades. Industrial and agricultural production were accompanying prices on the upward climb. After the depression of the middle 'nineties both industry and agriculture had entered upon new stages, each year recording new high levels in the volume of output of staple commodities. Markets were at the same time widened, and manufacturers were finding outlets at home and abroad for their expanding production.

Iron and steel played prominent parts in this economic expansion. The steel industry had been growing in relative importance for thirty years. By the end of the nineteenth century steel was definitely in the saddle, and dominated the American industrial situation. Conditions in the steel industry constituted the prime barometer of business. Following the Civil War our released national energies were devoted to railroad construction. By 1900 the peak of activity in this industry had been passed, but steel was needed as never before for equipping the new industrial plants, for providing new rolling stock, for use in building construction. With the intensification of our efforts in foreign fields, overseas markets for steel were open for exploitation. This era was marked by the accumulation of capital funds and the construction of capital equipment at a rapid rate, perhaps more rapid than ever before in this country's history, and steel was the leading beneficiary. It was no coincidence that the first billion dollar corporation in this country was formed in 1901, and that this was the United States Steel Corporation. Economic hegemony had passed from agriculture to steel, and the 'economic climate' of the early twentieth century experienced a corresponding change.

No summary of the general attributes of this period would be complete without reference to industrial combinations. Between 1899 and 1901 more combinations were formed than in any similar period in our history. The stimulus of widening markets and the benefits of mass production were powerful incentives to such combinations. The newer technological methods required an investment in plant and equipment far heavier than had been necessary under earlier conditions. The inducement to promoters and underwriters of quick, certain and large profits to be made through the pushing of a successful merger was another force working in the same direction. In 1901, the year with which this survey begins, Theodore Roosevelt's inaugural address dealt in considerable part with the evils of such combinations. The era of 'trust busting' was in prospect.

Perhaps most notable among the conditions characterizing the opening of this period was the optimism of the business world. The *Final Report* of the United States Industrial Commission, submitted in 1902, speaks in glowing terms of the fortunate state of affairs then prevailing. At the beginning of the nineteenth century, says the *Report,* "The people possessed neither wealth, knowledge, nor power. . . . For centuries the elements of applied science and of the modern arts had been germinating, concealed and unrecognized. At the commencement of the nineteenth century they began visibly to expand and the long-dormant industrial system reached large fruition in a single century." (p. 524)

In language even more strongly reminiscent of discussion during the recent post-war expansion, the *Report* deals with the effect of reduction of costs upon the extension of the market, and the reverse influence, upon production costs, of such extension. "Reduction of costs usually brings about a reduction of prices and an increase in amount and reliability of compensation of the producers. Every reduction of prices extends the market, often in much more than commensurate degree. Each extension of the market, by enlarging the scale of production, affords an opportunity still further to reduce costs and prices and to increase wages." (p. 536) The *Report* proceeds, "But the radical industrial changes of the nineteenth century and the crises and crashes, which at intervals of 10 to 20 years have been their accompaniment, are likely to be less severe in the future. Civilization and the industries are established upon a new basis, and progress hereafter will probably be smoother, although equally rapid." (p. 537) It is pointed out, further, that though temporary hardship may result from such improvement in methods of production, the increased consumption of goods which the cheapening of production makes possible will in the long run absorb the labor displaced. As an instance of this, "there are probably now demanded even a much larger number of horses merely for transporting people to and from the trains than were a century ago employed in the whole stage coach business." (p. 535) The frame of mind prevailing at the beginning of the twentieth century was marked by a buoyant optimism; there prevailed widespread confidence that a new path to plenty was open and that the way had been cleared to happiness and prosperity for all.

## A Survey of Major Tendencies

The preceding chapters have traced the changes occurring between the turn of the century and the outbreak of the World War in production, prices and production costs in the United States. A study of economic changes which runs in terms of production and prices alone does not, of course, include all the factors affecting economic processes. In tracing economic processes in the large we should like to measure changes in the volume and cost of capital and credit, in the volume and character of domestic and foreign trade, in the national income and its various elements, and in numerous other economic factors. These desires far exceed the scope of the data and the possibility of present treatment. We must be content with a more restricted view of economic events during the years immediately preceding the war.

Certain aspects of the changes which occurred in the American economy between 1901 and 1913, aspects which are capable of quantitative treatment, are defined by the measurements in the following table. A graphic representation of these changes is given in Figure 27.

These exhibits do not give a complete account of the economic changes occurring during the period 1901-1913, but so far as they go they furnish an interesting picture of a developing economy. As a basic factor underlying the economic changes of this era we

TABLE 48

MOVEMENTS OF CERTAIN ECONOMIC ELEMENTS IN THE UNITED STATES, 1901-1913

| (1) | (2) | (3) | (4) | (5) | (6) | (7) | (8) |
|---|---|---|---|---|---|---|---|
| | Absolute measurements | | | Index numbers | | Average annual rate of change (per cent) | Index of instability of growth |
| Economic element [a] | Unit | 1901 | 1913 | 1901 | 1913 | | |
| Population | million | 77 | 96 | 100 | 125 | +2.0 | 0.3 |
| Savings deposits | million dollars | 2,597 | 4,727 | 100 | 182 | +4.8 | 1.7 |
| Total loans and investments, all banks | " | 9,246 | 20,034 | 100 | 217 | +6.3 | 2.4 |
| Index of wholesale prices | | | | 100 | 126 | +1.8 | 2.2 |
| Index of production | | | | 100 | 156 | +3.1 | 3.7 |
| Ton miles of freight, railroads | billion ton miles | 147 | 302 | 100 | 205 | +5.5 | 4.3 |
| Bank clearings, outside New York City | billion dollars | 39 | 75 | 100 | 193 | +5.7 | 3.0 |
| Imports | million dollars | 903 | 1,894 | 100 | 210 | +6.0 | 4.6 |
| Exports | " | 1,355 | 2,330 | 100 | 172 | +4.8 | 4.8 |
| Employment (manufacturing industries) | thousand wage-earners | 5,184 | 7,277 | 100 | 140 | +2.7 | 2.7 |
| Average annual earnings of employed workers (excluding farm labor) | dollars | 508 | 675 | 100 | 133 | +2.2 | 1.4 |
| Cost of living index | | | | 100 | 127 | +1.8 | 1.4 |

[a] The population figures are based on estimates made by W. I. King, in which the available information on births, deaths, and migration is used in interpolating for inter-censal years. While an appreciable margin of error enters into the estimates for individual years, they are better adapted to our purpose than are estimates based upon straight-line interpolation between census years. Data on savings deposits in the United States are from the *Report* of the Comptroller of the Currency, 1914, I, p. 87. Loans and investments, from the same source, p. 74, include loans, discounts and overdrafts, and bonds, stocks, etc., listed as resources of state, savings, and private banks, loan and trust companies and national banks. The wholesale price index is that of the U. S. Bureau of Labor Statistics. Production changes are measured by the index number explained in Chapter I. Data on the number of tons of freight carried one mile have been taken from *Statistics of Railways in the United States*, 1915, p. 37. Bank clearings for 159 cities (excluding New York City) are from the annual number of the *Financial Review*, 1916, p. 64. The import and export series are those compiled by the Bureau of Foreign and Domestic Commerce, Department of Commerce. Employment data are from *Recent Economic Changes*, National Bureau of Economic Research, New York, 1929, II, p. 450; they are census-year figures for manufacturing employment, with interpolations for non-census years based on annual indexes of employment compiled by Professors Cobb and Douglas. Employees' earnings and the cost of living index are from Paul H. Douglas, *Real Wages in the United States*, Houghton Mifflin Co., Boston, 1930, pp. 60, 392.

## FIGURE 27
### MOVEMENTS OF CERTAIN ECONOMIC ELEMENTS IN THE UNITED STATES, 1901-1913

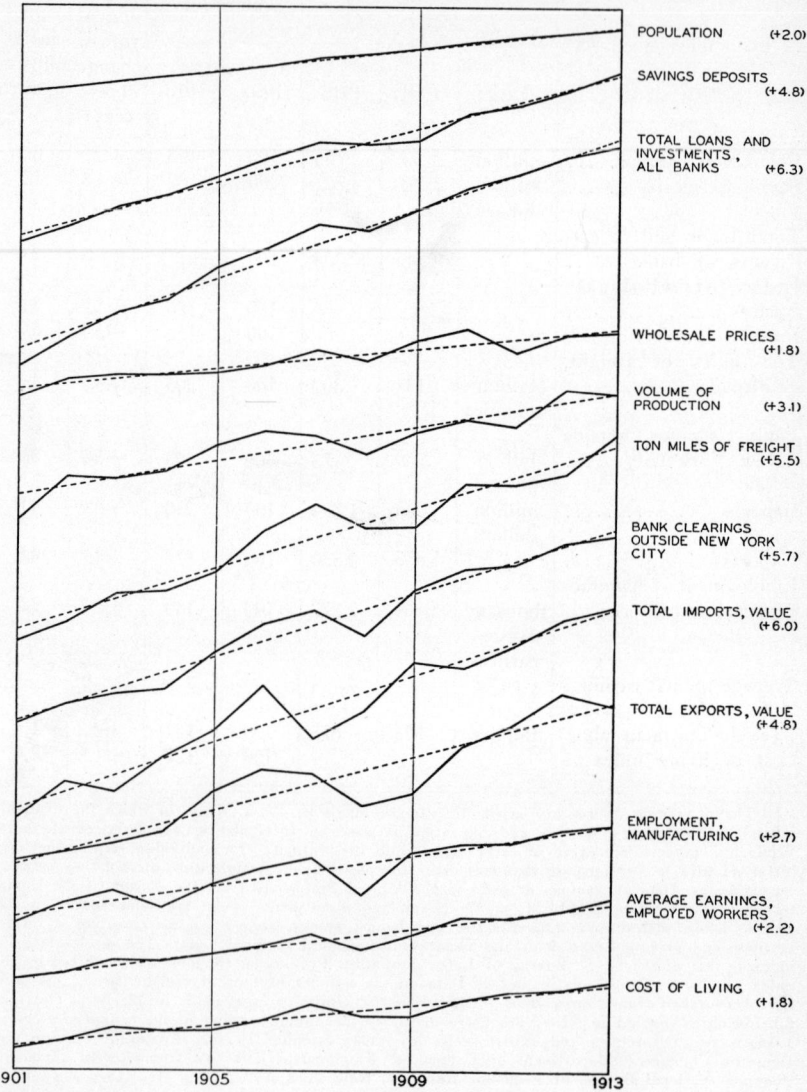

Plotted on ratio scale. The figures in parentheses define average annual rates of change (in percentage form).

have the steady advance of population, at a rate of 2.0 per cent a year. There were slight undulations in this steady growth, undulations with a mean annual amplitude approximating three-tenths of one per cent of the normal population.[1] These measurements of the rate of gain and of the oscillations in population define the scale of changes in the human factor, and furnish standards of comparison for use in evaluating economic changes.

In contrast to population changes we have the movements of the two factors already discussed, production and prices. While the human element increased at a rate of 2.0 per cent a year, with minor oscillations, the volume of physical goods increased at a rate of 3.1 per cent, a net gain per head of 1.1 per cent a year. Variations in the output of physical goods averaged 3.7 per cent a year, these swings having more than ten times the amplitude of the undulations in population. The relative movements of population and of the volume of physical goods are of obvious significance. From the relations between these two elements, growing at unequal rates, fluctuating over widely different ranges, are derived certain of the prime characteristics of an economic era. The price system, playing an instrumental but important rôle, was marked by a rising tendency. The rate of advance for wholesale prices was 1.8 per cent a year. Oscillations in the price level, defined by an index of 2.2, covered about eight times the average range of swings in population and about sixty per cent of the mean movement in the volume of production.

Of the other economic factors depicted in Figure 27, the important element of capital funds is represented by a single and inadequate series measuring deposits in the savings banks of the country. These deposits increased between 1901 and 1913 at a rate of 4.8 per cent a year, a figure which may well exceed the rate of growth of general capital funds during this period.[2]

---

[1] Deficiencies of the statistical record of births, deaths and migration during the period 1901-13 render it impossible to measure with any high degree of accuracy the year-to-year variations in the total population. The figure given, derived from King's estimates, is probably a maximum value, since it is based upon vital statistics for inter-censal years covering relatively small areas.

[2] In post-war years the rate of increase in total savings deposits was greater than the rate of increase in capital funds, as indicated by more comprehensive figures.

The production series treated in Chapter I throw some light on the growth of capital. Our rather limited sample indicated an average annual increase of 5.0 per cent in the production of goods to be used as capital equipment. The produc-

We are on firmer ground in dealing with the supply of credit. Data on book credits are not available, but the volume of bank credit, the most important element of the total, may be measured in terms of the total loans, discounts and investments of all banks in the United States. Between 1901 and 1913 the total volume of bank credit increased from 9,246 millions of dollars to 20,034 millions, the average annual rate of increase being 6.3 per cent. (The expansion of credit volume paralleled and, of course, was based in considerable part upon a steady increase in the world production of gold.) The figure defining the growth of credit can not be interpreted by itself, for it stands in close relation to changes in the volume of production and trade and in the level of prices. For the period 1901-1913 we have no direct and adequate measure of changes in the physical volume of domestic trade. If the rate of change in volume of production, which averaged 3.1 per cent a year, may serve as an indication of the rate of change in the number of physical units of goods changing hands, the increase in credit volume would appear to have been out of proportion to the demands of business. A rising price level accompanied the more rapid increase in credit volume.[1]

---

tion of such equipment includes additions to and replacements of an existing supply of capital goods. Changes in increments are, obviously, not the same as changes in aggregate supply. The production index refers to physical goods; savings deposits are in dollars of changing purchasing power.

[1] The relation is not a simple one between volume of production, volume of credit and wholesale price level, although these are probably the major factors. In the first place, trade of all sorts, rather than production, should be measured. The volume of trade was probably increasing at a somewhat more rapid rate than the volume of measurable production. This period was marked by increasing fabrication of materials of many types, and by the taking over, by the factory and by artisans, of work formerly done in the home. (Net ton miles of freight carried by railroads, an index of one type of trade, increased at an annual rate of 5.5 per cent between 1901 and 1913.) Again, credit employed in connection with security transactions constitutes, to some extent, a separate reservoir. This is not distinguished as a separate item for this period. Another factor was the apparent decline in the average monthly velocity of circulation of bank deposits. Studies of the Federal Reserve Bank of New York indicate a decline in the velocity of circulation of demand deposits in the United States at a rate averaging 2.5 per cent a year during this period. This would tend, of course, to lessen the effective volume of credit. Perhaps more important is the inadequacy of the wholesale price index as a measure of changes in the purchasing power of the dollar in all markets. Snyder's index of the general price level, based upon a wider sample of price transactions, increased at a rate of 2.4 per cent a year, an advance substantially greater than that recorded for the wholesale price index. These and other limitations of the data render it impossible to establish any

The flunctuations in credit volume, as measured by an index of instability of 2.4, were of about the same order of magnitude as the variations in the price level, and were considerably smaller than the average annual variation in aggregate physical production. The volume of goods produced was the most variable of the factors so far considered.

The volume of export trade kept approximate pace with the volume of domestic production between 1901 and 1913. An increase of 4.8 per cent a year in aggregate export values may be taken to represent an advance of about 3 per cent a year in physical volume. Aggregate import values rose by 6.0 per cent a year, which, at the prevailing rate of price advance, represents an increase of the physical volume of imports at a rate close to 4 per cent a year. Oscillations of both imports and exports appear to have been of about the same order of magnitude as the fluctuations of production.

Of series reflecting domestic trade we have two, net ton miles of freight carried by railroads and bank clearings in 159 cities outside New York. The former, a series in physical units, increased between 1901 and 1913 at a rate of 5.5 per cent a year, while bank clearings increased in volume at a rate of 5.7 per cent. If we make allowance for the effect of changing prices upon bank clearings (using Snyder's price index), we secure 3.3 per cent as the approximate rate of increase in the volume of physical transactions which are represented by such clearings.[1] These figures indicate that the volume of commercial transactions at large was increasing at a rate slightly greater than that at which physical output was increasing, while the advance in volume of railroad transportation exceeded by a wider margin the increase in physical production.

In dealing with the volume of employment we are hampered by lack of comprehensive and accurate data. The estimated number of wage-earners in manufacturing industries increased from 5,184 thousands in 1901 to 7,277 thousands in 1913; the annual rate of increase averaged 2.7 per cent. This figure, which substantially ex-

---

precise relations between changes in the series cited. The evidence is clear, however, that credit expansion occurred at a rate in excess of that required to finance the increasing volume of commercial transactions, and that an accompaniment, causal or consequential, was a rising price level.

[1] The assumption is here made that bank clearings outside New York represent, primarily, exchanges of physical goods. To some extent financial transactions affect such clearings.

ceeds the rate of gain in population, indicates that an increasing percentage of the population was employed in manufacturing industries. During this same period salaried workers engaged in manufacture increased in number at a rate of 5.0 per cent a year.

The data reviewed provide an outline picture of certain major tendencies of the pre-war era. We have measured the rate of change in population and have observed the minor oscillations as population changes from year to year. The major movements of production and exchange during this period show remarkable uniformity, when reduced to comparable terms. The physical volume of production, of domestic trade and of exports increased at rates close to 3 per cent a year. When aggregate values, not physical volumes, are measured, these rates run in the neighborhood of 5 per cent a year. The annual oscillations of the series relating to production, imports, exports, primary domestic distribution (represented by ton miles of freight carried) and employment do not differ widely in magnitude, averaging between 2.7 and 4.8 per cent. This is a range of variation from ten to fifteen times that characteristic of population. Such excess fluctuation of the economic series (excessive in relation to the changes in the number of producers and consumers for whom the economic system functions) may be taken to reflect instability arising from faults in the economic order, or defects inherent in an individualistic system of satisfying economic wants. Or it is, perhaps, a necessary accompaniment of economic growth and of a changing scale of human desires.

## Changes in Distributive Shares

We pass to a more detailed account of the economic developments of the period 1901-1913. Dealing, first, with various elements of income, it is possible to approximate the trend of wages and to estimate, with a larger margin of error, changes in the receipts of stockholders and bondholders.

### Wage Trends

The most comprehensive wage statistics compiled for this period are those of Paul H. Douglas.[1] They indicate that the per capita money earnings of employed workers of all groups, excluding farm labor, increased between 1901 and 1913 at an average rate of 2.2

[1] *Real Wages in the United States,* Houghton Mifflin Co., Boston, 1930.

per cent per year. (The index of wage level constructed by Carl Snyder agrees closely with this result, showing an average annual increase at a rate of 2.1 per cent.)[1] There is, of course, variation among the rates of change of earnings in different groups. For the most important single group, wage-earners in manufacturing plants, the average rate of increase in money earnings was 1.7 per cent a year. Brissenden's figures on the actual money earnings of factory workers, in which correction is made for unemployment, indicate the same rate of increase.[2]

If these earnings figures are to be compared with the physical volume series already presented, the effect of changing dollar values should be eliminated. This may be done with reasonable accuracy by means of Douglas' index, which shows an increase in the cost of living for working men's families at a rate of 1.8 per cent a year between 1901 and 1913.[3] Real earnings of all employed workers increased, therefore, at a rate of 0.4 per cent, while real earnings of manufacturing employees declined at a rate of 0.1 per cent. These movements are in sharp contrast with the concurrent increase in physical volume of production. Granted the accuracy of the wage and cost of living indexes, it would appear that increased industrial productivity did not result in any substantial addition to the real income of employed workers in general, while the real returns of manufacturing labor actually declined.[4]

[1] *Business Cycles and Business Measurements,* Macmillan Co., New York, 1927, p. 289.

[2] Paul F. Brissenden, *Earnings of Factory Workers, 1899-1927,* Census Monograph X, 1929.

[3] Douglas' cost of living index for the pre-war period is a combination of index numbers derived from quoted retail food prices and of estimates of changes in the retail prices of clothing, furniture, fuel and light, and tobacco and spirits based upon the wholesale prices of the commodities named. The adjustment of wholesale to retail prices has been based upon the divergence between the average wholesale and retail prices of 27 identical food commodities (from 1907 to 1914 this correction was made on the basis of the average wholesale and retail prices of 13 foods and of fuel and light, statistics on the cost of fuel and light becoming available in that year). Data on rents were not available. In view of the unavoidable deficiencies of the Douglas index, measurements relating to real earnings must be considered as subject to some degree of error. They remain, however, the best available estimates.

The use of this cost of living index as a deflator is open to question in cases in which remuneration in kind supplements money incomes. This is notably true of farm labor and of ministers. Estimates of changes in real earnings for these groups are probably least accurate.

[4] Different distributive shares are marked by differences in time lags in their adjustment to changing price levels. The real values of interest and dividend pay-

§ *Changes in earnings, by occupational groups.*—The general average of wage changes fails to reveal the diversities of the movements actually occurring among different employed groups. These movements are defined by the measurements in the following table, which are based, except where otherwise noted, upon the wage estimates of Paul H. Douglas. The series are shown graphically in Figures 28 and 29.

The three general measurements at the head of the table relate to somewhat different aspects of the problem. Douglas' index, purporting to measure the earnings of all groups of employed workers, exclusive of farm workers, shows an increase of money earnings at an average annual rate of 2.2 per cent, and of real earnings (i.e., in dollars of constant purchasing power) at a rate of 0.4 per cent. Snyder's index of wage level indicates an average annual increase in money wages at the rate of 2.1 per cent. The Bureau of Labor Statistics' index of hourly rates of pay among all employed workers, except agricultural workers, shows an increase of 2.4 per cent a year, which exceeds the rate of advance in earnings. The general trend of wages and earnings is clearly defined by those three independently constructed index numbers. Money earnings advanced at a rate slightly in excess of 2 per cent a year, while real earnings (earnings in terms of physical goods) increased at a rate somewhat less than 0.5 per cent a year. The advance of earnings fell slightly behind that of hourly wage rates, because of a shortening of the average working day during this period.

Among the main groups of employed workers the rates of advance in money earnings between 1901 and 1913 ranged from 0.6 per cent a year for government employees to 4.3 per cent for teachers. As regards absolute amounts, it is to be noted that teachers started at the lowest level in 1901, with annual average earnings of only $337, while government employees, in executive departments, started at the highest level, with average earnings of $1,047 a year. The real earnings of the latter group declined at the rate of 1.2 per cent a year; the real earnings of teachers increased at a rate of 2.5 per cent. Transportation workers and coal miners also increased their real earnings between 1901 and 1913. Postal employees, clerical and low salaried workers, manufacturing wage-earners, and ministers suffered slight declines in their real earnings. Least regular were the earnings of coal miners, for which the index of instability was 4.4 per cent. Government employees, with an average variation of only 0.3 per cent, had the most stable average income.[1]

---

ments are subject to wide variations when measured as percentages of the national income. Rents of natural resources change slowly in money value, as do also salaries and professional fees. Wages have still a different time lag, in relation to changes in general price levels. Accordingly, statements as to changes in real wages must be interpreted with reference to conditions, as to such lags, in the terminal years of the period covered.—M. C. Rorty.

[1] Since these figures relate to employed workers they do not furnish accurate indications of the variations in earnings which accompany periods of unemployment.

## TABLE 49
### CHANGES IN EARNINGS OF EMPLOYED WORKERS, 1901-1913

| (1) Occupational group | (2) (3) Wage index, or absolute earnings in dollars | | (4) Average annual rate of change (per cent) | (5) Index of instability | (6) Average annual rate of change in real earnings or in real wage rates [a] (per cent) |
| --- | --- | --- | --- | --- | --- |
| | 1901 | 1913 | | | |
| All groups of employed workers, excluding farm labor (Douglas) | $508 | $675 | +2.2 | 1.4 | +0.4 |
| Index of wage level (Snyder)[b] | 100 | 128 | +2.1 | 0.9 | +0.3 |
| Index of wages per hour, excluding farm labor (U. S. Bureau of Labor Statistics)[c] | 100 | 135 | +2.4 | 0.8 | +0.6 |
| Classes of employed workers (Douglas) | | | | | |
| Teachers | $337 | $547 | +4.3 | 0.8 | +2.5 |
| Railroad employees | $549 | $760 | +2.5 | 1.8 | +0.7 |
| Coal miners | $454 | $621 | +2.3 | 4.4 | +0.5 |
| Postal employees | $936 | $1,124 | +1.7 | 2.2 | −0.1 |
| Clerical and low salaried workers | $1,009 | $1,236 | +1.7 | 0.9 | −0.1 |
| Manufacturing wage-earners | $456 | $578 | +1.7 | 2.2 | −0.1 |
| Ministers | $730 | $899 | +1.7 | 1.5 | −0.1 |
| Government employees, executive departments | $1,047 | $1,136 | +0.6 | 0.3 | −1.2 |
| Manufacturing wage-earners (Douglas) | | | | | |
| Land vehicles | $500 | $772 | +3.4 | 3.1 | +1.5 |
| Clothing | $391 | $533 | +2.4 | 1.9 | +0.5 |
| Paper and printing | $503 | $664 | +2.1 | 1.8 | +0.3 |
| Leather and leather goods | $435 | $562 | +2.0 | 1.0 | +0.1 |
| Textiles | $325 | $416 | +1.8 | 2.5 | 0.0 |
| Iron and steel | $553 | $700 | +1.7 | 2.2 | −0.1 |
| Tobacco products | $395 | $453 | +1.0 | 1.5 | −0.8 |
| Lumber and its products | $413 | $527 | +0.8 | 4.5 | −1.0 |
| Unskilled workers: | | | | | |
| Index of weekly earnings of unskilled workers (Hurlin)[d] | 100 | 124 | +1.7 | 0.8 | −0.1 |
| Index of weekly earnings of unskilled workers, manufacturing industries (Coombs)[e] | 100 | 119 | +1.1 | 1.8 | −0.7 |
| Farm labor, wages without board (Douglas) | $255 | $360 | +2.7 | 1.9 | +0.8 |

[a] Douglas' cost of living index has been used in determining changes in real earnings.
[b] Snyder's index for this period (Snyder, *op. cit.*, pp. 137, 289) is a combination of the Department of Labor's index of the wages of unskilled labor and estimates, taken from Burgess' *Trend of School Costs*, of the wages of teachers and clerks.
[c] *Monthly Labor Review*, Feb. 1921, p. 74.
[d] Hurlin's estimates of the earnings of unskilled workers are based upon wage statistics for common labor in manufacturing industries, supplemented by data on the wages of building labor, railroad labor and farm labor without board. The index appears in Douglas, *op. cit.*, p. 175.
[e] Whitney Coombs, *Wages of Unskilled Labor in Manufacturing Industries*, p. 99.

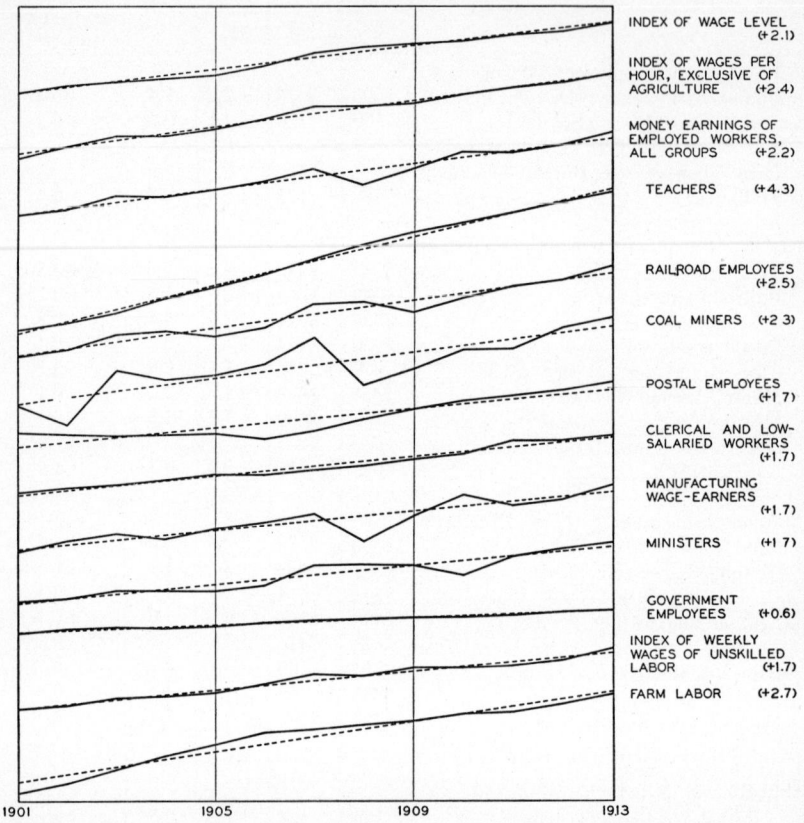

FIGURE 28

CHANGES IN MONEY EARNINGS OF EMPLOYED WORKERS IN THE UNITED STATES, 1901-1913

MAJOR GROUPS

Plotted on ratio scale. The figures in parentheses define average annual rates of change (in percentage form).

Measurements relating to the earnings of eight groups of workers in manufacturing industries are available. (See Figure 29.) For four of these, including workers in industries producing land vehicles, clothing, leather and leather goods, and in paper and printing establishments, real wages increased, at rates ranging from 0.1 to 1.5 per cent a year. Real earnings in textile industries showed no net change; there was a net decline in real wages in the iron and steel, tobacco products and lumber industries.

Two entries in the table relate to the earnings of unskilled workers. The real earnings of all unskilled labor declined slightly over this

## FIGURE 29
### CHANGES IN MONEY EARNINGS OF EMPLOYED WORKERS IN THE UNITED STATES, 1901-1913
#### MANUFACTURING INDUSTRIES

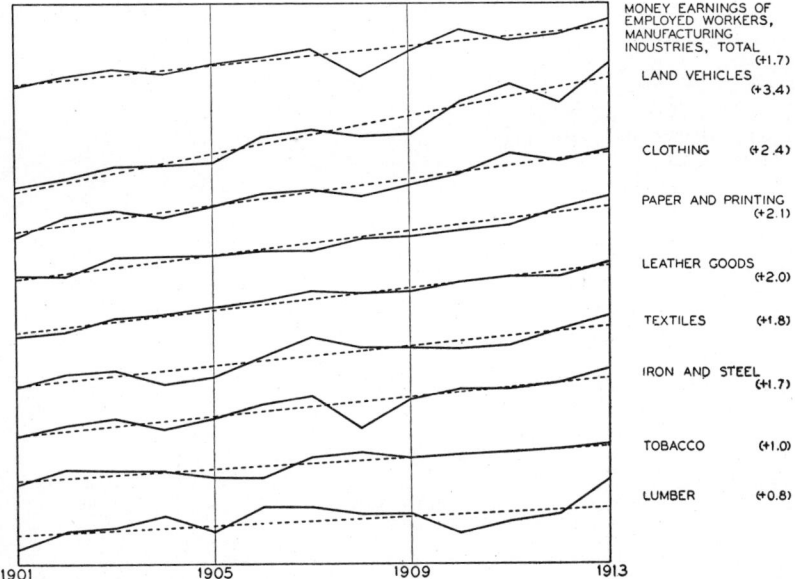

Plotted on ratio scale. The figures in parentheses define average annual rates of change (in percentage form).

period; for unskilled factory workers the decline was more substantial, at a rate of 0.7 per cent a year. Heavy immigration was an important factor in preventing an advance in wages in this field. The expanding production and rising wealth of the years preceding the war brought no real gain to the large numbers of unskilled workers.

Farm labor entered upon this period at a level of absolute earnings far below that of any of the other groups of employed workers. The advance in real earnings between 1901 and 1913 averaged 0.8 per cent a year.

In studying the instability of earnings in manufacturing industries we may make use of a set of index numbers constructed by Paul F. Brissenden, in which account is taken of variation in earnings due to loss of employment.[1] From these data we have computed for each industrial group an index of instability, measuring the average degree of departure from regularity of growth.

[1] *Earnings of Factory Workers, 1899-1927,* Census Monograph X, p. 108. In view of the difficulties facing Brissenden in making his estimates of year-to-year changes in earnings, the indexes of instability of growth given in the text, which reflect these year-to-year fluctuations, must be considered as approximations only.

## TABLE 50

MEASUREMENTS OF INSTABILITY OF GROWTH IN THE EARNINGS OF FACTORY WORKERS IN THE UNITED STATES, 1901-1913

| Industrial group | Index of instability of growth in per capita earnings |
|---|---|
| Tobacco products | 1.4 |
| Paper and wood pulp | 2.1 |
| Boots and shoes | 2.6 |
| Silk goods | 2.8 |
| Clothing, men's | 3.2 |
| Leather, tanned | 4.2 |
| Automobiles [a] | 4.4 |
| Cotton manufactures | 4.8 |
| Iron and steel: steel works and rolling mills | 5.9 |
| Woolen and worsted goods | 6.1 |
| Knit goods | 6.6 |
| Cars, steam railroad | 8.3 |
| All factory workers | 3.9 |

[a] Estimates of earnings in the automobile industry for inter-censal years prior to 1907 have been based upon changes in earnings in all industries. This has probably resulted in a measure which understates the actual degree of instability.

For all factory workers, the variation in annual per capita earnings averaged 3.9 per cent, as contrasted with average variations in the growth of the physical volume of manufacturing production amounting to some 4.7 per cent. Differences among industrial groups in respect of stability of growth are large. Greatest stability is found in the earnings of the workers in the tobacco industry. At the other extreme, fluctuations of earnings in the production of cars for steam railroads averaged 8.3 per cent a year.

### Cash Receipts and Capital Gains of Stockholders

How did changes in the average returns to stockholders between 1901 and 1913 compare with changes in the earnings of industrial and other laborers? We do not have a complete record of corporation dividend disbursements during this period, but such a comparison may be made with reference to returns secured from a reasonably comprehensive sample. This sample includes 93 corporations (66 industrial and public utility corporations and 27 railroads), with aggregate stock outstanding in January, 1901, of a par value of approximately 3,820 millions of dollars. The shares represented included over 60 per cent of those listed on the New York Stock Exchange in 1901.[1]

The present account runs in terms of total disbursements to those who in 1901 held stock in these companies. (The measurements apply also, of course, to one who held any given portion of the total stock outstanding in 1901.) Dividends paid on stock issued after 1901 (other than on stock dividends received by those holding stock in 1901) are excluded. Aggregate disbursements to stockholders, inclusive and exclusive of the cash values of subscription rights,[2] are shown in the following table.

TABLE 51

Cash Income Received from 1901 to 1913, inclusive, by the Holders of All Common Stock Outstanding on January 1, 1901

93 Industrial, Public Utility and Railroad Corporations [a]

| Year | Cash income (millions of dollars) | | Cash income, including rights, per $10,000 investment on January 1, 1901 (dollars) |
|---|---|---|---|
| | Including rights | Excluding rights | |
| 1901 | 218.4 | 171.3 | 603.8 |
| 1902 | 209.8 | 167.8 | 580.1 |
| 1903 | 196.2 | 182.4 | 542.5 |
| 1904 | 200.5 | 166.2 | 554.4 |
| 1905 | 194.7 | 173.8 | 538.6 |
| 1906 | 251.9 | 197.8 | 696.5 |
| 1907 * | 289.8 | 241.6 | 801.5 |
| 1908 | 218.3 | 208.3 | 603.6 |
| 1909 | 269.6 | 225.9 | 745.4 |
| 1910 | 261.1 | 247.0 | 721.9 |
| 1911 | 261.5 | 243.1 | 723.0 |
| 1912 | 254.1 | 248.6 | 702.6 |
| 1913 ** | 306.4 | 282.0 | 847.2 |
| Total receipts, thirteen years ............. | 3,132.3 | 2,755.8 | 8,661.1 |
| Average annual rate of change (per cent)... | +3.0 | +4.4 | +3.0 |
| Index of instability... | 8.2 | 5.1 | 8.2 |

The footnotes to this table appear on pp. 140 and 141.

[1] In later years the coverage is not as great, relatively, for the sample is limited to corporations in existence in 1901.

[2] It has been assumed that subscription rights were sold at market quotations and the proceeds added to the cash dividends received. Stock dividends have been considered as additions to the holdings of the investors.

Footnotes to Table 51.

\* These entries include a 200 per cent extra dividend of the Adams Express Co., amounting to 24 millions of dollars. This disbursement, which was in the form of collateral trust bonds, has here been treated as a cash dividend, though in some respects it was equivalent to a stock dividend. Rates of change in the aggregate figures would be only slightly modified if the disbursement had been treated as a stock dividend.

\*\* On February 15, 1913, some 39 millions of dollars were distributed to stockholders of the Standard Oil Co. of New Jersey as a result of the liquidation of loans necessitated by Federal dissolution proceedings. To prevent undue influence of such disbursements upon the averages, the weight given Standard Oil stock has been reduced (by one-half) to the approximate importance of these securities among all common stocks, as estimated from the listings on the New York Stock Exchange in 1901.

a Following are the corporations included in the sample.

| Industrials and utilities (66) | Market value of stock as of January 1, 1901 (millions of dollars) |
|---|---|
| Adams Express Co. | 18.0 |
| Amalgamated Copper Co. | 139.9 |
| American Agricultural Chemical Co. | 4.6 |
| American Beet Sugar Co. | 3.4 |
| American Car and Foundry Co. | 6.7 |
| American Chicle Co. | 5.2 |
| American Cotton Oil Co. | 6.3 |
| American Express Co. | 34.2 |
| American Hide and Leather Co. | 1.2 |
| American Ice Securities Co. | 9.0 |
| American Radiator Co. | 1.8 |
| American Shipbuilding Co. | 2.3 |
| American Smelting and Refining Co. | 26.8 |
| American Sugar Refining Co. | 53.6 |
| American Telephone and Telegraph Co. | 177.1 |
| American Tobacco Co. (American Tobacco Trust, 1904) | 61.0 |
| American Type Founders Co. | 2.3 |
| Barney and Smith Car Co. | 0.2 |
| Brooklyn Union Gas Co. | 26.8 |
| Calumet and Hecla Mining Co. | 82.3 |
| Celluloid Co. | 5.7 |
| Colorado Fuel and Iron Co. | 12.6 |
| Consolidated Gas Co. of New York | 142.0 |
| Consolidated Tobacco Co. (American Tobacco Trust, 1904) | 45.0 |
| Consolidation Coal Co., Md. | 6.1 |
| Continental Tobacco Co. (American Tobacco Trust, 1904) | 19.0 |
| (Wm.) Cramp and Sons' Ship and Engine Bldg. Co. | 3.8 |
| Crucible Steel Co. of America | 5.4 |
| Diamond Match Co. | 19.3 |
| Distilling Co. of America (Distillers' Securities Corp.) | 2.9 |
| General Chemical Co. | 4.2 |
| General Electric Co. | 41.4 |
| International Paper Co. | 4.3 |
| International Steam Pump Co. | 3.2 |
| Lehigh Coal and Navigation Co. | 18.1 |
| Mergenthaler Linotype Co. | 17.9 |
| National Biscuit Co. | 10.9 |
| National Enameling and Stamping Co. | 2.4 |
| National Lead Co. | 2.7 |
| New York Air Brake Co. | 9.7 |
| North American Co. | 7.5 |
| Otis Elevator Co. | 1.7 |
| Pacific Coast Co. | 4.0 |
| Peoples' Gas, Light and Coke Co. | 30.1 |
| Philadelphia Co. | 12.6 |
| Pressed Steel Car Co. | 6.3 |
| Proctor and Gamble Co. | 14.0 |
| Pullman Co. | 148.4 |
| Republic Iron and Steel Co. | 4.5 |
| Singer (Sewing Machine) Manufacturing Co. | 80.0 |
| Sloss-Sheffield Steel and Iron Co. | 1.7 |

## OTHER ECONOMIC CHANGES, PRE-WAR 141

Footnotes to Table 51—*cont.*

|  | Market value of stock as of January 1, 1901 (millions of dollars) |
|---|---|
| Standard Oil Co. of N. J. (one-half of the total stock outstanding) | 390.0 |
| Swift and Co. | 20.3 |
| Union Bag and Paper Co. | 2.8 |
| Union Ferry Co. | 0.9 |
| Union Typewriter Co. | 3.6 |
| United Fruit Co. | 16.1 |
| United Gas Improvement Co. | 57.2 |
| U. S. Cast Iron Pipe and Foundry Co. | 0.6 |
| U. S. Express Co. | 5.5 |
| U. S. Leather Co. (Central Leather Co.) | 9.3 |
| U. S. Rubber Co. | 6.9 |
| U. S. Steel Corp. | .... |
| Virginia-Carolina Chemical Co. | 6.9 |
| Wells Fargo and Co. | 11.0 |
| Western Union Telegraph Co. | 82.0 |
| Westinghouse Air Brake Co. | 40.1 |
| Total (excluding U. S. Steel Corp.) | 2,003.3 |
| *Railroads (27)* | |
| Atchison, Topeka and Santa Fe Ry. | 48.3 |
| Atlantic Coast Line R. R. | 11.5 |
| Baltimore and Ohio R. R. | 37.9 |
| Buffalo, Rochester and Pittsburgh Ry. | 4.8 |
| Canadian Pacific Ry. | 59.8 |
| Chesapeake and Ohio Ry. | 25.6 |
| Chicago, Milwaukee and St. Paul Ry. | 69.4 |
| Chicago and North Western Ry. | 67.3 |
| Chicago, Rock Island and Pacific Ry. | 60.8 |
| Delaware, Lackawanna and Western R. R. | 50.7 |
| Erie R. R. | 28.1 |
| Illinois Central R. R. | 87.4 |
| Lehigh Valley R. R. | 23.8 |
| Missouri, Kansas and Texas Ry. | 8.8 |
| Missouri Pacific Ry. | 36.0 |
| New York Central and Hudson River R. R. | 166.6 |
| New York, New Haven and Hartford R. R. | 115.4 |
| Northern Pacific Ry. | 68.1 |
| Pennsylvania R. R. | 225.7 |
| Pere Marquette R. R. | 4.2 |
| Reading Co. | 17.3 |
| St. Louis and San Francisco R. R. | 6.1 |
| Seaboard Air Line Ry. | 2.9 |
| Southern Pacific Co. | 86.8 |
| Southern Railway | 26.8 |
| Toledo, St. Louis and Western R. R. | 1.2 |
| Union Pacific R. R. | 76.9 |
| Total | 1,418.2 |
| Grand total (excluding U. S. Steel Corp.) | 3,421.5 |

The U. S. Steel Corporation, though not organized until February 25, 1901, was included in the sample, with an estimated weight based upon the stock outstanding on July 1, 1901. In this case it was assumed that the rate of return during the last two quarters prevailed during the entire year. The value of the investment as of January 1, 1901, (210.0 millions of dollars) was estimated on the basis of the change in the market value between January 1, 1901, and January 1, 1902, of the other stocks in the sample. In two other instances of considerable capital changes during the first part of 1901 (Amalgamated Copper Co. and American Telephone and Telegraph Co.) the stock outstanding at the middle of the year was taken as the weighting factor.

In measuring the results of the original investment in stock of the Standard Oil Co. and of the American Tobacco Trust, account has been taken of the returns accruing to securities received in the dissolution of parent companies in 1911.

Aggregate dividend payments and the cash value of rights on this group of stocks in 1901 amounted to some 218 millions of dollars. From this relatively high level there was some decline prior to 1905, and an irregular advance thereafter. Over the entire thirteen-year period the annual rate of gain in cash disbursements to stockholders averaged 3.0 per cent. The degree of irregularity in this advance is measured by an index of instability of 8.2.

Dividend payments alone show a more rapid and a more regular growth. From an aggregate sum of 171 millions of dollars in 1901, such disbursements increased to 282 millions in 1913, a gain at a rate of 4.4 per cent a year, with an instability index of 5.1.

The entries in the last column record the changes in the absolute amounts received in dividends and subscription rights by one who in 1901 invested $10,000 in the common stock of the corporations represented in the sample, distributed in proportion to the stock outstanding in 1901.[1] The rate of gain is, of course, the same as that shown by aggregate cash income of all stockholders. The

FIGURE 30

GRAPHIC REPRESENTATION OF INVESTMENT EXPERIENCE OF HOLDERS OF COMMON STOCK IN 93 CORPORATIONS, 1901-1913

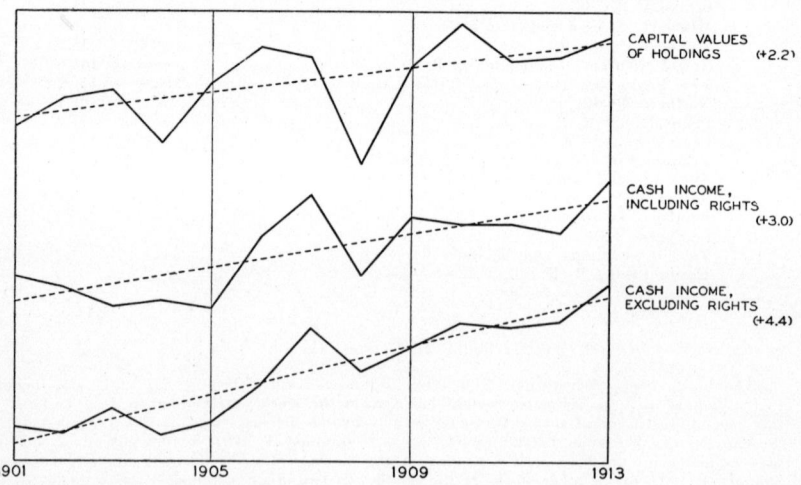

Plotted on ratio scale. The figures in parentheses define average annual rates of change (in percentage form).

---

[1] Except for the reduction in the weight given the Standard Oil Co. of New Jersey. See note to preceding table.

figures indicate that the return on the capital investment amounted to slightly more than six per cent in 1901, declined to about five and one-half per cent in 1903-4-5, and stood close to eight and one-half per cent in 1913.

This gain in the cash receipts of stockholders was accompanied by an appreciation in the capital value of the assets represented by the stock outstanding in 1901. Measurements of the aggregate value of these stocks (plus the value of stock dividends) are given in the following table, together with the annual cash receipts. The data of the preceding table have been converted to relative form, with the year 1901 as 100, to facilitate comparison with the changes in the capital value of the investment. They are plotted in Figure 30.

TABLE 52

RELATIVE NUMBERS DEFINING THE INVESTMENT EXPERIENCE OF HOLDERS OF ALL COMMON STOCK OUTSTANDING ON JANUARY 1, 1901

93 Industrial, Public Utility and Railroad Corporations

| Year | Cash income | | Capital value [a] |
|---|---|---|---|
| | Including rights | Excluding rights | |
| 1901 | 100 | 100 | 100 |
| 1902 | 96 | 98 | 110 |
| 1903 | 90 | 106 | 113 |
| 1904 | 92 | 97 | 94 |
| 1905 | 89 | 101 | 116 |
| 1906 | 115 | 115 | 131 |
| 1907 | 133 | 141 | 127 |
| 1908 | 100 | 122 | 87 |
| 1909 | 123 | 132 | 123 |
| 1910 | 120 | 144 | 143 |
| 1911 | 120 | 142 | 125 |
| 1912 | 116 | 145 | 127 |
| 1913 | 140 | 165 | 136 |
| Average annual rate of change (per cent)... | +3.0 | +4.4 | +2.2 |
| Index of instability... | 8.2 | 5.1 | 7.8 |

[a] The market price as of January 1 of each year has been used to determine the capital value of the investment. For each company this price is multiplied by the number of shares of common stock outstanding on January 1, 1901, plus shares representing stock dividends declared after that date.

Over the thirteen-year period here covered, the capital value of the stocks represented in the present sample increased 36 per cent. While cash income (dividends plus cash value of subscription rights) was increasing at a rate of 3.0 per cent a year, the capital value of the investment was advancing by 2.2 per cent a year. Both these gains exceeded the rate of advance in the level of wholesale prices (1.8 per cent a year).[1]

*Industrial and Public Utility Stocks.*—The experience of holders of industrial and public utility stocks over this period is recorded in the averages for 66 of the corporations included in the general

TABLE 53

CASH INCOME RECEIVED FROM 1901 TO 1913, INCLUSIVE, BY THE HOLDERS OF ALL COMMON STOCK OUTSTANDING ON JANUARY 1, 1901

66 Industrial and Public Utility Corporations [a]

| Year | Cash income (millions of dollars) | | Cash income, including rights, per $10,000 investment on January 1, 1901 (dollars) |
|---|---|---|---|
| | Including rights | Excluding rights | |
| 1901 | 123.2 | 120.6 | 555.5 |
| 1902 | 132.4 | 115.7 | 597.0 |
| 1903 | 128.7 | 120.8 | 580.3 |
| 1904 | 129.4 | 104.4 | 583.5 |
| 1905 | 107.5 | 106.0 | 484.7 |
| 1906 | 124.4 | 120.9 | 560.9 |
| 1907 | 157.1 | 152.2 | 708.4 |
| 1908 | 114.6 | 114.5 | 516.7 |
| 1909 | 126.8 | 126.6 | 571.7 |
| 1910 | 154.5 | 154.5 | 696.6 |
| 1911 | 150.2 | 138.8 | 677.7 |
| 1912 | 151.2 | 151.1 | 681.8 |
| 1913 | 189.8 | 189.5 | 855.4 |
| Total receipts, thirteen years .............. | 1,789.8 | 1,715.6 | 8,070.2 |
| Average annual rate of change (per cent)... | +2.8 | +3.6 | +2.8 |
| Index of instability... | 9.3 | 10.1 | 9.3 |

[a] See the footnote to Table 51 for a list of these corporations. Note is there made of exceptional disbursements in 1907 and 1913.

[1] Note should be made of the possibility of bias in any sample covering a period of years, and composed of a constant number of concerns. Concerns coming into existence during the period covered are of necessity excluded, as are also

sample.[1] Table 53 shows the cash disbursements to those who, in 1901, held the common stock of these corporations.

The average rate of increase in the cash income of stockholders in these corporations was slightly lower than the rate of gain for all common stockholders. The rate is + 2.8 per cent a year, including rights, + 3.6 per cent, excluding rights. Variations in the growth of income are pronounced, approximating 10 per cent a year.

TABLE 54

RELATIVE NUMBERS DEFINING THE INVESTMENT EXPERIENCE OF HOLDERS OF ALL COMMON STOCK OUTSTANDING ON JANUARY 1, 1901

66 Industrial and Public Utility Corporations

| Year | Cash income | | Capital value [a] |
|---|---|---|---|
| | Including rights | Excluding rights | |
| 1901 | 100 | 100 | 100 |
| 1902 | 107 | 96 | 100 |
| 1903 | 104 | 100 | 102 |
| 1904 | 105 | 87 | 86 |
| 1905 | 87 | 88 | 105 |
| 1906 | 101 | 100 | 119 |
| 1907 | 128 | 126 | 110 |
| 1908 | 93 | 95 | 75 |
| 1909 | 103 | 105 | 108 |
| 1910 | 125 | 128 | 127 |
| 1911 | 122 | 115 | 115 |
| 1912 | 123 | 125 | 116 |
| 1913 | 154 | 157 | 132 |
| Average annual rate of change (per cent)... | +2.8 | +3.6 | +2.1 |
| Index of instability... | 9.3 | 10.1 | 8.1 |

[a] As determined from market values as of January 1 of each year. These index numbers of capital values of industrial and public utility stocks may be compared with the Dow-Jones index of stock prices (*Wall Street Journal*). This index, based on monthly averages of high and low prices of 12 industrial stocks, showed an average annual increase of 2.8 per cent between 1901 and 1913, and an index of instability of 9.7.

concerns going out of business during this period. A complete account of the fortunes of corporate stockholders would include both of these excluded groups. It is probable that the exclusion of new concerns (notably those which represent new industries) is of more importance than the exclusion of concerns disappearing during the period. If there is any consistent bias in the sample, as regards rate of increase in stockholders' returns, it is probably downward.

[1] The aggregate par value in 1901 of the industrial and public utility stocks included in the sample was 3,820 million dollars, 55 per cent of the total. As to number of shares, these stocks made up 51 per cent of the total sample.

Cash returns on the 1901 market value of these stocks amounted to about 5.6 per cent in 1901, 8.6 per cent in 1913. All figures for 1913 are swelled by the heavy Standard Oil disbursements of that year.

Reducing these figures to relative form, they may be compared with changes in the aggregate market value of the original investment. The several series appear in Table 54, on the preceding page.

A gain at the rate of 2.8 per cent a year in cash income was accompanied by an advance of 2.1 per cent in the capital value of the investment. This gain in aggregate value exceeded by only a small margin the advance in the level of wholesale prices. Fluctuations in capital value, as measured with reference to the line of average growth, averaged 8.1 per cent a year.

§ *Returns to industrial stockholders, other records.*—Compilations of dividend disbursements by industrial corporations have been made by various students of investment conditions. Measurements derived from these smaller samples, selected according to various criteria and yielding widely different results, are here given as matters of interest. There is no reason to doubt that the results secured from the much larger sample represented in the preceding tables furnish a more accurate record of the actual returns to stockholders as a class.

The figures in the following table are derived from four samples of industrial corporations, those in the Dow-Jones list and three other groups selected by E. L. Smith. The entries in column (2) show the changes in cash dividends received by one who invested $10,000 on January 1, 1901, equally divided among the twelve stocks in the Dow-Jones list. It is assumed that the original fund, plus accruals in the form of stock dividends and subscription rights, was liquidated every six months and redistributed equally among the same group of stocks.[1] In column (3) are given the cash returns secured by one who invested $10,000 on January 1, 1901, equally distributed among the stocks on the Dow-Jones list, without change thereafter.[2] In this case the cash values of subscription rights have been included in the income figures. In both compilations stock dividends have been included in the capital sums.

[1] These figures are based on revised compilations of Dwight C. Rose, *Investment Management,* Harpers, New York, 1928, pp. 134-137, 371 ff. The treatment of subscription rights differs from that followed in the analysis described above, but for this period, and for these stocks, rights were not of great importance.

[2] Except when necessitated by changes in the Dow-Jones list. In such cases the entire market value of the holdings in the discontinued stock was invested in the new security.

The entries in columns (4), (5) and (6) relate to lists of securities selected by E. L. Smith[1] in tracing the returns to common stocks. Column (4) gives the returns on ten industrial stocks with the best

TABLE 55

Estimates of Cash Income from Each of Five Investments of $10,000 Made on January 1, 1901, in Industrial Common Stocks
1901-1913

| (1) | (2) | (3) | (4) | (5) | (6) |
|---|---|---|---|---|---|
| | Dow-Jones sample [a] | | E. L. Smith's selection | | |
| Year | Returns from investment redistributed semi-annually (12 corporations) | Returns from fixed investment (12 corporations) | Returns from fixed investment based on: | | |
| | | | dividend record (10 corporations) | market activity (10 corporations) | market activity, ten different industries (10 corporations) |
| 1901 | $ 264 | $ 360 | $ 615 | $ 818 | $ 616 |
| 1902 | 334 | 354 | 751 | 589 | 514 |
| 1903 | 344 | 402 | 687 | 563 | 595 |
| 1904 | 254 | 285 | 742 | 510 | 394 |
| 1905 | 401 | 341 | 762 | 702 | 480 |
| 1906 | 630 | 655 | 1,085 | 1,041 | 731 |
| 1907 | 813 | 904 | 809 | 876 | 672 |
| 1908 | 735 | 807 | 737 | 858 | 763 |
| 1909 | 766 | 783 | 875 | 908 | 824 |
| 1910 | 801 | 768 | 773 | 1,068 | 962 |
| 1911 | 811 | 746 | 699 | 868 | 812 |
| 1912 | 963 | 887 | 674 | 1,040 | 984 |
| 1913 | 1,056 | 985 | 838 | 1,051 | 1,048 |
| Total receipts, thirteen years .. | 8,172 | 8,277 | 10,047 | 10,892 | 9,395 |
| Average annual rate of change (per cent) .... | +11.7 | +9.5 | +0.7 | +4.6 | +6.5 |
| Index of instability | 13.4 | 16.4 | 9.6 | 12.5 | 10.8 |

[a] Not all the securities of the Dow-Jones sample over this period were common stocks. Exclusion of the few preferred stocks would not greatly alter the rate of growth. The entries in column (2) relate to cash dividends only, the values of subscription rights having been treated as additions to the capital sum.

[1] E. L. Smith, *Common Stocks as Long Term Investments*, Macmillan, New York, 1925, pp. 21-31. The data for these three samples (Tests 1, 2 and 3, respectively) were modified slightly to measure returns on a fixed investment of exactly $10,000.

dividend record for the period 1894-1900. The figures in column (5) measure returns on the ten industrial common stocks in which there had been the largest number of transactions for the week of January 12, 1901. The stocks in the third sample, column (6), were chosen to represent ten different industries; they were selected on the basis of market activity during the week of January 12, 1901. For each of the three samples an equal sum was invested in the ten stocks at the average price for the first week in January, and maintained throughout the period. The cash values of subscription rights and fractional stock dividends were added to cash income.

The Dow-Jones stocks yielded returns which showed a very rapid rate of increase between 1901 and 1913, a gain which was paralleled by a material advance in the capital value of the invested funds. Cash income increased at the high rate of 11.7 per cent a year, when the fund was redistributed semi-annually, and at the rate of 9.5 per cent a year when no such redistribution was made. The shifting of funds led to a relatively heavy concentration of investment from time to time in low-priced stocks, and these scored more rapid gains than high-priced shares.[1]

The rates of increase in cash income received by investors in the groups of securities represented in columns (4), (5) and (6) were distinctly lower than the rates derived from the Dow-Jones list of stocks. For the group selected on the basis of high yield, the gain was at the rate of 0.7 per cent a year; for the second group, selected on the basis of activity, the rate of gain was 4.6 per cent a year; for the third group, the gain averaged 6.5 per cent.

The risk to which the stockholder is traditionally subject is reflected in the measurements of instability relating to the series cited above. The average fluctuations in income from cash dividends ranged from 16.4 to 9.6 per cent a year. Fluctuations in capital value averaged 15.1 per cent a year for the redistributed funds represented by the entries in column (2), Table 55, and 8.1 per cent a year for the funds included in the large sample of 66 industrial corporations. In general, these fluctuations reflect variations in the rate of advance, not alternating gains and losses.

*Railroad Stocks.*—Turning now to railroads, we have the following record of cash received by those who on January 1, 1901, held all the outstanding stock of 27 leading roads. As in the case of industrial stocks, only cash dividends and the cash values of subscription rights have been included. Such rights constituted an important part of the income of railroad stockholders during this period.

[1] Differing modes of treating subscription rights would account for part of this difference.

## TABLE 56

Cash Income Received from 1901 to 1913, Inclusive, by the Holders of All Common Stock Outstanding on January 1, 1901

27 Railroads

| Year | Cash income (millions of dollars) | | Cash income, including rights, per $10,000 investment on January 1, 1901 (dollars) |
|---|---|---|---|
| | Including rights | Excluding rights | |
| 1901 | 95.2 | 50.7 | 671.3 |
| 1902 | 77.4 | 52.1 | 545.8 |
| 1903 | 67.5 | 61.6 | 476.0 |
| 1904 | 71.1 | 61.8 | 501.3 |
| 1905 | 87.2 | 67.8 | 614.9 |
| 1906 | 127.5 | 76.9 | 898.3 |
| 1907 | 132.7 | 89.4 | 935.7 |
| 1908 | 103.7 | 93.8 | 731.2 |
| 1909 | 142.8 | 99.3 | 1,006.9 |
| 1910 | 106.6 | 92.5 | 751.7 |
| 1911 | 111.3 | 104.3 | 784.8 |
| 1912 | 102.9 | 97.5 | 726.3 |
| 1913 | 116.6 | 92.5 | 822.2 |
| Total receipts, thirteen years .............. | 1,342.5 | 1,040.2 | 9,466.4 |
| Average annual rate of change (per cent)... | +3.4 | +5.8 | +3.4 |
| Index of instability... | 15.7 | 8.0 | 15.7 |

In 1901, the cash income (including the cash value of rights) on this group of stocks constituted 6.7 per cent of the market value of the stock outstanding, a figure materially higher than that for 66 industrial stocks.[1] The return declined to less than 5 per cent in 1903. The average rate of increase in cash income over the thirteen-year period was 3.4 per cent a year. (The chief advance was recorded prior to 1910.)

If we reduce these income figures to relative terms, they may be compared with corresponding measurements of changes in the capital value of the fund invested in 1901 in railroad stocks.

[1] If dividend payments alone be included, the return in 1901 was considerably higher for industrial stocks (5.4 per cent of the market value for industrials, as against 3.6 per cent for rails). Subscription rights, particularly those given by the Pennsylvania Railroad, raised the yield on railroad stocks to the high figure cited in the text.

## TABLE 57
RELATIVE NUMBERS DEFINING THE INVESTMENT EXPERIENCE OF HOLDERS OF ALL COMMON STOCK OUTSTANDING ON JANUARY 1, 1901

### 27 Railroads

| Year | Cash income | | Capital value [a] |
|---|---|---|---|
| | Including rights | Excluding rights | |
| 1901 | 100 | 100 | 100 |
| 1902 | 81 | 103 | 124 |
| 1903 | 71 | 121 | 130 |
| 1904 | 75 | 122 | 104 |
| 1905 | 92 | 134 | 132 |
| 1906 | 134 | 152 | 149 |
| 1907 | 139 | 176 | 150 |
| 1908 | 109 | 185 | 106 |
| 1909 | 150 | 196 | 145 |
| 1910 | 112 | 182 | 164 |
| 1911 | 117 | 206 | 140 |
| 1912 | 108 | 192 | 141 |
| 1913 | 122 | 182 | 140 |
| Average annual rate of change (per cent)... | +3.4 | +5.8 | +2.2 |
| Index of instability... | 15.7 | 8.0 | 10.2 |

[a] Determined from market values as of January 1 of each year.

The net advance between 1901 and 1913 in the capital value of the common stocks of these 27 railroads amounted to 40 per cent, as compared with a gain of 22 per cent in cash income (including rights).[1] The rate of gain in aggregate capital value averaged 2.2 per cent a year, a figure approximately the same as that for industrial stocks.

§ *Returns to railroad stockholders, other records.*—The above record may be supplemented by figures derived from five smaller samples of railroad stocks. These results are of interest, though they do not measure the actual experience of railroad stockholders at large as accurately as do figures derived from the more comprehensive sample previously cited.

[1] Cash income in 1901 included a considerable sum derived from the sale of subscription rights. The net advance between 1901 and 1913 in cash dividends alone amounted to over 80 per cent.

## TABLE 58

Estimates of Cash Income from Each of Five Investments of $10,000 Made on January 1, 1901, in Railroad Common Stocks
1901-1913

| (1) | (2) | (3) | (4) | (5) | (6) |
|---|---|---|---|---|---|
| | Dow-Jones sample [a] | | E. L. Smith's selection [b] | | |
| | | | Returns from fixed investment based on: | | |
| Year | Returns from investment redistributed semi-annually (20 corporations) | Returns from fixed investment (20 corporations) | size of stock issue (10 corporations) | dividend payments in 1900 (10 corporations) | failure to pay dividends in 1900 (10 corporations) |
| 1901 | $ 380 | $ 551 | $ 288 | $ 426 | $ 114 |
| 1902 | 406 | 557 | 316 | 464 | 135 |
| 1903 | 447 | 609 | 333 | 487 | 146 |
| 1904 | 414 | 482 | 331 | 490 | 146 |
| 1905 | 451 | 596 | 485 | 505 | 297 |
| 1906 | 502 | 772 | 631 | 563 | 406 |
| 1907 | 572 | 989 | 763 | 661 | 511 |
| 1908 | 532 | 637 | 884 | 747 | 754 |
| 1909 | 572 | 694 | 757 | 611 | 775 |
| 1910 | 618 | 724 | 852 | 635 | 876 |
| 1911 | 620 | 626 | 848 | 643 | 881 |
| 1912 | 601 | 716 | 847 | 628 | 764 |
| 1913 | 578 | 788 | 927 | 628 | 710 |
| Total receipts, thirteen years .. | 6,693 | 8,741 | 8,262 | 7,488 | 6,515 |
| Average annual rate of change (per cent) .... | +4.1 | +2.5 | +10.2 | +3.4 | +16.6 |
| Index of instability | 5.2 | 10.5 | 14.8 | 6.9 | 27.7 |

[a] The Dow-Jones sample (20 stocks) included some preferred stocks during the early years. The returns in column (2), which assume an equal redistribution of the fund every six months and the addition of the values of subscription rights to the capital sum, are based upon D. C. Rose's calculations (*Investment Management*, pp. 378-379). Column (3) gives the returns on a fixed investment of approximately equal sums in the several Dow-Jones stocks. In this case the values of rights have been treated as cash income.

[b] Columns (4), (5) and (6) contain results of E. L. Smith's investigations (*Common Stocks as Long Term Investments*, pp. 60-67). Column (4) gives the cash income from equal investments in the common stock of the ten railroads having the largest outstanding issues of common and preferred stocks; column (5) gives the cash income from equal investments in the common stock of the ten largest railroads paying dividends on common stock in 1900; column (6) gives the cash income from equal investments in the common stock of the ten largest railroads which paid no dividends in 1900. Slight adjustments have been made in the data to give returns on original investments of exactly $10,000.

## Investment Experience of Bondholders

The fortunes of one other important group of income recipients, bondholders, remain to be discussed. The compilations of Dwight C. Rose make it possible to measure the fluctuations in the value of a capital fund invested in the bonds included in the Dow-Jones index of bond prices,[1] and to determine the actual cash disbursements in the form of interest payments on such bonds.

TABLE 59

INVESTMENT EXPERIENCE OF A FUND OF $10,000 INVESTED IN BONDS IN JANUARY, 1901, AND REDISTRIBUTED SEMI-ANNUALLY TO MAINTAIN EQUAL DISTRIBUTION
1901-1913

(These bonds are those included in the Dow-Jones index of bond prices.)

| Year | Interest paid per year | Value of fund [a] |
|---|---|---|
| 1901 | $406 | $10,118 |
| 1902 | 408 | 10,198 |
| 1903 | 416 | 9,880 |
| 1904 | 420 | 9,716 |
| 1905 | 418 | 10,114 |
| 1906 | 418 | 10,046 |
| 1907 | 421 | 9,648 |
| 1908 | 424 | 9,066 |
| 1909 | 423 | 9,707 |
| 1910 | 431 | 9,544 |
| 1911 | 433 | 9,552 |
| 1912 | 436 | 9,375 |
| 1913 | 438 | 9,040 |
| Average annual rate of change (per cent) | +0.6 | −0.8 |
| Index of instability | 0.5 | 1.8 |

[a] Average of the market values as of January 1 and July 1 of each year.

The gain in actual cash return from this bond investment averaged 0.6 per cent a year between 1901 and 1913, while the value of the capital fund declined at a rate of 0.8 per cent a year. The changes in return are due to the shifting of the investment from

[1] For the first part of the period, the Dow-Jones index was based almost entirely upon railroad bonds, but later a number of public utility and industrial bonds were added to the sample. In 1901 the sample included fifteen bonds; by 1913, this had been increased to thirty-three bonds.

For the detailed record, see *Investment Management*, pp. 386-390.

lower to higher yielding bonds in the averaging process, as well as to changes in the sample.[1]

The notable steadiness of return, as evidenced by an index of instability of but 0.5, is a distinctive feature of bond investment. Fluctuations in the capital value of the invested funds were somewhat more pronounced (averaging 1.8 per cent per year), but the indexes of instability for both income and capital were distinctly lower than the corresponding measurements for equity securities.

## Summary of Changes in Distributive Shares

Figures relating to the disbursement of the product of industry among different classes of income recipients are now brought together for comparison. The index numbers in the table on the next page (shown graphically in Figure 31) are based upon the data previously presented, and are subject to the limitations already indicated. These measurements do not, of course, relate to aggregate disbursements, or to the total shares of different productive agents. They measure changes in the average earnings per employee among two groups of employed workers, in the cash receipts of persons investing fixed sums in industrial, public utility and railroad common stocks on January 1, 1901, and in the cash receipts of a person investing similarly in industrial, public utility and railroad bonds. (In discussing returns to holders of industrial and railroad stocks reference has been made to the aggregate stocks of selected corporations, but the measurements given may be taken to define average returns to individuals.) Capital gains or losses by the investor in stocks or bonds are not here included. The wage series listed relate to the earnings of employed workers; losses due to lack of employment do not enter into the wage index numbers.

The smallest advances in income were recorded for bondholders. The average bondholder who had invested a fixed amount in 1901 and whose funds had been periodically redistributed to maintain equality, received 8 per cent more in actual cash returns in 1913 than in 1901.[2] The average manufacturing wage-earner received

[1] There were no defaults in interest payments on any of the bonds included in the Dow-Jones sample during this period.

[2] Had the investment been maintained without change among a fixed group of interest-paying bonds, the actual cash return would, of course, have remained constant. Bond yields were advancing during this period, however, so that the figure cited probably describes the true situation more accurately than would a constant index.

## TABLE 60
### Index Numbers of Incomes Received by Wage-earners, Stockholders and Bondholders in American Industries, 1901-1913
(In current dollars)

| (1) | (2) | (3) | (4) | (5) | (6) | (7) |
|---|---|---|---|---|---|---|
| | Average earnings of employed workers [a] | | Cash receipts of holders of common stocks [b] | | | Cash receipts of bondholders [c] |
| Year | All groups | Manufacturing plants | All corporations | Industrial and public utility corporations | Railroads | |
| 1901 | 100 | 100 | 100 | 100 | 100 | 100 |
| 1902 | 102 | 104 | 96 | 107 | 81 | 100 |
| 1903 | 107 | 107 | 90 | 104 | 71 | 102 |
| 1904 | 106 | 105 | 92 | 105 | 75 | 103 |
| 1905 | 109 | 108 | 89 | 87 | 92 | 103 |
| 1906 | 112 | 111 | 115 | 101 | 134 | 103 |
| 1907 | 117 | 114 | 133 | 128 | 139 | 104 |
| 1908 | 111 | 104 | 100 | 93 | 109 | 104 |
| 1909 | 117 | 114 | 123 | 103 | 150 | 104 |
| 1910 | 124 | 122 | 120 | 125 | 112 | 106 |
| 1911 | 124 | 118 | 120 | 122 | 117 | 107 |
| 1912 | 127 | 121 | 116 | 123 | 108 | 107 |
| 1913 | 133 | 127 | 140 | 154 | 122 | 108 |
| Average annual rate of change (per cent) .. | +2.2 | +1.7 | +3.0 | +2.8 | +3.4 | +0.6 |
| Index of instability ...... | 1.4 | 2.2 (3.9)* | 8.2 | 9.3 | 15.7 | 0.5 |

[a] Paul H. Douglas, *Real Wages in the United States*, Houghton Mifflin Co., Boston, 1930, p. 392.
[b] Dividends plus cash value of rights. See Tables 52, 54 and 57.
[c] See Table 59 above.
* Brissenden's index of the actual money earnings of factory workers gives a measure of instability of 3.9. In the construction of Brissenden's index account is taken of unemployment, whereas Douglas' index relates to the earnings of employed workers alone. The index of instability of Brissenden's series is a more exact measure of the actual fluctuations in earnings.

27 per cent more, while among employed workers of all classes, the average advance amounted to 33 per cent. For the holder of railroad stocks, who had invested a fixed sum on January 1, 1901, the cash return in 1913 exceeded by 22 per cent the cash return in 1901. The average holder of industrial stocks who had invested a fixed sum on January 1, 1901, received 54 per cent more in cash dividends (plus rights) in 1913 than in 1901. The average holder

## FIGURE 31

CHANGES IN INCOMES RECEIVED BY WAGE-EARNERS, STOCKHOLDERS AND BONDHOLDERS IN AMERICAN INDUSTRIES, 1901-1913

(IN CURRENT DOLLARS)

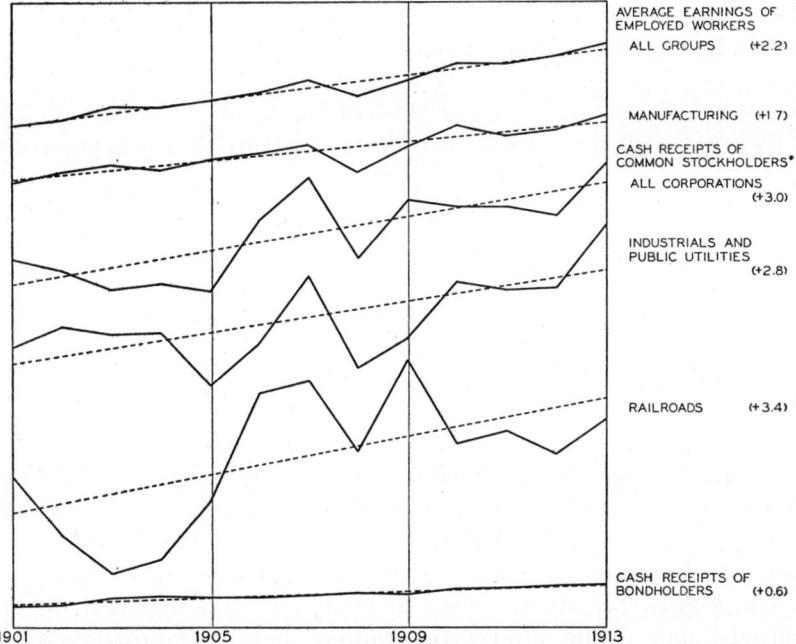

Plotted on ratio scale. The figures in parentheses define average annual rates of change (in percentage form).
* Index numbers derived from sample corporate returns.

of industrial and railroad stocks in combination received 40 per cent more in cash income in 1913 than in 1901.

It is clear from the annual figures that the 1913 returns to stockholders were exceptionally large. (They were affected by a special disbursement of 39 millions of dollars to stockholders of the Standard Oil Company of New Jersey.) In comparing the average annual rates of change given in the table, the distorting effect of a single exceptional figure is largely avoided. Lowest of these rates was the figure of 0.6 per cent for bondholders; highest was that of 3.4 per cent for railroad stockholders. Rates of gain in the earnings of manufacturing employees (1.7 per cent), for all workers (2.2 per cent) and for holders of common stocks in industrial and public utility corporations (2.8 per cent), fell between these limits.

Properly to interpret these income figures, we should consider also the accompanying changes in the values of capital assets. If we employ as base the value of each of these funds at the time of initial investment, January 1, 1901, and compare with this the liquidation value thirteen years later, on January 1, 1914, we have the index numbers given below.

TABLE 61

CHANGES IN THE VALUES OF CAPITAL ASSETS OF STOCKHOLDERS AND BONDHOLDERS, 1901-1914

| Date | Index numbers of capital values | | |
|---|---|---|---|
| | Industrial and public utility stocks | Railroad stocks | Bonds |
| Initial investment, January 1, 1901... | 100.0 | 100.0 | 100.0 |
| Liquidation value, January 1, 1914... | 119.0 | 116.9 | 90.3 |

Over this period the capital value of the original investment advanced 19.0 per cent for industrial and public utility stocks, and 16.9 per cent for railroad stocks. There was a decline of almost 10 per cent in the market value of the bonds included in the sample.[1] (The figures for stocks relate to relatively large samples, 66 industrial and public utility corporations and 27 railroads. Much greater appreciation is shown by certain of the smaller samples. Measurements relating to bonds are based upon a relatively small sample, ranging from 15 issues in 1901 to 33 issues in 1913.)

There are, of course, no corresponding measurements relating to the value of the capital assets of employed workers. There is probably some appreciation in such capital assets, in the form of acquired skill and experience, during the earlier years of a worker's active employment, but if the element of depreciation due to advancing age be considered the net change is almost certainly negative. (This loss has probably been more pronounced in recent years,

[1] It should be noted that the liquidation date is January 1, 1914, whereas all rates of change in capital values are computed for the period January 1, 1901, to January 1, 1913. Market conditions at these two dates were quite different. The Dow-Jones index of stock prices shows values on January 1, 1914, to have been 16 per cent below those on January 1, 1913. The later date is employed in computing liquidation values because dividend payments made in the year 1913 have been included in returns to stockholders.

with increasing mechanization, than it was in the early years of this century.)

If we take account of concurrent changes in cash income and in the value of capital assets during the period 1901-1913, we find bondholders and employed workers at one end of the scale and stockholders at the other. The former, with steadier income, gained slightly in cash receipts, but suffered actual losses in values of capital assets. Stockholders gained at materially higher rates, as regards cash income, and benefited also from the appreciated value of capital assets.

Steadiness of income is of obvious importance. Indexes of instability, which measure the average percentage deviation of actual receipts from the values which would have been recorded had the rate of change between 1901 and 1913 been constant, are lowest for bondholders, next highest for wage-earners, highest for stockholders. Among employed workers in general the average variation in earnings, from year to year, measured from the line of constant growth, was 1.4 per cent. For employed factory workers the variation averaged 2.2 per cent. (The figures relate, it must be recalled, to variations in *average earnings,* which are much more stable than the earnings of separate individuals.) If account be taken of losses due to periods of unemployment, the measure of instability for this group becomes 3.9, indicating that the average earnings of factory workers oscillated from year to year by an amount equal to about 4 per cent of normal earnings. This is of the same order of magnitude as the measure defining the range of fluctuations in the physical volume of production. The instability of economic processes is directly reflected in the earnings of wage-workers.[1]

Widest of all were the variations in the cash income received by stockholders. Profits, being of the nature of a residual, are the most variable element of distribution. Fluctuations in the receipts of railroad stockholders averaged 15.7 per cent a year, while the

[1] As we have seen, the average variation in the physical production of individual industries is greater than the variation in the total stream of production. Changes in the aggregate are reduced by the offsetting effects of contrary movements in the output of individual industries. The weighted average of the indexes of instability for 31 series relating to the output of fabricated goods was 8.0, considerably greater than the figure of 4.7 derived from the index of total production of manufacturing industries. Similarly, an index of instability of earnings derived from data for different industries would be greater than the index of 3.9 given above, which was computed from aggregate payrolls and the aggregate number of employees of all manufacturing industries.

variations in the cash receipts of industrial stockholders averaged 9.3 per cent. For industrial and railroad stocks, in combination, variations averaged 8.2 per cent. Data on actual earnings per share, if available, would show a wider range of variation than do the dividend disbursements which are here cited. It is, of course, common corporate practice to stabilize dividends through the agency of surplus and undivided profits.

### *Comparison of Changes in Distributive Shares, in Dollars of Constant Purchasing Power*

The index numbers in Table 60 measure changes in receipts in the form of current dollars, which were steadily declining in purchasing power between 1901 and 1913. A correction is needed if we are to measure changes in the actual command over goods represented by the dollars received by the different agents. Factors properly adapted to the correction of these several index numbers are not available. Douglas' cost of living index may be applied as deflator throughout, with the recognition that the corrections for the interest and dividend index numbers are probably not as accurate as the wage corrections. It is not likely, however, that cost trends during this period among articles for which the incomes of bondholders and stockholders were spent differed materially from the cost trends among articles entering into wage-earners' budgets. The index of wage-earners' living costs shows the same average annual rate of change between 1901 and 1913 as does the index of wholesale prices.

The corrected series, measuring changes in the purchasing power of the cash receipts of different economic agents, are given in Table 62.

With reference to consumable goods and services the person drawing his income from an investment in bonds, made in 1901, secured approximately 15 per cent less in 1913 than in 1901. The industrial wage-earner stood at approximately the same level in 1913 as in 1901, in respect to real income. A person representative of the average employed worker in all groups secured roughly 5 per cent more in 1913 than in 1901. The cash income of an investor in railroad stocks commanded 3 per cent less in 1913 than in 1901, though the rate of change over the thirteen-year period averaged

## TABLE 62

**Index Numbers of Incomes Received by Wage-earners, Stockholders and Bondholders in American Industries, 1901-1913** [a]

(In dollars of constant purchasing power)

| (1) | (2) | (3) | (4) | (5) | (6) | (7) |
|---|---|---|---|---|---|---|
| | Average earnings of employed workers | | Receipts of holders of common stock | | | Receipts of bond-holders |
| Year | All groups | Manufacturing plants | All corporations | Industrial and public utility corporations | Railroads | |
| 1901 | 100 | 100 | 100 | 100 | 100 | 100 |
| 1902 | 99 | 101 | 93 | 105 | 79 | 98 |
| 1903 | 100 | 99 | 84 | 97 | 66 | 95 |
| 1904 | 100 | 98 | 86 | 99 | 70 | 97 |
| 1905 | 102 | 102 | 84 | 82 | 86 | 97 |
| 1906 | 102 | 101 | 105 | 92 | 121 | 93 |
| 1907 | 100 | 98 | 114 | 109 | 119 | 89 |
| 1908 | 99 | 93 | 89 | 83 | 97 | 93 |
| 1909 | 104 | 101 | 110 | 92 | 134 | 93 |
| 1910 | 105 | 103 | 101 | 106 | 95 | 90 |
| 1911 | 101 | 96 | 98 | 100 | 96 | 87 |
| 1912 | 103 | 98 | 95 | 100 | 88 | 87 |
| 1913 | 105 | 100 | 111 | 121 | 97 | 85 |
| Average annual rate of change (per cent) .. | +0.4 | −0.1 | +1.2 | +0.9 | +1.7 | −1.2 |

[a] The entries are the index numbers in Table 60 deflated by Douglas' index of the cost of living.

+1.7 per cent a year.[1] The years immediately following fell well below 1901. The trend for the period as a whole was a rising one. The real income of an investor in industrial stocks was 21 per cent higher in 1913 than in 1901, if we may accept the sample of 66 corporations as representative. (For this group the 1913 figure was exceptionally high.) The holder of industrial and railroad stocks in combination received approximately 11 per cent more in purchasing power in 1913 than in 1901.

There is, of course, an element of uncertainty in each of the above index numbers. The cost of living index is not perfect, the

---

[1] The year 1901 was marked by exceptionally high returns to railroad stockholders, if account be taken of the values of subscription rights, notably those of the Pennsylvania Railroad.

indexes of earnings of employees are not thoroughly accurate, and the dividend and interest records are not in all respects representative. Yet the general picture which these index numbers give is probably a faithful one. During the period of rising prices and of advancing living costs between 1901 and 1913 the status of the industrial wage-earner was not materially changed. Increased earnings barely kept pace with rising living costs. Employed workers in general were under the same necessity of fighting against rising prices, but the general average of real earnings advanced slightly. All those drawing incomes from securities with fixed rates of return suffered a loss in their command over goods and services. With reference to the trend over the period as a whole, the gains of railroad stockholders were substantial, though declines set in during the closing years. Gains were also recorded by those holding equity rights in industrial corporations. Stockholders were the residual claimants in an era of industrial expansion, occurring under institutional conditions which definitely limited the rewards of the other groups whose fortunes we have been able to follow.

These statements relate to the returns secured by individuals, not to aggregate amounts. At a later point reference is made to changes in the aggregate disbursements to different economic agents.

§ *On changes in the purchasing power of the capital assets of stockholders and bondholders.*—The above measurements relate to the purchasing power of current income. But the capital sums representing the investments of stockholders and bondholders were also changing in purchasing power. The measurement of these changes constitutes a problem differing somewhat from that faced in dealing with the purchasing power of current income. A large proportion of current income must, for purposes of day-to-day living, be converted into consumable goods and services. Invested capital funds are not ordinarily so converted. Such goods and services are bought, in general, only when the income from the investment is spent. The yield, in terms of real income, is a prime consideration of the investor. Yet, from the point of view of the private investor, the convertibility of capital funds into commodities, and into the services of labor, enters very definitely into the determination of the real value of such funds. In any survey of long-term economic changes account must be taken of alterations in the 'conversion value' of the capital assets of stockholders and bondholders.

If we assume that the capital sums representing the investments of stockholders and bondholders were, upon liquidation on January 1, 1914, expended for goods entering into the cost of living index, we find that substantial declines occurred between 1901 and 1914 in the real values of the capital assets of all classes of security holders. This decline amounted to approximately eight per cent for holders of industrial and public utility stocks, nine per cent for holders of railroad stocks, and no less than 30 per cent for bondholders. It is true that the conversion of capital funds into consumable goods is a relatively rare occurrence, so that these figures do not, in general, represent realized losses. They do, however, represent potential losses in case of such conversion, and are therefore relevant to a consideration of the changing status of the investor.

If the conversion is to be made not into consumable goods but into tangible capital assets, the significant price changes are those relating to the services of labor and to the value of goods entering into capital equipment. An index of wages per hour (excluding the wages of farm labor) constructed by the U. S. Bureau of Labor Statistics, and an index of the prices of goods destined for use as capital equipment, constructed by the National Bureau of Economic Research, provide means of approximating changes in the value of capital funds when such conversion is contemplated. (These index numbers were averaged, with weights of 1 and 3, respectively, in securing the deflating index required.) Thus measured, we find that the purchasing power of the capital assets of holders of industrial and public utility stocks increased, over this period, by about four per cent; for railroad stockholders the gain amounted to about three per cent. During the same thirteen-year period the purchasing power of the capital assets of bondholders declined by approximately 20 per cent.

## Foreign Trade and the Balance of International Payments

### Changes in the Foreign Trade of the United States

Between 1901 and 1913 the value of aggregate imports of the United States increased from 903 to 1,894 millions of dollars, the average annual rate of increase being 6.0 per cent. Over the same period total exports increased from 1,355 to 2,330 millions of dollars, at an average rate of growth of 4.8 per cent a year. The general character of the changes occurring in our export and import trade is indicated by the two following tables and by Figures 32 and 33.

The five groups of imports increased between 1901 and 1913 at rates which ranged from 5.0 per cent a year for finished manufactures to 6.5 per cent a year for semi-manufactures. The degree of variation averaged about 6 per cent a year, except for semi-manufactures. In this group average annual deviations amounted to 9.9 per cent of the normal values.

Trends in our export trade were quite different from those

## TABLE 63
### Foreign Trade of the United States, 1901-1913
Changes in Aggregate Values of Imports, by Major Classes of Commodities

| (1) | (2) | (3) | (4) | (5) |
|---|---|---|---|---|
| | Absolute value [a] (millions of dollars) | | Average annual rate of change (per cent) | Index of instability of growth |
| Commodity group | 1901 | 1913 | | |
| All commodities | 903.3 | 1,893.9 | +6.0 | 4.6 |
| Semi-manufactures | 147.7 | 319.3 | +6.5 | 9.9 |
| Crude materials | 308.6 | 649.7 | +6.4 | 6.3 |
| Crude foodstuffs | 120.3 | 247.9 | +6.2 | 6.9 |
| Manufactured foodstuffs | 95.3 | 227.6 | +6.0 | 5.2 |
| Finished manufactures | 231.4 | 449.3 | +5.0 | 6.0 |

[a] Year beginning July 1.

### FIGURE 32
### FOREIGN TRADE OF THE UNITED STATES, 1901-1913
CHANGES IN AGGREGATE VALUES OF IMPORTS, BY MAJOR CLASSES OF COMMODITIES

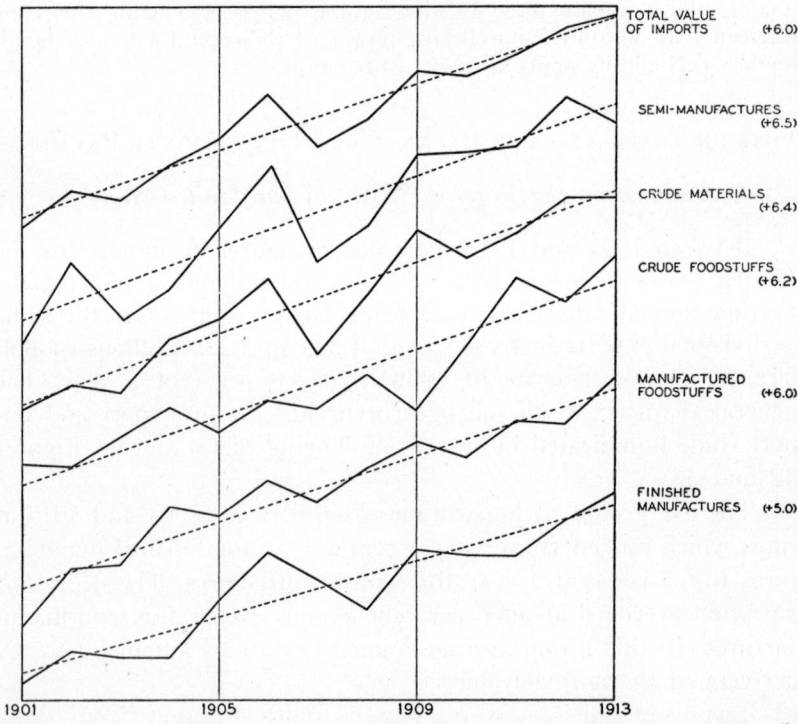

Plotted on ratio scale. The figures in parentheses define average annual rates of change (in percentage form).

## TABLE 64
### Foreign Trade of the United States, 1901-1913
Changes in Aggregate Values of Exports, by Major Classes of Commodities

| (1)<br>Commodity group | (2) (3)<br>Absolute value [a]<br>(millions of dollars) | | (4)<br>Average<br>annual rate<br>of change<br>(per cent) | (5)<br>Index of<br>instability<br>of growth |
|---|---|---|---|---|
| | 1901 | 1913 | | |
| All commodities | 1,355.5 | 2,329.7 | +4.8 | 4.8 |
| Semi-manufactures | 132.2 | 374.2 | +8.7 | 8.2 |
| Finished manufactures | 321.9 | 724.9 | +7.6 | 5.8 |
| Crude materials | 387.7 | 799.8 | +5.9 | 4.4 |
| Manufactured foodstuffs | 328.8 | 293.2 | −0.7 | 6.3 |
| Crude foodstuffs | 184.8 | 137.5 | −2.4 | 18.4 |

[a] Year beginning July 1.

### FIGURE 33
#### FOREIGN TRADE OF THE UNITED STATES, 1901-1913
CHANGES IN AGGREGATE VALUES OF EXPORTS,
BY MAJOR CLASSES OF COMMODITIES

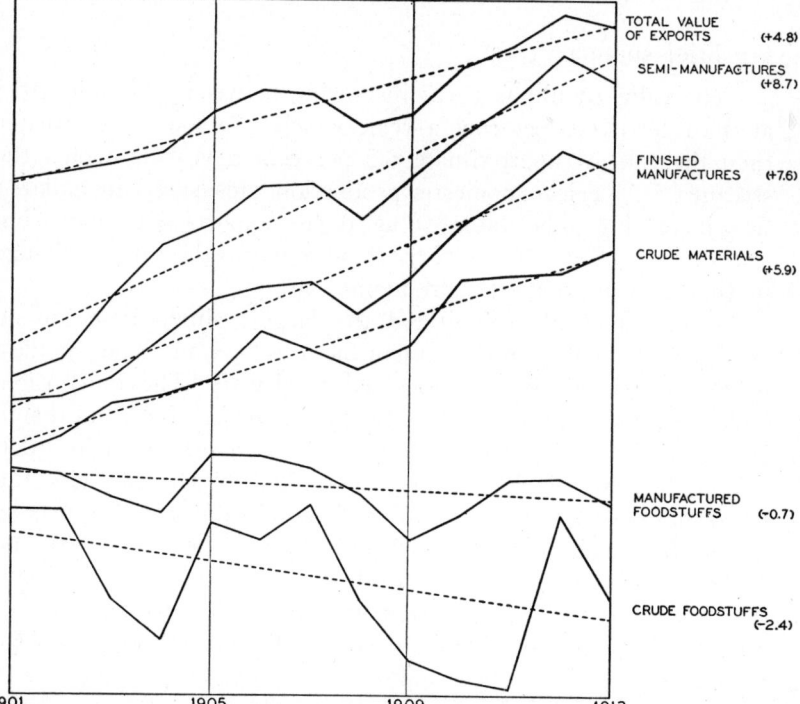

Plotted on ratio scale. The figures in parentheses define average annual rates of change (in percentage form).

prevailing among imports. Between 1901 and 1913 the exports of foodstuffs, both crude and manufactured, declined in value. Exports of all classes of non-foods increased at relatively high rates, ranging from 5.9 per cent a year for crude materials to 8.7 per cent a year for semi-manufactures. These unstable shifts are reflected in the changing composition of our export trade. Foodstuffs, which constituted 38 per cent of our total exports in 1901, made up only 18 per cent of the total in 1913. The proportion of the total consisting of crude materials increased from 29 to 34 per cent; the percentage of semi-manufactures increased from 10 to 16, while that of finished manufactures increased from 24 to 31.

The growth of export trade was most stable for crude materials, for which the index of instability was 4.4 per cent. For crude foodstuffs, at the other extreme, the average annual deviation from normal amounted to more than 18 per cent. This variation is due, presumably, to unstable world conditions of supply, an instability which imparts a highly speculative element to the production and marketing of agricultural products.

In brief summary:

The value of imports was increasing between 1901 and 1913 at the rate of 6.0 per cent a year, which was somewhat greater than the rate of approximately 5 per cent a year at which the stream of American domestic production (measured in dollars) was increasing. The value of aggregate exports was increasing at a rate of 4.8 per cent a year, about equal to the rate of change in the value of domestic production.

Crude materials constituted the largest single item among our imports, with finished manufactures second. The smallest portion consisted of manufactured foodstuffs. The most rapid increase between 1901 and 1913 was recorded for semi-manufactures, with crude materials and crude foodstuffs next in order. Among exports crude materials again bulked largest, with finished manufactures second and crude foodstuffs last. Exports of foodstuffs, crude and manufactured, declined between 1901 and 1913, while exports of semi-finished and finished manufactures rose most rapidly. These movements among commodities of import and export trade reflect, of course, the growth of American manufacturing industries and our declining importance as a source of raw food supplies for the world.

## The Balance of International Payments

There are not available for the pre-war period accurate figures on the 'invisible' factors in international trade. Yet, if we are to understand the general position of the United States in the world economy, the survey of merchandise movements should be supplemented by some reference to the balance of international payments prior to the World War. The following table contains estimates of the major items in our balance of payments during the period 1896-1914.

TABLE 65

BALANCE OF INTERNATIONAL PAYMENTS OF THE UNITED STATES, 1896-1914 [a]

(Aggregates for nineteen years, in millions of dollars)

|  | Credit | Debit |
|---|---|---|
| *Credit items* | | |
| Exports of merchandise and silver.......................... | 32,128 | |
| Exports of gold .......................................... | 1,219 | |
| New capital borrowings from abroad...................... | 2,000 | |
| Interest payments on American capital invested abroad.... | 760 | |
| Freight charges receivable ................................ | 86 | |
| *Debit items* | | |
| Imports of merchandise and silver........................ | | 22,866 |
| Imports of gold .......................................... | | 1,393 |
| New capital loans by the United States.................... | | 1,000 |
| Interest payments on total foreign capital invested in the United States ........................................... | | 3,800 |
| Tourists' expenditures ................................... | | 3,230 |
| Immigrants' remittances ................................. | | 2,850 |
| Freight charges payable ................................. | | 727 |
| Insurance premiums, commissions and miscellaneous items.. | | 570 |
|  | 36,193 | 36,436 |

[a] This table is taken from "The Balance of Trade in the United States" by Charles J. Bullock, John H. Williams and Rufus S. Tucker, *Review of Economic Statistics,* July, 1919, pp. 231-232.

The data are totals for the entire period, built up from various estimates. As is explained in the original memoir, a considerable margin of error was involved in the making of certain of these estimates. The difference between the debit and credit items represents an unexplained discrepancy. The credit items do not include the money brought by immigrants, which is estimated at 300 million dollars.

For purposes of comparison with corresponding data for postwar years, it will be useful to summarize these figures within four general classes—items relating to the movements of goods and services, items relating to the service of debts and to charitable and other remittances not arising out of the purchase of goods or services, items relating to the movement of capital, and items relating to gold and currency movements. These figures, reduced to annual averages, appear in the next table.

### TABLE 66
#### Summary of Pre-war Balance of International Payments of the United States
(Annual averages for the period 1896-1914)

| Class of transaction | Annual average (in millions of dollars) | |
|---|---|---|
| | Credit | Debit |
| Export balance of goods and services, net [a] | +254 | |
| Payment on debts, net [b] | | −310 |
| Net capital borrowings from abroad | + 53 | |
| Net imports of gold | | − 9 |
| | +307 | −319 |
| Correction for net discrepancy | + 12 | |

[a] The net balance of the following items:
- Excess of merchandise exports  + 488
- Tourist expenditures  − 170
- Net freight charges  − 34
- Insurance premiums, commissions, etc.  − 30

The plus sign on the net balance means that the United States exported more in the form of goods and services than it received.

[b] The sum of the following items:
- Immigrant remittances  − 150
- Net interest payable  − 160

The minus sign on this entry means that the United States paid more in the form of immigrant remittances and interest on debts than it received.

During this pre-war period of nineteen years the net balance on goods sold and services rendered by the United States averaged 254 millions of dollars a year. In addition, credits were established abroad to the amount of 53 millions of dollars a year through the borrowing of capital. Balancing these credits (with the discrepancy noted) were debits of 310 millions a year representing payments on debts (including immigrant remittances) and 9 millions a year covering gold importations. It is a balance sheet standing in interesting contrast to that of the post-war years.

### Changes in the Aggregate Rewards of Economic Classes

It is suggestive to think of the basic economic changes occurring during a given era in terms of three broad streams, moving at varying rates and oscillating with varying amplitudes. First is the stream of human energies and needs represented by population, which was increasing between 1901 and 1913 at a rate of 2.0 per cent a year, with an average annual variation from constancy of growth amounting to 0.3 per cent. Next is the stream of physical goods produced by and for this population, a stream which increased during this pre-war era at a rate approximating 3.1 per cent a year, with an average variation (on an annual basis) of about 3.7 per cent. These are the fundamental movements. But the actual flow of goods, in the process of distribution to domestic and foreign consumers, takes place through the agency of money. It is pecuniary values, not goods, which are infinitely divisible, which are capable of economic manipulation, and which are the subjects of the accounting records that are of the essence of business. The stream which is the actual object of economic regulation, and in terms of which economic activities are carried on, is a stream of monetary values. This element grew at a rate approximating 4.9 per cent a year, and its fluctuations averaged 4.9 per cent a year.[1]

In certain important respects changes in aggregate values and in the values of products of different types are more significant than are changes in production or prices. For it is the contribution of a given group in the form of dollars' worth of products or services, not in physical units, which determines the rewards of that group. (The value contribution may vary, of course, because of changes in the number of physical units or of hours of service contributed, or because of changes in the prices of these units.) If we are interested in the pecuniary rewards of different groups of producers, we must trace changes in aggregate values, not changes in per-unit prices or in total volume of production. And if interest attaches to total real rewards, the aggregate value of the contribution of each group must be 'deflated', must be divided by an index of the changing costs of the goods which constitute the real rewards of the various agents of production.

If we had accurate data on the constituent elements of the total value stream an illuminating study of economic changes might be made. The contributions and the rewards of agricultural and non-

[1] That values increased at a more rapid rate than did the volume of physical goods is due, of course, to a rise in the level of prices. This rise, which averaged 1.8 per cent a year, was facilitated, if not stimulated, by an increase in the amount of money in circulation at a rate of 3.8 per cent, and by an increase in the loans and investments of all banks at an average annual rate of 6.3 per cent.

agricultural producers, of producers of raw materials and of manufactured goods, of producers of consumers' goods and producers' goods, might then be traced in detail. In each case one would measure the relative importance of price and volume in effecting changes in monetary rewards. Again, changes in the proportion of the total value stream going to important groups of income recipients—to wage-earners, to recipients of dividends, of interest, and of rents—might be defined. Correcting these value figures by proper factors,[1] it would be possible to measure changes in the actual quantities of goods (and services) going to each of these groups and, in certain cases, to reduce these to a per capita basis.

The data available do not permit such changes to be measured in detail, nor with complete accuracy. As approximations to the desired measurements, figures defining certain of the broader movements of the period prior to the war are summarized in Table 67. The entries in columns (3), (4) and (5) are plotted in Figure 34.

Between 1901 and 1913 the total value stream increased, as we have seen, at a rate approximating 4.9 per cent a year. This may be broken into three components—the aggregate values of raw farm products, of raw mineral products and of the products of fabrication in manufacturing industries.[2] The value of raw mineral products increased most rapidly, at an average annual rate of 5.9 per cent. Raw farm products increased in total value at a rate of 4.0 per cent a year. The aggregate value of manufacturing production (i.e., 'value added' in manufacturing operations) increased at a rate of about 4.9 per cent a year.[3] This last element has two component parts—the value contribution of labor, as measured by wages paid, and the value contribution of ownership and management, as measured by 'overhead expenses plus profits'. During this period aggregate wages increased at an average annual rate of 4.8 per cent a year. Aggregate overhead expenses plus profits increased at a rate of 5.0 per cent a year.

[1] In each case the deflator should be an index of the prices of the goods actually purchased by the members of the group in question. Such special index numbers are not, in general, available; use must be made of deflators which are not altogether appropriate.

[2] Products of forests and fisheries are omitted because of lack of data.

[3] This figure is based upon records for all manufacturing industries covering the four census years 1899, 1904, 1909 and 1914. For raw farm and mineral products the data are annual, covering the years 1901 to 1913. There is thus not perfect comparability among the different series. For the purpose of comparing general trends, however, the materials available may be used.

TABLE 67

ESTIMATES OF PRE-WAR TENDENCIES AMONG PRODUCERS OF ECONOMIC GOODS

Changes in Values of Products and in Command over Goods

(Entries define average annual rates of change. For manufacturing industries the figures relate to the period 1899-1914, for other industries to the period 1901-1913.)

| (1) | (2) | (3) | (4) | (5) |
|---|---|---|---|---|
| | | | Change in command over goods and factors in such change | |
| Economic group | Change in aggregate value of product (per cent per year) | Change in aggregate command over goods [a] (per cent per year) | Change in command over goods attributable to alterations in | |
| | | | purchasing power per unit (per cent per year) | number of physical units (per cent per year) |
| All producers .............. | +4.9 | +3.1 | —— | +3.1 |
| Producers of: | | | | |
|   Raw farm products... | +4.0 | +2.2 | +0.5 | +1.7 |
|   Raw minerals ....... | +5.9 | +4.1 | —1.5 | +5.6 |
|   Manufactured goods: | | | | |
|     All agents of fabrication [b] .......... | +4.9 | +3.1 | —1.3 | +4.5 |
|     Labor .......... | +4.8 | +3.0 | —1.1 | +4.1 |
|     Ownership and management .. | +5.0 | +3.2 | —1.4 | +4.7 |

    [a] The index of wholesale prices of the U. S. Bureau of Labor Statistics has been used as a deflator throughout.
    [b] These entries relate to all manufacturing industries covered by the Census of Manufactures.
    The measurement of changes in the physical contributions of different agents of fabrication is discussed in Chapter III. The index numbers there described have been adjusted in order to secure comparability with other entries in the table. The procedure followed in the correction of these index numbers, which are based on a sample of all manufacturing industries, involves the assumption that changes in per-unit costs of labor and other agents of fabrication are the same for both the excluded and included industries.

Deflating these several figures by an index of general wholesale prices we secure approximations to the changes in actual command over goods enjoyed by each of these broad producing groups. In view of the rather wide margins of error in the data, and in the process of deflation, these changes should be discussed in general terms only, without suggesting a misleadingly high degree of numerical accuracy. Broadly speaking, then, we may say that in the

## FIGURE 34
### GRAPHIC REPRESENTATION OF PRE-WAR TENDENCIES AMONG PRODUCERS OF RAW MATERIALS AND MANUFACTURED GOODS*
AVERAGE RATES OF CHANGE IN PURCHASING POWER PER UNIT OF GOODS PRODUCED, IN AGGREGATE PHYSICAL PRODUCTION AND IN AGGREGATE COMMAND OVER GOODS

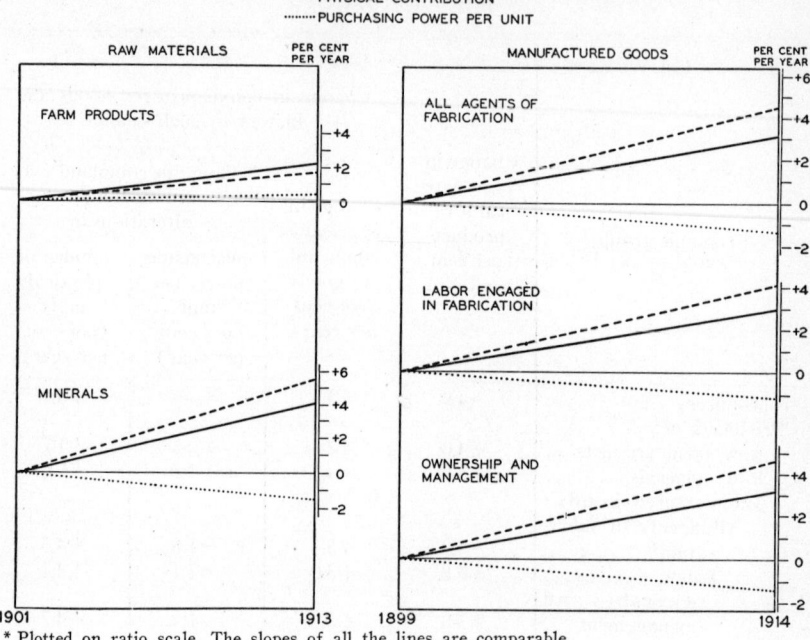

\* Plotted on ratio scale. The slopes of all the lines are comparable.

United States during the years preceding the war the volume of physical goods increased at a rate of some three per cent a year. That portion going to producers of farm products, in exchange for the sum total of their goods, increased at a rate of some two per cent a year; that going to producers of raw mineral products increased at a rate of about four per cent a year; the portion going to agents of fabrication increased at a rate of approximately three per cent a year. All groups shared in the increasing volume of goods, but a relatively larger proportion of the total went to mineral producers, a relatively smaller proportion to agricultural producers. The aggregate rewards of manufacturing producers increased at a rate about equal to the rate of advance in the total volume.

These changes in command over goods enjoyed by the different producers are due to the combined influence of two factors—changes in the actual number of physical units contributed to the total volume of production, and changes in the real value per unit (that is, in the purchasing power, per unit, in terms of commodities in general) of the physical goods thus contributed. (The component elements of aggregate purchasing power are graphically portrayed in Figure 34.) The gain of some 2.2 per cent a year in the total purchasing power of farmers was due to an advance of about 1.7 per cent a year in volume of goods produced, and to a gain of about 0.5 per cent a year in the real value, per unit, of these goods.[1] Both factors, one based on physical contributions, one on favorable market relations, contributed to the gain of agricultural producers.

Quite different were the factors affecting the returns to the other groups. The real values, per unit, of raw mineral products declined at a rate of about 1.5 per cent a year, but so rapid was the advance in physical output (at a rate of 5.6 per cent a year) that the total purchasing power of these goods advanced at a rate of approximately 4.1 per cent a year. Among manufacturing industries the real value of the services of agents of fabrication, per unit of product, declined between 1899 and 1914 at a rate of 1.3 per cent a year. Here again rapidly increasing physical output more than offset this decline, yielding a net advance in command over goods in general at a rate of 3.1 per cent a year.

The separate records of manufacturing labor and ownership (plus management) do not differ materially from their joint record. The aggregate command over goods exercised by manufacturing labor as a whole, and by ownership and management as a whole, increased at rates in the neighborhood of three per cent a year for the industries included. In each case this was the result of rapidly increasing physical output (at rates falling between 4.1 and 4.7 per cent a year) and of a material decline in the market value (in terms of goods) of the contribution of each of these factors to each unit of manufactured goods produced.

§ *A further view of factors affecting the aggregate purchasing power of agents of fabrication.*—In measuring changes in the command over physical goods exercised by manufacturing labor and by ownership and management, we have distinguished two factors—the number of

[1] These measures relate to the wholesale value of farm products. Adequate data on farm prices are not available for this period.

physical units produced and the real value in exchange, per unit. We might, instead, differentiate the number of working units and the reward secured by each unit. In the case of manufacturing labor we would measure changes in the number of men employed and in the real wages paid. The product of the two would be the aggregate real reward of manufacturing labor. Salaried workers may be treated in the same manner. The composite 'ownership and management' presents greater difficulties. If we subtract salaries, for separate treatment, the remainder includes such items as rent, depreciation, interest and taxes, together with profits. This residue cannot be broken up into its elements.

Following are the estimates of average annual rates of change which we derive from data covering the period 1899-1914. As in the preceding table these are based upon all census returns, not those included in the sample cited in earlier chapters.

TABLE 68

Changes in Aggregate Rewards of Agents of Fabrication, and Factors in such Changes, 1899-1914

Manufacturing Industries of the United States

(Entries define average annual rates of change between 1899 and 1914)

| (1) | (2) | (3) | (4) | (5) |
|---|---|---|---|---|
| | | \multicolumn{3}{l}{Change in command over goods and factors in such change} | | |
| Economic group | Change in aggregate receipts, in current dollars (per cent per year) | Change in aggregate command over goods $a$ (per cent per year) | Change in command over goods attributable to alterations in | |
| | | | real reward per worker (per cent per year) | number of workers (per cent per year) |
| Wage-earners ............ | +4.8 | +2.9 | +0.1 | +2.8 |
| Salaried workers ........ | +8.0 | +6.4 | —0.2 | +6.7 |
| Other recipients of income from manufacturing enterprises .............. | +4.2 | +2.3 | — | — |

$a$ Deflation has been effected by Douglas' index of cost of living. This is not entirely appropriate, since it was computed with reference to the budgets of wage-earners, but it may be used as a rough means of reduction to common terms.

Aggregate disbursements to wage-earners in manufacturing plants between 1899 and 1914 increased at an average annual rate of 4.8 per cent. This was equivalent to an increase of approximately 2.9 per cent a year in the aggregate volume of goods commanded by wage-earners.

The number of wage-earners increased at a rate of 2.8 per cent a year, however, so that the net gain in purchasing power (or real earnings) per wage-earner increased at a rate of but 0.1 per cent a year.[1]

For salaried workers aggregate money payments increased at a much more rapid rate, 8.0 per cent a year. This was equivalent to an increase of approximately 6.4 per cent a year in volume of goods commanded by these disbursements. Breaking this latter aggregate down into its elements, we find the number of salaried workers increasing at 6.7 per cent a year, real earnings per salaried worker dropping at a rate of 0.2 per cent a year.

Aggregate disbursements for overhead (less salaries) and profits increased at a rate of 4.2 per cent a year. This represents a gain in aggregate command over goods at a rate approximating 2.3 per cent a year, on the rather liberal assumption that the average cost of items for which these disbursements were expended changed at the same rate as did the elements of a workman's budget. Beyond this point we may not go at present. It would be illuminating if we could measure the actual change in the number of physical units of capital equipment employed in manufacturing industries during this period, and the change in the returns per unit. The improved and enlarged equipment of industry, made possible by new investment and by the ploughing back on an extensive scale of undistributed profits, is evidenced in part by the increased number of establishments, in part by the increased output per worker employed. But reasonably accurate estimates of the actual changes occurring in the amount of capital equipment in use are not now possible.[2]

## Changes in the Aggregate Physical Contributions of Economic Classes, in Relation to their Aggregate Physical Rewards

In the preceding section an attempt has been made to measure changes in the aggregate value contributions of certain economic groups and changes in the command over goods exercised by those groups, during the years preceding the war. In seeking to trace the economic tendencies of this period it is desirable to take one further step. An index of aggregate purchasing power in dollars of constant value measures changes in what the community is giving, in physical units, for the services of a given group of producers. It

---

[1] At an earlier point a figure corresponding to this but based upon annual data for the years 1901 to 1913, as compiled by Paul H. Douglas, has been cited. This figure indicated a *decrease* in real per capita earnings at a rate of 0.1 per cent a year. The slight difference is due to the difference in the periods covered.

[2] The index of production of capital equipment given in Chapter I provides estimates of annual changes in output of *new* capital equipment. It does not apply to the existing *stock* of such equipment.

defines changes in what is being taken out of the stream of goods by that group of producers. We may secure a measurement of considerable significance by setting against this index one which defines changes in the aggregate physical contribution of that group of producers. That is, we secure the ratio of the aggregate physical contribution of a given group to the aggregate physical rewards, or the aggregate withdrawals from the stream of physical production, of that group. Values above unity (or above 100, in relative form) would indicate increasing contributions, on the part of a given group, with reference to remuneration received, while values below unity would indicate declining contributions, with reference to goods commanded in exchange. These matters are illustrated by the materials in the following table, relating to selected manufacturing industries.

TABLE 69

Showing Alterations Occurring between 1899 and 1914 in the Terms of Exchange between Given Groups of Manufacturing Producers and All Producers [a]

| (1) Manufacturing group | (2) Physical volume of production (fabrication) in 1914 (1899=100) | (3) Aggregate purchasing power of 'value added by manufacture' in 1914 (1899=100) | (4) Ratio of aggregate production to aggregate purchasing power in 1914 (1899=100) |
|---|---|---|---|
| All manufacturing industries included in the sample... | 176.3 | 141.4 | 124.7 |
| Steel works and rolling mills | 178.6 | 121.8 | 146.6 |
| Cotton goods | 153.9 | 117.8 | 130.6 |
| Slaughtering and meat packing | 127.1 | 158.5 | 80.2 |

[a] These measurements relate to the specific products of fabrication, not to the total output. It is the contribution of agents of fabrication which is here in question. (This is the physical counterpart of 'value added by manufacture'.) Purchasing power is measured in terms of commodities in general, at wholesale, as these are represented in the index of wholesale prices of the U. S. Bureau of Labor Statistics.

For all manufacturing industries included in the sample (the list of commodities is given in Appendix IV) the physical volume of production increased 76.3 per cent between 1899 and 1914. The goods commanded in exchange increased in volume over the same period by 41.4 per cent. The ratio of 176.3 to 141.4 is 1.247, or, in relative form, 124.7. This is the ratio which, we may say, defines changes in the social contribution of the given agents of production. An increase in the ratio means that more is being added to the total volume of goods, in comparison with the amount taken out as payment. A decline means that less is being contributed, in comparison with rewards received: that is, that the community is paying proportionately more, in terms of goods, for the products of the group in question. In the present case the ratio indicates a 25 per cent increase, between 1899 and 1914, in the contribution of these manufacturing industries, measured in relation to the real costs of their products. For every unit of goods taken out of the total volume of produced goods, these industries contributed 25 per cent more in 1914 than in 1899.[1]

The term 'social contribution' is perhaps misleading, as used above, in that it may imply an ethical standard. Changes in the ratio cited do not necessarily furnish any indication of the relative profitability of different industries. An advancing ratio may reflect economies due to mass production, or to any of a number of other factors. Declines in the ratio may be due to rising material

[1] Several reservations should be made with reference to this figure. It is based not on the complete list of census industries but upon 35 industries, for which alone adequate statistics of quantities produced are available. Again, the figure relates to the contribution of agents of fabrication, not to the volume of manufactured goods in its entirety. Finally, the deflating instrument is the index of wholesale prices of the U. S. Bureau of Labor Statistics, an index into which the products of these 35 industries do not enter, or enter with weights different from those assigned to them in the present study.

As was noted in Chapter I, there is clear evidence that the production index derived from the 35 industries for which production statistics were available between 1899 and 1914 understates the true rate of gain in manufacturing production. On the assumption that fabrication costs per unit of product changed during this period at the same rate among the industries excluded from our sample as among the 35 industries included, we have derived index numbers of physical volume of production for all industries included in the Census of Manufactures. (In deriving the production index numbers described in Chapter I account was also taken of the records of output per capita.) Using these results, we have the following figures for all manufacturing industries:

|  | Physical volume of production in 1914 (1899 = 100) | Aggregate purchasing power of 'value added by manufacture' in 1914 (1899 = 100) | Ratio of aggregate production to aggregate purchasing power in 1914 (1899 = 100) |
|---|---|---|---|
| All manufacturing industries | 195.4 | 156.7 | 124.7 |

The ratio in the last column must, on the assumptions made, be equal to the ratio derived from the data for 35 industries.

costs, advancing costs of production, or to increasing profits per unit. The ratio itself is of considerable significance, as an indication of the contributions of different productive agents to the total volume of consumable goods, measured with reference to their real rewards, but reasons for specific changes in the ratio may not be assigned without detailed knowledge of individual industries.[1]

The three individual industries cited in Table 69 show considerable variations in the values of the ratios in column (4). Judged with reference to what the community paid for their products, in physical terms, steel works and rolling mills increased their contribution by the largest amount, almost 50 per cent, between 1899 and 1914. The real cost of these products was materially lowered. The cotton goods industry increased its contribution, similarly measured, by more than 30 per cent. There was a decline, however, of almost 20 per cent in the contribution of the slaughtering and meat packing industry, when set against the goods received in return.

[1] Another view of the meaning of this ratio is secured by considering the reciprocals of the measurements given. The reciprocal of 1.247 (the ratio from which the relative number 124.7 is derived) is .80. This ratio defines changes in the goods commanded by a given group, measured in relation to the physical contribution of that group. This is equivalent to an index of purchasing power per unit, in dollars of constant worth.

If we let $p$ represent the price of a certain product, expressed as relative, $q$ the physical amount produced, also in relative form, and $P$ an index of the general level of wholesale prices, the aggregate purchasing power of the product in question, relative to the base year, is given by

$$\frac{pq}{P}.$$

The ratio of this value to the physical production, $q$, of the product in question,

$$\frac{pq/P}{q}$$

reduces to $p/P$, which is the ratio of the price of the product to the general index of wholesale prices. This measures the purchasing power per unit of the product in question, in wholesale markets.

It is obvious, yet significant, that the ratio of the aggregate physical remuneration of a given group of producers to the aggregate physical contribution of that group is equivalent to the per-unit purchasing power of goods produced by that group. The forces which define the social costs of the contributions of different groups of producers are focused in the markets where prices are set. If we view these prices merely in monetary terms we overlook much of the story they tell. In attempting to trace broad economic movements it is illuminating to view such measures of per-unit purchasing power as ratios between physical aggregates—between the aggregate amounts which groups of producers are able to take out of the total volume of goods produced and the aggregate amounts they contribute to that total. Changes in these ratios measure economic movements of large importance.

The real cost to the community of the products of this industry increased.

In the following table we bring together for comparison a number of ratios of the type discussed above. (The groups represented are not mutually exclusive.) These ratios give a bird's-eye view of the changing status of different groups of producers, with respect to their contributions to the general community of producers and consumers.[1] The caution should be repeated that in judging and comparing these ratios no questions of merit or of demerit enter. We may not say, on the basis of this evidence alone, why certain producers contribute proportionately more to the common pot, while others contribute proportionately less.

TABLE 70

Showing Alterations Occurring between 1901 and 1913 in the Terms of Exchange between Given Groups of Producers and All Producers

| Economic group [a] | Ratio of aggregate physical contribution to aggregate physical withdrawal in 1913 (1901=100) |
|---|---|
| Producers of: | |
| Chemicals and drugs | 133 |
| Metals and metal products | 129 |
| House-furnishings | 110 |
| Textile products | 106 |
| Foods | 99 |
| Building materials | 99 |
| Farm products | 93 |
| Fuel and lighting | 92 |
| Hides and leather products | 91 |
| Mineral products | 114 |
| Farm crops | 101 |
| Animal products | 89 |
| Forest products | 86 |
| Products of American farms | 95 |
| All other products | 105 |
| Producers' goods | 102 |
| Consumers' goods | 98 |

[a] Most of the groups here listed contain both raw and processed goods.

[1] These ratios are based upon price quotations at wholesale. They differ from those given in Table 69, which relate to the specific services of fabricating agents.

The first nine entries are derived from the commodity classification employed in the construction of price index numbers by the United States Bureau of Labor Statistics. Four of these groups—producers of chemicals and drugs, metals and metal products, housefurnishings, and textile products—were increasing their contributions, with reference to their withdrawals from the common fund. The cost to the community of the aggregate contribution of each of five other groups—producers of foods, building materials, farm products, fuel and lighting, and hides and leather products—was rising. The four groups in the first set relate, in general, to products which have undergone a considerable degree of fabrication; those in the second set relate, in the main, to raw or slightly fabricated materials. The story of the pre-war era, as we have seen, is one of increasing social cost of raw materials, of declining social cost of fabrication charges.

The next division in the table distinguishes forest products, animal products, farm crops and mineral products, each group containing both raw and processed goods. (These entries are based upon price index numbers constructed by the National Bureau of Economic Research.) There was a material rise in the contribution of producers of mineral products, a very slight advance in that of producers and fabricators of farm crops. There was a decline, in relation to the social cost, in the contributions of producers of forest and animal products.

Lumping now all products of American farms, raw and processed, and all other products, raw and processed, we have the two next figures in the preceding table. These show an increase of 5 per cent, between 1901 and 1913, in the relative contribution of those producing and fabricating materials of non-farm origin, a decline of 5 per cent in the relative contribution of those producing and fabricating materials originating on American farms. (In each case the contribution is measured against aggregate rewards, in physical terms.)

In the final division, producers' goods and consumers' goods are distinguished. In 1913 the community was receiving more of the former type of goods, less of the latter, with reference to the goods given to producers as remuneration. The social cost of consumers' goods had increased, that of producers' goods had declined slightly. But the margin of difference is not pronounced.

§ *Contributions and rewards of agents of fabrication.*—This type of analysis may be applied to agents of production, as well as to industries, when the necessary data are available. This may be illustrated with reference to the contribution and the remuneration of manufacturing labor. A simple comparison may be set up by securing the ratio of the change in the aggregate contribution of labor [1] to the change in the aggregate remuneration of labor, between 1899 and 1914. (This is the reciprocal of the labor cost per unit of product, in dollars.) If we wish to shift the comparison to the level of physical contributions and rewards, the denominator of the fraction must be, not aggregate money wages, but the purchasing power of this aggregate. This change may be effected by dividing the aggregate wage figure by an index of living costs. The denominator thus secured measures changes in aggregate payments by the community to manufacturing wage-earners, in the form of consumable goods, housing, and other items entering into the cost of living. The ratio of the aggregate physical production of labor to aggregate physical rewards constitutes a measure similar to that employed in tracing alterations in the terms of exchange between different groups of industrial producers.[2]

The entries in the following table indicate the method of derivation and present results relating to wage-earners in selected manufacturing industries.

Between 1899 and 1914 the aggregate physical contribution of wage-earners in the 35 manufacturing industries here included increased 69.4 per cent,[3] while their aggregate reward (total wages corrected for changes in the cost of living) increased 38.1 per cent. The ratio of 169.4 to 138.1 is 1.227 or, in relative form, 122.7. The 'social contribution' of labor in these industries, measured with reference to the community's payments to labor, increased by some 23 per cent. For every unit of goods received as remuneration, manufacturing labor contributed

[1] In measuring changes in the quantities produced by wage-earners it is necessary to assume that the total contribution of labor, as of each of the other productive factors, increases proportionately with an increase of the volume of production in individual industries. Material alterations in methods of production may invalidate this assumption. It is true, of course, that improvements in the technical equipment of manufacturing industries have been a considerable factor in increasing the productivity of labor in recent years.

In combining data from different industries it is possible to take account of the varying importance of labor as a productive agent in the several industries, so that for manufacturing industries in general it is not necessary to assume equal increases in the output of the several productive agents. (See Chapter III for a series of index numbers defining changes in the physical output attributable to the several factors of production in manufacturing industries.)

[2] The reciprocal of this ratio is identical with an index of labor cost per unit of product, deflated by an index of the cost of living.

[3] We are here assuming that in individual industries the contribution of labor increases proportionately with an increase in the total output. Any increase recorded is, of course, a joint product of the several agents of production; we are not able to measure the specific productivity of the different agents.

## TABLE 71

SHOWING ALTERATIONS OCCURRING BETWEEN 1899 AND 1914 IN THE TERMS OF EXCHANGE BETWEEN MANUFACTURING LABOR AND ALL PRODUCERS

Ratios of Aggregate Quantities Produced by Manufacturing Wage-earners to their Aggregate Purchasing Power [a]

| Producing group | Physical volume of production in 1914 (1899=100) | Aggregate purchasing power of wages received in 1914 (1899=100) | Ratio of aggregate production to aggregate purchasing power in 1914 (1899=100) |
|---|---|---|---|
| Wage-earners in: | | | |
| All manufacturing industries included in the sample | 169.4 | 138.1 | 122.7 |
| Blast furnaces, iron and steel | 163.3 | 91.2 | 179.1 |
| Petroleum refining | 296.5 | 213.7 | 138.7 |
| Steel works and rolling mills | 178.6 | 136.1 | 131.3 |
| Cotton goods factories | 153.9 | 127.0 | 121.1 |
| Woolen and worsted goods factories | 145.4 | 125.3 | 116.0 |
| Flour and grist mills | 114.1 | 111.7 | 102.1 |
| Boot and shoe factories | 131.4 | 133.8 | 98.2 |
| Slaughtering and meat packing | 127.1 | 137.7 | 92.3 |

[a] Aggregate purchasing power refers to command over items included in the Douglas cost of living index.

23 per cent more in 1914 than in 1899. Viewing this inversely, the real cost to the community of the contribution of manufacturing labor declined approximately 19 per cent.

This ratio varies considerably from industry to industry, as is clear from the cases cited above. In slaughtering and meat packing the physical contribution increased less than did the aggregate purchasing power of wages received; the ratio defining the 'social contribution' declined from 100.0 to 92.3 between 1899 and 1914. In the production of pig iron (in which great technical improvements were made) the volume of production increased some 63 per cent, while the aggregate real rewards of labor declined about 9 per cent. The index based on the ratio between the two increased from 100.0 to 179.1.

The ratios relating to labor have not the clearly defined meanings that those relating to the separate industries have, for there is no separate contribution made by wage-earners which can be divorced from the facilitating services of tools of all sorts. All references to 'the contribution of labor' must be taken to mean 'the contribution of labor utilizing the technical equipment available in the industry'. This is the same reservation that applies to indexes of per capita productivity.

One further comparison of somewhat the same sort is of interest. Recognizing that we cannot measure separately the output of the different agents of production, we may yet treat certain of the data relating to sellers of materials, wage-earners and the composite element of 'overhead costs plus profits' as though such separation were possible. As between sellers of materials and the different agents of fabrication there is a fairly clear distinction, easier to make and to measure than is that between wage-earners and the equipment they utilize. Measurements relating to changes in the aggregate contributions of these different agents and in their aggregate physical rewards are given in the next table.

TABLE 72

SHOWING ALTERATIONS OCCURRING BETWEEN 1899 AND 1914 IN THE AGGREGATE PRODUCTION OF DIFFERENT AGENTS, AND IN THEIR AGGREGATE REWARDS

(Data relating to 35 manufacturing industries of the United States)

| Economic group | Physical contribution in 1914 (1899=100) | Aggregate purchasing power in 1914 [a] (1899=100) | Ratio of aggregate contribution to aggregate purchasing power in 1914 (1899=100) |
|---|---|---|---|
| All agents of production, manufacturing | 163.3 | 152.9 | 106.8 |
| Sellers of materials [b] | 157.8 | 153.0 | 103.2 |
| Agents of fabrication | 176.3 | 136.5 | 129.2 |
| Wage-earners | 169.4 | 138.1 | 122.7 |
| Others (represented in overhead costs plus profits) | 180.4 | 135.2 | 133.4 |

[a] In computing purchasing power, the wholesale price index of the Bureau of Labor Statistics has been used in dealing with the total products of manufacturing industries. Douglas' cost of living index has been used for the different productive agents. This index is strictly applicable only to wage-earners but in default of better it has been used for all entries except the first. It is adequate for purposes of a rough comparison. The figures given above for agents of fabrication are not consistent with those in Table 69, which were deflated by an index of wholesale prices.

[b] 'Materials', as that term is used in the Census of Manufactures, include semi-processed goods, fuel, containers, etc., as well as raw materials proper.

The increasing degree of fabrication of manufactured goods, and the growing proportion of heavily fabricated goods in the total products of manufacture, is shown by the rather wide difference between the index numbers of production relating to materials and to fabrication. These numbers indicate an increase between 1899 and 1914 of about 58 per cent in quantity of materials used, of some 76 per cent in the contribution of fabricating agents. Over the same interval the aggregate purchasing power of sellers of materials increased by 53 per cent, while that of agents of fabrication advanced by 36 per cent. The ratio which defines changes in aggregate contribution, in relation to changes in aggregate purchasing power, increased by 3 per cent for sellers of materials, by 29 per cent for agents of fabrication. (This latter figure is 25 per cent, if purchasing power be measured in terms of commodities at wholesale. The figure in the text relates to purchasing power in terms of items in the cost of living index.) The community was receiving much more in 1914 from agents of fabrication, in relation to their aggregate physical rewards, than in 1899. From sellers of materials (a term which here includes a considerable proportion of goods which are not raw materials proper) the gain was much less.

Among agents of fabrication a separation of contributions is largely fictitious, but it is possible to take some account of the increasing importance of the equipment represented by 'overhead'. The quantity index points to a gain of about 80 per cent in the volume of production attributable to ownership and management.[1] Setting this against the index measuring gain in aggregate purchasing power of this group, a ratio of 1.334 is secured. This is somewhat larger than the corresponding measure of 1.227 secured for wage-earners.[2]

In summary of these figures: From the point of view of the com-

[1] This is secured by weighting the production figures for separate industries, when combining them, by amounts proportioned to the importance of overhead costs plus profits in the several industries.

[2] As was pointed out in Chapter I, the physical volume of production of all manufacturing industries increased at a somewhat more rapid rate than did the output of the 35 industries for which statistics of production are available. On the assumption that prices and costs changed at the same rates among all industries as among the 35 we have studied, index numbers of production relating to all census industries may be constructed. Results based on these figures are given below. (In measuring changes in aggregate purchasing power use has been made of the same deflators employed in securing the entries in Table 72.)

Showing Alterations Occurring between 1899 and 1914 in the Aggregate Production of Different Agents and in the Aggregate Rewards of these Agents, Manufacturing Industries of the United States

| Economic group | Physical contribution in 1914 (1899 = 100) | Aggregate purchasing power in 1914 (1899 = 100) | Ratio of aggregate contribution to aggregate purchasing power in 1914 (1899 = 100) |
|---|---|---|---|
| All agents of production, manufacturing | 174.0 | 162.9 | 106.8 |
| Sellers of materials | 166.8 | 161.7 | 103.2 |
| Agents of fabrication | 195.4 | 151.3 | 129.2 |
| Wage-earners | 184.3 | 150.3 | 122.7 |
| Others (represented in overhead costs plus profits) | 202.8 | 152.0 | 133.4 |

The increases between 1899 and 1914 in the contribution and in the purchasing power of each of the several agents are higher than appears from the data for 35 industries. It is probably a necessary result of the increasing diversification of industry that an index of production based on standard commodities should understate the true rate of increase in physical output. The ratios which define the relation between changes in contributions and changes in rewards are identical with those relating to the samples of 35 industries, a fact which follows from the method employed in deriving the corrected quantity indexes.

munity at large, the aggregate contribution of manufacturing industries advanced during this fifteen-year pre-war period more rapidly than did the aggregate amount received by such industries in return for their wares. The community gained; the social cost of the services of manufacturing industries declined. The same is true with reference to the contributions and rewards of the several agents coöperating in these industries. The community's gain from the sellers of materials (which here includes semi-fabricated goods, fuel, etc.) was least. Substantial, however, were the gains from the services of wage-earners and of creditors, owners and managers. The aggregate contribution of wage-earners increased by about 23 per cent more than did the aggregate reward. The aggregate contribution of creditors, owners and managers increased some 33 per cent more than did the aggregate reward.[1] Difficulties of measurement affect both terms of these comparisons, physical output and purchasing power. The figures are not to be assumed to define accurately the changes taking place. The broad tendencies they reveal undoubtedly prevailed.

These various measurements of purchasing power changes bear upon, though they do not solve, a problem of considerable importance. During the pre-war period now under review expanding credit and increasing supplies of money stimulated, or permitted, a growth of aggregate values exceeding the growth in volume of physical goods and services. The volume of goods increased at a rate approximating 3.1 per cent a year between 1901 and 1913; aggregate values expanded at a rate of about 4.9 per cent a year. Rising prices account for the difference. New values not attributable to the production of goods or the rendering of services were created by this cheapening of money. Such new values carried with them command over goods just as potent as that carried by values attributable to the production of physical goods. To what economic groups did the values created by rising prices accrue? What economic groups lost in purchasing power as a result of the creation of these new values?

To answer these questions accurately and in detail would require a far more comprehensive knowledge of the economic processes of this period than we now possess. Changes in the individual rewards of different economic agents and in the aggregate rewards of different economic groups would occur with the passage of time, even though no change occurred in the value of money.

---

[1] The fact that the base year, 1899, was prosperous, while the given year, 1914, was depressed, would tend to raise this ratio. The rewards of this group were high in 1899, relatively low in 1914.

Fluctuations in the value of money constitute only one factor (though often a dominating one) in the interplay of forces affecting prices and values. We cannot disentangle this one factor from all other complicating influences. Yet certain of the alterations in purchasing power occurring during this era clearly reflect the influence of changing monetary values.

Our findings have indicated that between 1901 and 1913 the income of an average bondholder lost in purchasing power at a rate of 1.2 per cent a year, that the income of an average holder of common stocks increased in purchasing power at a rate of 1.2 per cent a year, and that the income of an average wage-earner increased in purchasing power at a rate of 0.4 per cent a year. That the real returns to bondholders declined, and that the real returns to wage-earners advanced so slowly, in spite of advancing productivity, is definitely attributable to the lagging of their monetary rewards during a period of rising prices. It is reasonable to assume that the gain in the real rewards of stockholders during this period is in part due to the same factor. When prices rise, and the real rewards of fixed claimants decline, the returns to the residual claimant are likely to advance.[1]

One could hazard opinions as to the part played by the monetary factor in effecting certain of the other changes in purchasing power which occurred during this period, changes affecting different industries, different income groups and different economic classes. But definite proof would be hard to give. The incidence of changing monetary values upon the structure of prices has never been charted. Indeed, the effects of inflation (or of deflation) are not necessarily the same at all times. A stream of new values may be poured into the economic system through various channels; the direction of pressure of the new values will vary correspondingly. But the addition (or subtraction) of such values may profoundly modify the distribution of the physical fruits of industry.

## DIVERSITY OF PRE-WAR ECONOMIC MOVEMENTS

The picture which remains in one's mind after a consideration of the various measurements presented is one of an economic

[1] This result is not inconsistent with the evidence that in manufacturing industries overhead costs plus profits declined, per unit of product, during this period. Increasing output might well lead to a gain in the rewards of stockholders, though profits, per unit of product, declined.

system surging forward on nearly all fronts, but with movements that were uneven and highly irregular when seen in detail. The various elements of the system were growing at widely different rates and fluctuating over widely different ranges. Population, production, the volume of credit, of capital, of foreign trade, the contributions and the rewards of different industrial groups and of different agents of production—all these were changing at diverse rates and with varying degrees of regularity. It was not a system which moved forward with its various elements in close agreement, with nicely coördinated reciprocal changes. It was a system in constant flux, whether viewed as a whole or in any of its parts.

The differing ranges of oscillation of the various elements of the economic system involve constant readjustment, constant shiftings, as new bases for the necessary coördination of working parts are sought. These are short-term adjustments, adaptations to swings which complete and return upon themselves with more or less regularity over a period of a few years. Of a different order are the readjustments called for by the divergent rates of growth of the various economic elements. Here are shifts which do not reverse themselves over such periods as that which is here studied. These tendencies persist, and adaptation to the changes they bring must involve more permanent alterations in the relations among working parts. How prompt and effective these short-term readjustments and these more permanent adaptations may be must depend upon the flexibility of the economic system.

The coördination of economic elements under a system of private enterprise and freedom of competition is left to the play of forces which are assumed to be automatic in character, and which work through the system of prices. The conditions under which prompt and complete readjustment to economic changes might be automatically effected have never been fully realized. At different times and in different places the degree of realization has varied. Such readjustment is presumably more difficult the less flexible the economy and the more severe the stresses to which the diversity of economic movements subjects it. In the comparison of pre-war and post-war epochs we shall be concerned, among other things, with this aspect of the problem of economic coördination.

# CHAPTER V

## *Interregnum*
## *Production, Price and Cost Changes, 1913-1923*

### *The End of an Era*

THE changed conditions which followed the outbreak of the World War brought certain immediate shifts in economic tendencies. Many of these changes were closely associated with the temporary conditions due to the war. Other changes were more enduring, and their effects persisted, to shape the direction of American economic development during the years which followed the signing of the Armistice.

The war altered the directions in which the productive energies of the United States were being expended. Even before our entrance the demands of the warring countries had placed heavy emphasis on the production of food, munitions, ships, clothing, chemicals and similar goods. The construction industries and other industries producing goods not directly necessary for subsistence or for the prosecution of war languished.

In the field of prices the moderate but persistent advance which had characterized the preceding eighteen years was quickened. Between 1914 and 1920 the level of wholesale prices in the United States advanced 127 per cent, as compared with an increase of 46 per cent between 1896 and 1914. Of greater importance than the rise in the price level were the abrupt changes which occurred in relations among the prices of important commodity groups. The slow secular divergences of prices in different groups which had characterized the two preceding decades were succeeded by sharply accentuated alterations in price relations, many of them reversing tendencies previously prevailing. In 1917 a further important factor, that of price control, was introduced. During the preceding quarter century the development of monopolies and semi-monopolies and the consummation of various formal and informal trade agreements had encroached upon the region of free prices. The area within which competitive forces of supply and of demand worked freely had been diminishing. The introduction of governmental price control in 1917 brought an immediate and material widening of the area of price regulation, and a consequent reduction in the area of price freedom.

Shifts in the character of our foreign trade reflected changing conditions of demand and of production resulting from the war. In addition, there was an enormous advance in the volume of exports, representing not only our own military efforts, but sales, credit advances and the out-flow of capital to allied and neutral nations.

The check to immigration, the drafting of men for military service and the increasing demand for labor brought substantial wage advances in most industries. During the war-time advance and, even more, during the sharp post-war deflation, labor improved its position to a degree perhaps never before approached during an equal period of time. Swelling business volume and rising prices increased profits, particularly among the industries benefiting from war-time demands.

Of the more enduring changes brought by the war probably the most important was the shift of the United States from a debtor to a creditor status in the family of nations. Foreign capital invested in this country during the many years of industrial development preceding was repatriated in substantial amounts by the warring countries in financing their military efforts. In addition, capital loans, both private and governmental, were made by this country in unprecedented amounts. Heavy long-term credits were built up abroad in amounts far out-balancing the foreign credits still remaining in this country. Enduring, also, were many of the changes in our foreign trade relations and in the character of our export trade. The withdrawal, in greater or less degree, of the fighting countries from foreign markets during the war made new openings for the export trade of the United States.

All these movements changed materially the make-up of the stream of currently-produced values, and altered the terms upon which goods and services were exchanged among different economic groups. These shifts we shall explore in succeeding pages.

It is not the purpose of this chapter to review in detail the numerous economic movements occurring during the war years.

We must, however, bridge the gap between the ending of the pre-war period and the beginning of the post-war epoch with which the following chapters are concerned. Because of the character of the data, many of which relate only to census years, and because of the unsettled conditions prevailing just prior to and just after the war, the precise limits of this interregnum are difficult to set. For the purposes of the following discussion one terminus will be 1913 or 1914, the other, 1922 or 1923. We shall briefly summarize certain of the major changes in production, prices and costs occurring between these years. No attempt will be made to deal with other economic elements.

## Production and Construction

The general course of production in the United States between 1913 and 1922 is indicated by the measurements in the following table, which are shown graphically in Figure 35.

### TABLE 73
Changes in Physical Volume of Production in the United States, 1913-1922 [a]

| (1) | (2) | (3) | (4) | (5) | (6) | (7) | (8) |
|---|---|---|---|---|---|---|---|
| | | Manufac- | American farm products | | All other products | | Total |
| Year | Raw materials | tured goods | | | | | volume of production |
| | | | Raw | Processed | Raw | Processed | |
| 1913 | 100 | 100 | 100 | 100 | 100 | 100 | 100 |
| 1914 | 109 | 96 | 112 | 101 | 94 | 93 | 102 |
| 1915 | 117 | 114 | 121 | 104 | 102 | 117 | 116 |
| 1916 | 107 | 137 | 105 | 107 | 116 | 144 | 123 |
| 1917 | 116 | 138 | 114 | 107 | 124 | 148 | 128 |
| 1918 | 115 | 138 | 112 | 109 | 125 | 146 | 127 |
| 1919 | 115 | 122 | 117 | 100 | 106 | 130 | 119 |
| 1920 | 124 | 130 | 124 | 92 | 122 | 145 | 127 |
| 1921 | 109 | 103 | 112 | 94 | 96 | 106 | 106 |
| 1922 | 119 | 129 | 123 | 107 | 102 | 137 | 124 |

[a] The index numbers of the output of raw materials are based upon computations of Stewart for the early years (1913-1919) and of the Federal Reserve Board and the Bureau of Agricultural Economics for the later period. (See Walter W. Stewart, "An Index of the Physical Volume of Production," *The American Economic Review*, Vol. XI, No. 1, March, 1921, pp. 57-70; *Federal Reserve Bulletin*, Vol. 13, No. 2, February, 1927, pp. 100-103; U. S. Department of Agriculture, *Yearbook of Agriculture, 1931*, p. 974.) The index numbers of the output of manufactured goods for the census years are averages secured from sample industries, adjusted, as in Chapter I, to represent all manufacturing industries. Interpolations for intercensal years have been based upon the index numbers of manufacturing production of Stewart and of the Federal Reserve Board.

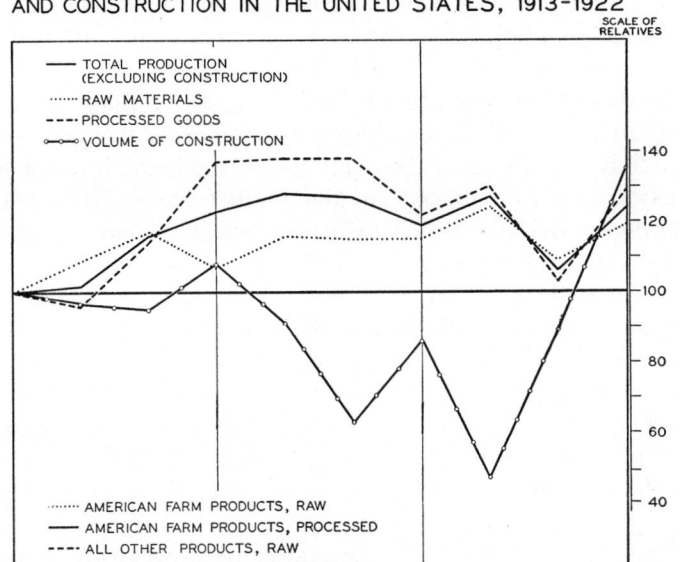

**FIGURE 35**

CHANGES IN PHYSICAL VOLUME OF PRODUCTION AND CONSTRUCTION IN THE UNITED STATES, 1913-1922

The aggregate volume of production increased rather rapidly between 1914 and 1917. Thereafter, to 1920, it remained close to a constant level approximately 27 per cent above the 1913 output. (A minor fall occurred in 1919.) The decline accompanying the recession of 1921 was pronounced, but a new advance was well under way by the following year.

The year 1922 marks the beginning of the post-war period to be studied in subsequent chapters. It is pertinent to inquire as to the relative level of production in that year. The figures in Table 73 indicate an advance of 24 per cent in physical volume of production between 1913 and 1922. In comparison, total production expanded by 42 per cent during the nine years from 1901 to 1910; from 1904 to 1913 there was a gain of 32 per cent in volume of physical output. It is clear that total production in 1922 did not stand at a particularly high level, with reference to output in 1913.[1]

The index numbers tracing changes in the output of raw and of processed goods show striking contrasts during the years of wartime activity. These years brought no exceptional increase in the production of raw materials in the United States. Between 1914 and 1919 the output of such materials ranged from a level 7 per cent above that of 1913 to a level 17 per cent above. Manufactured goods increased, by 1918, to a level 38 per cent above that of the base year. The sharp advance in the output of raw materials between 1919 and 1920 is notable, because of its bearing on the behavior of raw material prices during the recession which began in 1920. The terminal year, 1922, found the volume of production of manufactured goods 29 per cent above the 1913 level, while the production of raw materials was about 19 per cent greater than in 1913.

The war-time advance in the output of processed commodities not originating on American farms [2] materially exceeded that of any of the other groups represented in Table 73. The extreme drop in the output of this group during the recession of 1921, and the very slight change which this recession brought in the production of farm products, are to be noted. The index numbers of agricultural production show slight evidence of adaptation of production to changing conditions resulting from the post-war recession. The result of inflexibility of production was, inevitably, a severe price drop. Non-farm products, more flexible in production, were less severely affected by the general price recession.

In the terminal year, 1922, the output of raw products of American farms stood at a high level, 23 per cent above the 1913 base. This expansion in output, resulting from the war-time stimulus, coincided in time with an apparent shift of emphasis in consumer demand from articles of food and clothing to more durable con-

[1] The year 1922 was marked by expanding business; the peak of prosperity was not reached until 1923. The base year, 1913, was one of general business contraction.

[2] This group includes fabricated minerals, and processed forms of such materials as rubber, silk, lumber and wood pulp. Minerals are the most important element in the total.

sumption goods. Price weakness and economic distress were unavoidable resultants.

## Construction

During the war and immediate post-war years new building followed a course quite different from that of the production of movable goods. The following index, based upon the shipments of construction materials, traces the tendencies prevailing in this field. The series is plotted in Figure 35.

TABLE 74

VOLUME OF CONSTRUCTION IN THE UNITED STATES, 1913-1922 [a]

| Year | Volume of construction |
|------|------------------------|
| 1913 | 100 |
| 1914 | 97 |
| 1915 | 95 |
| 1916 | 108 |
| 1917 | 91 |
| 1918 | 63 |
| 1919 | 86 |
| 1920 | 47 |
| 1921 | 89 |
| 1922 | 135 |

[a] Compiled by Associated General Contractors from records of shipments of construction materials. The index is a simple average of structural steel bookings, common brick bookings, Portland cement shipments, loadings of sand, gravel and stone, face brick shipments and shipments of enameled sanitary ware. The index numbers given are averages of monthly figures. See *Survey of Current Business,* Annual Supplement, 1931.

Up to 1916 there was no sustained drop in construction, but during the succeeding five years construction was markedly subnormal. The level reached in 1920 was more than 50 per cent below that of 1913. Recovery began in 1921 and was well under way in 1922. The shortage of construction of all sorts which accumulated between 1917 and 1921 led to an abnormally rapid expansion of construction activities after 1921. The effects of this expansion were felt throughout the economic system during the years which followed.

The marked contrast between construction and volume of production in 1920 is important because of the strikingly different rôles played by construction in the recessions beginning in 1920 and in 1929. The former began with construction far below normal, while the recession of 1929 began with the volume of construction in general at excessively high levels.

## Volume of Manufacturing Production

The years in which the Census of Manufactures was taken are not most appropriately placed for a detailed study of changes in the volume of manufacturing production during the war and immediate post-war years. General changes during the entire period may be followed, however, by the use of census figures, which for the industries covered, are far more comprehensive than are the annual index numbers listed in preceding tables.[1]

TABLE 75

GROWTH OF MANUFACTURING PRODUCTION IN THE UNITED STATES, 1914-1923

Index Numbers of Physical Volume of Production, Number of Wage-earners and per Capita Output

| Year | Physical volume of production | Number of wage-earners | Output per wage-earner |
|---|---|---|---|
| 1914 | 100.0 | 100.0 | 100.0 |
| 1919 | 127.7 | 124.5 | 102.6 |
| 1921 | 105.7 | 100.1 | 105.6 |
| 1923 | 156.3 | 130.3 | 120.0 |

The advance in production to 1919, the drop in 1921 and the remarkable spurt from 1921 to 1923 are reflected in these index numbers, shown graphically in Figure 36. Viewing the changes in physical volume of production as net results of changes in the number of wage-earners employed and in output per wage-earner, it will be seen that the latter was a relatively constant element in the situation between 1914 and 1921. The advance in output from 1914 to 1919 was accomplished largely through an increase in the number of wage-earners; the drop from 1919 to 1921 reflected, primarily, a decline in the number of workers. There was an advance in

[1] These index numbers relate to a selected sample, representing approximately 45 per cent of the value of product of all manufacturing industries. The present measurements differ somewhat from the indexes of manufacturing production given in Table 73, which have been adjusted to the data of all census industries. In a later note (pp. 198-201) index numbers corresponding to those in Table 75, but adjusted to all census industries, are given.

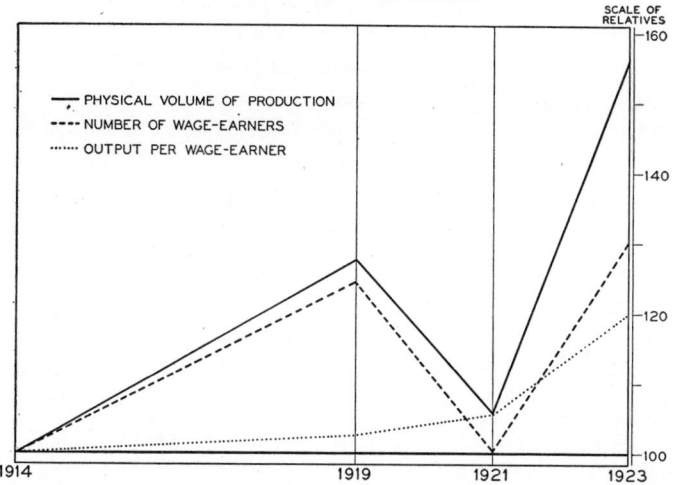

**FIGURE 36**

GROWTH OF MANUFACTURING PRODUCTION
IN THE UNITED STATES, 1914-1923

VOLUME OF PRODUCTION, NUMBER OF WAGE-EARNERS
AND OUTPUT PER WAGE-EARNER

productivity during the seven years from 1914 to 1921, but it was not great, in comparison with pre-war changes. Substantial gains in both factors contributed to the gain in aggregate output between 1921 and 1923. The number of wage-earners increased by 30.2 per cent over this two-year period, while output per wage-earner, which is attributable to technical and organizational improvements, as well as to enhanced skill, increased by 13.6 per cent.

§ *Changes in physical volume of production and in output per wage-earner, individual industries.*—Records relating to the physical volume of production and to output per wage-earner in individual manufacturing industries are given, for reference, in Tables 76 and 77, following. Averages derived from the central items of frequency distributions and designed to represent typical situations in manufacturing industries, are presented in these tables, in addition to the measurements relating to individual industries. The averages of physical output which appear at the foot of Table 76 are slightly lower than those obtained by the 'ideal' formula (see Table 75). Somewhat greater are the differences between similarly derived index numbers of output per wage-earner (see Tables 75 and 77). A typical manufacturing industry suffered a loss in productivity per worker between 1914 and 1921. Between 1921 and 1923, however, the gain in productivity shown by these averages was greater than the gain shown by the earlier index numbers. In 1923, for the typical manufacturing industry, output was greater by 45 per cent than in 1914, and output per worker was greater by almost 13 per cent.

TABLE 76

CHANGES IN PHYSICAL VOLUME OF MANUFACTURING PRODUCTION IN THE UNITED STATES, 1914-1923

Index Numbers for 52 Industries

| Industry | Index numbers of physical volume of production | | | |
|---|---|---|---|---|
| | 1914 | 1919 | 1921 | 1923 |
| Motor vehicles, including bodies and parts. | 100.0 | 408.7 | 304.9 | 637.2 |
| Rubber goods | 100.0 | 286.6 | 218.6 | 369.1 |
| Petroleum refining | 100.0 | 194.7 | 231.2 | 316.7 |
| Linoleum and asphalted-felt-base floor coverings | 100.0 | 187.9 | 185.6 | 288.0 |
| Coke, not including gas-house coke | 100.0 | 141.5 | 97.8 | 205.3 |
| Condensed and evaporated milk | 100.0 | 234.0 | 189.9 | 201.8 |
| Iron and steel: steel works and rolling mills | 100.0 | 145.8 | 87.7 | 186.3 |
| Ice, manufactured | 100.0 | 139.3 | 158.2 | 180.7 |
| Iron and steel: blast furnaces | 100.0 | 135.5 | 72.3 | 173.8 |
| Rice cleaning and polishing | 100.0 | 160.1 | 169.8 | 171.7 |
| Butter and cheese | 100.0 | 122.2 | 139.0 | 166.1 |
| Canning and preserving: fruits and vegetables; pickles, jellies, preserves, and sauces | 100.0 | 136.2 | 100.0 | 159.2 |
| Paints and varnishes | 100.0 | 127.3 | 107.1 | 158.4 |
| Woolen goods | 100.0 | 122.4 | 110.8 | 157.6 |
| Silk manufactures | 100.0 | 133.0 | 121.4 | 155.2 |
| Gas, manufactured, illuminating and heating | 100.0 | 135.6 | 128.6 | 152.7 |
| Cast-iron pipe | 100.0 | 70.1 | 77.6 | 151.2 |
| Paper and wood pulp | 100.0 | 119.5 | 101.4 | 147.1 |
| Carpets and rugs, wool, other than rag | 100.0 | 86.4 | 83.5 | 144.8 |
| Salt | 100.0 | 142.2 | 101.9 | 144.2 |
| Knit goods | 100.0 | 113.7 | 109.5 | 139.1 |
| Musical instruments: pianos | 100.0 | 128.7 | 83.7 | 138.4 |
| Wire, drawn from purchased bars or rods | 100.0 | 105.4 | 55.9 | 137.3 |
| Slaughtering and meat packing, wholesale. | 100.0 | 131.7 | 109.0 | 137.3 |
| Explosives | 100.0 | 126.3 | 88.1 | 137.1 |
| Soap | 100.0 | 127.2 | 114.8 | 132.7 |
| Sugar refining, cane | 100.0 | 106.1 | 113.0 | 132.5 |
| Cars, steam and electric railroad, not built in railroad repair shops | 100.0 | 105.9 | 58.2 | 131.5 |
| Sand-lime brick | 100.0 | 89.3 | 58.3 | 129.5 |
| Cotton goods | 100.0 | 106.9 | 98.5 | 127.5 |
| Wood distillation and charcoal manufacture | 100.0 | 124.2 | 52.7 | 127.1 |
| Cement | 100.0 | 93.2 | 97.8 | 126.6 |
| Clay products (other than pottery) and non-clay refractories | 100.0 | 76.1 | 72.9 | 126.3 |

TABLE 76—Continued

| Industry | Index numbers of physical volume of production | | | |
|---|---|---|---|---|
| | 1914 | 1919 | 1921 | 1923 |
| Hats, wool-felt | 100.0 | 139.7 | 88.5 | 125.9 |
| Wool shoddy | 100.0 | 119.1 | 56.2 | 118.2 |
| Lace goods, cotton | 100.0 | 88.9 | 77.1 | 112.6 |
| Turpentine and rosin | 100.0 | 71.6 | 98.0 | 110.5 |
| Worsted goods | 100.0 | 88.2 | 89.6 | 107.8 |
| Motorcycles, bicycles, and parts | 100.0 | 149.1 | 68.0 | 107.1 |
| Hats, fur-felt | 100.0 | 103.2 | 88.6 | 102.4 |
| Oilcloth | 100.0 | 62.1 | 78.0 | 101.9 |
| Sugar, beet | 100.0 | 98.0 | 140.2 | 99.9 |
| Lime | 100.0 | 82.2 | 63.1 | 99.5 |
| Flour and other grain-mill products | 100.0 | 105.7 | 91.0 | 96.2 |
| Lumber and timber products | 100.0 | 92.5 | 78.0 | 95.0 |
| Cordage and twine | 100.0 | 92.3 | 75.9 | 94.6 |
| Fertilizers | 100.0 | 92.0 | 68.6 | 87.2 |
| Jute and linen goods | 100.0 | 77.2 | 54.8 | 81.2 |
| Canning and preserving: fish, crabs, shrimps, oysters, and clams | 100.0 | 114.1 | 53.9 | 73.3 |
| Sugar, cane, not including products of refining | 100.0 | 95.6 | 92.0 | 63.1 |
| Musical instruments: organs | 100.0 | 74.2 | 81.7 | 59.0 |
| Oil, cake, and meal, cottonseed | 100.0 | 83.1 | 60.2 | 52.3 |
| Average [a] | 100.0 | 125.3 | 99.7 | 145.3 |

[a] An arithmetic average of the central items of a weighted frequency distribution, with weights based on 'value added', averaged for the base year and the given year. The central one-fifth of the items, by weight, were included in computing the average.

TABLE 77

Changes in Output per Wage-earner in Manufacturing Industries of the United States, 1914-1923

Index Numbers for 52 Industries

| Industry | Index numbers of physical volume of production per wage-earner | | | |
|---|---|---|---|---|
| | 1914 | 1919 | 1921 | 1923 |
| Motor vehicles, including bodies and parts | 100.0 | 151.2 | 181.7 | 199.5 |
| Rubber goods | 100.0 | 133.8 | 156.6 | 198.1 |
| Linoleum and asphalted-felt-base floor coverings | 100.0 | 153.7 | 144.3 | 160.6 |
| Gas, manufactured, illuminating and heating | 100.0 | 137.7 | 160.1 | 157.2 |
| Coke, not including gas-house coke | 100.0 | 101.8 | 128.3 | 152.6 |

TABLE 77—Continued

| Industry | Index numbers of physical volume of production per wage-earner | | | |
|---|---|---|---|---|
| | 1914 | 1919 | 1921 | 1923 |
| Ice, manufactured | 100.0 | 103.7 | 146.4 | 149.9 |
| Musical instruments: pianos | 100.0 | 133.8 | 126.1 | 148.7 |
| Condensed and evaporated milk | 100.0 | 102.7 | 120.5 | 146.0 |
| Iron and steel: blast furnaces | 100.0 | 91.9 | 113.5 | 139.0 |
| Explosives | 100.0 | 86.0 | 123.9 | 135.2 |
| Silk manufactures | 100.0 | 113.4 | 108.0 | 133.9 |
| Canning and preserving: fruits and vegetables; pickles, jellies, preserves, and sauces | 100.0 | 107.1 | 116.0 | 131.7 |
| Hats, fur-felt | 100.0 | 118.6 | 135.7 | 130.2 |
| Carpets and rugs, wool, other than rag | 100.0 | 118.0 | 114.1 | 128.8 |
| Rice cleaning and polishing | 100.0 | 95.0 | 109.7 | 122.0 |
| Sand-lime brick | 100.0 | 96.8 | 85.1 | 121.5 |
| Petroleum refining | 100.0 | 83.9 | 92.8 | 120.4 |
| Clay products (other than pottery) and non-clay refractories | 100.0 | 97.2 | 103.4 | 119.9 |
| Iron and steel: steel works and rolling mills | 100.0 | 96.7 | 92.6 | 119.3 |
| Wool shoddy | 100.0 | 99.8 | 102.7 | 118.7 |
| Lace goods, cotton | 100.0 | 102.0 | 89.7 | 114.7 |
| Wire, drawn from purchased bars or rods | 100.0 | 94.0 | 66.3 | 113.4 |
| Butter and cheese | 100.0 | 95.2 | 106.2 | 113.4 |
| Paints and varnishes | 100.0 | 95.1 | 95.3 | 111.3 |
| Soap | 100.0 | 88.0 | 97.9 | 110.1 |
| Motorcycles, bicycles, and parts | 100.0 | 91.3 | 105.2 | 108.5 |
| Paper and wood pulp | 100.0 | 92.9 | 85.1 | 107.8 |
| Knit goods | 100.0 | 98.9 | 101.6 | 107.5 |
| Salt | 100.0 | 110.6 | 85.8 | 106.8 |
| Woolen goods | 100.0 | 95.5 | 96.3 | 106.8 |
| Fertilizers | 100.0 | 79.5 | 92.4 | 106.8 |
| Flour and other grain-mill products | 100.0 | 90.5 | 99.7 | 105.9 |
| Sugar, beet | 100.0 | 66.6 | 82.4 | 105.5 |
| Jute and linen goods | 100.0 | 98.8 | 77.4 | 105.1 |
| Turpentine and rosin | 100.0 | 83.3 | 115.9 | 104.5 |
| Oilcloth | 100.0 | 67.2 | 100.7 | 103.6 |
| Cotton goods | 100.0 | 94.1 | 90.7 | 102.6 |
| Slaughtering and meat packing, wholesale | 100.0 | 80.8 | 92.0 | 102.2 |
| Cement | 100.0 | 101.9 | 104.0 | 100.7 |
| Sugar refining, cane | 100.0 | 65.6 | 82.2 | 97.7 |
| Lime | 100.0 | 87.5 | 73.2 | 97.1 |
| Musical instruments: organs | 100.0 | 116.7 | 106.1 | 97.0 |
| Worsted goods | 100.0 | 93.1 | 92.6 | 96.7 |
| Cars, steam and electric railroad, not built in railroad repair shops | 100.0 | 111.5 | 70.4 | 94.8 |
| Cordage and twine | 100.0 | 82.5 | 82.0 | 91.0 |
| Wood distillation and charcoal manufacture | 100.0 | 70.6 | 72.2 | 89.9 |
| Oil, cake, and meal, cottonseed | 100.0 | 67.7 | 81.2 | 89.5 |

INTERREGNUM

TABLE 77—Continued

| Industry | Index numbers of physical volume of production per wage-earner | | | |
|---|---|---|---|---|
| | 1914 | 1919 | 1921 | 1923 |
| Canning and preserving: fish, crabs, shrimps, oysters, and clams............ | 100.0 | 101.3 | 74.5 | 88.0 |
| Cast-iron pipe .......................... | 100.0 | 69.7 | 77.9 | 88.0 |
| Lumber and timber products............. | 100.0 | 87.4 | 94.9 | 84.9 |
| Sugar, cane, not including products of refining .................................. | 100.0 | 56.7 | 121.7 | 80.6 |
| Hats, wool-felt ......................... | 100.0 | 120.1 | 76.8 | 80.0 |
| Average *a* ............................. | 100.0 | 95.5 | 95.3 | 112.8 |

*a* An arithmetic average of the central items of a weighted frequency distribution, with weights based on 'value added', averaged for the base year and the given year. The central one-fifth of the items, by weight, were included in computing the average.

We pass now to the record of production in terms of establishments.

TABLE 78

Growth of Manufacturing Production in the United States, 1914-1923

Index Numbers of Physical Volume of Production, Number of Establishments and Output per Establishment

| Year | Physical volume of production | Number of establishments | Output per establishment |
|---|---|---|---|
| 1914 | 100.0 | 100.0 | 100.0 |
| 1919 | 127.7 | 112.6 | 113.5 |
| 1921 | 105.7 | 94.1 | 112.4 |
| 1923 | 156.3 | 98.7 | 158.4 |

From 1914 to 1919 the volume of production was increased by means of a substantial addition to the number of establishments in operation.[1] The recession of 1920-21 brought a decline of more than 16 per cent, a far greater drop in number of establishments than had been recorded in any census interval since 1899. During the two following years a slight increase occurred. Perhaps even more significant is the tremendous increase, amounting to approxi-

[1] This may reflect, in part, an increased coverage in the 1919 census. The exclusion from these averages of all establishments having an output valued at less than $5,000 would tend, however, to minimize the effect of wider coverage in that year. See the footnote to p. 37.

mately 41 per cent, in output per establishment between 1921 and 1923. This gain, exceeding any previous record, is a dramatic indication of the part played by large-scale production in the economic advance of the nineteen-twenties.

Breaking output per establishment into two constituent elements, we have the following record.

TABLE 79

Growth of Manufacturing Production in the United States, 1914-1923

Factors Affecting Output per Establishment

| Year | Output per establishment | Number of workers per establishment | Output per worker |
|------|--------------------------|-------------------------------------|-------------------|
| 1914 | 100.0 | 100.0 | 100.0 |
| 1919 | 113.5 | 110.6 | 102.6 |
| 1921 | 112.4 | 106.3 | 105.6 |
| 1923 | 158.4 | 132.0 | 120.0 |

The human element was called upon to swell production during the war-time emergency. The gain in output per establishment from 1914 to 1919 was due, primarily, to an increase in the number of workers per establishment. Technical improvements, which are reflected in growing output per worker, were not numerous during this period. In the revival following 1921 both human and technological factors were called upon to augment production, and we find workers per establishment and output per worker increasing notably.

§ *Volume of manufacturing production, revised measurements.*—In dealing with pre-war production movements reference was made to the problem presented by new industries and by industries the products of which cannot be enumerated. Current index numbers of production are necessarily limited to commodities for which quantity statistics are available. In correcting for this omission by deriving index numbers of volume of manufacturing production from census statistics of 'value added' and number of workers employed, we secured measurements which indicated a considerably more rapid growth of production between 1899 and 1914 than was shown by the index numbers based directly on physical units. A similar method may be employed for the period 1914-1923. The following figures indicate the relative rates of change in 'value added' in industries included in the sample, and in excluded industries.

## TABLE 80
### Changes in Value Added by Manufacture, 1914-1923

| (1) Year | (2) (3) 'Value added', all census industries | | (4) (5) 'Value added', industries included in sample | | (6) (7) 'Value added', industries not included in sample | |
|---|---|---|---|---|---|---|
| | In millions of dollars | In relatives | In millions of dollars | In relatives | In millions of dollars | In relatives |
| 1914 | 9,710 | 100.0 | 3,335 | 100.0 | 6,375 | 100.0 |
| 1919 | 24,809 | 255.5 | 9,365 | 280.8 | 15,444 | 242.3 |
| 1921 | 18,332 | 188.8 | 6,357 | 190.6 | 11,975 | 187.8 |
| 1923 | 25,850 | 266.2 | 9,782 | 293.3 | 16,068 | 252.0 |

Between 1914 and 1919 the value added by manufacturing industries included in the detailed enumeration increased approximately 181 per cent, as compared with an increase of 142 per cent among industries not included in the index. Over the seven-year period from 1914 to 1921 there was no appreciable difference between the two groups. When the comparison is carried to 1923 we again find a more rapid increase among the industries included in our index than among the excluded industries.

It is apparent that the included industries are not in all respects representative of the total. To correct for this defect we may derive, as in Chapter I, new index numbers designed to measure changes in the aggregate output of all manufacturing industries. These are given below.

## TABLE 81
### Derived Index Numbers of Physical Volume of Production, 1914-1923
### All Manufacturing Industries of the United States

| Year | Index numbers of physical production, derived from measurements of cost of fabrication, per unit of product | Index numbers of physical production, derived from measurements of output per capita |
|---|---|---|
| 1914 | 100.0 | 100.0 |
| 1919 | 119.3 | 133.9 |
| 1921 | 108.0 | 106.4 |
| 1923 | 146.9 | 152.7 |

Two different estimates of the change in volume of production among all manufacturing industries appear in this table. The first of these is based on the assumption that changes in the cost of fabrication, per unit of product, among all manufacturing industries, were the same as the changes occurring among the industries for which adequate quantity statistics are available. The second estimate proceeds from the assumption that changes in output per worker were the same among all industries as among the group included in the index.

The differences between the two derived index numbers are not wide, except for the year 1919. The difference for this date indicates, we may assume, that there was less uniformity among manufacturing industries during the disturbed years from 1914 to 1919 than is usually found. Changes in output per worker and in fabrication costs were less consistent from industry to industry than is usually the case. By 1921, however, something approaching uniformity was again attained, and no great divergence appears thereafter.

Averaging the two derived index numbers of production we secure the measurements given in column (3) below. These constitute our best estimate of the true course of production among all manufacturing industries between 1914 and 1923. These are contrasted with index numbers based directly on physical quantities produced in 52 industries, and on annual data.

TABLE 82

COMPARISON OF INDEX NUMBERS OF PHYSICAL VOLUME OF MANUFACTURING PRODUCTION, 1914-1923

| (1) | (2) | (3) | (4) |
|---|---|---|---|
| | Census index numbers of volume of fabrication | | |
| Year | Based on 52 industries | Derived from 'value added' and number of employees, all industries | Unadjusted annual index numbers of manufacturing output [a] |
| 1914 | 100.0 | 100.0 | 100.0 |
| 1919 | 127.7 | 126.6 | 132.6 |
| 1921 | 105.7 | 107.2 | 105.9 |
| 1923 | 156.3 | 149.8 | 159.6 |

[a] Stewart's index for the years 1914-1919, that of the Federal Reserve Board for the rest of the period.

These three index numbers follow the same general course between 1914 and 1923. No such clear divergence appears as was found among the measurements for the years preceding the war. The greatest difference occurs in 1923, when the derived (and most comprehensive) index is appreciably lower than the other measurements. The net advance in manufacturing production between 1914 and 1923 appears to have been less than is shown by index numbers based on the output of the standard commodities for which production statistics are readily available. This situation reverses that found to prevail in the pre-war period.

## Changes in Commodity Prices, 1913-1922

The numerous shifts in economic relations which resulted from the price revolution occurring between 1913 and 1922 may not here be traced in detail, but certain of the general price movements of this period may be followed. These movements were, of course, radical in character; their effects have persisted.

TABLE 83

Wholesale Price Movements, 1913-1922 [a]

| (1) Year | (2) Changes in level of wholesale prices (index of U. S. Bureau of Labor Statistics) | (3) Index of price dispersion | (4) Average monthly variability of wholesale prices |
|---|---|---|---|
| 1913 | 100.0 | 8.4 | 3.7 |
| 1914 | 97.6 | 7.4 | 4.4 |
| 1915 | 99.6 | 10.6 | 5.9 |
| 1916 | 122.5 | 13.7 | 8.7 |
| 1917 | 168.3 | 12.4 | 10.6 |
| 1918 | 188.1 | 14.2 | 7.3 |
| 1919 | 198.6 | 11.9 | 9.7 |
| 1920 | 221.2 | 15.7 | 10.8 |
| 1921 | 139.8 | 18.3 | 8.5 |
| 1922 | 138.5 | 11.7 | 6.5 |

[a] For an explanation of the index of dispersion see *The Behavior of Prices*, National Bureau of Economic Research, pp. 256 ff. The method of measuring monthly price variability is explained in the same volume, pp. 370 ff. The measurements in col. (3) are based upon 391 price series, those in col. (4) upon 214 price series.

The sharp rise in prices which began late in 1915, reaching a peak in 1920, and the ensuing rapid decline are phenomena still fresh in memory. Still remembered, also, are the prosperity which accompanied the war-time advance and the pains of readjustment which followed upon the collapse of prices in 1921. In 1922, the year which marks the beginning of the post-war advance reviewed in succeeding chapters, the level of wholesale prices stood some 40 per cent above that of 1913.

The index of dispersion and the index of monthly variability of prices, given in columns (3) and (4) above, define other aspects of the changes occurring during this period. The measures of dispersion indicate the degree of divergence of the prices of individual commodities at wholesale, that is, the degree of scattering of these prices from year to year. Starting with a relatively low degree of dispersion in 1913, the index rises to an abnormally high level in 1921. There was some decline between 1921 and 1922, but the figure for 1922 is still very high, judged with reference to prewar standards. For the entire period from 1915 to 1922 the degree of year-to-year dispersion was greater than that recorded in any year back to 1899. These high index numbers reflect a constant disruption of price relations. There was no crystallization of relationships, no attainment of that degree of stability which had prevailed before the war. The indexes in column (4), which measure the average degree of fluctuation, from month to month, of the prices of individual commodities, confirm this evidence. These averages are high between 1916 and 1922, higher than in any year between 1890 and 1915.

This fact has a direct bearing upon the character of the price decline which accompanied the recession of 1920-21, and helps to differentiate this recession from that which began in 1929. In May, 1920, commodity prices started downward after a sharp eleven-months' advance which had carried the general level up 23 per cent, and after a five-year advance amounting to 142 per cent. The level from which the decline started was not one which bore any of the aspects of permanence. The relations among different elements of the price structure which existed in May, 1920, had prevailed for only a short time. Flux had been the outstanding feature of the recent past. There had been no consolidation of the economic positions of different economic groups, no general making of long-term commitments on the basis of existing prices. As a result, when once the price decline was well under way the barriers to liquidation which are offered by a thoroughly consolidated position and a sense of permanence in commodity values were relatively weak. Within the eleven months of sharpest decline the drop amounted to 44 per cent, and the rate of decline per month averaged 5.1 per cent. Price recession was intense, but the violent change was concentrated within a period of less than a year.

The high index numbers of dispersion and variability are indicative of continuing instability of economic relations. Such conditions introduce uncertainty into business dealings and emphasize speculative factors in commercial transactions. This whole period was a time of such change in the relations of industries, one to another, as had not existed during the entire quarter-century preceding. By 1922 the tide of change had begun to subside. Order was being established and elements of speculative uncertainty were growing less pronounced in business dealings.

§ *The influence of price changes on the value stream, 1913-1922.*—
The steep advance and subsequent sharp decline of prices accentuated the changes which were occurring in volume of production. The accompanying alterations in total values of goods produced were of exceptional magnitude. These changes are indicated in the following table. The several index numbers are shown graphically in Figure 37.

TABLE 84

INDEX NUMBERS OF PHYSICAL VOLUME, PRICES AND AGGREGATE VALUES OF GOODS PRODUCED IN THE UNITED STATES, 1913-1922

| Year | Physical volume of production | Wholesale prices | Aggregate values [a] |
|---|---|---|---|
| 1913 | 100 | 100 | 100 |
| 1914 | 102 | 98 | 100 |
| 1915 | 116 | 100 | 116 |
| 1916 | 123 | 122 | 150 |
| 1917 | 128 | 168 | 215 |
| 1918 | 127 | 188 | 239 |
| 1919 | 119 | 199 | 237 |
| 1920 | 127 | 221 | 281 |
| 1921 | 106 | 140 | 148 |
| 1922 | 124 | 138 | 171 |

[a] The above price index (U. S. Bureau of Labor Statistics) measures changes in the average wholesale prices of units of goods, both raw and processed; the production index measures changes in output of units of raw and processed goods. The value series, derived by multiplying these index numbers together, measures changes in the aggregate value of transactions involved in the productive process. It does not relate to the total value of finished products alone.

The derivation of an index number of aggregate values from price and production index numbers represents a very rough approximation indeed, for the production and price index numbers are not based upon identical commodities. The general movements shown are probably correct, but the given figures for stated years should be looked upon only as estimates.

During the war the impression prevailed that the volume of production in this country attained exceptionally high levels. The above figures indicate that it was values and not physical quantities which were

## FIGURE 37

### CHANGES IN VOLUME OF PRODUCTION, AVERAGE PRICE AND AGGREGATE VALUE OF GOODS PRODUCED IN THE UNITED STATES, 1913-1922

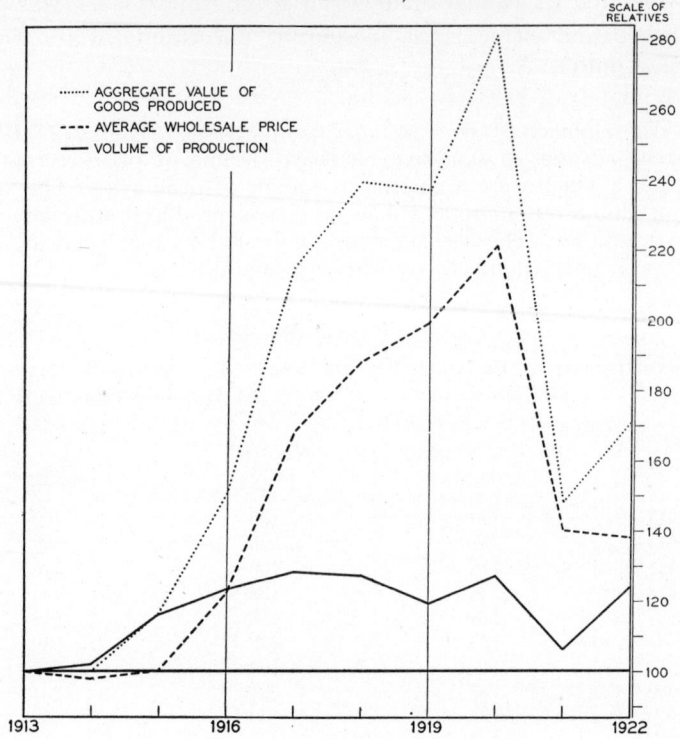

growing with an amazing rapidity.[1] By 1916 the output of goods had increased by 23 per cent over 1913; aggregate values were up by 50 per cent. The peak came in 1920, when aggregate output was 27 per cent greater and aggregate values were 181 per cent greater than in 1913. This increase in total values of 181 per cent in seven years may be contrasted with the gain of approximately 97 per cent during the 13 years from 1901 to 1913. With the stream of values growing to such flood-tide proportions it is small wonder that the impression of prosperity was so pronounced. In the main, of course, rising prices accounted for this growth of values. The recession of 1921 cut values in half, though volume of output was reduced by but one-fifth. The period to be discussed in later chapters opens in 1922 with aggregate values of goods produced some 71 per cent greater than in 1913.

[1] See also the production, price and value index numbers appearing in *History of Prices During the War,* War Industries Board, Price Bulletin No. 1, p. 45.

## Price Movements of Raw Materials and of Manufactured Goods

From 1901 to 1913 current prices of both raw materials and manufactured goods advanced, the former somewhat more rapidly. In terms of dollars of constant purchasing power the net increase for raw materials, per unit, during this thirteen-year period was approximately 3 per cent, while manufactured goods lost about 1 per cent in purchasing power. The situation prevailing at the end of the interregnum we are now studying was notably different, as is shown by the measurements in the next table, and by the graphs in Figure 38.

TABLE 85

RAW MATERIALS AND MANUFACTURED GOODS

Changes in Wholesale Prices and in Purchasing Power, 1913-1922 [a]

| Year | Index numbers of wholesale prices | | Index numbers of per-unit purchasing power | |
|---|---|---|---|---|
| | Raw materials | Manufactured goods | Raw materials | Manufactured goods |
| 1913 | 100.0 | 100.0 | 100.0 | 100.0 |
| 1914 | 98.7 | 97.8 | 100.5 | 99.6 |
| 1915 | 104.2 | 102.0 | 101.4 | 99.2 |
| 1916 | 127.9 | 129.4 | 99.1 | 100.2 |
| 1917 | 174.4 | 169.4 | 101.9 | 98.9 |
| 1918 | 188.9 | 198.4 | 96.5 | 101.4 |
| 1919 | 196.1 | 206.1 | 96.4 | 101.3 |
| 1920 | 202.2 | 239.5 | 88.7 | 105.1 |
| 1921 | 125.0 | 162.7 | 83.0 | 108.0 |
| 1922 | 133.2 | 154.8 | 89.8 | 104.4 |

[a] These index numbers are unweighted geometric averages of price relatives, constructed by the National Bureau of Economic Research. The number of price series in each group in 1922 is given below:
    Raw materials    136
    Manufactured goods    330

Up to 1917 no substantial differences appear between the prices of raw materials and of manufactured commodities. During the three succeeding years manufactured goods leaped upward in price, while raw materials, after scoring some advance between 1917 and 1918, remained for two years only slightly above the 1918 level. The price collapse of 1920-21 carried raw materials to much lower levels than were reached by the prices of manufactured goods.

These comparisons are of chief significance in their bearing

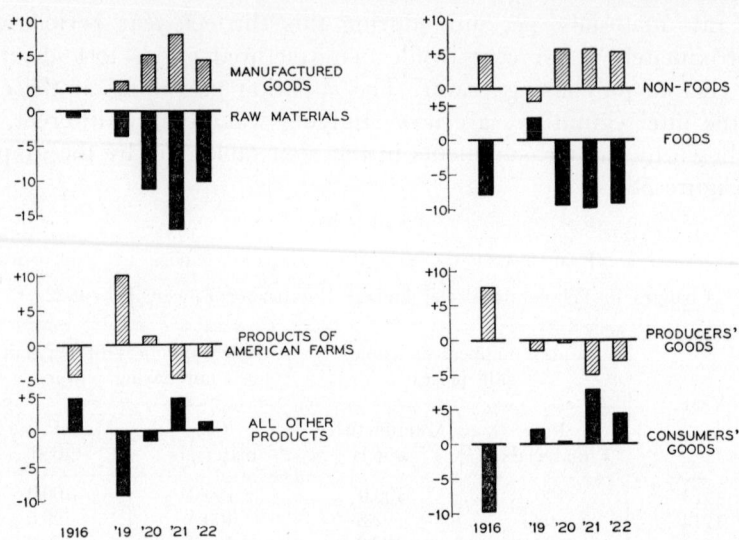

FIGURE 38

GRAPHIC REPRESENTATION OF CHANGES IN THE REAL VALUES, PER UNIT, OF COMMODITIES IN SELECTED GROUPS, 1913-1922

(CHANGES ARE MEASURED AS PERCENTAGE DEVIATIONS FROM 1913 PURCHASING POWER.)

on changes in the real per-unit values of goods of these two classes, in terms of commodities in general. By 1920, when wholesale prices had reached their peak, manufactured goods had gained, on the average, 5 per cent in purchasing power, while the per-unit value of raw materials had declined 11 per cent. Here was a distinct reversal of pre-war tendencies which had progressively enhanced the purchasing power of raw materials and had cheapened manufactured goods. The drop of prices in 1921 served still further to widen this margin. At average prices in that year the purchasing power of manufactured goods was 8 per cent higher than in 1913, while the purchasing power of raw materials was 17 per cent below the 1913 standard. The year 1922, which marks the end of the period here under review and the beginning of the period to be described in the following chapters, found manufactured goods still overvalued, in terms of pre-war standards, while the per-unit purchasing power of raw materials, although somewhat higher than in 1921, was still substantially lower than before the war. We shall have occasion later to discuss this reversal in greater detail. It was a change of profound significance, the effects of which were felt by producers throughout the world during the decade of the 'twenties.

The effect of the war on the price variability of commodities in these two groups is indicated by the entries in the following table.

TABLE 86

RAW MATERIALS AND MANUFACTURED GOODS

Measurements of Variability of Wholesale Prices, 1898-1913, 1914-1921

| Commodity group | Number of price series | Measurement of monthly variability of prices | | Measurement of frequency of price change | |
|---|---|---|---|---|---|
| | | 1898-1913 | 1914-1921 | 1898-1913 | 1914-1921 |
| Raw materials ..... | 49 | 8.2 | 10.9 | .82 | .83 |
| Manufactured goods. | 158 | 3.6 | 7.4 | .34 | .47 |

In both periods manufactured goods were distinctly less variable in price and were subject to less frequent price changes than were raw materials. The price disturbances of the war years increased somewhat the normally high variability of raw material prices. Far more pronounced, however, were their effects upon manufactured goods. For this group monthly price variability was more than doubled, and the frequency of price change was increased by approximately one-third.

It is a fact of very considerable importance that different elements of the price system possess different degrees of freedom to react to changes in conditions of supply or of demand. Certain elements are subject to a far higher degree of control and are far less sensitive to changing market conditions than are other price elements. These differences in rigidity, which have recently been so dramatically revealed, are clearly shown by the entries in the table above. Perhaps more striking is the fact that the prices of manufactured goods, which had tended to crystallize during the years before the war, were broken open by the war-time changes. These goods still remained far below raw materials in their sensitiveness to changing market conditions, but the degree of their flexibility, as measured by the present index numbers, was very much higher between 1914 and 1921 than it had been during the 15 years preceding. In the survey of subsequent changes it will be of interest to determine whether these prices again crystallized after the wave of war-time price changes had passed.

## Price Movements of Products of American Farms and Other Products

The period we are now studying brought a revolutionary alteration in the economic status of the American farmer. He was favored at first by the price advance of the war years, but the subsequent liquidation carried him to a lower economic level than he had known for many years. The fortunes of agricultural and other producers during these years are reflected in the movements of the index numbers of purchasing power changes given in the accompanying table. (Purchasing power here refers to command over goods in general in wholesale markets. Deflation, in other words, is based upon an index of commodity prices at wholesale.)[1]

TABLE 87

Products of American Farms and All Other Products
Index Numbers of Purchasing Power, in Wholesale Markets, 1913-1922 [a]

| (1) | (2) | (3) | (4) | (5) | (6) | (7) |
|---|---|---|---|---|---|---|
| Year | Products of American farms | | All other products | | All products of American farms | All other products |
| | Raw | Processed | Raw | Processed | | |
| 1913 | 100.0 | 100.0 | 100.0 | 100.0 | 100.0 | 100.0 |
| 1914 | 104.3 | 102.3 | 94.4 | 97.3 | 103.1 | 96.5 |
| 1915 | 104.0 | 99.9 | 97.2 | 98.8 | 101.4 | 98.3 |
| 1916 | 97.1 | 94.5 | 102.3 | 105.6 | 95.5 | 104.8 |
| 1917 | 106.3 | 100.6 | 95.2 | 97.6 | 102.7 | 97.2 |
| 1918 | 105.4 | 107.4 | 84.2 | 96.7 | 106.7 | 93.7 |
| 1919 | 109.1 | 110.6 | 79.4 | 94.4 | 110.0 | 90.8 |
| 1920 | 93.2 | 106.1 | 81.9 | 104.2 | 101.2 | 98.6 |
| 1921 | 82.4 | 103.5 | 83.9 | 111.7 | 95.2 | 104.7 |
| 1922 | 92.3 | 102.1 | 85.9 | 106.2 | 98.3 | 101.3 |

[a] The number of price series in each group in 1922 is given below:

| Products of American farms | | All other products | |
|---|---|---|---|
| Raw | 83 | Raw | 53 |
| Processed | 143 | Processed | 187 |
| Total | 226 | Total | 240 |

[1] The index numbers in the text are given in terms of purchasing power, since the significance of the changes shown is more readily apparent in this form. Corresponding index numbers, in current dollars, appear in Appendix III.

Index numbers relating to the two major groups are shown graphically in Figure 38.

The year 1919 marked the peak of values of farm products, in both raw and processed forms. The per-unit purchasing power of farm products, at wholesale, was approximately 10 per cent higher in that year than in 1913, while the purchasing power of non-farm products was about the same degree below the 1913 level. Liquidation brought a complete reversal of these relations. At average prices in 1921 the purchasing power of raw farm products was 18 per cent below the level of 1913 values. Raw non-farm products stood at a level almost as low. Processed farm products had a per-unit value some 3 per cent higher than in 1913, while the purchasing power of processed non-farm products had advanced almost 12 per cent. This latter group gained the most substantial advantage from the price shifts of liquidation.

The degree of disturbance of pre-war relations was lessened by 1922, but the positions of the indexes in that year still reflect significant departures from earlier relations. Farm products as a group were worth less than in 1913, while non-farm products had higher real values. In each group raw materials stand at the lower level, while products of manufacture show relatively improved economic position.[1]

§ *Prices and purchasing power of agricultural products at the farm.*—Index numbers of wholesale prices do not, of course, measure changes in the amounts received by farmers for their products or in the amounts

---

[1] We have noted that for commodities in general the developments of the war years enhanced the degree of variability of the prices of individual commodities. This is true also of the commodities in the groups defined above.

Comparison of Measurements of Monthly Variability
1898-1913, 1914-1921

| Commodity group | Number of price series | Measurement of monthly variability | |
|---|---|---|---|
| | | 1898-1913 | 1914-1921 |
| Products of American farms | | | |
| Raw | 24 | 9.0 | 12.5 |
| Processed | 83 | 3.7 | 8.2 |
| Total | 107 | 4.9 | 9.1 |
| All other products | | | |
| Raw | 25 | 5.4 | 9.4 |
| Processed | 75 | 3.4 | 6.6 |
| Total | 100 | 3.9 | 7.3 |

The relations among groups in respect of susceptibility to price changes were not altered by the war-time movements, but in all groups there was a notable increase in the degree of price fluctuation. These measurements indicate profound alterations in the ordinary operations of business; they give evidence of the introduction of severe disturbances into the processes of buying and selling.

which they must pay for commodities bought. The United States Bureau of Agricultural Economics has constructed comprehensive index numbers of prices actually received by farmers and of prices paid by farmers for articles used in living and production.[1] The ratio between these two indicates, more accurately than does the purchasing power index presented above, the actual changes occurring in the command of agricultural producers over the commodities they require.

TABLE 88

Showing Changes in Prices Received by Farmers, in Prices Paid by Farmers and in the Purchasing Power of Farm Products, 1913-1922

| (1) Year | (2) Index numbers of farm prices | (3) Prices paid by farmers for commodities bought | (4) Ratio of prices received to prices paid (in relative form) |
|---|---|---|---|
| 1913 | 100 | 100 | 100 |
| 1914 | 102 | 101 | 101 |
| 1915 | 100 | 106 | 95 |
| 1916 | 117 | 123 | 95 |
| 1917 | 176 | 150 | 118 |
| 1918 | 200 | 178 | 112 |
| 1919 | 209 | 205 | 102 |
| 1920 | 205 | 206 | 99 |
| 1921 | 116 | 156 | 75 |
| 1922 | 124 | 152 | 81 |

The farmer's relative position was not materially improved by high prices until 1917, when the purchasing power of the average unit of American farm products was some 18 per cent higher than in 1913. In 1919 and 1920 buying prices went up for the farmer; by 1920 he had lost all the advantage he had enjoyed during the two closing years of the war. The drop in 1921 carried him far below his pre-war levels. By 1922 the farmer was selling and buying under conditions such that each unit of product was worth about 19 per cent less than in 1913, in terms of goods a farmer needs. This is a somewhat darker, but truer, picture than that presented by the index numbers of wholesale prices.[2]

[1] U. S. Department of Agriculture, *Yearbook of Agriculture, 1930*, pp. 995, 996.
[2] These measurements, of course, define purchasing power per unit of product. The farmer's actual position is more accurately shown by measurements of aggregate purchasing power, for changing yields are important factors in the farmer's economic situation. Estimates of gross farm income made by the Bureau of Agricultural Economics indicate that the aggregate purchasing power of farmers in 1922 was about six per cent less than the aggregate purchasing power of farmers in 1913. Relatively high yields in 1922 furnished partial compensation for the loss in per-unit purchasing power.

Materials presented in preceding sections of this chapter help to explain some of the price movements with which we have just been dealing. Index numbers of production of farm products, after attaining a high level in 1915, remained below corresponding indexes for raw non-farm products during the three succeeding years. These were years of strong demand and the result was a highly favorable price situation for farmers. In 1919 and 1920 the output of raw farm products was carried to relatively high levels. There was some decline in production in 1921, but 1922 again was marked by heavy output of farm products. Here is an obvious explanation of the price and purchasing power changes we have just been discussing. The business recession in 1920-21, combined with the shifts which accompanied the ending of the war, brought a sharp drop in the demand for farm products, as it did, in greater or less degree, in the demand for all products. In contrast to the sharp decline in the production of non-farm products, particularly processed non-farm products, there was no prompt adaptation on the part of farmers to this change in conditions. From 1920 to 1921 the output of processed non-farm products decreased approximately 27 per cent as compared with a drop of 10 per cent in the output of raw farm products. This prompt adaptation on the part of producers of processed non-farm products to changed economic conditions meant, of course, sudden and violent liquidation and retrenchment, involving unemployment and, in many cases, financial reorganization. It did, however, lessen the severity of the price drop and left manufacturing interests with enhanced purchasing power per unit of product. Deferred liquidation on the part of agricultural interests, and failure to adjust output to new demand conditions, brought price weakness which has persisted to this day.

### *Price Movements of Farm Crops, Animal Products, Mineral Products and Forest Products*

From the turn of the century to the beginning of the war a progressive and persistent change was taking place in the price relations of various animal and mineral products and of farm crops. The real value of forest products was rising steadily, as was also that of animal products. Farm crops were about holding their own, while the real value, per unit, of mineral products was steadily dropping. The story of price changes among these groups during the troubled war years and the years which followed is somewhat different. Index numbers of purchasing power changes for commodities of these four classes are shown in the next table.[1]

TABLE 89

FARM CROPS, ANIMAL PRODUCTS, MINERAL PRODUCTS AND FOREST PRODUCTS
Index Numbers of Purchasing Power, in Wholesale Markets, 1913-1922 [a]

| Year | Farm crops | Animal products | Mineral products | Forest products |
|---|---|---|---|---|
| 1913 | 100.0 | 100.0 | 100.0 | 100.0 |
| 1914 | 103.0 | 101.8 | 96.5  | 97.1  |
| 1915 | 101.0 | 99.2  | 102.5 | 90.4  |
| 1916 | 95.2  | 93.9  | 114.6 | 87.0  |
| 1917 | 104.3 | 96.5  | 106.1 | 80.5  |
| 1918 | 107.9 | 101.0 | 99.9  | 79.8  |
| 1919 | 110.2 | 106.5 | 90.5  | 92.8  |
| 1920 | 104.2 | 93.5  | 97.8  | 117.2 |
| 1921 | 93.2  | 92.1  | 112.0 | 102.3 |
| 1922 | 95.8  | 96.4  | 105.1 | 105.3 |

[a] The number of price series in each group in 1922 is given below. (Nine price series included in the all commodities index have been omitted from these averages because of difficulty of classification.)

| | |
|---|---|
| Farm crops | 124 |
| Animal products | 122 |
| Mineral products | 158 |
| Forest products | 53 |

The war carried the prices of mineral products and farm crops to high levels, and the index numbers of per-unit purchasing power are correspondingly elevated. Forest products lagged behind, losing substantially in purchasing power. This loss was more than made up in 1920, when such products stood at a far higher level of real value than the commodities in any of the other groups. In 1922 forest products and mineral products had a higher per-unit purchasing power than in 1913, while the real values, per unit, of animal products and farm crops were appreciably lower. Comparing the period as a whole with the pre-war period, the most notable changes are found in the enhanced purchasing power of mineral products and the loss in purchasing power of animal products. Mineral products, which had been materially cheapened during the thirteen years before the war, possessed, in 1922, a per-unit purchasing

[1] The index numbers in the text are given in terms of purchasing power, since the significance of the changes shown is more readily apparent in this form. Corresponding index numbers, in current dollars, appear in Appendix III.

power more than 5 per cent greater than in 1913. We have here another of the revolutionary shifts brought by the recession of 1920-21, a shift which had enduring effects on developments during the succeeding years. Sellers of mineral products, who probably had most to gain from the improved productive efficiency which the post-war years were to bring, were exceptionally favored also in that the post-war readjustment left them in an exceedingly strong position in commodity markets.[1]

## Price Movements of Foods and Non-foods

The effect of the economic changes occurring from 1901 to 1913 was to enhance the purchasing power of foods, particularly of raw foods, and to lower that of non-foods, particularly of raw non-foods. In Table 90, on page 214, a similar comparison for the war years is presented.[2]

With minor exceptions during two or three years, non-foods gained in purchasing power over the period here under review, while foods lost. In 1922, non-foods had a purchasing power some 5 per cent greater than in 1913; that of foods was 9 per cent less. Here we have another reversal of tendencies prevailing during pre-war years. In both major groups we find that raw materials suffered the greater loss in purchasing power between 1913 and 1922. Processed non-foods were the only group to show a net advance in real value per unit during this nine-year period.[3] This group, it

---

[1] Among these groups, as among the others previously discussed, prices which had formerly been stabilized and prices which had formerly been lethargic were stimulated into new activity by the changes of this disturbed epoch. A comparison of measures of variability and of frequency of price change during the periods 1898-1913 and 1914-1921 follows:

| Commodity group | Number of price series | Monthly variability of prices 1898-1913 | 1914-1921 | Frequency of price change 1898-1913 | 1914-1921 |
|---|---|---|---|---|---|
| Farm crops | 69 | 4.9 | 9.9 | .52 | .62 |
| Animal products | 46 | 5.1 | 8.3 | .59 | .69 |
| Forest products | 20 | 3.9 | 7.5 | .32 | .45 |
| Mineral products | 63 | 3.7 | 6.9 | .36 | .43 |

Prices of farm products remain the most variable of all those compared, while the frequency of price change remains highest for animal products. All the measurements show a very considerable increase in the magnitude of price changes and in the frequency of price alterations. The crust of custom was broken in the field of prices as it had not been for many years.

[2] The index numbers in the text are given in purchasing power terms. Corresponding index numbers, in current dollars, appear in Appendix III.

[3] Automobiles, which constitute a distinctive class of commodities in respect of price movements during these years, are not included in the present index numbers.

## TABLE 90

### FOODS AND NON-FOODS

Index Numbers of Purchasing Power, in Wholesale Markets, 1913-1922 [a]

| (1) | (2) | (3) | (4) | (5) | (6) | (7) |
|---|---|---|---|---|---|---|
| Year | Foods | | Non-foods | | All foods | All non-foods |
| | Raw | Processed | Raw | Processed | | |
| 1913 | 100.0 | 100.0 | 100.0 | 100.0 | 100.0 | 100.0 |
| 1914 | 105.0 | 103.9 | 95.6 | 98.0 | 104.3 | 97.6 |
| 1915 | 101.5 | 101.4 | 101.2 | 98.5 | 101.4 | 99.1 |
| 1916 | 94.5 | 90.5 | 104.6 | 104.6 | 92.2 | 104.6 |
| 1917 | 98.3 | 96.6 | 105.6 | 100.1 | 97.3 | 101.5 |
| 1918 | 96.5 | 100.1 | 96.5 | 102.0 | 98.5 | 100.9 |
| 1919 | 103.7 | 102.9 | 88.9 | 100.9 | 103.2 | 98.2 |
| 1920 | 89.8 | 91.2 | 87.2 | 111.2 | 90.6 | 105.6 |
| 1921 | 84.1 | 95.6 | 81.5 | 113.5 | 90.2 | 105.6 |
| 1922 | 87.6 | 93.7 | 92.0 | 109.0 | 90.9 | 105.2 |

[a] The number of price series in each group in 1922 is given below:

| Foods | | Non-foods | |
|---|---|---|---|
| Raw | 71 | Raw | 65 |
| Processed | 90 | Processed | 240 |
| Total | 161 | Total | 305 |

should be remembered, declined approximately 2 per cent in per-unit purchasing power between 1901 and 1913, a figure which stands in contrast to the net gain of 9 per cent between 1913 and 1922. Here, again, we have a group of products for which, presumably, costs of production had been most heavily reduced as a result of technical improvements and changes in production methods during the pre-war years, and which was left in an extremely strong economic position by the recession of the high tide of prices in 1921. This group, moreover, stood to gain most if the technical advance characteristic of pre-war years were to be resumed. In the study of the changes occurring during the following years this condition must be borne in mind.

### Price Movements of Producers' Goods and Consumers' Goods

We have seen that the prices of goods in shape for final consumption show characteristic modes of behavior which differ from those of commodities destined for use as capital equipment or subject to further processing. The index numbers in the following table show changes in the purchasing power of these two classes of goods and of various sub-divisions of each during the period now under review.[1] A graphic representation of certain of these measurements is given in Figure 38.

TABLE 91

Producers' Goods and Consumers' Goods

Index Numbers of Purchasing Power, in Wholesale Markets, 1913-1922 [a]

| (1) | (2) | (3) | (4) | (5) | (6) | (7) | (8) | (9) | (10) | (11) |
|---|---|---|---|---|---|---|---|---|---|---|
| | Producers' goods | | | | Consumers' goods | | | | All producers' goods | All consumers' goods |
| Year | Raw | Processed | Foods | Non-foods | Raw | Processed | Foods | Non-foods | | |
| 1913 | 100.0 | 100.0 | 100.0 | 100.0 | 100.0 | 100.0 | 100.0 | 100.0 | 100.0 | 100.0 |
| 1914 | 99.6 | 97.1 | 105.2 | 96.2 | 103.7 | 102.3 | 103.9 | 100.7 | 98.1 | 102.6 |
| 1915 | 104.7 | 99.5 | 107.4 | 100.0 | 91.6 | 99.0 | 98.5 | 96.6 | 101.6 | 97.8 |
| 1916 | 99.8 | 112.2 | 96.7 | 110.2 | 89.5 | 90.2 | 90.0 | 90.2 | 107.4 | 90.2 |
| 1917 | 104.8 | 105.3 | 100.6 | 106.5 | 91.6 | 92.8 | 95.7 | 88.1 | 105.2 | 92.6 |
| 1918 | 99.1 | 103.1 | 100.5 | 101.9 | 87.9 | 99.5 | 97.4 | 97.3 | 101.6 | 97.4 |
| 1919 | 96.0 | 99.9 | 107.3 | 96.4 | 97.1 | 103.2 | 101.2 | 103.3 | 98.4 | 102.1 |
| 1920 | 88.2 | 107.5 | 90.0 | 102.3 | 89.5 | 102.5 | 90.9 | 115.1 | 99.7 | 100.2 |
| 1921 | 78.2 | 106.9 | 77.8 | 99.7 | 101.0 | 109.4 | 97.3 | 125.0 | 95.0 | 107.9 |
| 1922 | 85.8 | 104.4 | 82.3 | 100.9 | 103.8 | 104.4 | 95.6 | 117.9 | 97.0 | 104.4 |

[a] The number of price series in each group in 1922 is given below:

| Producers' goods | | Consumers' goods | |
|---|---|---|---|
| Raw | 105 | Raw | 31 |
| Processed | 179 | Processed | 151 |
| Foods | 54 | Foods | 107 |
| Non-foods | 230 | Non-foods | 75 |
| Total | 284 | Total | 182 |

Comparing first the entries in columns (10) and (11), it is to be noted that during the early years of the war the purchasing power of producers' goods was enhanced, while consumers' goods were cheapened. This reflects, presumably, the bidding of manufacturers for supplies to meet the war-time demand. Beginning with 1918 this situation was reversed. The recession of 1921 carried producers' goods to a level of real value approximately 5 per cent below that of 1913. Consumers' goods were worth, in terms of commodities, some 8 per cent more than in 1913. This margin was narrowed in 1922, but a major discrepancy still persisted. The era

[1] The index numbers in the text are given in terms of purchasing power. Corresponding index numbers, in current dollars, appear in Appendix III.

extending from 1922 to 1929, which we shall later subject to a detailed scrutiny, opens with producers' goods low-priced and consumers' goods high-priced, with reference to pre-war standards. This represents, of course, a favorable situation for those who buy in the markets for producers' goods and sell in the markets for consumers' goods.

The division of each of these groups into raw and processed categories [see columns (2), (3), (6) and (7)] reveals that both raw and processed producers' goods were carried to high levels of purchasing power by war-time demand, notably in 1917, but that raw producers' goods suffered most severely during the post-war deflation. In 1922 such goods had a real value, per unit, 14 per cent lower than in 1913. The other three groups of this division stood at higher levels in 1922 than in 1913.

Cutting across the categories of producers' and consumers' goods in another direction, we separate foods from non-foods. These index numbers [shown in columns (4), (5), (8) and (9)] reveal how quickly the wheel of fortune turned upon itself for producers of these several types of goods. The year 1916 finds non-foods among producers' goods with a purchasing power per unit 10 per cent higher than in 1913, while non-foods among consumers' goods stood 10 per cent below the earlier level. The shift in demand brought by the end of the war and the cataclysmic reversals accompanying the 1920-21 recession materially enhanced the purchasing power of consumers' non-foods. In 1921 the average purchasing power of goods in this class was approximately 25 per cent higher than in 1913. Producers' non-foods were then slightly below the 1913 level while food products in the producers' goods group were some 22 per cent lower in value than in 1913. These inequalities were reduced somewhat by 1922 but the range of difference, with reference to pre-war standards, was still pronounced. Most depressed were the real values of foods not yet in shape for final consumption (i.e., in the producers' goods class), while the purchasing power of non-foods in shape for sale to final consumers was approximately 18 per cent above the 1913 level.

In tracing price changes it is of interest to employ yet another grouping, differing slightly from that shown above. Articles of capital equipment classified among producers' goods have no counterpart among consumers' goods while, on the other hand, raw consumers' goods, which do not, of course, undergo fabrication before consumption, have no counterpart in the producers' goods group. If we form a new class composed of producers' goods destined for human consumption we shall have a group which may be set against processed consumers' goods. This does not mean that precisely identical commodities, at different stages of manufacture, are contained in these two groups. But we do have here representatives of two different stages along the path followed by goods in the course of their fabrication and distribution. Index numbers for these two groups, in purchasing power form, appear in the next table.[1] They are plotted in Figure 39.

TABLE 92

Producers' Goods Destined for Human Consumption and Processed Consumers' Goods

Index Numbers of Purchasing Power, in Wholesale Markets, 1913-1922 [a]

| Year | Producers' goods destined for human consumption | Processed consumers' goods |
| --- | --- | --- |
| 1913 | 100 | 100 |
| 1914 | 101 | 102 |
| 1915 | 105 | 99 |
| 1916 | 110 | 90 |
| 1917 | 108 | 93 |
| 1918 | 108 | 99 |
| 1919 | 104 | 103 |
| 1920 | 96 | 102 |
| 1921 | 82 | 109 |
| 1922 | 88 | 104 |

[a] The numbers of price series in these groups in 1922 are as follows:
    Producers' goods destined for human consumption    132
    Processed consumers' goods    151

In 1916, when war-time demand had attained full dimensions, producers' goods destined for ultimate consumption had an average real value, in terms of commodities in general, 10 per cent higher than they had enjoyed three years before, while processed consumers' goods had lost 10 per cent of their per-unit purchasing power. The recession of 1921 carried goods of the first class 18 per cent below the pre-war level, while processed consumers' goods had a per-unit purchasing power 9 per cent higher than in 1913. By 1922 the loss of the first group had been reduced to 12 per cent, while the gain for the second group had been reduced to 4 per cent.

[1] Index numbers in current dollars appear in Appendix III.

## FIGURE 39
### GRAPHIC REPRESENTATION OF CHANGES IN THE REAL VALUES, PER UNIT, OF COMMODITIES IN SELECTED GROUPS, 1913-1922
#### SELECTED CLASSES OF PRODUCERS' GOODS AND CONSUMERS' GOODS
(CHANGES ARE MEASURED AS PERCENTAGE DEVIATIONS FROM 1913 PURCHASING POWER.)

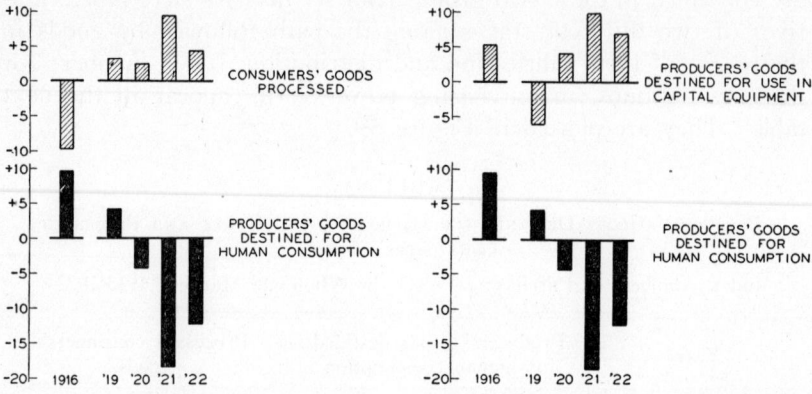

The post-war advance which was begun in 1922 starts, then, with an extremely wide margin between the respective purchasing powers of these two important classes of goods. Commodities intended for consumption, but requiring further fabrication before their ultimate sale to consumers, were selling at very low prices, while the prices paid by ultimate consumers for goods in their final form were well above pre-war levels. Here, obviously, was a situation which worked to the distinct advantage of fabricating agents. The prices at which they bought were low, the prices at which they sold were high. The manner in which this margin of advantage was utilized, and the degree to which the different agents of fabrication —employees, management and ownership—reaped the rewards of this advantageous condition remain to be discussed. It is clear at this stage, however, that fabricating agents were in a position of economic advantage such as they had not enjoyed for many years. (This advantage could not, of course, become a real one under conditions of acute depression. Favorable price margins mean nothing unless goods are being sold in sufficient quantities. But once the volume of sales picks up after depression, the full benefits of such price margins may be realized.)

One further classification of producers' goods is to be made. As we have seen, producers' goods intended for human consumption were greatly lowered in real value by the events which accompanied the recession of 1920-21. Was the same thing true of producers' goods intended for ultimate use as capital equipment? The following table permits an answer to this question.[1] The measurements are shown graphically in Figure 39.

TABLE 93

PRODUCERS' GOODS DESTINED FOR HUMAN CONSUMPTION AND FOR USE IN CAPITAL EQUIPMENT

Index Numbers of Purchasing Power, in Wholesale Markets, 1913-1922 [a]

| Year | Producers' goods destined for human consumption | Producers' goods destined for use in capital equipment |
|---|---|---|
| 1913 | 100 | 100 |
| 1914 | 101 | 95 |
| 1915 | 105 | 98 |
| 1916 | 110 | 105 |
| 1917 | 108 | 103 |
| 1918 | 108 | 97 |
| 1919 | 104 | 94 |
| 1920 | 96 | 104 |
| 1921 | 82 | 110 |
| 1922 | 88 | 107 |

[a] The numbers of price series in these groups in 1922 are as follows:
    Producers' goods destined for human consumption    132
    Producers' goods destined for use in capital equipment    152

The end of the war in 1918 found articles of capital equipment undervalued, in relation to the 1913 standard. The net effect of recession and of post-war revival was to carry their prices upward; by 1922 goods of this class had a purchasing power, in terms of goods in general, 7 per cent higher than in 1913. It was not all producers' goods, therefore, which were cheapened by the great post-war recession. In improving and extending his capital equipment the producer was forced to pay much higher prices, with reference to pre-war standards, than was necessary in buying materials for fabrication into consumers' goods. The manufacturer's distinct price advantage was restricted to goods of the latter class.

[1] Index numbers in current dollars are given in Appendix III.

## Changes in Prices and Costs in Manufacturing Industries, 1914-1923

It is possible to trace in greater detail certain changes occurring in selling prices and costs of fabrication among manufacturing industries. The basic data for a list of selected industries, for which comparable statistics on production, cost of materials, wages, etc., are available, appear in the following table.

### TABLE 94
Statistics of Selected Manufacturing Industries in the United States, 1914-1923 [a]

(All value figures in thousands of dollars)

| (1) | (2) | (3) | (4) | (5) | (6) | (7) | (8) |
|---|---|---|---|---|---|---|---|
| | Statistics relating to all products of industries represented in index of physical volume of production | | | | | Actual value of products entering into index of physical volume of production | Ratio of value of products entering into index to total value of products (7)/(2) |
| Year | Total value of products | Cost of materials | Cost of fabrication, plus profits | Total wages paid | Overhead expenses plus profits | | |
| 1914 | 9,306,464 | 6,558,680 | 2,747,784 | 1,188,443 | 1,559,341 | 8,364,314 | .899 |
| 1919 | 24,887,795 | 17,368,936 | 7,518,859 | 3,122,521 | 4,396,338 | 22,220,996 | .893 |
| 1921 | 15,956,026 | 10,876,326 | 5,079,700 | 2,384,286 | 2,695,414 | 14,312,703 | .897 |
| 1923 | 23,170,088 | 15,384,586 | 7,785,502 | 3,433,701 | 4,351,801 | 21,010,915 | .907 |

[a] The data for all years represented in this table relate to establishments reporting products of a value of $5,000 or more.

The products of the industries entering into this table constitute from 44 to 47 per cent, by value, of total products of all manufacturing industries; the sample with which we are working is a broad one.

If we reduce to relative numbers certain of the entries in the above table, we have the series appearing in Table 95. An index of physical volume of manufacturing production, based upon the output of the selected industries, is also given in this table. Having measurements of this type, relating to aggregate values and to quantities for identical industries, we are able to measure changes in selling price, per unit of product, and in the various elements of manufacturing cost, per unit of product.

## TABLE 95

### Relative Numbers Defining Changes in Important Elements of Manufacturing Production in the United States, 1914-1923

| (1) Year | (2) Physical volume of production (fabrication) | (3) Value of products | (4) Cost of materials | (5) Cost of fabrication, plus profits | (6) Total wages paid | (7) Overhead expenses plus profits |
|---|---|---|---|---|---|---|
| 1914 | 100.0 | 100.0 | 100.0 | 100.0 | 100.0 | 100.0 |
| 1919 | 127.7 | 267.4 | 264.8 | 273.6 | 262.7 | 281.9 |
| 1921 | 105.7 | 171.4 | 165.8 | 184.8 | 200.6 | 172.9 |
| 1923 | 156.3 | 249.0 | 234.6 | 283.3 | 288.9 | 279.1 |

§ *On changes in the apparent physical contributions of different agents of manufacturing production, 1914-1923.*—As was explained in Chapter III, it is necessary, in securing accurate measurements of changes in different cost elements, to employ different index numbers of physical volume of manufacturing production. The index numbers given in Table 95, which measure changes in the volume of fabrication, are not necessarily identical with index numbers measuring changes in the aggregate volume of output of manufacturing industries. For changes occur in the degree of fabrication in different industries, and industries in which raw materials undergo varying degrees of fabrication change in relative importance. Still other index numbers are necessary for measuring changes in the physical contributions of

## TABLE 96

### Index Numbers Measuring Changes in the Apparent Physical Contributions of Different Agents of Manufacturing Production, 1914-1923

| (1) Year | (2) Aggregate output (weights based on value of product) | (3) Volume of materials (weights based on cost of materials) | (4) Volume of fabrication (weights based on 'value added') | (5) Apparent contribution of labor (weights based on wages paid) | (6) Apparent contribution of ownership and management (weights based on overhead expenses plus profits) |
|---|---|---|---|---|---|
| 1914 | 100.0 | 100.0 | 100.0 | 100.0 | 100.0 |
| 1919 | 126.3 | 125.6 | 127.7 | 124.6 | 130.2 |
| 1921 | 103.3 | 102.2 | 105.7 | 101.4 | 109.1 |
| 1923 | 149.0 | 145.7 | 156.3 | 154.6 | 157.7 |

labor and of the other agents of fabrication. The various index numbers relating to volume of manufacturing production are summarized, for reference, in Table 96. (These do not purport, of course, to measure the specific contributions of the several productive agents.)

The elements involved in deriving index numbers of selling price, per unit of product, are shown in the next table.

TABLE 97

INDEX NUMBERS OF AGGREGATE VALUE, PRODUCTION AND PRICE, 1914-1923

Manufacturing Industries of the United States

| Year | Aggregate value of manufactured product | Physical volume of output [a] | Average selling price per unit, products of manufacture |
|---|---|---|---|
| 1914 | 100.0 | 100.0 | 100.0 |
| 1919 | 267.4 | 126.3 | 211.8 |
| 1921 | 171.4 | 103.3 | 166.0 |
| 1923 | 249.0 | 149.0 | 167.1 |

[a] Weights based on value of product.

The changes in volume of manufacturing production during the war-time advance, the recession in 1921 and the sharp rise thereafter, have been discussed. During the first five-year period selling price changes greatly overshadowed volume changes in swelling the total value of manufactured products. During the decline from 1919 to 1921 volume and prices fell by amounts which did not differ greatly. (Production declined 18 per cent, prices 22 per cent.) Thereafter, however, volume increased rapidly, while the great revival from 1921 to 1923 brought practically no change in the average selling price, per unit of product, of manufactured goods.[1]

[1] The index numbers of selling prices, given in Table 97, which are derived from statistics of aggregate values and quantities, and not from price quotations on individual commodities, may be compared with index numbers derived from such individual quotations. If we shift to the 1914 base the index numbers of wholesale prices of manufactured goods which were given in Table 85, adding a figure for 1923, we have the following measurements:

| | |
|---|---|
| 1914 | 100.0 |
| 1919 | 210.7 |
| 1921 | 166.4 |
| 1923 | 166.7 |

The degree of correspondence is very close, in view of the complete independence of the methods of computation.

§ *Selling prices, individual industries.*—We have already remarked upon the undesirability of trusting to general index numbers alone in tracing the diversified changes characteristic of manufacturing industries. At times the degree of diversity is so pronounced that an average is misleading. In the following table are brought together index numbers defining price movements in individual manufacturing industries between 1914 and 1923.

TABLE 98

CHANGES IN THE SELLING PRICES OF PRODUCTS OF MANUFACTURING INDUSTRIES OF THE UNITED STATES, 1914-1923

Index Numbers for 52 Industries

| Industry | Index numbers of selling price, per unit of product | | | |
|---|---|---|---|---|
| | 1914 | 1919 | 1921 | 1923 |
| Hats, wool-felt | 100.0 | 250.3 | 291.5 | 356.8 |
| Lime | 100.0 | 229.9 | 275.7 | 266.5 |
| Musical instruments: organs | 100.0 | 128.2 | 199.3 | 260.0 |
| Coke, not including gas-house coke | 100.0 | 225.4 | 228.0 | 253.7 |
| Lace goods, cotton | 100.0 | 250.2 | 255.1 | 240.6 |
| Knit goods | 100.0 | 242.7 | 224.0 | 235.9 |
| Worsted goods | 100.0 | 288.1 | 212.5 | 234.9 |
| Lumber and timber products | 100.0 | 215.8 | 169.5 | 230.4 |
| Cast-iron pipe | 100.0 | 269.0 | 214.3 | 229.9 |
| Wood distillation and charcoal manufacture | 100.0 | 261.2 | 180.0 | 229.1 |
| Cars, steam and electric railroad, not built in railroad repair shops | 100.0 | 256.0 | 285.0 | 223.9 |
| Woolen goods | 100.0 | 287.4 | 201.1 | 222.9 |
| Cotton goods | 100.0 | 293.9 | 191.9 | 220.5 |
| Oilcloth | 100.0 | 311.1 | 219.6 | 217.4 |
| Canning and preserving: fish, crabs, shrimps, oysters, and clams | 100.0 | 211.6 | 201.6 | 207.8 |
| Cement | 100.0 | 184.9 | 204.7 | 205.1 |
| Oil, cake, and meal, cottonseed | 100.0 | 329.9 | 170.1 | 204.1 |
| Sugar, cane, not including products of refineries | 100.0 | 279.4 | 115.6 | 199.5 |
| Carpets and rugs, wool, other than rag | 100.0 | 206.3 | 179.9 | 199.2 |
| Clay products (other than pottery) and non-clay refractories | 100.0 | 204.2 | 199.7 | 197.7 |
| Hats, fur-felt | 100.0 | 215.2 | 159.4 | 197.3 |
| Jute and linen goods | 100.0 | 228.7 | 199.9 | 193.2 |
| Silk manufactures | 100.0 | 203.9 | 189.4 | 193.2 |
| Sugar refining, cane | 100.0 | 238.1 | 142.7 | 189.4 |
| Sugar, beet | 100.0 | 243.0 | 158.5 | 189.3 |
| Sand-lime brick | 100.0 | 189.2 | 212.9 | 189.0 |
| Paper and wood pulp | 100.0 | 198.5 | 198.2 | 185.8 |
| Iron and steel: steel works and rolling mills | 100.0 | 211.2 | 183.9 | 184.3 |

TABLE 98—*Continued*

| Industry | Index numbers of selling price, per unit of product | | | |
| --- | --- | --- | --- | --- |
| | 1914 | 1919 | 1921 | 1923 |
| Wool shoddy | 100.0 | 253.4 | 157.3 | 183.7 |
| Iron and steel: blast furnaces | 100.0 | 191.5 | 182.8 | 182.5 |
| Salt | 100.0 | 188.1 | 232.1 | 182.3 |
| Paints and varnishes | 100.0 | 183.7 | 176.1 | 175.4 |
| Wire, drawn from purchased bars or rods | 100.0 | 188.0 | 218.6 | 174.7 |
| Soap | 100.0 | 194.9 | 163.7 | 163.1 |
| Turpentine and rosin | 100.0 | 369.9 | 119.4 | 159.8 |
| Butter and cheese | 100.0 | 202.5 | 137.7 | 157.7 |
| Cordage and twine | 100.0 | 241.9 | 166.2 | 156.2 |
| Canning and preserving: fruits and vegetables; pickles, jellies, preserves, and sauces | 100.0 | 193.1 | 176.2 | 156.0 |
| Ice, manufactured | 100.0 | 165.6 | 170.3 | 154.5 |
| Linoleum and asphalted-felt-base floor coverings | 100.0 | 159.2 | 148.8 | 153.5 |
| Petroleum refining | 100.0 | 211.5 | 188.5 | 142.9 |
| Fertilizers | 100.0 | 199.9 | 171.7 | 137.1 |
| Motorcycles, bicycles, and parts | 100.0 | 160.6 | 153.1 | 135.8 |
| Gas, manufactured, illuminating and heating | 100.0 | 110.5 | 145.6 | 134.2 |
| Condensed and evaporated milk | 100.0 | 209.8 | 134.6 | 134.1 |
| Explosives | 100.0 | 176.8 | 162.2 | 132.1 |
| Musical instruments: pianos | 100.0 | 132.6 | 140.2 | 128.0 |
| Flour and other grain-mill products | 100.0 | 222.1 | 148.5 | 124.9 |
| Rice cleaning and polishing | 100.0 | 244.1 | 105.3 | 119.0 |
| Slaughtering and meat packing, wholesale | 100.0 | 195.2 | 122.3 | 114.0 |
| Motor vehicles, including bodies and parts | 100.0 | 116.2 | 109.0 | 98.7 |
| Rubber products | 100.0 | 132.0 | 107.2 | 86.3 |
| Average [a] | 100.0 | 208.4 | 175.1 | 182.2 |

[a] An arithmetic average of the central items of a weighted frequency distribution, with weights based on value of product, averaged for the base year and the given year. The central one-fifth of the items, by weight, were included in computing the average.

Detailed consideration of the price changes occurring in these industries is not necessary. It is significant that the averages given at the foot of this table differ in certain respects from the index numbers of selling prices in Table 97. Heavily weighted industries with exceptional price movements, notably meat packing in 1921 and 1923, exert a very strong influence upon a mathematical average of the type of the 'ideal' index. This is desirable for certain purposes, but it may give results which are not typical of manufacturing industries in general. The averages at the foot of Table 98, which are probably more representative of the fortunes of typical manufacturing industries than are those previously presented, indicate a slightly lower level of selling prices in 1919, a somewhat higher level in 1921 and 1923.

The present procedure permits the derivation of measurements of cost of materials, per unit of product, and of fabrication costs, plus profits, per unit of product. These several index numbers, expressed first in current dollars and then in dollars of constant purchasing power in wholesale markets, appear in the next table. Figure 40 presents a graphic portrayal of the changes in these costs.[1]

TABLE 99

Changes in Selling Price, Cost of Materials and Fabrication Costs, plus Profits, 1914-1923

Manufacturing Industries of the United States

(All measurements relate to changes per unit of product)

| (1) | (2) | (3) | (4) | (5) | (6) | (7) |
|---|---|---|---|---|---|---|
| | In current dollars | | | In dollars of constant purchasing power | | |
| Year | Selling price | Cost of materials | Fabrication costs, plus profits | Selling price | Cost of materials | Fabrication costs, plus profits |
| 1914 | 100.0 | 100.0 | 100.0 | 100.0 | 100.0 | 100.0 |
| 1919 | 211.8 | 210.8 | 214.2 | 104.1 | 103.6 | 105.2 |
| 1921 | 166.0 | 162.2 | 174.9 | 115.8 | 113.2 | 122.0 |
| 1923 | 167.1 | 161.0 | 181.2 | 113.1 | 109.0 | 122.7 |

The great rise in prices of manufactured goods between 1914 and 1919 reflected rising material costs and rising fabrication costs in almost equal degree. In the ensuing drop of 1921 costs of materials fell to lower levels, relatively, than did fabrication costs. During the two years of revival following 1921, a revival which increased the total physical output of manufacturing industries by 48 per cent, material costs dropped fractionally, while fabrication costs, plus profits, per unit of product advanced almost 4 per cent.

The picture is clearer if we trace the changes in dollars of constant purchasing power. Here we may see manufacturing industries as a whole, and the two elements distinguished above, against the background of general market changes. As already observed, the

[1] Reduction to dollars of constant purchasing power has been effected through division by the wholesale price index of the U. S. Bureau of Labor Statistics. Since this is not a perfect deflator in the present case, attention should be paid to the relative movements of the different index numbers, rather than to absolute figures.

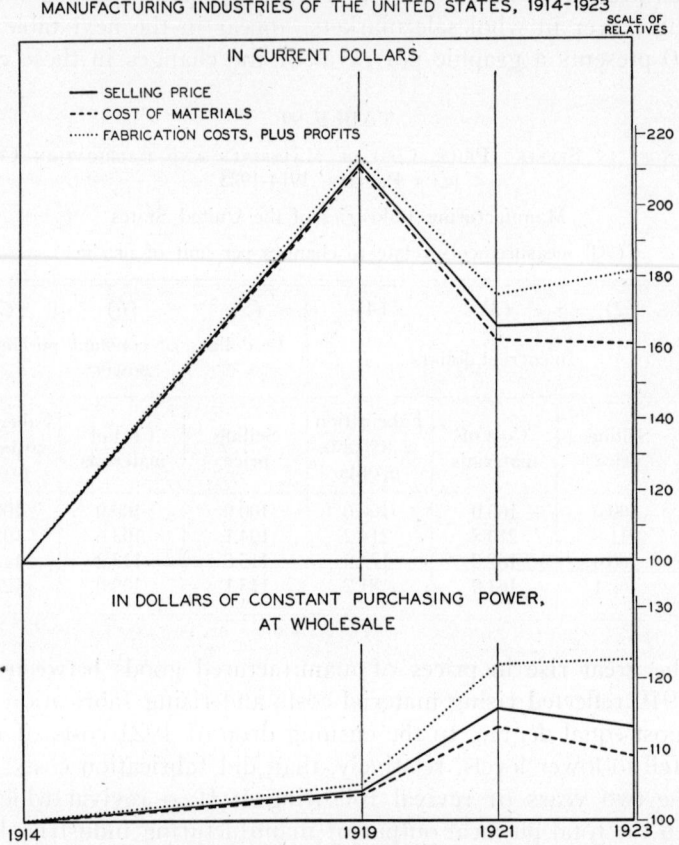

FIGURE 40

CHANGES IN AVERAGE SELLING PRICE, COST OF MATERIALS
AND FABRICATION COSTS, PLUS PROFITS,
PER UNIT OF PRODUCT

MANUFACTURING INDUSTRIES OF THE UNITED STATES, 1914-1923

effect of war-time and post-war developments was to reverse the trend toward steadily cheapening manufactured goods which had prevailed before the war. The purchasing power of manufactured goods, per unit, stood very much higher in 1921 than in 1914, and this advantage was only slightly impaired by 1923. Sellers of materials (and these, it must be remembered, include not only sellers of raw materials proper, but sellers of semi-processed goods, fuel, supplies, etc., for use in manufacturing) gained also, though the index numbers relating to this group are lower throughout than those defining selling price changes. It is fabrication costs which show the most pronounced divergence from their pre-war tendencies. These costs (in dollars of constant purchasing power) declined steadily from 1899 to 1914, being in 1914, 19.8 per cent lower, per unit of manufactured product, than in 1899. The record of changes after 1914 is one of unbroken advance. The liquidation of 1920-21 was much less severe for fabricating agents than for most other economic elements, and the net result was a very high level of real fabrication costs in 1921. These costs, which here include profits, rose fractionally during the remarkable spurt of activity between 1921 and 1923.

§ *Material costs and fabrication costs, individual industries.*—We shall do well at this point to note the diversity of cost movements among manufacturing industries between 1914 and 1923. Space considerations preclude extended comment, but the reader will find it enlightening to trace the changes in material costs and in fabrication costs among the manufacturing industries listed in the two following tables.

TABLE 100

CHANGES IN MATERIAL COSTS, MANUFACTURING INDUSTRIES OF THE UNITED STATES, 1914-1923

Index Numbers for 52 Industries

| Industry | Index numbers of cost of materials, per unit of product | | | |
|---|---|---|---|---|
| | 1914 | 1919 | 1921 | 1923 |
| Hats, wool-felt | 100.0 | 271.6 | 284.8 | 363.8 |
| Lime | 100.0 | 234.5 | 306.2 | 269.3 |
| Coke, not including gas-house coke | 100.0 | 229.2 | 249.6 | 249.4 |
| Knit goods | 100.0 | 256.4 | 224.7 | 237.6 |
| Lace goods, cotton | 100.0 | 259.0 | 258.7 | 228.8 |
| Cars, steam and electric railroad, not built in railroad repair shops | 100.0 | 250.8 | 262.8 | 227.0 |
| Lumber and timber products | 100.0 | 183.9 | 177.5 | 221.0 |
| Silk manufactures | 100.0 | 202.3 | 192.6 | 213.7 |
| Worsted goods | 100.0 | 277.6 | 170.9 | 213.7 |
| Sand-lime brick | 100.0 | 186.0 | 248.3 | 211.1 |
| Oil, cake, and meal, cottonseed | 100.0 | 329.5 | 178.9 | 208.7 |
| Sugar, cane, not including products of refineries | 100.0 | 289.6 | 115.6 | 208.6 |
| Cotton goods | 100.0 | 276.9 | 166.4 | 208.5 |
| Canning and preserving: fish, crabs, shrimps, oysters, and clams | 100.0 | 229.5 | 198.0 | 205.4 |
| Wood distillation and charcoal manufacture | 100.0 | 244.1 | 190.6 | 203.0 |

## TABLE 100—Continued

| Industry | Index numbers of cost of materials, per unit of product | | | |
|---|---|---|---|---|
| | 1914 | 1919 | 1921 | 1923 |
| Woolen goods | 100.0 | 279.8 | 170.6 | 200.9 |
| Hats, fur-felt | 100.0 | 230.1 | 175.3 | 199.0 |
| Sugar refining, cane | 100.0 | 236.4 | 143.0 | 194.9 |
| Clay products (other than pottery) and non-clay refractories | 100.0 | 209.5 | 222.2 | 194.1 |
| Cast-iron pipe | 100.0 | 214.0 | 181.9 | 190.7 |
| Iron and steel: steel works and rolling mills | 100.0 | 195.1 | 193.9 | 185.8 |
| Paper and wood pulp | 100.0 | 183.4 | 206.4 | 183.0 |
| Oilcloth | 100.0 | 275.2 | 182.5 | 183.0 |
| Salt | 100.0 | 179.8 | 257.0 | 182.4 |
| Iron and steel: blast furnaces | 100.0 | 179.6 | 188.8 | 179.9 |
| Musical instruments: organs | 100.0 | 112.4 | 172.5 | 179.4 |
| Paints and varnishes | 100.0 | 192.9 | 181.1 | 177.9 |
| Wire, drawn from purchased bars or rods | 100.0 | 172.8 | 198.8 | 172.8 |
| Sugar, beet | 100.0 | 214.4 | 210.0 | 171.3 |
| Wool shoddy | 100.0 | 254.4 | 150.4 | 169.8 |
| Gas, manufactured, illuminating and heating | 100.0 | 151.9 | 205.7 | 163.7 |
| Carpets and rugs, wool, other than rag | 100.0 | 183.7 | 141.9 | 159.2 |
| Turpentine and rosin | 100.0 | 372.0 | 121.9 | 156.4 |
| Motorcycles, bicycles, and parts | 100.0 | 159.8 | 139.2 | 154.2 |
| Butter and cheese | 100.0 | 204.2 | 133.0 | 153.4 |
| Cement | 100.0 | 164.2 | 201.4 | 153.2 |
| Ice, manufactured | 100.0 | 176.6 | 187.2 | 149.4 |
| Soap | 100.0 | 211.2 | 147.5 | 147.4 |
| Petroleum refining | 100.0 | 197.1 | 183.8 | 138.4 |
| Condensed and evaporated milk | 100.0 | 216.8 | 125.2 | 137.0 |
| Canning and preserving: fruits and vegetables; pickles, jellies, preserves, and sauces | 100.0 | 190.8 | 172.8 | 136.5 |
| Fertilizers | 100.0 | 186.7 | 195.8 | 136.0 |
| Musical instruments: pianos | 100.0 | 145.2 | 158.8 | 134.6 |
| Jute and linen goods | 100.0 | 168.2 | 145.0 | 134.6 |
| Cordage and twine | 100.0 | 223.0 | 140.5 | 130.0 |
| Flour and other grain-mill products | 100.0 | 227.0 | 145.9 | 123.1 |
| Motor vehicles, including bodies and parts | 100.0 | 135.0 | 132.3 | 117.8 |
| Rice cleaning and polishing | 100.0 | 232.2 | 97.6 | 113.6 |
| Explosives | 100.0 | 141.9 | 135.8 | 112.5 |
| Linoleum and asphalted-felt-base floor coverings | 100.0 | 143.6 | 122.8 | 112.4 |
| Slaughtering and meat packing, wholesale | 100.0 | 199.2 | 118.9 | 109.9 |
| Rubber products | 100.0 | 127.2 | 106.0 | 83.3 |
| Average [a] | 100.0 | 200.6 | 163.3 | 174.1 |

[a] An arithmetic average of the central items of a weighted frequency distribution, with weights based on cost of materials, averaged for the base year and the given year. The central one-fifth of the items, by weight, were included in computing the average.

## TABLE 101

CHANGES IN FABRICATION COSTS, PLUS PROFITS, MANUFACTURING INDUSTRIES OF THE UNITED STATES, 1914-1923

Index Numbers for 52 Industries

| Industry | Index numbers of cost of fabrication, plus profits, per unit of profit | | | |
|---|---|---|---|---|
| | 1914 | 1919 | 1921 | 1923 |
| Oilcloth | 100.0 | 470.3 | 384.0 | 370.2 |
| Hats, wool-felt | 100.0 | 228.5 | 298.4 | 349.7 |
| Jute and linen goods | 100.0 | 383.3 | 339.9 | 343.0 |
| Musical instruments: organs | 100.0 | 139.7 | 218.9 | 319.2 |
| Cast-iron pipe | 100.0 | 364.6 | 270.6 | 298.3 |
| Wood distillation and charcoal manufacture | 100.0 | 293.9 | 159.5 | 278.9 |
| Worsted goods | 100.0 | 308.7 | 294.4 | 276.7 |
| Lime | 100.0 | 226.7 | 254.3 | 264.6 |
| Coke, not including gas-house coke | 100.0 | 216.4 | 178.2 | 263.3 |
| Carpets and rugs, wool, other than rag | 100.0 | 241.9 | 239.7 | 262.3 |
| Cement | 100.0 | 206.5 | 208.1 | 259.4 |
| Woolen goods | 100.0 | 299.4 | 249.3 | 257.6 |
| Lace goods, cotton | 100.0 | 243.7 | 252.5 | 249.5 |
| Cotton goods | 100.0 | 323.7 | 236.6 | 241.4 |
| Lumber and timber products | 100.0 | 237.0 | 164.1 | 236.7 |
| Knit goods | 100.0 | 224.7 | 223.2 | 233.9 |
| Cordage and twine | 100.0 | 293.0 | 235.6 | 226.7 |
| Linoleum and asphalted-felt-base floor coverings | 100.0 | 186.9 | 195.1 | 226.4 |
| Sugar, beet | 100.0 | 298.8 | 58.0 | 224.3 |
| Cars, steam and electric railroad, not built in railroad repair shops | 100.0 | 266.6 | 331.1 | 217.3 |
| Wool shoddy | 100.0 | 251.4 | 172.5 | 214.5 |
| Canning and preserving: fish, crabs, shrimps, oysters, and clams | 100.0 | 182.5 | 207.5 | 211.6 |
| Clay products (other than pottery) and non-clay refractories | 100.0 | 201.7 | 189.2 | 199.4 |
| Soap | 100.0 | 157.6 | 200.7 | 198.9 |
| Hats, fur-felt | 100.0 | 202.7 | 146.3 | 195.9 |
| Iron and steel: blast furnaces | 100.0 | 250.7 | 153.1 | 195.1 |
| Canning and preserving: fruits and vegetables; pickles, jellies, preserves, and sauces | 100.0 | 197.8 | 182.9 | 194.1 |
| Paper and wood pulp | 100.0 | 225.5 | 183.7 | 190.8 |
| Butter and cheese | 100.0 | 190.5 | 171.9 | 189.2 |
| Salt | 100.0 | 194.7 | 212.0 | 182.1 |
| Iron and steel: steel works and rolling mills | 100.0 | 240.2 | 165.7 | 181.8 |
| Wire, drawn from purchased bars or rods | 100.0 | 221.5 | 262.1 | 179.0 |
| Oil, cake, and meal, cottonseed | 100.0 | 332.6 | 119.3 | 177.2 |
| Sand-lime brick | 100.0 | 190.8 | 193.5 | 177.0 |
| Sugar, cane, not including products of refineries | 100.0 | 250.6 | 115.6 | 174.1 |

## TABLE 101—Continued

| Industry | Index numbers of cost of fabrication, plus profits, per unit of profit | | | |
|---|---|---|---|---|
| | 1914 | 1919 | 1921 | 1923 |
| Paints and varnishes.................... | 100.0 | 169.5 | 168.4 | 171.7 |
| Silk manufactures ...................... | 100.0 | 206.0 | 185.1 | 166.1 |
| Rice cleaning and polishing............. | 100.0 | 345.6 | 171.0 | 164.8 |
| Explosives ............................ | 100.0 | 233.2 | 204.9 | 164.0 |
| Petroleum refining ..................... | 100.0 | 277.8 | 210.0 | 163.7 |
| Turpentine and rosin.................... | 100.0 | 369.2 | 118.6 | 161.0 |
| Ice, manufactured ..................... | 100.0 | 161.0 | 163.3 | 156.6 |
| Slaughtering and meat packing, wholesale.. | 100.0 | 167.3 | 145.2 | 141.9 |
| Fertilizers ............................ | 100.0 | 231.5 | 114.1 | 139.8 |
| Flour and other grain-mill products....... | 100.0 | 192.3 | 164.5 | 136.1 |
| Sugar refining, cane.................... | 100.0 | 256.4 | 139.9 | 132.3 |
| Musical instruments: pianos............. | 100.0 | 121.7 | 124.2 | 122.3 |
| Condensed and evaporated milk........... | 100.0 | 181.0 | 173.6 | 122.1 |
| Gas, manufactured, illuminating and heating | 100.0 | 89.6 | 113.4 | 118.4 |
| Motorcycles, bicycles, and parts.......... | 100.0 | 161.3 | 166.6 | 118.1 |
| Rubber products ....................... | 100.0 | 137.6 | 108.5 | 89.8 |
| Motor vehicles, including bodies and parts.. | 100.0 | 100.9 | 90.1 | 83.2 |
| Average [a] ............................ | 100.0 | 230.2 | 175.9 | 187.6 |

[a] An arithmetic average of the central items of a weighted frequency distribution, with weights based on 'value added', averaged for the base year and the given year. The central one-fifth of the items, by weight, were included in computing the average.

The weighted averages at the foot of each of these tables, averages designed to measure changes in typical manufacturing industries, without giving excessive weight to the fortunes of exceptionally circumstanced industries, differ from the index numbers of costs which appear in Table 99. Material costs, per unit of product, are shown as somewhat lower in 1919, somewhat higher in 1923, than appears from the first set of index numbers. Fabrication costs appear to have been much higher in 1919 for the average manufacturing industry than the weighted index of all industries suggests. For the two later census years the differences are not great.

Changes in two major elements of fabrication costs—labor costs and a composite which includes overhead, salaries and profits—may be traced separately. Index numbers of these costs, which are given in the following table, are plotted in Figure 41.

Both elements of fabrication costs advanced rapidly between 1914 and 1919, but they diverged markedly during the two years following. In 1921 labor costs, per unit of product, were approxi-

## TABLE 102

Changes in Total Fabrication Costs, Labor Costs and Overhead Costs plus Profits, 1914-1923

Manufacturing Industries of the United States

(All measurements relate to changes per unit of product)

| (1) | (2) | (3) | (4) | (5) | (6) | (7) |
|---|---|---|---|---|---|---|
| | In current dollars | | | In dollars of constant purchasing power | | |
| Year | Fabrication costs, plus profits | Labor costs | Overhead costs plus profits | Fabrication costs, plus profits | Labor costs | Overhead costs plus profits |
| 1914 | 100.0 | 100.0 | 100.0 | 100.0 | 100.0 | 100.0 |
| 1919 | 214.2 | 210.8 | 216.4 | 105.2 | 103.6 | 106.3 |
| 1921 | 174.9 | 197.9 | 158.4 | 122.0 | 138.1 | 110.5 |
| 1923 | 181.2 | 186.9 | 176.9 | 122.7 | 126.5 | 119.8 |

mately 98 per cent higher than in 1914, while overhead costs plus profits, per unit of product, were only 58 per cent higher. The subsequent revival brought some reduction in labor costs but carried the composite of overhead costs and profits to a much higher level.

Here, again, index numbers expressed in dollars of constant purchasing power are perhaps more illuminating. In using these, we may think of the community as paying in goods for the services of the different productive agents. Between 1914 and 1919, there was an advance of about 5 per cent in the cost of the services of fabricating agents. The subsequent recession, in which wages suffered a smaller decline than those recorded for most other prices, brought a sharp increase in real labor costs, per unit of product. In 1921, these costs were 38 per cent above the 1914 level. The reduction in labor costs that followed the business advance from 1921 to 1923 left these costs still high, more than 26 per cent above the 1914 standard.[1]

Overhead costs and profits show no such great advance as labor costs between 1914 and 1921. There was a substantial increase,

---

[1] When we speak of the community as paying in goods for the services of fabricating agents, we are referring to goods as priced in wholesale markets. Changes in the real rewards of labor are not here in question, for labor's income is not spent in wholesale markets. Since manufactured goods are first disposed of in wholesale markets, however, it seems proper to measure changes in these various costs in terms of purchasing power at wholesale.

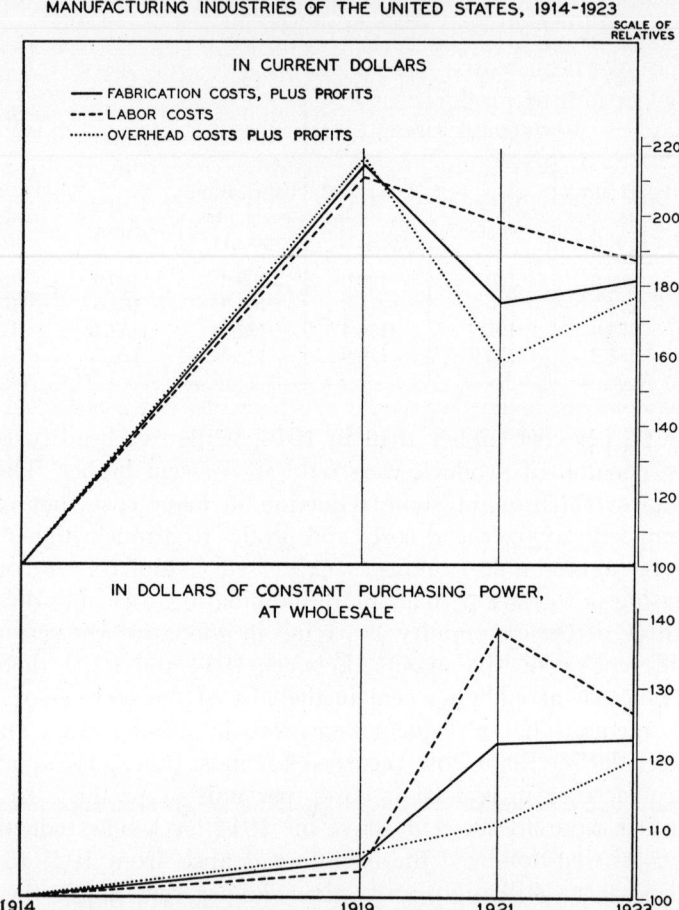

FIGURE 41

CHANGES IN AVERAGE FABRICATION COSTS, LABOR COSTS AND OVERHEAD COSTS PLUS PROFITS, PER UNIT OF PRODUCT

MANUFACTURING INDUSTRIES OF THE UNITED STATES, 1914-1923

however, carrying overhead costs plus profits in 1921 to a level 10 per cent higher, in terms of dollars of constant purchasing power, than in 1914. Recovery in 1922 and 1923 advanced these costs (including profits) to a level about 20 per cent above that of 1914.[1]

[1] The advance in 'overhead costs plus profits' between 1914 and 1921 was due, in part, to increasing taxes during this period. Data published by the Bureau of the Census, supplemented by estimates based on compilations of the Bureau of

It is unfortunate that we cannot separate overhead costs and profits, for it is certain that during some of this period these two elements moved in different directions. In 1921 overhead costs proper were relatively high, per unit of product, while profits, per unit, were low. Increasing production from 1921 to 1923 probably lowered overhead costs, per unit, but brought distinctly higher profits, per unit of product.

It is of interest to compare the changes in production costs which were occurring during the fifteen years from 1899 to 1914 with those which took place from 1914 to 1923. During the decade and a half which preceded the war there was a substantial decline in both elements of fabrication costs, as measured in dollars of constant purchasing power. The community was giving progressively less, in terms of goods at wholesale, for the contributions of labor

---

Internal Revenue, may be used in measuring changes in certain of the component elements of 'overhead costs plus profits'. The following percentages relate to all manufacturing industries in the United States.

| Item of cost | Percentage of total 'overhead cost plus profits' | | | |
|---|---|---|---|---|
| | 1914 | 1919 | 1921 | 1923 |
| Taxes, total | 7.6 | 14.3 | 9.2 | 7.5 |
| Salaries | 22.0 | 19.9 | 25.3 | 18.9 |
| Payments for contract work | 3.4 | 3.2 | 4.5 | 4.2 |
| Elements other than taxes, salaries and contract work | 67.0 | 62.6 | 61.0 | 69.4 |
| Overhead costs plus profits, total | 100.0 | 100.0 | 100.0 | 100.0 |

Payments for contract work constituted a fairly constant proportion of the total during this period. Salaries constituted a smaller proportion of all overhead costs plus profits during the prosperous years 1919 and 1923 than during the depressed years 1914 and 1921. The advance of this item in 1921 is particularly marked. Taxes almost doubled in relative importance between 1914 and 1919, and remained relatively high in 1921.

The index of overhead costs plus profits, per unit of product, reflects, of course, the increase in tax payments. If taxes be excluded from overhead costs plus profits, the index numbers in column (4) of Table 102 will be modified somewhat. A corrected index follows. This relates to costs in current dollars.

| Year | Overhead costs plus profits per unit of product, manufacturing industries (excluding all taxes) |
|---|---|
| 1914 | 100 |
| 1919 | 201 |
| 1921 | 156 |
| 1923 | 177 |

We are not dealing with accurately measurable quantities here, but the differences between the original and the revised measurements indicate the relative importance of war-time and post-war taxes, as factors in overhead costs. The elimination of taxes reduces the 1919 index of overhead costs plus profits, per unit of product, from 216 to 201. In subsequent years the differences between the original and the corrected measurements are slight.

and of management to each unit of manufactured goods. In 1914 real labor costs, per unit of product, were 16 per cent below the 1899 level, while the composite of overhead costs and profits was 22 per cent below that level. The steady cheapening of manufactured goods which was a characteristic tendency of the pre-war period was due, of course, to the declining unit cost of fabrication. We had come to think of this steady cheapening of manufactured goods as an invariable accompaniment of an increasing volume of fabrication and of improving technical methods. One of the most striking results of the changes which came with the economic revolution occurring between 1914 and 1923 was the reversal of this persistent pre-war tendency. The ability of fabricating agents to resist liquidation, their greater flexibility in the face of changed market conditions, and the weakness of raw material producers in the face of liquidation were factors in this reversal. This change involved a momentous shift in purchasing power, a major modification of the relations among important elements of our economic structure. It is a fact of very considerable importance that this change occurred and that, as a result, we entered upon the period of post-war expansion with manufacturing labor, management and ownership in such strong strategic positions.

§ *Labor costs and other fabrication costs, individual industries.*—Turning from the average changes in labor and overhead costs defined by the above index numbers to the detailed figures for individual industries, we again find wide differences. Labor costs and overhead costs, per unit of product, advanced sharply for certain industries and but slightly, or not at all, for others. The actual changes in all their diversity are shown by the measurements in the two following tables.

TABLE 103

CHANGES IN LABOR COSTS, MANUFACTURING INDUSTRIES OF THE UNITED STATES, 1914-1923

Index Numbers for 52 Industries

| Industry | Index numbers of labor costs, per unit of product | | | |
| --- | --- | --- | --- | --- |
| | 1914 | 1919 | 1921 | 1923 |
| Oilcloth | 100.0 | 317.8 | 281.6 | 286.9 |
| Hats, wool-felt | 100.0 | 166.2 | 255.9 | 267.5 |
| Worsted goods | 100.0 | 222.3 | 241.6 | 243.1 |
| Jute and linen goods | 100.0 | 235.2 | 277.5 | 240.4 |

## TABLE 103—Continued

| Industry | Index numbers of labor costs, per unit of product | | | |
|---|---|---|---|---|
| | 1914 | 1919 | 1921 | 1923 |
| Cast-iron pipe | 100.0 | 296.7 | 239.4 | 234.0 |
| Lime | 100.0 | 224.1 | 266.4 | 233.2 |
| Woolen goods | 100.0 | 225.0 | 235.0 | 229.3 |
| Cordage and twine | 100.0 | 227.8 | 243.7 | 229.0 |
| Carpets and rugs, wool, other than rag | 100.0 | 190.4 | 233.5 | 227.7 |
| Musical instruments: organs | 100.0 | 134.3 | 206.3 | 227.4 |
| Lumber and timber products | 100.0 | 232.8 | 181.3 | 226.0 |
| Cars, steam and electric railroad, not built in railroad repair shops | 100.0 | 177.4 | 277.8 | 224.0 |
| Cement | 100.0 | 195.9 | 193.5 | 215.9 |
| Wood distillation and charcoal manufacture | 100.0 | 274.9 | 227.7 | 213.4 |
| Cotton goods | 100.0 | 227.6 | 228.1 | 212.9 |
| Canning and preserving: fish, crabs, shrimps, oysters, and clams | 100.0 | 205.2 | 244.1 | 208.8 |
| Lace goods, cotton | 100.0 | 197.3 | 232.2 | 207.0 |
| Knit goods | 100.0 | 184.7 | 202.5 | 203.0 |
| Wire, drawn from purchased bars or rods | 100.0 | 252.1 | 289.1 | 197.3 |
| Wool shoddy | 100.0 | 210.4 | 212.2 | 196.5 |
| Slaughtering and meat packing, wholesale | 100.0 | 256.1 | 226.0 | 196.5 |
| Soap | 100.0 | 206.9 | 204.0 | 194.5 |
| Paper and wood pulp | 100.0 | 213.2 | 235.4 | 193.5 |
| Sugar refining, cane | 100.0 | 273.6 | 220.2 | 193.4 |
| Salt | 100.0 | 171.3 | 232.7 | 187.0 |
| Paints and varnishes | 100.0 | 186.4 | 214.3 | 185.9 |
| Clay products (other than pottery) and non-clay refractories | 100.0 | 190.9 | 189.3 | 183.4 |
| Iron and steel: steel works and rolling mills | 100.0 | 232.5 | 196.9 | 182.0 |
| Flour and other grain-mill products | 100.0 | 199.7 | 197.5 | 180.7 |
| Fertilizers | 100.0 | 262.8 | 222.4 | 178.7 |
| Oil, cake, and meal, cottonseed | 100.0 | 292.4 | 241.5 | 178.2 |
| Sugar, cane, not including products of refineries | 100.0 | 269.4 | 161.1 | 176.8 |
| Turpentine and rosin | 100.0 | 294.4 | 121.4 | 174.7 |
| Hats, fur-felt | 100.0 | 158.0 | 148.9 | 174.7 |
| Silk manufactures | 100.0 | 172.9 | 198.7 | 173.7 |
| Sand-lime brick | 100.0 | 177.8 | 195.9 | 170.6 |
| Petroleum refining | 100.0 | 237.6 | 228.0 | 169.0 |
| Coke, not including gas-house coke | 100.0 | 209.4 | 170.7 | 164.1 |
| Canning and preserving: fruits and vegetables; pickles, jellies, preserves, and sauces | 100.0 | 187.0 | 167.1 | 163.0 |
| Motorcycles, bicycles, and parts | 100.0 | 181.0 | 154.9 | 158.2 |
| Sugar, beet | 100.0 | 245.6 | 244.7 | 153.2 |
| Butter and cheese | 100.0 | 160.8 | 163.9 | 150.8 |
| Iron and steel: blast furnaces | 100.0 | 247.6 | 178.4 | 148.8 |
| Explosives | 100.0 | 220.9 | 167.4 | 148.3 |

## TABLE 103—Continued

| Industry | Index numbers of labor costs, per unit of product | | | |
|---|---|---|---|---|
| | 1914 | 1919 | 1921 | 1923 |
| Gas, manufactured, illuminating and heating | 100.0 | 145.9 | 155.6 | 146.5 |
| Musical instruments: pianos | 100.0 | 126.1 | 143.8 | 141.3 |
| Linoleum and asphalted-felt-base floor coverings | 100.0 | 133.2 | 149.1 | 141.0 |
| Condensed and evaporated milk | 100.0 | 166.7 | 148.8 | 137.0 |
| Ice, manufactured | 100.0 | 168.0 | 143.6 | 135.0 |
| Rice cleaning and polishing | 100.0 | 186.7 | 155.6 | 124.3 |
| Rubber products | 100.0 | 153.1 | 128.1 | 111.7 |
| Motor vehicles, including bodies and parts | 100.0 | 118.1 | 102.8 | 101.9 |
| Average [a] | 100.0 | 225.1 | 205.1 | 188.6 |

[a] An arithmetic average of the central items of a weighted frequency distribution, with weights based on wages, averaged for the base year and the given year. The central one-fifth of the items, by weight, were included in computing the average.

## TABLE 104
Changes in Overhead Costs plus Profits, Manufacturing Industries of the United States, 1914-1923
Index Numbers for 52 Industries

| Industry | Index numbers of overhead costs plus profits, per unit of product | | | |
|---|---|---|---|---|
| | 1914 | 1919 | 1921 | 1923 |
| Jute and linen goods | 100.0 | 688.2 | 468.6 | 554.4 |
| Hats, wool-felt | 100.0 | 333.2 | 370.0 | 487.8 |
| Cast-iron pipe | 100.0 | 546.0 | 354.4 | 470.2 |
| Musical instruments: organs | 100.0 | 146.4 | 234.3 | 431.3 |
| Oilcloth | 100.0 | 578.0 | 456.3 | 429.0 |
| Coke, not including gas-house coke | 100.0 | 222.6 | 185.0 | 352.6 |
| Wood distillation and charcoal manufacture | 100.0 | 309.7 | 102.7 | 333.3 |
| Worsted goods | 100.0 | 417.4 | 360.8 | 318.9 |
| Carpets and rugs, wool, other than rag | 100.0 | 304.5 | 247.2 | 304.4 |
| Lime | 100.0 | 230.0 | 239.1 | 303.9 |
| Woolen goods | 100.0 | 412.3 | 271.0 | 300.6 |
| Lace goods, cotton | 100.0 | 283.2 | 269.8 | 285.8 |
| Linoleum and asphalted-felt-base floor coverings | 100.0 | 224.2 | 226.9 | 285.5 |
| Cement | 100.0 | 212.6 | 216.5 | 284.3 |
| Cotton goods | 100.0 | 465.8 | 249.3 | 283.6 |
| Knit goods | 100.0 | 270.2 | 246.7 | 269.1 |
| Sugar, beet | 100.0 | 322.9 | —[a] | 256.5 |
| Lumber and timber products | 100.0 | 242.0 | 143.9 | 249.4 |

## TABLE 104—Continued

| Industry | Index numbers of overhead costs plus profits, per unit of product | | | |
|---|---|---|---|---|
| | 1914 | 1919 | 1921 | 1923 |
| Iron and steel: blast furnaces............. | 100.0 | 253.0 | 134.0 | 229.8 |
| Wool shoddy ............................ | 100.0 | 283.5 | 141.4 | 228.7 |
| Hats, fur-felt ........................... | 100.0 | 267.5 | 142.5 | 226.7 |
| Cordage and twine....................... | 100.0 | 342.8 | 229.5 | 224.9 |
| Clay products (other than pottery) and non-clay refractories ................... | 100.0 | 217.0 | 189.2 | 222.0 |
| Canning and preserving: fish, crabs, shrimps, oysters, and clams............. | 100.0 | 171.7 | 190.2 | 212.9 |
| Butter and cheese........................ | 100.0 | 205.6 | 176.0 | 208.7 |
| Canning and preserving: fruits and vegetables; pickles, jellies, preserves, and sauces | 100.0 | 202.7 | 190.1 | 208.4 |
| Cars, steam and electric railroad, not built in railroad repair shops.................. | 100.0 | 438.0 | 433.2 | 204.6 |
| Soap ................................... | 100.0 | 144.8 | 199.8 | 200.1 |
| Paper and wood pulp..................... | 100.0 | 235.4 | 141.7 | 188.5 |
| Sand-lime brick ......................... | 100.0 | 203.6 | 191.2 | 183.2 |
| Iron and steel: steel works and rolling mills | 100.0 | 250.8 | 123.7 | 181.5 |
| Rice cleaning and polishing............... | 100.0 | 403.3 | 176.5 | 179.5 |
| Salt .................................... | 100.0 | 209.8 | 199.0 | 179.1 |
| Oil, cake, and meal, cottonseed............ | 100.0 | 347.7 | 73.5 | 176.9 |
| Sugar, cane, not including products of refineries ............................... | 100.0 | 243.6 | 98.4 | 173.0 |
| Explosives .............................. | 100.0 | 238.2 | 219.8 | 170.3 |
| Paints and varnishes ..................... | 100.0 | 165.9 | 158.5 | 168.7 |
| Ice, manufactured ....................... | 100.0 | 157.3 | 173.7 | 168.0 |
| Wire, drawn from purchased bars or rods. | 100.0 | 198.0 | 241.5 | 165.0 |
| Petroleum refining ...................... | 100.0 | 292.8 | 203.2 | 161.7 |
| Silk manufactures ....................... | 100.0 | 230.9 | 174.8 | 160.4 |
| Turpentine and rosin..................... | 100.0 | 458.1 | 115.2 | 144.6 |
| Fertilizers .............................. | 100.0 | 222.0 | 81.4 | 128.1 |
| Flour and other grain-mill products....... | 100.0 | 190.5 | 156.6 | 125.4 |
| Slaughtering and meat packing, wholesale.. | 100.0 | 130.1 | 111.4 | 119.1 |
| Condensed and evaporated milk........... | 100.0 | 186.3 | 182.9 | 116.5 |
| Gas, manufactured, illuminating and heating | 100.0 | 75.3 | 103.8 | 112.0 |
| Musical instruments: pianos .............. | 100.0 | 117.8 | 107.0 | 105.8 |
| Sugar refining, cane...................... | 100.0 | 248.7 | 104.0 | 105.0 |
| Motorcycles, bicycles, and parts........... | 100.0 | 147.1 | 175.1 | 89.1 |
| Rubber products ........................ | 100.0 | 130.2 | 99.2 | 79.5 |
| Motor vehicles, including bodies and parts. | 100.0 | 90.8 | 82.6 | 72.4 |
| Average *b* ............................. | 100.0 | 235.8 | 164.8 | 187.5 |

*a* 'Value added', less wages, was a negative quantity for this industry in 1921.
*b* An arithmetic average of the central items of a weighted frequency distribution, with weights based on overhead costs plus profits, averaged for the base year and the given year. The central one-fifth of the items, by weight, were included in computing the average.

## Summary of Price Changes, 1913-1922

The period under review ends in 1922 with the level of wholesale prices approximately 40 per cent above that prevailing in 1913. But all price elements did not rise in the same degree, as we have seen. These inequalities may be most effectively described if we measure the degree of change in purchasing power, or in command over goods in general, at wholesale, among the several commodity groups.

Raw materials lost approximately 10 per cent in purchasing power, per unit, between 1913 and 1922, while the average unit of manufactured goods gained 4 per cent. (The index of selling prices of manufactured goods derived from census data reveals an even greater advance in the per-unit purchasing power of manufactured goods.)

Raw products of American farms lost 8 per cent in purchasing power per unit during this period; raw non-farm products lost 14 per cent. Processed products of American farms gained 2 per cent, while processed non-farm products gained over 6 per cent in purchasing power, per unit.

Foods lost approximately 9 per cent in purchasing power per unit, while non-foods gained correspondingly. (The gain was restricted to processed non-foods.)

Perhaps more important, with reference to the possibilities of profit on the part of manufacturers, were the changes in the relations of producers' and consumers' goods. Producers' goods experienced a drop of 3 per cent in their real value, per unit, while goods in shape for consumption became some 4 per cent more expensive, in terms of commodities in general. Those producers' goods which were intended for ultimate human consumption or direct use lost 12 per cent in purchasing power, while consumers' goods which had passed through processes of fabrication gained 4 per cent.

The brief recital of these changes between 1913 and 1922 does not sufficiently emphasize their profound importance. At one extreme we have a sharp fall in the real value, per unit, of raw materials, at the other, a sharp rise in the real cost to consumers of the goods they require. The intervening margin, which defines the cost to the country at large of the contribution of agents of fabrication, was materially widened. These measurements indicate that raw material producers were receiving less, per unit of goods produced, while consumers were paying distinctly more, the net result being a great increase in the real cost of manufacturing. This is the more remarkable because it represents a reversal of the steady cheapening of the services of agents of fabrication which had prevailed before the war.

An analysis of the statistics compiled by the Census of Manufacturers bears out the conclusions of the preceding survey. The average selling price of products of manufacture, when expressed in dollars of constant purchasing power, was approximately 13 per cent higher in 1923 than in 1914.[1] Tracing constituent elements of selling price (expressed in dollars of constant purchasing power at wholesale) we find that in 1923 fabrication costs were 23 per cent higher, per unit, than in 1914. Labor costs were 27 per cent higher, and overhead costs plus profits were 20 per cent higher.

Making full allowance for the possible margin of error in each of these results, they may be accepted as furnishing confirmation and explanation of certain of the important shifts noted on earlier pages. The price changes which occurred between 1914 and 1923 had the effect of increasing substantially the cost to the consumer of the services of agents of fabrication. Which way the causal influences ran—whether prices of manufactured goods were high because fabrication costs were high, or whether the price advantage enjoyed by manufactured goods permitted the payment of high wages, high salaries, and high profits—we do not here inquire. We are concerned only with the final effect, which was to offset the cheapening tendency prevailing in earlier years and to add a considerable amount to the prices paid by buyers everywhere for the services rendered by fabricating agents.

[1] This figure is appreciably higher than that for 1922, which was secured in the analysis of annual data. The two measurements are, of course, independently derived, and different deflators have been used in reducing the original measurements to purchasing power form. We should emphasize, in particular, that the deflating index employed on the census materials is that of the Bureau of Labor Statistics and that the prices of manufactured goods which enter into that index are not those derived from the census data. The actual figure of 13 per cent which we have given above should not, therefore, be looked upon as possessing absolute accuracy; but there is no reason to doubt that the general movement of the prices of manufactured goods, with reference to all prices, was in the direction shown by this index.

The effects of these price changes were felt over a wide range of economic activity. An economy habituated to slowly changing relations among its elements was first stimulated by the sharp price advance occurring between 1915 and 1920 and then subjected to a violent shaking up which, in the course of less than two years, profoundly modified relations established through decades of slow growth. Looking backward now we can see that the shaking-up process did not prevent, and perhaps stimulated, a notable economic advance. There remains a question as to whether anything approaching complete adaptation to the new order was attained before or during this advance.

## CHAPTER VI

## *Changes in the Volume and Character of Production in the United States, 1922-1929*

A PERIOD of sustained prosperity opened in the United States after the major recession of 1920-21. This prosperity was interrupted by a recession of some magnitude in 1924, and by a relatively slight fall in 1927. The recovery from each of these checks was rapid. Not until the year 1929 was well on its way was there recorded a general and widespread decline in the volume and intensity of operations in the financial and industrial structure of the country at large. The period of post-war expansion, extending from 1922 to 1929, constitutes a relatively homogeneous era which is of particular economic interest. Certain of the tendencies and conditions characteristic of this era are to be reviewed in the present and following chapters.

In Chapter I, which deals with production tendencies during the years preceding the war, reference has been made to certain problems of general interest in following the trend of production in a given country. The rate of increase in the physical volume of production, the regularity of flow of the stream of production, the relative changes occurring in extractive and fabricating industries, in agricultural and non-agricultural industries, in industries producing consumption goods and in those producing articles of capital equipment—all these concern us in tracing the course of events during the period leading up to the 1929 recession. For it was an era unique in many ways, marked by conditions widely different from those prevailing during the period immediately preceding, and in certain important respects unlike those characteristic of the years before the war. Points of similarity and of difference between the pre-war and post-war periods will be emphasized as the discussion proceeds.

In following the changes occurring between 1922 and 1929 we must bear in mind the events of the war years and the conditions prevailing at the beginning of this post-war period. At the wartime peak, in 1917 and 1918, the volume of physical production, excluding products of the construction industries, stood some 28 per cent above the 1913 level. After a decline in 1919, output stood again in 1920 at a level close to that of the war years. The drop in 1921 carried production almost down to the 1913 average. Much of this loss had been made up by 1922; in that year the volume of production had increased to a level approximately 24 per cent above the 1913 figure.

If we go beyond the averages to certain of the details, we find that in 1922 agricultural production was about 23 per cent above the 1913 level, mineral production some 2 per cent above, and manufacturing production about 29 per cent above. The standing of various other classes of goods has been indicated in the preceding chapter.

The volume of construction followed a quite different course. Dropping in 1914 and 1915 somewhat below the 1913 level, there was an advance in 1916 to a volume about 8 per cent above that base. Thereafter there was a decline, interrupted only in 1919, until in 1920 the volume of construction was only 47 per cent of that in 1913. There was a substantial increase in 1921, and in 1922 (the year from which recent movements are traced) the volume of construction was about 35 per cent greater than in 1913. In seven of the nine years which had elapsed since 1913, however, the amount of construction work done had been below that of the base year. With a rapidly expanding population this meant a large accumulated shortage, a shortage which placed its impress upon the events of the following decade.

The measurements of production and other changes occurring in the United States between 1922 and 1929 relate, as has been noted, to a period of expansion. This period opens with business reviving from relatively deep depression; it ends in a year of high prosperity. In a very real sense it constitutes a single phase of economic expansion, rather than a rounded record of the gamut of business experience. The pre-war period surveyed in earlier chapters opened in prosperity and ended with a year of declining activity. It was marked, too, by a sharp business break in 1907-08, exceeding in magnitude any of the interruptions to expansion that occurred between 1922 and 1929. In comparing the developments of these two periods no assumption of identity of conditions can be made. Yet the comparison is significant, for the earlier period provides standards of reference to employ in measuring and appraising the events that led up to the recession of 1929. Such standards are particularly desirable in tracing changes in the physical volume of production.

### CHANGES IN THE VOLUME OF PRODUCTION, 1922-1929
### GENERAL MEASUREMENTS

Post-war production movements may be traced, first, in terms of movable goods (i.e., construction is excluded). The quantitative record follows.

TABLE 105

GROWTH OF PHYSICAL VOLUME OF PRODUCTION IN THE UNITED STATES, 1922-1929 [a]

| Year | Volume of production (excluding construction) | Year-to-year change in volume of production (per cent) |
|---|---|---|
| 1922 | 100 | — |
| 1923 | 112 | +12 |
| 1924 | 109 | − 3 |
| 1925 | 117 | + 7 |
| 1926 | 124 | + 6 |
| 1927 | 123 | − 1 |
| 1928 | 129 | + 5 |
| 1929 | 134 | + 4 |

Average annual rate of change (per cent) .......................... +3.8
Index of instability of growth ...... 2.1

[a] The process employed in the construction of these index numbers is similar to that used in compiling the pre-war measurements (see Appendix I). Annual index numbers of agricultural production and of the production of raw minerals have been combined with an annual index of manufacturing production (that of the Federal Reserve Board), adjusted to corrected biennial index numbers of manufacturing production based upon census records. In this correction and adjustment account has been taken of the output of non-standard commodities for which statistics of output in physical units are not generally available. (See pp. 39-43 for an explanation of the method of correction.)

These measurements, with corresponding population figures, are plotted in Figure 42.

## FIGURE 42
### GROWTH OF POPULATION AND OF PHYSICAL VOLUME OF PRODUCTION IN THE UNITED STATES, 1922-1929

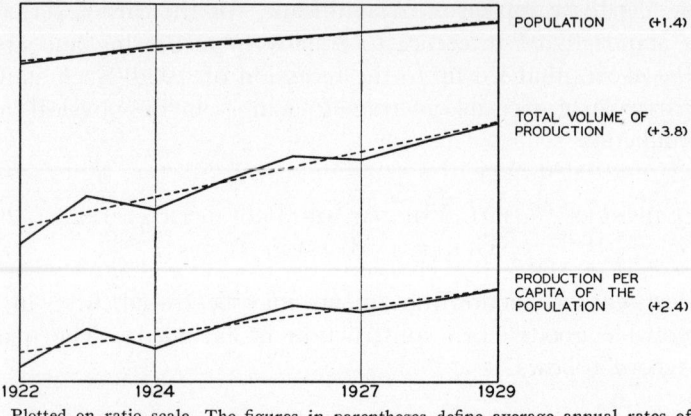

Plotted on ratio scale. The figures in parentheses define average annual rates of change (in percentage form).

Comparing with pre-war figures the rate of growth in production shown by these index numbers, and the corresponding rate of population increase, we have the following exhibit:

|  | Average annual rate of increase in: | | |
|---|---|---|---|
| Year | Volume of production (per cent) | Population (per cent) | Production per capita of population (per cent) |
| 1901-1913 | +3.1 | +2.0 | +1.1 |
| 1922-1929 | +3.8 | +1.4 | +2.4 |

Between 1922 and 1929 the aggregate output of movable goods in the United States increased 34 per cent—slightly more than one-third. The rate of increase in volume of output (3.8 per cent a year) was distinctly higher than the pre-war rate (3.1 per cent a year). The expansion of 1922-29 is clearly reflected in the comprehensive records of agricultural, mineral and manufacturing production which are summarized in Table 105.

This advance is the more impressive if account be taken of post-war retardation of the rate of growth of population. Prior to the war the physical volume of goods which might have been allocated yearly to each member of the population was increasing at a rate of 1.1 per cent a year. Between 1922 and 1929 the individual's 'share' in annual output (a purely hypothetical share, of course, since goods of all sorts are included, and since distribution is not equal) increased at a rate of 2.4 per cent a year. If we consider that the annual per capita increment, in these terms, is more than twice as great in the later period, the significance of the change is apparent. Viewed in another way, a doubling of the annual share theoretically available for distribution to every inhabitant of the country would have required 63 years, under pre-war conditions. Between 1922 and 1929 rates of population and production change were such that the doubling of the individual's portion would have required only 29 years.[1] Since the rate of advance in production was not maintained after 1929 these figures may appear fictitious, but it is a matter of considerable moment that conditions so full of promise for the future welfare of the population of this country prevailed during the years now under survey. We have not yet garnered all the fruits of that experience.

The index numbers of production given in Table 105 are based upon the output of raw agricultural and mineral products, and of manufactured goods of all types. Productive services rendered directly, and not embodied in goods, are necessarily excluded. There is reason to believe that 'production' of this non-material type was growing in relative importance during this period, but the degree of advance cannot be estimated with any accuracy.[2] The growth of construction during this period is also omitted from these records. This is a defect which may be corrected for the post-war years, for it is possible to approximate with reasonable accuracy changes in the volume of construction of various types. In a later section of the present chapter detailed figures on construction are

[1] These figures relate, of course, to pure statistical averages. No account is taken of systems of distribution, nor of the relative importance of capital goods and consumption goods in the aggregate output.

[2] That the output of service industries increased more rapidly than that of industries producing physical commodities is indicated by figures of the Census of Occupations, 1930. In 1920 the production of physical commodities (agriculture, forestry, fishing, extraction of minerals, manufacturing and mechanical industries) absorbed approximately 65 per cent of all persons gainfully employed in the United States. (Persons engaged in clerical occupations, who cannot readily be classified either under service or non-service industries, have been excluded from both groups, as well as from the total, in the computation of these percentages. See footnote, p. 419.) In 1930 the corresponding figure was 58 per cent. The service industries (transportation, trade and finance, public and professional service, and domestic and personal service) absorbed 35 per cent in 1920 and 42 per cent in 1930. The classifications are rough, but the trend is unmistakable.

presented. At this point we consider only the course of total production, including construction of all sorts.

TABLE 106

INDEX NUMBERS OF PRODUCTION AND CONSTRUCTION IN THE UNITED STATES, 1922-1929

| (1) Year | (2) Production of movable goods [a] | (3) Volume of construction [b] | (4) Total production and construction [c] |
|---|---|---|---|
| 1922 | 100 | 100 | 100 |
| 1923 | 112 | 93 | 110 |
| 1924 | 109 | 103 | 109 |
| 1925 | 117 | 136 | 119 |
| 1926 | 124 | 143 | 126 |
| 1927 | 123 | 143 | 125 |
| 1928 | 129 | 149 | 131 |
| 1929 | 134 | 131 | 134 |
| Average annual rate of change (per cent)... | +3.8 | +6.1 | +4.1 |
| Index of instability of growth | 2.1 | 8.9 | 2.1 |

[a] From Table 105.

[b] Based on the F. W. Dodge Corporation estimates for the entire United States, with correction for changes in construction costs. See pp. 266-269.

[c] Weighted average of columns (2) and (3). Weights are based upon the approximate total value of physical production and upon an estimate (50 per cent of total contracts awarded) of 'value added' in construction, in 1923 and 1925.

The index numbers in column (4) represent our best estimate of the actual course of physical production, including construction, in the United States between 1922 and 1929. It indicates a remarkably steady growth. Checks to the advance were felt in 1924 and 1927, but these brought no appreciable decline in aggregate physical output. The effect of the introduction of construction is to yield a somewhat higher average annual rate of increase (4.1 per cent a year, as against 3.8 per cent for the production index alone).

§ *On the stability of productive processes, 1922-1929.*—Of equal significance with changes in aggregate and per capita production is the stability of flow of the stream of physical goods. From 1901 to 1913, as we have seen, the fluctuations in the aggregate output of physical goods averaged 3.7 per cent per year.[1] These variations in the stream

[1] This index defines the degree of departure from a constant rate of change. It is not absolute variation from year to year which is measured, but deviations from constancy of growth.

of production are to be contrasted with fluctuations in population growth, which were estimated to average 0.3 per cent per year. Oscillations in the growth of physical production materially exceeded oscillations in population growth. The post-war record now being studied extends over a somewhat shorter period, and one marked by no recession as severe as that of 1907-08. Yet the comparison is significant, in any effort to summarize the characteristics of the eight years between 1922 and 1929. This period fell between two major economic storms (the recession of 1920-21 and that which began in 1929) and the working of the economic system during these years is of more than average interest. How stable and regular were economic processes during this era?

The index of aggregate production shows variations from a constant rate of growth averaging 2.1 per cent a year between 1922 and 1929, as contrasted with variations of 3.7 per cent a year for the pre-war period. In so far as our data are comparable,[1] these figures indicate a decrease of some 43 per cent in the amplitude of oscillations of total production. The greater stability of the flow of physical goods in the eight years from 1922 to 1929 is clearly revealed in the charts on which the different index numbers of production are plotted. (See Figures 1 and 42.) Instability of population growth during the recent period is measured by an index of 0.3, which is equal to the corresponding pre-war figure.[2]

The stability of processes of production is not capable of definition solely in terms of aggregate production. The output of constituent elements may be highly variable, while the total stream shows but slight variations. From many points of view the behavior of individual elements may be more significant than the behavior of the aggregate. For the post-war period we have measures of instability relating to 80 production series. The weighted mean of these measurements indicates an average annual fluctuation (i.e., departure from constancy of

[1] The stability of an index number of the type cited above is in part dependent upon the number of series included. When the fluctuations of economic series do not agree perfectly in timing, their movements tend to offset one another, when averaged, and this offsetting influence is the greater the larger the number of series included.

For both the pre-war and post-war periods the series relating to the production of raw materials represent practically the total production of these goods. The number of series in the post-war sample is somewhat greater than in the earlier period, but the additional commodities are chiefly minor agricultural products. For manufactures the basic samples are more comprehensive in the post-war period, but in the process of adjustment to the corrected census index numbers an attempt was made in both periods to approximate the relative stability of aggregate manufacturing production. Under these conditions there is no reason for believing that the greater stability of the index numbers for the post-war period is due to the offsetting influence of the larger number of series included in the sample.

[2] Inter-censal population estimates are based upon less satisfactory materials for the pre-war than for the post-war years.

growth) in the output of individual commodities of 6.4 per cent.[1] This may be taken as a measure of the degree of regularity of change among basic productive processes during an era of general prosperity.

For the period 1901-1913 the average of the indexes of instability relating to 59 production series was 8.2 per cent. The data for the more recent period indicate that the growth of production was substantially more stable between 1922 and 1929 than it was between 1901 and 1913. If we may take the two averages to be comparable (they do not relate to precisely the same list of commodities), they would indicate that the instability of production growth was 22 per cent less between 1922 and 1929 than between 1901 and 1913.[2]

## Changes in the Character of Physical Production, 1922-1929

We turn now to the make-up of the total stream of production. Raw materials and manufactured goods, foods and non-foods, capital equipment and consumption goods—all these change in volume of production at varying rates, and in their differing rates of change are found clues to the direction in which an economy is moving.

[1] This figure relates, of course, to a single eight-year period of economic expansion, a period which terminated in a major recession. If the various series studied were extended into the recession, the measure of instability would be much greater. For our present purpose we are accepting the period 1922-1929 as a distinct economic entity.

[2] The individual measurements entering into the pre-war average have been given in Chapter I. Following are the indexes of instability of growth relating to the 80 production series studied for the period 1922-1929:

| Series relating to production of materials | Index of instability of growth | Series relating to processes of fabrication | Index of instability of growth |
|---|---|---|---|
| Sheep, total slaughter | 1.2 | Sheep, Federal inspected slaughter | 1.2 |
| Wool | 1.4 | Flour, wheat | 1.5 |
| Milk | 1.5 | Cigars | 1.6 |
| Gold | 2.4 | Newsprint consumption | 1.9 |
| Poultry products | 2.7 | Cigarettes | 2.0 |
| Sugar, domestic | 4.0 | Fuel oil | 2.4 |
| Petroleum, crude | 4.4 | Gasoline | 2.5 |
| Natural gas | 4.6 | Boots and shoes | 3.1 |
| Cement | 4.9 | Wood pulp, chemical | 3.2 |
| Silver | 5.3 | Book paper | 3.2 |
| Corn | 5.4 | Lubricating oil | 3.4 |
| Calves, total slaughter | 5.5 | Kerosene | 3.8 |
| Stone | 5.7 | Fine paper | 4.0 |
| Cattle, total slaughter | 5.8 | Newsprint production | 4.2 |
| Hay | 6.0 | Wool machinery activity | 4.6 |
| Wheat | 6.3 | Silk loom activity | 4.8 |
| Tobacco | 6.7 | Tires, pneumatic | 4.8 |
| Swine, total slaughter | 6.8 | Cotton consumption | 4.8 |
| Sand | 6.9 | Wool rug and loom activity | 4.9 |
| Bituminous coal | 7.3 | Cement | 4.9 |
| Lead, crude | 7.4 | Silk deliveries | 5.3 |

(*Footnote continued on following page*)

## Production of Raw Materials and of Manufactured Goods

Index numbers defining changes in the output of raw materials and of manufactured goods appear in Table 107, on the following page. These are shown graphically in Figure 43.

As in the pre-war period, the output of manufactured goods increased at a rate substantially higher than that at which the production of raw materials increased—at a rate of $+4.5$ per cent a year, as compared with $+2.5$ per cent for raw materials. Corresponding pre-war figures were $+3.9$ and $+2.2$ per cent. The difference between the two rates of change is greater in the later period.

Some reasons for the sharper advance in the output of manufactured goods have been suggested at an earlier point. The general group of raw materials includes many articles of food which are consumed in a raw or but slightly processed form, and the rate of increase in the output of these commodities would not be expected materially to exceed the rate of growth of population. The rapid increase in the proportion of processed goods in our export trade

*(Footnote continued from preceding page)*

| Series relating to production of materials | Index of instability of growth | Series relating to processes of frabrication | Index of instability of growth |
|---|---|---|---|
| Zinc, slab | 7.5 | Sugar meltings | 5.7 |
| Oats | 8.6 | Tin deliveries | 5.8 |
| Copper, mine production | 8.7 | Wood pulp, mechanical | 5.8 |
| Iron ore | 8.9 | Steel ingots | 6.1 |
| Potatoes | 9.1 | Lumber | 6.3 |
| Rice | 9.9 | Cattle, Federal inspected slaughter | 6.3 |
| Barley | 10.1 | Wool consumption | 6.4 |
| Apples | 13.8 | Plate glass | 6.4 |
| Anthracite coal | 13.9 | Upper leather | 6.7 |
| Oranges | 14.1 | Calves, Federal inspected slaughter | 6.7 |
| Cottonseed | 14.3 | Copper, blister | 7.3 |
| Cotton | 14.3 | Lead, crude | 7.4 |
| Peaches | 15.4 | Zinc, slab | 7.5 |
| Rye | 15.6 | Pig iron | 8.5 |
| Flaxseed | 23.4 | Common brick | 8.7 |
| | | Hogs, Federal inspected slaughter | 8.9 |
| | | Coke, total | 9.1 |
| | | Sole leather | 9.4 |
| | | Inner tubes | 9.5 |
| | | Flooring | 10.4 |
| | | Motor vehicles | 11.4 |
| | | Vessels built | 17.3 |
| | | Locomotives, railroad | 27.4 |

These 80 production series, with a few minor additions, are the components of the annual index numbers utilized in securing the final production estimates given in Table 105. Three series (relating to the production of cement, crude lead and slab zinc) are included both among the series measuring the output of raw materials and manufactured products.

Descriptions of these production series, with statements of sources, appear in Appendix V.

## TABLE 107

### Raw Materials and Manufactured Goods

Index Numbers of Physical Volume of Production in the United States, 1922-1929 [a]

| Year | Raw materials | Manufactured goods |
|---|---|---|
| 1922 | 100 | 100 |
| 1923 | 112 | 112 |
| 1924 | 115 | 106 |
| 1925 | 115 | 118 |
| 1926 | 122 | 125 |
| 1927 | 119 | 125 |
| 1928 | 122 | 132 |
| 1929 | 124 | 140 |
| Average annual rate of change (per cent) .............. | +2.5 | +4.5 |
| Index of instability of growth. | 2.5 | 2.4 |

[a] The index numbers of manufacturing production have been adjusted to take account of the increasing diversification of manufacturing industries. The procedure is similar to that employed for the pre-war years. Details are given in Appendix I.

## FIGURE 43

### GROWTH OF PHYSICAL VOLUME OF PRODUCTION IN THE UNITED STATES, 1922-1929

RAW MATERIALS AND MANUFACTURED GOODS

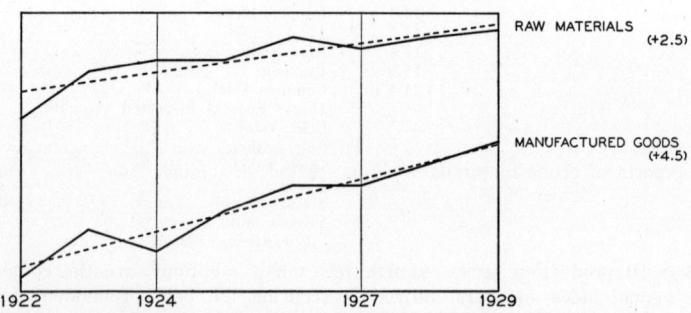

Plotted on ratio scale. The figures in parentheses define average annual rates of change (in percentage form).

has affected somewhat the character of domestic production.[1] Finally, the increased degree of fabrication of many classes of goods, and the performance outside the home of many operations formerly performed within the home, would also result in a more rapid increase in the output of manufactured goods. The records indicate that increasing fabrication, with a corresponding increase in the diversification of manufacturing production, has been a marked characteristic of the period 1922-1929.[2]

§ *Unrevised index numbers of physical production.*—The index numbers of manufacturing production shown in Table 105 were secured by a process of adjustment, designed to take account of the output of commodities generally excluded from index numbers of physical production. As was suggested on an earlier page, there are periods of expanding production and increasing variety of demand when index numbers based upon standard commodities, the output of which is subject to definite measurement, understate the true rate of production growth. At other times, of which the war years furnish an example, there is a decrease in the diversification of manufacturing output, and at such times the true rate of production increase may be less than is indicated by a study of standard commodities. The corrected index numbers previously presented necessarily lack the accuracy, in detail, of indexes based on the definitely measurable output of standard commodities, but there is no reason to doubt that they give a closer approximation to the actual course of production between 1922 and 1929. Unrevised index numbers, based directly upon physical quantities, are of interest, however. These are given in Table 108.

[1] Between 1922 and 1929 the aggregate values of exported goods in each of the major classes changed at the following average annual rates:

| | |
|---|---|
| Manufactured foodstuffs | —3.8 per cent |
| Crude foodstuffs | —3.5 " " |
| Crude materials | +0.9 " " |
| Semi-manufactures | +5.9 " " |
| Finished manufactures | +9.3 " " |

Exports of finished manufactures were increasing at a more rapid rate than during pre-war years (the rate between 1901 and 1913 was 7.6 per cent a year), while exports of crude materials were increasing at a much lower rate (the pre-war rate was 5.9 per cent). Manufactured foodstuffs constitute an exception to the general tendency for exports of manufactures to increase.

[2] The correction of the index of manufacturing production, to take account of the output of new types of goods, and of goods for which statistics of physical quantities are not available, involved a stepping-up of the apparent rate of increase of this index from 3.7 per cent to 3.9 per cent, for the period 1901-1913. For the period 1922-1929 this correction involved a stepping-up from a rate of increase of 3.7 per cent a year to a rate of 4.5 per cent a year. The increased margin in recent years is probably evidence of greater diversification, beyond the range of standard, readily-enumerated physical units.

## TABLE 108

### Index Numbers of the Physical Output of Movable Goods, 1922-1929

(These index numbers are based directly upon records of physical production.)

| Year | Production of raw materials | Manufacturing production [a] | Total production [b] |
|---|---|---|---|
| 1922 | 100 | 100 | 100 |
| 1923 | 112 | 116 | 115 |
| 1924 | 115 | 108 | 111 |
| 1925 | 115 | 121 | 120 |
| 1926 | 122 | 124 | 124 |
| 1927 | 119 | 122 | 121 |
| 1928 | 122 | 129 | 127 |
| 1929 | 124 | 137 | 133 |
| Average annual rate of change (per cent)... | +2.5 | +3.7 | +3.3 |

[a] Index constructed by the Federal Reserve Board from data relating to 23 industrial groups.

[b] This index was secured by combining the index numbers of manufacturing production and raw material production given in the two columns to the left. The index of production of raw materials is the same as that appearing in Table 107. The wide coverage of the sample of raw materials, the output of which is capable of direct enumeration, made it unnecessary to correct this index by the method employed for manufactured goods.

This index of total production shows a rate of increase of but 3.3 per cent a year, between 1922 and 1929, as compared with the figure of 3.8 per cent derived from the corrected records. For manufacturing production, the above rate of advance of 3.7 per cent per year falls materially below the corrected rate of 4.5 per cent. It is significant, however, that during the period 1923-1925 the index relating to standard commodities shows a higher level of production, with reference to 1922, than does the more comprehensive adjusted index. During the first phase of this post-war expansion somewhat greater emphasis appears to have been placed on the production of the staples which are currently enumerated in physical units. After 1925 there is evidence of increasing diversification, with greater emphasis on the output of the numerous non-standard commodities which come into popularity during a period of generally high purchasing power and of consumer optimism. The narrowing of demand, and the concentration of production on a smaller number of necessary commodities which characterized the war years, was reversed during this period. As a result, the true rate of gain in manufacturing production appears to have been somewhat higher than the rate shown by a study of those commodities amenable to direct statistical treatment.

The index numbers which are based directly upon statistics of physical output are fundamental records in any study of the course of production. That they clearly understate the true rate of increase between 1922 and 1929, and require correction, is shown in the detailed discussion of manufacturing production in the later pages of this chapter.

Other index numbers of manufacturing production, based upon different samples of commodities and different methods of construction, are marked by rates of growth fairly close to that of the uncorrected index given above. An extension of Day's annual index of manufactures [1] shows an increase of 3.3 per cent a year. An index of manufacturing production computed by Y. S. Leong, with sixty component series,[2] indicates an average annual advance of 3.5 per cent.

In the discussion of production changes during the years 1901-1913 some emphasis was placed on the divergence of tendencies prevailing in different industries. These divergences were distinctly more marked among fabricated goods than among raw materials. Similar differences are found for the period 1922-1929.

When we say that the total volume of physical production increased at a rate of 3.8 per cent a year we are speaking, of course, with reference to an aggregate. This aggregate is made up of a large number of elements growing, often, at widely discrepant rates. These elements may be grouped into broad classes, as in the present classification of raw and processed goods. We secure the most realistic picture of the course of production, however, when we view these elements in all the diversity of their separate movements. The original data relating to 80 production series (36 raw materials, 44 processed goods) are plotted in Figure 44. The divergence of rates of change is illustrated graphically in Figure 45.[3]

[1] Warren M. Persons, *Forecasting Business Cycles*, John Wiley and Sons, New York, 1931, p. 171.

[2] "Indexes of the Physical Volume Production of Producers' and Consumers' Goods," *Journal of the American Statistical Association*, XXVII, No. 177, March 1932, pp. 21-37.

[3] Following are measures of the rates of change in the individual series studied. (These series, it is to be noted, are not the precise ones entering into the production indexes cited above.)

| Series relating to production of materials | Average annual rate of change, 1922-1929 (per cent) | Series relating to processes of fabrication | Average annual rate of change, 1922-1929 (per cent) |
|---|---|---|---|
| Natural gas | +11.8 | Gasoline | +15.9 |
| Sand | +10.1 | Cigarettes | +11.2 |
| Barley | +10.0 | Tires, pneumatic | + 9.0 |
| Stone | + 8.6 | Plate glass | + 8.9 |
| Copper, mine production | + 7.3 | Silk deliveries | + 8.8 |
| Petroleum, crude | + 7.1 | Fuel oil | + 7.8 |
| Zinc, slab | + 5.4 | Copper, blister | + 7.5 |

(*Footnote continued on page 256*)

## FIGURE 44
CHANGES IN PHYSICAL VOLUME OF PRODUCTION OF INDIVIDUAL COMMODITIES IN THE UNITED STATES, 1922-1929
A- RAW MATERIALS

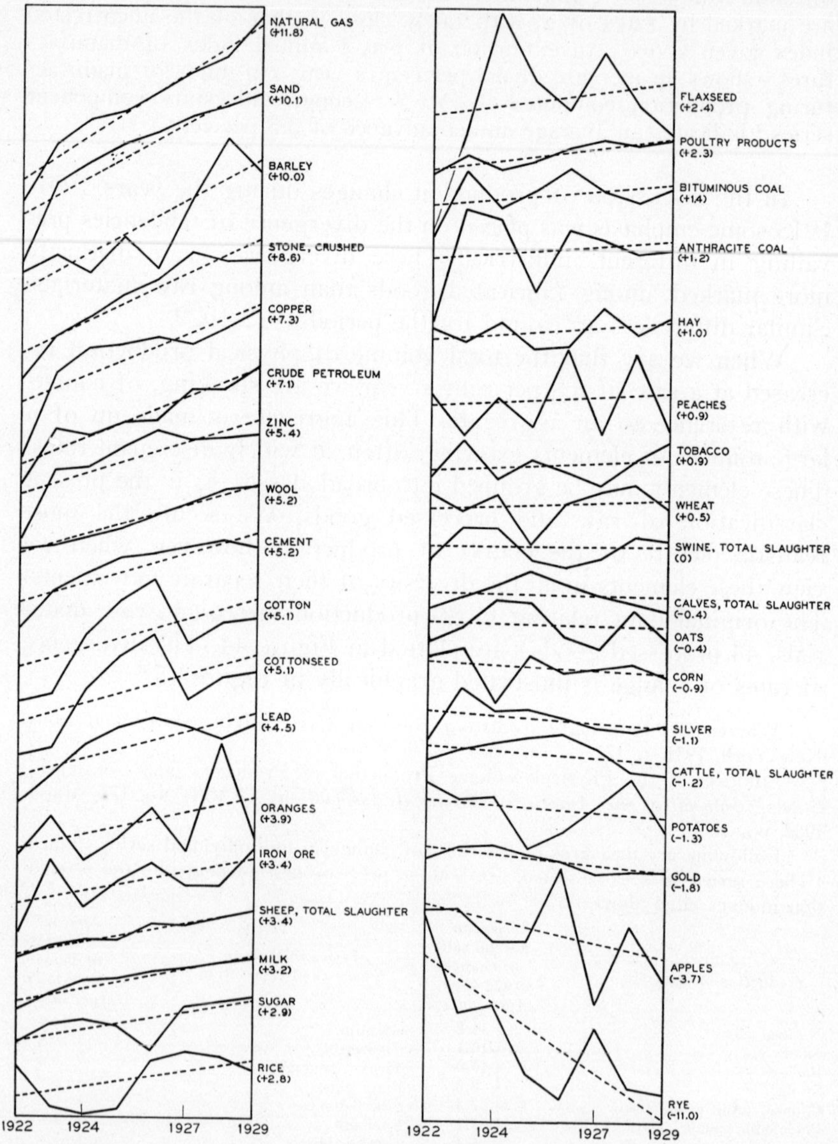

PLOTTED ON RATIO SCALE. THE FIGURES IN PARENTHESES DEFINE AVERAGE ANNUAL RATES OF CHANGE

## FIGURE 44 (CONT.)

### CHANGES IN PHYSICAL VOLUME OF PRODUCTION OF INDIVIDUAL COMMODITIES IN THE UNITED STATES, 1922-1929

#### B- PROCESSED GOODS

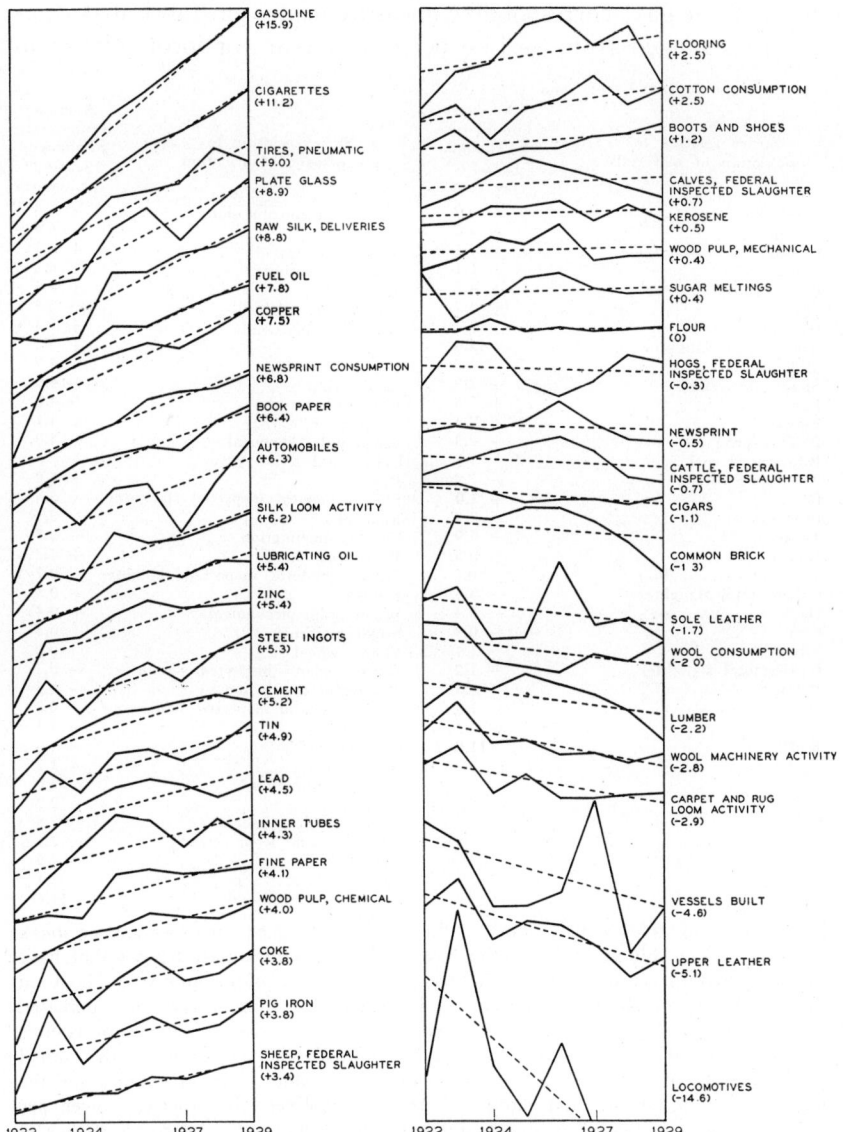

PLOTTED ON RATIO SCALE. THE FIGURES IN PARENTHESES DEFINE AVERAGE ANNUAL RATES OF CHANGE.

256  ECONOMIC TENDENCIES

Here are widely divergent movements, surprisingly divergent for a period of general expansion such as that falling between 1922 and 1929. Within the group of raw materials average annual rates of change ranged from — 11.0 per cent for rye to + 11.8 per cent for natural gas; corresponding measurements for fabricated commodities ranged from — 14.6 per cent a year for locomotives [1] to

*(Footnote continued from page 253)*

| Series relating to production of materials | Average annual rate of change, 1922-1929 (per cent) | Series relating to processes of fabrication | Average annual rate of change, 1922-1929 (per cent) |
|---|---|---|---|
| Wool | + 5.2 | Newsprint consumption | + 6.8 |
| Cement | + 5.2 | Book paper | + 6.4 |
| Cotton | + 5.1 | Motor vehicles | + 6.3 |
| Cottonseed | + 5.1 | Silk loom activity | + 6.2 |
| Lead, crude | + 4.5 | Zinc, slab | + 5.4 |
| Oranges | + 3.9 | Lubricating oil | + 5.4 |
| Iron ore | + 3.4 | Steel ingots | + 5.3 |
| Sheep, total slaughter | + 3.4 | Cement | + 5.2 |
| Milk | + 3.2 | Tin deliveries | + 4.9 |
| Sugar, domestic | + 2.9 | Lead, crude | + 4.5 |
| Rice | + 2.8 | Inner tubes | + 4.3 |
| Flaxseed | + 2.4 | Fine paper | + 4.1 |
| Poultry products | + 2.3 | Wood pulp, chemical | + 4.0 |
| Bituminous coal | + 1.4 | Coke, total | + 3.8 |
| Anthracite coal | + 1.2 | Pig iron | + 3.8 |
| Hay | + 1.0 | Sheep, Federal inspected slaughter | + 3.4 |
| Peaches | + 0.9 | Flooring | + 2.5 |
| Tobacco | + 0.9 | Cotton consumption | + 2.5 |
| Wheat | + 0.5 | Boots and shoes | + 1.2 |
| Swine, total slaughter | 0.0 | Calves, Federal inspected slaughter | + 0.7 |
| Calves, total slaughter | — 0.4 | Kerosene | + 0.5 |
| Oats | — 0.4 | Wood pulp, mechanical | + 0.4 |
| Corn | — 0.9 | Sugar meltings | + 0.4 |
| Silver | — 1.1 | Flour, wheat | 0.0 |
| Cattle, total slaughter | — 1.2 | Hogs, Federal inspected slaughter | — 0.3 |
| Potatoes | — 1.3 | Newsprint production | — 0.5 |
| Gold | — 1.8 | Cattle, Federal inspected slaughter | — 0.7 |
| Apples | — 3.7 | Cigars | — 1.1 |
| Rye | —11.0 | Common brick | — 1.3 |
| | | Sole leather | — 1.7 |
| | | Wool consumption | — 2.0 |
| | | Lumber | — 2.2 |
| | | Wool machinery activity | — 2.8 |
| | | Wool rug and loom activity | — 2.9 |
| | | Vessels built | — 4.6 |
| | | Upper leather | — 5.1 |
| | | Locomotives, railroad | —14.6 |

[1] For locomotives a mere count of the number produced furnishes a poor index of the physical volume of production because of the substantial changes that have occurred within recent years in the weight and power of locomotives. The total tractive power of all steam locomotives in service for Class I railroads increased at an average rate of 0.6 per cent a year over this period. (This is, of course, an aggregate, and is not necessarily inconsistent with a sharp decline in the annual increments to the total.) With the scrapping of the older types of engines and the introduction of heavier and more powerful locomotives, the tractive power per locomotive has increased at an average rate of 2.5 per cent a year. (*Statistics of Railways in the United States*, 1930, p. S-117.)

### FIGURE 45

### ILLUSTRATING THE DIVERGENCE OF PRODUCTION TRENDS IN THE UNITED STATES, 1922-1929*

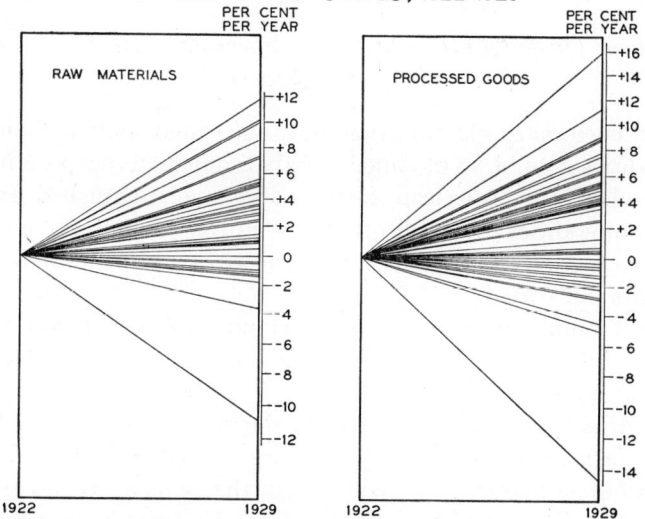

* Plotted on ratio scale. The lines here plotted relate to the commodities listed in footnote on pp. 253 and 256, in the order of that listing.

+ 15.9 per cent a year for gasoline. As in the pre-war period, the degree of divergence is somewhat greater among processed goods (weighted standard deviation of rates of change 3.9) than among raw materials (weighted standard deviation of rates of change 3.1).

Comparison of pre-war and post-war periods with respect to degree of divergence is difficult. If we use rates of change relating to identical commodities in the two periods we are restricted in the later period to industries which, in the main, have passed through their most rapid stage of growth. If we include in the post-war period industries not appearing in the earlier records we cannot be sure of the comparability of our groups. If the coverage were complete in both periods the question of comparability in detail would not have to be faced, but this is far from being the case. Taking the figures as they stand, as providing the basis of a rough comparison, we note that the degree of divergence appears to have been somewhat greater among raw materials between 1922 and 1929 than between 1901 and 1913, and that divergence was less among fabricated goods in the recent period than it was in the earlier period.[1]

## *Physical Output of Products of American Farms and of All Other Products*

The customary classification into cultivated and non-cultivated commodities should be modified for the immediate purpose in order that products of American farms may be distinguished from all other commodities. The 'all other' group thus includes a few products such as silk goods and pneumatic tires, the raw materials of which are cultivated.

Index numbers of the physical volume of production of commodities in these two groups are given in the next table. They appear graphically in Figure 46.

There is a wide margin between the rates at which the production of farm products and of non-farm products increased during this period—a margin even wider than that which divides the rates of growth of raw and processed goods. As against an advance of 2.0 per cent a year for the group of farm products, the output of non-farm products increased at a rate averaging 5.1 per cent a year. The production of farm products kept comfortably ahead of the growth of population (1.4 per cent a year), while the output of commodities not originating on American farms expanded at a rate far in excess of the rate of population growth. The wants which have been expanding in recent years, and which augmented incomes and improvements of consumer credit have provided means of satisfying, have not, in general, been those which farm products could fill.

[1] These statements are based on the following measurements:

|  | Number of production series | Weighted standard deviation of rates of change |
|---|---|---|
| 1901-1913 |  |  |
| Raw materials | 28 | 2.1 |
| Manufactured goods | 31 | 5.7 |
| 1922-1929 |  |  |
| Raw materials | 36 | 3.1 |
| Manufactured goods | 44 | 3.9 |

Weights have been based upon the value of materials at the farm and mine and upon the 'value added by manufacture' in 1909 and in 1923 and 1925. The influence of the exceptionally rapid growth in the production of motor vehicles during the pre-war period (45 per cent a year) has been reduced by adjusting the weight given this industry in the sample on the basis of its relative importance in total manufacturing production.

## TABLE 109

### Products of American Farms and All Other Products
Index Numbers of Physical Volume of Production in the United States, 1922-1929 [a]

| (1) Year | (2) (3) Products of American farms | | (4) (5) All other products [b] | | (6) All products of American farms | (7) All other products |
|---|---|---|---|---|---|---|
| | Raw | Processed | Raw | Processed | | |
| 1922 | 100 | 100 | 100 | 100 | 100 | 100 |
| 1923 | 105 | 106 | 137 | 115 | 105 | 119 |
| 1924 | 110 | 102 | 130 | 108 | 107 | 111 |
| 1925 | 110 | 111 | 133 | 121 | 110 | 122 |
| 1926 | 116 | 112 | 144 | 131 | 114 | 133 |
| 1927 | 110 | 118 | 147 | 128 | 113 | 131 |
| 1928 | 116 | 114 | 146 | 138 | 115 | 140 |
| 1929 | 114 | 121 | 159 | 147 | 116 | 149 |
| Average annual rate of change (per cent) | +1.7 | +2.6 | +4.6 | +5.1 | +2.0 | +5.1 |
| Index of instability of growth | 2.2 | 2.0 | 4.7 | 3.0 | 1.2 | 3.1 |

[a] A description of the procedure followed in the construction of these index numbers is given in Appendix I, Section 2. The index numbers of the output of processed products have been adjusted to measurements representing all manufacturing industries.

[b] The commodities which have been included in the sample of raw materials not originating on American farms are all minerals. In addition to mineral products in the processed group there have been included series relating to the fabrication of lumber and of imported cultivated materials.

Within each of these two main groups the production of processed goods was increasing between 1922 and 1929 at rates which exceeded the growth in output of raw materials.[1]

A comparison of these rates with those prevailing between 1901 and 1913 is suggestive. For all farm products (raw and processed) the rates of growth, pre-war and post-war, are practically identical—2.1 and 2.0 per cent a year. However, the pre-war advance occurred with population increasing at 2.0 per cent a year, while the rate of population growth in the recent period was but 1.4 per cent a year. Here is a material difference, the effects of

---

[1] The apparent discrepancy between the average annual rates of change in the production of non-farm products, raw, processed and total, is due to the fact that the weights given to processed goods in this group are much heavier than the weights given to raw materials.

## FIGURE 46
### GROWTH OF PHYSICAL VOLUME OF PRODUCTION IN THE UNITED STATES, 1922-1929
#### PRODUCTS OF AMERICAN FARMS AND ALL OTHER PRODUCTS

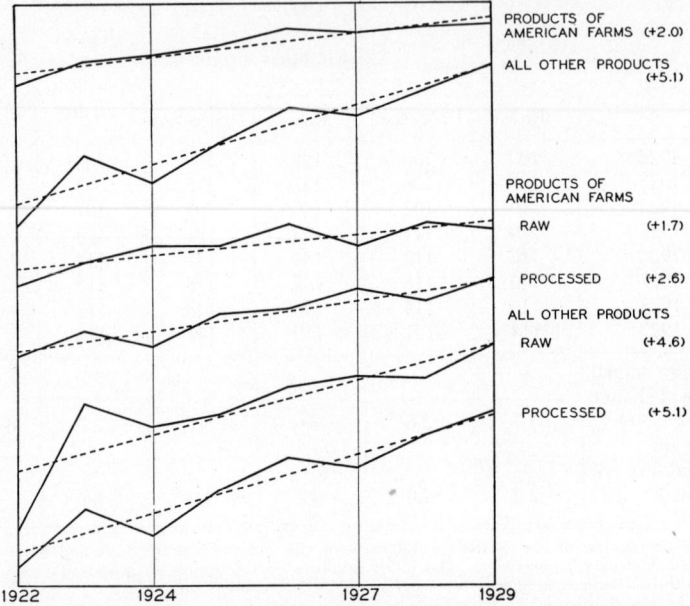

Plotted on ratio scale. The figures in parentheses define average annual rates of change (in percentage form).

which on the market for farm products were intensified by the changes occurring in the character of our foreign trade. Exports of both crude and manufactured foodstuffs were declining at rapid rates between 1922 and 1929, after the temporary stimulus of the war and immediate post-war years.

The more rapid advance of aggregate production in the recent period, as contrasted with 1901-1913, is attributable to the expanding output of commodities not originating on American farms. The post-war rate of 5.1 per cent a year exceeds materially the pre-war figure of 4.3 per cent. It was on non-farm products that new demands were concentrated during the expansion of the last decade.

§ *Comparison of identical commodities, pre-war and post-war.*—In the preceding comparisons of the periods 1901-1913 and 1922-1929 with respect to the movements of production, use has been made of index numbers and averages not based upon identical commodities. If index numbers representative of conditions in each of the periods are to be used, it is, indeed, inevitable that there should be some differences among the commodities included. New industries come into being, and commodities change in relative importance with the passage of time. Nevertheless, it is desirable that we supplement the comparison of general but dissimilar index numbers and averages by a study of the behavior of identical commodities during the two periods. Relevant measurements relating to 48 commodities are given in Table 110, on page 262.

Of the 16 raw farm products on the list, seven have post-war rates of increase which exceed the pre-war rates. Comparative rates are shown for six series relating to the production of processed products originating on American farms. For only one, cottonseed consumption, did the post-war rate of increase exceed the pre-war rate. Two of the six show declining post-war rates.

Among raw products of non-farm origin (minerals) only three out of 11 were marked by rates of post-war increase exceeding the pre-war rates. Of 15 comparable series representing the production of processed products of primarily non-farm origin, four show higher post-war rates; for the other 11 post-war rates were lower than the pre-war figures.

Of the total 48 production series compared, only 15 were increasing during the period between 1922 and 1929 at rates in excess of those prevailing between 1901 and 1913. This evidence seems clearly at variance with the conclusion given at an earlier point, namely, that the rate of increase in the volume of production was somewhat greater in post-war than in pre-war years. The explanation is found in the varying importance of particular series at different times (notably, in the present case, the declining importance of agricultural products and the increasing importance of industrial products), and in the fact that series representative of the general stream of production at one time are not representative at another.

Most series measuring the production of particular commodities begin to decline in rates of growth at relatively early dates in the histories of those commodities. It is to be expected, then, that comparisons of rates of growth of identical series at different periods should in general show lower rates during the later period. But an individual series may be increasing at a lower rate during a later period, and at the same time may be contributing to a more rapid advance of the aggregate physical volume of production. Thus the output of motor vehicles increased at an annual rate of 45.0 per cent between 1901 and 1913, and at only 6.3 per cent between 1922 and 1929. But motor vehicles were almost a negligible element in aggregate production during the early part of the century, whereas they have been a dominating factor in recent years. A given percentage increase represents a far larger increment, of course, when the annual aggregate is large than it does when the absolute annual production is small.

Again, the comparison of identical series necessitates the omission

## TABLE 110

### Average Annual Rates of Change in the Production of Identical Commodities

#### 1901-1913 and 1922-1929 [a]

| (1) Products of American farms | (2) | (3) | (4) All other products | (5) | (6) |
|---|---|---|---|---|---|
| Commodity | Average annual rate of change (per cent) | | Commodity | Average annual rate of change (per cent) | |
|  | 1901-1913 | 1922-1929 |  | 1901-1913 | 1922-1929 |
| Raw materials | | | Raw materials | | |
| Sugar, domestic .... | +5.1 | +2.9 | Cement, total ...... | +13.8 | +5.2 |
| Sheep, total slaughter | +3.6 | +3.4 | Petroleum, crude ... | +9.8 | +7.1 |
| Potatoes ........... | +3.1 | −1.3 | Natural gas ........ | +7.1 | +11.8 |
| Cotton ............. | +2.8 | +5.1 | Zinc ............... | +7.0 | +5.4 |
| Tobacco ........... | +2.7 | +0.9 | Copper ............ | +5.8 | +7.3 |
| Barley ............. | +2.7 | +10.0 | Bituminous coal .... | +5.7 | +1.4 |
| Oats ............... | +2.4 | −0.4 | Iron ore ........... | +5.5 | +3.4 |
| Cottonseed ......... | +1.9 | +5.1 | Lead ............... | +3.9 | +4.5 |
| Corn ............... | +1.9 | −0.9 | Anthracite coal .... | +3.4 | +1.2 |
| Cattle, total slaughter | +1.7 | −1.2 | Gold ............... | +1.8 | −1.8 |
| Swine, total slaughter | +1.1 | 0.0 | Silver ............. | +1.2 | −1.1 |
| Hay ................ | +0.4 | +1.0 | Manufactured goods | | |
| Wool ............... | +0.3 | +5.2 | Motor vehicles ..... | +45.0 | +6.3 |
| Apples ............. | −0.2 | −3.7 | Cement, total ...... | +13.8 | +5.2 |
| Wheat ............. | −0.3 | +0.5 | Silk imports ....... | +7.2 | +8.8 |
| Flaxseed ........... | −3.0 | +2.4 | Steel ingots and castings ............ | +7.1 | +5.3 |
| Manufactured goods | | | Zinc consumption ... | +6.9 | +5.6 |
| Cigarettes ......... | +17.2 | +11.2 | Coke ............... | +5.7 | +3.8 |
| Cottonseed consumption ............. | +3.9 | +7.5 | Pig iron ........... | +5.0 | +3.8 |
| Cotton consumption . | +3.1 | +2.5 | Copper consumption. | +4.8 | +8.4 |
| Wool consumption .. | +1.2 | −2.0 | Passenger cars, railroad ............. | +4.1 | +0.8 |
| Cigars ............. | +1.1 | −1.1 | Sugar, total supply.. | +3.9 | +1.7 |
| Flour, wheat ....... | +0.3 | 0.0 | Lead, available for consumption ..... | +2.6 | +4.0 |
| | | | Steel rails ......... | +1.1 | +1.8 |
| | | | Common brick sold.. | 0.0 | −1.3 |
| | | | Freight cars ....... | −0.6 | −8.5 |
| | | | Vessels built ....... | −3.7 | −4.6 |

[a] In some cases the post-war measurements here given differ slightly from those cited in earlier tables. For the present purpose we have sought series identical with those used for pre-war years.

of new series relating to commodities just coming into production, and perhaps playing important parts during the later of the two periods compared. Radios, electric refrigerators and similar commodities are recent examples of such novelties. A valid and adequate comparison of aggregate production during two periods can not, then, be based upon identical commodities, with identical weights. Adequate representation of the total stream of production in each period must be sought. It is notable that index numbers of manufacturing output based on standard commodities show no greater rate of increase for the post-war period than for the pre-war period, until adjustment is made to measurements reflecting the output of non-standard fabricated products. The comparison of individual commodities throws interesting light on the course of production during the two periods, but it does not tell the whole story.

## The Value and Volume of Construction

During the war emphasis was placed on the production of immediately necessary articles of food and clothing, and war supplies. At the end of the first post-war depression there existed an accumulated shortage of construction, representing deferred construction of residences, roads, public works of all sorts, and commercial and industrial buildings. By 1922 the productive forces of the country were turning to the filling of this gap. This movement, and its consequences, deeply affected the course of economic events between 1922 and 1929 and played an important rôle in the subsequent recession.

The measurement of the volume of construction presents difficulties, for appropriate physical units of measurement are lacking. We may determine the amount of certain important building materials turned out, we may measure the floor space of certain types of buildings constructed, but these data fall far short of reflecting the great variety of construction of roads, bridges, dams, power plants, and industrial, commercial and residential buildings which took place during this period. Records in terms of values, with their admitted imperfections, are the most comprehensive available. We turn first to these, as given in Table 111, for a general survey of construction movements. The series are plotted in Figure 47.

From an estimated figure of 4,330 millions of dollars in 1922, total construction contracts awarded increased in value to 7,295 millions in 1928. There was a drop to 6,421 millions in 1929. The average annual rate of increase over the eight-year period was 6.7 per cent. This exceeds materially the rate of approximately 3.3 per

## TABLE 111
### Growth of Construction in the United States, 1922-1929
#### Estimated Values of Total Contracts Awarded[a]
#### (In millions of dollars)

| (1) Year | (2) Commercial buildings | (3) Industrial buildings | (4) Public and institutional buildings | (5) Apartments and hotels[b] | (6) 1 and 2 family houses | (7) Public works and utilities | (8) Total construction |
|---|---|---|---|---|---|---|---|
| 1922 | 642 | 421 | 804 | 836 | 899 | 728 | 4,330 |
| 1923 | 619 | 541 | 745 | 1,037 | 1,037 | 789 | 4,768 |
| 1924 | 691 | 413 | 887 | 1,212 | 1,188 | 846 | 5,237 |
| 1925 | 976 | 550 | 1,112 | 1,621 | 1,455 | 1,009 | 6,724 |
| 1926 | 1,020 | 744 | 1,082 | 1,627 | 1,331 | 1,259 | 7,062 |
| 1927 | 1,053 | 562 | 1,123 | 1,503 | 1,376 | 1,404 | 7,022 |
| 1928 | 974 | 699 | 1,081 | 1,513 | 1,556 | 1,472 | 7,295 |
| 1929 | 1,038 | 845 | 1,006 | 933 | 1,206 | 1,394 | 6,421 |
| Average annual rate of change (per cent) .. | +8.1 | +9.3 | +4.7 | +3.7 | +5.1 | +11.4 | +6.7 |
| Index of instability of growth ..... | 10.1 | 10.8 | 8.2 | 18.2 | 9.7 | 6.4 | 9.2 |

[a] These estimates of building and engineering construction have been made by the F. W. Dodge Corporation upon the basis of contracts ($5,000 and over per project) awarded in 37 states. (In 1923 36 states were covered, in 1922, 27.) They represent total construction in the United States, the data having been raised to include the omitted eleven western states by the application of correction factors based upon estimates of population and certain types of construction.

The constitution of certain of the above groups requires further definition:
*Commercial:* Banks, airports, garages, offices, offices and banks, stores, warehouses.
*Industrial:* Mineral extraction, food products, chemical industries, leather, power plants, iron and steel, vehicles, petroleum, paper and pulp, printing and binding, rubber, textile, lumber, non-ferrous metals, miscellaneous.
*Public and institutional:* Schools, colleges, libraries, museums, gymnasiums, hospitals, institutions, military and naval buildings, municipal buildings, post offices, churches, convents, memorial buildings, auditoriums and halls, clubs and lodges, parks, park buildings, theatres.
*Public works and utilities:* Waterfront developments, bridges, incinerators, lighting systems, railroad construction, railway buildings, sewerage systems, highways, water supply systems.

[b] The average rate of growth and the index of instability for construction of apartments and hotels do not indicate the true movement of this series. The rapid rise during the first part of the period and the subsequent decline are not adequately described by a compound interest curve.

cent [1] which measures the increasing aggregate value of the production of movable goods during this period.

The most important element of the total in 1922 was the con-

[1] Estimated on the basis of an average increase in general production at a rate of 3.8 per cent per year, and a decrease in wholesale prices at a rate of 0.5 per cent per year.

## FIGURE 47
### GROWTH OF CONSTRUCTION IN THE UNITED STATES, 1922-1929
ESTIMATED VALUES OF TOTAL CONTRACTS AWARDED, 48 STATES

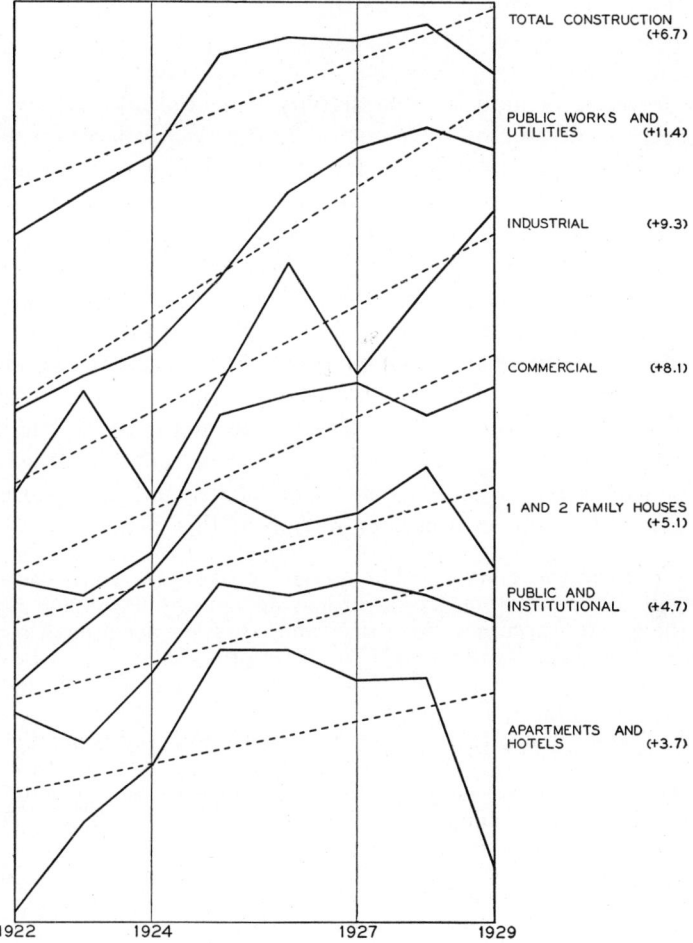

Plotted on ratio scale. The figures in parentheses define average annual rates of change (in percentage form).

struction of 1 and 2 family houses, with apartments and hotels next. These classes grew most rapidly up to 1925. With minor fluctuations the values of these two groups of residential buildings remained fairly constant at relatively high levels thereafter, through

1928, but declined markedly in 1929. Commercial buildings, industrial buildings, public and institutional buildings and public works and utilities made their most rapid gains after 1924. One group only, industrial buildings, reached its value peak in 1929, advancing 50 per cent during the two years from 1927 to 1929.

These figures, estimates though they be, indicate how rapid was the rush to fill the gaps existing in the field of construction after the war years. A high level of activity had been attained by 1925. The aggregate value of construction in that year approximated 6.7 billions of dollars, as compared with 26.8 billions of dollars, the total value contribution ('value added') of all manufacturing industries of the country. This rapid advance is understandable, in view of the deficiencies of our equipment after the war, but the maintenance of construction activity at this level during the four succeeding years furnishes the most striking feature of the record. It is now clear that there occurred in this field a piling up of utilities the enjoyment of which would necessarily be spread over a considerable period of time. This condition affected not only the industries and financial agents directly concerned, but also the direction and intensity of subsequent consumer demand. More attention is given to this subject in a later section of this chapter.

§ *Construction volume.*—The preceding figures, which relate to aggregate values of contracts awarded, do not define volume changes with the greatest accuracy, for prices and costs did not remain constant during this period. It is possible to correct the value figures by index numbers of construction costs, but the results must be accepted with reservations. Changes in costs are not uniform throughout the country, or for all enterprises. It is of dubious validity to apply generally index numbers of costs based upon sample studies. If we recognize these limitations, we may make use of 'deflated' value series as approximations to the volume index numbers we should like to have. Figures derived in this fashion appear in Table 112.

Rising construction costs served to swell the values of contracts awarded between 1922 and 1929, and correction for this factor reduces the figures for the various years. Total construction gained at an average annual rate of 6.1 per cent, as compared with 6.7 per cent for the value series. The other series (except apartments and hotels) are reduced correspondingly, but the general picture is still one which shows the construction industry making a great forward leap after 1924, and remaining at a high and slightly rising level of activity until 1928. All groups except industrial buildings had passed their peaks prior to 1929.

Still further evidence on the changing volume of construction is afforded by statistics of the area of floor surface recorded in connection

## TABLE 112

GROWTH OF CONSTRUCTION IN THE UNITED STATES, 1922-1929 [a]

Index Numbers of Volume of Construction Secured by Deflating Aggregate Values of Contracts Awarded

| (1) Year | (2) Commercial buildings | (3) Industrial buildings | (4) Public and institutional buildings | (5) Apartments and hotels | (6) 1 and 2 family houses | (7) Public works and utilities | (8) Total construction |
|---|---|---|---|---|---|---|---|
| 1922 | 100.0 | 100.0 | 100.0 | 100.0 | 100.0 | 100.0 | 100.0 |
| 1923 | 78.6 | 108.2 | 75.6 | 108.2 | 104.9 | 88.3 | 93.3 |
| 1924 | 87.2 | 84.2 | 89.5 | 127.7 | 122.5 | 94.2 | 103.0 |
| 1925 | 128.3 | 113.8 | 116.8 | 177.6 | 152.3 | 117.0 | 136.5 |
| 1926 | 133.1 | 152.5 | 112.9 | 180.8 | 137.9 | 145.1 | 143.0 |
| 1927 | 138.7 | 117.5 | 118.3 | 168.7 | 141.9 | 163.3 | 143.3 |
| 1928 | 127.9 | 147.8 | 113.5 | 169.9 | 161.2 | 170.7 | 149.0 |
| 1929 | 136.2 | 179.4 | 105.5 | 104.7 | 125.0 | 161.6 | 131.0 |
| Average annual rate of change (per cent) .. | +7.0 | +8.9 | +3.6 | +4.0 | +4.7 | +10.5 | +6.1 |
| Index of instability of growth ..... | 11.8 | 11.2 | 9.8 | 18.6 | 9.3 | 9.3 | 8.9 |

[a] These are the value series presented in Table 111, deflated, and put into relative form with 1922 as 100. (The index of total construction is a weighted average of the indexes in columns (2) to (7) inclusive.) The deflating index employed varies with the series in question. The general construction cost index of the *Engineering News Record* has been used to correct for price changes in the commercial, public and institutional, and public works and utilities groups. The index of factory building costs, compiled by the Aberthaw Construction Company, was used to deflate the values of industrial buildings. For residential construction the special indexes of the American Appraisal Company were employed as deflators; an index based on costs of construction of a brick and steel frame building was applied to hotel and apartment house contracts, and a similar index for frame buildings was used for the series on 1 and 2 family houses. These index numbers follow:

INDEX NUMBERS OF CONSTRUCTION COSTS

| Year | General construction (Engineering News Record) | Factory buildings (Aberthaw Construction Company) | Brick, steel frame (American Appraisal Company) | Frame (American Appraisal Company) |
|---|---|---|---|---|
| 1922 | 100 | 100 | 100 | 100 |
| 1923 | 123 | 119 | 115 | 110 |
| 1924 | 123 | 116 | 114 | 108 |
| 1925 | 118 | 115 | 109 | 106 |
| 1926 | 119 | 116 | 108 | 107 |
| 1927 | 118 | 114 | 106 | 108 |
| 1928 | 118 | 112 | 106 | 107 |
| 1929 | 119 | 112 | 106 | 107 |

These index numbers are all published in the *Survey of Current Business*.

with contracts awarded in 36 states (F. W. Dodge Corporation figures), and by an index of total construction based upon shipments of building materials by the Associated General Contractors of America. These are given in the next table.

## TABLE 113

GROWTH OF CONSTRUCTION IN THE UNITED STATES, 1922-1929

Index Numbers of Contracts Awarded, by Floor Surface Areas, and of Building Materials Booked and Shipped

| (1) Year | (2) Building contracts, floor space [a] | (3) | (4) | (5) Index of construction based on shipments of materials [b] |
|---|---|---|---|---|
| | Residential | Commercial | Industrial | |
| 1922 | 100.0 | 100.0 | 100.0 | 100 |
| 1923 | 114.4 | 97.4 | 94.9 | 116 |
| 1924 | 123.6 | 100.6 | 64.7 | 121 |
| 1925 | 157.9 | 134.5 | 87.2 | 131 |
| 1926 | 146.0 | 125.9 | 101.8 | 133 |
| 1927 | 138.6 | 117.6 | 88.0 | 139 |
| 1928 | 160.4 | 133.9 | 118.3 | 146 |
| 1929 | 108.8 | 135.0 | 137.5 | 145 |
| Average annual rate of change (per cent) .... | +3.0 | +4.9 | +5.8 | +4.9 |
| Index of instability of growth ..... | 11.9 | 6.0 | 13.8 | 3.0 |

[a] Contracts awarded in 36 states, compiled by the F. W. Dodge Corporation, by area of floor surface. The 1922 figure is estimated from reports from 27 states.

[b] Compiled by Associated General Contractors of America. The index is a simple average of structural steel bookings, common brick bookings, Portland cement shipments, loading of sand, gravel and stone, shipments of face brick and shipments of enameled sanitary ware. (1931 Annual Supplement, *Survey of Current Business,* p. 190.)

The index of total construction, being based upon the bookings and shipments of selected building materials, is not directly comparable with the figures given in earlier tables. Lumber movements do not enter into the index. The materials included in the index show an average annual rate of increase, during this period, of 4.9 per cent.

Index numbers based on areas of floor surface of different types of buildings under construction are, of course, far less comprehensive in scope than the value figures previously discussed. In so far as the groupings are comparable, the area figures show much the same year-to-year variations as do the value figures, but rather lower rates of increase. The very great drop in floor area of residential buildings in 1929 (a drop of 32 per cent) reduced the rate of growth for the period as a whole to 3.0 per cent a year. For the years 1922-1928 the annual rate of advance averaged 7.0 per cent. The construction of industrial buildings, which surged forward most rapidly between 1927 and 1929, increased at an average rate of 5.8 per cent a year during the whole period. Among commercial buildings the gain in floor area was at a rate of 4.9 per cent a year.

Of the various measures presented, deflated value figures probably give the best approximation to the actual changes occurring in aggregate volume of construction of all sorts. There are admitted difficulties encountered in the deflating process, but the more comprehensive character of the value compilations impels one to accept these in preference to the much more restricted statistics of areas. Further use is made of these data in later sections.

## Physical Output of Finished Products, 1922-1929 Consumption Goods and Capital Equipment

In passing to categories of goods destined for human consumption and goods intended for use as capital equipment, certain difficulties of measurement are encountered. Capital goods, by their nature, are not readily enumerated, and much of this type of equipment falls outside the field covered by current statistics. In summarizing available materials, records of output in physical units will be supplemented by data measuring changes in values. This will be done only where it is reasonable to assume that the value series do not overstate the rate of advance in the physical volume of production, or where deflation by suitable price index numbers is possible.

The measurements described in the present section have been designed to indicate changes in the volume of production of *finished* goods—to measure the flow of such products in the form of ultimate consumption goods or of finished capital equipment. Immediate interest lies not in the sources of these goods but in the uses to which they are put. For this reason raw materials and partly fabricated goods have been excluded from the averages. Weights assigned to the component series have been based upon the values of the finished products. These index numbers do not measure the total productive effort of the country, except in so far as the output of raw materials is transformed into finished products ready for consumption or capital use. In this respect the averages are of the nature of indexes of consumption, rather than indexes of production, though in the long run the rates of growth of these two series must not be greatly different.[1]

---

[1] The exact agreement, as regards rates of change, of the index of total production of finished goods given in this section with the general production index presented on earlier pages is a fortuitous result, though the relationship is bound to be close.

## Non-durable Consumption Goods

Changes in the output of non-durable consumption goods are traced in the following table, and in Figure 48.

TABLE 114

NON-DURABLE CONSUMPTION GOODS

Index Numbers of Physical Volume of Production of Finished Goods, 1922-1929 [a]

| Year | Foods | Other non-durable consumption goods | Total non-durable consumption goods |
|---|---|---|---|
| 1922 | 100 | 100 | 100 |
| 1923 | 106 | 121 | 108 |
| 1924 | 107 | 129 | 110 |
| 1925 | 106 | 132 | 110 |
| 1926 | 110 | 149 | 116 |
| 1927 | 110 | 159 | 118 |
| 1928 | 113 | 171 | 122 |
| 1929 | 113 | 185 | 124 |
| Average annual rate of change (per cent) .... | +1.6 | +8.3 | +2.8 |
| Index of instability of growth ..... | 1.3 | 2.5 | 1.4 |

[a] The series included in the index of production of food products relate to the following commodities, or groups of commodities: Flour, meat products, poultry products, fruits and vegetables, truck crops, milk, butter, ice cream, beverages (value series), sugar, tobacco, cottonseed oil, fresh fish. Six series make up 'other non-durable consumption goods'. These relate to the production of gasoline, manufactured gas, anthracite coal, druggists' preparations (a value series), kerosene, and to the consumption of newsprint. A description of these index numbers is given in Appendix I.

The output of perishable consumption goods increased at a rate of 2.8 per cent a year between 1922 and 1929, which is below the average rate of advance in volume of production. This figure conceals a sharp divergence of the index numbers for foods and for other non-durable consumption goods. The volume of foods produced increased at a rate of 1.6 per cent a year, the 1929 aggregate being only 13 per cent greater than that for 1922. The advance in food production is barely above the rate of population increase, which averaged 1.4 per cent a year between 1922 and 1929. This condition would indicate on its face a slight increase in per capita consumption of foods. During this period there was, undoubtedly, a movement toward a more varied diet, as well as a general re-direction of consumer expenditure in which foods have declined in relative importance. The food series used above, however, are not

**FIGURE 48**

GROWTH OF PRODUCTION OF FINISHED GOODS
IN THE UNITED STATES, 1922-1929

NON-DURABLE CONSUMPTION GOODS

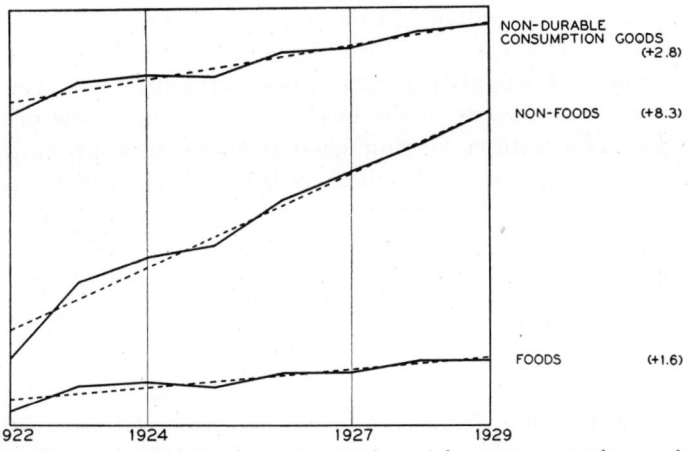

Plotted on ratio scale. The figures in parentheses define average annual rates of change (in percentage form).

general enough to provide a complete picture of the changes in food habits which are known to have taken place. The figures are affected, too, by the declining importance of food exports, in both raw and processed forms.[1]

[1] The following figures relate to exports and imports of food products during the period 1922-1929:

|  | Average annual rate of change (per cent) | Index of instability |
|---|---|---|
| Exports |  |  |
| Crude foodstuffs, value | —3.5 | 14.2 |
| Manufactured foodstuffs, value | —3.8 | 3.7 |
| Imports |  |  |
| Crude foodstuffs, value | +7.1 | 6.4 |
| Manufactured foodstuffs, value | —1.6 | 8.1 |

The change in our trade position, in regard to the movement of food products, has been pronounced. Imports of crude foodstuffs were increasing in aggregate value at the very high rate of 7.1 per cent a year between 1922 and 1929, while exports of both crude and manufactured foodstuffs were declining at substantial rates. The decline in exports represents, in part, a drop from the somewhat inflated levels attained in the immediate post-war years, when large volumes of food were going from this country to the war-ravaged areas of Europe. This is one aspect of a more general alteration in the international economic relations of the United States, a change already evident in the figures for the period 1901-1913. Food exports, which bulked so large in our earlier history, have been declining, while manufactured goods, particularly manufactured non-foods, have become increasingly important in our export trade.

The output of other perishable consumption goods, including gasoline, kerosene, anthracite coal, manufactured gas, druggists' preparations and newsprint, increased at a rate of 8.3 per cent a year during this period. Gasoline, which was being produced in sharply increasing volume (15.9 per cent a year), dominates this group; newsprint consumption, advancing at the rate of 6.8 per cent a year, and druggists' preparations, increasing by 7.6 per cent a year, were also factors in the increase. If gasoline, newsprint and druggists' preparations be eliminated from the total group of non-durable consumption goods, there is left a group which distinctly lagged behind in the general advance of this period. With the exceptions noted (and possibly others of lesser importance), perishable consumers' goods were not the commodities for which demand was increasing rapidly between 1922 and 1929.

## Semi-durable Consumption Goods

Textile products, boots and shoes, and rubber tires constitute a group of semi-durable consumption goods. Changes in the output of these commodities are shown by the following index numbers, which are plotted in Figure 49.

TABLE 115

SEMI-DURABLE CONSUMPTION GOODS

Index Numbers of Physical Volume of Production of Finished Goods, 1922-1929

| (1) Year | (2) Textile products | (3) Boots and shoes | (4) Rubber tires | (5) Total semi-durable consumption goods |
|---|---|---|---|---|
| 1922 | 100 | 100 | 100 | 100 |
| 1923 | 106 | 109 | 112 | 107 |
| 1924 | 92 | 97 | 127 | 96 |
| 1925 | 105 | 100 | 151 | 109 |
| 1926 | 105 | 100 | 151 | 109 |
| 1927 | 114 | 106 | 157 | 117 |
| 1928 | 108 | 107 | 187 | 116 |
| 1929 | 116 | 112 | 175 | 122 |
| Average annual rate of change (per cent) .... | +2.2 | +1.2 | +8.6 | +2.9 |
| Index of instability of growth ..... | 3.7 | 3.1 | 5.0 | 2.7 |

### FIGURE 49
### GROWTH OF PRODUCTION OF FINISHED GOODS IN THE UNITED STATES, 1922-1929
#### SEMI-DURABLE CONSUMPTION GOODS

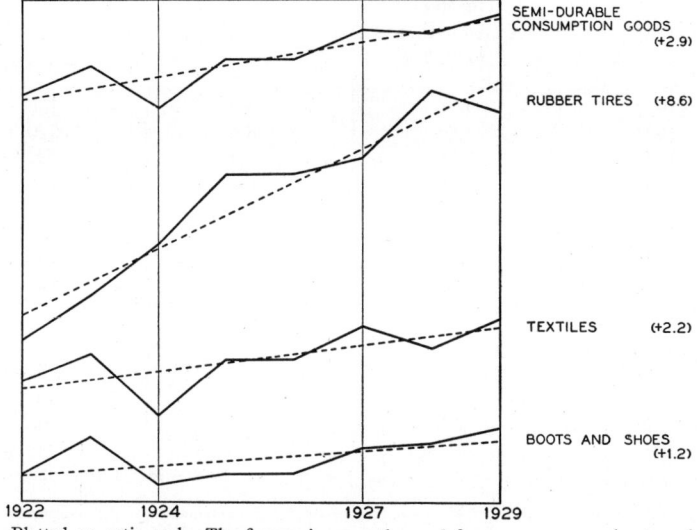

Plotted on ratio scale. The figures in parentheses define average annual rates of change (in percentage form).

The total output of semi-durable consumption goods increased at a rate approximately equal to that at which perishable consumption goods advanced, but lower than the rate of growth of total production. Such goods as a class did not feel the pressure of the new demand. The volume of production of textiles and, notably, of boots and shoes, lagged conspicuously behind the general procession in the economic advance of the 'twenties. One type of semi-durable consumption goods spurted forward, however. The expanding output of rubber tires, growing at a rate of 8.6 per cent a year during this period, reflected the phenomenal growth of the automobile industry.

### Durable Consumption Goods

We turn now to durable consumption goods,[1] with which is included residential construction.

[1] The line between semi-durable and durable goods is not readily drawn in all cases. For the present purpose we have placed in the durable group articles with a period of useful service exceeding approximately two years.

## TABLE 116

### Durable Consumption Goods

Index Numbers of Physical Volume of Production of Finished Goods, 1922-1929

| Year | Durable consumption goods [a] | Residential construction [b] | Durable consumption goods, including residential construction |
|---|---|---|---|
| 1922 | 100 | 100 | 100 |
| 1923 | 127 | 106 | 120 |
| 1924 | 120 | 125 | 122 |
| 1925 | 140 | 165 | 148 |
| 1926 | 151 | 159 | 154 |
| 1927 | 136 | 155 | 142 |
| 1928 | 154 | 165 | 158 |
| 1929 | 172 | 115 | 153 |
| Average annual rate of change (per cent) .... | +6.3 | +4.3 | +5.6 |
| Index of instability of growth ..... | 6.2 | 13.9 | 6.2 |

[a] The index of production of durable consumption goods is constructed from the following series:

*Automobiles.* Index numbers of automobile production constructed by the National Bureau of Economic Research from data compiled by the Census of Manufactures have been used, with interpolations for inter-censal years. In the construction of these index numbers an attempt has been made to adjust for changes in the type of automobiles produced.

*Furniture.* The furniture series has been secured from statistics of the aggregate value of household furniture production, as reported in the Census of Manufactures, interpolated for inter-censal years by means of the Federal Reserve Board's index of furniture sales, and deflated by the Bureau of Labor Statistics' index of wholesale furniture prices.

*Electrical equipment.* The electrical equipment series is an index based upon estimates of sales (in units) of vacuum cleaners, washing machines, sewing machines and electric refrigerators made by C. E. Persons from data presented in *Electrical Merchandising* (*Quarterly Journal of Economics,* November, 1930, p. 111).

*Carpets.* This series has been secured from statistics of the aggregate value of carpet and rug production as reported in the Census of Manufactures, interpolated for inter-censal years on the basis of carpet and rug loom activity.

*Mattresses.* The production of mattresses is represented by a series secured from the undeflated value of product as compiled by the Census of Manufactures, with estimates for inter-censal years based on the sales of one of the larger manufacturers.

*Phonographs and radios.* This series is based upon statistics of the value of phonographs manufactured and total retail radio sales (reduced by 50 per cent to approximate values at the factory). Changes in the size and quality of phonographs and radio receiving sets introduce an unknown bias into a series based upon number alone. The records of dollar values do not in this case exaggerate the growth of the industry, for the price of comparable units had undoubtedly fallen during the period.

*Pianos.* This series has been secured from statistics compiled by the Census of Manufactures; estimates for inter-censal years have been based upon employment in industries producing musical instruments.

[b] The index of residential construction is based upon the F. W. Dodge Corporation estimates of contracts awarded for construction of apartments, hotels, and 1 and 2 family houses for the entire United States, deflated by construction cost indexes of the American Appraisal Company.

The two elements of this total follow quite different courses during the years covered above, as is clear from the graphs in Figure 50. Durable consumption goods, not including residences, rose steadily in volume of output, with slight checks in 1924 and 1927. The index for 1929 was 172, with reference to 100 in 1922, and the average annual rate of advance was 6.3 per cent. Residential construction rose sharply to a high point in 1925, dropped some-

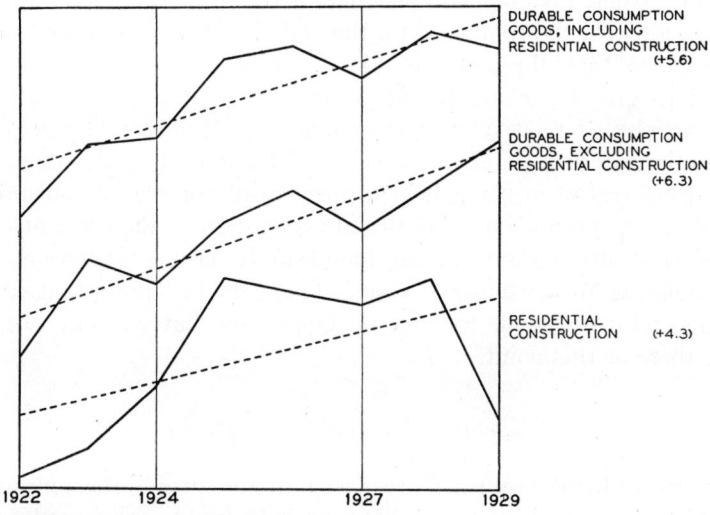

FIGURE 50
GROWTH OF PRODUCTION OF FINISHED GOODS
IN THE UNITED STATES, 1922-1929
DURABLE CONSUMPTION GOODS

Plotted on ratio scale. The figures in parentheses define average annual rates of change (in percentage form).

what during the next two years, but reached a new peak in 1928. From that height, 65 per cent above the base, the volume of such construction fell in 1929 to a level only 15 per cent above the 1922 standard. The average annual rate of increase, over the entire period, was 4.3 per cent. (Between 1922 and 1928 the average rate was 8.8 per cent, a truer indication of the general tendency during the time of expansion.) Combining the two series, we have an index of the changes in production of all types of durable consumption goods. This shows an advance of 53 per cent in the production of goods of this type between 1922 and 1929, at an average annual rate of 5.6 per cent.

Clearly, it was among durable consumption goods that the expansion of output was most pronounced between 1922 and 1929. Consumers were not increasing the proportions of their incomes spent for foods, clothing, or shoes. As regards certain of these groups there may have been positive retrenchment. The rapid increase of consumer expenditures occurred, in the main, in the markets for goods which are more or less durable, for automobiles, electrical equipment, radios and houses. (Gasoline, newsprint, tobacco and automobile tires constitute the chief exceptions to this rule.) A sharp check occurred in the construction of residences after 1928, but the growing volume of production of other durable consumption goods kept the total well up through 1929. It is a fact of some significance that these goods, the swelling production of which helped to give the characteristic tone to this period of expansion, were articles of relatively long periods of usefulness. The growing proportion of such goods in consumers' budgets meant that unconsumed utilities were being held in increasing volume by consumers. A decreasing proportion of the total production of the economy was being currently consumed, an increasingly large 'inventory' was accumulating in consumers' hands. This fact has important implications, with reference to later developments, but we may not explore these at this point.

### Elements of Capital Equipment

More difficult problems are faced in measuring the output of capital goods. Much of this equipment is in highly fabricated form, for which suitable measurements of volume of production are lacking. Computations based upon the production of basic materials entering into capital equipment are of doubtful validity, for differences in degree of fabrication are of the highest importance in relation to volume of capital goods produced. In the present case basic raw materials have been omitted from the calculations. The index numbers given relate to changes in the amount of *finished* equipment produced. In the absence of adequate measurements of physical volume of such equipment, a number of value series have been used. Where possible, correction for changes in the price factor have been made. In other cases value series have been used outright, on

## FIGURE 51
### GROWTH OF PRODUCTION OF FINISHED GOODS IN THE UNITED STATES, 1922-1929
#### ELEMENTS OF CAPITAL EQUIPMENT

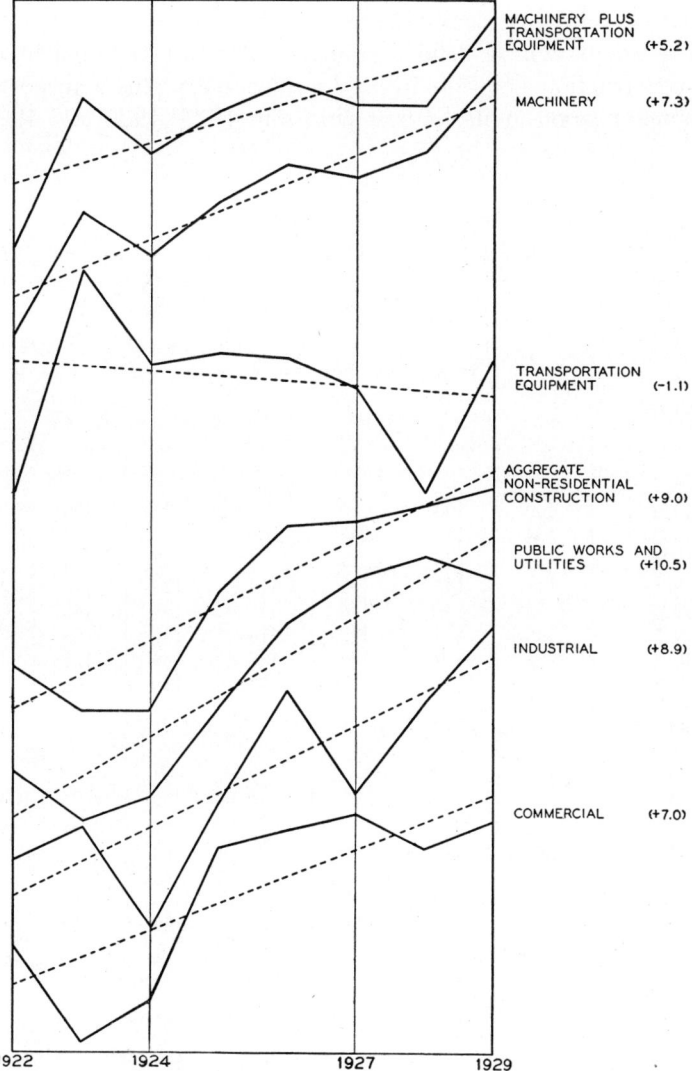

Plotted on ratio scale. The figures in parentheses define average annual rates of change (in percentage form).

the assumption that the prices of capital equipment did not, in general, show rising trends between 1922 and 1929. The level of wholesale prices declined, on the average, over this period.

Measurements of changes in the output of various forms of capital equipment appear in the next table. They are plotted in Figure 51, on the preceding page.

The index which defines changes in capital equipment other than construction (i.e., the index for machinery plus transportation equipment) stood at its highest points in 1923, 1926 and 1929. A

TABLE 117

ELEMENTS OF CAPITAL EQUIPMENT

Index Numbers of Physical Volume of Production of Finished Goods, 1922-1929

| (1) | (2) | (3) | (4) | (5) | (6) | (7) | (8) |
|---|---|---|---|---|---|---|---|
| | | | Machinery plus transportation equipment | Non-residential construction [c] | | | |
| Year | Machinery [a] | Transportation equipment [b] | | Industrial | Commercial | Public works and utilities | Total |
| 1922 | 100 | 100 | 100 | 100 | 100 | 100 | 100 |
| 1923 | 134 | 175 | 145 | 108 | 79 | 88 | 89 |
| 1924 | 121 | 136 | 125 | 84 | 87 | 94 | 89 |
| 1925 | 138 | 141 | 139 | 114 | 128 | 117 | 120 |
| 1926 | 153 | 139 | 150 | 153 | 133 | 145 | 142 |
| 1927 | 146 | 129 | 142 | 118 | 139 | 163 | 144 |
| 1928 | 157 | 99 | 142 | 148 | 128 | 171 | 150 |
| 1929 | 191 | 139 | 177 | 179 | 136 | 162 | 157 |
| Average annual rate of change (per cent) .. | +7.3 | −1.1 | +5.2 | +8.9 | +7.0 | +10.5 | +9.0 |
| Index of instability of growth ..... | 6.6 | 12.7 | 8.1 | 11.2 | 11.8 | 9.3 | 7.6 |

[a] The index of production of machinery is based upon the following items:

*Agricultural equipment.* Domestic sales as reported to the Bureau of the Census, deflated by the Bureau of Labor Statistics' index of wholesale prices of agricultural implements.

*Foundry equipment.* Value of shipments. Figures for 1922-1924 are estimated on the basis of new orders. Data from Foundry Equipment Manufacturers' Association, covering about 65 to 70 per cent of the industry.

*Stokers.* Sales in horsepower from data collected by the Bureau of the Census.

*Machine tools.* Shipments (number of machines) for the years 1925-1929; estimates for 1922-1924 on the basis of new orders. The data, compiled by the National Machine Tool Builders' Association, cover about one-third of the industry.

*Electrical equipment.* The value of output of stationary electric motors (rated at one horsepower and over), transformers, generators, and miscellaneous industrial and commercial apparatus, as given by the Census of Manufactures. Figures for inter-censal years have been

rapid advance occurred between 1922 and 1923; thereafter there were oscillations about the 1923 level, until the notable advance between 1928 and 1929. Over the whole period the annual rate of increase averaged 5.2 per cent. The three series relating to non-residential construction,[1] combined in a weighted average, show a steady advance from a low of 89 in 1923 and 1924 (on the 1922 base) to a high of 157 in 1929. The high rate of increase in this type of construction, an increase averaging 9.0 per cent per year, reflects the temporarily low levels at which this index stood in 1923 and 1924. Subsequently, non-residential construction advanced with a rush. The index for machinery and transportation equipment was high, in relation to 1922, during the entire period from 1923 on.

## Capital Equipment, Consumption Goods and all Finished Goods

The union of these two series gives us the index of production of total capital equipment, including construction, which appears in the table following. The present figures differ from data relating to changes in the volume of capital funds, discussed in Chapter

[1] Public and institutional buildings, such as schools and museums, are not included in the average.

interpolated on the basis of the Federal Reserve Board's index numbers of employment in the manufacture of electrical machinery.

*Wood working machinery.* Number of machines shipped, as compiled by the Association of Manufacturers of Wood Working Machinery, representing about fifty per cent of the industry.

*Textile machinery.* Value of product as reported in the Census of Manufactures, with figures for inter-censal years estimated on the basis of activity in the textile industry.

*Engines, turbines, and waterwheels.* Value of product as reported in the Census of Manufactures, with estimates for inter-censal years.

*Pumps, steam, power and centrifugal.* Value of shipments of 23 identical firms, believed to represent about two-thirds of the industry, compiled by the Hydraulic Society.

*Foundry and machine shop products.* Value of product for census years, deflated by an average of the index numbers of wholesale prices of iron and steel, agricultural implements, and 'other metal products' compiled by the U. S. Bureau of Labor Statistics. Figures for inter-censal years have been estimated on the basis of factory employment in the machinery industry.

b The index of production of transportation equipment is based upon five component series:
    Motor trucks and commercial vehicles
    Shipbuilding, gross tons completed
    Locomotives, number completed
    Railroad freight cars, number
    Railroad passenger cars, number
As a result of the exceptionally high peak in 1923 and the sharp drop in 1928 the average tendency during these years is downward. If information were available on the production of railroad rolling stock in terms of capacity or weight, the average rate of decline would be somewhat less. Construction of railroad trackage, stations, etc., is included in the estimates of construction of public works and utilities.

c The construction series are estimates of the F. W. Dodge Corporation relating to value of contracts awarded in the United States (48 states) for commercial, industrial, and public works and utilities construction. (The value figures have been deflated by the index numbers of construction costs constructed by the *Engineering News Record* (commercial buildings, public works and utilities) and by the Aberthaw Construction Company (industrial construction).

IX, in that they relate to volume of capital equipment and, more particularly, in that they deal with annual increments, not aggregate amounts. These are the annual additions to, and replacements of, existing capital equipment. Incremental figures of this type may properly be compared with the annual flow of consumption goods. Index numbers measuring changes in the output of finished consumption goods and in all finished goods are also given in this table.

TABLE 118

CONSUMPTION GOODS, CAPITAL EQUIPMENT AND TOTAL PRODUCTION

Index Numbers of Physical Volume of Production of Finished Goods, 1922-1929

| Year | Consumption goods, total, including residential construction | Capital equipment, total, including non-residential construction and public works | Total production of finished goods |
| --- | --- | --- | --- |
| 1922 | 100 | 100 | 100 |
| 1923 | 111 | 125 | 113 |
| 1924 | 110 | 112 | 110 |
| 1925 | 120 | 132 | 122 |
| 1926 | 125 | 147 | 128 |
| 1927 | 124 | 143 | 127 |
| 1928 | 130 | 145 | 132 |
| 1929 | 131 | 170 | 137 |
| Average annual rate of change (per cent) .... | +3.7 | +6.4 | +4.1 |
| Index of instability of growth ..... | 2.3 | 5.7 | 2.7 |

These index numbers are shown graphically in Figure 52.

The output of both consumption goods and capital equipment advanced in three spurts between 1922 and 1929, these spurts being far more pronounced for capital equipment than for goods ready for consumption and use. The year 1923 marks the peak of one advance, 1926 another and 1929 a third. In percentage terms, these three movements brought gains of 11, 14, and 6 per cent in the output of consumption goods, of 25, 31, and 19 per cent in the production of capital equipment. The sharp gain of capital equipment between 1928 and 1929, when the production of consumption goods remained practically constant in volume, is notable. For the

## FIGURE 52
### GROWTH OF PRODUCTION OF FINISHED GOODS IN THE UNITED STATES, 1922-1929
#### TOTAL PRODUCTION, CAPITAL EQUIPMENT AND CONSUMPTION GOODS

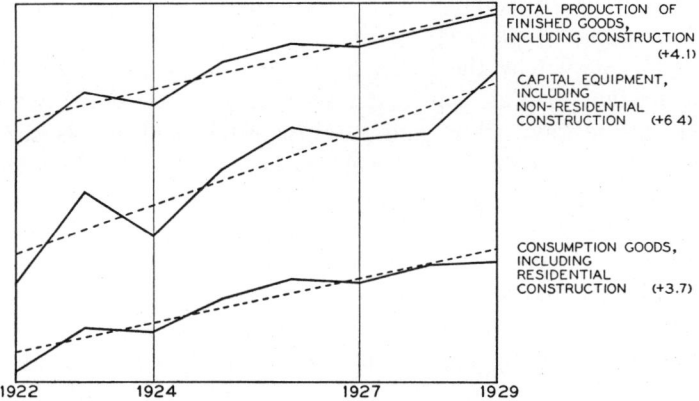

Plotted on ratio scale. The figures in parentheses define average annual rates of change (in percentage form).

period 1922-1929, as a whole, the output of consumption goods increased at a rate of 3.7 per cent a year, while the volume of additions to capital equipment rose at an average annual rate of 6.4 per cent a year.

The present index numbers show an appreciably more rapid growth of those products of economic activity which may be called procreative, than of end-products in the form of consumption goods. The equipment for producing goods for ultimate consumption was being augmented year by year at an exceptionally rapid rate. An increasing proportion of our total annual output of goods took the form of equipment designed to further the processes of roundabout production. So wide a margin of difference raises a question as to whether too large a proportion of the country's productive energies was being devoted to the construction of capital equipment. The subsequent collapse, and the phenomena of excess capacity of which there were signs even before the break in 1929, would suggest that this was so. We lack a criterion, however, for determining the optimum relations between output of consumption goods and of capital equipment, relations which may conduce to equilibrium. Here we require a greater knowledge of economic processes than we now possess if we are to set up standards for the division of our labor between these two types of production.[1]

The index of total production of finished goods which is secured by combining the two series just compared shows an increase of output between 1922 and 1929 at a rate of 4.1 per cent a year. This happens to agree precisely with the rate of advance in general production shown by the index first constructed (see Table 106). In the present case all raw materials, except those which are consumed in the raw state, and semi-manufactured goods are excluded.[2] (The distribution of weights is correspondingly altered.) We are dealing here with the output of end-products, ready for consumption, and of capital equipment ready for use in production. If comprehensive records were available this would perhaps be the form which all index numbers of total production should take. It is of interest that index numbers so derived should come so close to agreement, year by year, with index numbers of aggregate production based upon raw and semi-finished as well as finished goods.

## Durable and Non-durable Goods

For the purpose of a final comparison we group together all durable consumption goods and capital equipment, including in this combination all construction, residential and non-residential.[3] This class contains all those goods which contain stored up utilities, which render their services to producers or to consumers over a period of years. Against this group we set a combination of perish-

[1] If full account were taken of the trends of exports and imports during this period, one would be in a better position to appraise domestic processes. The export of foods, as we have seen, was declining steadily. Capital equipment shared in the general advance in the exports of finished manufactures. Figures which are uncorrected for movements of foreign trade probably over-emphasize somewhat the margin between the rates of change of consumption goods and capital equipment. But there is no reason to think that the picture would be materially different if full correction were made for such movements of trade. Between 1923 and 1929, when exports of manufactures were increasing steadily, the proportion of domestic manufactures exported advanced from 7 per cent to 8 per cent. In absolute terms the increase was considerable, but it exerted no profound influence on the make-up of total domestic production.

An economy which devotes a large part of its resources to the production of capital equipment is subject to wide variations of activity with changing business conditions. This is true whether the capital equipment be exported or sold at home.

[2] Certain finished commodities such as lumber, cement, paints, and structural steel are also excluded, to avoid duplication in the construction indexes.

[3] Excluding public and institutional construction.

able and semi-durable consumption goods—foods, gasoline, tobacco, textiles, tires, shoes, etc. These series are shown graphically in Figure 53.

TABLE 119

Comparison of Production Tendencies, 1922-1929

Durable and Non-durable Goods

| Year | Durable goods [a] | Non-durable goods (including semi-durable goods) | All finished goods |
|---|---|---|---|
| 1922 | 100 | 100 | 100 |
| 1923 | 122 | 108 | 113 |
| 1924 | 118 | 106 | 110 |
| 1925 | 142 | 109 | 122 |
| 1926 | 151 | 114 | 128 |
| 1927 | 142 | 118 | 127 |
| 1928 | 153 | 120 | 132 |
| 1929 | 159 | 123 | 137 |
| Average annual rate of change (per cent) .... | +5.9 | +2.8 | +4.1 |
| Index of instability of growth ..... | 5.5 | 1.1 | 2.7 |

[a] This group includes all construction, and the production of machinery, ships, locomotives, railroad cars, automobiles, trucks, furniture, and electrical equipment.

The output of goods which are completely consumed over a short period of time increased without great variation from 1922 to 1929. The volume of production in 1929 was 23 per cent greater than in 1922. The average annual rate of advance was 2.8 per cent, comfortably in excess of the rate of growth of population (1.4 per cent). Average annual variation from a constant rate of growth amounted to but 1.1 per cent. Quite different is the story of durable goods. The output of such goods in 1929 was 59 per cent greater than in 1922; the average rate of advance was 5.9 per cent a year. Variation from constancy of growth averaged 5.5 per cent a year. These figures tell a great deal about the character of the economic advance which occurred between 1922 and 1929. The pressure of advertising, of installment selling, of all the devices which tended to speed up buying during this period, had their richest fruits in the marketing of durable consumption goods.[1] Combined with this

[1] Gasoline, tobacco, druggists' preparations and newsprint, commodities from the non-durable group, shared in this advance.

## FIGURE 53
### GROWTH OF PRODUCTION OF FINISHED GOODS IN THE UNITED STATES, 1922–1929
#### TOTAL PRODUCTION, DURABLE GOODS AND NON-DURABLE GOODS

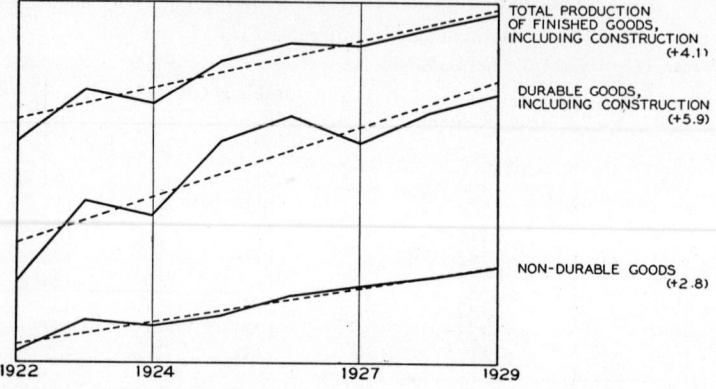

Plotted on ratio scale. The figures in parentheses define average annual rates of change (in percentage form).

was a great advance in the production of capital equipment, also durable in character.

It is probably true, in general, that wants for perishable goods are not highly expansible. An economy which finds its productive powers suddenly enhanced,[1] as was the case in the United States after 1921, is not likely to devote these new powers to the multiplication of foods, or of other goods which are used up in a short time. It will turn out more capital equipment and will seek to encourage demand for new types of consumer goods. Demand for food and clothing is stable, not varying greatly in amount. There are no great possibilities of expansion of wants here, even under strong pressure on the part of sellers, while, conversely, consumers are not in a position materially to reduce the volume of their buying except under the pressure of the strongest necessity. But by the introduction of new goods and the clever 'education' of consumers the 'damned wantlessness' of the natural man may be effectively over-

[1] This form of statement probably reverses, in part, the true course of events. Productive powers were enhanced as a result of the development of new industries, in which high productivity per worker was possible. Had the same energies gone into the production of greater quantities of foods and clothing the same increase in productivity would not have been recorded.

come.[1] It is perhaps not inevitable that such expansion should be felt primarily in the demand for durable consumption goods. Effective advertising might create an insistent demand for soap bubbles. During the decade under review, however, the new demand was directed toward durable goods—automobiles, electric household conveniences, radios, new houses.

From 1922 to 1929 the army of sellers pushed forward on this new front. Wants were stimulated, and the new goods were turned out in ever-increasing volume. The most effective selling methods ever employed were directed against consumers. High profits, high industrial wages, the availability of credit in unprecedented volume provided the means of purchasing. The sense of constantly advancing wealth was encouraged, moreover, by rising values of urban real estate and of securities.

Consumer resistance during this period was quiescent. But it is of the highest importance that so much of this buying was directed toward the purchase of durable goods. To a large extent the new buying of consumers, as well as the buying of equipment by producers, involved a storing up of utilities. In a very real sense the existence of unused utilities in the form of durable consumption goods and capital equipment represents inventories of goods, inventories in the hands of consumers and of producers. The possibility of a material diminution in the volume of buying is very much greater when a large percentage of current purchases goes to the buying of durable goods than it is when perishables are relatively more important. After heavy buying of durable goods consumers may retire from the market for a longer period than is possible when the average consumer's budget is made up almost exclusively of non-durable goods. In this respect the output of durable consumption goods may be expected to resemble in many ways the production of capital goods, which is notoriously highly variable, and which reflects in exaggerated degree the cyclical ups and downs of business.

It is not the present purpose to follow economic changes through the period of the depression, but it is proper to indicate the bearing upon the character of the depression of the rapid growth of durable goods during the years preceding. What brought about the check to buying we do not here consider. But once the check was given,

[1] Nineteenth century German traders in the backward regions of the world cursed the *verdammte Bedürfnislosigkeit* of the natives.

the existence of the stored-up utilities embodied in the heavy preceding production of durable goods made it possible for current purchases to suffer a great and prolonged decline. Consumers had a back-log, and whether necessity or desire persuaded them to utilize it, they did so, to a degree never approached in recent years. At the same time the buying of capital equipment was checked. Previous heavy installation and construction of such goods added its weight to the influence of diminishing sales of end-products. An economy geared to produce durable goods to a greater degree than ever before was bound to be deeply affected by such a cessation of buying on the part both of final consumers and of users of capital equipment.

§ *On changes in the relative importance of certain types of commodities.*—Changes in the character of aggregate output may be traced in another manner, by measuring the relative importance of goods of different types, at different periods. The division into durable and non-durable goods may be first employed. In the first category are included all durable consumption goods, as well as articles of capital equipment. Non-durable goods include perishable and semi-durable consumption goods. The following table presents data on the total value of production of agricultural, mineral and manufacturing industries at four different dates, with estimated aggregate values of the output of durable and non-durable goods at each of these dates. Fisheries and the construction industries are omitted, because of deficiencies of data or difficulties of comparison.

TABLE 120

COMPARATIVE VALUES OF DURABLE AND NON-DURABLE GOODS PRODUCED IN THE UNITED STATES, 1899, 1914, 1923 AND 1929

(In tens of millions of dollars)

| (1) Year | (2) Value of total production [a] | (3) Value of durable goods | (4) Value of non-durable goods (including semi-durable goods) | (5) Value of durable goods as percentage of total value |
|---|---|---|---|---|
| 1899 | 914 | 242 | 672 | 26.5 |
| 1914 | 1,949 | 494 | 1,455 | 25.3 |
| 1923 | 4,094 | 1,386 | 2,708 | 33.9 |
| 1929 | 4,795 | 1,688 | 3,107 | 35.2 |

[a] Based upon the estimated value of raw agricultural and mineral products and the 'value added' in the fabrication of these materials. Data are from issues of *Mineral Resources of the United States, Yearbook of Agriculture* and publications of the Census of Manufactures and the Census of Mines and Quarries.

These figures show a slight decline in the relative importance of durable goods in total output between 1899 and 1914, a drop from 26.5 per cent to 25.3 per cent of the aggregate.[1] By 1923 the output of durable goods had attained new high levels, and the advance continued to 1929. Of the production here included 35.2 per cent consisted of durable goods in 1929, as against 26.5 per cent in 1899 and 25.3 per cent in 1914. This represents a substantial and significant change. Whatever the reasons—changing consumer habits, increasing industrial diversification, changing character of foreign trade—the figures indicate that an increasing percentage of our economic energies was being devoted to the production of goods which render service to producer or consumer over a considerable period. The consumption (and the productive use) of such goods may be stimulated in times of prosperity, but the reverse is also true. Buyers of such goods are in position to withdraw from the market for considerable periods, even though their purchasing power be unimpaired. This is not so likely to be true of buyers of non-durable consumption goods. There is here further evidence of a change in the national economy which rendered it particularly subject to such a drying-up of demand as occurred in many lines after the stock market break of 1929 and the subsequent economic demoralization.[2]

We may approach the same problem from a somewhat different angle by attempting to estimate the relative importance of articles of food and clothing in aggregate national production. It is possible to secure the approximate value of the total production of food and clothing by combining with the total value of raw farm products which enter into foods and clothing the 'value added' in the manufacture of food and clothing. The aggregate with which this figure is compared is the same as that employed above, with, of course, the same restrictions.

[1] Corresponding percentages for 1904 and 1909 are 26.7 and 26.5. The relatively low figure for 1914 may be due to the existence of depression in that year, a condition which reduces the output of capital equipment more sharply than it does the production of non-durable consumption goods.

[2] The omissions from the above table are so numerous that conclusions must be drawn with caution. On the one hand the great growth of service industries and the increasing importance of distributive agencies are not measured by the figures we have included. Such services partake of many of the characteristics of perishable goods. (Certain of these services differ from the bulk of perishable consumers' goods, which consists of foods and clothing, in that they are conveniences or luxuries, rather than necessities.) On the other hand the exclusion of data on construction, for which adequate pre-war figures are lacking, tends to reduce the apparent growth of production of durable goods.

The index of production of durable goods presented in Table 119, which includes construction, indicates a greater increase between 1923 and 1929 than do the aggregate values of these goods as given in the table above (30 per cent, as against 22 per cent). This apparent discrepancy is due in part to the influence of the construction series, and to the dampening effect upon the aggregate value of durable goods of a decline in the prices of these commodities. That the earlier index refers only to end-products is also of some significance.

## TABLE 121

Comparative Values of Food and Clothing Produced in the United States, 1899, 1914, 1923 and 1929

(In tens of millions of dollars)

| (1) Year | (2) Value of farm products, raw [a] | (3) 'Value added' by manufacture of food and clothing | (4) Total value, food and clothing | (5) Total value, all production | (6) Value of food and clothing as percentage of total |
|---|---|---|---|---|---|
| 1899 | 371 | 158 | 529 | 914 | 57.9 |
| 1914 | 816 | 326 | 1,142 | 1,949 | 58.6 |
| 1923 | 1,079 | 790 | 1,869 | 4,094 | 45.7 |
| 1929 | 1,191 | 898 | 2,089 | 4,795 | 43.6 |

[a] Excludes crops fed to animals.

In general, the demand for articles of food and clothing is relatively inelastic. These are the commodities which the consumer must have, and which he will buy so long as his income permits. Growing diversification and increasing economic power probably always bring a decline in the relative importance of such commodities in total national output. Such a tendency also means that the ability of the consumer to withdraw from the market for a considerable time is growing. This may not necessarily mean that a less stable economic condition is developing. But it would appear that economic equilibrium under such conditions would be potentially less stable, more subject to starts and stoppages with the alternating stimulation and retardation of consumer demand for more durable and less essential goods.

Over the thirty-year period between 1899 and 1929 the percentage of aggregate production (as here measured) which consisted of articles of food and clothing declined from 57.9 per cent to 43.6 per cent. These figures indicate that the change occurred between 1914 and 1929, for the 1914 percentage of food and clothing was somewhat greater than that for 1899. (A condition of business depression in 1914 probably tended to increase the percentage somewhat.) Here is evidence, even clearer than that previously presented, bearing on the character of the economic shift occurring during the decade of the 'twenties. The national economy was ministering in decreasing degree to demands for non-durable goods immediately essential to existence. The tie between demands for the current necessities of life and the working of the productive mechanism appears to have been less direct during the post-war period under review than it was during the years immediately preceding the war. The maintenance of equilibrium becomes a progressively more delicate task as the bonds between the working economy and primal human needs become more tenuous.

## Physical Output and Productivity of Manufacturing Industries, 1923-1929

From the detailed records compiled by the Census of Manufactures additional light may be thrown on the course and character of manufacturing production during the years prior to the recession of 1929. In the preceding chapter we have briefly noted the course of manufacturing production between 1914 and 1923—the rise during the war years, the drop that accompanied the recession of 1920-1921, and the notable increase in output between 1921 and 1923. This last advance, which swelled the volume of manufacturing production by about 48 per cent in two years, was effected through an increase of 30 per cent in number of workers employed and a gain of almost 14 per cent in per capita output. We start in 1923, therefore, at a very high level of production and with an exceptionally high standard of working efficiency among manufacturing employees.

Changes in the physical volume of manufacturing production and in certain related elements between 1923 and 1929 are defined by the index numbers in the next table. These are shown graphically in Figure 54.[1]

Over the six-year period which preceded the 1929 break the physical volume of manufacturing production, as measured by the present index numbers, increased 13.0 per cent. (This period begins, it must be remembered, with production at a very high level in 1923.) There was a concurrent decline of 7.4 per cent in number of wage-earners employed in the industries included in the sample studied. More than off-setting this drop in the human factor was the gain of 22.0 per cent in general productive efficiency, as recorded in per capita productivity. This advance occurred on top of an

---

[1] Adequate data relating to physical output are not available for all census industries. The size of the present sample, in relation to the total coverage of the census, is indicated by the following summary:

| Year | Total value of products reported in Census of Manufactures (thousands of dollars) | Value of products in industries represented by index numbers of physical volume of production (thousands of dollars) | Percentage of total value of manufactured products represented in index numbers |
|---|---|---|---|
| 1923 | 60,555,998 | 28,281,117 | 46.7 |
| 1925 | 62,713,714 | 29,091,937 | 46.4 |
| 1927 | 62,718,347 | 27,532,655 | 43.9 |
| 1929 | 70,137,459 | 29,476,380 | 42.0 |

For an explanation of the method employed in the construction of index numbers based on census data, see Chapter III.

## TABLE 122
### Growth of Manufacturing Production in the United States, 1923-1929
Index Numbers of Physical Volume of Production, Number of Wage-earners and per Capita Output

| Year | Physical volume of production | Number of wage-earners | Output per wage-earner |
|---|---|---|---|
| 1923 | 100.0 | 100.0 | 100.0 |
| 1925 | 102.4 | 95.4 | 107.3 |
| 1927 | 104.2 | 92.3 | 113.0 |
| 1929 | 113.0 | 92.6 | 122.0 |
| Average annual rate of change (per cent) .... | +2.0 | —1.3 | +3.3 |

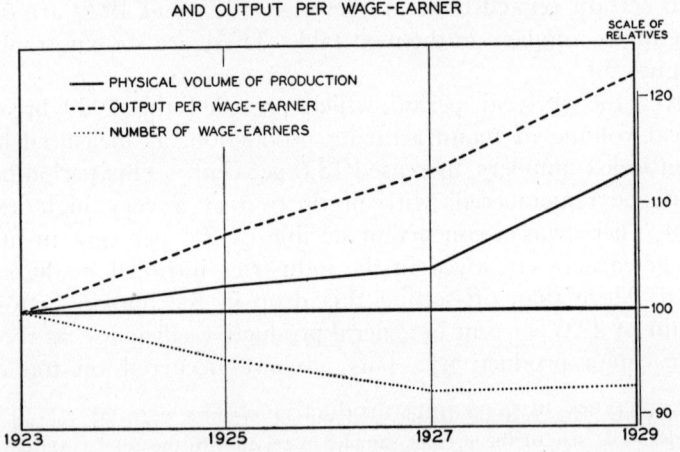

FIGURE 54

GROWTH OF MANUFACTURING PRODUCTION IN THE UNITED STATES, 1923-1929

VOLUME OF PRODUCTION, NUMBER OF WAGE-EARNERS AND OUTPUT PER WAGE-EARNER

increase of 13.6 per cent in per capita output between 1921 and 1923.

Advancing productivity was, of course, a conspicuous feature of the last decade. From 1919 to 1929 output per worker employed increased approximately 43 per cent among the industries in the present sample. The work that required 100 men in 1919 could be done by 70 in 1929. Thirty out of 100 could have been dispensed with, on the evidence of this index, if no increase in aggregate output had been desired. Productivity per worker increased between 1919 and 1929 at an average annual rate of 3.8 per cent. This is substantially greater than the corresponding figure of 1.7 per cent for the fifteen-year period from 1899 to 1914, which itself represents a notable advance in productive efficiency.

The character of these changes is more clearly revealed when they are followed by biennial periods:

| Census interval | Increase in volume of manufacturing production (per cent) | Change in number of wage-earners (per cent) | Increase in output per wage-earner (per cent) |
|---|---|---|---|
| 1923-1925 | +2.4 | −4.6 | +7.3 |
| 1925-1927 | +1.8 | −3.3 | +5.2 |
| 1927-1929 | +8.4 | +0.3 | +8.0 |

Between 1923 and 1925, years of prosperity which straddle a minor recession in 1924, there was an increase of over 7 per cent in output per employee, a decline of 4.6 per cent in number of workers and a net gain of 2.4 per cent in volume of output. During the next two years, which ended in the slightly depressed year, 1927, the process continued, with productivity increasing, number employed declining and aggregate output advancing. With the stimulus of renewed prosperity per capita output again spurted, after 1927, increasing 8 per cent during the next two years. The aggregate volume of production increased by more than 8 per cent. This notable advance brought only a slight increase (0.3 per cent) in the number of wage-earners employed in the industries included in the present sample.

If we carry this story back thirty years by census periods we note the highly suggestive fact that not once has there been a check to the increase in per capita productivity. The rate of advance has varied greatly, but the tendency toward increasing productive efficiency has persisted, in good years and bad. In general, however, the chief factor in expanding production prior to 1923 was an enlarged body of wage-earners. This was true during the great advances from 1904 to 1909, from 1914 to 1919, from 1921 to 1923. Since 1923, however, better technical equipment, improved organization and enhanced skill on the part of the working force seem definitely to have supplanted numbers as instruments of expanding production. The persistence of this tendency must compel men to consider its implications for the future.

§ *Changes in physical volume of production and in output per wage-earner, individual industries.*—The index numbers discussed above are, of course, averages. But between 1923 and 1929 there were diverse movements among the manufacturing industries of the United States. There is no thoroughly satisfactory method of representing these diverse movements by a single set of index numbers. A truer picture of the actual course of events during this period may be secured from the following records, relating to changes in volume of production in 62 industries.

TABLE 123

CHANGES IN PHYSICAL VOLUME OF MANUFACTURING PRODUCTION IN THE UNITED STATES, 1923-1929

Index Numbers for 62 Industries, with Average Annual Rates of Change

| Industry | Index numbers of physical volume of production | | | | Average annual rate of change 1923-1929 (per cent) |
|---|---|---|---|---|---|
| | 1923 | 1925 | 1927 | 1929 | |
| Bone black, carbon black, and lamp-black.. | 100.0 | 144.8 | 138.9 | 214.1 | +12.1 |
| Canning and preserving: fish, crabs, shrimps, oysters, and clams............. | 100.0 | 131.4 | 140.6 | 197.4 | +11.3 |
| Asphalted-felt-base floor coverings......... | 100.0 | 131.3 | 185.1 | 169.4 | + 9.5 |
| Petroleum refining ....................... | 100.0 | 129.6 | 143.5 | 177.1 | + 9.4 |
| Oilcloth ................................. | 100.0 | 107.7 | 128.8 | 162.5 | + 8.8 |
| Hats, wool-felt .......................... | 100.0 | 101.4 | 120.9 | 140.5 | + 6.3 |
| Canning and preserving: fruits and vegetables; pickles, jellies, preserves, and sauces | 100.0 | 123.0 | 125.0 | 149.5 | + 6.3 |
| Paints and varnishes..................... | 100.0 | 115.1 | 128.3 | 142.5 | + 6.0 |
| Condensed and evaporated milk.......... | 100.0 | 103.6 | 120.9 | 136.5 | + 5.7 |
| Firearms ................................ | 100.0 | 91.2 | 120.7 | 130.1 | + 5.6 |
| Paper and pulp .......................... | 100.0 | 113.9 | 128.0 | 137.8 | + 5.5 |
| Oil, cake, and meal, cottonseed........... | 100.0 | 154.5 | 174.1 | 143.2 | + 5.4 |
| Rubber products ........................ | 100.0 | 118.6 | 126.5 | 139.1 | + 5.3 |
| Silk manufactures ....................... | 100.0 | 119.1 | 125.6 | 136.3 | + 4.9 |
| Sugar, beet ............................. | 100.0 | 144.7 | 120.9 | 146.8 | + 4.7 |
| Sand-lime brick ......................... | 100.0 | 151.4 | 152.6 | 137.6 | + 4.3 |
| Fertilizers .............................. | 100.0 | 113.9 | 117.2 | 130.7 | + 4.2 |
| Salt .................................... | 100.0 | 100.1 | 107.5 | 122.3 | + 3.5 |
| Iron and steel: steel works and rolling mills | 100.0 | 100.7 | 101.2 | 124.2 | + 3.5 |
| Corn syrup, corn oil, and starch.......... | 100.0 | 103.3 | 124.8 | 118.2 | + 3.5 |
| Cement ................................. | 100.0 | 118.7 | 126.9 | 123.5 | + 3.4 |
| Coke, not including gas-house coke........ | 100.0 | 90.3 | 92.3 | 121.8 | + 3.4 |
| Ice, manufactured ....................... | 100.0 | 113.6 | 114.4 | 124.8 | + 3.4 |
| Wood distillation and charcoal manufacture | 100.0 | 109.2 | 116.2 | 122.1 | + 3.3 |
| Gas, manufactured, illuminating and heating | 100.0 | 102.3 | 118.0 | 117.7 | + 3.2 |
| Chocolate and cocoa products.............. | 100.0 | 109.4 | 113.7 | 119.2 | + 2.8 |
| Oil, cake, and meal, linseed............... | 100.0 | 119.7 | 113.4 | 123.3 | + 2.8 |

TABLE 123—*Continued*

| Industry | Index numbers of physical volume of production | | | | Average annual rate of change 1923-1929 (per cent) |
|---|---|---|---|---|---|
| | 1923 | 1925 | 1927 | 1929 | |
| Motor vehicles, including bodies and parts. | 100.0 | 103.3 | 90.3 | 123.3 | + 2.8 |
| Turpentine and rosin...................... | 100.0 | 109.5 | 122.9 | 114.6 | + 2.6 |
| Soap ...................................... | 100.0 | 99.9 | 105.1 | 115.1 | + 2.4 |
| Rice cleaning and polishing............... | 100.0 | 80.9 | 106.2 | 104.6 | + 2.0 |
| Explosives ............................... | 100.0 | 97.9 | 101.3 | 110.3 | + 1.7 |
| Butter and cheese........................ | 100.0 | 106.9 | 112.1 | 109.8 | + 1.6 |
| Hats, fur-felt ........................... | 100.0 | 93.1 | 114.5 | 103.8 | + 1.6 |
| Sugar refining, cane...................... | 100.0 | 122.2 | 115.6 | 115.2 | + 1.3 |
| Cast-iron pipe ........................... | 100.0 | 120.2 | 122.2 | 108.6 | + 1.2 |
| Cotton goods ............................ | 100.0 | 98.1 | 109.7 | 104.6 | + 1.2 |
| Iron and steel: blast furnaces............. | 100.0 | 91.3 | 90.8 | 106.7 | + 1.0 |
| Sugar, cane, not including products of refineries ................................ | 100.0 | 78.4 | 41.8 | 117.6 | + 1.0 |
| Musical instruments: organs.............. | 100.0 | 106.1 | 128.1 | 97.8 | + 0.7 |
| Linoleum ................................. | 100.0 | 87.0 | 93.3 | 101.6 | + 0.6 |
| Slaughtering and meat packing, wholesale.. | 100.0 | 94.7 | 97.5 | 100.9 | + 0.3 |
| Cordage and twine........................ | 100.0 | 100.5 | 99.4 | 101.8 | + 0.2 |
| Clay products (other than pottery) and non-clay refractories .................... | 100.0 | 106.9 | 107.1 | 100.5 | + 0.1 |
| Tanning materials, natural dyestuffs, mordants and assistants, and sizes........... | 100.0 | 95.1 | 97.8 | 98.1 | — 0.1 |
| Lumber and timber products............... | 100.0 | 108.0 | 100.4 | 101.6 | — 0.1 |
| Carpets and rugs, wool, other than rag.... | 100.0 | 94.1 | 86.3 | 101.4 | — 0.2 |
| Lime ..................................... | 100.0 | 109.2 | 99.0 | 100.2 | — 0.5 |
| Flour and other grain-mill products........ | 100.0 | 95.3 | 96.6 | 94.5 | — 0.8 |
| Jute and linen goods...................... | 100.0 | 97.2 | 94.5 | 94.1 | — 1.0 |
| Lace goods, cotton........................ | 100.0 | 86.8 | 88.5 | 92.6 | — 1.1 |
| Knit goods ............................... | 100.0 | 94.6 | 95.4 | 91.8 | — 1.2 |
| Wool shoddy ............................. | 100.0 | 113.4 | 73.1 | 102.8 | — 1.6 |
| Buttons .................................. | 100.0 | 95.5 | 82.3 | 86.0 | — 3.0 |
| Woolen goods ............................ | 100.0 | 98.0 | 89.1 | 83.5 | — 3.1 |
| Worsted goods ........................... | 100.0 | 84.8 | 81.5 | 75.5 | — 4.4 |
| Motorcycles, bicycles, and parts........... | 100.0 | 75.9 | 67.4 | 77.2 | — 4.7 |
| Musical instruments: pianos............... | 100.0 | 94.5 | 73.9 | 48.9 | —10.5 |
| Carriages, wagons, sleighs, and sleds...... | 100.0 | 63.8 | 52.5 | 50.1 | —11.6 |
| Cars, steam and electric railroad, not built in railroad repair shops.................. | 100.0 | 62.3 | 43.7 | 42.4 | —14.7 |
| Wire, drawn from purchased bars or rods.. | 100.0 | 93.2 | 103.1 | — | — |
| Felt goods, wool or hair.................. | 100.0 | 102.3 | 96.3 | — | — |
| Average [a] ............................... | 100.0 | 101.5 | 103.6 | 119.0 | + 2.8 |

[a] An arithmetic average of the central items of a weighted frequency distribution, with weights based on 'value added', averaged for the base year and the given year. The central one-fifth of the items, by weight, were included in computing the average.

During this six-year period of general economic advance 13 of the 60 industries for which complete data are available showed net declines. In the extreme case, that of steam and electric railroad cars, the rate

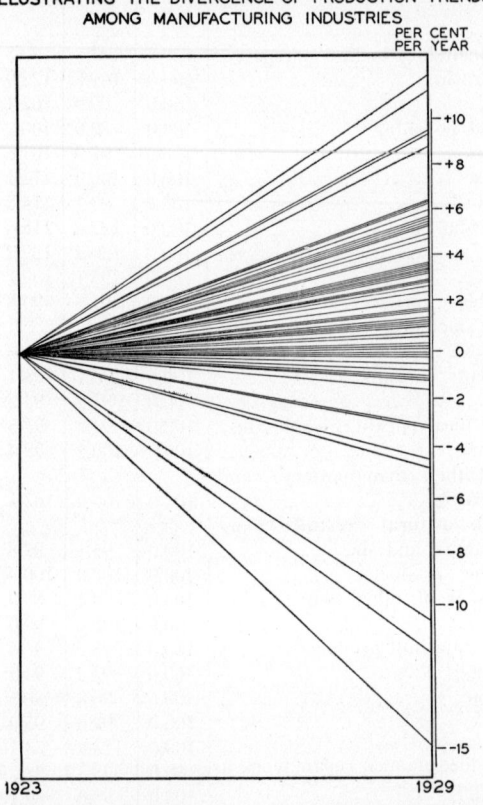

**FIGURE 55**

GROWTH OF MANUFACTURING PRODUCTION
IN THE UNITED STATES, 1923-1929*

ILLUSTRATING THE DIVERGENCE OF PRODUCTION TRENDS
AMONG MANUFACTURING INDUSTRIES

* Plotted on ratio scale. The lines here plotted relate to the industries listed in Table 123, in the order of that listing.

of fall averaged almost 15 per cent a year.[1] At the other limit we have an advance (in the production of bone black, carbon black and lampblack) averaging 12 per cent a year. The degree of divergence is shown graphically in Figure 55, in which rates of change in production in

[1] The capacity, rather than the number of railroad cars, would give a far better index of the output of this type of equipment, but this information is not available. Aggregate capacity of freight cars in service on Class I steam railroads increased

different industries are represented by lines diverging from a common point. The standard deviation of these rates of change is 3.7, somewhat less than the corresponding pre-war value of 5.7.[1]

Reference has already been made to the problems arising out of sharply divergent rates of growth and decline among the elements of the industrial structure. Interchange of men and capital, adaptation of related industries and of instruments of distribution to changing conditions are necessary. Flexibility is a prime requirement of an economic system in these circumstances, if adaptation is to be made easily and without friction. The figures cited indicate that the degree of divergence was somewhat less between 1923 and 1929 than between 1899 and 1914. One extreme case, the rapidly-growing motor vehicle industry, distorts the standard deviation for the years 1899-1914. Excluding this industry [2] the pre-war standard deviation becomes 2.5, as compared with the more recent figure (correspondingly corrected) of 3.8.

There are obvious difficulties in the way of a comparison of economic periods, with respect to degree of divergence of prevailing tendencies. If identical industries are studied, the influence exerted by newly developed commodities and rapidly advancing new industries is ignored. If identical series are not used, doubts arise as to the comparability of the data employed, unless thoroughly comprehensive records for the two periods are available. The measurements last given indicate greater divergence among manufacturing industries in recent years, a condition which would make greater demands upon the productive system in the way of adaptability to changing conditions. But this is an indication which must be checked before its implications may be accepted. We shall return to this subject in a later discussion of employment shifts among manufacturing industries of the United States.

Turning to the record of changes in per capita output in the several industrial groups, we have available the detailed measurements appearing in Table 124.

---

slightly between 1922 and 1929 (at an average annual rate of 0.8 per cent), but this is not necessarily inconsistent with a sharp decline in the annual additions to the total. It is also true that much railroad car construction was included under car repairs. Adequate quantity figures are not available for construction of this type. The value added in such repair work as was reported shows a decline of some 3.3 per cent per annum, between 1923 and 1929, as contrasted with an annual rate of decline of 10.9 per cent in the value added in railroad car construction. While a figure showing an average decline of 15 per cent a year perhaps overstates the rate of fall in this industry, all the evidence indicates the reality of the fall.

[1] The two measurements do not relate to the same list of industries, nor to equal periods of time.

[2] The exclusion is justified solely because of the deficiencies of the standard deviation. A single extreme value affects this measure to a degree not proportionate to the relative weight of that entry.

## TABLE 124

**Changes in Output per Wage-earner in Manufacturing Industries of the United States, 1923-1929**

Index Numbers for 62 Industries, with Average Annual Rates of Change

| Industry | Index numbers of physical volume of production per wage-earner | | | | Average annual rate of change 1923-1929 (per cent) |
|---|---|---|---|---|---|
| | 1923 | 1925 | 1927 | 1929 | |
| Coke, not including gas-house coke........ | 100.0 | 110.4 | 124.2 | 165.4 | +8.8 |
| Salt ...................................... | 100.0 | 108.1 | 122.8 | 154.4 | +7.7 |
| Condensed and evaporated milk............ | 100.0 | 120.6 | 135.7 | 148.4 | +6.6 |
| Carriages, wagons, sleighs, and sleds...... | 100.0 | 107.0 | 125.6 | 144.1 | +6.6 |
| Iron and steel: blast furnaces............. | 100.0 | 114.8 | 119.2 | 149.0 | +6.5 |
| Sugar, cane, not including products of refineries .................................. | 100.0 | 107.1 | 121.4 | 143.0 | +6.3 |
| Oilcloth ................................. | 100.0 | 111.6 | 144.6 | 138.4 | +6.2 |
| Bone black, carbon black, and lamp-black.. | 100.0 | 125.4 | 116.5 | 151.4 | +6.1 |
| Sugar, beet .............................. | 100.0 | 123.5 | 123.6 | 148.3 | +6.1 |
| Soap ..................................... | 100.0 | 110.3 | 133.0 | 139.3 | +6.0 |
| Cement .................................. | 100.0 | 108.4 | 122.6 | 139.9 | +5.9 |
| Tanning materials, natural dyestuffs, mordants and assistants, and sizes.......... | 100.0 | 123.7 | 131.4 | 144.3 | +5.8 |
| Petroleum refining ....................... | 100.0 | 132.4 | 134.4 | 146.6 | +5.7 |
| Asphalted-felt-base floor coverings......... | 100.0 | 89.6 | 127.5 | 126.1 | +5.4 |
| Silk manufactures ....................... | 100.0 | 112.6 | 123.2 | 135.4 | +5.1 |
| Chocolate and cocoa products ............. | 100.0 | 105.5 | 121.6 | 131.0 | +4.9 |
| Paper and pulp .......................... | 100.0 | 111.0 | 125.2 | 130.8 | +4.7 |
| Hats, wool-felt .......................... | 100.0 | 106.7 | 107.9 | 130.5 | +4.3 |
| Rubber products ......................... | 100.0 | 115.3 | 122.9 | 129.8 | +4.2 |
| Sand-lime brick ......................... | 100.0 | 110.0 | 112.4 | 129.8 | +4.1 |
| Flour and other grain-mill products....... | 100.0 | 104.8 | 113.4 | 125.8 | +4.0 |
| Canning and preserving: fish, crabs, shrimps, oysters, and clams.............. | 100.0 | 114.1 | 101.6 | 132.3 | +3.8 |
| Lime .................................... | 100.0 | 111.0 | 111.6 | 126.3 | +3.6 |
| Iron and steel: steel works and rolling mills | 100.0 | 105.4 | 108.7 | 122.7 | +3.3 |
| Sugar refining, cane...................... | 100.0 | 128.5 | 126.0 | 126.2 | +3.2 |
| Butter and cheese........................ | 100.0 | 124.3 | 116.7 | 126.6 | +3.1 |
| Explosives ............................... | 100.0 | 109.7 | 111.5 | 122.0 | +3.1 |
| Lumber and timber products.............. | 100.0 | 114.7 | 120.3 | 120.3 | +3.0 |
| Rice cleaning and polishing............... | 100.0 | 110.1 | 123.0 | 117.6 | +3.0 |
| Gas, manufactured, illuminating and heating | 100.0 | 92.0 | 102.9 | 116.2 | +2.9 |
| Oil, cake, and meal, linseed............... | 100.0 | 116.9 | 109.8 | 123.2 | +2.8 |
| Wool shoddy ............................ | 100.0 | 108.8 | 92.7 | 124.1 | +2.7 |
| Corn syrup, corn oil, and starch........... | 100.0 | 104.0 | 117.0 | 114.7 | +2.7 |
| Fertilizers ............................... | 100.0 | 107.7 | 117.0 | 116.0 | +2.6 |

TABLE 124—*Continued*

| Industry | Index numbers of physical volume of production per wage-earner | | | | Average annual rate of change 1923-1929 (per cent) |
|---|---|---|---|---|---|
| | 1923 | 1925 | 1927 | 1929 | |
| Cordage and twine....................... | 100.0 | 107.0 | 107.9 | 118.2 | +2.6 |
| Cotton goods ........................... | 100.0 | 103.9 | 110.7 | 115.2 | +2.5 |
| Jute and linen goods..................... | 100.0 | 97.2 | 106.8 | 113.5 | +2.4 |
| Buttons ................................ | 100.0 | 98.4 | 101.3 | 114.4 | +2.2 |
| Cast-iron pipe .......................... | 100.0 | 112.6 | 115.2 | 115.4 | +2.2 |
| Oil, cake, and meal, cottonseed........... | 100.0 | 121.5 | 120.4 | 117.0 | +2.2 |
| Firearms ............................... | 100.0 | 126.5 | 122.2 | 118.0 | +2.2 |
| Ice, manufactured ...................... | 100.0 | 122.4 | 138.9 | 109.8 | +2.0 |
| Canning and preserving: fruits and vegetables; pickles, jellies, preserves, and sauces | 100.0 | 103.9 | 112.0 | 111.5 | +2.0 |
| Linoleum ............................... | 100.0 | 111.9 | 108.9 | 114.7 | +1.9 |
| Paints and varnishes..................... | 100.0 | 103.1 | 104.3 | 112.5 | +1.9 |
| Motor vehicles, including bodies and parts. | 100.0 | 98.1 | 99.0 | 111.5 | +1.7 |
| Slaughtering and meat packing, wholesale. | 100.0 | 104.4 | 108.7 | 110.5 | +1.7 |
| Hats, fur-felt ........................... | 100.0 | 102.7 | 120.2 | 105.9 | +1.7 |
| Clay products (other than pottery) and non-clay refractories .................... | 100.0 | 106.8 | 109.0 | 108.9 | +1.4 |
| Motorcycles, bicycles, and parts........... | 100.0 | 119.1 | 113.8 | 111.8 | +1.4 |
| Wood distillation and charcoal manufacture | 100.0 | 106.7 | 105.6 | 108.5 | +1.2 |
| Worsted goods ......................... | 100.0 | 105.5 | 107.5 | 106.5 | +1.0 |
| Carpets and rugs, wool, other than rag.... | 100.0 | 97.8 | 92.5 | 108.0 | +0.9 |
| Woolen goods .......................... | 100.0 | 105.8 | 104.4 | 106.6 | +0.9 |
| Musical instruments: pianos.............. | 100.0 | 104.5 | 99.0 | 105.6 | +0.6 |
| Lace goods, cotton....................... | 100.0 | 90.5 | 99.7 | 99.0 | +0.3 |
| Knit goods ............................. | 100.0 | 98.4 | 97.4 | 96.9 | —0.5 |
| Turpentine and rosin..................... | 100.0 | 127.8 | 111.2 | 96.3 | —1.3 |
| Cars, steam and electric railroad, not built in railroad repair shops................. | 100.0 | 99.7 | 92.6 | 91.5 | —1.7 |
| Musical instruments: organs.............. | 100.0 | 80.0 | 85.8 | 77.0 | —3.6 |
| Wire, drawn from purchased bars or rods. | 100.0 | 107.1 | 110.6 | — | — |
| Felt goods, wool or hair.................. | 100.0 | 114.0 | 101.3 | — | — |
| Average[a] ............................. | 100.0 | 105.3 | 109.7 | 117.8 | +2.7 |

[a] Arithmetic average of the central items of a weighted frequency distribution, with weights based on 'value added', averaged for the base year and the given year. The central one-fifth of the items, by weight, were included in computing the average.

Of the 60 industries for which complete data are available 25 showed increases of more than 25 per cent in per capita output between 1923 and 1929. That this advance could have taken place over a period of six years is one of the most striking features of the period under review. Only five industries showed declines in per capita output in 1929, as compared with 1923.

Here again there is evidence of the extraordinary diversity of the influences affecting manufacturing industries. In terms of average annual movements we find rates of change in output per wage-earner which range from +8.8 per cent for coke, to —3.6 per cent for organs. (We are not now concerned with the reasons for these changing rates, reasons which lie in changing marketing conditions, as well as in technical aspects of production.) The standard deviation of the rates of change in output per worker is 1.9 for the period 1923-1929, a figure almost identical with that for the period 1899-1914. The divergence of these changes is illustrated graphically in Figure 56, in which trend lines of per capita output in different industries are plotted.

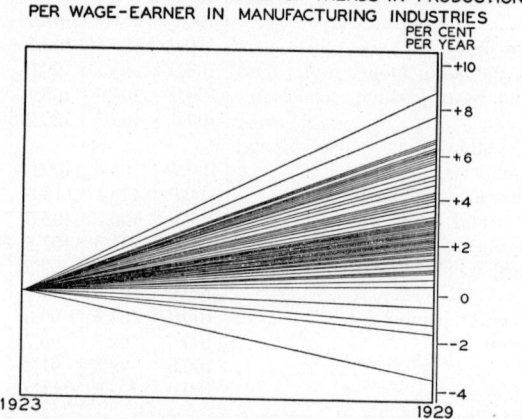

**FIGURE 56**

GROWTH OF MANUFACTURING PRODUCTION IN THE UNITED STATES, 1923-1929*

ILLUSTRATING THE DIVERGENCE OF TRENDS IN PRODUCTION PER WAGE-EARNER IN MANUFACTURING INDUSTRIES

\* Plotted on ratio scale. The lines here plotted relate to the industries listed in Table 124, in the order of that listing.

Beneath the two preceding tables are given series of averages, defining changes in production and in per capita output as recorded among central and representative manufacturing industries. These differ somewhat from the index numbers previously presented, which were derived by methods which give consistent and mathematically more elegant results. The averages just cited are probably more representative of typical conditions. These are summarized in Table 125.

Up to 1927 the record of these averages, in respect of volume of production, follows that of the index numbers previously given. Between 1927 and 1929 the stories diverge. The present averages indicate an advance in output of 15 per cent among typical American industries

### TABLE 125
GROWTH OF MANUFACTURING PRODUCTION IN THE UNITED STATES, 1923-1929
Averages of Aggregate Production and of per Capita Output
(Derived from the central items of frequency distributions)

| Year | Physical volume of production | Output per wage-earner |
|---|---|---|
| 1923 | 100.0 | 100.0 |
| 1925 | 101.5 | 105.3 |
| 1927 | 103.6 | 109.7 |
| 1929 | 119.0 | 117.8 |
| Average annual rate of change (per cent) .............. | +2.8 | +2.7 |

between those two years, as against the gain of 8.4 per cent shown by the 'ideal' index.

The productivity index based on central items in the frequency tables shows a somewhat lower range of values than were secured by the 'ideal' index. The story is sufficiently impressive, however, indicating a gain in per capita output among representative manufacturing industries of 17.8 per cent in six years. By far the most rapid gain occurred in the two years from 1927 to 1929.

## Manufacturing Establishments and Volume of Manufacturing Production

Turning from workers and output per worker to establishments and the records of output per establishment, new aspects of recent movements in the manufacturing field may be traced. Relevant index numbers are given below, and are plotted in Figure 57.

### TABLE 126
GROWTH OF MANUFACTURING PRODUCTION IN THE UNITED STATES, 1923-1929
Index Numbers of Physical Volume of Production, Number of Establishments and Output per Establishment

| Year | Physical volume of production | Number of establishments | Output per establishment |
|---|---|---|---|
| 1923 | 100.0 | 100.0 | 100.0 |
| 1925 | 102.4 | 93.0 | 110.1 |
| 1927 | 104.2 | 88.7 | 117.4 |
| 1929 | 113.0 | 93.8 | 120.5 |
| Average annual rate of change (per cent) .... | +2.0 | −1.2 | +3.1 |

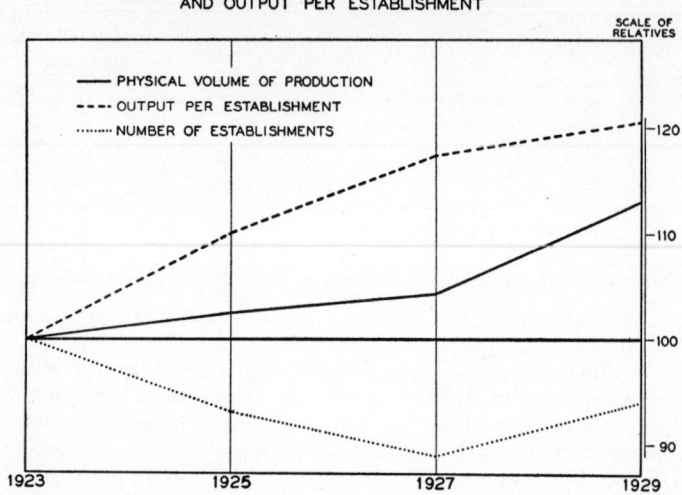

### FIGURE 57
#### GROWTH OF MANUFACTURING PRODUCTION IN THE UNITED STATES, 1923-1929
VOLUME OF PRODUCTION, NUMBER OF ESTABLISHMENTS AND OUTPUT PER ESTABLISHMENT

The pre-war record was one of an increasing number of establishments, and a much more rapidly advancing output per establishment. Between 1914 and 1923 there was a net decline in number of establishments. (The actual loss took place during the period 1919-1921.) Output per establishment advanced throughout the war, suffered a slight check (1 per cent) from 1919 to 1921, and increased by the phenomenal figure of 41 per cent between 1921 and 1923. Taking up the story in 1923, the above table indicates a drop of 6.2 per cent between 1923 and 1929 in number of establishments, with a gain of 20.5 per cent in production per establishment.

The tendency toward large scale production is more clearly revealed if we survey a longer period. Among the industries here studied, the number of establishments was slightly higher in 1929 than in 1899, thirty years before. (The index for 1929 is 104.6 on the 1899 base.) Output per establishment was 198 per cent greater. During the decade from 1919 to 1929 the number of establishments declined 18 per cent; output per establishment increased 68 per cent. Integration, and the concentration of production in establishments turning out constantly larger quantities of goods, have proceeded more rapidly during the last decade than in any similar period we have covered.

This movement continued uninterruptedly during the six-year period from 1923 to 1929, except for a check to the decline in the number of establishments between 1927 and 1929.[1] Changes by inter-censal periods are shown by the following figures:

| Census interval | Increase in volume of manufacturing production (per cent) | Change in number of establishments (per cent) | Increase in output per establishment (per cent) |
|---|---|---|---|
| 1923-1925 | +2.4 | −7.0 | +10.1 |
| 1925-1927 | +1.8 | −4.6 | + 6.7 |
| 1927-1929 | +8.4 | +5.7 | + 2.6 |

§ *Changes in output per establishment, individual industries.*—There have been wide differences among industries in respect to changes in output per establishment. To trace these we must turn from the index numbers to the records for individual industries, which appear in Table 127.

We shall not here comment in detail upon the entries in this table, significant though they be. The fact that in 15 out of 60 industries output per establishment was increased by more than 50 per cent during a short six years indicates how drastic were the changes occurring in American industry. Twenty-seven of the 60 industries increased output per establishment by more than 25 per cent over the same period, a period which opens, be it remembered, after a great advance in productivity (from 1921 to 1923) which is not here considered. This was an era of dynamic change in the structure and methods of manufacturing industries in the United States.

The averages at the foot of Table 127, which are based upon the central items in the several columns, are designed to measure the changes taking place among representative industries. They do not differ materially from the index numbers given in Table 126.

This remarkable advance in output per establishment calls for further consideration. A given establishment may increase its output by adding to the number of workers employed, or by increasing productivity per worker through improved organization, better equipment or greater skill on the part of the workers. To which of

[1] The increase in number of establishments in 1929 is in part due to the more complete canvass in the decennial census of that year.

## TABLE 127

CHANGES IN OUTPUT PER ESTABLISHMENT IN MANUFACTURING INDUSTRIES OF THE UNITED STATES, 1923-1929

Index Numbers for 62 Industries, with Average Annual Rates of Change

| Industry | Index numbers of output per establishment | | | | Average annual rate of change 1923-1929 (per cent) |
|---|---|---|---|---|---|
| | 1923 | 1925 | 1927 | 1929 | |
| Coke, not including gas-house coke........ | 100.0 | 99.8 | 141.5 | 221.6 | +16.0 |
| Sugar, cane, not including products of refineries ............................. | 100.0 | 101.8 | 96.2 | 204.9 | +13.3 |
| Motor vehicles, including bodies and parts. | 100.0 | 154.2 | 151.1 | 217.6 | +12.1 |
| Carriages, wagons, sleighs, and sleds...... | 100.0 | 166.2 | 177.6 | 220.5 | +12.1 |
| Canning and preserving: fish, crabs, shrimps, oysters, and clams............. | 100.0 | 148.7 | 150.6 | 203.6 | +11.1 |
| Bone black, carbon black, and lamp-black.. | 100.0 | 149.2 | 140.9 | 199.4 | +10.5 |
| Salt ..................................... | 100.0 | 107.3 | 139.0 | 163.8 | + 9.2 |
| Oilcloth ................................. | 100.0 | 107.7 | 144.9 | 162.5 | + 9.2 |
| Iron and steel: blast furnaces............. | 100.0 | 126.5 | 132.3 | 175.2 | + 9.1 |
| Petroleum refining ...................... | 100.0 | 137.9 | 154.9 | 173.4 | + 8.8 |
| Wood distillation and charcoal manufacture | 100.0 | 126.7 | 162.5 | 165.0 | + 8.8 |
| Hats, wool-felt .......................... | 100.0 | 96.8 | 149.3 | 148.7 | + 8.4 |
| Gas, manufactured, illuminating and heating | 100.0 | 104.5 | 133.8 | 154.6 | + 8.2 |
| Motorcycles, bicycles, and parts........... | 100.0 | 82.2 | 90.7 | 150.5 | + 7.9 |
| Silk manufactures ....................... | 100.0 | 114.7 | 121.8 | 151.9 | + 6.9 |
| Oil, cake, and meal, linseed............... | 100.0 | 123.3 | 116.8 | 149.7 | + 6.0 |
| Rubber products ......................... | 100.0 | 118.4 | 129.7 | 143.4 | + 5.9 |
| Paper and pulp .......................... | 100.0 | 111.3 | 125.0 | 140.5 | + 5.9 |
| Sugar, beet ............................. | 100.0 | 136.6 | 128.5 | 150.4 | + 5.7 |
| Firearms ................................ | 100.0 | 95.7 | 126.7 | 130.1 | + 5.5 |
| Rice cleaning and polishing............... | 100.0 | 88.6 | 122.2 | 124.4 | + 5.0 |
| Oil, cake, and meal, cottonseed............ | 100.0 | 147.6 | 162.6 | 136.5 | + 4.7 |
| Flour and other grain-mill products....... | 100.0 | 113.0 | 125.3 | 127.7 | + 4.2 |
| Butter and cheese........................ | 100.0 | 117.3 | 126.3 | 125.5 | + 3.7 |
| Asphalted-felt-base floor coverings......... | 100.0 | 107.4 | 138.8 | 117.2 | + 3.7 |
| Knit goods .............................. | 100.0 | 110.6 | 118.6 | 123.4 | + 3.5 |
| Iron and steel: steel works and rolling mills | 100.0 | 104.1 | 101.8 | 125.3 | + 3.5 |
| Lime .................................... | 100.0 | 116.1 | 114.6 | 126.1 | + 3.4 |
| Canning and preserving: fruits and vegetables; pickles, jellies, preserves, and sauces | 100.0 | 124.8 | 125.1 | 126.5 | + 3.4 |
| Carpets and rugs, wool, other than rag.... | 100.0 | 107.8 | 104.8 | 125.2 | + 3.4 |
| Explosives .............................. | 100.0 | 100.7 | 107.4 | 120.5 | + 3.2 |
| Lumber and timber products .............. | 100.0 | 110.2 | 125.6 | 73.9 | + 3.1 |
| Corn syrup, corn oil, and starch........... | 100.0 | 106.7 | 148.8 | 107.8 | + 2.9 |
| Buttons ................................. | 100.0 | 111.0 | 120.8 | 117.5 | + 2.8 |

## TABLE 127—Continued

| Industry | Index numbers of output per establishment | | | | Average annual rate of change 1923-1929 (per cent) |
|---|---|---|---|---|---|
| | 1923 | 1925 | 1927 | 1929 | |
| Cotton goods ........................... | 100.0 | 98.8 | 112.0 | 114.2 | + 2.7 |
| Soap .................................. | 100.0 | 99.2 | 110.8 | 113.4 | + 2.5 |
| Chocolate and cocoa products............. | 100.0 | 105.8 | 95.6 | 119.2 | + 2.3 |
| Fertilizers ............................. | 100.0 | 111.2 | 108.1 | 117.4 | + 2.3 |
| Wool shoddy ........................... | 100.0 | 98.4 | 78.4 | 121.3 | + 2.2 |
| Slaughtering and meat packing, wholesale.. | 100.0 | 104.2 | 109.0 | 113.3 | + 2.1 |
| Paints and varnishes..................... | 100.0 | 103.0 | 105.3 | 113.6 | + 2.1 |
| Clay products (other than pottery) and non-clay refractories .................... | 100.0 | 109.3 | 115.1 | 112.8 | + 2.0 |
| Tanning materials, natural dyestuffs, mordants and assistants, and sizes........... | 100.0 | 95.1 | 100.2 | 110.4 | + 1.8 |
| Turpentine and rosin..................... | 100.0 | 130.8 | 128.6 | 114.5 | + 1.8 |
| Hats, fur-felt ........................... | 100.0 | 103.9 | 127.8 | 103.2 | + 1.6 |
| Sugar refining, cane..................... | 100.0 | 116.4 | 110.1 | 109.7 | + 1.0 |
| Cordage and twine...................... | 100.0 | 103.1 | 103.6 | 105.3 | + 0.8 |
| Cast-iron pipe .......................... | 100.0 | 113.9 | 108.8 | 107.1 | + 0.8 |
| Worsted goods ......................... | 100.0 | 87.1 | 95.6 | 97.8 | + 0.1 |
| Cement ................................ | 100.0 | 108.9 | 104.8 | 102.0 | + 0.1 |
| Ice, manufactured ...................... | 100.0 | 114.4 | 112.1 | 100.8 | 0.0 |
| Condensed and evaporated milk........... | 100.0 | 97.4 | 98.5 | 99.3 | 0.0 |
| Linoleum .............................. | 100.0 | 101.6 | 93.3 | 101.6 | − 0.2 |
| Sand-lime brick ........................ | 100.0 | 114.5 | 105.1 | 101.6 | − 0.2 |
| Musical instruments: organs.............. | 100.0 | 109.8 | 120.0 | 94.6 | − 0.3 |
| Woolen goods .......................... | 100.0 | 100.0 | 97.0 | 96.0 | − 0.8 |
| Musical instruments: pianos .............. | 100.0 | 106.5 | 95.3 | 96.5 | − 1.1 |
| Jute and linen goods .................... | 100.0 | 87.7 | 85.2 | 94.1 | − 1.1 |
| Lace goods, cotton ...................... | 100.0 | 80.6 | 80.2 | 88.1 | − 2.0 |
| Cars, steam and electric railroad, not built in railroad repair shops................. | 100.0 | 61.5 | 45.0 | 43.3 | −14.2 |
| Felt goods, wool or hair.................. | 100.0 | 108.4 | 102.1 | — | — |
| Wire, drawn from purchased bars or rods.. | 100.0 | 87.8 | 90.4 | — | — |
| Average [a] ............................. | 100.0 | 107.3 | 114.9 | 124.4 | + 3.7 |

[a] Arithmetic average of the central items of a weighted frequency distribution, with weights based on 'value added', averaged for the base year and the given year. The central one-fifth of the items, by weight, were included in computing the average.

these factors has the recent advance in output per establishment been due? The entries in Table 128 throw light on this problem.

The answer to the question we have just raised is clear. During the entire period the number of workers in the average estab-

## TABLE 128
### Growth of Manufacturing Production in the United States, 1923-1929
Factors Affecting Output per Establishment

| Year | Output per establishment | Number of workers per establishment | Output per worker |
|---|---|---|---|
| 1923 | 100.0 | 100.0 | 100.0 |
| 1925 | 110.1 | 102.5 | 107.3 |
| 1927 | 117.4 | 104.0 | 113.0 |
| 1929 | 120.5 | 98.7 | 122.0 |
| Average annual rate of change (per cent) .... | +3.1 | −0.1 | +3.3 |

lishment decreased 1.3 per cent,[1] output per worker increased by 22.0 per cent. In this marked preponderance of the mechanical and organizational factor the recent period is unique. Between 1899 and 1914 the gain in output per establishment was due to both factors. In 1914, 20.4 per cent more workers were employed per factory than in 1899, while output per worker was 29.6 per cent greater. From 1914 to 1923 increasing output per establishment was due to an advance of 32 per cent in number of workers per establishment, of 20 per cent in output per worker. During the six years ending in 1929 an absolute decrease in workers per establishment accompanied a notable increase in productivity per worker, an increase attributable to better equipment, better organization and enhanced personal skill. Here is further evidence of the strength of the tendency toward the use of mechanical and organizational factors, as instruments for augmenting production. We have not yet solved the problems that this movement has brought with it.

Changes by census periods are shown by the following summary:

| Census interval | Increase in output per establishment (per cent) | Change in number of workers per establishment (per cent) | Increase in output per worker (per cent) |
|---|---|---|---|
| 1923-1925 | +10.1 | +2.5 | +7.3 |
| 1925-1927 | + 6.7 | +1.4 | +5.2 |
| 1927-1929 | + 2.6 | −5.0 | +8.0 |

[1] Again a reservation must be entered because of the probably greater coverage of the 1929 census.

In each of the census periods the elements reflected in output per wage-earner were prime factors in stimulating production per establishment.

§ Records by industries of the changes in number of wage-earners per establishment between 1923 and 1929 are shown in the following table. The story they tell, and the contrasts between industries, are sufficiently clear without comment at this point.

TABLE 129

Changes in Number of Wage-earners per Establishment in Manufacturing Industries of the United States, 1923-1929

Index Numbers for 62 Industries, with Average Annual Rates of Change

| Industry | Index numbers of wage-earners per establishment | | | | Average annual rate of change 1923-1929 (per cent) |
|---|---|---|---|---|---|
| | 1923 | 1925 | 1927 | 1929 | |
| Motor vehicles, including bodies and parts. | 100.0 | 157.1 | 152.6 | 195.2 | +9.8 |
| Wood distillation and charcoal manufacture | 100.0 | 118.7 | 153.8 | 152.2 | +7.6 |
| Canning and preserving: fish, crabs, shrimps, oysters, and clams............ | 100.0 | 130.3 | 148.2 | 153.9 | +7.0 |
| Motorcycles, bicycles, and parts.......... | 100.0 | 69.1 | 79.7 | 134.6 | +6.2 |
| Coke, not including gas-house coke........ | 100.0 | 90.4 | 113.9 | 134.0 | +5.9 |
| Sugar, cane, not including products of refineries ................................ | 100.0 | 95.1 | 79.3 | 143.3 | +5.6 |
| Carriages, wagons, sleighs, and sleds...... | 100.0 | 155.3 | 141.4 | 153.0 | +5.4 |
| Gas, manufactured, illuminating and heating | 100.0 | 113.6 | 130.1 | 133.1 | +5.0 |
| Bone black, carbon black, and lamp-black.. | 100.0 | 119.0 | 121.0 | 131.7 | +4.2 |
| Hats, wool-felt ......................... | 100.0 | 90.8 | 138.4 | 113.9 | +4.1 |
| Knit goods ............................. | 100.0 | 112.4 | 121.8 | 127.3 | +4.0 |
| Turpentine and rosin.................... | 100.0 | 102.4 | 115.6 | 118.9 | +3.3 |
| Oil, cake, and meal, linseed.............. | 100.0 | 105.4 | 106.4 | 121.5 | +3.1 |
| Firearms .............................. | 100.0 | 75.7 | 103.7 | 110.2 | +3.1 |
| Petroleum refining ..................... | 100.0 | 104.2 | 115.2 | 118.3 | +3.1 |
| Musical instruments: organs............. | 100.0 | 137.3 | 139.8 | 122.8 | +2.9 |
| Oilcloth ............................... | 100.0 | 96.4 | 100.3 | 117.4 | +2.7 |
| Oil, cake, and meal, cottonseed........... | 100.0 | 121.5 | 135.1 | 116.7 | +2.7 |
| Iron and steel: blast furnaces............ | 100.0 | 110.1 | 111.0 | 117.5 | +2.5 |
| Carpets and rugs, wool, other than rag.... | 100.0 | 110.2 | 113.3 | 116.0 | +2.4 |
| Rice cleaning and polishing.............. | 100.0 | 80.5 | 99.4 | 105.8 | +1.9 |
| Rubber products ....................... | 100.0 | 102.7 | 105.6 | 110.5 | +1.7 |
| Silk manufactures ...................... | 100.0 | 101.9 | 98.8 | 112.2 | +1.6 |
| Salt ................................... | 100.0 | 99.3 | 113.2 | 106.1 | +1.5 |
| Canning and preserving: fruits and vegetables; pickles, jellies, preserves, and sauces | 100.0 | 120.1 | 111.7 | 113.4 | +1.4 |

TABLE 129—*Continued*

| Industry | Index numbers of wage-earners per establishment | | | | Average annual rate of change 1923-1929 (per cent) |
|---|---|---|---|---|---|
| | 1923 | 1925 | 1927 | 1929 | |
| Paper and pulp | 100.0 | 100.3 | 99.8 | 107.4 | +1.1 |
| Clay products (other than pottery) and non-clay refractories | 100.0 | 102.3 | 105.6 | 103.6 | +0.7 |
| Buttons | 100.0 | 112.9 | 119.3 | 102.7 | +0.7 |
| Butter and cheese | 100.0 | 94.4 | 108.2 | 99.1 | +0.6 |
| Slaughtering and meat packing, wholesale | 100.0 | 99.8 | 100.2 | 102.5 | +0.4 |
| Flour and other grain-mill products | 100.0 | 107.8 | 110.5 | 101.5 | +0.3 |
| Corn syrup, corn oil, and starch | 100.0 | 102.6 | 127.2 | 93.9 | +0.3 |
| Paints and varnishes | 100.0 | 100.0 | 101.0 | 101.0 | +0.2 |
| Cotton goods | 100.0 | 95.0 | 101.2 | 99.2 | +0.2 |
| Iron and steel: steel works and rolling mills | 100.0 | 98.7 | 93.7 | 102.1 | +0.1 |
| Explosives | 100.0 | 91.8 | 96.3 | 98.8 | 0.0 |
| Sugar, beet | 100.0 | 110.6 | 104.0 | 101.4 | —0.1 |
| Lime | 100.0 | 104.7 | 102.7 | 99.9 | —0.1 |
| Hats, fur-felt | 100.0 | 101.2 | 106.3 | 97.5 | —0.1 |
| Fertilizers | 100.0 | 103.2 | 92.5 | 101.2 | —0.4 |
| Wool shoddy | 100.0 | 90.4 | 84.6 | 97.7 | —0.7 |
| Worsted goods | 100.0 | 82.6 | 88.9 | 91.8 | —1.0 |
| Cast-iron pipe | 100.0 | 101.2 | 94.4 | 92.9 | —1.4 |
| Asphalted-felt-base floor coverings | 100.0 | 119.8 | 108.9 | 93.0 | —1.5 |
| Musical instruments: pianos | 100.0 | 101.9 | 96.3 | 91.3 | —1.6 |
| Woolen goods | 100.0 | 94.5 | 93.0 | 90.1 | —1.6 |
| Cordage and twine | 100.0 | 96.4 | 96.0 | 89.1 | —1.7 |
| Ice, manufactured | 100.0 | 93.4 | 80.8 | 91.8 | —2.0 |
| Linoleum | 100.0 | 90.8 | 85.7 | 88.6 | —2.1 |
| Lace goods, cotton | 100.0 | 89.0 | 80.5 | 89.0 | —2.3 |
| Sugar refining, cane | 100.0 | 90.5 | 87.4 | 86.9 | —2.3 |
| Chocolate and cocoa products | 100.0 | 100.2 | 78.6 | 91.0 | —2.6 |
| Jute and linen goods | 100.0 | 90.2 | 79.8 | 82.9 | —3.4 |
| Soap | 100.0 | 89.9 | 83.3 | 81.4 | —3.5 |
| Sand-lime brick | 100.0 | 104.1 | 93.5 | 78.2 | —4.0 |
| Tanning materials, natural dyestuffs, mordants and assistants, and sizes | 100.0 | 76.9 | 76.3 | 76.5 | —4.2 |
| Cement | 100.0 | 100.5 | 85.5 | 72.9 | —5.2 |
| Lumber and timber products | 100.0 | 96.1 | 104.4 | 61.5 | —5.8 |
| Condensed and evaporated milk | 100.0 | 80.7 | 72.6 | 61.3 | —7.6 |
| Cars, steam and electric railroad, not built in railroad repair shops | 100.0 | 61.6 | 48.6 | 47.3 | —12.7 |
| Felt goods, wool or hair | 100.0 | 95.1 | 100.8 | — | — |
| Wire, drawn from purchased bars or rods | 100.0 | 81.9 | 81.7 | — | — |
| Average [a] | 100.0 | 99.9 | 101.2 | 102.3 | +0.4 |

[a] Arithmetic average of the central items of a weighted frequency distribution, with weights based on 'value added', averaged for the base year and the given year. The central one-fifth of the items, by weight, were included in computing the average.

§ *On the diversification of manufacturing production: A revision of index numbers of output.*—All attempts to measure changes in the volume of physical production are, of necessity, approximations to the truth. The output of many types of goods, particularly highly fabricated goods, is not subject to enumeration. Again, the numerous new products which are constantly appearing on the market must be omitted from an index based upon the production of standardized units over a period of years. The more diversified the economy, the more dynamic the industrial structure, the less adequate are the conventional index numbers which trace changes in the output of standard and readily-enumerated products. These conditions have been strongly-marked features of our economic development during the last decade. New commodities of a thousand types have been marketed; 'consumer education' to the use of new modes of refrigeration, heating, cooking, sanitation and recreation has been proceeding apace. And an increasing proportion of the manufactured goods produced has consisted of highly fabricated articles of constantly changing quality and character. The measurement of alteration in physical output under these conditions presents far greater difficulties than it would in an economy producing few and simple commodities of standard type.

It is a fair assumption that an index number of the conventional type, designed to measure changes in volume of output, will understate the actual rate of growth over a period of years. (This would not necessarily be true in the rebound from a period of depression, during which the output of basic commodities is likely to have been subject to sharp reduction.) The figures in Table 130 bear on this point.

Over the six-year period the value of the services of agents of fabrication of all census industries, as measured by 'value added', in-

TABLE 130
CHANGES IN VALUE ADDED BY MANUFACTURE, 1923-1929

| (1) | (2) | (3) | (4) | (5) | (6) | (7) |
|---|---|---|---|---|---|---|
| Year | 'Value added', all census industries | | 'Value added', industries included in sample [a] | | 'Value added', industries not included in sample | |
| | In millions of dollars | In relatives | In millions of dollars | In relatives | In millions of dollars | In relatives |
| 1923 | 25,850 | 100.0 | 9,961 | 100.0 | 15,889 | 100.0 |
| 1925 | 26,778 | 103.6 | 10,196 | 102.4 | 16,582 | 104.4 |
| 1927 | 27,585 | 106.7 | 9,729 | 97.7 | 17,856 | 112.4 |
| 1929 [b] | 31,844 | 123.2 | 11,147 | 113.7 | 20,697 | 129.2 |

[a] These figures give the full 'value added' for all industries included in the index, without correction for adjustment of weights.

[b] In the construction of the index of production relatives were first obtained on 1927 as base, and then shifted to 1923 as 100. The entries for 1929 (preliminary) as given in the table are not directly comparable with the figures for earlier years.

creased by 23.2 per cent, while the increase for industries included in the index numbers presented on earlier pages amounted to but 13.7 per cent. It is significant that the chief divergence occurred between 1925 and 1927. The limited group of industries heretofore included dropped 4.6 per cent in 'value added' during the minor recession of 1927, while all manufacturing industries increased 3.0 per cent.[1] From 1927 to 1929 the general group and the limited group advanced at much the same rate.

But value figures do not define changes in physical production. For industries covered by the Census of Manufactures such physical changes may be approximated in two different ways, one based on the assumption that the cost of fabrication, per unit of product, changed at the same rate among all manufacturing industries as among the selected group for which quantity statistics are available, the other on the assumption that output per wage-earner changed among all manufacturing industries in the same degree as among the group of industries included in the sample. The procedure followed is illustrated in the next table.

TABLE 131

ILLUSTRATING THE DERIVATION OF INDEX NUMBERS OF THE PHYSICAL VOLUME OF MANUFACTURING PRODUCTION, 1923-1929

All Census Industries

| (1) | (2) | (3) | (4) | (5) | (6) | (7) | (8) | (9) |
|---|---|---|---|---|---|---|---|---|
| | Derivation of index numbers based upon 'value added' | | | | Derivation of index numbers based upon number of wage-earners employed | | | |
| Year | Total 'value added', all census industries | | 'Value added' per unit of product, industries included in sample | Derived index of physical volume of production | Number of wage-earners, all census industries | | Index of per capita production, industries included in sample | Derived index of physical volume of production |
| | In millions of dollars | In relatives | | | In thousands | In relatives | | |
| 1923 | 25,850 | 100.0 | 100.0 | 100.0 | 8,778 | 100.0 | 100.0 | 100.0 |
| 1925 | 26,778 | 103.6 | 97.3 | 106.4 | 8,384 | 95.5 | 107.3 | 102.5 |
| 1927 | 27,585 | 106.7 | 92.4 | 115.4 | 8,350 | 95.1 | 113.0 | 107.4 |
| 1929 | 31,844 | 123.2 | 96.8 | 127.3 | 8,808 | 100.3 | 122.0 | 122.4 |

[1] It will be remembered that in the upswing from the depression of 1921 'value added' for all census industries increased by only 41 per cent (i.e., 'value added' in 1923 exceeded 'value added' in 1921 by 41 per cent), while 'value added' for the industries included in the index advanced by 54 per cent. Cyclical swings of business are more severe among the basic industries for which production statistics are readily available than among manufacturing industries at large.

The derived index numbers in columns (5) and (9) of the above table both show greater gains in physical production than are shown by the index based upon actual statistics of output. The two series of derived measurements follow the same general course, but with appreciable differences in all years. To secure the most satisfactory approximation to the actual changes in the volume of manufacturing production we may average the two. The results are given in column (3) of the next table. In column (2) appears the index based on actual production statistics, for census years. The Day-Thomas index in column (4) represents a different combination of census data. The other two indexes are based upon annual statistics of quantities produced.

TABLE 132

COMPARISON OF INDEX NUMBERS OF PHYSICAL VOLUME OF MANUFACTURING PRODUCTION IN THE UNITED STATES, 1923-1929

| (1) | (2) | (3) | (4) | (5) | (6) |
|---|---|---|---|---|---|
| | Census index numbers of volume of fabrication | | | Index numbers based upon annual data | |
| Year | Based on 62 industries | Derived from 'value added' and number of employees, all industries | Day and Thomas [a] | Federal Reserve Board [b] | Day and Persons [c] |
| 1923 | 100.0 | 100.0 | 100.0 | 100.0 | 100.0 |
| 1925 | 102.4 | 104.4 | 104.9 | 104.0 | 103.1 |
| 1927 | 104.2 | 111.4 | 105.6 | 105.0 | 102.4 |
| 1929 | 113.0 | 124.8 | — | 117.8 | 113.6 |

[a] *The Growth of Manufacturers, 1899-1923*, U. S. Department of Commerce, Census Monograph VIII, 1928, p. 194. The index for 1927 was prepared at the Division of Research and Statistics of the Federal Reserve Board by Aryness Joy, with the collaboration of V. S. Kolesnikoff.
[b] Annual averages of monthly index numbers. For complete data see the *Federal Reserve Bulletin*, Sept. 1931, p. 507.
[c] Warren M. Persons, *Forecasting Business Cycles*, John Wiley and Sons, New York, 1931, p. 171.

In 1927 and 1929 the derived index number of volume of manufacturing production is appreciably higher than the other four indexes. Over the entire six-year period a gain of approximately 25 per cent is shown by this index, as against gains of from 13 to 18 per cent indicated by the other measurements. The marked difference between the index numbers develops between 1925 and 1927. For this two-year period the other index numbers, based on standard commodities, record only slight advances, reflecting the check to business experienced in 1927. (One index shows a slight loss.) The all-inclusive census index shows a gain of 6.7 per cent, in spite of the recession. There is reason to accept this record as accurate, for the depression of 1927 was not widespread. It was felt by the basic industries, but producers in general were not materially affected.

Index numbers of manufacturing production which have been adjusted to take account of diversification of output during this period have been used in the construction of the general index numbers given in earlier pages of this chapter.

## Summary: Production Tendencies in the United States, Post-war

If attention be concentrated upon standard and readily-enumerated commodities little difference is found between the periods 1901-1913 and 1922-1929, in respect to the rate of increase in aggregate production. Available records indicate a pre-war gain at a rate of 2.9 per cent a year, a post-war gain at a rate of 3.3 per cent a year in the volume of output of such commodities. If, however, we take account of industrial diversification, and attempt to include the great variety of commodities which are not included in current physical records of production, the estimates for both periods are raised. The pre-war rate of advance, thus corrected, becomes 3.1 per cent a year, while the post-war rate is 3.8 per cent a year. (Construction is excluded for both periods.) Making allowance now for the rate of change in population, we obtain an estimate of 2.4 per cent as the average annual rate of increase in physical output per head of the population between 1922 and 1929, as compared with a rate of 1.1 per cent between 1901 and 1913. Expressed in other terms, these figures indicate that, at the pre-war rate, 63 years would have been required for a doubling of the individual's share in the annual output of the country, while, at the rate of increase prevailing between 1922 and 1929, such doubling would have required only 29 years.

In terms of cold figures the margin between average rates of gain of 3.1 per cent and of 3.8 per cent, between rates of 1.1 per cent and 2.4 per cent, may not look impressive. But the difference is of the highest significance. Over an eight-year period the American economy was moving forward at a rate perhaps never surpassed, a rate which represented a potential doubling of the physical income of the average citizen once every 29 years. For a period of almost a decade a rate of advance was achieved which gave promise of material comforts for the citizens at large on a broader scale than had ever before been attained. The combination of circumstances which permitted this rate of increase in the flow of physical goods to be maintained calls for searching investigation, if we are to wring the full meaning out of the events of this period.

Not only was the rate of increase in total production volume impressively high; it was also impressively stable, in contrast with earlier experience. The fluctuations in aggregate output between 1922 and 1929 (expressed as deviations from the output which would have been recorded had a constant rate of change prevailed) averaged but 2.1 per cent a year. The amplitude of the swings in total production was 43 per cent less than that prevailing during the thirteen pre-war years. Production records for individual commodities reveal the same tendency toward increasing stability.

Going beneath the surface of the aggregate stream of goods and tracing the movements of its major constituents, a truer conception of the actual course of events in recent years is secured. As regards domestic production the record does not indicate an exceptionally rapid advance in the output of raw materials. From 1922 to 1929 the total volume of raw material production increased 24 per cent, at an average annual rate of 2.5 per cent. The output of manufactured goods, on the other hand, increased in volume some 40 per cent over the same period, at an average rate of 4.5 per cent a year. (These figures are based upon the revised index numbers of manufacturing production, corrected to allow for the increasing diversification of output shown by statistics of value of output.) The expenditure of labor in increasing degree on refinements of fabrication, the production of an ever more diversified stream of ultimate products—these were characteristic features of the period preceding the last recession.[1]

Separating products of American farms from all other commodities, we find an even sharper divergence of production trends. Farm products, raw and processed, increased in output between 1922 and 1929 by 16 per cent, the average annual rate of advance being 2.0 per cent. The aggregate output of other products advanced by 49 per cent over the same period, at an annual rate of 5.1 per

---

[1] It was, of course, for these diversified, highly fabricated products that demand was increasing most rapidly. The less rapid advance in output of raw materials did not necessarily mean that the production of these materials was more closely adapted to market conditions. There were many factors other than domestic production, factors having to do with demand, and with world supply, which affected market values. The figures we have cited are not inconsistent with the fact that price weakness first appeared in the raw material markets of the world.

cent. Higher standards of living, the tapping of strata of less insistent wants, meant a swelling of demand for non-agricultural products. The farmer ministers to essential but relatively inelastic wants. Here is one important reason for the failure of agriculturists to keep pace with other groups of producers during the advance of the 'twenties.[1]

The rapidity of the advance both in volume and value of construction has been emphasized in the preceding brief survey. A notable feature of these developments was the extremely rapid growth in the volume of residential construction after 1923, and the sharp termination of this movement after 1928. For reasons which are to be found in part in the conditions left by the war years, in part in the more immediate conditions surrounding the financing of construction work, the construction industry provided one of the major channels for the economic expansion which preceded the last recession.

During the period 1922-1929 the aggregate production of capital equipment, including non-residential construction, increased 70 per cent (i.e., the 1929 total was 170 per cent of the 1922 total); the average annual rate of advance was 6.4 per cent. This was materially higher than the rate of gain in total production. Our energies were being devoted in increasing degree to the production of those durable goods which are used in the production of other goods. During this same period the volume of production of perishable consumers' goods increased at a rate of 2.8 per cent a year, while the volume of production of semi-durable consumers' goods (textile, leather and rubber products) advanced at approximately the same rate. If we now bring into the picture durable consumers' goods (residences, automobiles, house-furnishings, radios, etc.) we find a group which, in respect of rate of change, belongs with capital equipment, rather than with other consumption goods. The output of these goods increased at a rate of 5.6 per cent a year between 1922 and 1929. Here is striking evidence of the change in consumer habits. The rate of increase in the production of food, clothing, and other perishable and semi-durable goods exceeded by no great margin the rate of increase in population. Our productive energies, in excess of those necessary to maintain existing standards

[1] Slow adaptation of agricultural production to changing conditions, a tardiness due to social as well as economic conditions of rural life, is, of course, another and related factor.

of food consumption and of dress for a constantly expanding population, were devoted in the main to augmenting the aggregate supply of durable goods—capital equipment and durable articles of consumption.

If we lump together all durable goods we secure a group which increased 59 per cent in volume of output between 1922 and 1929, at an average annual rate of 5.9 per cent. Semi-durable and perishable goods together constitute a group which increased in aggregate volume by approximately 23 per cent over the same period, at an average rate of 2.8 per cent. The current flow of goods which had a useful life, either procreative or for consumption purposes, well in excess of two years was increasing at a rate more than twice that at which perishable and semi-durable goods were increasing. This rapid increase in the output of durable goods represented a tremendous storing up of utilities, either in the form of productive capacity or of potential enjoyment through direct consumption. A reservoir was being filled, an immense reserve supply created, which was not recorded in current inventories of stocks of goods on hand. Heavy buying in prosperity always leads to such an accumulation of stocks in consumers' hands and of equipment in the hands of producers. The distinctive feature of the years preceding the recession was that this accumulation continued over such a relatively long period, and that the production of goods of relatively long life was advancing at a rate so much greater than was the production of goods necessarily used up over a short period of time. The accumulation of such stocks of durable goods in the hands of producers and consumers was a potent factor, of course, in the subsequent curtailment of buying.

Additional evidence of the changing character of consumption is furnished by statistics on the comparative values of articles of food and clothing produced in the United States at different census periods. Figures in round numbers (precise records are not available) indicate that food and clothing constituted about 58 per cent, by value, of total production in the United States (excluding construction) in 1899, about 59 per cent in 1914, and only 44 per cent in 1929. The great drop from 1914 to 1929 is in part explained by the fact that the former was a year of depression, the latter one of prosperity, and in part by the declining importance of articles of food in our export trade. But it is probably safe to say that changes in the character of consumption and the heavy expenditure for capital equipment characteristic of recent years were the chief factors in this remarkable shift.

The study of statistics compiled by the Census of Manufactures reveals certain striking aspects of recent production movements. With a steadily advancing volume of production, the number of wage-earners and the number of manufacturing establishments declined, while output per wage-earner and output per establishment showed notable gains. Most impressive of these changes is the gain in productivity per worker. Over the fifteen years from 1899 to 1914 output per wage-earner increased approximately 30 per cent—notable evidence of the growing efficiency of both the human and mechanical factors of production. Great as this gain was, it was exceeded during the decade from 1919 to 1929. Output per worker increased no less than 43 per cent during these ten years, gaining in every biennial period. The sharpest advance—approximately 14 per cent—occurred between 1921 and 1923, with a gain of 8 per cent between 1927 and 1929 next in order of magnitude.

In discussing pre-war tendencies a distinction was made between numbers of workers on the one hand and technical, mechanical and organizational elements on the other, as two factors which might be called upon, alternatively or in combination, when increases in production were sought. There was evidence that before the war technical and organizational elements, as these are reflected in output per capita, were being utilized in increasing degree in expanding production. These elements, in abeyance during the years from 1914 to 1919, have since been clearly dominant in the manufacturing industries of this country. Over large areas of economic endeavor the human factor, as an agency for expanding production, has been subordinated to the mechanical. The social and economic problems raised by this development are among the most urgent issues of the day. How the productive power thus released is to be efficiently and equitably used, how human labor is to be economized in production without dispossessing workers, how time thus gained by the relaxing of economic pressure may be fruitfully expended—these are questions pressing for solution. The economic difficulties which were precipitated in 1929 have not removed these problems; they have accentuated them.

## CHAPTER VII

## *Price Movements, 1922-1929*

THE generation of men whose business experience covered the quarter century that ended in 1920 had become accustomed, in all their business dealings, to the nourishing influence of rising prices. First there was the relatively gentle rise from the middle 'nineties to the outbreak of the World War, a rise that served nicely to keep labor costs and fixed costs down, that gave that sense of well-being which comes from steadily appreciating capital values and inventories, that gently but persistently lifted business from the doldrums of occasional depression without necessitating liquidation that cut to the heart. Later the stronger stimulus of sharply rising prices carried profits to new levels, swelled the stream of values which is of prime concern to business men, and gave to many the heady experience of sudden wealth.

To a generation thus habituated came in 1920 and 1921 the profound shock of a drop in values more sudden and severe than any they had ever known, a drop which altered overnight the values of the counters in terms of which business is conducted, and changed radically the positions and holdings of all the players in the game. There ensued eight years of comparative calm, during which the conditions left by the readjustment were explored and favorable opportunities were exploited, while those countries and classes unfavorably affected became somewhat inured to the adverse forces released by the war and post-war storms. Then came another catastrophic drop in prices, distorting values, altering profoundly the relative positions of different economic agents, and introducing new uncertainties into business dealings.

An earlier chapter has dealt with some of the consequences of the first great post-war drop in commodity values. Subsequent studies of the National Bureau will be concerned with the character and the effects of the most recent storm. Our present interest lies in the conditions and tendencies prevailing between these two major recessions.

## Movements of the Level of Wholesale Prices. Price Trends and Cycles

Changes in the general level of prices between 1922 and 1929 are defined by the following measurements.

TABLE 133

Changes in the Level of Wholesale Prices in the United States, 1922-1929

| Year | Index numbers of wholesale prices [a] | Year-to-year change in wholesale prices (per cent) |
|---|---|---|
| 1922 | 100.0 | — |
| 1923 | 104.0 | +4.0 |
| 1924 | 101.4 | −2.5 |
| 1925 | 107.0 | +5.5 |
| 1926 | 103.4 | −3.4 |
| 1927 | 98.7 | −4.5 |
| 1928 | 100.0 | +1.3 |
| 1929 | 98.6 | −1.4 |

[a] The index numbers are those of the U. S. Bureau of Labor Statistics, with base shifted to 1922.

The net movement of the level of wholesale prices between 1922 and 1929 was slightly downward, the rate of decline averaging 0.5 per cent a year. But this average does not describe with accuracy the actual course of prices, which were rising from 1922 to 1925, and declining thereafter at an average annual rate of 2.0 per cent. This declining trend of commodity prices, contrasting so sharply with the advance which had persisted during the preceding quarter century, is one of the most striking characteristics of the post-war economic situation. The causes of this movement are both complex and obscure. A decline in the rate of increase in world production of gold, an increasing demand for gold as the restoration of stable monetary standards proceeded, a distribution of gold stocks not accurately proportioned to the monetary and commercial needs of the world, increasing productivity of labor and falling costs in the production of both raw and manufactured goods, a constantly growing volume of production of world staples, and, in the United States at least, the concentration in the markets for securities and for urban realty of much of the new purchasing power represented by expanding credit—these probably contributed in varying degrees to the decline of wholesale prices which persisted even during the prosperous times preceding the recession of 1929.

This movement, considered in relation to general price changes after 1920, bears the earmarks of a secular trend. We may not say whether this movement will continue, but it is pertinent to inquire into the relation between the trend of average prices and the behavior of commodity prices during periods of business expansion and recession. In doing this we take no account of the prolonged recession which began in 1929. The present study deals only with the record of events occurring prior to 1930.

Between May, 1897, and February, 1919, there were six complete cycles in American business, each including a period of advancing prices and a period of declining prices. The average duration of the period of advancing prices was 31 months. The average duration of the period of falling prices was 12 months. The typical price cycle consisted of two and one-half years of rising prices and one year of falling prices.

Between February, 1919, and May, 1927, three price cycles may be traced. During these cycles the upward movement of prices continued for sixteen months, on the average, while the downswing averaged seventeen months in duration. The price recession which began in 1929 followed sixteen months of advancing prices and ten months of slightly sagging prices.

It is reasonable to conclude that the difference between these records arises out of the differing trends of the level of prices. A persistent secular advance, such as that prevailing between 1897 and 1920, expresses itself in prolonged periods of cyclical price rise, curtailed periods of cyclical decline. Declining prices represent brief intermissions in an era of general advance. A falling price level is similarly manifest in shortened periods of cyclical rise, extended periods of cyclical decline. (Between May, 1892, and May, 1897, there were two cycles, with the period of price advance averaging eight months in duration, the period of price decline averaging twenty-two months.) Under these conditions, it is rising prices which appear as brief departures from the prevailing trend.

§ *World movements of wholesale prices.*—Confirmatory evidence on the prevailing trend of prices is found in the movements of prices abroad. In preparing the following table the records of price changes in twenty-nine countries between 1923 and the beginning of the price drop associated with the recession of 1929 have been surveyed, and the high point of prices during this period noted in each case. All index numbers cited are on the 1926 base.

TABLE 134

PRE-RECESSION BEHAVIOR OF WHOLESALE PRICES IN 29 COUNTRIES, 1923-1929

| (1) | (2) | (3) | (4) | (5) | (6) | (7) |
|---|---|---|---|---|---|---|
| | Pre-recession high | | Recession high | | Pre-recession decline [a] | |
| Country | Date | Price index 1926=100 | Date | Price index 1926=100 | Duration (in months) | Percentage |
| | 1923 | | | | | |
| Australia | July | 112.0 | Sept. 1929 | 101.4 | 74 | 9.5 |
| Dutch East Indies | Dec. | 110.7 | May 1929 | 94.3 | 65 | 14.8 |
| | 1924 | | | | | |
| Switzerland | Feb. | 123.8 | July 1929 | 98.8 | 65 | 20.2 |
| New Zealand | Sept. | 108.1 | Sept. 1929 | 96.5 | 60 | 10.7 |
| British India | Oct. | 119.2 | Sept. 1929 | 96.6 | 59 | 19.2 |
| British South Africa | Oct. | 108.1 | Jan. 1929 | 97.6 | 51 | 9.7 |
| Japan | Nov. | 119.8 | Dec. 1928 | 97.1 | 49 | 18.9 |
| Netherlands | Nov. | 111.0 | Mar. 1929 | 101.4 | 52 | 8.6 |
| Hungary | Dec. | 129.0 | Mar. 1929 | 109.7 | 51 | 15.0 |
| Spain | Dec. | 109.4 | Nov. 1928 | 97.2 | 47 | 11.2 |
| | 1925 | | | | | |
| Austria | Jan. | 119.5 | May 1929 | 109.8 | 52 | 8.1 |
| Canada | Jan. | 106.0 | Aug. 1929 | 98.4 | 55 | 7.2 |
| Czechoslovakia | Jan. | 109.9 | Feb. 1929 | 100.9 | 49 | 8.2 |
| Denmark | Jan. | 149.1 | Feb. 1929 | 97.5 | 49 | 34.6 |
| Great Britain | Jan. | 115.5 | Mar. 1929 | 94.6 | 50 | 18.1 |
| Egypt (Cairo) | Feb. | 122.0 | Nov. 1928 | 97.7 | 45 | 19.9 |
| Norway | Feb. | 141.9 | Aug. 1928 | 81.8 | 42 | 42.4 |
| Sweden | Feb. | 113.4 | May 1928 | 102.0 | 39 | 10.1 |
| Bulgaria | Feb. | 117.6 | May 1929 | 120.0 | 51 | +2.1 [b] |
| Estonia | Mar. | 112.3 | Mar. 1929 | 107.9 | 48 | 3.9 |
| Poland | Mar. | 133.3 | Mar. 1929 | 111.6 | 48 | 16.3 |
| Lithuania | Apr. | 114.9 | Apr. 1929 | 102.2 | 48 | 11.1 |
| Finland | Aug. | 105.0 | Aug. 1928 | 103.0 | 36 | 1.9 |
| Germany | Sept. | 107.4 | Mar. 1929 | 103.9 | 42 | 3.3 |
| United States | Nov. | 104.5 | July 1929 | 96.5 | 44 | 7.7 |
| | 1926 | | | | | |
| Belgium | July | 117.7 | Mar. 1929 | 116.8 | 32 | 0.8 |
| France | July | 119.0 | Mar. 1929 | 91.0 | 32 | 23.4 |
| Italy | Aug. | 115.7 | Mar. 1929 | 76.3 | 31 | 27.8 |
| | 1927 | | | | | |
| Peru | May | 102.0 | Mar. 1929 | 93.1 | 22 | 8.7 |

[a] To date of beginning of price decline associated with current recession. In most cases this was not a persistent decline, but included some advances.
[b] In Bulgaria the net movement of prices was upward over this period.

It is a noteworthy fact that in each of these twenty-nine countries, with the single exception of Bulgaria, wholesale prices reached a level, at some date prior to 1928-1929, higher than that from which the recession of 1929 began. In nearly all cases this high point was attained in 1924 or 1925, so that before the cyclical recession began prices had been declining for from three to five years. The degree of pre-recession decline of prices ranged from less than one per cent (in Belgium) to more than 40 per cent (in Norway).

These price movements should be viewed in relation to the postwar resumption of the gold standard, which restored the ties between gold and commodity prices. This process began in 1919, when the United States removed war-time restrictions upon gold exports. During the chaos of the years 1920-1923 little more was done, but in 1924 the movement was resumed. By 1927 most of the industrial countries previously on a gold standard were again within the fold and, in addition, certain other countries not previously on a gold standard had sought stability in the same direction. The sequence of restoration is indicated by the following summary:

| Country | Date of restoration (or establishment) of gold standard | Date of restoration of stability of exchange on New York |
|---|---|---|
| United States [a] | June 1919 | — |
| Lithuania | Aug. 1922 | Aug. 1922 |
| Latvia | Nov. 1922 | Mar. 1922 |
| Austria * [b] | Jan. 1923 | Sept. 1922 |
| Sweden | Apr. 1924 | Aug. 1922 |
| Germany * | Oct. 1924 | June 1924 |
| Switzerland * | Nov. 1924 | Nov. 1924 |
| Netherlands | Apr. 1925 | Nov. 1924 |
| United Kingdom | May 1925 | May 1925 |
| Australia | May 1925 | May 1925 |
| New Zealand | May 1925 | May 1925 |
| Union of South Africa | May 1925 | May 1925 |
| Hungary * [c] | May 1925 | Jan. 1925 |
| Finland * | Dec. 1925 | Mar. 1924 |
| Chile * | Jan. 1926 | Oct. 1925 |
| Czechoslovakia * | Apr. 1926 | Feb. 1923 |
| Canada | July 1926 | July 1924 |
| Belgium * | Oct. 1926 | Oct. 1926 |
| Bulgaria * | Jan. 1927 | Jan. 1924 |
| Denmark | Jan. 1927 | Mar. 1926 |
| British India * | Mar. 1927 | May 1925 |
| Argentina | Aug. 1927 | Mar. 1927 |
| Poland * | Oct. 1927 | Nov. 1926 |
| Italy * | Dec. 1927 | Dec. 1927 |
| Estonia * | Jan. 1928 | Nov. 1924 |
| Norway | May 1928 | Sept. 1927 |
| Greece * | May 1928 | Jan. 1927 |
| France | June 1928 | Dec. 1926 |
| Rumania * | Feb. 1929 | Feb. 1929 |

\* Redemption permitted in gold exchange.
[a] Restrictions on export of gold removed.
[b] National Bank under obligation to keep its notes at gold par.
[c] Stabilized with reference to the British pound, Aug. 1924.

All cyclical price declines have certain common characteristics. The prices of some commodities are more sensitive than others to the forces of recession. Raw materials react more sharply than manufactured goods; producers' goods (i.e., goods not yet in shape for final consumption) feel the influence of price changes more promptly than do consumers' goods (goods ready for consumption or use by final consumers). It is among manufactured goods, and particularly, among manufactured consumers' goods, that the process of liquidation is most painful. For among these goods relatively inflexible costs and established prices play far more important parts than they do among raw materials and producers' goods in general. The difficulty of reducing overhead charges in manufacturing and distribution, obstacles to the reduction of labor costs, the inertia of established prices among packaged and trade-marked goods all tend to retard liquidation among fabricated goods and consumers' goods. Yet in a time of general price recession some decline there must be among the prices of these goods in order that reduced aggregate incomes of producers of raw materials, of industrial laborers and of other classes of consumers may be adequate to the moving of goods offered for sale.

These characteristics of periods of price recession are familiar. What is of exceptional interest now, in view of the possibility that the force of a secular price decline is accentuating the cyclical price recession, is the difference between the problems of liquidation during eras of rising and of falling prices. When the long-term movement of prices is upward, lagging liquidation of the prices of manufactured goods is in part compensated by forces related to the long-term trend. For under these conditions the cyclical phase of falling prices is brief, and only a moderate degree of price decline appears to be necessary before readjustment of price relations is established. Drastic price-cutting and forced readjustment of costs by manufacturers are not so essential, because the upward push of cheapening money will help to check the fall of raw materials and of producers' goods, and to start their prices again advancing. For it is just these commodities which are most sensitive to changes in the value of money. The secular force of rising prices serves both as a cushion during recession and as a springboard during revival to these more sensitive commodity groups.

These conditions are reversed during a recession which occurs when the trend of prices is declining. The more sensitive raw materials and producers' goods still fall first and fall farther during such a recession, but the cushion to the drop and the springboard to revival are no longer there. In their place is an intensification of the cyclical forces responsible for the price decline, an intensification due to the long-term tendency toward a lower price level. If the prices of manufactured goods and of consumers' goods are to stay within hailing distance of those first to fall, reduction of fixed costs and of standard selling prices is essential. For these groups, also, the difficulties of price readjustment are aggravated at such a time. A longer period of liquidation, more severe price declines and the absence of the cushioning influence of a rising trend all serve to accentuate the problem which manufacturers and dealers face. Indeed, the prolongation of the period of cyclical recession during eras of declining prices is probably due in considerable part to the excessive difficulties of price liquidation and cost reduction at such times.

The difficulties of readjusting the prices of manufactured goods to a lower general level will be more severe the greater the investment in capital equipment, the more important the element of overhead costs in the expenses of production. It is these costs which are most difficult to reduce when prices are falling. Because our present investment in industrial equipment is much heavier than at any earlier time, it is probable that the stresses of a continual readjustment among prices and costs necessitated by a protracted period of falling prices would place a more severe strain on the industrial system than did any of the price declines of the eighteenth or nineteenth centuries. In tracing the record of recent price changes we should bear in mind the probability that a secular price decline is accentuating cyclical recessions and intensifying the difficulties of readjustment which prevail after a major check to business prosperity.

## The Influence of Price Changes on Aggregate Values, 1922-1929

During the period preceding the outbreak of the World War a steadily rising volume of production was converted into a still more rapidly swelling stream of values through the agency of advancing prices. This process, a generally happy one for producers and traders, continued at a sharply accelerated pace until 1920. During the following year price liquidation cut the stream of values in half, intensifying the losses which accompanied declining physical output.

The net effect of general price changes in the period now under review was to cause the stream of values to rise less rapidly than physical production. Changes in aggregate values are approximated by the estimates in the following table. These series are plotted in Figure 58.

TABLE 135

INDEX NUMBERS OF PHYSICAL VOLUME, PRICES AND AGGREGATE VALUES OF GOODS PRODUCED IN THE UNITED STATES, 1922-1929

| Year | Physical volume of production (excluding construction) | Wholesale prices | Aggregate values in wholesale markets |
|---|---|---|---|
| 1922 | 100 | 100 | 100 |
| 1923 | 112 | 104 | 116 |
| 1924 | 109 | 101 | 111 |
| 1925 | 117 | 107 | 125 |
| 1926 | 124 | 103 | 128 |
| 1927 | 123 | 99 | 121 |
| 1928 | 129 | 100 | 129 |
| 1929 | 134 | 99 | 132 |
| Average annual rate of change (per cent) .... | +3.8 | —0.5 | +3.3 |
| Index of instability | 2.1 | 2.0 | 3.9 |

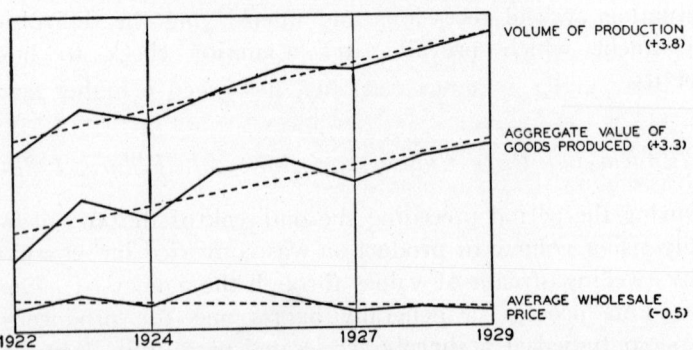

FIGURE 58

CHANGES IN VOLUME OF PRODUCTION, AVERAGE PRICE AND AGGREGATE VALUE OF GOODS PRODUCED IN THE UNITED STATES, 1922-1929

Plotted on ratio scale. The figures in parentheses define average annual rates of change (in percentage form).

Between 1922 and 1925 both production and price factors served to swell commercial values; thereafter increasing volume of output alone contributed to expanding values, and the rate of advance was correspondingly reduced. The net rate of gain in aggregate values over the period averaged 3.3 per cent a year, as against a pre-war rate of 4.9 per cent. To one thinking in terms of aggregate values growth was more rapid in pre-war years. But there was more substance to the growth of 1922-29, a more rapid advance in the output of physical goods.

## Price Stability and Economic Flexibility

In an individualistic, competitive economy prices perform the rôle that would fall to a dictator under a completely centralized system. The allocation of productive energies among the various fields of economic endeavor, the division of labor among the thousands of occupations practiced in a modern industrial economy, the apportionment of capital, the distribution of goods in time and space so that supply and demand may be properly balanced against each other in each of the tens of thousands of consumption centers of the world—all these are tasks which prices perform. Faultless coördination has, of course, never been attained. Feasts and famines, lean years and fat, plenty here and scarcity there, unemployed capital and unemployed labor—these have always alternated, or rubbed shoulders. But it has been supposed that with the spread of the money economy (and the concomitant development of modern agencies for the dissemination of information, the transportation of goods, the transference of capital) these economic maladjustments would progressively diminish. There is good reason to believe that the general tendency has been in this direction; industrial civilization, under a money economy, has given a higher standard of living to the average man, and has brought greater uniformity and stability of economic standards over broad areas. Instability and uncertainty—the vagaries of weather and of war and the accidents of trade—have persisted, it is true, but in a long view their importance has declined. The price system, developing with modern industrialism, has served to coördinate with a surprising degree of accuracy the elements of the highly complex structure of interdependent parts that constitutes the world economy.

The effective performance of this function is dependent upon the existence of a number of conditions. Freedom of competition, the full mobility of labor and of capital and, as a condition to which these contribute, the existence of free and uncontrolled prices of commodities, services, capital and credit—all these are essential to the coördination of economic processes in an individualistic and capitalistic economy.[1] To the extent that these conditions are not realized, a nice adjustment of the working parts of national economies and of the world economy will not be attained.

It is difficult to set up standards for determining the degree to which these conditions prevail at given times. It is possible, as we have seen, to measure the variability of prices. In earlier chapters a sustained decline in price variability during pre-war years and a sharp rise in price variability during the war and immediate post-war years have been traced. That the high price variability of the war years was followed by an era of more stable prices is readily demonstrated. But we cannot, on the basis of the statistical evidence alone, define the point at which stability becomes rigidity, nor say when sensitivity to market changes is lost. The pre-war decline in price variability, the excessive instability of the war years and the decreasing variability characteristic of the years between 1922 and 1929 are revealed by the measurements given in Table 136. The indexes of variability are supplemented by an index of year-to-year dispersion.

The entries in column (2) are averages of measurements relating to approximately 200 series of wholesale price quotations. For each of these series the mean deviation of the monthly prices about the average price for the year has been computed, and it is these individual mean deviations which have been averaged to secure the measurements given in the table. The sharp drop in variability which followed the troubles of 1920-21, a drop which carried the index to levels comparable with the lowest prevailing before the war, is the most striking feature of the table.[2]

Inequalities or variations in the year-to-year price movements of the several hundred individual commodities entering into the

[1] Such full mobility and freedom of competition may entail other difficulties, not here discussed. The above statement of the conditions theoretically essential to the working of a competitive economy does not imply that these conditions represent a state of economic perfection, nor that the attainment of a perfectly free price system is necessarily a desirable objective of economic policy.

[2] The rising trend of prices prior to the war would tend to increase slightly (by something less than 0.5) the pre-war measurement of average variability.

## TABLE 136
### Monthly Variability and Dispersion of Wholesale Prices in the United States, 1890-1929

| (1) | (2) | (3) | (4) |
|---|---|---|---|
| Period or year | Average of measurements of monthly variability, individual commodities [a] | Monthly variability, index of U. S. Bureau of Labor Statistics [a] | Index of year-to-year price dispersion [b] |
| 1890-1897 | 4.6 | 2.2 | 9.1 * |
| 1898-1905 | 4.7 | 1.9 | 8.7 |
| 1906-1913 | 4.2 | 1.7 | 7.7 |
| 1914-1921 | 8.3 | 4.3 | 13.0 |
| 1922-1925 | 5.3 | 1.8 | 10.6 |
| 1926-1929 | 4.0 | 0.9 | 7.9 |
| 1922 | 6.6 | 3.1 | 11.7 |
| 1923 | 4.8 | 2.0 | 11.0 |
| 1924 | 5.5 | 1.6 | 8.3 |
| 1925 | 4.4 | 0.7 | 11.5 |
| 1926 | 4.2 | 1.1 | 8.9 |
| 1927 | 4.8 | 1.0 | 9.2 |
| 1928 | 3.4 | 0.7 | 7.8 |
| 1929 | 3.7 | 0.8 | 5.6 |

* 1891-1897.

[a] The measure of monthly variability is the mean deviation of average monthly prices from the average price for the year, expressed as a percentage of the annual mean. See *The Behavior of Prices*, pp. 39-49. The entries in column (2) are the unweighted arithmetic averages of such measurements relating to 207 price series for the periods between 1890 and 1922, and to 201 price series for the years 1922 to 1929.

[b] The index of dispersion is the antilogarithm of a fractional part (.6745) of the logarithmic standard deviation. It defines, in percentage form, the approximate limits of the zone within which would fall 50 per cent of the price relatives at a given date, and on a given base. Thus a value of 10 for a given date means that, on that date, approximately half the price relatives deviated from the geometric mean of all the relatives by less than 10 per cent. For a full description of this measure see *The Behavior of Prices*, pp. 256-262. The entries in col. (4) relate to 195 price series for the years 1891 to 1902, to 205 price series for the years 1903 to 1913, and to 391 price series for the years 1914 to 1929.

general index are measured by the index of dispersion. The larger the index the greater the inequalities represented and, presumably, the greater the disturbance of established business relations. The average value of the indexes of dispersion for the period 1922-1929 is 9.2, which is somewhat greater than the average of 8.1 for the years 1901-1913. This comparison would indicate greater internal disturbance of the price structure in recent years than during the period before the war. In so far as the average tells the story, this appears to have been the case. The relatively stable price level prevailing between 1922 and 1929 concealed rather wide individual movements. The declining trend of the index of dispersion is significant, however. From 11.7 in 1922 the index drops to 5.6 in 1929, the lowest value recorded during the 39 years for which this index has been constructed. Inequalities of price movements among individual commodities, which were pronounced during the early post-war years, had been materially reduced by 1929.

The stability of the level of wholesale prices during the years immediately preceding the recent recession is evidenced by the entries in column (3). Not only was the general price level less variable than during any preceding period of expansion; it was less variable than at any previous period covered by the present records, which extend back by years to 1890. The price system bore no sign of a rising economic fever prior to the collapse of 1929.[1]

These various measurements tell a story of stability of the price level and of steadily increasing stability among the individual elements of the price structure. The customary signs of inflation in commodity markets were absent, and individual prices were moving within relatively narrow limits. If weaknesses were developing within the price structure before the recession of 1929 they are not immediately discernible in the records we have cited. There remains the possibility that increasing stability concealed underlying faults, that rigidity, not stability, was developing. We have said that within a competitive economy prices play the rôle that would fall to a dictator in a centralized, non-competitive economy. Theirs is the task of securing that delicate adjustment between the working parts of the economy which is essential to the maintenance of equilibrium. When prices lose something of their freedom there may be no immediate signs of faulty adjustment. Under these conditions movements toward disequilibrium may go further before corrective processes are stimulated. There are some reasons for thinking that the price system had become less sensitive to changes in market conditions during the years preceding the recession of 1929, and that the economic system had lost in flexibility and adaptability as a result.[2]

---

[1] The inclusion of an increasing number of commodities in the index in recent years would tend to reduce the variability of the price index.

[2] The fact that earlier events are viewed from the perspective of 1932 is, of course, an element in this interpretation.

## PRICE MOVEMENTS, POST-WAR

Perhaps the most obvious of the factors which have tended to decrease the sensitiveness of prices are the various valorization agencies which have been established in recent years. Efforts have been made to maintain at constant levels the prices of a large number of raw materials. The powerful aid of governments has been extended to associations of producers in these efforts. Some typical valorization schemes in operation during the period under review are listed in the following summary.

### TABLE 137
#### Summary of Valorization Schemes

| Commodity | Period of valorization project | Participants in project | Nature of price control |
|---|---|---|---|
| Crude rubber | 1922-28 | Great Britain, colonial governments (Stevenson plan) | Restriction of exports from producing areas under British control. |
| Coffee | 1922— | Sao Paulo Coffee Institute, backed by State of Sao Paulo (and Brazilian government to 1924) | Regulation of coffee shipments from interior, financing of stocks held by producers. |
| Wheat | 1923—<br>1929— | Canadian coöperative pools<br>United States Federal Farm Board | Storage, centralized marketing. Government financing of purchase and storage of excess supply. Attempts to obtain voluntary curtailment of production. |
| Silk | 1914-22<br>1926-28<br>1929— | Japan, producers, with government coöperation | Curtailment of production and withdrawal of excess stocks from market. |
| Sugar | 1925-28<br>1929— | Cuban government<br>Cuban government | Restriction of production, export selling agency.<br>Compulsory single selling agency. |
| Cotton<br>Long staple<br>Short staple | 1921-30<br>1929— | Egyptian government<br>United States Federal Farm Board | Several occasions of restriction of acreage, government purchase at a fixed price.<br>Government financing of purchase and storage of excess supply. |

TABLE 137—*Continued*

| Commodity | Period of valorization project | Participants in project | Nature of price control |
|---|---|---|---|
| Copper | 1926-30 | Copper Exporters, Inc., backed by 90 per cent of world production | Regulation of American export price, other prices at fixed differentials; no longer effective due to defection of smaller producers. |
| | 1929— | Copper producers | Attempts at voluntary curtailment of production. |
| Nitrates | 1919-27 | Chilean Nitrate Producers' Association | Limitation of exports and fixing of price. |
| | 1928— | Chilean Nitrate Producers' Association | Selling agency for all Chilean production; manipulation of export tax to meet foreign competition. |
| | 1929— | International agreement of Chilean, British and German producers | Price convention. |
| Potash | 1924-25 | Agreement of German and Alsatian cartels | Allotment of sales for several countries. |
| | 1926— | International cartel of German and Alsatian producers | Joint commission of control and common sales agencies for all countries. |
| Mercury | 1928— | International cartel sanctioned by Spanish and Italian governments | Allocation of production of Spanish and Italian mines and establishment of joint sales bureau. |
| Sulphur | 1923— | Agreement of Italian and American producers | Allocation of output, division of markets. |
| Sisal | 1920— | Mexican and Yucatan governments with producers' association | Regulation of production and fixing of prices. |
| Quinine | 1913— | Association of most producers and all manufacturers outside United States; dominated by Dutch | Regulation of production and prices of cinchona bark and prices of quinine. |
| Camphor | 1899— | Japanese and Formosan governments | Government monopoly controlling production; weakened in recent years by competition of synthetic camphor. |

TABLE 137—Continued

| Commodity | Period of valorization project | Participants in project | Nature of price control |
|---|---|---|---|
| Major international cartels, not directly affecting prices in the United States ||||
| Steel | 1926— | Producers of Belgium, France, Germany, Luxemburg and Saar Basin and from 1927 Czechoslovakia, Austria and Hungary | Production allotted, with excess production and exports subject to penalty. |
| Aluminum | 1926— | French, British, Swiss and German producers | Allocation of markets. |
| Margarine | 1927— | English and Dutch trusts | Same officers head both companies; joint purchasing and common sales policy. |
| Rayon | 1927-29 | English, German, Italian, Dutch and Belgian producers | Agreement restricting process of production and allocating markets; occasional price agreements. |
| Zinc | 1928— | Belgian, Dutch, French, German, Polish, British and Spanish producers | Control of production and markets. |

Valorization efforts do not by any means constitute the only developments tending toward greater price stability. The growth of coöperative marketing has reduced price competition among certain groups of producers.[1] Mergers, combines, semi-monopolies and monopolies which are able to enforce price control tend to limit the variability of prices. We lack definite information as to the importance of such combinations today, but there is reason to believe

[1] The total business done by farmers' coöperative associations in the United States, as reported by the U. S. Department of Agriculture, increased from approximately $636,000,000 in 1915 to $2,500,000,000 in the crop year 1929-30 (*Yearbook of Agriculture, 1931,* p. 1080).

Orderly marketing through coöperation may be, of course, quite different from valorization. Coöperation may, indeed, make prices no less sensitive to changing market conditions, though the change in size of the marketing unit may prevent minor fluctuations. It is hard to draw a line between stabilization which reduces variation, without reducing the due sensitivity of prices to market changes, and stabilization which represents loss of freedom to react to market changes.

that their number and scope have been expanding.[1] Trade agreements among producers, the interchange of price and cost information among members of trade associations, informal 'following of the leader', may have somewhat similar results in reducing the flexibility of prices.[2]

Of a different type is that increasing rigidity of the price system which results from the extension of the services of public utilities. The growing use of gas and electricity for heating, lighting, cooking and refrigeration and as sources of industrial power has brought an enormous extension of the area within which regulated rates prevail. If we add to these services those of transportation and other utilities we have a wide range of prices marked by a very high degree of rigidity.

These various pieces of evidence suggest that in recent years the price system may have been less effective as an instrument of economic coördination than at earlier times and that, both internationally and domestically, this may have contributed to the development of a condition of disequilibrium. Internationally, the breakdown of the gold standard as a result of the war, and the failure to re-establish it in full operating efficiency, impeded the attainment of a smoothly-working world economy after the war.[3]

[1] The exemption from the Sherman Anti-trust Law of associations engaged in export trade is a notable development in the direction of price control, and one of increasing importance. Exports by such associations increased from 4.3 per cent of the national total in 1926 to 14.0 per cent in 1929. (L. B. Zapoleon, "International and Domestic Commodities and the Theory of Prices," *Quarterly Journal of Economics,* May, 1931, p. 454.) These associations may fix prices, allocate sales, determine spheres of influence, and become parties to international cartels—all activities tending to reduce price competition. The influence of such associations upon prices has not been restricted to foreign markets.

[2] Without attempting to indicate the precise conditions which give rise to inflexibility in the following cases, we may cite them as illustrations of the stability of prices of various types of products under modern marketing conditions. Prices are those compiled by the U. S. Bureau of Labor Statistics.

| Year | Bread, loaf before baking, pound, N. Y. | Steel rails, standard, gross ton, mill, open hearth | Hammers, Maydole, dozen, N. Y. | Gloves, dozen pairs, factory, men's | Shingles, 16 in. long, M, mill, cypress | Tobacco, smoking, granulated, 1 oz. bags, per gross, N. Y. |
| --- | --- | --- | --- | --- | --- | --- |
| 1925 | $0.070 | $43.000 | $12.243 | $33.840 | $5.804 | $8.320 |
| 1926 | .070 | 43.000 | 11.400 | 33.840 | 5.825 | 8.320 |
| 1927 | .070 | 43.000 | 11.400 | 33.840 | 5.833 | 8.320 |
| 1928 | .070 | 43.000 | 11.400 | 33.840 | 5.750 | 8.320 |
| 1929 | .066 | 43.000 | 11.400 | 33.840 | 5.750 | 8.320 |

[3] Defective working of international credit instruments should doubtless be coupled with the failure of the gold standard, in explaining the faults in inter-

This failure is manifest in the condition of the world price structure during the decade of the 'twenties. Domestically, we possessed, and still possess, a price system half slave and half free. The area of controlled and regulated prices had been steadily expanding during the years preceding the war, while the fixed element of costs had been growing. This movement was speeded up after the war. If we take account of the growth of public utilities, the increasing variety of services rendered by municipalities and other public bodies, with their expanding armies of employees, the combination movement, the growth of trade associations and coöperative bodies, the increasing emphasis upon non-price factors in merchandising, the various valorization schemes recently attempted and still unliquidated, we may not doubt that the system of mobile and freely competing economic agents and of fluid economic forces envisaged by the classical economists was far from realization in our post-war economy.

The possible consequences of such a situation are numerous. Rigidity in one part of the price structure may involve excessively wide fluctuations in other parts. The variability characteristic of the prices of raw materials, and the exceptional fluctuations to which those prices have recently been subject, may be in part the result of price rigidity elsewhere. More important is the possibility of serious maladjustment among economic factors. When the nervous system of prices is functioning smoothly slight faults lead immediately to corrective action. A price system rigid and inelastic over wide areas may permit discordant and unbalanced developments to proceed until the task of rectification is of major proportions.

The statistical record does not definitely establish the existence of harmful price rigidity. We have no test for distinguishing between inelasticity and stability. It is clear that during the period 1922-1929 there was a steady decline in the degree of movement occurring in the prices of individual commodities. This trend may have resulted from increasing stability. But other evidence supports the conclusion that necessary sensitivity to changing market conditions was being lost. Many of the troubles arising out of the present

---

national price coördination. The pre-war system for the dissemination and control of capital and credit, centering at London, had been evolved through years of growth. Shifts of political and economic power resulting from the war dislocated this system. A smoothly-working alternative system had not been developed prior to the difficulties of 1929. The weakness of the existing instruments was a factor of no small importance in the international collapse of prices.

world depression, and out of our domestic difficulties, had their origin in the failure of the price system to preserve an efficient adjustment of the working parts of the world economy and of the national economy of the United States, at a time when there were no adequate alternative instruments of coördination.

## Price Movements, Major Commodity Groups

We know that the general trends defined by index numbers of production, of prices and of values are in some degree mathematical abstractions, only distantly related to the many-sided realities of economic life. We pass now to some of the more realistic details of post-war price changes.

### Raw Materials and Manufactured Goods

Index numbers measuring changes in the average prices of raw and manufactured goods between 1922 and 1929 are given in the following table.[1] These are shown graphically in Figure 59.

[1] These index numbers, constructed by the National Bureau of Economic Research from price quotations compiled by the U. S. Bureau of Labor Statistics, are unweighted geometric averages of relative prices. The reduction to purchasing power form (that is, to measurements in terms of dollars of constant purchasing power) has been effected by dividing the group index numbers by an 'all commodities' price index, constructed from the same set of quotations and by the same method.

The Bureau of Labor Statistics publishes index numbers of the prices of raw materials, semi-finished and finished goods. These, with base shifted to 1922, are given below.

| Year | Raw materials | Semi-finished goods | Finished goods |
|---|---|---|---|
| 1922 | 100.0 | 100.0 | 100.0 |
| 1923 | 102.6 | 119.9 | 102.8 |
| 1924 | 101.7 | 109.9 | 99.8 |
| 1925 | 111.1 | 106.5 | 104.2 |
| 1926 | 104.2 | 101.1 | 103.6 |
| 1927 | 100.5 | 95.3 | 98.4 |
| 1928 | 103.2 | 95.6 | 99.4 |
| 1929 | 101.6 | 94.9 | 97.9 |

As regards raw materials, the explanation of the differences between these measurements and those in the text lies, primarily, in differences in the weights employed. The index numbers of the National Bureau are geometric averages of relative prices, unweighted except through the use of several quotations on important commodities; those of the Bureau of Labor Statistics are weighted aggregates of actual prices, weights being based upon quantities entering into trade. The effect of the latter system is to give to eight commodities (wheat, corn, cattle, hogs, cotton, anthracite and bituminous coal and crude petroleum) some 60 per cent of the total weight for all raw materials. For certain purposes this method

(*Footnote continued on page 334*)

## TABLE 138

INDEX NUMBERS MEASURING CHANGES IN THE PRICES AND PURCHASING POWER OF RAW MATERIALS AND OF MANUFACTURED GOODS, 1922-1929 [a]

| (1) | (2) | (3) | (4) | (5) |
|---|---|---|---|---|
| | Index numbers of wholesale prices | | Index numbers of per-unit purchasing power [b] | |
| Year | Raw materials | Manufactured goods | Raw materials | Manufactured goods |
| 1922 | 100.0 | 100.0 | 100.0 | 100.0 |
| 1923 | 106.3 | 105.3 | 100.8 | 99.8 |
| 1924 | 105.5 | 102.8 | 101.9 | 99.3 |
| 1925 | 114.8 | 104.9 | 106.6 | 97.4 |
| 1926 | 107.9 | 101.7 | 104.3 | 98.4 |
| 1927 | 105.2 | 98.2 | 105.0 | 98.1 |
| 1928 | 108.1 | 98.9 | 106.7 | 97.6 |
| 1929 | 105.6 | 97.9 | 105.6 | 97.9 |
| Average annual rate of change (per cent) .... | +0.5 | —0.7 | +0.9 | —0.3 |

[a] The numbers of items in these commodity groups varied between 136 and 142 price series for raw materials, between 330 and 350 series for manufactured goods.

[b] As measured in terms of the 'all commodities' index constructed by the National Bureau of Economic Research. This index declined at an average annual rate of 0.4 per cent between 1922 and 1929.

## FIGURE 59

### MOVEMENTS OF WHOLESALE PRICES IN THE UNITED STATES, 1922-1929

RAW MATERIALS AND MANUFACTURED GOODS

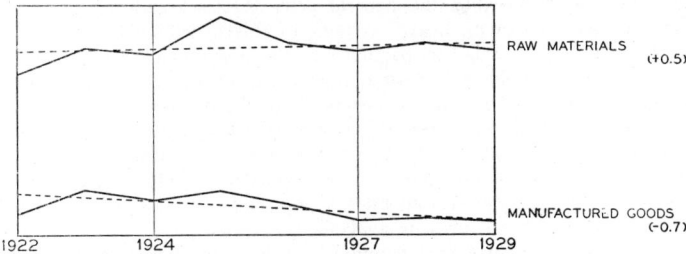

Plotted on ratio scale. The figures in parentheses define average annual rates of change (in percentage form).

The record of price changes over this eight-year period is in some respects like that of the years 1901-1913. Raw materials gained in purchasing power, while manufactured goods declined. The margin of advantage of raw materials, on the basis of net

*(Footnote continued from page 332)*
of weighting is proper, but it gives somewhat insufficient weight to the commodities which bulk large as materials of fabrication.

In addition, it is to be noted that the raw materials index of the National Bureau includes certain commodities classed as semi-finished by the Bureau of Labor Statistics.

There are more important differences between the index numbers of prices of manufactured goods, as constructed by the National Bureau and by the Bureau of Labor Statistics, and these differences affect the 'purchasing power' measurements. Among processed goods, the commodities entering into the National Bureau's index numbers are those classed as finished products by the Bureau of Labor Statistics, and some of those classed as semi-finished. Automobiles, which are given heavy weight in the index of the Bureau of Labor Statistics, are excluded, however, while a selected list from a rather numerous group of commodities for which prices are gathered by the Bureau of Labor Statistics but which are not used in the construction of that Bureau's index, have been included in the commodities entering into the present calculations. This latter group provides more adequate representation of lumber and of an important class of finished goods, primarily steel products, such as trowels, saws and hammers. Commodities of this class are relatively inflexible in price.

It is difficult to measure with any high degree of accuracy changes in the prices of automobiles over such a period as that from 1913 to 1930. Important quality changes have occurred, and there have been striking shifts in the proportion of cars of different price classes marketed. Taking the figures as they stand, they show a material reduction (amounting to about 25 per cent) in the average price of automobiles between 1913 and 1929. The omission of this commodity tends to make the general index higher, with reference to the 1913 base, and to increase the index numbers of prices of manufactured goods, consumers' goods, non-foods, and all other groups into which automobiles would go.

The exceptional character of automobile price movements since 1913 constitutes another important reason for omitting automobiles from the present index numbers. No other commodity of like importance declined 25 per cent in average price between 1913 and 1929, when the general price level was advancing by some 40 per cent. The inclusion, with heavy weights, of this exceptional commodity would tend to distort an index number, particularly the index number of a sub-group in which automobiles would be of predominant importance. The prices of other manufactured goods, and of other consumers' goods, did not follow the course of automobile prices. It is, of course, of great economic significance that automobile prices were reduced so drastically, but it does not seem proper to allow such an exceptional movement to dominate the various group index numbers computed in the present investigation. Automobiles, then, are to be considered a class apart; they do not enter into the present analysis.

The inclusion of a considerable number of finished steel products has tended to raise the index numbers of the groups into which these products fall. Though marked by fairly fixed prices, these commodities should be included as representative of the important group of tools and hardware.

average annual gain, was greater in the recent period. (The pre-war rates of change in purchasing power were + 0.3 per cent a year for raw materials, − 0.1 per cent for manufactured goods.) But we are not justified in considering the post-war period in isolation. We have seen that the events of 1914-1921 profoundly modified many economic relations, among them the price relations prevailing among producers of raw materials and agents of fabrication. Changes of recent years must be seen against this background. Index numbers of purchasing power on the 1913 base provide a broader view of these developments.

| Commodity group | Index numbers of purchasing power, per unit | | | | | |
|---|---|---|---|---|---|---|
| | 1913 | 1919 | 1920 | 1921 | 1922 | 1929 |
| Raw materials | 100.0 | 96.4 | 88.7 | 83.0 | 89.8 | 94.9 |
| Manufactured goods | 100.0 | 101.3 | 105.1 | 108.0 | 104.4 | 102.2 |

These measurements are plotted in Figure 60.

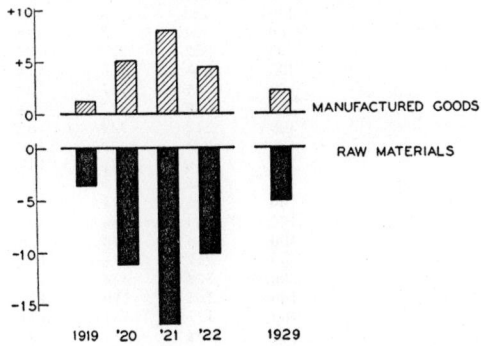

FIGURE 60

CHANGES IN THE REAL VALUES, PER UNIT, OF RAW MATERIALS AND OF MANUFACTURED GOODS, 1913-1929

(CHANGES ARE MEASURED AS PERCENTAGE DEVIATIONS FROM 1913 PURCHASING POWER.)

The story of the decline in the real per-unit value of raw materials has been told in an earlier chapter. In 1921 each unit of raw materials was worth approximately 17 per cent less than in 1913, in exchange for goods in general, while each unit of manufactured goods was worth approximately 8 per cent more. The margin had been narrowed by 1922, but it is clear that the advance recorded in the prices of raw materials between 1922 and 1929 was a movement which started from a level of values far below that of 1913. The year 1929 found the per-unit purchasing power of raw materials still some 5 per cent below the pre-war standard. The decline from 1922 to 1929 for manufactured goods, on the other hand, was a drop from the position of superior advantage in which the recession of 1920-21 had left goods of this class. In some degree this advantage continued through 1929.[1]

[1] Index numbers, like all averages, sometimes conceal more than they reveal. For this reason it is well to follow the changes occurring between 1913 and 1929 in the prices of specific raw materials, in comparison with changes in the average prices of commodity groups. (These index numbers relate to actual prices and not to purchasing power, as in the preceding text.)

|  | 1913 | 1919 | 1920 | 1921 | 1922 | 1929 |
|---|---|---|---|---|---|---|
| All commodities index (National Bureau of Economic Research) | 100 | 203 | 228 | 151 | 148 | 148 |
| All manufactured goods | 100 | 206 | 240 | 163 | 155 | 151 |
| All raw materials | 100 | 196 | 202 | 125 | 133 | 141 |
| Aluminum | 100 | 140 | 141 | 91 | 79 | 101 |
| Anthracite coal | 100 | 156 | 179 | 198 | 200 | 204 |
| Apples | 100 | 268 | 227 | 190 | 212 | 190 |
| Bananas | 100 | 263 | 198 | 174 | 147 | 115 |
| Barley | 100 | 195 | 202 | 102 | 101 | 98 |
| Beans | 100 | 202 | 186 | 130 | 191 | 250 |
| Bituminous coal | 100 | 187 | 266 | 207 | 236 | 154 |
| Cattle | 100 | 206 | 170 | 103 | 111 | 159 |
| Clover seed | 100 | 295 | 218 | 114 | 122 | 166 |
| Cocoa bean | 100 | 147 | 134 | 66 | 76 | 101 |
| Coffee | 100 | 189 | 145 | 79 | 109 | 168 |
| Copper, ingot | 100 | 122 | 114 | 80 | 85 | 115 |
| Copra | 100 | 84 | 87 | 46 | 44 | 43 |
| Corn | 100 | 257 | 227 | 92 | 100 | 151 |
| Cotton | 100 | 251 | 260 | 111 | 161 | 146 |
| Cottonseed | 100 | 301 | 237 | 102 | 161 | 160 |
| Crushed stone | 100 | 189 | 212 | 214 | 188 | 365 |
| Eggs | 100 | 212 | 229 | 162 | 139 | 148 |
| Ferromanganese | 100 | 244 | 332 | 136 | 123 | 179 |
| Flaxseed | 100 | 336 | 281 | 137 | 184 | 205 |
| Gravel | 100 | 193 | 224 | 203 | 180 | 183 |
| Hay | 100 | 225 | 214 | 142 | 144 | 173 |
| Hemp | 100 | 164 | 174 | 89 | 79 | 121 |
| Hides | 100 | 214 | 170 | 76 | 98 | 93 |
| Hogs | 100 | 217 | 174 | 105 | 115 | 126 |
| Hops | 100 | 323 | 426 | 115 | 81 | 81 |
| Iron ore | 100 | 165 | 190 | 177 | 155 | 131 |
| Lead, pig | 100 | 131 | 184 | 104 | 132 | 155 |
| Lemons | 100 | 95 | 75 | 90 | 117 | 149 |
| Milk | 100 | 190 | 191 | 169 | 164 | 194 |
| Nitrate of soda | 100 | 144 | 142 | 100 | 103 | 87 |
| Oats | 100 | 186 | 212 | 103 | 105 | 129 |
| Onions | 100 | 228 | 135 | 155 | 239 | 189 |
| Oranges | 100 | 109 | 142 | 118 | 178 | 148 |
| Peanuts | 100 | 208 | 229 | 149 | 118 | 139 |
| Pepper | 100 | 186 | 131 | 84 | 93 | 317 |
| Petroleum, crude | 100 | 244 | 364 | 185 | 192 | 132 |
| Phosphate rock | 100 | 147 | 268 | 164 | 90 | 91 |
| Pig iron | 100 | 189 | 280 | 157 | 169 | 125 |
| Potatoes | 100 | 232 | 424 | 175 | 165 | 157 |
| Poultry | 100 | 204 | 225 | 190 | 161 | 186 |
| Quicksilver | 100 | 214 | 190 | 106 | 139 | 291 |

(*Footnote continued on following page*)

## PRICE MOVEMENTS, POST-WAR

These figures represent one of the most remarkable reversals of economic tendencies which has occurred in modern times. As we have seen, the story of the years before the war was a story of constantly cheapening manufactured goods. Refinement of technical methods, development of mass production, improvement of management, were all tending to lower the prices paid by consumers for the services of fabricating agents. Raw materials as a class, on the other hand, were rising in value, relatively to manufactured goods. The margin of production was being pushed further out, and no widespread improvements of technique at all comparable to those so familiar in manufacturing had been developed. After 1913 the reversal we have noted occurred. Productive technique improved in the cultivation and extraction of raw products. Rich new territories were exploited; temporary war demands and a sharply rising price level stimulated rapid expansion in the output of certain of these goods. The termination of the war checked these temporary demands. Perhaps more important, the world-wide deflation of prices in 1920-21 found raw material producers unprepared for or unable to adapt themselves to a new order through prompt liquidation, readjustment of costs and adjustment of production to changed demand conditions.

The ending of war demand and the deflation of prices struck manufacturing interests just as sharp a blow as that suffered by raw material producers. Manufacturing producers, however, were able to liquidate more promptly, and to adapt production schedules to marketing possibilities more readily. In some degree, also, manufacturing producers readjusted costs to the new price level. But, partly because of the weak position of raw material producers, a thoroughgoing readjustment of costs was not necessary. Labor costs

*(Footnote continued from preceding page)*

|  | 1913 | 1919 | 1920 | 1921 | 1922 | 1929 |
|---|---|---|---|---|---|---|
| Rubber, crude | 100 | 59 | 44 | 20 | 21 | 25 |
| Rye | 100 | 241 | 294 | 191 | 139 | 160 |
| Sand | 100 | 178 | 203 | 182 | 159 | 154 |
| Sheep | 100 | 207 | 204 | 128 | 169 | 176 |
| Silk, raw | 100 | 232 | 232 | 159 | 193 | 135 |
| Spiegeleisen | 100 | 168 | 280 | 125 | 135 | 130 |
| Sugar, raw | 100 | 215 | 372 | 135 | 133 | 107 |
| Sulphur | 100 | 127 | 108 | 72 | 64 | 82 |
| Tankage | 100 | 233 | 277 | 106 | 159 | 155 |
| Tin, pig | 100 | 146 | 112 | 66 | 72 | 101 |
| Wheat | 100 | 276 | 280 | 151 | 138 | 134 |
| Wood pulp | 100 | 158 | 296 | 157 | 115 | 114 |
| Wool | 100 | 148 | 82 | 54 | 101 | 92 |
| Zinc, slab | 100 | 127 | 139 | 88 | 104 | 117 |

remained high, being, in 1923, some 87 per cent above the 1914 level. Tendencies prevailing thereafter reduced these price disparities somewhat but, by and large, manufactured goods enjoyed a distinct advantage, during the ensuing six or seven years, and sellers of raw materials were at a corresponding disadvantage.[1]

§ *Price variability of raw and processed goods.*—In earlier pages (Chapters II and V) raw materials and manufactured goods have been compared in respect of price variability. The measurements given confirmed everyday experience in showing that the prices of raw materials are distinctly more variable, and are subject to more frequent changes,

[1] This conclusion is supported by index numbers of the prices of 'identical' goods in raw and processed form, formerly computed by the U. S. Bureau of Labor Statistics. In purchasing power form, these give us the following results:

| Commodity group | Index numbers of purchasing power, per unit | | | | | |
|---|---|---|---|---|---|---|
| | 1913 | 1919 | 1920 | 1921 | 1922 | 1926 |
| Raw materials | 100.0 | 100.3 | 97.8 | 92.1 | 97.4 | 95.9 |
| Goods manufactured from these raw materials | 100.0 | 99.6 | 103.5 | 112.2 | 104.2 | 106.4 |

These index numbers show the marked decline in the real values of industrial raw materials in 1920-21. In 1926, the last year covered by these index numbers, the per-unit purchasing power of these materials was 4 per cent below the level of 1913, while the purchasing power of manufactured goods, per unit, was 6 per cent above the 1913 level.

Twenty-seven price series are included in the index of raw material prices, seventy in the index of prices of manufactured goods.

Index numbers secured from the Bureau of Labor Statistics classification of commodities into raw, semi-finished and finished goods do not yield the same results for the later years of the period. The existence of a special group of semi-finished goods prevents direct comparison of the raw and processed groups in the two classifications. The group of semi-finished goods has shown persistent price weakness in the post-war era. Certain important commodities in this group (notably pig iron) have been classed as raw materials in the division made by the National Bureau. The removal of these commodities from the Bureau of Labor Statistics raw materials group gives relatively more weight in that group to raw consumers' goods, which, as we have seen, gained materially in purchasing power since 1921.

One defect of the general comparison made above is that manufactured goods as a class are not well represented. Complicated machines, which vary in character and quality from time to time, cannot well be included in index numbers of the usual type. The commodities here included among manufactured goods are limited, in the main, to standardized goods not subject to great changes in quality. As regards such goods the conclusions suggested above are probably valid. They do not hold with the same force for those classes of mechanical equipment (of which the automobile is an outstanding example) which have been materially improved in quality since 1913 and which, in many cases, were actually reduced in price during the general advance from the pre-war level. Further consideration is given in the next chapter to price changes among a broader sample of manufacturing goods.

than are the prices of manufactured goods. The rather significant fact was noted, however, that the margin between the two groups was narrowed during the disturbed years from 1914 to 1921. The crystallized prices of processed goods were broken open by the fluctuations of the war years, and under the exigencies of those revolutionary times these goods acquired a new degree of price flexibility. Subsequent developments are of more than passing interest for the light they may throw on the presence of new tendencies toward more stable (or more firmly controlled) prices, under recent economic conditions.

TABLE 139

VARIABILITY OF PRICES OF RAW MATERIALS AND OF MANUFACTURED GOODS UNDER PRE-WAR, WAR-TIME AND POST-WAR CONDITIONS [a]

| (1) Period | (2) (3) Measurements of monthly variability of prices [b] | | (4) (5) Measurements of frequency of price change [c] | |
|---|---|---|---|---|
| | Raw materials | Manufactured goods | Raw materials | Manufactured goods |
| 1898-1913 | 8.2 | 3.6 | .82 | .34 |
| 1914-1921 | 10.9 | 7.4 | .83 | .47 |
| 1922-1929 | 7.8 | 3.7 | .83 | .42 |
| 1922-1925 | 9.0 | 4.0 | .88 | .44 |
| 1926-1929 | 6.5 | 3.3 | .79 | .40 |

[a] The numbers of price series upon which these measurements are based are as follows:

|  | 1898-1921 | 1922-1929 |
|---|---|---|
| Raw materials | 49 | 46 |
| Manufactured goods | 158 | 148 |

[b] Each measurement is an average of the mean percentage deviations of monthly prices of individual commodities about their annual averages. See *The Behavior of Prices*, pp. 39-49.

[c] Each measurement is an average of measurements for individual commodities. For each commodity the measure is the ratio of the number of times a price changed, from month to month, to the total possible number of changes. See *The Behavior of Prices*, pp. 56-60.

A movement toward post-war price stability is indicated by these measurements. For raw materials, the average of the monthly variability measurements for the years 1926-29 is 21 per cent below the average of the pre-war figures; the last entry for manufactured goods is 8 per cent below the average of the earlier figures. In respect of frequency of change the differences are less pronounced. For manufactured goods, indeed, the evidence indicates more frequent changes (but narrower fluctuations) than during the pre-war era.

These measurements define a movement, but they do not reveal the forces back of it. An extension of the area of control within the field of prices would bring just such reductions in amplitude of variations as the measurements indicate. But whether these reductions are mani-

340    ECONOMIC TENDENCIES

festations of a desirable stability, or of an undesirable loss of sensitivity to changing conditions of supply and demand, this evidence does not tell us.

## Products of American Farms and Other Products

In surveying events of the period 1901-13, we traced alterations in the terms of exchange between domestic agricultural producers and other producers. Corresponding price data for the post-war period appear in the following table. These index numbers are plotted in Figure 61.

TABLE 140

PRODUCTS OF AMERICAN FARMS AND ALL OTHER PRODUCTS

Index Numbers of Wholesale Prices in the United States, 1922-1929 [a]

| (1) | (2) | (3) | (4) | (5) | (6) | (7) |
|---|---|---|---|---|---|---|
| Year | Products of American farms | | All other products | | All products of American farms | All other products |
| | Raw | Processed | Raw | Processed | | |
| 1922 | 100.0 | 100.0 | 100.0 | 100.0 | 100.0 | 100.0 |
| 1923 | 104.8 | 103.7 | 108.7 | 106.6 | 104.1 | 106.9 |
| 1924 | 106.8 | 104.2 | 104.1 | 101.7 | 105.2 | 102.1 |
| 1925 | 116.4 | 111.7 | 112.9 | 99.9 | 113.4 | 102.6 |
| 1926 | 105.3 | 106.0 | 112.1 | 98.4 | 105.8 | 101.3 |
| 1927 | 105.6 | 104.9 | 105.2 | 93.2 | 105.1 | 95.7 |
| 1928 | 113.8 | 107.7 | 100.9 | 92.4 | 109.9 | 94.2 |
| 1929 | 109.9 | 105.2 | 100.2 | 92.5 | 106.9 | 94.1 |
| Average annual rate of change (per cent) | | | | | | |
| In price ..... | +1.1 | +0.6 | —0.4 | —1.8 | +0.8 | —1.5 |
| In purchasing power ..... | +1.5 | +1.0 | 0.0 | —1.4 | +1.2 | —1.1 |

[a] The maximum and minimum numbers of price series included in each of the commodity groups are given below:

Products of American farms
    Raw              83
    Processed    143 to 152
    Total          226 to 235

All other products
    Raw           53 to 59
    Processed    187 to 198
    Total       240 to 257

The index of American farm products shown above covers not only all raw materials produced on American farms, but processed

## FIGURE 61

### MOVEMENTS OF WHOLESALE PRICES IN THE UNITED STATES, 1922-1929

PRODUCTS OF AMERICAN FARMS AND ALL OTHER PRODUCTS

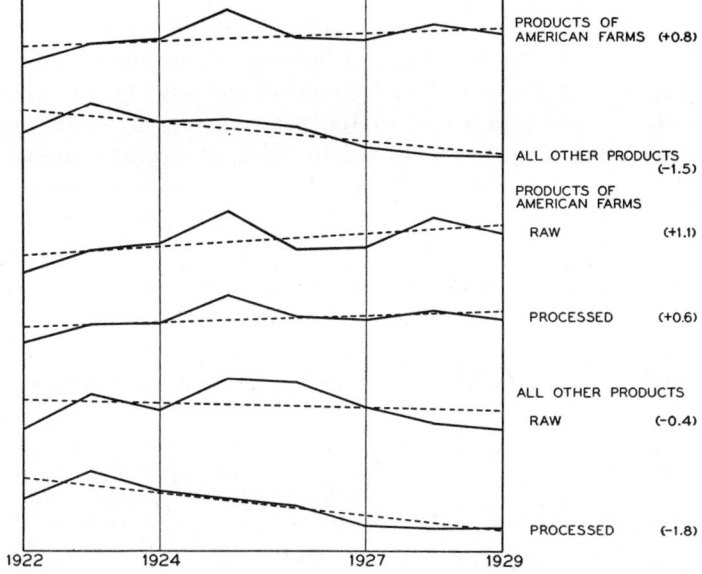

Plotted on ratio scale. The figures in parentheses define average annual rates of change (in percentage form).

forms of these materials as well.[1] Considering first this combination of raw and processed goods, we find an increase in average price per unit at an annual rate of 0.8 per cent. This represents an increase in purchasing power (in terms of commodities in general at wholesale) at a rate of 1.2 per cent.[2] For all products not originating on

[1] The Bureau of Agricultural Economics has constructed an index of agricultural prices from a weighted combination of the Bureau of Labor Statistics index numbers of the wholesale prices of farm products, foods and cattle feed. Processed articles such as textiles and leather products, which have been included in the National Bureau's averages, have been classed as non-agricultural. This index shows an average annual increase of 1.5 per cent in the wholesale prices of agricultural products between 1922 and 1929, and a decrease of 2.2 per cent for non-agricultural products.

[2] In determining the change in purchasing power, the index of all commodities constructed by the National Bureau of Economic Research has been employed. This index showed a net decline between 1922 and 1929 at a rate of 0.4 per cent a year, as compared with a rate of 0.5 per cent for the U. S. Bureau of Labor Statistics index.

American farms the movement of prices was downward between 1922 and 1929 at a rate of 1.5 per cent a year, a loss in purchasing power, per unit of product, at an average annual rate of 1.1 per cent.

More illuminating are the results secured when each of these major groups is broken into raw and processed classes. Raw farm products were rising in price, at wholesale, at an annual rate of 1.1 per cent between 1922 and 1929; goods of the same type in processed form rose in price at a rate of 0.6 per cent a year. Both raw and fabricated non-farm products fell in price, at average annual rates of 0.4 and 1.8 per cent a year. It was, thus, raw farm products and processed non-farm products which dominated price movements in the general groups of raw and manufactured goods, giving them their respective advancing and declining trends during this period.

To measure changes in the real rewards of these groups, movements must be followed in terms of purchasing power. These are summarized below, with corresponding pre-war measurements.

| Commodity group | Average annual rate of change in purchasing power | | | |
|---|---|---|---|---|
| | 1901-1913 (per cent) | | 1922-1929 (per cent) | |
| Products of American farms | | | | |
| Raw | +1.0 | | +1.5 | |
| Processed | +0.6 | | +1.0 | |
| Total | | +0.7 | | +1.2 |
| All other products | | | | |
| Raw | —0.4 | | 0.0 | |
| Processed | —0.8 | | —1.4 | |
| Total | | —0.7 | | —1.1 |

As regards the two main groups the records of purchasing power changes during the two periods are somewhat similar. For farm products per-unit purchasing power was advancing, while non-farm products showed corresponding declines. Among farm products, both raw and processed commodities gained in real value; processed non-farm products declined. Raw non-farm products lost in purchasing power in the pre-war era, remained constant in the later era.

The reason for the cheapening of non-farm products in both periods is found, in part, in the growing importance of large-scale production, the widening of markets and the accompanying lowering of manufacturing costs, per unit of product. In some degree, however, the post-war movements of both farm and non-farm prices are direct outgrowths of the situation left by the recession and price adjustment of 1920-21, which was described in an earlier chapter. As is well known, war-time conditions stimulated the demand for farm products in general, but the withdrawal of this stimulus brought a reaction which put agricultural prices at a lower level, relatively, than that which had prevailed before the war. These changes are shown by the following table, in which the prices of products of American farms and of all products not originating on American farms are expressed in terms of dollars of constant purchasing power, for certain selected years.

| Commodity group | Index numbers of purchasing power, per unit | | | | | |
|---|---|---|---|---|---|---|
| | 1913 | 1919 | 1920 | 1921 | 1922 | 1929 |
| Products of American farms... | 100 | 110.0 | 101.2 | 95.2 | 98.3 | 105.1 |
| All other products............ | 100 | 90.8 | 98.6 | 104.7 | 101.3 | 95.3 |

In 1919 products of American farms stood, in real value, 10 per cent above the 1913 level, while other products, on the average, had lost some 9 per cent in purchasing power. In 1921 the situation was reversed. Farm products were then almost 5 per cent below the 1913 level, in purchasing power, while the real per-unit value of products of non-farm origin was enhanced by a corresponding amount. The rise in the prices of farm products between 1921 and 1929, and the decline recorded for non-farm products, again altered these relations, carrying the average purchasing power of all goods originating on American farms to a level some 5 per cent above that of 1913, while the purchasing power of goods of non-farm origin was reduced to a point about 5 per cent below that level.

Each of the above groups includes both raw and processed goods, and the averages define the composite position of raw material producers and of manufacturers. Movements of the separate elements should be followed. Changes in purchasing power for the four constituent groups are shown below. The measurements are plotted in Figure 62.

| Commodity group | Index numbers of purchasing power, per unit | | | | | |
|---|---|---|---|---|---|---|
| | 1913 | 1919 | 1920 | 1921 | 1922 | 1929 |
| Products of American farms | | | | | | |
|   Raw ...................... | 100 | 109.1 | 93.2 | 82.4 | 92.3 | 101.4 |
|   Processed ................ | 100 | 110.6 | 106.1 | 103.5 | 102.1 | 107.3 |
| All other products | | | | | | |
|   Raw ...................... | 100 | 79.4 | 81.9 | 83.9 | 85.9 | 86.1 |
|   Processed ................ | 100 | 94.4 | 104.2 | 111.7 | 106.2 | 98.2 |

### FIGURE 62

GRAPHIC REPRESENTATION OF CHANGES IN THE REAL VALUES, PER UNIT, OF COMMODITIES IN SELECTED GROUPS, 1913-1929

PRODUCTS OF AMERICAN FARMS AND ALL OTHER PRODUCTS

(CHANGES ARE MEASURED AS PERCENTAGE DEVIATIONS FROM 1913 PURCHASING POWER.)

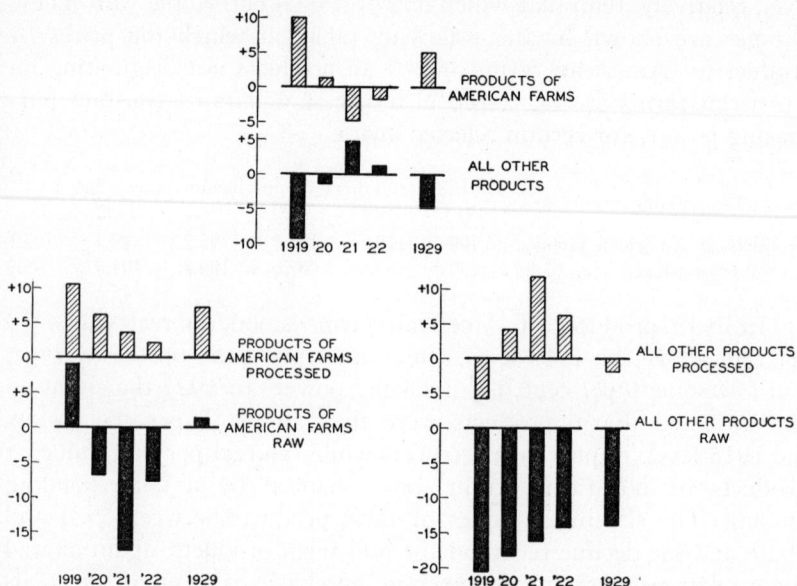

This table puts recent changes in a somewhat different light. Raw farm products, the prices of which are of far more concern to agricultural producers than are the prices of processed goods, fell sharply from the favored position they occupied in 1919, when they commanded almost 9 per cent more in terms of other goods than they had in 1913. By 1921 the per-unit value of these products, at wholesale, was almost 18 per cent below the 1913 level. In 1922, when the record of the earlier tables begins, they were still some 8 per cent below the pre-war level of purchasing power. The recovery following that date, as recorded by the gain in purchasing power at a rate of 1.5 per cent a year, had brought these products in 1929 to a level slightly more than one per cent above that of 1913.

Processed farm products shared the war-time gain with raw materials, but the recession of 1920-21 left them in 1922 with a per-unit purchasing power more than 2 per cent above the 1913 level. The gain since then has been a real one. In 1929 the prices of processed farm products represented a purchasing power 7 per cent above that which they possessed in 1913. The difference in the price behavior of raw and processed goods in the group of products originating on American farms provides an illuminating example of the play of economic forces, and of the incidence of economic change.

The striking decline which occurred during the 'twenties in the prices of manufactured goods of non-farm origin was emphasized in preceding pages. The above figures permit a just interpretation of this movement. In 1919 such goods possessed a per-unit purchasing power almost 6 per cent below that of 1913. This loss was rectified in good measure during the ensuing readjustment. By 1921 processed non-farm products had a per-unit purchasing power almost 12 per cent above that of 1913. From 1919 to 1921 the command over commodities in general exercised by the average unit of goods of this type had increased by more than 18 per cent. Producers of goods of this type (and this group includes, of course, industrial workers, as well as the owners of industrial plants) were most favored by the conditions following in the wake of the great recession. The nominal and actual cheapening of processed non-farm products between 1922 and 1929 constituted a restoration of the relations prevailing in 1913 between the prices of these goods and of other commodities at wholesale.

Notable among the four groups represented above are raw products of non-farm origin. In 1916 such goods possessed an average per-unit purchasing power slightly exceeding that of 1913. In no year since 1916 has this been true. Prices prevailing in 1921 represented a purchasing power for such goods 16 per cent below that of 1913. The slight gain in value recorded between 1921 and 1929 left this group in 1929 with per-unit purchasing power 14 per cent below the 1913 standard. The weakness of this general group of raw materials in recent months has, of course, been an outstanding feature of the current depression.

§ *Price variability of farm and other products.*—The increased variability imparted to prices by the disturbances of the war years and of the post-war recession has been described, and the return to later stability noted. The following measurements relate to the groups now under discussion.

## TABLE 141

### Products of American Farms and All Other Products
Comparison of Measurements of Monthly Price Variability, 1898-1929 [a]

| (1) | (2) | (3) | (4) | (5) | (6) | (7) |
|---|---|---|---|---|---|---|
| | Measurements of monthly price variability, products of American farms | | | Measurements of monthly price variability, all other products | | |
| Period | Raw | Processed | Total | Raw | Processed | Total |
| 1898-1913 | 9.0 | 3.7 | 4.9 | 5.4 | 3.4 | 3.9 |
| 1914-1921 | 12.5 | 8.2 | 9.1 | 9.4 | 6.6 | 7.3 |
| 1922-1929 | 9.7 | 4.0 | 5.3 | 5.8 | 3.2 | 3.9 |
| 1922-1925 | 10.4 | 4.3 | 5.6 | 7.5 | 3.8 | 4.7 |
| 1926-1929 | 8.9 | 3.7 | 4.9 | 4.1 | 2.7 | 3.1 |

[a] The numbers of price series upon which these measurements are based are as follows:

| Products of American farms | 1898-1921 | 1922-1929 | | All other products | 1898-1921 | 1922-1929 |
|---|---|---|---|---|---|---|
| Raw | 24 | 23 | | Raw | 25 | 23 |
| Processed | 83 | 81 | | Processed | 75 | 67 |
| Total | 107 | 104 | | Total | 100 | 90 |

Products of American farms returned, between 1926 and 1929, to precisely the points on the scale of variability that they had occupied during the sixteen pre-war years. The prices of non-farm products moved to much more stable positions during the four years preceding the 1929 recession. Indexes defining the magnitudes of month-to-month price fluctuations among non-farm products were lower in these years than in any earlier period covered by the record. The average decline in variability, from the pre-war to the most recent period, amounted to approximately 21 per cent for all goods of non-farm origin. It was among these classes of commodities, if anywhere in the price structure, that price rigidity was increasing.

*Changes in Farm Prices.*—Changes in the economic situation of the farmer are not necessarily reflected in the movements of wholesale prices, for these are not the prices the farmer actually receives, nor the prices he pays. There are available index numbers of farm prices, and of the prices paid by farmers for commodities used in production and for family maintenance, which define more accurately the effect of price changes upon the actual economic life of the farmer.[1] These are given in the following table. They are plotted in Figure 63.

[1] These index numbers are constructed by the U. S. Bureau of Agricultural Economics. *Yearbook of Agriculture, 1931*, pp. 1018, 1021.

### TABLE 142

Index Numbers Measuring Changes in Farm Prices and in the Per-unit Purchasing Power of Farm Products, 1922-1929

| Year | Farm prices (30 commodities) | Prices paid by farmers [a] | Purchasing power of farm products |
|---|---|---|---|
| 1922 | 100.0 | 100.0 | 100.0 |
| 1923 | 108.9 | 100.7 | 108.1 |
| 1924 | 108.1 | 101.3 | 106.7 |
| 1925 | 118.5 | 104.6 | 113.3 |
| 1926 | 109.7 | 102.6 | 106.9 |
| 1927 | 105.6 | 101.3 | 104.2 |
| 1928 | 112.1 | 102.6 | 109.3 |
| 1929 | 111.3 | 102.0 | 109.1 |
| Average annual rate of change (per cent) | +0.9 | +0.3 | +0.6 |

[a] Retail prices paid by farmers for commodities used in living and production.

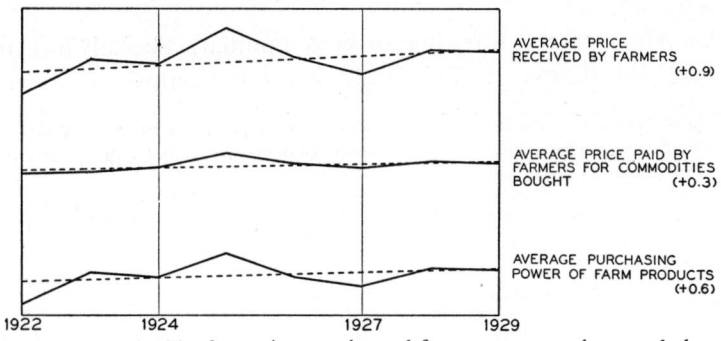

FIGURE 63

CHANGES IN FARM PRICES AND IN THE PURCHASING POWER OF FARM PRODUCTS, 1922-1929

AVERAGE PRICE RECEIVED BY FARMERS (+0.9)

AVERAGE PRICE PAID BY FARMERS FOR COMMODITIES BOUGHT (+0.3)

AVERAGE PURCHASING POWER OF FARM PRODUCTS (+0.6)

Plotted on ratio scale. The figures in parentheses define average annual rates of change (in percentage form).

Prices received by farmers increased between 1922 and 1929 at a rate somewhat lower than that at which the prices of raw farm products at wholesale advanced, and the gain in purchasing power, measured in terms of the commodities actually bought by farmers, was smaller. This gain, per unit of product, was at the rate of + 0.6 per cent a year.[1]

Here, again, we secure only a distorted picture if we restrict ourselves to the developments of recent years. The violent change which occurred between 1920 and 1921 in the economic status of the American farmer must appear in the background of any comprehensive view of the farm situation. With reference to an earlier base, we have the following record.

TABLE 143

INDEX NUMBERS MEASURING CHANGES IN FARM PRICES AND IN THE PER-UNIT PURCHASING POWER OF FARM PRODUCTS, 1913-1929

| Year | Farm prices | Prices paid by farmers | Purchasing power of farm products |
|---|---|---|---|
| 1913 | 100 | 100 | 100 |
| 1917 | 176 | 150 | 118 |
| 1920 | 205 | 206 | 99 |
| 1921 | 116 | 156 | 75 |
| 1922 | 124 | 152 | 81 |
| 1929 | 138 | 155 | 89 |

The index numbers in the last column are shown graphically in Figure 64.

The story of the war-time drop is familiar. The advance indicated by the figures in Table 142 is of the nature of a partial

---

[1] There was considerable variation among farm products in respect of trends in farm prices between 1922 and 1929. Measurements relating to the prices of six groups of products follow.

| Commodity group | Average annual rate of change, 1922-1929 (per cent) |
|---|---|
| Meat animals | + 5.7 |
| Grains | + 1.5 |
| Poultry products | + 1.1 |
| Fruits and vegetables | + 0.5 |
| Dairy products | + 0.1 |
| Cotton and cottonseed | − 5.0 |

Cotton and cottonseed suffered the sharpest decline. Meat animals, at the other extreme in trend, rose in price at a rate of 5.7 per cent a year. The wide diversity of conditions among agricultural producers, and the difficulty of treating this group as a whole, are emphasized by these differences in price trends.

## FIGURE 64
### CHANGES IN THE AVERAGE PER-UNIT PURCHASING POWER OF FARM PRODUCTS, 1913-1929
BASED ON PRICES RECEIVED AND PRICES PAID BY FARMERS
(CHANGES ARE MEASURED AS PERCENTAGE DEVIATIONS FROM 1913 PURCHASING POWER.)

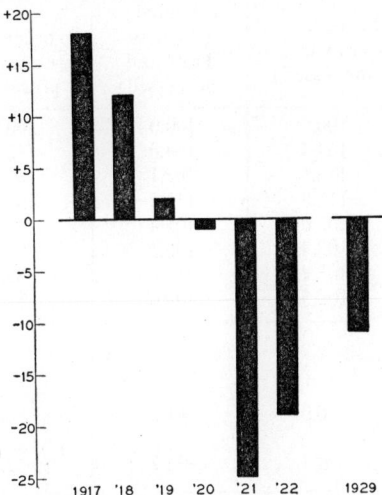

recovery from a position of marked disadvantage for farmers. The net result of the improvement which took place between 1921 and 1929 was to leave the farmer with products worth some 11 per cent less, in terms of purchasing power per unit, than in 1913, and approximately 25 per cent less than at the peak of agricultural prosperity in 1917. Since 1929 the hole out of which the farmer was painfully climbing has again been deepened.

*Farm Crops, Animal Products, Mineral Products and Forest Products*

Notable among the changes occurring in the pre-war era was a cheapening of mineral products, raw and processed, and an enhancement of the per-unit purchasing power of farm crops, animal products and forest products. (See Tables 28 and 29, Chapter II.) Index numbers showing the post-war price movements of these commodity groups are given below. They are presented graphically in Figure 65.

## TABLE 144
### Farm Crops and Animal, Forest and Mineral Products
Index Numbers of Wholesale Prices in the United States, 1922-1929 [a]

| (1)<br>Year | (2)<br>Farm crops<br>(raw and<br>processed) | (3)<br>Animal<br>products<br>(raw and<br>processed) | (4)<br>Forest<br>products<br>(raw and<br>processed) | (5)<br>Mineral<br>products<br>(raw and<br>processed) |
|---|---|---|---|---|
| 1922 | 100.0 | 100.0 | 100.0 | 100.0 |
| 1923 | 104.4 | 104.0 | 112.4 | 105.4 |
| 1924 | 108.6 | 102.1 | 100.2 | 101.8 |
| 1925 | 116.0 | 111.2 | 102.2 | 100.7 |
| 1926 | 107.0 | 105.4 | 97.3 | 100.6 |
| 1927 | 103.4 | 106.1 | 91.1 | 95.5 |
| 1928 | 105.2 | 112.6 | 88.2 | 94.6 |
| 1929 | 102.5 | 109.0 | 87.3 | 95.7 |
| Average annual rate of change (per cent) | | | | |
| In price | 0.0 | +1.3 | −2.9 | −1.2 |
| In purchasing power | +0.4 | +1.7 | −2.5 | −0.8 |

[a] The numbers of price series in the various groups are given below:
Farm crops 124
Animal products 122 to 131
Forest products 53 to 55
Mineral products 158 to 171

### FIGURE 65
### MOVEMENTS OF WHOLESALE PRICES IN THE UNITED STATES, 1922-1929
ANIMAL PRODUCTS, FARM CROPS, FOREST PRODUCTS AND MINERAL PRODUCTS

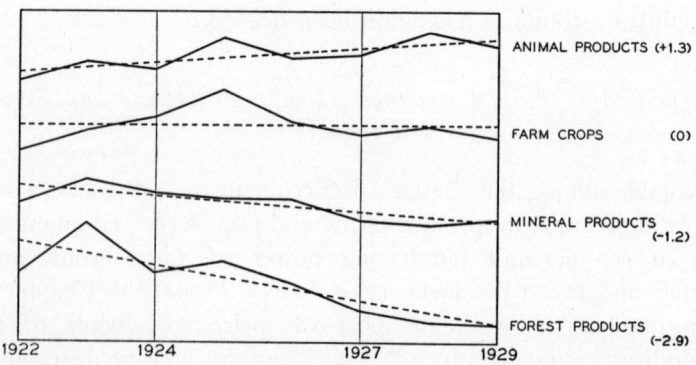

Plotted on ratio scale. The figures in parentheses define average annual rates of change (in percentage form).

As in the period 1901-1913, the per-unit real value (i.e., the purchasing power) of farm crops and of animal products increased between 1922 and 1929, while that of mineral products declined. The only reversal of tendency appears in the movements of forest products. An average annual increase in purchasing power at a rate of 1.2 per cent in pre-war years was succeeded by an average annual decline of 2.5 per cent from 1922 to 1929. But we shall do well to study separately the movements of raw and processed goods in each of these divisions.

TABLE 145

FARM CROPS AND ANIMAL, FOREST AND MINERAL PRODUCTS
RAW AND PROCESSED

Index Numbers of Wholesale Prices in the United States, 1922-1929 [a]

| (1) Year | (2) Farm crops Raw | (3) Farm crops Processed | (4) Animal products Raw | (5) Animal products Processed | (6) Forest products Raw | (7) Forest products Processed | (8) Mineral products Raw | (9) Mineral products Processed |
|---|---|---|---|---|---|---|---|---|
| 1922 | 100.0 | 100.0 | 100.0 | 100.0 | 100.0 | 100.0 | 100.0 | 100.0 |
| 1923 | 104.8 | 104.2 | 105.9 | 103.3 | 138.0 | 110.5 | 105.3 | 105.6 |
| 1924 | 112.4 | 106.3 | 103.4 | 101.7 | 114.0 | 99.0 | 100.3 | 102.5 |
| 1925 | 125.3 | 110.7 | 111.1 | 111.5 | 190.4 | 97.2 | 103.0 | 100.0 |
| 1926 | 114.0 | 102.9 | 101.5 | 107.9 | 157.5 | 93.5 | 104.4 | 99.4 |
| 1927 | 110.6 | 99.2 | 103.5 | 107.9 | 133.2 | 88.2 | 99.0 | 94.4 |
| 1928 | 113.6 | 100.5 | 114.6 | 111.8 | 101.1 | 87.1 | 96.5 | 94.0 |
| 1929 | 111.5 | 97.2 | 108.3 | 109.5 | 97.6 | 86.3 | 97.1 | 95.2 |
| Average annual rate of change (per cent) In price ..... | +1.2 | —0.8 | +1.0 | +1.4 | —1.6 | —3.1 | —0.8 | —1.4 |
| In purchasing power ..... | +1.6 | —0.4 | +1.5 | +1.8 | —1.2 | —2.7 | —0.4 | —1.0 |

[a] The numbers of price series in the various commodity groups are as follows:

Farm crops
  Raw    47
  Processed    77
Animal products
  Raw    47
  Processed    75 to 84

Forest products
  Raw    4
  Processed    49 to 51
Mineral products
  Raw    38 to 44
  Processed    120 to 127

As regards changes in purchasing power, the most pronounced divergence of trends among raw and processed goods appears in the group of farm crops. Between 1922 and 1929 there was a distinct gain in the real per-unit value of raw farm crops, a net loss in the per-unit value of goods of this type in processed form. Among mineral and forest products, the loss of per-unit purchasing power was greater for processed goods than for raw materials.[1] Processed animal products emerged with a net gain exceeding that of raw animal products.

As in dealing with price changes in other commodity groups, recent movements must be interpreted against the background of war-time changes and of pre-war relations. In the next table purchasing power changes of commodities in the groups listed above are referred to a pre-war base.

TABLE 146

FARM CROPS AND ANIMAL, FOREST AND MINERAL PRODUCTS

Index Numbers of Purchasing Power in Relation to a Pre-war Base, Selected Years

| Commodity group | 1913 | 1919 | 1920 | 1921 | 1922 | 1929 |
|---|---|---|---|---|---|---|
| Farm crops | 100.0 | 110.2 | 104.2 | 93.2 | 95.8 | 98.2 |
| Animal products | 100.0 | 106.5 | 93.5 | 92.1 | 96.4 | 105.0 |
| Forest products | 100.0 | 92.8 | 117.2 | 102.3 | 105.3 | 91.9 |
| Mineral products | 100.0 | 90.5 | 97.8 | 112.0 | 105.1 | 100.5 |
| Farm crops | | | | | | |
| Raw | 100.0 | 110.2 | 98.7 | 85.5 | 91.4 | 102.0 |
| Processed | 100.0 | 110.2 | 107.9 | 98.3 | 98.7 | 96.0 |
| Animal products | | | | | | |
| Raw | 100.0 | 103.5 | 82.8 | 75.1 | 88.5 | 96.0 |
| Processed | 100.0 | 108.2 | 100.8 | 104.6 | 101.5 | 111.1 |
| Forest products | | | | | | |
| Raw | 100.0 | 46.4 | 54.6 | 39.3 | 35.6 | 34.8 |
| Processed | 100.0 | 99.5 | 126.5 | 112.1 | 116.6 | 100.5 |
| Mineral products | | | | | | |
| Raw | 100.0 | 81.2 | 89.4 | 98.3 | 98.9 | 96.0 |
| Processed | 100.0 | 93.7 | 100.7 | 116.8 | 107.0 | 101.9 |

We have seen that the per-unit purchasing power of farm crops and animal products stood in 1922 some 4 per cent below the 1913 level, while that of forest and mineral products was about 5 per cent above that standard. The changes occurring between 1922 and

[1] The group of raw forest products includes only four price series, two quotations for crude rubber (latex crêpe, and plantation, ribbed, smoked sheets), and two for wood pulp (mechanical and sulphite). The sample is too small to justify detailed comparison of index numbers for raw and processed goods of this type.

1929 carried animal products to a level 5 per cent above 1913 parity, while the purchasing power of forest products was reduced to 8 per cent below the pre-war standard. The advance in the real value of farm crops and the decline of mineral values left these groups very close to the relations with all commodities which had prevailed in 1913.

The commodities in these groups include both raw and processed goods. Index numbers for the sub-groups are more illuminating. (These index numbers do not relate, however, to identical commodities in raw and processed forms.) Changes occurring between 1913 and 1929 in the purchasing power of goods in each of these sub-groups may be followed in detail in the table. We may note, in summary, that the advances between 1922 and 1929 in the purchasing power, at wholesale, of raw farm crops carried these goods slightly above their pre-war value; the advance in raw animal products left them, in 1929, 4 per cent below their 1913 purchasing power. Processed animal products were lifted to exceptionally high levels in 1929. In general, the effect of the changes occurring during the eight-year period was to narrow the margins which existed in 1921 and 1922 between the purchasing power of raw and processed goods in the same broad categories. Only among animal products was this not true.[1]

## Foods and Non-Foods

The division between foods and non-foods is one which is of importance rather from the point of view of the consumer than of the producer. In some respects it corresponds to a preceding classification, since the majority of farm products fall in the group of food products, but the differences are pronounced enough to render the separate consideration of the two divisions desirable. Index numbers of prices for the post-war period are given in Table 147, following. They are shown graphically in Figure 66.

The period under review was characterized by a sharp divergence between the trends of food and of non-food prices. In current dollars the prices of foods rose at a rate of 1.6 per cent a year, while the prices of non-foods declined at a rate of 1.5 per cent a year.

---

[1] The striking margin between the purchasing power of raw and processed forest products is not as significant as it appears to be. The group of processed goods of this class is not properly comparable with the very small group of raw materials, in which rubber predominates.

## TABLE 147

### Foods and Non-foods

Index Numbers of Wholesale Prices in the United States, 1922-1929 [a]

| (1) | (2) | (3) | (4) | (5) | (6) | (7) |
|---|---|---|---|---|---|---|
| Year | Food products | | Non-food products | | All foods | All non-foods |
| | Raw | Processed | Raw | Processed | | |
| 1922 | 100.0 | 100.0 | 100.0 | 100.0 | 100.0 | 100.0 |
| 1923 | 102.4 | 100.1 | 109.8 | 107.4 | 101.1 | 108.0 |
| 1924 | 107.6 | 101.5 | 103.1 | 103.4 | 104.1 | 103.3 |
| 1925 | 120.9 | 112.4 | 108.5 | 102.2 | 116.0 | 103.5 |
| 1926 | 113.5 | 108.9 | 102.0 | 99.1 | 110.9 | 99.7 |
| 1927 | 111.9 | 107.3 | 98.4 | 94.8 | 109.2 | 95.6 |
| 1928 | 117.8 | 109.3 | 98.7 | 95.1 | 112.9 | 95.9 |
| 1929 | 117.5 | 106.5 | 94.4 | 94.8 | 111.1 | 94.7 |
| Average annual rate of change (per cent) | | | | | | |
| In price ..... | +2.2 | +1.2 | −1.3 | −1.5 | +1.6 | −1.5 |
| In purchasing power ..... | +2.6 | +1.6 | −0.9 | −1.1 | +2.0 | −1.1 |

[a] The numbers of price series upon which the above index numbers are based varied within the limits given below:

| Foods | | Non-foods | |
|---|---|---|---|
| Raw | 71 | Raw | 65 to 71 |
| Processed | 90 to 96 | Processed | 240 to 254 |
| Total | 161 to 167 | Total | 305 to 325 |

These figures define with precision the actual tendencies of the two groups of commodities, as is clearly shown by the graphs in Figure 66. The per-unit purchasing power of commodities in the food group was rising at a rate of 2.0 per cent a year; the corresponding movement of non-foods was downward at a rate of 1.1 per cent a year. The explanation of this divergence is to be found, in part, in conditions of production and of marketing. The expanding wants of this period were wants for articles other than food, and the conditions of mass production which conduce to the lowering of price were more fully realized among non-foods. But in part, as we have seen, the explanation is to be found in the situation left by the recession of 1920-21.

The advance in prices was distinctly greater for raw than for processed foods; raw and processed non-foods declined by about the same amounts.

## FIGURE 66
### MOVEMENTS OF WHOLESALE PRICES IN THE UNITED STATES, 1922-1929
#### FOODS AND NON-FOODS

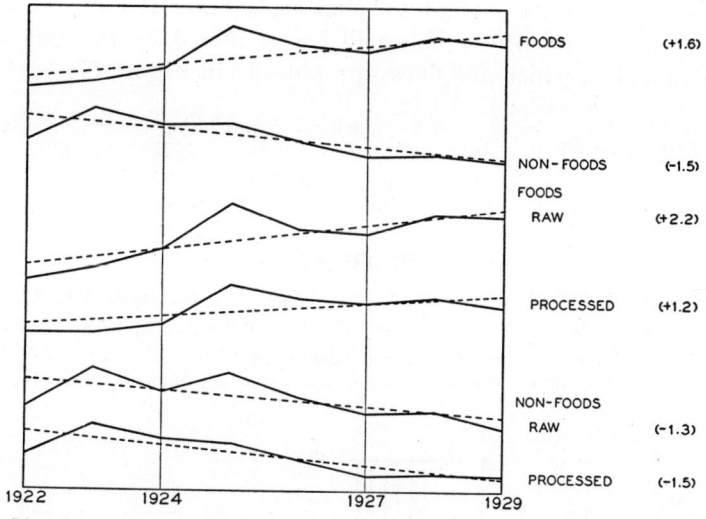

Plotted on ratio scale. The figures in parentheses define average annual rates of change (in percentage form).

These various measurements must be set against the corresponding pre-war figures.

| Commodity group | Average annual rate of change in purchasing power | |
|---|---|---|
| | 1901-1913 (per cent) | 1922-1929 (per cent) |
| Foods | +0.7 | +2.0 |
| Non-foods | —0.3 | —1.1 |
| Foods, raw | +1.3 | +2.6 |
| Foods, processed | +0.4 | +1.6 |
| Non-foods, raw | —0.6 | —0.9 |
| Non-foods, processed | —0.2 | —1.1 |

Rising food values (i.e., real values), per unit, and declining values of non-foods were characteristic of both pre-war and post-war periods. The margin of difference was much wider in the recent than in the earlier period. Both raw and processed foods gained in purchasing power between 1922 and 1929 at rates exceeding the pre-war rates. Processed non-foods declined at a much higher rate in the period just passed. Pre-war tendencies seem to have persisted in recent years, with enhanced force.

In a survey of the situation prevailing immediately after the recession of 1920-21 we find a partial explanation of the intensification of these tendencies. This will be facilitated by the following index numbers, which are shown graphically in Figure 67.

| Commodity group | Index numbers of purchasing power, per unit | | | | | |
| --- | --- | --- | --- | --- | --- | --- |
|  | 1913 | 1919 | 1920 | 1921 | 1922 | 1929 |
| Foods | 100.0 | 103.2 | 90.6 | 90.2 | 90.9 | 101.0 |
| Non-foods | 100.0 | 98.2 | 105.6 | 105.6 | 105.2 | 99.6 |

### FIGURE 67
GRAPHIC REPRESENTATION OF CHANGES IN THE REAL VALUES, PER UNIT, OF COMMODITIES IN SELECTED GROUPS, 1913-1929
FOODS AND NON-FOODS
(CHANGES ARE MEASURED AS PERCENTAGE DEVIATIONS FROM 1913 PURCHASING POWER.)

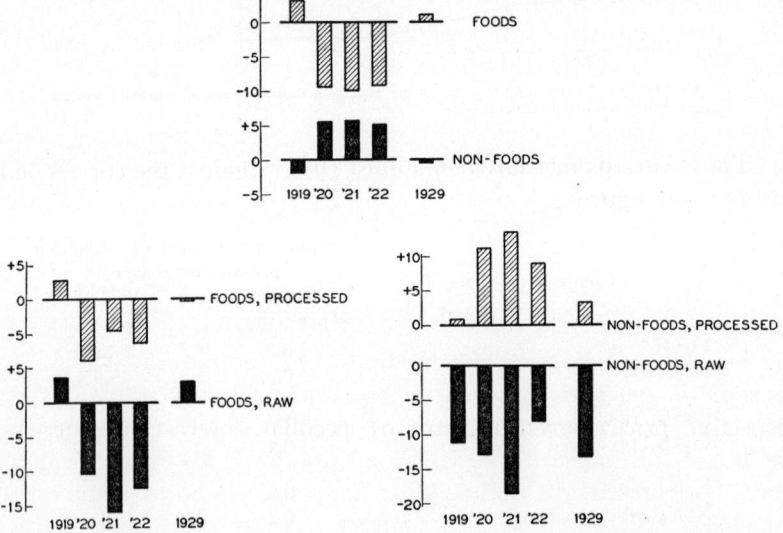

The pronounced increase in the per-unit purchasing power of food products between 1922 and 1929, and the corresponding decline of non-foods from the particularly advantageous position in which they were left by the recession of 1920-21, served approximately to restore the relations prevailing in 1913 between foods and non-foods. The statistics for the sub-groups help to define these changes.

| Commodity group | Index numbers of purchasing power, per unit | | | | | |
|---|---|---|---|---|---|---|
| | 1913 | 1919 | 1920 | 1921 | 1922 | 1929 |
| Foods | | | | | | |
| Raw | 100.0 | 103.7 | 89.8 | 84.1 | 87.6 | 103.0 |
| Processed | 100.0 | 102.9 | 91.2 | 95.6 | 93.7 | 99.8 |
| Non-foods | | | | | | |
| Raw | 100.0 | 88.9 | 87.2 | 81.5 | 92.0 | 86.9 |
| Processed | 100.0 | 100.9 | 111.2 | 113.5 | 109.0 | 103.4 |

The purchasing power in wholesale markets of raw foods, in terms of commodities in general, increased from 84.1 to 103.0 between 1921 and 1929 (the situation in 1913 being represented by 100). Processed food products suffered much less severely during the recession of 1920-21, and gained thereafter by a much smaller amount. The notable decline after 1921 in the per-unit purchasing power of processed non-foods did no more than carry these goods from a position in which the average unit commanded 13 per cent more of commodities in general than in 1913 to a position in which it commanded only 3 per cent more than in 1913. Raw non-food products were persistently below all other groups after 1919. The decline in their purchasing power between 1922 and 1929 intensified a position that was relatively bad at the beginning. This group contains most of the commodities falling in the class of raw materials not originating on American farms, changes in which have already been commented upon.

## Producers' Goods and Consumers' Goods

The classification of commodities into producers' goods and consumers' goods is of obvious economic significance, and their respective price movements are of peculiar interest. Consumers' goods are, of course, those which are in shape for final consumption. Their prices at wholesale are not the prices at which final consumers will purchase them, but no further processing charges will be incurred before they are marketed. Producers' goods are the materials of industry, raw or semi-processed, to be fabricated further before consumption or to be used in the construction of articles of capital equipment. Producers' goods are bought for purposes of profit, and the buyers are business men, not ultimate consumers.

(The present distinction between producers' goods and consumers' goods is not strictly a division between goods bought for profit and goods bought for use, because we are dealing with wholesale prices throughout, but it is an approach to such a classification.) The two classes of consumers' goods, raw and processed, are, of course, mutually exclusive. They do not represent different stages at which the same goods are priced, but two quite different types of goods—those consumed in a raw state and those consumed in a fabricated form.

Index numbers for the period 1922-1929 are given in the following table. Net movements are defined by the average annual rates of change cited in the table. The measurements are plotted in Figure 68.

TABLE 148

PRODUCERS' GOODS AND CONSUMERS' GOODS

Index Numbers of Wholesale Prices in the United States, 1922-1929 [a]

| (1) Year | (2) Producers' goods Raw | (3) Producers' goods Processed | (4) Consumers' goods Raw | (5) Consumers' goods Processed | (6) All producers' goods | (7) All consumers' goods |
|---|---|---|---|---|---|---|
| 1922 | 100.0 | 100.0 | 100.0 | 100.0 | 100.0 | 100.0 |
| 1923 | 107.8 | 108.2 | 101.9 | 102.2 | 108.0 | 102.1 |
| 1924 | 105.7 | 103.6 | 105.4 | 102.1 | 104.3 | 102.7 |
| 1925 | 113.5 | 102.4 | 119.7 | 108.0 | 106.3 | 109.8 |
| 1926 | 106.0 | 99.2 | 114.4 | 104.7 | 101.6 | 106.3 |
| 1927 | 104.3 | 94.9 | 108.6 | 101.9 | 98.3 | 103.0 |
| 1928 | 107.5 | 95.1 | 110.3 | 103.2 | 99.5 | 104.4 |
| 1929 | 103.3 | 94.8 | 113.6 | 101.6 | 97.9 | 103.5 |
| Average annual rate of change (per cent) | | | | | | |
| In price ..... | +0.1 | −1.6 | +1.6 | +0.1 | −0.9 | +0.4 |
| In purchasing power ..... | +0.5 | −1.1 | +2.0 | +0.6 | −0.5 | +0.8 |

[a] The numbers of price series included in the above groups varied within the limits given below:

Producers' goods
  Raw                   105 to 108
  Processed      179 to 184
  Total               284 to 292

Consumers' goods
  Raw                   31 to 34
  Processed      151 to 166
  Total               182 to 200

Producers' goods showed a net decline in price between 1922 and 1929, at a rate of 0.9 per cent a year. Consumers' goods rose in

## FIGURE 68
### MOVEMENTS OF WHOLESALE PRICES IN THE UNITED STATES, 1922-1929
#### PRODUCERS' GOODS AND CONSUMERS' GOODS

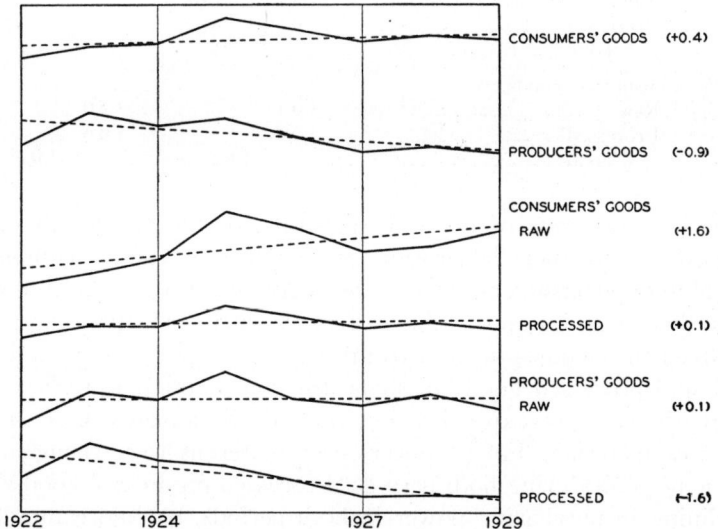

Plotted on ratio scale. The figures in parentheses define average annual rates of change (in percentage form).

price at a rate of 0.4 per cent. In terms of purchasing power producers' goods decreased at a rate of 0.5 per cent a year, while consumers' goods increased at a rate of 0.8 per cent. These purchasing power trends represent a wider margin than that which was opening up between 1901 and 1913.

Among the sub-groups, both classes of raw materials rose in price, the sharpest advance occurring in those which were in shape for consumption. The prices of processed producers' goods declined markedly, while prices advanced for manufactured consumers' goods. But all these figures must be interpreted with reference to purchasing power changes, and to earlier trends, if we are to appreciate their significance. The summary table at the top of page 360 permits this interpretation.

These figures indicate that during both periods consumers were giving every year a little more, in terms of goods in general, for the articles they purchased. The rate of advance was more rapid in the recent period. Producers, on the other hand, were giving a

|  | Average annual rate of change in purchasing power | |
|---|---|---|
| Commodity group | 1901-1913 (per cent) | 1922-1929 (per cent) |
| Producers' goods | | |
| Raw | +0.4 | +0.5 |
| Processed | −0.5 | −1.1 |
| Total | −0.2 | −0.5 |
| Consumers' goods | | |
| Raw | +0.1 | +2.0 |
| Processed | +0.2 | +0.6 |
| Total | +0.2 | +0.8 |

little less, in terms of goods in general, for the articles they purchased for further fabrication or for use in capital equipment. Breaking up consumers' goods into the two classes shown, it appears that there was no appreciable difference during the pre-war period between the changes in the two groups. In the post-war period both raw and processed goods in shape for consumption were becoming increasingly more expensive, but the rate of advance was sharper for raw materials. For producers, raw materials were rising in real value per unit during both periods. Processed producers' goods were declining in purchasing power in both periods, but more rapidly in the second.

Again we need information as to the conditions prevailing immediately before the post-war period begins. The following index numbers of changes in purchasing power, for selected years between 1913 and 1919, furnish this information and provide a tie between the pre-war and post-war records. They are shown graphically in Figure 69.

| Commodity group | Index numbers of purchasing power, per unit | | | | | |
|---|---|---|---|---|---|---|
| | 1913 | 1919 | 1920 | 1921 | 1922 | 1929 |
| Producers' goods | 100.0 | 98.4 | 99.7 | 95.0 | 97.0 | 94.9 |
| Consumers' goods | 100.0 | 102.1 | 100.2 | 107.9 | 104.4 | 108.0 |

Boom conditions in 1919 found consumers paying some 2 per cent more, in terms of dollars of constant purchasing power, for the articles they purchased,[1] while producers were paying somewhat less than they had paid, per unit, in 1913. By 1921 the margin had been materially widened, with producers' goods 5 per cent lower in

[1] For convenience of exposition, the assumption is made that actual consumers were buying at the quoted prices. Since the prices with which we are dealing are quotations in wholesale markets, this is not strictly true.

## FIGURE 69

### GRAPHIC REPRESENTATION OF CHANGES IN THE REAL VALUES, PER UNIT, OF COMMODITIES IN SELECTED GROUPS, 1913-1929

PRODUCERS' GOODS AND CONSUMERS' GOODS

(CHANGES ARE MEASURED AS PERCENTAGE DEVIATIONS FROM 1913 PURCHASING POWER.)

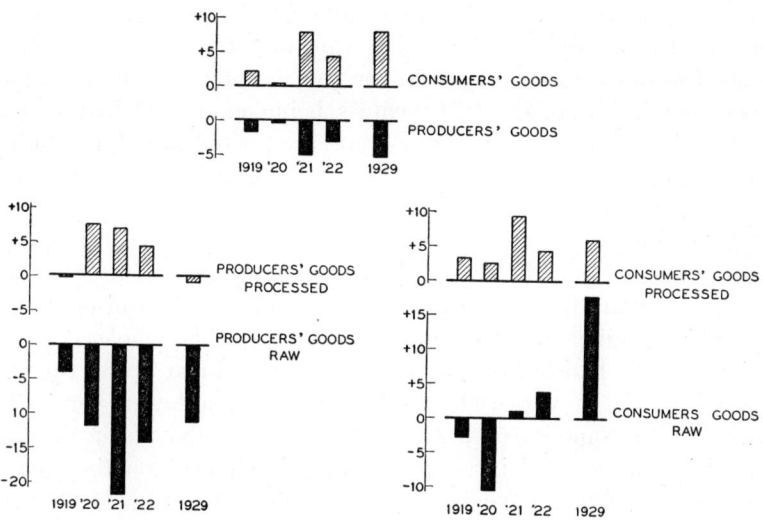

real value than in 1913, and consumers' goods about 8 per cent higher. The effect of the recession had been to cheapen substantially goods not yet in shape for final consumption, and to add materially to the per-unit real cost to consumers of goods in shape for consumption. This situation obviously favored manufacturing interests, once the necessary readjustment to the new price situation had been completed.

The story, thus far, resembles that relating to farm and non-farm products. The recession of 1920-21 left farm products, particularly raw farm products, undervalued, with reference to the 1913 situation, and non-farm products correspondingly overvalued. From this point on the stories differ. The tendencies prevailing between 1922 and 1929 served to restore, by 1929, the approximate relations prevailing in 1913 between the prices, at wholesale, of goods of agricultural and of non-agricultural origin. But there was no such restoration of the pre-war relations between producers' goods and consumers' goods. Between 1921 and 1922 the values of producers' goods, in dollars of constant purchasing power, advanced slightly, and the values of consumers' goods declined slightly, but from 1922 to 1929 there was a resumption of the downward movement in the purchasing power of producers' goods, and of the upward movement in the purchasing power of consumers' goods. In 1929 producers' goods were approximately 5 per cent cheaper, in terms of commodities in general, than in 1913. That is, the manufacturer, buying raw materials or semi-finished goods for fabrication, or goods for use in capital equipment, paid 5 per cent less than in 1913 (values being expressed in terms of 1913 dollars). The dealer buying goods at wholesale for retailing to the final consumer paid 8 per cent more per unit (again in terms of 1913 dollars).

This situation is clearly one which has favored manufacturing profits during the whole period we are studying. The dollar expended by manufacturers for materials, raw and semi-processed, has had a higher purchasing power during this whole post-war period than it had before the war, while the dollar spent for consumers' goods in wholesale markets has had a lower purchasing power. If the samples used are representative,[1] the results indicate that rising wages and increasing purchasing power on the part of ultimate consumers have been very essential features of the economic processes of this period.[2]

The details of this situation deserve notice.

| Commodity group | Index numbers of purchasing power, per unit | | | | | |
|---|---|---|---|---|---|---|
| | 1913 | 1919 | 1920 | 1921 | 1922 | 1929 |
| Producers' goods | | | | | | |
| Raw | 100.0 | 96.0 | 88.2 | 78.2 | 85.8 | 88.6 |
| Processed | 100.0 | 99.9 | 107.5 | 106.9 | 104.4 | 99.1 |
| Consumers' goods | | | | | | |
| Raw | 100.0 | 97.1 | 89.5 | 101.0 | 103.8 | 117.9 |
| Processed | 100.0 | 103.2 | 102.5 | 109.4 | 104.4 | 106.0 |

These figures appear graphically in Figure 69.

[1] For the post-war period the number of price series employed has varied from 284 to 292 for producers' goods, from 182 to 200 for consumers' goods.

[2] These figures relate, of course, only to commodities, not to the numerous services for which a goodly percentage of consumer income is spent. Furthermore, greater efficiency in merchandising may have made it possible for the retailer to pay the higher prices which have prevailed for consumers' goods without putting the ultimate consumer in the position of relative disadvantage which the present figures suggest. Index numbers of living costs, however, indicate that the cost of living has gone up at least as much since 1913 as the prices of consumers' goods at wholesale. (The index of general living costs constructed by the U. S. Bureau

The low price of raw materials has kept down the general average for producers' goods. At the low point in 1921 the raw materials used in manufacture were worth, in dollars of constant purchasing power, almost 22 per cent less than in 1913. There was some advance thereafter, but in 1929 these goods remained more than 11 per cent below the 1913 standard, in terms of real values. Cheap industrial raw materials were an important feature of the post-war business situation.

There is is a sharp contrast between the price movements of raw materials entering into manufacture and those of raw materials ready for final consumption without change of form. In 1919 and 1920 raw consumers' goods were almost on terms of equality with raw producers' goods, with reference to the 1913 base. The recession of 1920-21 left raw consumers' goods about one per cent above parity with goods in general (judged with reference to a 1913 base), and by 1929 they stood 18 per cent above that level. It would be interesting to inquire into the precise conditions which caused raw materials in shape for final consumption to increase in purchasing power, per unit, 32 per cent between 1920 and 1929, while the real value of raw materials requiring fabrication remained practically constant, at a level well below pre-war parity with other commodities. Differences in the conditions under which producers' and consumers' goods are marketed, as well as differences in the conditions of supply, have probably been influential factors in this divergence of movement.

### Goods Entering into Capital Equipment and Articles of Human Consumption

In dealing with producers' and consumers' goods we were concerned with the immediate form of certain classes of goods quoted, whether in shape for consumption, or requiring further fabrication. We now inquire into the ultimate purpose for which goods will be used—for direct consumption by human beings, or for the purpose of building up (or replacing) capital equipment. Whether a good is or is not in final form for consumption does not affect its classification in this case. There is not, of course, a clear line of demarcation

---

of Labor Statistics averaged 170.8 for 1929, on the 1913 base. The index of prices of consumers' goods, at wholesale, for 1929, on the same base, was 160.2. The cost of living index number constructed by the National Industrial Conference Board averaged 161.3 for 1929, on the base July, 1914.)

between goods which will be used for capital equipment and goods which will be used directly by consumers but, though some trouble is experienced with border-line cases, the classification may be made.[1]

Index numbers of prices of these two groups of commodities, with subdivisions into raw and processed forms, are given in the following table. They are plotted in Figure 70.

TABLE 149

GOODS ENTERING INTO CAPITAL EQUIPMENT AND ARTICLES OF HUMAN CONSUMPTION

Index Numbers of Wholesale Prices in the United States, 1922-1929 [a]

| (1) | (2) | (3) | (4) | (5) | (6) | (7) |
|---|---|---|---|---|---|---|
| | Goods entering into capital equipment | | Articles of human consumption | | All goods entering into capital equipment | All articles of human consumption |
| Year | Raw | Processed | Raw | Processed | | |
| 1922 | 100.0 | 100.0 | 100.0 | 100.0 | 100.0 | 100.0 |
| 1923 | 108.1 | 110.2 | 105.6 | 102.7 | 109.8 | 103.5 |
| 1924 | 100.2 | 104.5 | 107.3 | 101.9 | 103.5 | 103.6 |
| 1925 | 103.8 | 103.1 | 118.5 | 105.9 | 103.3 | 109.8 |
| 1926 | 104.2 | 101.3 | 109.1 | 101.9 | 101.9 | 104.2 |
| 1927 | 100.1 | 96.4 | 106.9 | 99.1 | 97.1 | 101.6 |
| 1928 | 97.1 | 95.9 | 111.9 | 100.5 | 96.2 | 104.1 |
| 1929 | 97.5 | 97.0 | 108.3 | 98.5 | 97.0 | 101.5 |
| Average annual rate of change (per cent) | | | | | | |
| In price ..... | −0.8 | −1.4 | +0.9 | −0.4 | −1.3 | 0.0 |
| In purchasing power ..... | −0.4 | −1.0 | +1.3 | 0.0 | −0.9 | +0.4 |

[a] The numbers of price series entering into the various group averages ranged between the limits given below:

| Goods entering into capital equipment | | Articles of human consumption | |
|---|---|---|---|
| Raw | 32 to 35 | Raw | 104 to 107 |
| Processed | 120 to 125 | Processed | 210 to 225 |
| Total | 152 to 160 | Total | 314 to 332 |

Articles entering into capital equipment declined in price between 1922 and 1929 at a rate of 1.3 per cent a year; the drop in purchasing power averaged 0.9 per cent a year. For articles of human consumption the price index for 1929 was 1.5 per cent higher than in

[1] Details of this and of other classifications of commodities here employed are given in Appendix II.

### FIGURE 70
### MOVEMENTS OF WHOLESALE PRICES
### IN THE UNITED STATES, 1922-1929
ARTICLES OF HUMAN CONSUMPTION AND GOODS ENTERING INTO CAPITAL EQUIPMENT

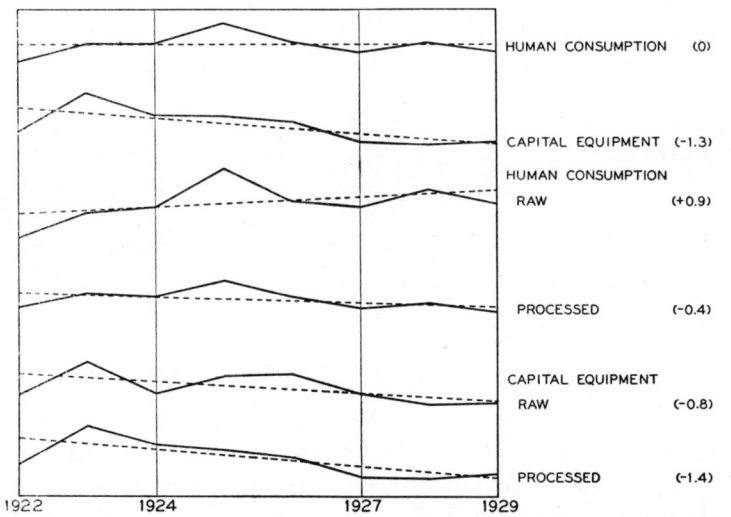

Plotted on ratio scale. The figures in parentheses define average annual rates of change (in percentage form).

1922. The intervening years were marked by a rise of almost 10 per cent between 1922 and 1925, a decline thereafter. The line defining the price tendency over the whole eight-year period shows no net change. In terms of purchasing power there was a net annual advance of 0.4 per cent. Processed goods in both groups became relatively cheaper, but among raw materials the trends diverged. Raw materials destined for human consumption increased in real value; raw materials destined for use as capital equipment showed a small net downward movement.

These movements gain significance from comparison with pre-war tendencies. Relevant figures appear at the top of page 366.

In both periods articles entering into capital equipment were cheapened, in terms of real values, while articles intended for ultimate human consumption were rising in value. (Measurements of post-war tendencies among articles of human consumption define net changes, rather than persistent trends. The year 1925 marked a clear turning point in price movements among goods of this class.) The terms of exchange between these two broad groups of com-

| Commodity group | Average annual rate of change in purchasing power | |
|---|---|---|
| | 1901-1913 (per cent) | 1922-1929 (per cent) |
| Goods entering into capital equipment | | |
| Raw | −1.0 | −0.4 |
| Processed | −0.4 | −1.0 |
| Total | −0.5 | −0.9 |
| Articles of human consumption | | |
| Raw | +0.8 | +1.3 |
| Processed | +0.1 | 0.0 |
| Total | +0.2 | +0.4 |

modities were subject to the same general tendencies in the two periods. Investment in capital equipment was facilitated by a cheapening of capital goods, while the real per-unit value of consumers' goods showed net advances.

But again we must know what occurred during the war years, and during the first great post-war recession. The following measurements, which define changes in purchasing power, per unit, of goods falling in the two main classes, tell this story. These changes are shown graphically, for the sub-groups as well as the totals, in Figure 71.

| Commodity group | Index numbers of purchasing power, per unit | | | | | |
|---|---|---|---|---|---|---|
| | 1913 | 1919 | 1920 | 1921 | 1922 | 1929 |
| Articles of capital equipment | 100.0 | 93.9 | 104.1 | 109.9 | 107.0 | 103.8 |
| Articles of human consumption | 100.0 | 102.9 | 98.3 | 95.9 | 97.0 | 98.4 |

There is not found here the same contrast that existed between producers' and consumers' goods. The boom prices of 1919 carried the prices of articles destined ultimately for human consumption above those of articles entering into capital equipment, but this situation was reversed in the following year. Deflation in 1920 and 1921 left articles of capital equipment almost 10 per cent higher, in purchasing power, than in 1913, and articles entering into consumption some 4 per cent below the 1913 level. After 1921 the two groups moved somewhat closer toward pre-war parity. The post-war decline in the prices of articles destined for use in capital equipment has been, therefore, a movement toward the price relations prevailing in 1913, not, as in the case of producers' goods in general, a widening of the price differences prevailing in 1922.

## FIGURE 71

GRAPHIC REPRESENTATION OF CHANGES IN THE REAL VALUES, PER UNIT, OF COMMODITIES IN SELECTED GROUPS, 1913-1929

ARTICLES OF HUMAN CONSUMPTION AND GOODS ENTERING INTO CAPITAL EQUIPMENT
(CHANGES ARE MEASURED AS PERCENTAGE DEVIATIONS FROM 1913 PURCHASING POWER.)

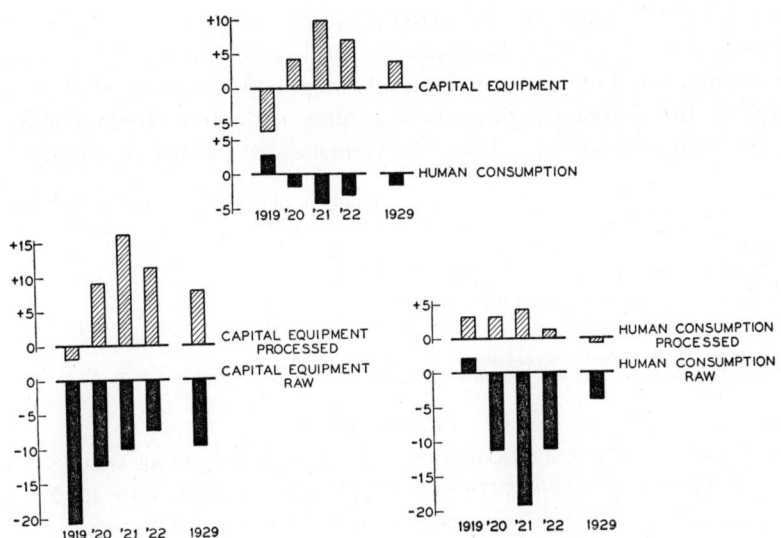

Changes in purchasing power occurring among the raw and processed sub-groups of these major classes are shown by the following measurements.

| Commodity group | Index numbers of purchasing power, per unit | | | | | |
| --- | --- | --- | --- | --- | --- | --- |
|  | 1913 | 1919 | 1920 | 1921 | 1922 | 1929 |
| Articles of capital equipment | | | | | | |
| Raw | 100.0 | 79.4 | 87.6 | 90.0 | 92.6 | 90.3 |
| Processed | 100.0 | 98.2 | 109.1 | 116.1 | 111.3 | 107.9 |
| Articles of human consumption | | | | | | |
| Raw | 100.0 | 102.2 | 88.9 | 80.9 | 88.9 | 96.2 |
| Processed | 100.0 | 103.2 | 103.2 | 104.2 | 101.1 | 99.6 |

The most striking feature of this exhibit is that raw materials of both groups have been consistently below pre-war parity with processed goods of corresponding types since 1919. The gap was widest in 1921, and has narrowed since then. Among articles of capital equipment the margin remained wide in 1929. The weakness of raw material prices, notably those of industrial raw materials, has, of course, been an outstanding characteristic of the recent economic situation.

The marked difference between the price relations among the above categories and those prevailing between producers' and consumers' goods calls for some comment. The broad group of producers' goods is made up of two divisions—articles which will ultimately enter into capital equipment and articles intended for human consumption, but not yet in final shape. Over the period under review the prices of these two groups of commodities followed quite different courses. These movements are plotted in Figure 72.

| Commodity group | Index numbers of purchasing power, per unit | | | | | |
| --- | --- | --- | --- | --- | --- | --- |
| | 1913 | 1919 | 1920 | 1921 | 1922 | 1929 |
| Producers' goods destined for human consumption [a] | 100.0 | 104.2 | 95.9 | 81.6 | 87.9 | 86.9 |
| Producers' goods destined for use in capital equipment [b] | 100.0 | 93.9 | 104.1 | 109.9 | 107.0 | 103.8 |

[a] Index numbers based on 132 price series.
[b] Index numbers based on samples of from 152 to 160 price series.

### FIGURE 72
GRAPHIC REPRESENTATION OF CHANGES IN THE REAL VALUES, PER UNIT, OF COMMODITIES IN SELECTED GROUPS, 1913-1929
SELECTED CLASSES OF PRODUCERS' GOODS AND CONSUMERS' GOODS
(CHANGES ARE MEASURED AS PERCENTAGE DEVIATIONS FROM 1913 PURCHASING POWER.)

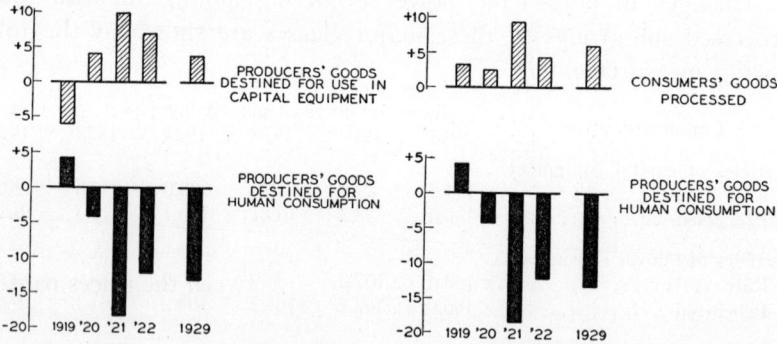

The recession of 1920-21 carried to a point 18 per cent below the 1913 level the purchasing power of goods meant for human consumption, but not yet in final shape. By 1929 this margin had been reduced to 13 per cent, but commodities of this class were still materially below their pre-war real value, per unit. Goods to be used in the construction of capital equipment were low in value in 1919, but during the next ten years were consistently above pre-war parity with goods in general.

This last comparison suggests another line to follow, in attempting to trace significant price relations during the post-war period. The price quotations on producers' goods meant for ultimate human consumption refer to prices paid by producers (or by middlemen acting for them) on goods to be fabricated further before final sale to consumers. With the index numbers of these prices we may compare index numbers of prices of processed consumers' goods— prices of manufactured goods which are in shape for final consumption. The prices employed do not refer necessarily to the same goods in different stages of fabrication, but they do refer to two distinct stages in the manufacturing-merchandising process leading up to the sale of goods to the final consumer. The changes in the price relations between these two stages are shown in Figure 72; the index numbers appear in the following table.

| Commodity group | Index numbers of purchasing power, per unit | | | | | |
|---|---|---|---|---|---|---|
| | 1913 | 1919 | 1920 | 1921 | 1922 | 1929 |
| Producers' goods destined for human consumption [a] | 100.0 | 104.2 | 95.9 | 81.6 | 87.9 | 86.9 |
| Consumers' goods, processed [b] | 100.0 | 103.2 | 102.5 | 109.4 | 104.4 | 106.0 |

[a] Index numbers based on 132 price series.
[b] Index numbers based on samples of from 151 to 166 price series.

Both groups of goods shared in the revival of 1919, and had their purchasing power raised above the 1913 level. In the ensuing recession goods meant for consumption but not yet in final shape lost 22 per cent of their per-unit purchasing power (i.e., declined 22 per cent further between 1919 and 1921 than did goods in general), while fabricated consumers' goods gained an additional 6 per cent in per-unit purchasing power. This constitutes a very wide divergence, for the figures relate to purchasing power, not to actual price movements. The opening of this spread between the prices paid by producers for important materials and the prices received by producers for finished goods meant greatly widened profit margins, once revival got under way and the volume of trade picked up. It is a notable feature of this exhibit that the margin persisted, although it was narrowed somewhat during the later years of the period under review.[1]

[1] If in 1913 producers' goods destined for human consumption had been relatively high-priced, while processed consumers' goods had been relatively low-priced,

*On the Levels of Operating and Capital Costs, 1922-1929.*—
If we consider the costs of the manufacturing producer under two
heads, those involved in normal operating processes and those involved in the construction or extension of capital equipment, we find
a rather sharp contrast prevailing during the period 1922-1929. The
available evidence indicates that, as regards current productive
operations, the average producer was in a relatively strong position
in these years. Material costs, as measured by index numbers of the
prices of raw materials and of producers' goods destined for human
consumption, were low, in comparison with earlier standards, and
selling prices of processed consumers' goods were high. Labor costs,
as we shall see in the next chapter, were high, but these were declining rapidly under the stimulus of a sharp increase in productivity.
Here were conditions conducing to large operating profits, and such
profits were in fact realized.[1]

As regards the cost of capital equipment the picture is quite different. The prices of goods entering into such equipment, particularly processed goods, stood at a high level during this whole period.
Some decline occurred between 1922 and 1929, but the period ends
with the real values of such goods well above pre-war parity with
other goods. If we take account also of the relatively high costs of
construction during this period [2] we have an impressive picture of
the changes involved in constructing or extending capital equipment.

The figures relating to the production of capital equipment
which were cited in the preceding chapter take on added significance
in the light of these price and cost records. The construction of capital equipment increased at a rate of 6.4 per cent a year between
1922 and 1929. The volume of such construction in 1929 was 70
per cent greater than in 1922. The productive energies of the country were being devoted to the production of capital equipment to a
degree not approached in pre-war years, or during the war. And

---

the condition prevailing between 1922 and 1929 might not be significant. In fact,
goods of the first class were in 1913 slightly lower in price than processed consumers' goods, with reference to the years preceding. On 1901 as base, the index
of wholesale prices for producers' goods destined for human consumption stood
in 1913 at 117.9; the index for processed consumers' goods was 119.6.

[1] See Chapter IX.

[2] The *Engineering News Record's* index shows a high level of construction costs
during this period:

| | | | |
|---|---|---|---|
| 1922 | 100 | 1926 | 119 |
| 1923 | 123 | 1927 | 118 |
| 1924 | 123 | 1928 | 118 |
| 1925 | 118 | 1929 | 119 |

this tremendous volume of capital equipment was being constructed on a high price and high cost basis. We shall not understand the developments of this period, nor the events which followed, if we fail to take account of these facts. For the existence of a large volume of high-cost capital equipment contributed materially to the weight of the subsequent debt burden and to the difficulties in the way of prompt liquidation and of ready readjustment of costs to lower price levels.

§ *Other commodity groups.*—We may, finally, compare pre-war and post-war price changes among the various commodity groups appearing in the classification of the United States Bureau of Labor Statistics. To simplify comparison, these changes have been expressed as variations in purchasing power, per unit.

TABLE 150

COMPARISON OF AVERAGE ANNUAL RATES OF CHANGE IN PURCHASING POWER, 1901-1913 AND 1922-1929

Commodity Groups of the United States Bureau of Labor Statistics

| Commodity group | Average annual rate of change in purchasing power | |
|---|---|---|
| | 1901-1913 | 1922-1929 |
| Foods | +0.5 | +2.3 |
| Hides and leather products | +0.8 | +2.0 |
| Farm products | +0.9 | +1.7 |
| Chemicals and drugs | −2.2 | −0.5 |
| Metals and metal products | −2.2 | −0.8 |
| Building materials | +0.4 | −0.8 |
| House-furnishing goods | −0.9 | −1.4 |
| Miscellaneous | −0.5 | −1.5 |
| Textiles | −0.7 | −1.7 |
| Fuel and lighting | −1.4 | −2.6 |

Commodities falling in three commodity groups, food products, farm products, and hides and leather products, gained in purchasing power, on the average, between 1922 and 1929. All other groups declined in purchasing power, with the fuel and lighting group losing in relative position at the rate of 2.6 per cent a year. The three groups that gained in the post-war period advanced also between 1901 and 1913. Building materials gained slightly during the earlier period, declined in the later period. Metals and metal products, chemicals and drugs, house-furnishing goods, fuel and lighting, textiles, and commodities in the miscellaneous group were becoming steadily cheaper, in terms of other goods, during both periods.

To complete the picture we need to trace recent changes against a pre-war base.

| Commodity group | Index numbers of purchasing power, per unit | | | | | |
|---|---|---|---|---|---|---|
| | 1913 | 1919 | 1920 | 1921 | 1922 | 1929 |
| Foods | 100.0 | 101.6 | 96.7 | 100.9 | 98.5 | 114.0 |
| Hides and leather products | 100.0 | 128.8 | 113.7 | 114.7 | 110.9 | 117.4 |
| Farm products | 100.0 | 111.0 | 95.3 | 88.4 | 94.7 | 107.5 |
| Chemicals and drugs | 100.0 | 98.6 | 92.9 | 102.6 | 90.3 | 86.1 |
| Metals and metal products | 100.0 | 72.6 | 74.4 | 92.6 | 81.8 | 81.1 |
| Building materials | 100.0 | 102.7 | 119.7 | 122.9 | 123.9 | 123.3 |
| House-furnishing goods | 100.0 | 94.7 | 113.9 | 143.6 | 132.7 | 122.7 |
| Miscellaneous | 100.0 | 75.2 | 81.3 | 83.9 | 72.0 | 65.0 |
| Textiles | 100.0 | 118.9 | 130.0 | 118.0 | 126.3 | 115.6 |
| Fuel and lighting | 100.0 | 85.6 | 120.7 | 112.9 | 126.4 | 99.2 |

The post-war boom of 1919 found metals, fuel and lighting, house-furnishings and the group of miscellaneous goods materially lower in purchasing power than in 1913. Chemicals and drugs were slightly below that standard. All other groups had higher purchasing power per unit than in 1913, with hides and leather products and textiles standing in particularly favorable positions. In the depression year, 1921, farm products, metal products and the 'miscellaneous' group stood below pre-war parity with other goods. The shifts occurring between 1921 and 1929 elevated farm products and improved the standing of foods.[1] Chemicals and drugs and fuel and lighting declined notably. In 1929 these two groups, together with metals and miscellaneous goods, were at a disadvantage, with reference to the 1913 standard, while all other groups were better off. Highest in unit value, in terms of commodities in general, were building materials, house-furnishings, hides and leather products, textiles and foods.

The price averages for the major industrial groups show substantial changes in relative position over the sixteen-year period here covered. These changes have been important factors in shaping the flow of monetary payments upon which prosperity depends. But they have not been the only factors; the condition of various groups of producers cannot be determined from the evidence of price movements alone. We return later to this subject.

## Summary: Post-war Movements of Commodity Prices

A general characterization of the post-war period, in respect to the trends and changing relations of commodity prices, is deferred to the final chapter. Only a brief summary is given at this point.

Post-war production tendencies, we have seen, represented a

[1] The group of American farm products, raw and processed, which appears in an earlier classification, includes commodities which here fall among foods, farm products, hides and leather products and textiles.

continuation of tendencies prevailing before the war. The recent period was not unlike the earlier, except as regards the tempo of change and the degree of difference among the rates of change in the production of goods of different categories. In the realm of prices certain pre-war tendencies continued, but in the main the story of recent years is sharply different from that of the earlier period. The persistent upward movement of the price level, a rise that played a leading rôle in the economic processes of the years before the war, was succeeded by a declining movement, world-wide in its reach. Relatively favorable exchange conditions for raw material producers in general, and for farmers in particular, were replaced by unfavorable conditions which prevailed, despite some improvement, during the entire decade. Agents of fabrication, on the other hand, improved their status materially in post-war years. Gains due to the steadily advancing productivity of manufacturing industries were substantial. In addition, the real values of manufactured products had been increased during the general price recession of 1920-21, and a large part of this advantage persisted during the years which followed. Economic groups drawing their incomes from these industries stood in positions of relative advantage during the post-war decade.

Another aspect of the same change is seen in the widened margin between the prices of producers' goods and of consumers' goods which marked this period. In general, producers' goods were cheapened by the price shifts of the 1920-21 recession, while the real per-unit value of consumers' goods was enhanced. This meant that the incomes of those selling materials to manufacturers were reduced (in so far as per-unit returns were concerned), while the real cost of goods sold to final consumers was raised. The charge to consumers for the services of fabrication and distribution represented by the margin between the prices of these two broad classes of goods was higher than before. What is perhaps most significant here is that there was no apparent tendency for this particular margin to be reduced during the years from 1922 to 1929. Consumers' goods remained high in price, in relation to other goods, over this entire period. Not all producers' goods were low in real cost during these years, however. The cost of capital equipment was relatively high, and remained high to the end of the period. Abundant capital and an optimistic business attitude toward the future combined to stimulate a heavy program of capital construction under these high-cost conditions. A swelling debt burden, the weight of which was acutely felt during the subsequent liquidation, was an accompaniment of this expansion.

The consequences of these shifting price relations were far-reaching. They affected capital values and investment opportunities and rewards; they altered the terms of exchange between city and country, and between industrial centers and raw material producing areas the world over. The course of events during the decade of the 'twenties was profoundly influenced by the changes in economic relations represented by movements of prices and costs, and by the alterations of rewards which accompanied them.

During these years divergent production trends, involving continual shifts of labor and of capital, were placing upon our economic system requirements of flexibility and adaptability. But, concurrently, constantly greater capital investment, a constantly widening area of regulated and controlled prices, a steady reduction of the area within which free price competition prevailed were tending, apparently, to reduce the flexibility of prices. Though unequivocal quantitative evidence of this change is not available, and though a precise distinction between decreasing flexibility and increasing stability cannot be drawn, yet the existence of this tendency during the years prior to 1929 may hardly be doubted. Internationally and domestically prices were becoming less effective as instruments of economic coördination. In the absence of alternative instruments of social control, the maintenance of working relations among the elements of the economic structure was becoming correspondingly more difficult. The problem posed by these circumstances persists, for the present generation to face in the years beyond the depression.

CHAPTER VIII

## *Price and Cost Changes in Manufacturing Industries of the United States, 1923-1929*

ALTERATIONS in quoted prices of the type cited in the last chapter are the outward manifestations of a great variety of changes in the conditions of supply and of demand, most of which are not open to definite measurement. Within one important industrial area, that which includes the manufacturing industries of the United States, it is possible to press more deeply into the complex of conditions which, on the supply side, lie back of observable market changes.

*Changes in Physical Output and in Aggregate Values and Costs, Manufacturing Industries*

Certain of the statistics to be utilized in the study of price and cost changes are summarized in Table 151, on the following page. The statistics there given relate to selected industries for which comparable data on physical output and on aggregate values and costs are available. The entries in column (7) define the values of the products entering into the index of physical volume of production, described in Chapter VI. The entries in column (2) give the values of the products to which the entries in columns (3) to (6) relate. The ratios in column (8) serve as a measure of the degree of comparability of the original data relating to physical output, on the one hand, and to number of establishments, number of wage-earners, aggregate value of product and aggregate costs, on the other. It appears that the quantity data employed in constructing the physical volume index relate to approximately 90 per cent, by value, of the goods represented by the data in columns (2) to (6), a relation sufficiently high to justify confidence in the measurements to be derived from a comparison of these various series. As has been explained in detail in a preceding section [1] a correction based upon

[1] Chapter III.

## TABLE 151

### Statistics of Selected Manufacturing Industries of the United States, 1923-1929 [a]

(All value figures in thousands of dollars)

| (1) | (2) | (3) | (4) | (5) | (6) | (7) | (8) |
|---|---|---|---|---|---|---|---|
| Year | Statistics relating to all products of industries represented in index of physical volume of production | | | | | Actual value of products entering into index of physical volume of production | Ratio of actual value of products entering into index to total value of products of industries represented (7) ÷ (2) |
| | Total value of products | Cost of materials | Cost of fabrication, plus profits | Total wages paid | Overhead expenses plus profits | | |
| 1923 | 28,281,117 | 18,320,242 | 9,960,875 | 4,377,966 | 5,582,909 | 25,379,316 | .897 |
| 1925 | 29,091,937 | 18,895,686 | 10,196,251 | 4,272,439 | 5,923,812 | 26,331,034 | .905 |
| 1927* | 27,532,655 | 17,804,133 | 9,728,522 | 4,136,866 | 5,591,656 | 24,603,710 | .894 |
| 1927** | 27,532,655 | 17,804,133 | 9,728,522 | 4,136,866 | 5,591,656 | 24,602,896 | .894 |
| 1927*** | 27,189,717 | 17,609,634 | 9,580,083 | 4,068,522 | 5,511,561 | 24,371,727 | .896 |
| 1929 | 29,476,380 | 18,329,657 | 11,146,723 | 4,197,782 | 6,948,941 | 26,536,632 | .900 |

\* The statistics for 1927 which appear on this line are comparable with the data for 1923.
\*\* The statistics for 1927 which appear on this line are comparable with the data for 1925.
\*\*\* The statistics for 1927 which appear on this line are comparable with the data for 1929.

[a] Definitions of the terms used by the Bureau of the Census are given in a footnote to Table 37, Chapter III. Essentially no changes were made prior to the 1929 Census. In the report for that year manufacturers were directed for the first time (a) to omit the cost of mill or shop supplies from the cost of materials, (b) to report either the cost of materials used or purchased, and (c) to report as the value of product the selling value of the goods actually sold.

These changes in the schedules for 1929 were designed to facilitate the making of the returns. For this reason manufacturers in certain industries (76 in all) were permitted to report value of products as at former censuses. While no information is to be had on the extent to which the comparability of the census data has been impaired by these various changes, the impairment is believed to have been slight in most industries.

Some of the statistics relating to the Census of 1929 are preliminary figures.

these 'adequacy ratios' has been made, in constructing the index of physical production, to validate this comparison.

Ratios similar to those in column (8) above have been computed for the various individual industries for which census statistics are compiled. The industries for which this ratio fell below .60 have been excluded from the computations. The data in Table 151 relate to 62 major industries (60 for 1929) for which the ratio exceeded .60. Those included, enumerated in a later section, constituted somewhat more than 40 per cent of all census industries, by value of product.[1]

Comparison of these various series is more readily made when the data are in relative form.

TABLE 152

RELATIVE NUMBERS DEFINING CHANGES IN IMPORTANT ELEMENTS OF MANUFACTURING PRODUCTION IN THE UNITED STATES, 1923-1929 [a]

| (1) Year | (2) Physical volume of production (fabrication) | (3) Value of products | (4) Cost of materials | (5) Cost of fabrication, plus profits | (6) Total wages paid | (7) Overhead expenses plus profits |
|---|---|---|---|---|---|---|
| 1923 | 100.0 | 100.0 | 100.0 | 100.0 | 100.0 | 100.0 |
| 1925 | 102.4 | 101.1 | 101.8 | 99.6 | 96.0 | 102.4 |
| 1927 | 104.2 | 95.8 | 95.5 | 96.3 | 93.3 | 98.7 |
| 1929 | 113.0 | 102.0 | 98.3 | 109.3 | 94.3 | 121.0 |

[a] The entries in Table 152 have not been derived directly from the data given in Table 151. Weights for four industries have been reduced to the approximate proportion they would have if all census products were included in the sample. This was necessary, for pre-war years, for industries producing automobiles, forest products and petroleum products. The rubber industry has been added to this list for the post-war period. These four industries, heavily represented in the sample, would have had undue influence upon the averages if this adjustment had not been made.

[1] The importance of the industries included in the present computations, in relation to all industries covered by the Census of Manufactures, is indicated by the following summary.

| Year | Total value of products reported in Census of Manufactures (thousands of dollars) | Value of products in industries represented by index numbers of physical volume (thousands of dollars) | Percentage of total value of manufactured products represented in index numbers |
|---|---|---|---|
| 1923 | 60,555,998 | 28,281,117 | 46.7 |
| 1925 | 62,713,714 | 29,091,937 | 46.4 |
| 1927* | 62,718,347 | 27,532,655 | 43.9 |
| 1927** | 62,718,347 | 27,189,717 | 43.4 |
| 1929 | 70,137,459 | 29,476,380 | 42.0 |

* Statistics comparable with 1925 and 1923.
** Statistics comparable with 1929.

378                    ECONOMIC TENDENCIES

From the above measurements of changes in values and quantities (measurements relating to identical industries) we may derive index numbers measuring alterations in average selling price and in the several elements of manufacturing cost, per unit of product.[1] These are the measurements with which we are at present concerned.

## Changes in the Selling Prices of Manufactured Goods

The following table shows the elements which are utilized in securing estimates of the changes in the average per-unit selling price of manufactured goods in the United States between 1923 and 1929. The index numbers there given, which relate, of course, to the 62 industries for which adequate quantity statistics are available, are shown graphically in Figure 73.

Between 1923 and 1929 the aggregate value of manufactured products, for the industries here represented, remained practically constant, except for the sharp drop from 1925 to 1927 and the rise in 1929 to the earlier level. Volume of output increased without a check, however, rising most rapidly between 1927 and 1929. Average price per unit suffered a slight drop from 1923 to 1925,

[1] As explained in Chapter III, the method of weighting employed in constructing the index numbers of physical volume must be appropriate to the particular purpose. In deriving an index of selling price per unit of product, the aggregate value of product must be divided by an index of physical output in the construction of which weights based upon value of product have been employed. Similarly, in deriving an index of cost of fabrication, per unit of manufactured product, an index of physical output the elements of which are weighted according to 'value added' must be employed. We need, therefore, various index numbers of physical production, measuring changes in the apparent physical contributions of the various agents represented by the aggregate value figures compiled by the Bureau of the Census. Following are the several index numbers required:

Index Numbers Measuring Changes in the Apparent Physical Contributions of Different Agents of Manufacturing Production, 1923-1929

| Year | Aggregate output (weights based on value of product) | Volume of materials (weights based on cost of materials) | Volume of fabrication (weights based on 'value added') | Apparent contribution of labor (weights based on wages paid) | Apparent contribution of ownership and management (weights based on overhead expenses plus profits) |
|---|---|---|---|---|---|
| 1923 | 100.0 | 100.0 | 100.0 | 100.0 | 100.0 |
| 1925 | 102.0 | 101.8 | 102.4 | 101.0 | 103.7 |
| 1927 | 104.2 | 104.1 | 104.2 | 101.9 | 106.2 |
| 1929 | 112.3 | 111.8 | 113.0 | 110.0 | 115.5 |

## TABLE 153

### Index Numbers of Aggregate Value, Production and Price, 1923-1929
Manufacturing Industries of the United States

| Year | Aggregate value of manufactured products | Physical volume of output [a] | Average selling price per unit, products of manufacture |
|---|---|---|---|
| 1923 | 100.0 | 100.0 | 100.0 |
| 1925 | 101.1 | 102.0 | 99.0 |
| 1927 | 95.8 | 104.2 | 91.9 |
| 1929 | 102.0 | 112.3 | 90.8 |

[a] Weights based on value of product.

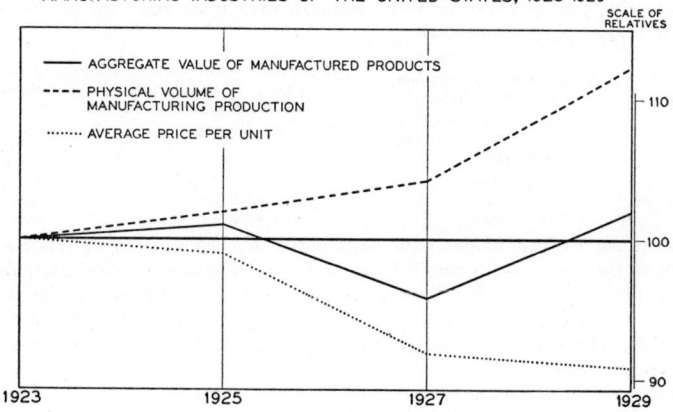

### FIGURE 73
CHANGES IN AGGREGATE VALUE, VOLUME OF PRODUCTION AND AVERAGE PRICE OF PRODUCTS
MANUFACTURING INDUSTRIES OF THE UNITED STATES, 1923-1929

experienced a substantial loss in 1927, and declined somewhat further during the business revival that occurred between 1927 and 1929. This confirms quite definitely the evidence furnished by other index numbers concerning the declining trend of prices of manufactured goods during these years.[1]

Though we are here concerned primarily with the movements of prices and costs since 1923, the changes of this period must be

[1] There are available two other series of index numbers of prices of manufactured goods, index numbers computed directly from quoted prices. A comparison

seen against the background of earlier events, as these have been sketched in the preceding chapters. For the present purpose it is sufficient to recall that in 1923 the volume of manufacturing output was approximately 49 per cent greater than in 1914 and 44 per cent greater than in 1921,[1] while selling price per unit of product was some 67 per cent higher than in 1914 and one per cent higher than in 1921. From 1923 to 1929 production moved upward from one of the highest peaks previously attained, while prices continued at a slower pace a downward movement which dates from 1919.

§ *Selling prices, individual industries.*—Any index number is an abstraction from reality, for the diversity of movement that characterizes industrial change, seen in detail, is necessarily lost to view when attention centers on a single figure. This is particularly true in the present instance, because of the wide differences among the price movements occurring in manufacturing industries. The individual records appear in the following table.[2]

of these with the indexes derived independently, from data of production and aggregate value, is of interest.

| Year | Index of average selling price per unit of product, manufacturing industries (derived from data of output and aggregate value) | Index numbers of prices of manufactured goods (derived from market price quotations) | |
|---|---|---|---|
| | | National Bureau of Economic Research | U. S. Bureau of Labor Statistics |
| 1923 | 100.0 | 100.0 | 100.0 |
| 1925 | 99.0 | 99.6 | 99.3 |
| 1927 | 91.9 | 93.2 | 93.0 |
| 1929 | 90.8 | 92.9 | 92.6 |

(The National Bureau index is an unweighted geometric mean of relative prices, based upon the quotations compiled by the U. S. Bureau of Labor Statistics. The index of the Bureau of Labor Statistics, as given above, is an average of the index numbers of prices of finished and semi-finished goods, with weights of 6 and 1, respectively. The base has been shifted from 1926 to 1923 for the purpose of the above comparison.)

There are differences in detail among the movements shown by these three index numbers, but in view of the widely different methods of derivation the agreement is convincingly close.

[1] These figures relate to the index of manufacturing production weighted by value of product. When 'value added' weights are employed the increase in manufacturing production (fabrication) is 56 per cent between 1914 and 1923, 48 per cent between 1921 and 1923.

[2] The validity of these and all similar measurements relating to production, price and cost changes in individual industries rests upon the accuracy and upon the inter-censal comparability of census enumerations. A correction is made for variations in the proportion of the total value of products for which quantity statistics are secured (correction for a varying *adequacy ratio*) but in all other respects the census figures as published are utilized.

## TABLE 154

### Changes in the Selling Prices of Products of Manufacturing Industries of the United States, 1923-1929

Index Numbers for 62 Industries, with Average Annual Rates of Change

| Industry | Index numbers of selling price, per unit of product | | | | Average annual rate of change 1923-1929 (per cent)[a] |
|---|---|---|---|---|---|
| | 1923 | 1925 | 1927 | 1929 | |
| Hats, fur-felt | 100.0 | 114.4 | 115.3 | 129.5 | +4.0 |
| Slaughtering and meat packing, wholesale.. | 100.0 | 124.6 | 121.2 | 130.2 | +3.7 |
| Cars, steam and electric railroad, not built in railroad repair shops | 100.0 | 103.7 | 118.3 | 120.8 | +3.5 |
| Musical instruments: organs | 100.0 | 120.5 | 125.5 | 119.5 | +2.8 |
| Corn syrup, corn oil, and starch | 100.0 | 110.4 | 92.4 | 120.5 | +2.1 |
| Chocolate and cocoa products | 100.0 | 102.0 | 113.0 | 106.0 | +1.4 |
| Linoleum | 100.0 | 98.4 | 96.8 | 107.3 | +1.0 |
| Knit goods | 100.0 | 101.0 | 100.9 | 103.7 | +0.5 |
| Buttons | 100.0 | 103.8 | 108.0 | 101.3 | +0.4 |
| Flour and other grain-mill products | 100.0 | 129.9 | 113.4 | 104.4 | —0.1 |
| Butter and cheese | 100.0 | 97.7 | 99.6 | 97.1 | —0.3 |
| Ice, manufactured | 100.0 | 99.9 | 98.1 | 98.3 | —0.3 |
| Paints and varnishes | 100.0 | 101.2 | 100.1 | 97.8 | —0.4 |
| Tanning materials, natural dyestuffs, mordants and assistants, and sizes | 100.0 | 101.6 | 101.4 | 97.4 | —0.4 |
| Motor vehicles, including bodies and parts.. | 100.0 | 97.9 | 99.7 | 95.4 | —0.6 |
| Motorcycles, bicycles, and parts | 100.0 | 99.1 | 98.6 | 95.8 | —0.7 |
| Gas, manufactured, illuminating and heating | 100.0 | 98.9 | 97.3 | 95.7 | —0.7 |
| Soap | 100.0 | 100.8 | 98.8 | 95.4 | —0.8 |
| Firearms | 100.0 | 94.2 | 91.2 | 95.6 | —0.8 |
| Worsted goods | 100.0 | 100.7 | 90.8 | 97.7 | —0.9 |
| Canning and preserving: fruits and vegetables; pickles, jellies, preserves, and sauces | 100.0 | 97.2 | 88.8 | 96.4 | —1.0 |
| Fertilizers | 100.0 | 99.2 | 88.7 | 97.2 | —1.0 |
| Sand-lime brick | 100.0 | 103.1 | 98.4 | 93.7 | —1.2 |
| Cordage and twine | 100.0 | 113.2 | 101.7 | 95.5 | —1.2 |
| Carpets and rugs, wool, other than rag | 100.0 | 100.0 | 97.0 | 92.3 | —1.3 |
| Woolen goods | 100.0 | 101.2 | 92.8 | 94.0 | —1.4 |
| Explosives | 100.0 | 94.9 | 95.4 | 90.1 | —1.5 |
| Rice cleaning and polishing | 100.0 | 140.5 | 108.2 | 98.3 | —1.7 |
| Jute and linen goods | 100.0 | 108.1 | 96.5 | 91.7 | —1.8 |
| Wool shoddy | 100.0 | 111.0 | 103.2 | 89.4 | —1.9 |
| Clay products (other than pottery) and non-clay refractories | 100.0 | 93.7 | 89.5 | 89.1 | —2.0 |

## TABLE 154—Continued

| Industry | Index numbers of selling price, per unit of product | | | | Average annual rate of change 1923-1929 (per cent)[a] |
|---|---|---|---|---|---|
| | 1923 | 1925 | 1927 | 1929 | |
| Carriages, wagons, sleighs, and sleds | 100.0 | 104.6 | 99.0 | 87.4 | —2.2 |
| Turpentine and rosin | 100.0 | 110.0 | 92.4 | 91.2 | —2.2 |
| Oil, cake, and meal, cottonseed | 100.0 | 84.5 | 70.1 | 91.7 | —2.2 |
| Lace goods, cotton | 100.0 | 99.3 | 86.2 | 88.2 | —2.6 |
| Iron and steel: steel works and rolling mills | 100.0 | 92.7 | 87.1 | 85.7 | —2.6 |
| Paper and pulp | 100.0 | 94.1 | 88.7 | 85.4 | —2.6 |
| Rubber products | 100.0 | 110.9 | 101.0 | 84.2 | —2.9 |
| Salt | 100.0 | 92.9 | 86.7 | 83.6 | —3.0 |
| Lumber and timber products | 100.0 | 88.0 | 80.9 | 83.8 | —3.1 |
| Wood distillation and charcoal manufacture | 100.0 | 78.0 | 80.1 | 81.7 | —3.1 |
| Canning and preserving: fish, crabs, shrimps, oysters, and clams | 100.0 | 91.8 | 91.5 | 81.1 | —3.1 |
| Condensed and evaporated milk | 100.0 | 88.4 | 88.4 | 81.2 | —3.1 |
| Oil, cake, and meal, linseed | 100.0 | 103.7 | 86.9 | 84.1 | —3.4 |
| Musical instruments: pianos | 100.0 | 96.3 | 91.9 | 80.1 | —3.4 |
| Cast-iron pipe | 100.0 | 90.6 | 84.0 | 81.0 | —3.5 |
| Petroleum refining | 100.0 | 102.2 | 83.2 | 83.1 | —3.7 |
| Hats, wool-felt | 100.0 | 102.1 | 89.8 | 79.5 | —3.9 |
| Cement | 100.0 | 96.0 | 87.6 | 78.2 | —4.0 |
| Lime | 100.0 | 98.4 | 88.9 | 77.4 | —4.2 |
| Oilcloth | 100.0 | 93.5 | 77.3 | 80.3 | —4.2 |
| Cotton goods | 100.0 | 91.9 | 75.1 | 75.6 | —5.1 |
| Iron and steel: blast furnaces | 100.0 | 83.2 | 77.5 | 71.9 | —5.3 |
| Coke, not including gas-house coke | 100.0 | 81.1 | 80.0 | 66.8 | —6.0 |
| Asphalted-felt-base floor covering | 100.0 | 98.0 | 72.9 | 72.3 | —6.1 |
| Silk manufactures | 100.0 | 89.2 | 78.5 | 67.6 | —6.3 |
| Bone black, carbon black, and lampblack | 100.0 | 68.9 | 70.4 | 66.3 | —6.3 |
| Sugar, beet | 100.0 | 77.3 | 73.4 | 62.5 | —7.2 |
| Sugar refining, cane | 100.0 | 68.4 | 71.2 | 60.7 | —7.4 |
| Sugar, cane, not including products of refineries | 100.0 | 63.0 | 70.5 | 57.3 | —8.0 |
| Felt goods, wool or hair | 100.0 | 101.8 | 103.5 | — | — |
| Wire, drawn from purchased bars or rods | 100.0 | 100.7 | 94.2 | — | — |
| Average [b] | 100.0 | 97.2 | 90.6 | 90.3 | —1.9 |

[a] Average rates of change for the period 1923-1929 are given in this and following tables, as a ready means of comparing the movements of different series. Such rates for the period 1923-1929 are not strictly comparable with similar figures for the period 1922-1929. Differences of conditions in terminal years may materially affect such rates over short periods of time.

[b] Arithmetic average of the central items of a weighted frequency distribution, with weights based on value of product, averaged for the base year and the given year. The central one-fifth of the items, by weight, were included in computing the average.

Of the 60 industries for which complete records were available, per-unit selling prices were higher in 1929 than in 1923 for 10, lower for 50. Reducing the changes to an average annual basis, we find wide variation, ranging from an upward movement of 4.0 per cent a year in the price of the products of the industry designated 'hats, fur-felt' to a downward movement of 8.0 per cent a year in the prices of sugar cane products (excluding products of refineries). This variation in the rates of change of per-unit selling price is shown graphically in Figure 74. The degree of divergence in price movements among manufacturing

### FIGURE 74
#### ILLUSTRATING THE DIVERGENCE OF PRICE TRENDS AMONG 60 MANUFACTURING INDUSTRIES OF THE UNITED STATES, 1923-1929.
AVERAGE RATES OF CHANGE IN SELLING PRICES, PER UNIT OF PRODUCT*

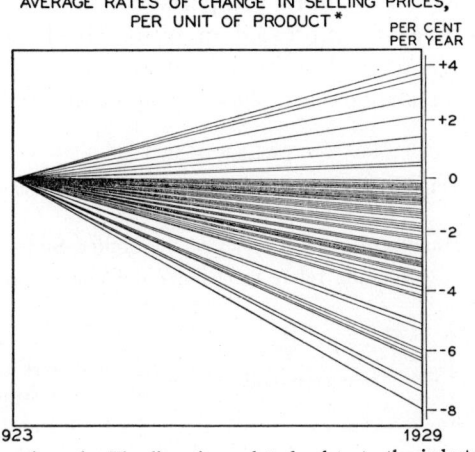

* Plotted on ratio scale. The lines here plotted relate to the industries listed in Table 154, in the order of that listing. The last two entries are omitted.

industries between 1923 and 1929 was distinctly greater than the divergence between 1899 and 1914. The standard deviation (weighted) of rates of change is 3.0 for the post-war period, as compared with 1.7 for the pre-war period. In respect of price trends there was greater ferment working among manufacturing industries in recent years than in pre-war days. Diversity of fortunes was more pronounced.

In one respect the post-war record resembles that of the pre-war years. There was somewhat less diversity among price trends than among production trends, for manufacturing industries. (The standard deviation of production trends between 1923 and 1929 is 3.7, as against 3.0 for prices.)

At the foot of Table 154 are given averages of the selling price index numbers, averages derived from the central items of weighted frequency distributions for the several years. These are in some respects more representative of the fortunes of a typical manufacturing industry than are the 'ideal' index numbers previously cited. For the years here covered the two sets of measurements differ but slightly.

## Changes in Material Costs and in Fabrication Costs, Manufacturing Industries

Selling price alterations are the net resultants of changes in material costs and in fabrication costs (including, in the latter, profits). Employing appropriately weighted index numbers of physical volume, we may derive from the statistics of aggregate material costs and aggregate 'value added' index numbers defining changes in these cost factors, per unit of product. These are given in the next table. To facilitate comparison with similar indexes for other periods they are expressed in terms of dollars of constant purchasing power, as well as in current dollars.[1] Index numbers of purchasing power changes are shown graphically in Figure 75.

TABLE 155

Changes in Selling Price, Cost of Materials and Fabrication Costs, plus Profits, 1923-1929

Manufacturing Industries of the United States

(All measurements relate to changes per unit of product)

| (1) | (2) | (3) | (4) | (5) | (6) | (7) |
|---|---|---|---|---|---|---|
| | In current dollars | | | In dollars of constant purchasing power | | |
| Year | Selling price | Cost of materials | Fabrication costs, plus profits | Selling price | Cost of materials | Fabrication costs, plus profits |
| 1923 | 100.0 | 100.0 | 100.0 | 100.0 | 100.0 | 100.0 |
| 1925 | 99.0 | 100.0 | 97.3 | 96.3 | 97.2 | 94.6 |
| 1927 | 91.9 | 91.7 | 92.4 | 96.9 | 96.7 | 97.5 |
| 1929 | 90.8 | 87.9 | 96.8 | 95.9 | 92.8 | 102.1 |
| Average annual rate of change (per cent) ..... | —1.8 | —2.3 | —0.7 | —0.6 | —1.1 | +0.5 |

[1] As in handling other indexes, reduction to constant terms has been effected through division by the U. S. Bureau of Labor Statistics index numbers of wholesale prices. It is recognized that this is not a perfect instrument for this purpose, but it provides the best available means of reducing dollar measurements for different periods to reasonably comparable terms.

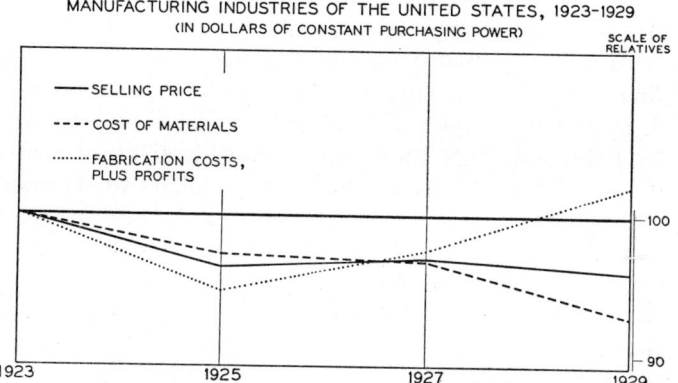

**FIGURE 75**

CHANGES IN AVERAGE SELLING PRICE, COST OF MATERIALS AND FABRICATION COSTS, PLUS PROFITS, PER UNIT OF PRODUCT

MANUFACTURING INDUSTRIES OF THE UNITED STATES, 1923-1929
(IN DOLLARS OF CONSTANT PURCHASING POWER)

Between 1923 and 1929 both elements of the selling price of manufactured goods declined, though somewhat unevenly. Over the six-year period the net decline in material costs (a decline of 12.1 per cent) substantially exceeded the drop in fabrication costs (3.2 per cent).[1] When these changes are measured in terms of a constant standard of value it is seen that material costs declined without a

[1] The returns relating to cost of materials in 1929 differ in one important respect from the returns for previous census periods. Mill and shop supplies were included among materials costs in all census enumerations up to and including that of 1927. In 1929 mill and shop supplies were expressly excluded from material costs. They would thus be included in that residual item which we have called overhead costs plus profits. In some degree the decline in material costs shown by the index numbers is attributable to this change in practice.

It is impossible to determine the precise degree of influence of this change. The Bureau of the Census reports that in census enumerations prior to that of 1929 some manufacturers found it impossible to segregate the cost of such supplies, and either estimated them or omitted them. To the extent that they were omitted, no change was involved in adopting the 1929 procedure.

It is reported, furthermore, that the cost of supplies is probably insignificant, or of very little importance, in comparison with the cost of materials proper except for a few industries of which the most important is that designated 'steel works and rolling mills'. For this industry the costs of relining and other repairing of furnaces and ladles, the replacement of stools, molds and rolls, and general repairs to equipment were included under cost of materials in census enumerations prior to that of 1929, but were excluded from material costs in the Census of 1929. This change would tend to lower material costs and raise 'overhead plus profits' for that industry in 1929. The record actually reveals a decline of almost 9 per cent in material costs, per unit of product, between 1927 and 1929, and an advance of 29 per cent in

break, while the drop in fabrication costs was restricted to the two-year period from 1923 to 1925. Thereafter the real cost of the services of fabricating agents advanced.

Properly to appraise these movements, and to appreciate their distinctive features, comparison should be made with the changes which occurred during earlier periods. Tables similar to that above, containing measurements covering the years 1899 to 1914 and 1914 to 1923, appear in Chapter III (p. 103) and Chapter V (p. 225). Between 1914 and 1923 there was a considerable advance in the price of manufactured goods, expressed in dollars of constant purchasing power. The recent period resembles the pre-war period in that the real price of manufactured products was declining. There is this notable difference, however. Between 1899 and 1914 the real price of manufactured goods declined because of a substantial reduction in fabrication costs, per unit of product. Material costs (in dollars of constant purchasing power) stood at the same level in 1914 as in 1899. Between 1923 and 1929 the drop in real prices of manufactured goods was due entirely to declining material costs. Fabrication costs showed a net increase over the period of 2.1 per cent.

As in every use of index numbers, the peculiarities of the base year must be remembered in interpreting these price and cost measurements. In 1923 the average selling price of manufactured goods, in dollars of constant purchasing power, stood 13.1 per cent above the 1914 level; cost of materials, per unit of product, was 9 per cent higher than in 1914, while fabrication costs (including profits) were 22.7 per cent higher than in 1914. From 1923 to 1929 manufactured goods declined somewhat from what was, relatively, a very high level of per-unit purchasing power. The cost of materials (including semi-finished goods) dropped from a level almost equally high. Fabrication costs increased fractionally from an unprecedentedly high point in 1923. From 1921 to 1929, in fact, the

---

overhead costs plus profits, per unit of product, for steel works and rolling mills. These movements are probably due in considerable part to the change in reporting practice.

We should note, also, that in 1929 manufacturers had the option of reporting either the cost of materials purchased or the cost of materials consumed during the year, whereas in former enumerations the cost of materials consumed in the manufacture of products made during the year was requested. Here, again, we are at a loss to determine the influence of this change on the reported statistics, but it was probably slight.

costs to the community of the services of fabricating agents of all sorts (including those whose rewards take the form of profits) was practically constant, at a level never before attained, so far as may be judged from present records.

These various changes may be viewed in graphic form, with reference to a pre-war base, in Figure 76.

### FIGURE 76
### CHANGES IN AVERAGE SELLING PRICE, COST OF MATERIALS AND FABRICATION COSTS, PLUS PROFITS
MANUFACTURING INDUSTRIES OF THE UNITED STATES, 1914-1929
(PERCENTAGE DEVIATIONS FROM 1914 PARITY, IN DOLLARS OF CONSTANT PURCHASING POWER)

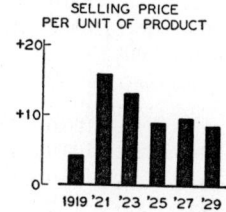
SELLING PRICE PER UNIT OF PRODUCT

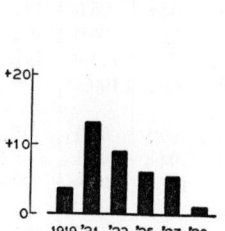
COST OF MATERIALS PER UNIT OF PRODUCT

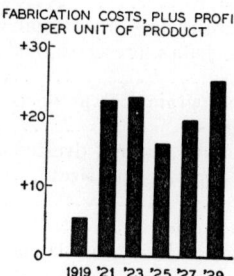
FABRICATION COSTS, PLUS PROFITS PER UNIT OF PRODUCT

§ *Material costs and fabrication costs, individual industries.*— Widely divergent movements were found when we traced changes in the selling prices of manufactured products by individual industries. Comparable index numbers measuring changes in material costs and in fabrication costs, in current dollars, are given in the two following tables. The divergence of the rates of change of these index numbers is shown graphically in Figure 77.

From an advance of 53 per cent to a decline of 50 per cent within a six-year period—this is the amazing range of variation in changing costs of materials, per unit of product, among manufacturing industries. The extreme cases are, of course, exceptional, but they serve to emphasize how diverse are the forces affecting American industries. The degree of divergence of trends in material costs (if we may speak of trends over a six-year period) was materially higher between 1923 and

## TABLE 156

CHANGES IN MATERIAL COSTS, MANUFACTURING INDUSTRIES OF THE UNITED STATES, 1923-1929

Index Numbers for 62 Industries, with Average Annual Rates of Change

| Industry | Index numbers of cost of materials, per unit of product | | | | Average annual rate of change 1923-1929 (per cent) |
|---|---|---|---|---|---|
| | 1923 | 1925 | 1927 | 1929 | |
| Hats, fur-felt .......................... | 100.0 | 125.2 | 129.6 | 153.1 | +6.7 |
| Slaughtering and meat packing, wholesale.. | 100.0 | 127.4 | 125.5 | 133.9 | +4.2 |
| Cars, steam and electric railroad, not built in railroad repair shops................. | 100.0 | 103.2 | 115.7 | 119.6 | +3.3 |
| Chocolate and cocoa products............. | 100.0 | 110.4 | 130.7 | 111.2 | +2.4 |
| Musical instruments: organs.............. | 100.0 | 126.0 | 125.2 | 113.2 | +1.7 |
| Corn syrup, corn oil, and starch........... | 100.0 | 121.0 | 97.8 | 118.5 | +1.5 |
| Linoleum ............................... | 100.0 | 84.1 | 95.2 | 99.2 | +0.5 |
| Buttons ................................. | 100.0 | 98.2 | 103.4 | 99.9 | +0.2 |
| Turpentine and rosin..................... | 100.0 | 121.0 | 110.4 | 102.7 | —0.1 |
| Canning and preserving: fruits and vegetables; pickles, jellies, preserves, and sauces | 100.0 | 104.8 | 95.0 | 102.3 | —0.1 |
| Worsted goods .......................... | 100.0 | 112.2 | 96.0 | 102.9 | —0.4 |
| Flour and other grain-mill products....... | 100.0 | 133.3 | 113.6 | 101.7 | —0.6 |
| Butter and cheese........................ | 100.0 | 100.7 | 100.3 | 96.4 | —0.6 |
| Tanning materials, natural dyestuffs, mordants and assistants, and sizes........... | 100.0 | 99.5 | 98.1 | 95.2 | —0.8 |
| Fertilizers .............................. | 100.0 | 94.6 | 92.1 | 95.6 | —0.8 |
| Jute and linen goods..................... | 100.0 | 117.0 | 98.9 | 99.8 | —0.9 |
| Bone black, carbon black, and lampblack... | 100.0 | 73.7 | 89.4 | 89.4 | —0.9 |
| Firearms ............................... | 100.0 | 95.5 | 114.7 | 86.8 | —1.0 |
| Woolen goods ........................... | 100.0 | 111.2 | 96.2 | 97.0 | —1.2 |
| Paints and varnishes .................... | 100.0 | 102.6 | 96.4 | 93.2 | —1.3 |
| Carriages, wagons, sleighs, and sleds...... | 100.0 | 107.9 | 108.6 | 90.0 | —1.4 |
| Cordage and twine....................... | 100.0 | 124.0 | 105.3 | 95.9 | —1.4 |
| Canning and preserving: fish, crabs, shrimps, oysters, and clams............. | 100.0 | 96.0 | 98.3 | 86.9 | —1.9 |
| Knit goods .............................. | 100.0 | 99.2 | 91.9 | 89.9 | —2.0 |
| Wool shoddy ............................ | 100.0 | 123.7 | 102.7 | 92.7 | —2.0 |
| Carpets and rugs, wool, other than rag.... | 100.0 | 113.6 | 101.8 | 88.9 | —2.2 |
| Soap ................................... | 100.0 | 106.6 | 94.5 | 87.5 | —2.5 |
| Gas, manufactured, illuminating and heating | 100.0 | 91.3 | 93.9 | 82.7 | —2.6 |
| Motor vehicles, including bodies and parts. | 100.0 | 82.5 | 88.9 | 81.8 | —2.7 |
| Rice cleaning and polishing............... | 100.0 | 141.0 | 108.8 | 90.6 | —2.7 |
| Asphalted-felt-base floor coverings ........ | 100.0 | 124.4 | 95.7 | 89.2 | —2.9 |

PRICES AND COSTS, POST-WAR 389

TABLE 156—*Continued*

| Industry | Index numbers of cost of materials, per unit of product | | | | Average annual rate of change 1923-1929 (per cent) |
|---|---|---|---|---|---|
| | 1923 | 1925 | 1927 | 1929 | |
| Oil, cake, and meal, cottonseed............ | 100.0 | 80.1 | 64.0 | 88.6 | —3.0 |
| Rubber products ....................... | 100.0 | 121.4 | 104.1 | 83.3 | —3.2 |
| Clay products (other than pottery) and non-clay refractories ................... | 100.0 | 90.6 | 90.2 | 80.1 | —3.3 |
| Motorcycles, bicycles, and parts........... | 100.0 | 89.1 | 83.8 | 81.1 | —3.4 |
| Paper and pulp......................... | 100.0 | 92.7 | 83.8 | 79.6 | —3.9 |
| Condensed and evaporated milk............ | 100.0 | 87.8 | 85.7 | 77.3 | —3.9 |
| Lime ................................. | 100.0 | 93.2 | 88.6 | 77.2 | —4.0 |
| Petroleum refining ..................... | 100.0 | 102.3 | 85.7 | 80.5 | —4.0 |
| Explosives ............................ | 100.0 | 98.0 | 92.2 | 76.1 | —4.2 |
| Cement ............................... | 100.0 | 95.4 | 93.9 | 74.4 | —4.2 |
| Oil, cake, and meal, linseed............... | 100.0 | 99.1 | 83.9 | 79.0 | —4.2 |
| Hats, wool-felt ........................ | 100.0 | 113.3 | 88.8 | 79.7 | —4.4 |
| Sand-lime brick ....................... | 100.0 | 86.4 | 80.2 | 75.3 | —4.6 |
| Iron and steel: steel works and rolling mills [a] ............................... | 100.0 | 88.0 | 81.7 | 74.7 | —4.7 |
| Lace goods, cotton ..................... | 100.0 | 105.2 | 88.0 | 74.4 | —5.0 |
| Musical instruments: pianos.............. | 100.0 | 96.3 | 84.7 | 73.5 | —5.0 |
| Sugar, beet ........................... | 100.0 | 84.9 | 92.3 | 68.2 | —5.0 |
| Lumber and timber products.............. | 100.0 | 93.6 | 85.8 | 72.0 | —5.1 |
| Ice, manufactured ..................... | 100.0 | 84.4 | 76.5 | 72.9 | —5.2 |
| Oilcloth .............................. | 100.0 | 103.5 | 75.4 | 75.5 | —5.6 |
| Wood distillation and charcoal manufacture | 100.0 | 83.9 | 76.8 | 70.3 | —5.7 |
| Coke, not including gas-house coke........ | 100.0 | 86.9 | 87.7 | 66.3 | —5.7 |
| Salt .................................. | 100.0 | 84.0 | 82.8 | 67.5 | —5.8 |
| Iron and steel: blast furnaces............. | 100.0 | 81.7 | 77.1 | 68.8 | —5.8 |
| Cast-iron pipe ......................... | 100.0 | 83.3 | 80.9 | 66.8 | —6.0 |
| Cotton goods ......................... | 100.0 | 95.7 | 69.2 | 73.8 | —6.0 |
| Silk manufactures ..................... | 100.0 | 84.9 | 74.0 | 60.1 | —7.9 |
| Sugar refining, cane..................... | 100.0 | 66.0 | 70.0 | 55.9 | —8.5 |
| Sugar, cane, not including products of refineries ............................. | 100.0 | 70.5 | 66.5 | 49.6 | —10.8 |
| Felt goods, wool or hair.................. | 100.0 | 107.8 | 101.2 | — | — |
| Wire, drawn from purchased bars or rods. | 100.0 | 101.9 | 92.8 | — | — |
| Average [b] ............................. | 100.0 | 98.1 | 90.3 | 83.8 | —3.0 |

[a] See footnote pp. 385-6.

[b] Arithmetic average of the central items of a weighted frequency distribution, with weights based on cost of materials, averaged for the base year and the given year. The central one-fifth of the items, by weight, were included in computing the average.

## FIGURE 77
### ILLUSTRATING THE DIVERGENCE OF COST TRENDS AMONG 60 MANUFACTURING INDUSTRIES OF THE UNITED STATES, 1923-1929
#### AVERAGE RATES OF CHANGE IN MATERIAL COSTS AND IN FABRICATION COSTS, PLUS PROFITS, PER UNIT OF PRODUCT*

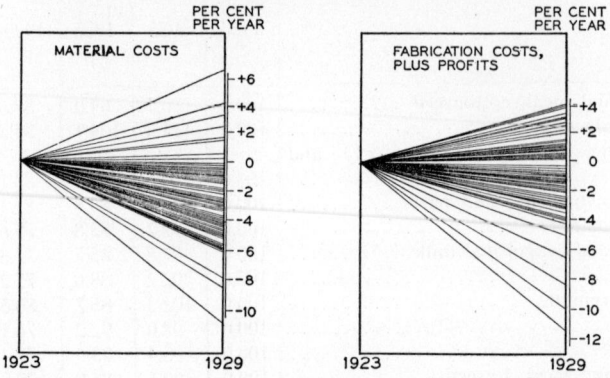

* Plotted on ratio scale. The lines here plotted relate to the industries listed in Tables 156 and 157, in the order of those listings. The last two entries are omitted.

1929 than it was between 1899 and 1914. This is indicated by a standard deviation (of the rates of change) of 3.7, as against 1.7, pre-war.

The weighted averages given at the foot of the table show the same general changes as do the 'ideal' index numbers previously derived. A somewhat greater decline in material costs in 1929 is indicated by the averages derived from the entries in Table 156.

In fabrication costs, again, there is variation from industry to industry. Such variation is to be expected in this case, for we are including in costs of fabrication the elusive element of profits. Here, again, we find a greater degree of divergence among manufacturing industries than is shown by the pre-war record. The standard deviation of the rates of change is 2.5, as against 1.9 for the earlier period.

We must make certain reservations in drawing conclusions from this comparison, but it is clearly to be inferred from the data of this and the preceding tables that post-war manufacturing conditions were less settled, less uniform from industry to industry, than was the case before the war. The difference, of course, is one of degree only, for variation within the manufacturing field has been too great, before as well as after the war, to justify one in speaking of uniformity or homogeneity of conditions.

The averages of central items given at the foot of Table 157 indicate declining fabrication costs, per unit of product, between 1923 and 1927, and a considerable advance from 1927 to 1929. This advance reflects, presumably, the higher profits of the latter year. These averages are higher than the 'ideal' index numbers previously presented.

## TABLE 157

### Changes in Fabrication Costs, plus Profits, Manufacturing Industries of the United States, 1923-1929

Index Numbers for 62 Industries, with Average Annual Rates of Change

| Industry | Index numbers of cost of fabrication, plus profits, per unit of product | | | | Average annual rate of change 1923-1929 (per cent) |
|---|---|---|---|---|---|
| | 1923 | 1925 | 1927 | 1929 | |
| Sugar refining, cane | 100.0 | 104.7 | 89.4 | 134.5 | +4.2 |
| Rice cleaning and polishing | 100.0 | 138.0 | 105.0 | 143.3 | +4.1 |
| Cars, steam and electric railroad, not built in railroad repair shops | 100.0 | 104.9 | 124.1 | 123.3 | +4.0 |
| Knit goods | 100.0 | 103.4 | 113.0 | 121.9 | +3.5 |
| Corn syrup, corn oil, and starch | 100.0 | 91.7 | 82.9 | 124.1 | +3.2 |
| Musical instruments: organs | 100.0 | 118.3 | 125.7 | 122.0 | +3.2 |
| Oil, cake, and meal, linseed | 100.0 | 148.8 | 115.5 | 134.1 | +2.8 |
| Flour and other grain-mill products | 100.0 | 111.4 | 112.1 | 118.9 | +2.6 |
| Motorcycles, bicycles, and parts | 100.0 | 111.6 | 117.4 | 114.3 | +2.2 |
| Soap | 100.0 | 90.9 | 106.2 | 108.6 | +2.0 |
| Oil, cake, and meal, cottonseed | 100.0 | 115.1 | 112.0 | 112.4 | +1.6 |
| Linoleum | 100.0 | 113.9 | 98.6 | 116.0 | +1.5 |
| Motor vehicles, including bodies and parts | 100.0 | 115.7 | 111.1 | 111.0 | +1.3 |
| Hats, fur-felt | 100.0 | 105.2 | 103.2 | 109.6 | +1.3 |
| Explosives | 100.0 | 91.4 | 98.9 | 105.7 | +1.2 |
| Ice, manufactured | 100.0 | 106.1 | 106.7 | 108.3 | +1.2 |
| Paints and varnishes | 100.0 | 99.0 | 106.1 | 105.1 | +1.1 |
| Butter and cheese | 100.0 | 79.8 | 95.4 | 101.0 | +1.0 |
| Slaughtering and meat packing, wholesale | 100.0 | 109.6 | 98.5 | 110.5 | +1.0 |
| Iron and steel: steel works and rolling mills [a] | 100.0 | 101.5 | 97.0 | 105.9 | +0.7 |
| Sand-lime brick | 100.0 | 113.9 | 110.2 | 105.6 | +0.6 |
| Gas, manufactured, illuminating and heating | 100.0 | 104.6 | 99.8 | 105.4 | +0.6 |
| Buttons | 100.0 | 107.6 | 111.2 | 102.2 | +0.5 |
| Wood distillation and charcoal manufacture | 100.0 | 69.7 | 84.5 | 97.5 | +0.4 |
| Condensed and evaporated milk | 100.0 | 91.0 | 100.9 | 99.4 | +0.4 |
| Tanning materials, natural dyestuffs, mordants and assistants, and sizes | 100.0 | 105.8 | 107.9 | 102.0 | +0.4 |
| Sugar, cane, not including products of refineries | 100.0 | 37.9 | 83.8 | 83.5 | −0.2 |
| Carpets and rugs, wool, other than rag | 100.0 | 87.0 | 92.4 | 95.6 | −0.4 |
| Paper and pulp | 100.0 | 96.3 | 96.9 | 95.6 | −0.6 |
| Cordage and twine | 100.0 | 96.5 | 96.1 | 95.0 | −0.8 |
| Firearms | 100.0 | 93.9 | 85.1 | 97.9 | −0.8 |
| Chocolate and cocoa products | 100.0 | 87.3 | 81.9 | 96.9 | −0.8 |

[a] See footnote, pp. 385-6.

## TABLE 157—Continued

| Industry | Index numbers of cost of fabrication, plus profits, per unit of product | | | | Average annual rate of change 1923-1929 (per cent) |
|---|---|---|---|---|---|
| | 1923 | 1925 | 1927 | 1929 | |
| Lace goods, cotton.......................... | 100.0 | 95.2 | 85.0 | 97.7 | —0.9 |
| Salt ....................................... | 100.0 | 100.1 | 89.8 | 96.6 | —1.1 |
| Oilcloth ................................... | 100.0 | 71.8 | 81.4 | 90.7 | —1.1 |
| Cast-iron pipe ............................. | 100.0 | 98.7 | 87.4 | 96.8 | —1.1 |
| Fertilizers ................................ | 100.0 | 109.9 | 80.9 | 101.0 | —1.3 |
| Clay products (other than pottery) and non-clay refractories .................... | 100.0 | 95.1 | 89.3 | 93.2 | —1.4 |
| Woolen goods .............................. | 100.0 | 89.0 | 88.7 | 90.4 | —1.6 |
| Worsted goods ............................. | 100.0 | 83.2 | 82.9 | 89.8 | —1.7 |
| Wool shoddy ............................... | 100.0 | 88.7 | 104.0 | 83.6 | —1.8 |
| Lumber and timber products............... | 100.0 | 84.6 | 77.9 | 91.2 | —1.9 |
| Musical instruments: pianos............... | 100.0 | 96.4 | 98.8 | 86.4 | —2.0 |
| Canning and preserving: fruits and vegetables; pickles, jellies, preserves, and sauces | 100.0 | 86.6 | 80.3 | 88.2 | —2.3 |
| Rubber products ........................... | 100.0 | 99.3 | 97.6 | 85.2 | —2.4 |
| Petroleum refining ........................ | 100.0 | 101.9 | 73.6 | 93.2 | —2.6 |
| Jute and linen goods....................... | 100.0 | 99.1 | 94.1 | 83.6 | —2.8 |
| Iron and steel: blast furnaces............. | 100.0 | 90.0 | 79.1 | 86.0 | —2.9 |
| Carriages, wagons, sleighs, and sleds ...... | 100.0 | 101.3 | 89.5 | 84.8 | —3.0 |
| Turpentine and rosin...................... | 100.0 | 106.3 | 86.2 | 87.3 | —3.0 |
| Hats, wool-felt ............................ | 100.0 | 90.1 | 90.8 | 79.2 | —3.4 |
| Cotton goods .............................. | 100.0 | 86.2 | 84.1 | 78.3 | —3.8 |
| Silk manufactures ......................... | 100.0 | 96.6 | 86.0 | 80.2 | —3.8 |
| Cement ................................... | 100.0 | 96.3 | 83.7 | 80.5 | —3.9 |
| Lime ...................................... | 100.0 | 102.0 | 89.2 | 77.6 | —4.3 |
| Canning and preserving: fish, crabs, shrimps, oysters, and clams............. | 100.0 | 85.2 | 80.8 | 71.8 | —5.1 |
| Coke, not including gas-house coke........ | 100.0 | 68.6 | 63.4 | 68.0 | —6.6 |
| Asphalted-felt-base floor coverings ........ | 100.0 | 83.1 | 60.0 | 62.8 | —8.5 |
| Bone black, carbon black, and lampblack... | 100.0 | 66.1 | 59.5 | 53.2 | —10.1 |
| Sugar, beet ............................... | 100.0 | 65.9 | 45.1 | 53.9 | —11.5 |
| Felt goods, wool or hair................... | 100.0 | 93.9 | 106.5 | — | — |
| Wire, drawn from purchased rods or bars.. | 100.0 | 98.2 | 97.2 | — | — |
| Average [b] ................................ | 100.0 | 99.2 | 96.3 | 101.4 | +0.1 |

[b] Arithmetic average of the central items of a weighted frequency distribution, with weights based on 'value added', averaged for the base year and the given year. The central one-fifth of the items, by weight, were included in computing the average.

## Changes in Labor Costs and in Other Fabrication Costs, Manufacturing Industries

We now break fabrication cost into its two constituent elements—labor costs and a combination of overhead costs, salaries and profits. Movements of index numbers measuring the cost of these services, per unit of product, between 1923 and 1929, are shown graphically in Figure 78. The index numbers plotted are those which define changes in terms of dollars of constant purchasing power.

TABLE 158

Changes in Total Fabrication Costs, Labor Costs and Overhead Costs plus Profits, 1923-1929

Manufacturing Industries of the United States

(All measurements relate to changes per unit of product)

| (1) | (2) | (3) | (4) | (5) | (6) | (7) |
|---|---|---|---|---|---|---|
| | In current dollars | | | In dollars of constant purchasing power | | |
| Year | Fabrication costs, plus profits | Labor costs | Overhead costs plus profits | Fabrication costs, plus profits | Labor costs | Overhead costs plus profits |
| 1923 | 100.0 | 100.0 | 100.0 | 100.0 | 100.0 | 100.0 |
| 1925 | 97.3 | 95.0 | 98.8 | 94.6 | 92.4 | 96.0 |
| 1927 | 92.4 | 91.6 | 92.9 | 97.5 | 96.6 | 97.9 |
| 1929 | 96.8 | 85.7 | 104.8 | 102.1 | 90.5 | 110.6 |
| Average annual rate of change (per cent) ..... | −0.7 | −2.5 | +0.4 | +0.5 | −1.3 | +1.7 |

For the present purpose we should perhaps center attention on the index numbers defining cost changes in terms of dollars of constant purchasing power. Granting the accuracy of the deflating medium (the wholesale price index of the United States Bureau of Labor Statistics) these measures indicate the real changes in the costs of fabrication, expressed in terms of commodities.

Real fabrication costs, we have noted, fell by more than five per cent between 1923 and 1925, and advanced almost eight per cent between 1925 and 1929. The present table shows that the two component elements of these costs followed strikingly divergent

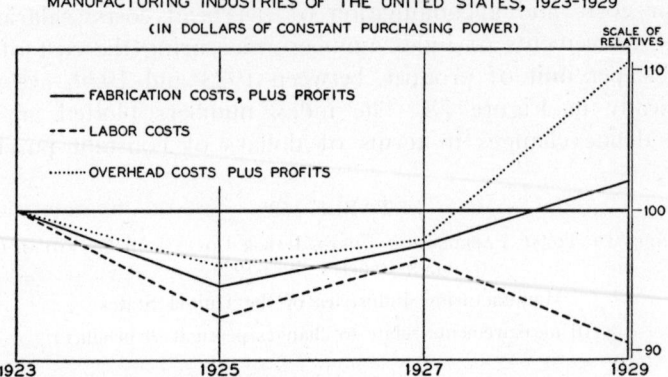

**FIGURE 78**

CHANGES IN AVERAGE FABRICATION COSTS, LABOR COSTS
AND OVERHEAD COSTS PLUS PROFITS,
PER UNIT OF PRODUCT

MANUFACTURING INDUSTRIES OF THE UNITED STATES, 1923-1929

(IN DOLLARS OF CONSTANT PURCHASING POWER)

courses. Labor costs per unit of product declined by almost ten per cent over this six-year period. The cost of overhead, management and ownership, per unit of product, declined four per cent between 1923 and 1925, advanced fifteen per cent during the next four years.[1]

Here, again, we must view these changes against the background of earlier tendencies. Real fabrication costs declined appreciably from 1899 to 1914, advanced sharply from 1914 to 1923. This is also the story of the changes in labor costs and in overhead costs plus profits. The pre-war decline was more pronounced

[1] Between 1923 and 1929 taxes constituted a declining proportion of the elements we have lumped under the heading 'overhead costs plus profits'. The following figures, based on data published by the Census Bureau, supplemented by estimates based on compilations of the Bureau of Internal Revenue, indicate the changes occurring in taxes and salaries, as component parts of the total.

| Item of cost | Percentage of total overhead costs plus profits | | | |
| --- | --- | --- | --- | --- |
| | 1923 | 1925 | 1927 | 1929 |
| Taxes, total | 7.5 | 7.4 | 6.5 | 5.8 |
| Salaries | 18.9 | 18.2 | 19.3 | 17.7 |
| Elements other than taxes and salaries | 73.6 | 74.4 | 74.2 | 76.5 |
| Overhead costs plus profits, total | 100.0 | 100.0 | 100.0 | 100.0 |

(Data relating to rent and to payments for contract work, which appeared in similar summaries for earlier years, are not available for the period 1923-1929. Payments for contract work, for which we have figures for part of the period, made up 4.2 per cent of the total in 1923, 3.7 per cent in 1925.)

In addition to the drop in taxes, it is to be noted that the amounts paid in

for overhead costs (including profits), while the war-time advance was greater for labor costs. The record of the six years from 1923 to 1929, then, is one of labor costs declining from a conspicuously high level (the peak of labor costs came in 1921), of charges for the services of management and ownership advancing from a level already relatively high in 1923.

We have noted the highly significant reversal, after 1914, of the tendency toward constantly lower fabrication costs (i.e., real costs) which had prevailed during the decade and a half preceding the war. There is no doubt that the rising trend of prices, and the accompanying lag of various production costs, played an important part in this cheapening of manufactured goods. Insistent war-time demands, and the ability of agents of fabrication to resist price liquidation and to make prompt adaptation to the changed conditions brought by the recession of 1920-21, served to place these agents in a position of advantage, in relation to raw material producers, in the ensuing years. The movement toward lower real costs set in again, after 1921, but from the evidence presented above there emerges the rather remarkable fact that the composite of amounts going to overhead, management and ownership failed to decline from the high level reached in 1923. Minor reductions in 1925 and 1927 were offset by a renewed advance in 1929 to a level more than ten per cent higher, per unit of product, than in the preceding peak year, 1923.[1]

---

salaries declined, as a fractional part of overhead costs plus profits, except during the minor depression of 1927.

If taxes be excluded from overhead costs plus profits, the index numbers in column (4) of Table 158 will be altered. A corrected index, expressed in current dollars, follows.

| Year | Overhead costs plus profits, per unit of product, manufacturing industries (excluding all taxes) |
|---|---|
| 1923 | 100 |
| 1925 | 99 |
| 1927 | 94 |
| 1929 | 107 |

The correction modifies the original index numbers only slightly.

[1] The fact that the costs of 'mill and shop supplies', which were, in general, classified among material costs in census compilations prior to 1929, are included among 'overhead costs plus profits' in the returns for 1929 would account for a slight advance in this item between 1927 and 1929. (See footnote, p. 385.) But the weight of this item among all overhead costs plus profits is small, in manufacturing industries at large.

To the extent that distributive costs enter into the manufacturer's 'value of product' a somewhat uncertain element is introduced into 'overhead costs plus profits'

These changes, with reference to a 1914 base, are graphically portrayed in Figure 79.

The figures we have cited point to one of the most curious features of the post-war situation. It is the accepted view that the position of the manufacturer is most happy when prices are rising.

### FIGURE 79
#### CHANGES IN AVERAGE FABRICATION COSTS, LABOR COSTS AND OVERHEAD COSTS PLUS PROFITS
MANUFACTURING INDUSTRIES OF THE UNITED STATES, 1914-1929
(PERCENTAGE DEVIATIONS FROM 1914 PARITY, IN DOLLARS OF CONSTANT PURCHASING POWER)

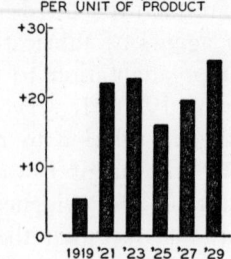

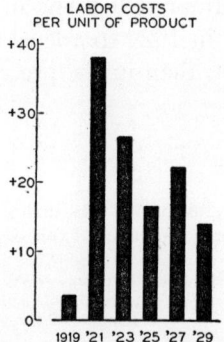
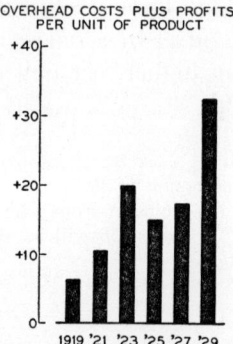

His labor costs and overhead costs, it has been assumed, rise less rapidly than his selling prices. Raw materials, traditionally sensitive to changes in the value of money, might rise more rapidly, but

---

for recent years. Certain tendencies have worked toward lower merchandising costs, but in the case of luxury goods such costs have remained high, and have perhaps risen. For goods of this class (as well as for certain trade-marked non-luxuries) advertising and selling costs constitute a large proportion of the final value of product, and such costs have not reflected the gain in efficiency registered in manufacturing operations.

the gains resulting from lagging labor and overhead costs might be expected to outweigh the advance in material prices. Per unit of product, this situation is assumed to swell the margin between manufacturing costs and selling prices.

So far as we may judge from the present figures this margin was expanded between 1923 and 1929, but this occurred under conditions of falling general prices rather than with advancing prices. Increasing output and rapidly increasing productivity brought substantial declines in labor costs per unit of product, even with high and rising wages. Conditions in world markets for raw materials favored the buyer, and gave the manufacturer the benefit of relatively low prices for such materials. In this situation labor costs, per unit of manufactured goods, and material costs, per unit, declined more rapidly than selling prices. The gap in our information has to do with the course of overhead costs. During this period capital investments in manufacturing plant and equipment were increasing at a fairly rapid rate. These investments, we have seen, were made at relatively high prices. It is thus not impossible that overhead costs per unit of product were advancing toward the close of this period, despite a swelling volume of manufacturing production. But if such advance occurred there is no evidence that it offset other gains sufficiently to curtail profits per unit of product. In most manufacturing industries falling general prices between 1923 and 1929 brought to the producer the gains he has been supposed to reap under conditions of advancing prices and brought, in addition, declining raw material prices. These fortunate conditions combined to maintain, and in many industries to swell, profit margins. During this period we appear to have had in the majority of manufacturing industries the curious and perhaps unprecedented condition of falling general prices and falling prices of manufactured goods, combined with an expanding margin between costs and selling prices of manufactured goods, and with manufacturing profits which increased not only in the aggregate, but per unit of product as well.

## A Comparison of Sales and Profits, Manufacturing Corporations

It is regrettable that census statistics of manufacturing industries do not permit a separation of profits from overhead costs proper. Relevant supplementary information is furnished by recent compilations of the Department of Commerce.[1] The following data relate to 2,046 large manufacturing corporations, the aggregate net profits of which constituted approximately 60 per cent of the total net profits of all manufacturing corporations.

TABLE 159

SALES AND PROFITS, 2,046 MANUFACTURING CORPORATIONS, 1922-1929

(In millions of dollars)

| Year | Sales | Profits [a] |
|---|---|---|
| 1922 | 18,103 | 1,784 |
| 1923 | 22,538 | 2,210 |
| 1924 | 22,850 | 2,023 |
| 1925 | 25,736 | 2,564 |
| 1926 | 27,309 | 2,759 |
| 1927 | 27,057 | 2,252 |
| 1928 | 28,219 | 2,736 |
| 1929 * | —— | 3,395 |

\* The entry for 1929 is estimated from data relating to 71 manufacturing corporations. The records for the 71 corporations are sufficiently close to those for the larger sample to justify the making of estimates for the larger group for 1929.

[a] Net profit is defined by R. C. Epstein as "taxable net income, plus non-taxable items where present (i.e., dividends from other corporations and tax-exempt interest), after all charges but, unless otherwise stated, before Federal taxes."

Our immediate interest is in profits in relation to physical output. Here, again, we are thrown upon methods of approximation. From the data on dollar value of sales we may derive an index of physical volume, correcting the sales record by an index of prices of manufactured goods. Data and results appear in the following table. Certain of these series are shown graphically in Figure 80.

These estimates indicate that the physical volume of sales of the manufacturing establishments here represented increased at the notable rate of 7.3 per cent a year between 1922 and 1929.[2] Profits kept pace with this rapidly expanding volume of production, and, in fact, advanced at a fractionally higher rate. This means that profit per unit of product, as shown in the last column, showed a slight net advance [3] during this era of economic expansion. The

[1] *A Source-Book for the Study of Industrial Profits,* R. C. Epstein and F. M. Clark, U. S. Department of Commerce, 1932.

[2] This is a higher rate than that at which manufacturing production in general increased. The difference is probably due to the fact that the present sample of 2,046 manufacturing concerns is heavily weighted by large concerns.

[3] The computed rate of change is fractionally above zero, though the figure, as rounded off in Table 160, is 0.0.

## TABLE 160

### Index Numbers of Sales, Prices, Profits and Output, 1922-1929
### 2,046 Manufacturing Corporations

| (1) Year | (2) Sales (dollar value) | (3) Prices ᵃ (wholesale) | (4) Estimated physical volume of sales | (5) Profits | (6) Estimated profit per unit of product sold |
|---|---|---|---|---|---|
| 1922 | 100.0 | 100.0 | 100.0 | 100.0 | 100.0 |
| 1923 | 124.5 | 105.7 | 117.8 | 123.9 | 105.2 |
| 1924 | 126.2 | 101.5 | 124.3 | 113.4 | 91.2 |
| 1925 | 142.2 | 104.7 | 135.8 | 143.7 | 105.8 |
| 1926 | 150.9 | 103.2 | 146.2 | 154.7 | 105.8 |
| 1927 | 149.5 | 97.7 | 153.0 | 126.2 | 82.5 |
| 1928 | 155.9 | 98.2 | 158.8 | 153.4 | 96.6 |
| 1929 | 167.7 * | 96.9 | 173.1 | 190.3 | 109.9 |
| Average annual rate of change (per cent) | +6.3 | —0.8 | +7.3 | +7.4 | 0.0 |

\* Estimated from gross sales, all manufacturing corporations, as reported to the Bureau of Internal Revenue.

ᵃ Simple average of an index of prices of manufactured goods based upon value of product per unit, as derived from the Census of Manufactures, and a combination of the Bureau of Labor Statistics indexes of wholesale prices of semi-manufactured and finished products, weighted one and six, respectively. This index, which differs slightly from that cited in the preceding chapter, is the most appropriate available deflator.

average rate of growth is small because of the declines of 1927 and 1928, but if we compare terminal years alone we note that the period ends in 1929 with profits per unit of product higher by 10 per cent than in 1922, while the physical volume of sales was greater by 73 per cent. There is here no evidence that, among the manufacturing industries represented, an increasing volume of output was accompanied by reductions in profits per unit of product and corresponding declines in selling price.[1]

---

[1] Since the detailed compilations in *A Source-Book for the Study of Industrial Profits* extend only through 1928, it has been necessary to estimate 1929 sales and profits for the 2,046 manufacturing corporations included in the Department of Commerce sample. The corporations in this sample are large ones, and therefore Epstein has based his estimate of 1929 profits upon returns for 71 large corporations, rather than upon all corporate returns. (Previous records of the 71 corporations resembled those of the larger sample of 2,046.) It is this estimate which has been used in the tables and text, above.

A series of measurements on profits per unit of product sold may be derived from the returns to the Bureau of Internal Revenue on the profits and gross sales

## FIGURE 80
### CHANGES IN ESTIMATED PHYSICAL VOLUME OF SALES, IN AGGREGATE PROFITS AND IN PROFIT PER UNIT OF PRODUCT

MANUFACTURING INDUSTRIES OF THE UNITED STATES, 1922-1929

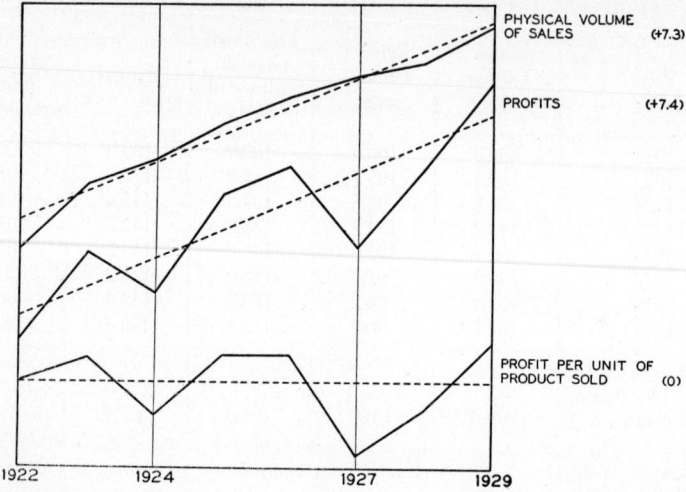

Plotted on ratio scale. The figures in parentheses define average annual rates of change (in percentage form).

These figures may not be the most significant we may secure. The compilations of the Department of Commerce indicate that corporations in certain industrial classes suffered declining profits of all manufacturing corporations, the dollar value of sales being deflated, as in Table 160. Data on profits and sales are, presumably, comparable, though the number of reporting corporations varies from year to year. These measurements follow.

| Year | Index of estimated net profit, per unit of goods sold, manufacturing corporations |
|---|---|
| 1922 | 100 |
| 1923 | 112 |
| 1924 | 89 |
| 1925 | 110 |
| 1926 | 106 |
| 1927 | 83 |
| 1928 | 100 |
| 1929 | 104 |

The year-to-year variations in profits per unit of goods sold are pronounced, for this group. The 1929 figure is four per cent greater than that for 1922, but, as a result of high values in 1923 and 1925, the general trend declines slightly over the eight-year period. The average annual rate of decline of the series is 0.6 per cent. It should be noted that, for this group, net profits are equivalent to taxable net income. Epstein's definition is a broader one.

during this period. These corporations, a distinct minority of the total studied, depress the aggregate somewhat. If we eliminate this group, including 815 corporations and representing 28 industries,[1] we have left a sample representing 45 industries. These industries did approximately 85 per cent of the total business of manufacturing corporations (by sales) in 1928, and contained approximately 83 per cent of the invested capital. For this group the record for the years 1922 to 1929 is a most prosperous one. Relevant data and derived measurements appear in the next table. The data are plotted in Figure 81.

TABLE 161
SALES, PRICES, PROFITS AND OUTPUT, 1922-1929
1,231 Corporations in 45 Manufacturing Industries of the United States

| (1) | (2) | (3) | (4) | (5) | (6) | (7) | (8) |
|---|---|---|---|---|---|---|---|
| Year | Sales (dollar value) | | Prices (wholesale) | Estimated physical volume of sales | Profits | | Estimated profit per unit of product sold |
| | In millions of dollars | In relatives | In relatives | In relatives | In millions of dollars | In relatives | In relatives |
| 1922 | 14,763 | 100.0 | 100.0 | 100.0 | 1,359 | 100.0 | 100.0 |
| 1923 | 18,288 | 123.9 | 105.7 | 117.2 | 1,653 | 121.6 | 103.8 |
| 1924 | 18,957 | 128.4 | 101.5 | 126.5 | 1,607 | 118.2 | 93.4 |
| 1925 | 21,646 | 146.6 | 104.7 | 140.0 | 2,144 | 157.8 | 112.7 |
| 1926 | 23,085 | 156.4 | 103.2 | 151.6 | 2,335 | 171.8 | 113.3 |
| 1927 | 23,012 | 155.9 | 97.7 | 159.6 | 1,891 | 139.1 | 87.2 |
| 1928 | 24,080 | 163.1 | 98.2 | 166.1 | 2,377 | 174.9 | 105.3 |
| 1929 | —— | 175.5* | 96.9 | 181.1 | 2,965** | 218.2** | 120.5 |
| Average annual rate of change (per cent) .. | | +7.0 | —0.8 | +8.1 | | +9.8 | +1.5 |

* Estimated from data relating to all manufacturing corporations.
** Estimated on the basis of returns for 71 corporations.

[1] The 28 industries in which profit rates showed definitely declining trends are the following: dairy products, canned foods, cotton converting, weaving woolens, silk weaving, carpets, knit goods, miscellaneous textiles, lumber manufacturing, planing mills, millwork, furniture (non-metal), miscellaneous lumber, blank paper, miscellaneous paper, book and music publishing, paints, toilet preparations, ceramics, glass, Portland cement, heating machinery, textile machinery, engines, railroad equipment, hardware, pianos, miscellaneous special manufacturing industries.

## FIGURE 81

### CHANGES IN ESTIMATED PHYSICAL VOLUME OF SALES, IN AGGREGATE PROFITS AND IN PROFIT PER UNIT OF PRODUCT

#### FORTY-FIVE SELECTED MANUFACTURING INDUSTRIES, 1922-1929

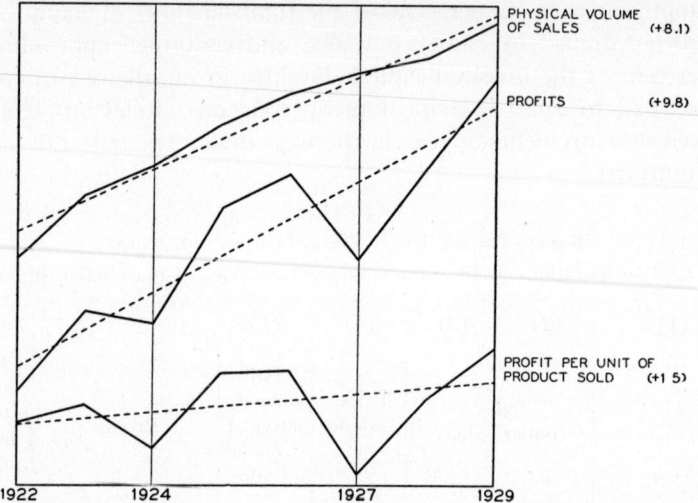

Plotted on ratio scale. The figures in parentheses define average annual rates of change (in percentage form).

For this group of corporations in the more profitable industries, profits per unit of product advanced about 13 per cent between 1922 and 1926, with one check in 1924. The recession of 1927 brought a considerable decline, but during the next two years a rapid advance carried the index to the high point for the period, more than 20 per cent above the 1922 base. (The figure for 1929 is an estimate based upon records of sales for all manufacturing industries and upon profits in a sample group of 71 corporations.) The rate of advance in profits per unit of product between 1922 and 1929 averaged 1.5 per cent a year.[1]

That the years between the two great post-war depressions were prosperous ones for manufacturing corporations requires no demonstration. Of immediate significance is the fact that profits,

[1] Net profits, as they enter into the above calculations, include dividends received from other corporations. In measuring changes in profits per unit of product, manufacturing profits proper are of chief concern. On the basis of data available in the *Source-Book* we may make a correction for dividends received by manufacturing corporations from other domestic corporations. Corrections for the 45 industries entering into the above calculations appear below. The last figure

per unit of product, showed no decline between 1922 and 1929 among the industries here represented. The rate of change per annum was fractionally above zero for the entire group, and + 1.5 per cent for corporations from the 45 industries in which profit rates advanced, or were maintained, during this period. A check to this advance occurred in 1924, a still more serious check in 1927,[1] but the upward push over-rode these, and in 1929 profits per unit of product were apparently at a higher level than in 1922 and indeed, for many corporations, were higher than at any time during the years included in our study.

A variable volume of business played a part, of course, in these fluctuations in profits. Modern industry, with its large capital investment and heavy overhead charges, is to a great extent dependent for profits upon a full volume of production. An increase in output reduces the overhead cost borne by each unit of goods produced. But that profits per unit of goods sold should have advanced, for this group of corporations, in the face of the strong competition which is assumed to have prevailed during this period, remains a curious fact. The explanation may lie in the expansion of consumer credit at a rate which permitted sales to continue without the full price reduction which might otherwise have accompanied declining

---

in column (2) is estimated from Treasury statistics for all manufacturing corporations.

| (1) Year | (2) Amounts received as dividends (millions of dollars) | (3) Net profits less dividends received (millions of dollars) | (4) Net profits less dividends (relative numbers) | (5) Net profits less dividends, per unit of product (relative numbers) |
|---|---|---|---|---|
| 1922 | 154 | 1,205 | 100.0 | 100.0 |
| 1923 | 154 | 1,499 | 124.4 | 106.1 |
| 1924 | 145 | 1,462 | 121.3 | 95.9 |
| 1925 | 234 | 1,910 | 158.5 | 113.2 |
| 1926 | 288 | 2,047 | 169.9 | 112.1 |
| 1927 | 248 | 1,643 | 136.3 | 85.4 |
| 1928 | 330 | 2,047 | 169.9 | 102.3 |
| 1929 | 446 | 2,519 | 209.0 | 115.4 |

During this period surplus funds were invested in the stock of other corporations in increasing degree, and dividends constitute an increasing percentage of total net profits. The entries in the last column indicate, however, that manufacturing profits proper increased more rapidly than volume of output, over the period as a whole. Rather sharp recessions appear in 1924 and in 1927, but the rate of change averaged +0.6 per cent per year, for the period.

[1] It is a significant fact that aggregate profits and profits per unit of product declined far more sharply in 1927 than in 1924, though the business recession of 1927 was distinctly less severe than that of 1924. It is possible that by 1926-27 the basis of profits was less sound than in 1923-24, and that a slighter check to expansion had more serious effects.

material costs and falling labor costs. Again, the swelling of purchasing power through the reaping of non-recurrent, but considerable, speculative profits may have been a factor in the maintenance of prices and the growth of profits. But be the reason what it may, the fact is clear that in a large percentage of manufacturing industries profit margins expanded during the general price decline of the nineteen-twenties. An ultimate explanation of the economic collapse which was precipitated in 1929 must give full weight to this striking fact.

§ *Labor costs and other fabrication costs, individual industries.*—Supplementing the general averages given in Table 158, we have the following record of changes in labor costs, per unit of product, in each of 62 manufacturing industries. The divergent movements of these index numbers, which are expressed in terms of current dollars, are illustrated in Figure 82.

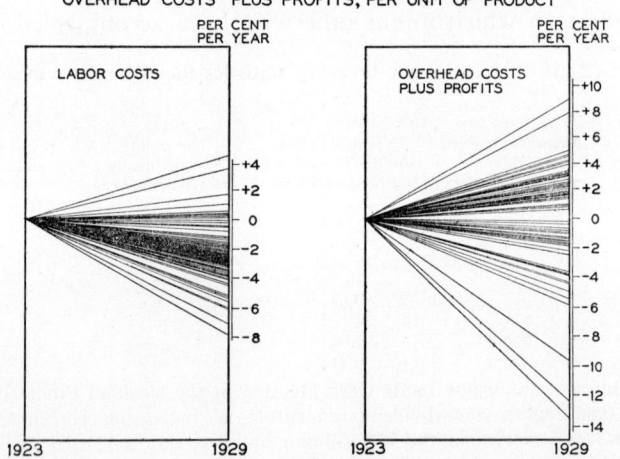

FIGURE 82

ILLUSTRATING THE DIVERGENCE OF COST TRENDS AMONG 60 MANUFACTURING INDUSTRIES OF THE UNITED STATES, 1923-1929

AVERAGE RATES OF CHANGE IN LABOR COSTS AND IN OVERHEAD COSTS PLUS PROFITS, PER UNIT OF PRODUCT*

* Plotted on ratio scale. The lines here plotted relate to the industries listed in Tables 162 and 163, in the order of those listings. The last two entries are omitted.

The general sweep of the tendency toward lower labor costs in manufacturing industries is attested by the fact that in 1929 only six industries out of 60 showed higher labor costs, per unit of product, than in 1923. Increasing volume of production, more efficient equipment, enhanced skill and improvements in organization undoubtedly

## TABLE 162

CHANGES IN LABOR COSTS, MANUFACTURING INDUSTRIES OF THE UNITED STATES, 1923-1929

Index Numbers for 62 Industries, with Average Annual Rates of Change

| Industry | Index numbers of labor costs, per unit of product | | | | Average annual rate of change 1923-1929 (per cent) |
|---|---|---|---|---|---|
| | 1923 | 1925 | 1927 | 1929 | |
| Musical instruments: organs.............. | 100.0 | 127.8 | 128.0 | 136.9 | +4.6 |
| Knit goods ............................ | 100.0 | 106.0 | 117.2 | 122.5 | +3.6 |
| Cars, steam and electric railroad, not built in railroad repair shops................. | 100.0 | 95.9 | 107.4 | 107.5 | +1.7 |
| Linoleum ............................. | 100.0 | 87.7 | 104.7 | 100.6 | +1.0 |
| Motorcycles, bicycles, and parts.......... | 100.0 | 93.1 | 100.8 | 101.0 | +0.5 |
| Lace goods, cotton...................... | 100.0 | 108.6 | 106.1 | 102.2 | +0.2 |
| Rice cleaning and polishing.............. | 100.0 | 98.4 | 105.5 | 98.8 | +0.2 |
| Wood distillation and charcoal manufacture | 100.0 | 91.2 | 94.3 | 100.0 | +0.2 |
| Oil, cake, and meal, cottonseed........... | 100.0 | 93.4 | 103.6 | 97.1 | +0.1 |
| Musical instruments: pianos.............. | 100.0 | 96.9 | 105.4 | 96.4 | —0.1 |
| Paints and varnishes.................... | 100.0 | 103.0 | 104.9 | 98.3 | —0.2 |
| Slaughtering and meat packing, wholesale. | 100.0 | 100.4 | 98.9 | 97.3 | —0.5 |
| Hats, fur-felt ......................... | 100.0 | 102.1 | 92.9 | 99.9 | —0.5 |
| Firearms .............................. | 100.0 | 80.7 | 86.6 | 93.2 | —0.8 |
| Worsted goods ........................ | 100.0 | 94.6 | 92.0 | 92.9 | —1.3 |
| Bone black, carbon black, and lampblack... | 100.0 | 81.4 | 100.9 | 85.6 | —1.3 |
| Buttons ............................... | 100.0 | 101.6 | 102.1 | 90.6 | —1.4 |
| Motor vehicles, including bodies and parts. | 100.0 | 104.8 | 102.9 | 90.2 | —1.6 |
| Corn syrup, corn oil, and starch.......... | 100.0 | 99.9 | 92.5 | 91.9 | —1.6 |
| Ice, manufactured ..................... | 100.0 | 88.0 | 81.4 | 91.3 | —1.8 |
| Oil, cake, and meal, linseed.............. | 100.0 | 94.0 | 100.0 | 85.4 | —2.0 |
| Woolen goods ......................... | 100.0 | 96.3 | 92.7 | 88.2 | —2.0 |
| Explosives ............................ | 100.0 | 86.7 | 88.1 | 86.7 | —2.1 |
| Clay products (other than pottery) and non-clay refractories .................. | 100.0 | 96.1 | 92.0 | 87.5 | —2.2 |
| Flour and other grain-mill products....... | 100.0 | 99.9 | 93.2 | 87.9 | —2.2 |
| Lumber and timber products............. | 100.0 | 88.8 | 86.5 | 87.1 | —2.2 |
| Iron and steel: steel works and rolling mills | 100.0 | 95.7 | 93.1 | 86.5 | —2.3 |
| Turpentine and rosin.................... | 100.0 | 89.8 | 89.3 | 85.8 | —2.3 |
| Wool shoddy .......................... | 100.0 | 94.1 | 107.3 | 80.0 | —2.4 |
| Hats, wool-felt ........................ | 100.0 | 97.7 | 94.2 | 85.7 | —2.4 |
| Carpets and rugs, wool, other than rag.... | 100.0 | 95.0 | 100.4 | 82.4 | —2.5 |
| Butter and cheese...................... | 100.0 | 82.7 | 90.3 | 82.3 | —2.5 |
| Sand-lime brick ....................... | 100.0 | 105.9 | 98.7 | 85.3 | —2.6 |
| Asphalted-felt-base floor coverings........ | 100.0 | 115.4 | 90.6 | 90.2 | —2.7 |
| Cast-iron pipe ......................... | 100.0 | 91.2 | 85.0 | 85.2 | —2.8 |

TABLE 162—*Continued*

| Industry | Index numbers of labor costs, per unit of product | | | | Average annual rate of change 1923-1929 (per cent) |
|---|---|---|---|---|---|
| | 1923 | 1925 | 1927 | 1929 | |
| Fertilizers .............................. | 100.0 | 95.2 | 92.0 | 83.6 | —2.8 |
| Gas, manufactured, illuminating and heating | 100.0 | 110.6 | 97.2 | 85.1 | —2.9 |
| Chocolate and cocoa products............. | 100.0 | 94.5 | 83.5 | 85.5 | —3.0 |
| Cordage and twine....................... | 100.0 | 92.0 | 90.9 | 81.9 | —3.0 |
| Jute and linen goods..................... | 100.0 | 96.1 | 91.9 | 81.5 | —3.2 |
| Rubber products ........................ | 100.0 | 88.5 | 86.0 | 81.2 | —3.3 |
| Lime ................................... | 100.0 | 94.8 | 91.1 | 79.7 | —3.5 |
| Canning and preserving: fruits and vegetables; pickles, jellies, preserves, and sauces | 100.0 | 95.9 | 87.2 | 80.8 | —3.6 |
| Soap ................................... | 100.0 | 89.2 | 90.3 | 77.9 | —3.6 |
| Silk manufactures ....................... | 100.0 | 94.5 | 87.9 | 79.7 | —3.7 |
| Sugar, cane, not including products of refineries .............................. | 100.0 | 104.1 | 88.5 | 80.8 | —3.9 |
| Paper and pulp.......................... | 100.0 | 92.8 | 83.6 | 79.8 | —3.9 |
| Cotton goods ........................... | 100.0 | 90.9 | 87.5 | 77.7 | —3.9 |
| Cement ................................. | 100.0 | 91.3 | 84.2 | 78.0 | —4.1 |
| Sugar refining, cane..................... | 100.0 | 77.4 | 76.4 | 77.3 | —4.1 |
| Canning and preserving: fish, crabs, shrimps, oysters, and clams ............. | 100.0 | 89.1 | 93.3 | 72.3 | —4.4 |
| Tanning materials, natural dyestuffs, mordants and assistants, and sizes........... | 100.0 | 82.6 | 79.9 | 75.1 | —4.5 |
| Oilcloth ................................ | 100.0 | 87.4 | 76.1 | 74.1 | —5.2 |
| Carriages, wagons, sleighs, and sleds...... | 100.0 | 97.4 | 86.1 | 71.9 | —5.3 |
| Petroleum refining ...................... | 100.0 | 77.7 | 76.3 | 71.3 | —5.3 |
| Iron and steel: blast furnaces............. | 100.0 | 84.2 | 82.7 | 68.4 | —5.6 |
| Sugar, beet ............................. | 100.0 | 82.7 | 79.5 | 67.5 | —6.0 |
| Salt .................................... | 100.0 | 89.2 | 81.4 | 67.2 | —6.1 |
| Condensed and evaporated milk........... | 100.0 | 80.0 | 75.1 | 62.9 | —7.1 |
| Coke, not including gas-house coke........ | 100.0 | 84.6 | 76.9 | 58.7 | —7.9 |
| Felt goods, wool or hair.................. | 100.0 | 94.4 | 104.1 | — | — |
| Wire, drawn from purchased bars or rods. | 100.0 | 96.7 | 97.6 | — | — |
| Average [a] .............................. | 100.0 | 95.4 | 92.5 | 86.6 | —2.3 |

[a] Arithmetic average of the central items of a weighted frequency distribution, with weights based on aggregate wages paid, averaged for the base year and the given year. The central one-fifth of the items, by weight, were included in computing the average.

contributed to this reduction of labor costs. But these factors operated, it must be recalled, under the conditions of very high labor costs which were left by the recession and depression of 1920-21. There was room for a reduction of labor costs.

More varied than the changes in labor costs were the movements of overhead costs plus profits among manufacturing industries between 1923 and 1929. The rates of change of these index numbers are plotted in Figure 82.

TABLE 163

CHANGES IN OVERHEAD COSTS PLUS PROFITS, MANUFACTURING INDUSTRIES OF THE UNITED STATES, 1923-1929

Index Numbers for 62 Industries, with Average Annual Rates of Change

| Industry | Index numbers of overhead costs plus profits, per unit of product | | | | Average annual rate of change 1923-1929 (per cent) |
|---|---|---|---|---|---|
| | 1923 | 1925 | 1927 | 1929 | |
| Sugar cane, refining.................... | 100.0 | 127.2 | 100.1 | 181.6 | +9.0 |
| Cars, steam and electric railroad, not built in railroad repair shops................ | 100.0 | 123.8 | 159.1 | 156.5 | +7.9 |
| Rice cleaning and polishing............. | 100.0 | 147.9 | 104.9 | 154.4 | +4.9 |
| Oil, cake, and meal, linseed............. | 100.0 | 179.1 | 123.8 | 161.0 | +4.6 |
| Corn syrup, corn oil, and starch.......... | 100.0 | 89.4 | 80.3 | 133.0 | +4.6 |
| Iron and steel: steel works and rolling mills $^a$ ............................... | 100.0 | 109.2 | 102.3 | 132.2 | +4.1 |
| Flour and other grain-mill products....... | 100.0 | 115.4 | 118.6 | 129.6 | +4.1 |
| Motorcycles, bicycles, and parts.......... | 100.0 | 135.4 | 138.6 | 131.3 | +3.9 |
| Knit goods ............................ | 100.0 | 101.1 | 109.4 | 121.4 | +3.4 |
| Motor vehicles, including bodies and parts. | 100.0 | 124.7 | 117.8 | 128.0 | +3.3 |
| Soap ................................. | 100.0 | 91.3 | 110.3 | 116.4 | +3.3 |
| Sand-lime brick ....................... | 100.0 | 121.3 | 120.7 | 124.1 | +3.1 |
| Hats, fur-felt ......................... | 100.0 | 108.6 | 114.7 | 120.4 | +3.1 |
| Condensed and evaporated milk.......... | 100.0 | 95.8 | 112.3 | 115.4 | +3.0 |
| Buttons .............................. | 100.0 | 115.7 | 123.5 | 117.8 | +2.7 |
| Explosives ............................ | 100.0 | 93.0 | 102.6 | 112.2 | +2.3 |
| Ice, manufactured ..................... | 100.0 | 113.7 | 117.4 | 115.5 | +2.3 |
| Musical instruments: organs............. | 100.0 | 112.1 | 124.1 | 112.4 | +2.2 |
| Butter and cheese...................... | 100.0 | 78.8 | 97.2 | 107.9 | +2.2 |
| Tanning materials, natural dyestuffs, mordants and assistants, and sizes.......... | 100.0 | 116.7 | 121.0 | 114.6 | +2.2 |
| Oil, cake, and meal, cottonseed........... | 100.0 | 123.3 | 115.2 | 118.1 | +2.0 |
| Slaughtering and meat packing, wholesale. | 100.0 | 115.9 | 98.2 | 119.6 | +1.9 |
| Linoleum ............................. | 100.0 | 126.9 | 95.6 | 123.7 | +1.8 |
| Salt .................................. | 100.0 | 107.3 | 95.4 | 116.2 | +1.8 |
| Paper and pulp........................ | 100.0 | 99.2 | 108.1 | 108.7 | +1.7 |
| Sugar, cane, not including products of refineries ............................. | 100.0 | 12.4 | 82.0 | 84.5 | +1.7 |
| Gas, manufactured, illuminating and heating | 100.0 | 102.8 | 100.6 | 111.5 | +1.6 |
| Carpets and rugs, wool, other than rag..... | 100.0 | 79.8 | 85.1 | 107.6 | +1.5 |

$a$ See footnote, pp. 385-6.

## TABLE 163—Continued

| Industry | Index numbers of overhead costs plus profits, per unit of product | | | | Average annual rate of change 1923-1929 (per cent) |
|---|---|---|---|---|---|
| | 1923 | 1925 | 1927 | 1929 | |
| Paints and varnishes | 100.0 | 98.0 | 106.4 | 106.7 | +1.4 |
| Cast-iron pipe | 100.0 | 108.7 | 90.7 | 112.3 | +0.9 |
| Oilcloth | 100.0 | 64.5 | 83.9 | 98.5 | +0.9 |
| Cordage and twine | 100.0 | 99.9 | 100.1 | 105.2 | +0.8 |
| Wood distillation and charcoal manufacture | 100.0 | 58.3 | 79.3 | 96.1 | +0.6 |
| Chocolate and cocoa products | 100.0 | 85.2 | 81.4 | 100.2 | —0.2 |
| Clay products (other than pottery) and non-clay refractories | 100.0 | 93.8 | 86.1 | 99.9 | —0.4 |
| Fertilizers | 100.0 | 116.1 | 76.2 | 108.3 | —0.7 |
| Firearms | 100.0 | 109.6 | 83.4 | 103.3 | —0.8 |
| Carriages, wagons, sleighs, and sleds | 100.0 | 105.1 | 92.8 | 97.7 | —1.0 |
| Woolen goods | 100.0 | 80.4 | 84.0 | 92.9 | —1.0 |
| Wool shoddy | 100.0 | 85.1 | 101.8 | 86.1 | —1.3 |
| Lumber and timber products | 100.0 | 80.0 | 68.7 | 95.5 | —1.4 |
| Petroleum refining | 100.0 | 111.4 | 72.6 | 101.8 | —1.7 |
| Lace goods, cotton | 100.0 | 86.9 | 71.9 | 94.9 | —1.7 |
| Iron and steel: blast furnaces | 100.0 | 92.8 | 77.4 | 94.6 | —1.7 |
| Canning and preserving: fruits and vegetables; pickles, jellies, preserves, and sauces | 100.0 | 83.3 | 77.8 | 90.9 | —1.8 |
| Rubber products | 100.0 | 106.5 | 105.3 | 87.8 | —1.9 |
| Worsted goods | 100.0 | 72.3 | 74.3 | 86.8 | —2.2 |
| Jute and linen goods | 100.0 | 101.8 | 96.1 | 85.5 | —2.5 |
| Cotton goods | 100.0 | 80.9 | 80.3 | 78.9 | —3.7 |
| Cement | 100.0 | 98.4 | 83.5 | 81.6 | —3.8 |
| Silk manufactures | 100.0 | 98.4 | 84.4 | 80.6 | —3.9 |
| Turpentine and rosin | 100.0 | 130.0 | 81.6 | 89.5 | —3.9 |
| Hats, wool-felt | 100.0 | 83.2 | 87.7 | 73.0 | —4.4 |
| Musical instruments: pianos | 100.0 | 95.7 | 91.1 | 74.7 | —4.4 |
| Lime | 100.0 | 109.0 | 87.4 | 75.6 | —5.0 |
| Canning and preserving: fish, crabs, shrimps, oysters, and clams | 100.0 | 83.4 | 75.0 | 71.6 | —5.5 |
| Coke, not including gas-house coke | 100.0 | 61.9 | 57.7 | 71.8 | —5.9 |
| Asphalted-felt-base floor coverings | 100.0 | 78.0 | 55.1 | 58.5 | —9.7 |
| Bone black, carbon black, and lampblack | 100.0 | 63.3 | 51.8 | 47.1 | —12.4 |
| Sugar, beet | 100.0 | 61.4 | 35.8 | 50.2 | —13.5 |
| Felt goods, wool or hair | 100.0 | 93.6 | 107.9 | — | — |
| Wire, drawn from purchased bars or rods | 100.0 | 99.6 | 96.9 | — | — |
| Average [b] | 100.0 | 100.9 | 99.6 | 110.1 | +1.4 |

[b] Arithmetic average of the central items of a weighted frequency distribution, with weights based on overhead costs plus profits, averaged for the base year and the given year. The central one-fifth of the items, by weight, were included in computing the average.

These measurements reveal in an illuminating fashion how diverse were the fortunes affecting manufacturing industries during the prosperity of the last decade. This diversity, while slightly less than that found for material costs per unit, exceeds the variation found among other elements of manufacturing costs. It is notable, too, that the divergence among index numbers of overhead costs plus profits was substantially greater between 1923 and 1929 than between 1899 and 1914. (The standard deviation of rates of changes in these indexes was 3.4 for the recent period, as against a figure of 2.4 for the pre-war period.) In considerable part, of course, the variations among industries are due to the influence of fluctuations in profits, an important element of this composite.[1] But whatever the changes among the separate elements of these costs, the evidence clearly indicates that the six years preceding the recession of 1929 made up a period of discordant and altogether uneven changes among manufacturing industries. The stability of economic conditions revealed by certain other data is not attested by this set of records.

## On the Relative Importance of Different Elements of Cost as Factors in Price Changes, 1923-1929

The preceding account has dealt with changes in three major elements of the selling price of manufactured goods—material costs, labor costs and overhead costs (including profits). Considering now only the terminal years of the period studied, we have noted the following changes in prices and costs, per unit of manufactured product. The index numbers relate to current dollars.

| Year | Selling price | Cost of materials | Labor costs | Overhead costs plus profits |
|---|---|---|---|---|
| 1923 | 100.0 | 100.0 | 100.0 | 100.0 |
| 1929 | 90.8 | 87.9 | 85.7 | 104.8 |

The three cost elements are of unequal importance, as is shown in the following summary:

| Year | Elements of cost as decimal fractions of value of product | | |
|---|---|---|---|
| | Materials | Labor | Overhead costs plus profits |
| 1923 | .663 | .148 | .189 |

---

[1] The change in census practice which placed the cost of mill and shop supplies among overhead charges in 1929, instead of with material costs, as in earlier enumerations, plays some part in the movements noted. The change is believed to have had but slight effect, except in certain industries. See footnote pp. 385-6.

These two sets of data permit us to determine the relative importance of changes in the different elements of cost, as factors in changing selling prices.[1] (In expressing the results it is convenient to speak of the changes in costs, including profits, as though they determined selling price changes. This, of course, is not necessarily true. In many cases elements of cost reflect changes that have their origin in the final market for the product.)

In summary, the results take the following form:

72.7 per cent of the gross change in the per-unit selling price of manufactured goods between 1923 and 1929 is attributable to falling material costs.
19.1 per cent of the gross change is attributable to falling labor costs.
8.2 per cent of the gross change is attributable to rising overhead costs (including profits).

In the present instance changes in two of the cost factors tended toward lower selling prices, while the change in the third factor tended toward higher prices. The net influence was markedly down-

---

[1] The decline of 9.2 per cent in selling price is the net result of a decline of 12.11 per cent in material costs, a decline of 14.25 per cent in labor costs, and an advance of 4.76 per cent in overhead costs plus profits. The base of the percentage figures which define the degree of influence of the several cost elements upon selling price is, of necessity, the numerical sum of the changes in the several elements (each factor properly weighted), this sum being taken without regard to sign. It is the *algebraic sum* of these changes which defines the actual movement of the price of the product, or the *net change*. The numerical sum measures the aggregate price-affecting changes among the several elements of cost, without reference to possible offsetting when the changes are in opposite directions. It is this aggregate, here called the *gross change,* which is significant for the present purpose, and it is to this aggregate that the percentages and ratios relate.

The detailed computations, upon which the measurements in the text are based, are given below.

Computation of influence of cost factors upon price change per unit of product, 1923-1929

| Element of cost | Degree of change in cost (per cent) | | Weight | | Contribution to change in selling price | Percentage distribution of elements of gross change in selling price |
|---|---|---|---|---|---|---|
| Materials | − 12.11 | × | .663 | = | − 8.03 | 72.7 |
| Labor | − 14.25 | × | .148 | = | − 2.11 | 19.1 |
| Overhead costs plus profits | + 4.76 | × | .189 | = | + .90 | 8.2 |
| Gross change (sum of items disregarding signs) | | | | | 11.04 | 100.0 |
| Net change (algebraic sum) | | | | | −9.24 | |

ward, with the influence of reduced material costs and labor costs far outweighing the advance in the third factor.

It is to be noted that materials, which in the aggregate constitute about 66 per cent of the total value of manufactured goods, accounted for almost 73 per cent of the gross change in price between 1923 and 1929, while labor costs, which make up 15 per cent of the aggregate value, accounted for slightly more than 19 per cent of the gross change. Changes in these two elements exerted exceptional influence upon selling price changes during this period, while changes in overhead costs plus profits were of 'subnormal' influence. Conveniently to summarize the rôle of each cost element in selling price changes, we have employed *activity* (or *sensitivity*) *ratios,* defining the relation between the actual influence and the 'expected influence' of each factor. Expectancy is based upon the ratio of aggregate costs of each type to the aggregate value of manufactured products. These measurements, relating to gross changes, in current dollars, between 1923 and 1929, follow:

| Element of manufacturing cost | Activity ratio |
|---|---|
| Materials | 72.7/66.3 = 1.10 |
| Labor | 19.1/14.8 = 1.29 |
| Overhead costs plus profits | 8.2/18.9 = .43 |

For the period 1899-1914 (when the movement of selling prices was upward) corresponding ratios for materials, labor, and overhead costs plus profits, were 1.37, .45 and .06, respectively. The most conspicuous difference is found in the more active rôle played by labor in the recent period.[1]

[1] In treating of price and cost changes during the pre-war period it was considered advisable to measure the influence of each cost factor upon selling price changes when these changes were expressed in terms of dollars of constant purchasing power, as well as in current dollars. Between 1899 and 1914 the changes in current dollars and in constant dollars were significantly different, for manufactured goods. The difference is much less pronounced for the recent period, and extended discussion of the measurements relating to constant dollars is unnecessary. Briefly, we may note that between 1923 and 1929 the average unit of manufactured goods declined 4.1 per cent in purchasing power. This was the net resultant of falling material costs, falling labor costs, and rising overhead costs plus profits, all expressed in dollars of constant purchasing power.

Of the gross change in per-unit purchasing power of manufactured goods, 59 per cent was due to falling material costs, 17 per cent was due to falling labor costs, while 24 per cent was due to rising overhead costs plus profits.

For this period, and with reference to changes in terms of dollars of constant purchasing power, the activity ratio for material costs was .88, for labor costs 1.16, for overhead costs plus profits 1.29.

## SUMMARY: PRICE AND COST MOVEMENTS IN MANUFACTURING INDUSTRIES

Notable changes have taken place within the last decade in the market values of manufactured goods and in the costs of the services of the several agents contributing to their production. Still more pronounced have been the shifts occurring within the last two decades. In summarizing recent movements, therefore, we shall at the same time pass in review the changes that may be seen against more distant bases. To avoid the confusion which arises from a shifting standard of monetary values we employ throughout a commodity standard of value. That is, prices and costs are measured in dollars of constant purchasing power in wholesale markets. These figures are presented in the following table, and are graphically portrayed in Figure 83.

TABLE 164

Changes in Unit Prices and Unit Costs, Products of Manufacturing Industries of the United States, 1899-1929

(In dollars of constant purchasing power)

| Year | Selling price | Cost of materials | Labor costs | Overhead costs plus profits |
|---|---|---|---|---|
| 1899 | 100 | 100 | 100 | 100 |
| 1914 | 94 | 100 | 84 | 78 |
| 1914 | 100 | 100 | 100 | 100 |
| 1923 | 113 | 109 | 127 | 120 |
| 1923 | 100 | 100 | 100 | 100 |
| 1929 | 96 | 93 | 91 | 111 |
| 1914 | 100 | 100 | 100 | 100 |
| 1929 | 108 | 101 | 115 | 132 |

It is convenient to divide the three decades covered by these records into two fifteen-year periods, those covered by the first and last pairs of entries in the above table. During the period which preceded the war the average per-unit value of products of manufacture, in terms of commodities in general, declined 6 per cent. This was an era when processed goods were being steadily cheapened. Changes in material costs (which here include cost of fuel,

## FIGURE 83

### CHANGES IN AVERAGE SELLING PRICE, COST OF MATERIALS, LABOR COSTS AND OVERHEAD COSTS PLUS PROFITS, PER UNIT OF PRODUCT

MANUFACTURING INDUSTRIES OF THE UNITED STATES, 1899-1914 AND 1914-1929

(IN DOLLARS OF CONSTANT PURCHASING POWER)

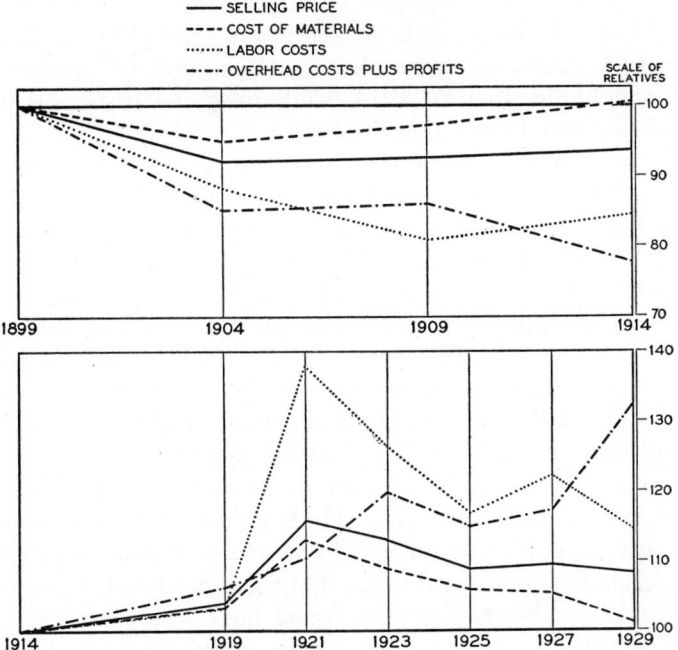

power, containers and semi-processed materials, as well as raw materials proper) played no part in this cheapening. Steadily declining costs of the services of the agents of fabrication were the dominating factors. Labor costs, per unit of product, declined 16 per cent, while the cost of management, as represented by overhead costs plus profits, dropped no less than 22 per cent between 1899 and 1914.[1] These index numbers suggest that, in general, the consumers rather than the producers of manufactured goods benefited most from the advances of the pre-war era.

[1] The explanation of the pronounced drop in overhead costs plus profits is found, in part, in the sharp differences between business conditions in 1899 and 1914. Profits were high in the former year, low in the latter. There was a declining trend in this item, however, regardless of the state of affairs in the terminal years.

During the fifteen-year period which opens with the war and ends with the termination of post-war prosperity in 1929, the net change in the real per-unit value of manufactured goods was in the other direction. The value of each unit, in terms of goods in general, advanced 8 per cent. Again material costs played a neutral part. Labor costs and overhead costs plus profits were the active factors,[1] but in this case their influence was exerted in the direction of enhanced values. In 1929 labor costs per unit of product were 15 per cent higher than in 1914, while overhead costs plus profits stood 32 per cent higher than in 1914.[2]

This reversal of the relative positions of manufactured goods and of other goods has been commented upon in the preceding chapter. That it was a shift of profound significance is not to be doubted. As one result, the post-war period saw new economic classes lifted into positions of dominance, while the status of other classes was definitely lowered. Through his increased purchasing power the industrial wage-earner exerted an influence during the decade of the 'twenties which was never his before. Instead of fighting to hold his own against a constantly rising cost of living, as he did during the pre-war era, he substantially elevated his consumption standards, and his demands shaped the course of post-war investment and production. High industrial profits helped to lay a foundation for the interest in securities which generated the great speculative boom of this era. On the other hand, farmers and raw material producers generally found their worlds turned upside down when the favorable market conditions they had known before the war were replaced by adverse relations. The intangible forces which fix market values altered the scales in which processed goods and raw materials are equated for purposes of exchange, requiring less in kind from the one side, and more from the other, for the goods which are necessary for production and for living.

Though we have dealt with the fifteen years between 1914 and 1929 as a unit, we must note that within this period a significant change in tendencies occurred. The selling prices of manufactured goods (in dollars of constant purchasing power) reached a peak in 1921, and declined thereafter. Labor costs per unit of product

[1] Or the factors profiting most from selling price changes, if we think of the causal sequence as originating in the final market.

[2] In this comparison the base year is one with a record of depression, the terminal year one of prosperity. These conditions emphasize fluctuations in the profit element in this composite.

reached an extremely high peak in 1921, and declined thereafter. Overhead costs plus profits rose between 1914 and 1923 and fell to lower levels during the next four years. Under the influence of the most recent era of prosperity, these costs attained in 1929 a new peak, some eleven per cent above that of 1923. We may say, then, that for costs which represent the services of ownership and management the decade of the 'twenties was table land, well above the level of the valley which lay on the other side. For labor costs, and for the real per-unit values of manufactured goods, this decade was a gentle downward slope from the peak to which the economic earthquake of 1920-21 had lifted them. The effects of the volcanic explosion of 1929 on the topographic features of this economic realm remain to be determined.

## CHAPTER IX

# Other Economic Changes, 1922-1929

THE first phase of the economic era which was ushered in by the World War ended, for the United States, in 1921. The next phase, falling between 1922 and 1929, was a period of prosperity, marked by increasing industrial productivity, rising living standards, generally advancing wages and rapidly increasing profits. The preceding chapters have described changes in production and prices occurring during this period. It remains to consider movements in certain factors which in part conditioned, in part reflected, the changes already discussed.

A detailed treatment of the complex economic movements of this period is not here possible. The discussion must be restricted to four or five elements of dominant importance. We shall consider, in turn, changes in total population and shifts in industrial employment, alterations in the volume and cost of capital and credit, movements of foreign trade, and changes in the aggregate values of the contributions of various productive agents and in their shares in the national income. Reference will be made throughout to the production and price movements already considered, and to the conditions and tendencies prevailing during the pre-war period discussed in earlier chapters.

### POPULATION CHANGES AND INDUSTRIAL DISPLACEMENT

Movements of population and of certain related series are defined by measurements in the following table. The original series are plotted, for the post-war years, in Figure 84.

One of the most important of post-war developments has been a slowing up in the rate of increase of population. The data [1] indicate

---

[1] The measurements for the recent period relate to annual estimates of the population of continental United States made by P. K. Whelpton of The Scripps Foundation. (See "Trends in Population Increase and Distribution during 1920-30", *American Journal of Sociology*, May, 1931, p. 867.) The series is based upon census tabulations for 1920 and 1930, and upon statistics of births, deaths and migration for inter-censal years. The general trend is doubtless well reflected in these estimates, but year-to-year fluctuations in the actual population may not be

## TABLE 165
MEASUREMENTS RELATING TO THE GROWTH OF POPULATION IN THE UNITED STATES, 1922-1929, WITH CORRESPONDING FIGURES FOR THE PERIOD 1901-1913

| (1) Element of population | (2) Average annual rate of change 1922-1929 (per cent) | (3) Index of instability 1922-1929 | (4) Average annual rate of change 1901-1913 (per cent) | (5) Index of instability 1901-1913 |
|---|---|---|---|---|
| Total population | + 1.4 | 0.3 | +2.0 | 0.3 |
| Number of wage-earners, manufacturing plants | + 1.0 | 2.9 | +2.7 | 2.7 |
| Farm population [a] | − 1.3 | 0.4 | — | — |
| Immigration [b] | −12.3 | 15.3 | +2.4 | 15.8 |

[a] No estimates of farm population are available for the pre-war period.

[b] A more exact measure of population movement is afforded by figures on net immigration (immigration less emigration). Net immigration declined at an average rate of 14.1 per cent between 1922 and 1929. The lack of statistics on emigration prior to 1907 prevents a comparison with the pre-war years.

It is to be noted that the data of immigration relate to increments, whereas the three other series in the table relate to aggregates.

### FIGURE 84
CHANGES IN THE TOTAL POPULATION OF THE UNITED STATES, IN THE FARM POPULATION AND IN THE NUMBER OF WAGE-EARNERS IN MANUFACTURING INDUSTRIES, 1922-1929

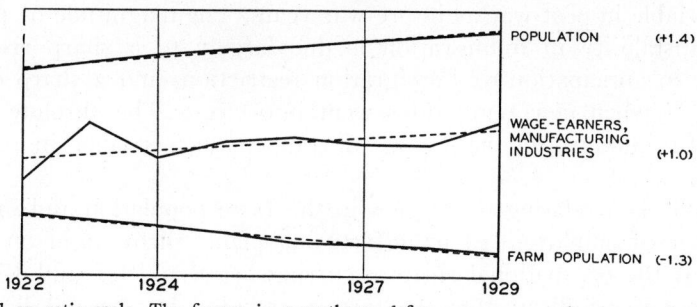

Plotted on ratio scale. The figures in parentheses define average annual rates of change (in percentage form).

so faithfully depicted. The estimates (revised), as of July 1 for the years 1922-1929, are as follows:

|  | (In thousands) |
|---|---|
| 1922 | 110,328 |
| 1923 | 112,243 |
| 1924 | 114,415 |
| 1925 | 116,137 |
| 1926 | 117,707 |
| 1927 | 119,307 |
| 1928 | 120,682 |
| 1929 | 121,888 |

a rate of increase of 1.4 per cent a year between 1922 and 1929, distinctly less than the average annual rate of 2.0 per cent which prevailed during the thirteen years preceding the war. The declining rate of population increase is due in part to immigration restriction. Immigration declined, between 1922 and 1929, at a rate of 12.3 per cent a year (net immigration declined by 14.1 per cent a year). That there is a more fundamental cause is suggested by recent researches of Drs. Louis I. Dublin and Alfred Lotka, of the Metropolitan Life Insurance Company. Their studies [1] indicate that the true rate of natural increase of the population of the United States in 1928 was 2.3 per 1000, instead of 7.8 per 1000, the apparent rate. The apparent rate is deceptively high because of the relatively large proportion of our population at present in the reproducing groups, as a result of the higher birth rates of two to three decades ago and of the unrestricted immigration then prevailing. Conditions in the United States, it is held by these authorities, are not far from those characteristic of a stationary population.

The measurements in column (3) of Table 165 indicate the same degree of stability in the growth of population for both pre-war and post-war periods.[2] Slightly less stability is shown during recent years in the series measuring the number of industrial wage-earners. Immigration, always highly unstable, appears to have been as variable in post-war as in pre-war years. The magnitude of post-war instability in immigration is due largely to a sharp rise in 1923, in anticipation of immigration restriction, and a sharp drop in 1924 when new regulations went into effect. The absolute volume of immigration has been, of course, much smaller in recent years.

The data relating to changes in the farm population and in the number of employees of manufacturing plants throw light on certain of the occupational shifts occurring between 1922 and 1929.[3] These series indicate that the farm population has been declining,

---

[1] "On the True Rate of Natural Increase", *Journal of the American Statistical Association,* Vol. XX, No. 152, September, 1925, pp. 305-339, and "The True Rate of Natural Increase of the Population of the United States", *Metron,* Vol. VIII, No. 4, July, 1930, pp. 107-119.

[2] It must be recalled that all inter-censal population figures are estimates, and that the pre-war estimates are based on fragmentary data. Greater confidence attaches to the measures of population trends than to the measures of instability.

[3] Farm population figures are estimates made by the U. S. Department of Agriculture. The series relating to manufacturing employees was secured from biennial census figures, with annual interpolations based on the factory employ-

while at the same time the industrial population (the employees of manufacturing establishments) has been increasing at a rate lower than that at which the entire population has been growing. The reason for this apparent inconsistency is probably found in the very rapid increase in the number of those rendering personal service and engaged in the distribution of goods. Estimates based upon compilations of the Census of Occupations indicate that the number of persons employed in the service industries (transportation, trade and finance, public service, professional service and domestic and personal service) increased from 35 per cent of the total number of persons gainfully employed in 1920 to 42 per cent in 1930.[1] While no precise statistics covering these occupations are available, there is clear evidence of a rapid increase in the number of persons thus employed. These three related shifts—an absolute decline in the farm population, a relative decline in the number of industrial employees, and a marked increase in the number of those engaged in mercantile pursuits and in personal service occupations—are important aspects of economic tendencies in the United States during post-war years.

§ *On the extent of industrial displacement, 1899-1929.*—A more detailed study of these industrial shifts, which have been speeded up with the increasing pace of economic growth, throws further light on recent tendencies. The present figures relate to changes occurring among manufacturing industries. Variations, by census periods, in the total number of employees (wage-earners) of manufacturing plants in the United States are measured by the entries at the top of page 420.

These figures reveal an uninterrupted increase in number of manufacturing employees between 1899 and 1919, decline and recovery during the next two periods, followed by two periods of decline and a final period of advance from 1927 to 1929. But this picture fails to show the actual displacements of labor occurring during these years, the shifts from factory to factory and from industry to industry that were taking place even during periods of general advance. We do not possess records by factories which would show the actual movements of labor, but it is possible to trace the shifts among industries, and to measure the degree of industrial readjustment which such shifts necessitated.

ment index of the Federal Reserve Board. The interpolation of the pre-war census data on employment is based on annual estimates of Cobb and Douglas (*American Economic Review, Supplement,* March, 1928, p. 148).

[1] Persons engaged in clerical occupations are not included either in this group or in the total. If they be included in the service industries the above figures become 40 and 47. If they be included among persons in industries producing physical commodities the above percentages become 33 and 39.

| Census period | Net gain or loss in number employed in identical industries [1] |
|---|---|
| 1899-1904 | + 750,972 |
| 1904-1909 | +1,161,467 |
| 1909-1914 | + 406,590 |
| 1914-1919 | +2,105,141 |
| 1919-1921 | −2,018,903 |
| 1921-1923 | +1,826,048 |
| 1923-1925 | − 411,637 |
| 1925-1927 | − 59,294 |
| 1927-1929 | + 365,132 |

[1] The coverage of decennial census tabulations (1899, 1909, 1919, 1929) is somewhat greater than that of other census tabulations. This makes a considerable difference in the number of establishments recorded, since a larger proportion of small establishments is included in the decennial tabulations, but is not believed materially to affect the records of total wage-earners employed.

The data given in this and the following tables have been secured from a comparison by census periods of the returns for identical industries. Industries for which comparable statistics are not available for successive census periods are omitted. For the period 1899 to 1919 the figures include employees of establishments reporting a value of product over $500; for later years the limit is $5,000.

These shifts are measured by the following figures. Accession and separation rates are shown graphically in Figure 85.

TABLE 166

ACCESSIONS AND SEPARATIONS OF WAGE-EARNERS, MANUFACTURING INDUSTRIES OF THE UNITED STATES, 1899-1929

| (1) | (2) | (3) | (4) | (5) | (6) | (7) |
|---|---|---|---|---|---|---|
| Census period | Number of industries | Average number of wage-earners [a] | Accessions | Separations | Accession rate [b] | Separation rate [c] |
| 1899-1904 | 295 | 5,076,197 | 820,322 | 69,350 | 16.2 | 1.4 |
| 1904-1909 | 316 | 6,105,264 | 1,247,920 | 86,453 | 20.4 | 1.4 |
| 1909-1914 | 338 | 6,933,670 | 637,310 | 230,720 | 9.2 | 3.3 |
| 1914-1919 | 353 | 8,305,476 | 2,368,496 | 263,355 | 28.5 | 3.2 |
| 1919-1921 | 306 | 7,819,308 | 36,989 | 2,055,892 | 0.5 | 26.3 |
| 1921-1923 | 318 | 7,766,304 | 1,912,916 | 86,868 | 24.6 | 1.1 |
| 1923-1925 | 320 | 8,483,768 | 234,554 | 646,191 | 2.8 | 7.6 |
| 1925-1927 | 323 | 8,267,736 | 263,539 | 322,833 | 3.2 | 3.9 |
| 1927-1929 | 321 | 8,514,427 | 626,267 | 261,135 | 7.4 | 3.1 |

[a] Average of numbers employed in the two years compared. The entries relating to the period prior to 1919 include the employees of establishments with output valued at more than $500. For later years the limit is $5,000.

[b] Accessions as percentage of average number employed.

[c] Separations as percentage of average number employed.

## FIGURE 85
### ACCESSION AND SEPARATION RATES BY INDUSTRIES
WAGE-EARNERS IN MANUFACTURING INDUSTRIES OF THE UNITED STATES

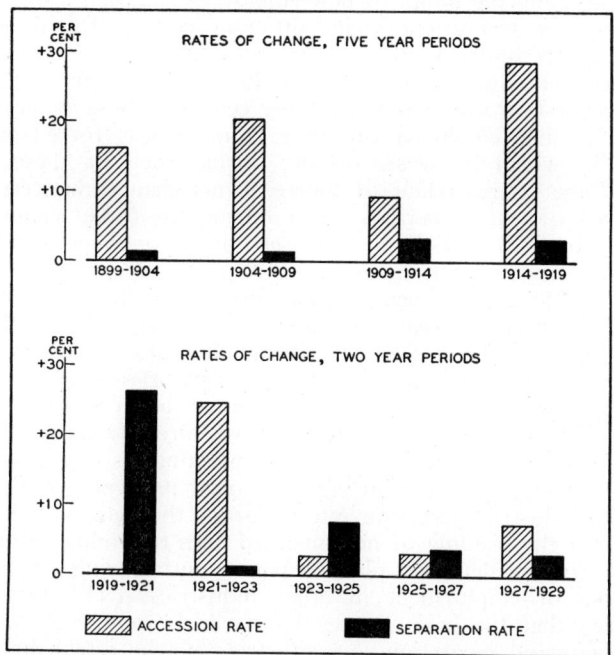

The comparisons set up in the preceding table are affected somewhat by the change in the length of the census period from five to two years after 1919, but account may be taken of this change in interpreting the results. For the present purpose we may neglect the periods between 1914 and 1923, concentrating attention on the first three and the last three census periods.

During the three pre-war periods absolute accessions (i.e., entrances of wage-earners into new manufacturing industries) averaged 901,851 during a census period of five years. The average accession rate was 14.9 per cent. On the average, during each of these periods, approximately one new man was brought in for each seven men on the payroll. During the three most recent periods (biennial periods) absolute accessions averaged 373,787. The average accession rate was 4.5 per cent. During each of these census periods, on the average, one new man was brought in for each 22 men on the payroll. Making due allowance for the difference in the length of the census interval, it is clear that there has been a marked reduction in the relative number of accessions. If we accept the accession rate as a measure of the demands placed upon industry for the training of new men, for the fitting of new men into the working mechanism of factory life, we may conclude that these demands have been lightened in recent years. The era of rapid growth, in respect of number employed, has been followed by one of comparative stability, and the influx of new employees has been lessened.

A study of separations yields different results. During the three pre-war census intervals absolute separations (i.e., reductions in the number of men employed in specific industries) averaged 128,841. The average separation rate was but 2.1 per cent. On the average, only one of every 48 men employed withdrew from or was forced out of the industry in which he was working, during each of these five-year periods. (The figures relate, of course, to net changes between the terminal years of census periods.) But during the three biennial census periods from 1923 to 1929 absolute separations averaged 410,053 men. Separations from specific industries during an average two-year period were more than three times as great, in absolute terms, as they were during an average five-year period before the war. (Again, the figures are based on net changes between terminal years of census periods.) The average separation rate was 4.9 per cent between 1923 and 1929. During each two-year period, on the average, between 1923 and 1929, 49 men out of every thousand employees withdrew from or were forced out of the industry in which they were working, as compared with 21 men out of every thousand during a five-year pre-war period.

As the industrial accession rate measures the demands placed upon industry for the training of new men, so does the industrial separation rate measure the demands placed upon manufacturing employees for the finding of employment in other industries. (The fact must be emphasized that the basic figures from which we are working relate to accessions and separations *by industries,* not by establishments. The unit of study is the individual industry, e.g., petroleum refining. The net change in employment in each of some three hundred odd industries constitutes a single observation, for the present purpose. Separations, then, measure the number of men actually forced to find employment in other industries, not in other plants within the same industry. The demands of readjustment are, accordingly, more severe than they would be if the data related to individual plants.) It is an impressive fact that under the prosperous industrial conditions prevailing between 1923 and 1929 one individual worker out of 20 was forced, every two years, to seek employment in a new manufacturing industry, or in a non-manufacturing industry. These conditions placed lighter demands upon industry for the training of new men, but placed much heavier demands upon wage-earners, and enforced a degree of adaptability not required under pre-war conditions. This marked lessening of the permanence of job tenure must be borne in mind, along with the wage changes, if we are to secure a just appreciation of the situation of industrial labor during the last decade.

There is not space here to trace the record through by large industrial groups. Data on separations, which are most significant as regards the strain of readjustment placed on wage-earners, are summarized below for six major groups.

TABLE 167

SEPARATIONS OF WAGE-EARNERS BY INDUSTRIAL GROUPS, 1899-1914, 1923-1929
(All figures, absolute and relative, relate to average changes during census intervals. Such intervals were of five years' duration during the period 1899-1914, of two years' duration during the period 1923-1929.)

| (1) | (2) | (3) | (4) | (5) |
|---|---|---|---|---|
| | Separations, 1899-1914 | | Separations, 1923-1929 | |
| Industrial group (manufacturing) | Average number | As percentage of average number employed | Average number | As percentage of average number employed |
| Foods | 3,888 | 1.0 | 18,869 | 2.8 |
| Textiles | 19,096 | 1.5 | 78,073 | 4.8 |
| Products of petroleum and coal | 3,672 | 5.0 | 4,523 | 3.2 |
| Iron and steel | 7,473 | 1.5 | 33,991 | 4.0 |
| Machinery | 1,427 | 0.2 | 23,787 | 2.6 |
| Transportation | 21,590 | 4.2 | 62,897 | 11.5 |

Separations increased during the post-war period, both absolutely and in relation to the number of wage-earners employed, among all but one of the industrial groups listed above. These groups do not cover the entire industrial field, but they are sufficiently comprehensive to indicate that permanence of tenure had declined for wage-workers in a large proportion of manufacturing industries. They do not, of course, tell the whole story; many types of industrial displacement are not reflected in such measurements of net change between large industrial groups. This record under-emphasizes the difficulties of workers in manufacturing industries, under modern industrial conditions.

## AVAILABILITY OF CAPITAL AND CREDIT

Capital and credit stand at the very center of the complex of inter-related elements which condition the working of a modern economic system. In the post-war development of the American economy they were particularly active factors. Conditions prevailing in markets for capital and credit help to explain many of the distinctive developments of this era. In the present brief survey there are brought together certain currently available materials bearing on changes in the supply and cost of capital and of various types of credit during this period.

## Supply of Capital

Since no accurate measurements of the total invested capital of the United States or of the amount of new capital funds available for investment each year are available, it is impossible to secure definitive figures as to the rate of increase in capital accumulation. However, there are a number of series which reflect, directly or indirectly, changes in the supply of savings and of capital available for business and industrial uses. Measurements of the rates of change and of the degree of instability of certain of these series are shown in Table 168. These are divided into two classes, those which relate to increments, or annual additions to capital funds, and those which relate to aggregate amounts, or funds. (No attempt is here made to correct for over-lapping among the various items.) The series listed are plotted in Figure 86.

### FIGURE 86
#### CHANGES IN CERTAIN ELEMENTS OF THE SUPPLY OF CAPITAL FUNDS IN THE UNITED STATES, 1922-1929

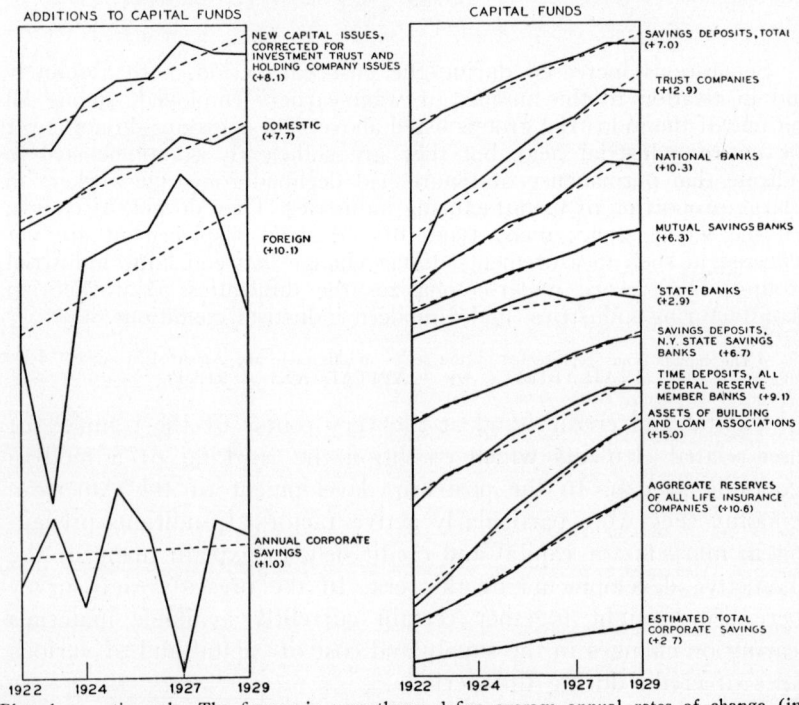

Plotted on ratio scale. The figures in parentheses define average annual rates of change (in percentage form).

## TABLE 168

Showing Changes in Certain Elements of the Supply of Capital Funds and in Annual Additions to Capital Funds in the United States, 1922-1929 [a]

| Sources or elements of capital funds [b] | Absolute values (in millions of dollars) | | Average annual rate of change (per cent) | Index of instability |
|---|---|---|---|---|
| | 1922 | 1929 | | |
| *Additions to Capital Funds* | | | | |
| New capital flotations | | | | |
| New capital issues, corrected for investment trust and holding company issues | 4,304 | 7,052 | + 8.1 | 6.9 |
| Domestic issues, total, corrected. | 3,669 | 6,294 | + 7.7 | 3.8 |
| Foreign issues, total | 635 | 758 | +10.1 | 27.4 |
| Annual corporate savings (estimated) | 1,747 | 2,320 | + 1.0 | 22.2 |
| *Capital Funds* | | | | |
| Total savings deposits [c] | 17,579 | 28,261 | + 7.0 | 2.3 |
| 'State' banks | 6,105 | 7,413 | + 2.9 | 2.9 |
| Mutual savings banks | 5,818 | 8,904 | + 6.3 | 0.8 |
| National banks | 4,074 | 7,889 | +10.3 | 2.8 |
| Trust companies | 1,525 | 4,023 | +12.9 | 6.9 |
| Savings deposits, New York State savings banks | 2,800 | 4,419 | + 6.7 | 1.1 |
| Time deposits of all Federal reserve member banks | 7,161 | 13,279 | + 9.1 | 3.2 |
| Aggregate reserves, life insurance companies | 7,176 | 14,272 | +10.6 | 0.7 |
| Assets of building and loan associations [d] | 3,117 | 8,356 | +15.0 | 2.8 |
| Total corporate savings (estimated) | 73,818 | 88,840 | + 2.7 | 0.3 |

[a] The capital funds represented by the series in this table are measured in current dollars, but no material distortion is introduced thereby. The period covered was marked by only a slight secular change in the value of the dollar.

[b] New capital flotations are from *The Commercial and Financial Chronicle*, supplemented by special compilations made for the National Bureau of Economic Research; details are given in Table 169. Total savings deposits, as of June 30, are derived from figures collected by the Savings Bank Division of the American Bankers Association. The figures for savings deposits of New York State savings banks are monthly averages, as published in the *Survey of Current Business*, 1931 Annual Supplement, p. 210. Time deposits of Federal reserve member banks are averages of the figures given on 'call dates'; they are from the *Annual Report* of the Federal Reserve Board, 1930, p. 95. The December 31 figures for reserves of life insurance companies as published in the *Insurance Yearbook*, 1930, The Spectator Co., p. 516, have been averaged to give figures as of June 30, as have the figures for assets of building and loan associations, from the *Statistical Abstract of the United States*, 1931, p. 279. (The latter figures were originally compiled by the United States Building and Loan League.) Additions to corporate savings and total corporate savings are from tables below.

[c] Includes the relatively small savings deposits of private banks.

[d] The assets of building and loan associations constitute a 'revolving fund' of savings, rather than an aggregate fund of capital in the proper sense.

Of the series listed in this table the following are of chief significance as indexes of the volume of savings proper in the United States:

Annual increments to total capital supply:
    New capital issues, corrected by the elimination of issues covering financing by investment trusts and holding corporations.
    Additions to aggregate corporate savings.
Elements of total capital supply:
    Total savings deposits, all banks.
    Total reserves, life insurance companies.
    Assets of building and loan associations.
    Total corporate savings.

Each of these requires some attention.

*Annual Increments to Capital Funds: New Issues.*—The first two of these series represent additions to existing capital funds, a fact which must be considered in interpreting their rates of change. Thus if new capital issues were constant in amount from year to year, it would mean that absolute annual increments to existing funds were constant. Total funds would be increasing under these conditions. Rates of change in such increments may not properly be compared with rates of change in total volumes.

Flotations of new capital issues are partly financed, in the first instance, out of bank credit. But this is ordinarily a passing phase of the process of flotation, for in the ultimate absorption of the securities true savings are called forth.[1] It is probable that this ultimate absorption by investors was somewhat longer delayed, during the period immediately preceding the 1929 recession, than it was under earlier conditions. In part, the volume of new security flotations was doubtless carried out of the reservoir of credit connected with the stock market, a reservoir which was greatly increased between 1922 and 1929. Accordingly, we should probably not consider the volume of new issues within recent years to be as accurate an index of savings proper as in earlier years when the reservoir of stock market credit was more stable in volume.

In tracing changes in capital issues we should deduct, from the total amount of new issues, amounts representing refunding issues

[1] If the volume of credit has been such as to cause price inflation this may not be true. The 'saving' out of which capital has been derived may in such a case have been involuntary—'automatic lacking', in D. H. Robertson's phrase (*Banking Policy and the Price Level,* King, London, 1926, p. 47).

and issues floated by investment trusts and trading and holding companies for the purchase of securities. Between 1922 and 1929 an increasing proportion of stock issues consisted of the offerings of investment trusts and of various types of holding companies. The proceeds of issues of this sort are not used to increase the capital equipment of the country, or to swell the country's circulating capital. The amounts of such issues, and corrected figures for issues from which the creation of capital goods proper may be expected, are shown in the following table. Three of these series are plotted in Figure 86.

TABLE 169

New Capital Issues in the United States, and Issues of Investment Trusts, Trading and Holding Companies, 1922-1929 [a]

(In millions of dollars)

| (1) Year | (2) Total new capital issues [b] | (3) Issues of investment trusts, trading and holding companies | (4) Net new capital issues | (5) Foreign issues, total new capital | (6) Domestic net new capital issues |
|---|---|---|---|---|---|
| 1922 | 4,304 | — | 4,304 | 635 | 3,669 |
| 1923 | 4,304 | 11 | 4,293 | 280 | 4,013 |
| 1924 | 5,593 | 59 | 5,534 | 997 | 4,537 |
| 1925 | 6,220 | 46 | 6,174 | 1,086 | 5,088 |
| 1926 | 6,344 | 102 | 6,242 | 1,145 | 5,097 |
| 1927 | 7,791 | 271 | 7,520 | 1,561 | 5,959 |
| 1928 | 8,114 | 1,033 | 7,081 | 1,319 | 5,762 |
| 1929 | 10,183 | 3,131 | 7,052 | 758 | 6,294 |
| Average annual rate of change (per cent) .. | +13.0 | — | +8.1 | +10.1 | +7.7 |
| Index of instability ....... | 5.1 | — | 6.9 | 27.4 | 3.8 |

[a] Data are from *The Commercial and Financial Chronicle*. The entries in column (3), which were compiled for the National Bureau of Economic Research by W. M. Cahill of *The Commercial and Financial Chronicle*, represent issues clearly intended for 'unproductive' purposes. Entries in other columns include municipal and other governmental issues but exclude Federal issues.
[b] Excluding refunding issues.

The series listed in column (4), in which our present interest lies, increased between 1922 and 1929 at a rate of 8.1 per cent a year, with an index of instability of 6.9. The aggregate amount of new issues in 1929, corrected by the subtraction of investment trust and holding company issues, was 7,052 millions of dollars. The magnitude of this figure may be realized when it is recalled that this represents an annual increment, not an existing volume. Foreign issues showed a much more rapid increase than domestic issues, for the period as a whole. The margin of difference would have been much greater had the period studied terminated in 1928. Between 1922 and 1928 the rate of increase in foreign capital issues in the United States averaged 19.0 per cent per year—a phenomenally rapid rise. This rapidly swelling volume of foreign issues played an important rôle in both domestic and international economic developments during this period. We shall touch upon this again.[1]

*Annual Increments to Capital Funds: Corporate Savings.*— Corporate savings, in the form of additions to surplus and undivided profits, constitute another important source of new capital. The amount of such savings may be estimated from corporate returns to the Bureau of Internal Revenue, by subtracting Federal taxes and cash dividends from net profits, with due correction for losses suffered by corporations showing no net profits. These figures appear in the next table.

Savings of this type show no marked increase during this period. A maximum value of almost three billions of dollars was registered in 1925, with the entries for 1923, 1928 and 1926 next in order of magnitude. In 1925, indeed, additions to corporate capital funds through this process of ploughing back profits amounted to 58 per cent of reported net domestic capital issues. For the entire period of eight years corporate savings amounted to 42

[1] The reduction of the public debt of the Federal government was a factor of some importance in augmenting the volume of savings during this period. Taxation which provides funds for the retirement of a public debt representing consumptive expenditure in the first place is a form of compulsory creation of new capital funds. For in the retirement of the debt, funds secured by taxation are made available for investment in private enterprise, or in state or municipal securities.

Between 1922 and 1929 the gross debt of the Federal government was reduced by approximately six billions of dollars. It is reasonable to assume that practically all of this was reinvested. Part of this sum would doubtless have been saved by the original recipients, if it had not been absorbed in taxes. But the swelling of the large volume of corporate and private saving by the addition of this huge sum representing, in some part, forced saving on the part of tax-payers contributed to the growth of capital funds and to the favorable conditions in capital markets which characterized this period.

## TABLE 170

Estimates of Corporate Savings in the United States
Annual Additions to Surplus and Undivided Profits, 1922-1929 [a]

| Year | Estimated corporate savings (in millions of dollars) |
|---|---|
| 1922 | 1,747 |
| 1923 | 2,528 |
| 1924 | 1,575 |
| 1925 | 2,957 |
| 1926 | 2,335 |
| 1927 | 1,115 |
| 1928 | 2,479 |
| 1929 | 2,320 |
| Average annual rate of change (per cent).... | +1.0 |
| Index of instability........................ | 22.2 |

[a] *Statistics of Income*, for 1922-1929, Bureau of Internal Revenue. The figures represent net profits, less taxes and cash dividends.

per cent of net domestic capital issues and to 51 per cent of net new capital issues floated for domestic corporations, as recorded in current compilations.[1] This would indicate that about 34 per cent of the new capital requirements of American corporations were met out of corporate savings. But this figure is subject to a considerable margin of error, since the degree of coverage of the relevant statistics cannot be determined exactly.[2]

We pass to a consideration of certain of the elements of total capital supply, dealing now with funds and not with annual increments.

*Savings Deposits.*—Total savings deposits of all banks in the United States, as compiled and published by the Savings Bank Division of the American Bankers Association, show an increase

[1] See Table 173.
[2] Between December 31, 1928, and December 31, 1929, total capital stock, plus bonds and mortgages, of corporations submitting balance sheets to the U. S. Bureau of Internal Revenue increased by 17,183 millions of dollars. New domestic capital issues (including investment trust, trading and holding corporations) as compiled by *The Commercial and Financial Chronicle*, amounted to 9,425 millions of dollars during the year 1929. Making due allowance for stock dividends and for possible variations in the coverage of the Federal statistics, it is clear that current compilations of new security issues, though carefully made, fail to include all additions to outstanding corporate stocks and mortgage obligations.

between 1922 and 1929 at an average annual rate of 7.0 per cent. (See Table 168 in connection with this figure, and those cited below.) The figure 7.0 is probably somewhat too high if taken as a measure of the rate of accumulation of funds in savings deposits proper. The totals on which it is based include the time deposits of Federal reserve member banks and certain deposits of other banks, which do not represent savings, exclusively. Reference to the figures for certain of the constituent items in this total reveals important differences among their rates of change. Savings in 'state' banks increased at a relatively low rate (2.9 per cent a year). Deposits in mutual savings banks increased at a rate of 6.3 per cent a year, with a measure of instability of but 0.8. This steady, regular growth probably indicates rather accurately the true rate of change in savings in that section of the country in which mutual savings banks are located (the New England states, New York, New Jersey, Delaware and Maryland). Deposits which are classed as 'savings' have increased much more rapidly in national banks and in trust companies. For the former, the average annual rate of change was 10.3 per cent, for the latter 12.9 per cent. Both figures are to be accepted with reservations arising from the growth of time deposits in member banks of the Federal Reserve System, and from the relatively rapid increase in the number of trust companies in recent years.

Time deposits of all member banks increased during this period at an annual rate of 9.1 per cent. The fact that such deposits are subject to lower reserve requirements than are demand deposits has induced banks to encourage the building up of time accounts. There is reason to believe that a considerable proportion of these time deposits do not represent accumulations of savings, or true primary deposits of the type found among mutual savings banks, but arise from the conversion of slow demand accounts into time accounts. In so far as these are derivative deposits resulting from lending operations, rather than primary deposits of true savings, they cannot be accepted as an accurate index of capital accumulation; accordingly, the relatively rapid rate of change in time deposits of all member banks, as well as the figure for total savings deposits cited above, must be discounted somewhat.

Savings deposits in New York state banks, which increased at an annual rate of 6.7 per cent during this period, are not subject to the defects pointed out above. Here, as in the case of the mutual savings banks, we have a steady growth marked by only slight variations from year to year. For the eastern part of the country the true rate of increase in this form of capital accumulation was probably in the neighborhood of six per cent a year.

Properly to interpret these figures it is necessary to have some idea of the magnitudes involved, since a given percentage rate of growth is more significant for a series of large magnitude than for one of small magnitude. For all banks, savings and time deposits in 1929 amounted to 28,261 millions of dollars. Of this aggregate almost nine billions of dollars was in mutual savings banks, over seven billions in state savings banks, close to eight billions in national banks, and four billions in trust companies.

*Reserves of Life Insurance Companies.*—Another important source of capital accumulation is found in premiums paid to life insurance companies. Changes in capital funds coming from this source are best measured in terms of the reserves of life insurance companies. These, which in 1929 amounted to over 14 billions of dollars, increased between 1922 and 1929 at a rate of 10.6 per cent a year, with an index of variability of 0.7. (See Table 168.) Here was a pronounced and steady rise in one of the highly important sources of new capital.

*Assets of Building and Loan Associations.*—Assets of this type, which represent, primarily, funds invested in residential construction, increased between 1922 and 1929 at a rate of 15.0 per cent a year, with an index of instability of 2.8. The aggregate value of such assets amounted, in 1929, to 8,356 millions of dollars. This remarkable increase was in part a reflection of the great expansion in residential building during this period. (It may be noted, by reference to Figure 86, that the line of trend does not in this case define the true rate of growth accurately throughout. In the earlier years the rate exceeded 15.0 per cent, while toward the end of the period there was an appreciable decline in the rate of increase.)

*Corporate Savings.*—The elements of total capital supply discussed above are all important, but their absolute magnitude, in combination, is exceeded by the aggregate savings of corporations. Such savings, appearing in the first instance as additions to corporate surplus, or to undivided profits, and perhaps later passing into the capital stock account through the medium of stock dividends, are a major factor in capital accumulation.[1] Figures defining the *annual* amounts of corporate savings have been given in an earlier section; our present problem is the more difficult one of determining the aggregate capital fund accumulated through corporate savings, and the rate of increase of this fund between 1922 and 1929. Estimated figures appear in the next table. The entries in the last column are plotted in Figure 86.

TABLE 171

ESTIMATES OF AGGREGATE CORPORATE SAVINGS, AND OF ANNUAL CORPORATE SAVINGS, 1922-1929

(In billions of dollars)

| Year | Additions to corporate savings during year | Total corporate savings at end of year | Total corporate savings at middle of year |
| --- | --- | --- | --- |
| 1921 | — | 73 | — |
| 1922 | 1.7 | 75 | 74 |
| 1923 | 2.5 | 77 | 76 |
| 1924 | 1.6 | 79 | 78 |
| 1925 | 3.0 | 82 | 80 |
| 1926 | 2.3 | 84 | 83 |
| 1927 | 1.1 | 85 | 85 |
| 1928 | 2.5 | 88 | 86 |
| 1929 | 2.3 | 90 | 89 |

§ *On the method of estimating the volume and rate of increase of corporate savings.*—(a) Between 1923 and 1929 [2] approximately 15 billions of dollars were added to corporate capital funds by corporate savings, as shown in Table 170 above. Of this sum about 5 billions,

[1] Economists have differed somewhat as to the extent to which additions to corporate surplus may be accounted true savings. Oswald W. Knauth, after an investigation of this subject, concludes that "between 80 per cent and 90 per cent of the reported surpluses may be considered to be real savings." ("The Place of Corporate Surplus in the National Income," *Journal of the American Statistical Association*, June, 1922, p. 161.) Colonel M. C. Rorty is inclined to believe that this figure is too high, in that insufficient account is taken of the possibility of drafts on surpluses to meet contingencies. In the present study the full amount of reported corporate surpluses has been included. If some portions of these surpluses do not constitute real savings, the absolute figures should be correspondingly reduced. The rate of growth of this element of capital would not be materially modified by such a change.

[2] While data are available for 1922 they are excluded because of the exceptional amount of stock dividends declared in that year. Stock dividends (amounting to 3,348 millions of dollars) were considerably in excess of corporate savings for the same year (1,747 millions).

as reported by the Bureau of Internal Revenue, were transferred to capital account through the medium of stock dividends, leaving 10 billions as additions to surplus and undivided profits. Such additions thus included only two-thirds of all corporate savings between 1923 and 1929.

(b) On December 31, 1929, surplus and undivided profits (less deficits) of all corporations in the United States amounted to approximately 60 billions of dollars.[1]

(c) If we assume that this figure constitutes two-thirds of all savings by corporations prior to December 31, 1929 [it was noted under point (a) that this proportion prevailed between 1923 and 1929] we have 90 billions of dollars as the approximate aggregate value of such savings as of December 31, 1929. Of this amount approximately 60 billions represented funds then classified as surplus and undivided profits, while approximately 30 billions represented funds previously transferred from surplus to the capital stock account, through the agency of stock dividends.

(d) From the total of 90 billions for December 31, 1929, are deducted the successive amounts shown annually in the table representing additions to corporate surplus and undivided profits. This procedure gives a series of figures representing total corporate savings as of December 31, for the years from 1921 to 1929.

(e) Total corporate savings as of June 30, each year, are computed from the December 31 figures. Figures thus centered at the middle of each year are more directly comparable with our other data than are figures relating to December 31 of each year. (To avoid a fictitious appearance of accuracy, the figures in the last two columns are given only to the nearest billion.)

We should note that the annual increments to corporate savings have been determined, with a fairly high degree of accuracy, from corporate returns to the Treasury. The margin of error attaching to estimates of total corporate savings is much greater. The process of stepping up, by ten per cent, surplus and undivided profits reported by corporations submitting balance sheets, as a means of correcting for unreported items, involves an error of indeterminable magnitude. The assumption that one-third of corporate savings was distributed in the form of stock dividends, because that was the approximate fraction prevailing between 1923 and 1929, involves a similar error. The assumption that corporate surplus and undivided profits consist only of corpo-

[1] The precise figure given in the 398,815 balance sheets submitted was 55,111 millions. But 456,021 income tax returns were made by active corporations for 1929. Since most of the corporations not filing balance sheets are small, we are not justified in estimating capital funds of all corporations on the basis of a simple proportion, that is, by multiplying the given figure by 456,021/398,815. A reasonable approximation is made by increasing by ten per cent the figure derived from the balance sheets submitted. This gives an estimated total surplus and undivided profits of 60 billions of dollars in 1929.

rate savings is not entirely accurate. Again, the process of working backward from an estimated value of corporate savings as of December 31, 1929, makes the range of absolute values of the entire series rest upon the magnitude of the 1929 estimate. However, the present purpose will be served by an approximation to the absolute magnitude of aggregate corporate savings. Our immediate interest is in the rate of growth of this series. Having accurate data on annual increments, this rate may be determined with reasonable accuracy even though the estimate of the absolute magnitude of the series be subject to a considerable error. Thus we have 2.7 per cent as the rate of increase in corporate savings between 1922 and 1929. If one assumes that the 1929 estimate of the magnitude of aggregate savings is subject to an error of as much as 20 per cent, this means that the true rate of gain in corporate savings is not less than 2.2 per cent a year, and not more than 3.4 per cent. These limits may be accepted as reasonable, in view of the nature of the present estimates.

There is reason to think that the fraction of corporate savings distributed in the form of stock dividends was greater between 1923 and 1929 than during earlier periods. If this is so, the present method overestimates corporate savings prior to 1922, and gives absolute figures for total corporate savings (as in Table 171) which are too large. It is likely that any error in these estimates lies in this direction. If such an error is present, the 1922-29 rate of growth of corporate savings, as given in the text, is too low.

As of December 31, 1921, total savings of corporations in the United States, as represented by surplus and undivided profits, or by prior disbursements of stock dividends, amounted to approximately 73 billions of dollars. This figure had increased by December 31, 1929, to approximately 90 billions. Shifting the data to June 30th of each year, to improve comparability with other series, we find an average increase of 2.7 per cent a year, with an index of instability of 0.3. In magnitude, this item materially exceeds the other elements of total capital supply listed above, and the rate of increase falls below those of the other items. Yet, because of the magnitude of the item, and the relative importance of this source of capital, the rate of advance is notable. It materially exceeds the figure of 1.4 per cent, which defines the growth of another important social 'fund'—aggregate population.

The four series discussed represent four important elements in the total savings of the country. Accepting these as constituting a fair sample of the aggregate, and summarizing them, we have the following picture of the growth of savings in the United States between 1922 and 1929. A graphic portrayal appears in Figure 87.

## TABLE 172

GROWTH OF CERTAIN ELEMENTS OF CAPITAL FUNDS IN THE UNITED STATES, 1922-1929

| Series | Absolute values, 1929 (millions of dollars) | Average annual rate of increase 1922-1929 (per cent) | Index of instability of growth |
|---|---|---|---|
| Corporate savings (estimated) | 88,840 | + 2.7 | 0.3 |
| Savings deposits, all banks | 28,261 | + 7.0 | 2.3 |
| Aggregate reserves, life insurance companies | 14,272 | +10.6 | 0.7 |
| Assets of building and loan associations | 8,356 | +15.0 | 2.8 |
| Total, four preceding items | 139,729 | + 4.7 | 0.5 |

FIGURE 87

GROWTH OF CERTAIN ELEMENTS OF AGGREGATE CAPITAL FUNDS, 1922-1929

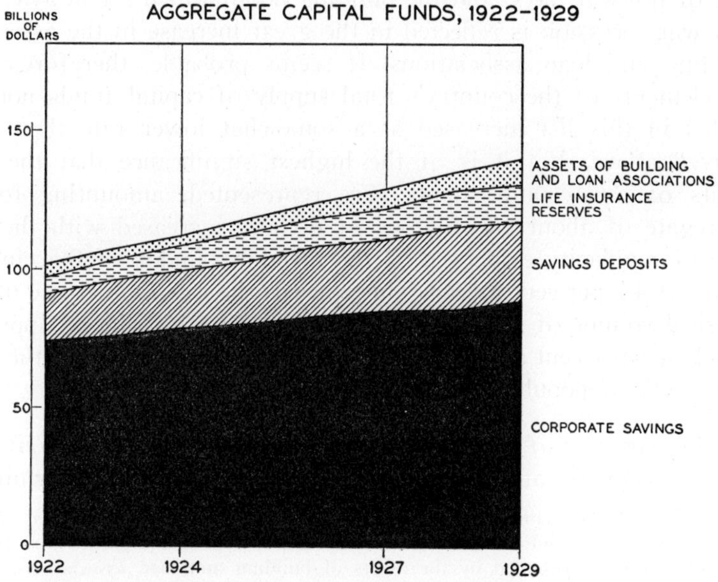

The rates of increase of the four series are inversely correlated with their absolute magnitudes. This is a reasonable relationship, since a given rate of increase involves greater absolute gains for a series of large magnitude than for one of small magnitude.

Judged with reference to the other economic series studied, two of the series listed (corporate savings and life insurance reserves) have been marked by notable stability of growth between 1922 and 1929.

There is probably little overlapping among the items in the above series, and it appears not illegitimate to add them and to measure the rate of change and the stability of the aggregate. When this is done we secure a series which amounted in 1929 to 139,729 millions of dollars and which increased between 1922 and 1929 at a rate of 4.7 per cent a year, with an index of instability of 0.5.

This aggregate falls short, of course, of including all the accumulated savings of the country. It is probable that the figure 4.7 overstates the rate of increase in the capital funds of the country as a whole. Of the elements included in the above total, two were subject to somewhat exceptional forces during the period under review. Sales of life insurance increased at a rate much higher than that of pre-war days, and the building boom which set in after the post-war recession is reflected in the great increase in the assets of building and loan associations. It seems probable, therefore, that the elements of the country's total supply of capital funds not included in this list increased at a somewhat lower rate than that derived above. Yet it is of the highest significance that the elements of our capital supply here represented, amounting to an aggregate of about 140 billions of dollars, increased with the degree of regularity evidenced by the instability index of 0.5, and at a rate of 4.7 per cent a year. This exceeds the rate of increase in the physical volume of production and construction (a rate of approximately 4.1 per cent a year) and is substantially greater than the rate of growth of population.[1]

*An Estimate of the Growth of Aggregate Corporate Capital.—* We may employ another approach to the problem of determining

[1] It is to be recognized, of course, that not all the savings included in the above figures went into the creation of industrial capital equipment. Practically the entire sum represented by the assets of building and loan associations, some 40 per cent of the resources of life insurance companies, and a considerable part of the savings deposits of banks were loaned on real estate mortgages. The proceeds of a large proportion of such loans were used to finance the construction of private residences. It is probable, too, that an increasing proportion of the surpluses and undivided profits of corporations remained in liquid form during this period.

the rate of gain in one important element of the capital funds of the United States—corporate capital. On December 31, 1929, total corporate bonds and stocks, as reported to the United States Treasury [1] in 398,815 corporate returns amounted to 156,501 millions of dollars. There were, however, 57,206 corporations filing income tax returns but not submitting balance sheets. As explained in the preceding section (see footnote, p. 433) we may take rough account of those not reporting by stepping up the total for December 31, 1929, by 10 per cent. (Only approximate accuracy is required in this total, since interest attaches to the rate of increase, not to absolute amounts.) The estimated total of corporate bonds and stocks outstanding, as of December 31, 1929, is 172.2 billions of dollars. (There is, it may be assumed, a certain amount of water in this total, but since it is unlikely that the percentage of stock issues not represented by actual investment changed materially between 1921 and 1929, this may be ignored.) By adding to the estimated figure for bonds and stocks outstanding on December 31, 1929, the estimated total of corporate surplus and undivided profits, we secure 232.8 billions of dollars as the estimated total of corporate capital funds on that date.[2]

It is desired to carry this series back, by years, to December 31, 1921. For each year of this period data on the additions to corporate capital funds are available. Thus, between December 31, 1928, and December 31, 1929, there were added to aggregate corporate capital funds 2.3 billions of dollars through additions to corporate surplus and undivided profits,[3] and 8.0 billions of dollars through the flotation of domestic corporate securities.[4] Subtracting the sum of these items from total corporate capital funds as of December 31,

---

[1] *Statistics of Income for 1929,* Bureau of Internal Revenue, p. 25.

[2] The combination of statistics of corporate stocks with those of surplus and undivided profits avoids any error arising from the existence of no-par stock.

[3] Net profits, less total taxes and total cash dividends paid, and less deficits on the part of corporations suffering losses.

[4] Since the capital funds of investment trusts and holding companies are included in the Treasury statistics, the issues of such companies are included in the total given. Refunding issues have been deducted.

The procedure here employed rests on the assumption that the Treasury data and the compilations on new issues are comparable. In detail, there are doubtless discrepancies, in addition to those for which correction has been made. But for the purposes of approximating the general magnitude of the sums involved, and of estimating the rate of growth of these funds, minor discrepancies may be ignored.

1929, we secure 222.5 billions of dollars as the total of corporate capital funds on December 31, 1928. The same procedure was followed for earlier years, successive annual increments being subtracted from year-end totals. The results (rounded off to the nearest billion) are shown in columns (5) and (6) of the following table.

TABLE 173

ESTIMATED GROWTH OF CORPORATE CAPITAL FUNDS IN THE UNITED STATES, 1922-1929

(In billions of dollars)

| (1) Year | (2) Through corporate savings | (3) Through sales of new securities [a] | (4) Total | (5) Total corporate capital funds at end of year | (6) Total corporate capital funds at middle of year |
|---|---|---|---|---|---|
| 1921 | — | — | — | 182 | — |
| 1922 | 1.7 | 2.4 | 4.1 | 186 | 184 |
| 1923 | 2.5 | 2.8 | 5.3 | 191 | 189 |
| 1924 | 1.6 | 3.1 | 4.7 | 196 | 194 |
| 1925 | 3.0 | 3.7 | 6.7 | 203 | 199 |
| 1926 | 2.3 | 3.8 | 6.2 | 209 | 206 |
| 1927 | 1.1 | 4.6 | 5.7 | 215 | 212 |
| 1928 | 2.5 | 5.4 | 7.8 | 222 | 219 |
| 1929 | 2.3 | 8.0 | 10.3 | 233 | 228 |

Columns (2), (3), (4) are headed: Additions to total corporate capital funds during year.

[a] Data on sales of new securities are the figures for domestic corporate issues, as compiled by *The Commercial and Financial Chronicle,* plus new issues of joint-stock land banks. Since financing by closed corporations and by small corporations would not find its way into the investment market, this series understates the absolute amount of financing through sales of new securities.

These are, of course, only estimates, and are to be looked upon merely as approximations to the figures desired. They indicate that the aggregate capital at the disposal of American corporations increased from approximately 182 billions of dollars at the end of 1921 to 233 billions of dollars at the close of 1929. The annual increase in aggregate capital during this period averaged about 6.4 billions of dollars. The year 1929, when something in excess of ten billions of dollars was added to corporate capital funds, marked the maximum increase.[1]

[1] Duplications affect this figure, since investment trust and holding company issues are included in the annual increments and in the aggregate fund. To the extent that industrial corporations in general employed surplus and undivided

The figures of greatest interest for our present purpose are those defining the rate of increase and the stability of aggregate capital funds at the disposal of corporations. Such aggregate funds (values computed as of the middle of each year) increased at an average annual rate of 3.1 per cent, and their oscillations averaged only four-tenths of one per cent. This estimate of the rate of growth of corporate capital funds has a much broader statistical base than had the data relating to separate elements of the capital supply, cited above. One may be confident that if it errs it is on the side of understatement.[1] It is an impressive figure, in view of the magnitude of the accumulations represented. The capital supply at the disposal of corporations was increasing during the period through which we have just passed at a rate more than twice that at which population was growing. These facts indicate that the innumerable and complicated instruments of round-about production were being

---

profits in the purchase of securities of other corporations, instead of utilizing these funds in their own business, a further duplication is introduced into the above calculations.

Difficulties arise, also, because of lack of complete information concerning the retirement of bond issues during the period covered, and because of the probability that some of the proceeds of new issues were used for refunding purposes, though not specifically so designated. However, errors due to these causes, which would tend to increase the apparent rate of growth of corporate capital funds, were undoubtedly more than balanced by errors due to incomplete coverage of data relating to new issues.

[1] The possibility of duplication through utilization of corporate surpluses in the purchase of new securities has been noted. Another source of possible error lies in the necessarily incomplete coverage of the current statistics of new issues. Figures previously cited (footnote, p. 429) indicate that the actual annual additions to the total stock and bond issues of domestic corporations rather materially exceed the values given in the compilations of *The Commercial and Financial Chronicle*. Many issues of closed and of small corporations would naturally be excluded from this record. If we make the assumption that the current statistics of new issues require a stepping-up of 50 per cent, and correct the figures in Table 173 correspondingly, we secure a series for total corporate capital funds which increases between 1922 and 1929 at a rate of 4.4 per cent a year.

Professor S. H. Nerlove, in his study *A Decade of Corporate Incomes* (University of Chicago Press, 1932), gives two series of estimates of the invested capital of all corporations in the United States. One of these shows a rate of increase of 4.3 per cent per year between 1922 and 1929, the other a rate of 5.0 per cent. (Nerlove's 'invested capital' is not equivalent to our 'corporate capital funds', since he is dealing with equity values only.)

For various reasons, then, it is safe to say that the estimates of corporate capital funds given in the text err on the side of conservatism, as regards their rate of growth. We may conclude that the true rate of increase in these funds, between 1922 and 1929, was in excess of 3.0 per cent and was probably in the neighborhood of 4.0 per cent per year.

created in ever greater volume during this period. The rate of increase, in fact, was one which, if maintained, would have resulted in a doubling of the total supply of these instruments in from 16 to 23 years. Whether this rate of increase in capital funds would be likely to engender unstable conditions, whether, in fact, it contributed to the recession which terminated this period of advance, is a natural question, but one which cannot at this stage of our knowledge be definitely answered.

The remarkable stability of this capital fund is worthy of note. The fluctuations in the aggregate were only slightly greater than the variations from year to year in population, and were distinctly smaller than the oscillations in any other economic series we have studied.

Independent evidence as to the rate of change in the aggregate capital funds at the disposal of corporations is furnished by the following index of the aggregate assets of American industrial corporations, compiled by the Statistical Division of the American Telephone and Telegraph Company.[1] This series, together with estimated corporate capital funds, is plotted in Figure 88.

TABLE 174

INDEX NUMBERS MEASURING CHANGES IN THE ASSETS OF AMERICAN INDUSTRIAL CORPORATIONS, 1922-1929

| Year | Index of corporate assets |
|---|---|
| 1922 | 100.0 |
| 1923 | 104.6 |
| 1924 | 106.7 |
| 1925 | 111.9 |
| 1926 | 116.4 |
| 1927 | 119.4 |
| 1928 | 127.3 |
| 1929 | 137.8 |

These data indicate a change in the aggregate assets of industrial corporations at an average annual rate of $+ 4.4$ per cent, between 1922 and 1929. This series and that which has just been

[1] This index has been placed at our disposal through the courtesy of Mr. Seymour L. Andrew, Chief Statistician. It is constructed from the published reports of somewhat over 400 important corporations, by the process of chaining links based on identical companies for pairs of successive years.

## FIGURE 88
### GROWTH OF ASSETS OF INDUSTRIAL CORPORATIONS AND OF TOTAL CORPORATE CAPITAL FUNDS IN THE UNITED STATES, 1922-1929

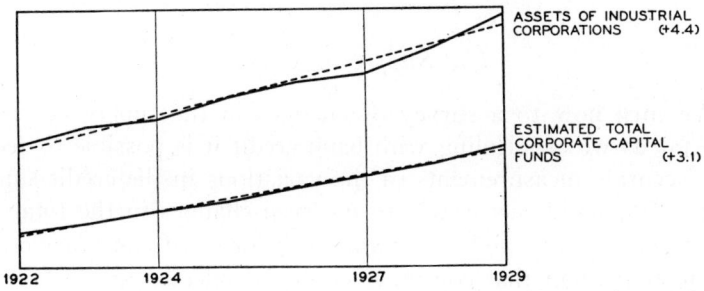

Plotted on ratio scale. The figures in parentheses define average annual rates of change (in percentage form).

discussed are drawn from different sides of the balance sheets of industrial corporations and are based upon somewhat different corporate groups. The rates of change derived from them differ somewhat, but are of the same general order of magnitude. A figure in the neighborhood of four per cent a year may be taken to define the rate of increase in corporate capital funds during the period between the recessions of 1920 and 1929.

The index of instability for industrial assets is 1.4, materially greater than the corresponding measurement for aggregate capital funds. Variations in inventories and in other liquid assets which vary with business conditions would affect industrial assets, from year to year, without there being any necessary change in aggregate capital.

It is clear from the preceding discussion that, with respect to the volume of capital available to American industry, no restriction was placed upon industrial expansion. Though the precise rate of increase in our capital resources may not be determined, for reasons pointed out above, the evidence indicates that the most important single element in the total supply has been increasing at a rate close to four per cent a year. Various other elements of the capital supply have increased at rates materially greater than this. The aggregate in Table 172 (which overlaps the above series to some extent, since corporate surpluses were included) shows an increase at the rate of 4.7 per cent a year. These various bits of evidence, supplementing data relating to the physical volume of production of capital equipment, indicate that a constantly increasing percentage of the total national income was diverted, during the period 1922-1929, to the replacement and accumulation of capital goods, and to the building up of circulating capital.[1]

## The Supply of Credit

We turn now to a survey of changes in the supply of credit. In so far as we are dealing with bank credit it is possible to secure fairly accurate measurements of the variations in the credit supply, but it is impossible accurately to measure changes in the total volume of book credit [2] and of certain other forms of consumer credit. Only to the extent that consumer credit is reflected in the business of commercial banks, therefore, does this highly important element enter into this survey.

It will be useful in tracing credit changes to distinguish between what may be called *primary funds,* funds available for use

[1] Chapter VI contains data relating to the production of capital goods which may be compared with the present statistics of capital funds.

Lack of data render it impossible to include in the above summary investments by individuals in farm improvements, farm equipment, drainage and similar additions to capital equipment, investments which were not financed by public offerings of securities.

[2] The U. S. Bureau of Internal Revenue has published statistics of notes and accounts receivable for all reporting corporations for the years 1926 to 1929. (See *Statistics of Income.*) For all corporations, excluding the finance group (in which banks fall) we have the following figures:

|  | Notes and accounts receivable (in millions of dollars) |
|---|---|
| Dec. 31, 1926 | 17,761 |
| Dec. 31, 1927 | 18,829 |
| Dec. 31, 1928 | 21,775 |
| Dec. 31, 1929 | 22,682 |

The magnitude of this item is apparent, if we compare it with a figure of 58,474 millions of dollars representing total bank credit (loans and investments of all banks in the United States) as of June 29, 1929. Equally striking is the fact that such notes and accounts receivable increased by almost 5 billions of dollars over a period of but three years.

Notes and accounts payable, for the same body of reporting corporations, increased from 17,360 millions of dollars on December 31, 1926, to 20,799 millions on December 31, 1929. Of the total for December 31, 1926, accounts payable made up 8,056 millions, notes payable made up 9,304 millions. On the broad assumption that all notes payable were for bank loans, we have, as the approximate amount of net receivables on December 31, 1926, 17,761 millions less 8,056 millions, or almost 10 billions of dollars. Though these are not definitive figures, they suggest the general order of magnitude of this particular form of credit.

as bank reserves and, in part, as media of circulation, and *secondary funds,* the latter consisting of credit extended by all banks other than Federal reserve banks. Our first concern is with changes in the supply of and in the demand for primary funds during the period 1922-1929.

*Primary Funds.*—In the following table are shown the elements of the total supply of primary funds. These are plotted in Figure 89.

TABLE 175

CHANGES IN AGGREGATE PRIMARY FUNDS IN THE UNITED STATES AND IN THE CONSTITUENT ELEMENTS OF THIS AGGREGATE, 1922-1929 [a]
(Averages of daily figures, in millions of dollars)

| (1) Year | (2) Stock of money gold | (3) Treasury currency outstanding | (4) Total Federal reserve bank credit outstanding | (5) Aggregate primary funds |
|---|---|---|---|---|
| 1922 | 3,802 | 1,604 | 1,226 | 6,632 |
| 1923 | 4,061 | 1,736 | 1,205 | 7,002 |
| 1924 | 4,439 | 1,757 | 996 | 7,192 |
| 1925 | 4,381 | 1,755 | 1,195 | 7,331 |
| 1926 | 4,452 | 1,743 | 1,258 | 7,453 |
| 1927 | 4,564 | 1,774 | 1,175 | 7,513 |
| 1928 | 4,206 | 1,783 | 1,505 | 7,494 |
| 1929 | 4,283 | 1,785 | 1,459 | 7,527 |
| Average annual rate of change (per cent) | +1.3 | +1.1 | +3.6 | +1.6 |
| Index of instability | 4.4 | 1.6 | 7.5 | 1.6 |

[a] The data in this table are from the *17th Annual Report of the Federal Reserve Board* (1930), p. 31.

The stock of money gold [1] is the major element of the primary funds of the United States, constituting 57.3 per cent of the aggregate in 1922, 56.9 per cent in 1929. This is available for use either in the form of bank reserves, in which it may form the basis of expansion of secondary funds, or as circulating media. Next in

[1] This stock consists of gold coin in circulation, plus gold held by the Treasury and by Federal reserve banks, except gold earmarked for foreign account. See *Federal Reserve Bulletin,* July, 1929, pp. 432-438.

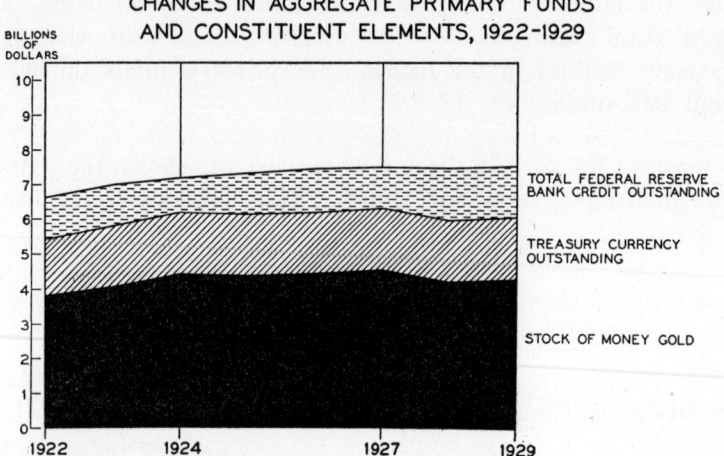

FIGURE 89

CHANGES IN AGGREGATE PRIMARY FUNDS AND CONSTITUENT ELEMENTS, 1922-1929

importance is Treasury currency, or Treasury credit,[1] constituting slightly less than one-quarter of the aggregate. This element, again, is available for use either in the form of bank reserves, or as part of the circulating media. The third element of the total volume of primary funds consists of Federal reserve bank credit, credit which is emitted in various ways. This credit constitutes the primary source of member bank reserve balances. Reserve bank credit made up slightly less than one-fifth of the total volume of primary funds in the United States between 1922 and 1929.

In absolute magnitude secondary funds are far more important than are primary funds. As compared with a total of 7,527 millions of dollars of primary funds in 1929, secondary funds (loans and investments of all banks in the United States) amounted to 58,474 millions,[2] almost eight times as much. But the growth of secondary funds, which supply the major part of the credit needs of the country, is conditioned by the available supply of primary funds, and, accordingly, the latter occupy a place of strategic importance in the credit and monetary structure of the country.

The relative importance of different elements in aggregate pri-

[1] This is made up of silver coin, silver certificates, Treasury notes of 1890, Federal reserve bank notes, national bank notes, United States notes, and minor coin, less Treasury holdings of cash.

[2] As of June 29, 1929. The daily average of primary funds for the week ending June 29 was 7,402 millions of dollars.

mary funds and the major changes in these elements are shown clearly by Figure 89. The stock of money gold increased substantially between 1922 and 1924 with imports of gold from abroad, and reserve bank credit contracted. Aggregate primary funds increased 560 millions of dollars. During the next two years the aggregate increased by about 260 millions of dollars, practically all of this coming from expanding reserve bank credit. Between 1926 and 1927 the stock of money gold again increased, by something over 100 millions of dollars, and reserve bank credit contracted by a slightly smaller amount. From 1927 to 1928 the stock of money gold dropped sharply, the loss amounting to over 350 millions of dollars, and reserve credit expanded, by an almost equal amount. Changes between 1928 and 1929 were slight.

These movements illustrate very well the rôle of Federal reserve credit as a factor regulating the total supply of primary funds. The stock of money gold, the largest element in the supply of these funds, moves, in the main, in response to forces not immediately connected with domestic business conditions and with domestic currency and credit requirements. Treasury credit, in total volume more important than reserve bank credit, has been a similarly insensitive factor. The elastic portion of this important aggregate of primary funds has consisted of reserve bank credit, the smallest element in the total. It is this element which must not only respond to the demands of business but must also correct the aggregate for such fluctuations in the other factors as are ill-adapted to the immediate needs of domestic business.

Total primary funds increased between 1922 and 1929 at an average annual rate of 1.6 per cent. The sharpest relative increase occurred in reserve bank credit, which rose at an average rate of 3.6 per cent a year, as against rates of 1.3 per cent and 1.1 per cent for the stock of money gold and Treasury credit. In absolute figures, however, the greatest addition to the aggregate came from the swelling stock of gold.

The other side of the picture is revealed by a study of the uses to which primary funds have been put, or, in other words, by a survey of the demand factors. Table 176, on the following page, shows the volume of primary funds flowing into each of four channels.

## TABLE 176
### Uses of Primary Funds in the United States, 1922-1929
(Averages of daily figures, in millions of dollars) [a]

| (1) Year | (2) Money in circulation | (3) Member bank reserve balances | (4) Non-member deposits in Federal reserve banks | (5) Unexpended capital funds, Federal reserve banks | (6) Aggregate primary funds |
|---|---|---|---|---|---|
| 1922 | 4,535 | 1,781 | 30 | 286 | 6,632 |
| 1923 | 4,822 | 1,873 | 27 | 280 | 7,002 |
| 1924 | 4,879 | 2,023 | 27 | 263 | 7,192 |
| 1925 | 4,869 | 2,167 | 31 | 264 | 7,331 |
| 1926 | 4,932 | 2,209 | 28 | 284 | 7,453 |
| 1927 | 4,892 | 2,290 | 31 | 300 | 7,513 |
| 1928 | 4,783 | 2,355 | 29 | 327 | 7,494 |
| 1929 | 4,763 | 2,358 | 30 | 376 | 7,527 |
| Average annual rate of change (per cent)..... | +0.4 | +4.2 | +0.8 | +4.1 | +1.6 |
| Index of instability | 2.0 | 2.3 | 4.6 | 6.4 | 1.6 |

[a] 17th Annual Report of the Federal Reserve Board (1930), p. 31.

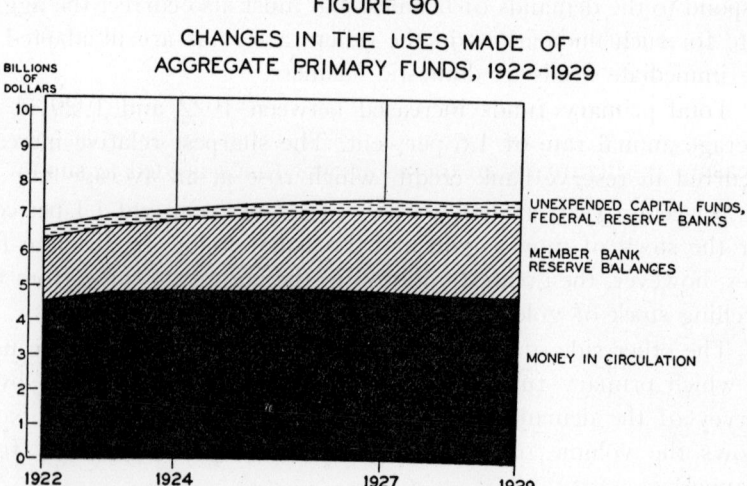

FIGURE 90
CHANGES IN THE USES MADE OF AGGREGATE PRIMARY FUNDS, 1922-1929

The constitution of the aggregate, with reference to the uses to which primary funds are put, is shown graphically in Figure 90.

By far the largest portion of aggregate primary funds (about two-thirds of the total) is used to provide media of circulation. An additional five per cent is practically withdrawn from the market, appearing as unexpended capital funds of the reserve banks. Nonmember deposits make up a very small portion (less than one-half of one per cent) of the total. The balance, averaging some 30 per cent of the total, is used to provide member bank reserve balances at Federal reserve banks. These balances provide the basis of the major portion of the credit supply of the country.

From 1922 to 1926 aggregate primary funds increased by something over 800 millions of dollars. Approximately half of this was used to provide additional money in circulation, while half went to augment member bank reserve balances. From 1926 to 1929 total primary funds increased by approximately 70 millions of dollars. Money in circulation had declined, during this period, by 170 millions of dollars, making available, altogether, some 240 millions of dollars of primary funds. About 150 millions of this went to swell member bank reserve balances, while about 90 millions were withdrawn through the increase in unexpended capital funds of reserve banks. The major part of the increase in primary funds over the whole period was used to increase member bank balances, the average rate of increase per year in this series being 4.2 per cent.

The story of the changes in primary funds between 1922 and 1929 is, therefore, fairly simple. For the first four years the net change in reserve bank credit was negligible; the inflow of gold from abroad, plus an increase of about 150 millions of dollars in Treasury credit, furnished the additional funds needed to supply an expansion of money in circulation and a steady advance in member bank balances. During the remainder of the period primary funds were released by a declining volume of money in circulation. There was a still greater decline, however, in the stock of money gold, owing to heavy exports. Additional Federal reserve credit was needed to supply funds for expanding member bank reserves, and to replace funds withdrawn through the increase in unexpended capital funds of the reserve banks. Reserve bank credit in 1929 was 200 millions of dollars greater than in 1926, and almost 300 millions of dollars greater than in 1927.

*Secondary Funds.*—We turn to the changes occurring between 1922 and 1929 in the volume of secondary funds, that is, in the volume of bank credit available to the business community. For purposes of comparison there are brought together in the following table series relating to aggregate primary funds, to that portion of total primary funds flowing into member bank reserve balances and hence serving directly as a basis of secondary funds, to member bank credit and to total bank credit.

TABLE 177

ELEMENTS OF THE MONEY AND CREDIT STRUCTURE, 1922-1929

(In millions of dollars)

| (1) | (2) | (3) | (4) | (5) |
|---|---|---|---|---|
| | | | Secondary funds | |
| Year | Aggregate primary funds (daily average) [a] | Member bank balances (daily average) | Member bank credit [b] (June 30) | Total credit, all banks [c] (June 30) |
| 1922 | 6,632 | 1,781 | 24,182 | 39,956 |
| 1923 | 7,002 | 1,873 | 26,507 | 43,738 |
| 1924 | 7,192 | 2,023 | 27,167 | 45,180 |
| 1925 | 7,331 | 2,167 | 29,518 | 48,830 |
| 1926 | 7,453 | 2,209 | 31,184 | 51,562 |
| 1927 | 7,513 | 2,290 | 32,756 | 53,750 |
| 1928 | 7,494 | 2,355 | 35,061 | 57,265 |
| 1929 | 7,527 | 2,358 | 35,711 | 58,474 |
| Average annual rate of change (per cent) | +1.6 | +4.2 | +5.8 | +5.6 |

[a] Stock of money gold, Treasury currency outstanding and Federal reserve credit.
[b] Loans and investments of all member banks.
[c] Loans and investments of all banks in the United States.

These series are shown graphically in Figure 91.

As a basic element we have the aggregate mass of primary funds, increasing at an average annual rate of 1.6 per cent between 1922 and 1929. More definitely linked to the credit superstructure is that portion of this aggregate (some thirty per cent) which is used as legal reserve balances by member banks. This portion increased by 577 millions of dollars between 1922 and 1929, at an average annual rate of 4.2 per cent.

Of a different order is the mass of bank credit directly avail-

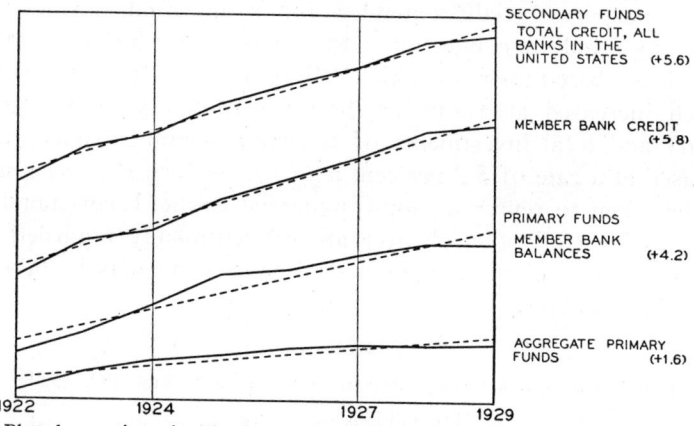

**FIGURE 91**

CHANGES IN ELEMENTS OF THE MONEY AND CREDIT STRUCTURE OF THE UNITED STATES, 1922-1929

Plotted on ratio scale. The figures in parentheses define average annual rates of change (in percentage form).

able to the business community. About sixty per cent of the total bank credit of the country consists of member bank credit, and this rests directly upon the member bank reserve balances. Member bank credit increased from 24,182 millions of dollars on June 30, 1922, to 35,711 millions on June 29, 1929, the average annual rate of increase being 5.8 per cent. Total bank credit increased over the same period from 39,956 millions of dollars to 58,474 millions, at an average annual rate of 5.6 per cent.

It is this last figure which measures the increase in the volume of credit actually available to the business world, an increase of more than 18,500 millions of dollars in seven years. The rate of increase, it should be noted, is materially greater than the rate of increase in the physical volume of production of movable goods during this period (approximately 3.8 per cent) and still greater than the rate of increase in the aggregate value of goods produced (approximately 3.3 per cent). It exceeds, also, the rates of increase in the capital funds and in the industrial assets of corporations.

It is possible to investigate the nature of this increase by studying some of the details given in the reports of certain Federal reserve member banks, a group which constitutes approximately 38 per cent of the banking strength of the country. For this group of reporting member banks the average annual rate of increase in volume of credit extended between 1922 and 1929 was 5.9 per cent, slightly above the rate for the banks of the country at large. The total may be broken up into two elements significant for the present purposes, credit extended for commercial purposes and credit employed in connection with security purchases or arising out of loans based upon securities.[1] By combining loans on securities (which increased at a rate of 10.5 per cent a year during this period) and total investments of reporting member banks (which increased at a rate of 5.2 per cent a year), we secure a series which may be taken to represent non-commercial credit. Loans not based on securities ('all other' loans) are conventionally regarded as a measure of the volume of commercial credit, and may be here employed for that purpose.

TABLE 178

GROWTH OF BANK CREDIT, REPORTING MEMBER BANKS, 1922-1929 [a]

(In millions of dollars)

| (1) Year | (2) Loans on securities | (3) Total investments | (4) Loans on securities plus total investments | (5) All other loans |
|---|---|---|---|---|
| 1922 | 3,863 | 4,086 | 7,949 | 7,261 |
| 1923 | 4,117 | 4,473 | 8,590 | 7,750 |
| 1924 | 4,456 | 4,747 | 9,203 | 8,001 |
| 1925 | 5,336 | 5,219 | 10,555 | 8,248 |
| 1926 | 5,722 | 5,250 | 10,972 | 8,588 |
| 1927 | 6,166 | 5,560 | 11,726 | 8,679 |
| 1928 | 6,894 | 6,052 | 12,946 | 8,909 |
| 1929 | 7,651 | 5,717 | 13,368 | 9,230 |
| Average annual rate of change (per cent) | +10.5 | +5.2 | +7.9 | +3.2 |
| Index of instability | 1.8 | 2.8 | 1.7 | 1.1 |

[a] The entries in this table are based upon monthly averages of weekly figures, as given in the *17th Annual Report of the Federal Reserve Board*, p. 98.

These series are plotted in Figure 92.

[1] The classification of total loans into loans on securities and 'all other' loans is not available for all Federal reserve member banks for the full period under review. Loans and investments of reporting member banks constitute, however, over 60 per cent of the total loans and investments of all member banks; the average annual rates of change are practically identical.

## FIGURE 92
### GROWTH OF BANK CREDIT IN THE UNITED STATES, 1922-1929
#### REPORTING MEMBER BANKS

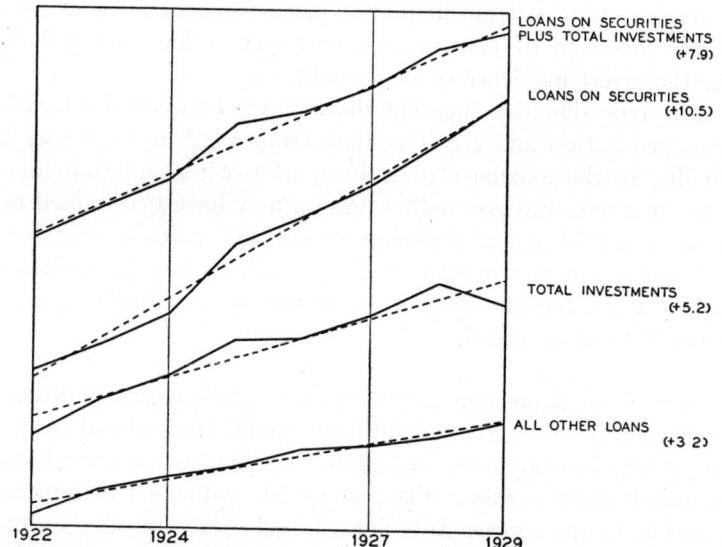

Plotted on ratio scale. The figures in parentheses define average annual rates of change (in percentage form).

This division reveals a pronounced difference between the courses taken by commercial and by non-commercial credit between 1922 and 1929. The volume of commercial credit increased at a rate of 3.2 per cent a year; the volume of credit connected with the security markets increased at a rate of 7.9 per cent a year. The former rate is actually lower than the figures measuring the trends of industrial production and of the volume of distribution of goods. The second rate stands close to the measurements defining the course of events in the security markets.

There are differing views as to the extent to which credit extended in connection with security transactions may flow into channels of commercial use. We need not here debate the question. It seems clear, however, that the full force of the purchasing power represented by a volume of credit increasing at a rate of 5.6 per cent a year was not felt in commodity markets. For if it had been, this figure is hardly consistent with a rate of increase of 3.8 per cent in the volume of production of movable goods and a rate of decline of 0.5 per cent in the level of wholesale prices. The state of demand was such, during this period, that the effect of the new credit was felt in certain markets (notably markets for securities and for urban realty) and not to the same extent in others. Credit may be free to flow from market to market but the state of demand and the direction of consumers' (or buyers') interests will determine the direct incidence of new credit.

It is true that the apparent discrepancy between the trends of prices, production and credit volume from 1922 to 1929 may have been due to the existence of a form of masked inflation in commodity markets. Excess credit emission may have maintained prices during a period when declining production costs tended toward lower prices. Such a tendency did prevail, as has been shown in Chapter VIII, but the drop in costs was not sufficient to account for the divergence noted.

*Increase in Mortgage Indebtedness.*—The preceding discussion has dealt solely with commercial bank credit. In a related field, that of mortgage indebtedness, important developments occurred during the period under review.[1] The last decade witnessed a tremendous expansion in the aggregate value of real estate mortgages in the United States, particularly of urban real estate mortgages. We are not justified in considering the increase in mortgage values to be exclusively due to credit expansion. The very considerable investments of life insurance companies, of building and loan associations and of mutual savings banks represent, primarily, the flow of savings. To the extent that real estate security offerings have been purchased by ultimate investors the same is true. In this field we are dealing with an expansion which combined elements of both credit and savings.

Changes in some of the elements of the total mortgage indebtedness of the country are indicated by the entries in the following table. It should be recognized that certain of the figures are estimates, subject to considerable margins of error. These series are charted in Figure 93.

Total estimated holdings of urban real estate mortgages more than doubled between 1922 and 1929. From an estimated value of approximately 13 billions of dollars in 1922, urban mortgage hold-

---

[1] See "Credit Expansion, 1920 to 1929, and its Lessons", Charles E. Persons, *Quarterly Journal of Economics,* Vol. XLV, November, 1930, pp. 94-130, for a discussion of this subject.

TABLE 179

ELEMENTS OF MORTGAGE INDEBTEDNESS IN THE UNITED STATES, 1922-1929
Estimated Holdings of Urban Real Estate Mortgages [a]
(In millions of dollars)

| (1) Year | (2) Commercial banks | (3) Mortgage bonds outstanding | (4) Mutual savings banks | (5) Life insurance companies | (6) Building and loan associations | (7) Total |
|---|---|---|---|---|---|---|
| 1922 | 3,393 * | 682 | 4,250 * | 1,634 * | 3,065 * | 13,024 |
| 1923 | 2,677 * | 900 | 4,375 * | 1,825 * | 3,627 * | 13,404 |
| 1924 | 3,449 * | 1,190 | 4,500 * | 2,019 | 4,384 * | 15,542 |
| 1925 | 4,221 * | 1,883 | 4,625 * | 2,507 | 5,085 | 18,321 |
| 1926 | 4,993 * | 2,654 | 4,750 * | 3,153 | 5,827 | 21,377 |
| 1927 | 5,767 | 3,305 | 4,875 * | 3,701 | 6,583 | 24,231 |
| 1928 | 6,221 | 3,972 | 5,000 * | 4,290 | 7,336 | 26,819 |
| 1929 | 5,195 | 4,169 | 5,125 * | 4,831 | 7,787 * | 27,107 |
| Average annual rate of change (per cent) .. | +10.7 | +29.0 | +2.7 | +18.0 | +14.0 | +12.5 |

* Estimated.
[a] From Charles E. Persons, op. cit., p. 104.

FIGURE 93

CHANGES IN THE ESTIMATED HOLDINGS OF URBAN REAL ESTATE MORTGAGES IN THE UNITED STATES, 1922-1929

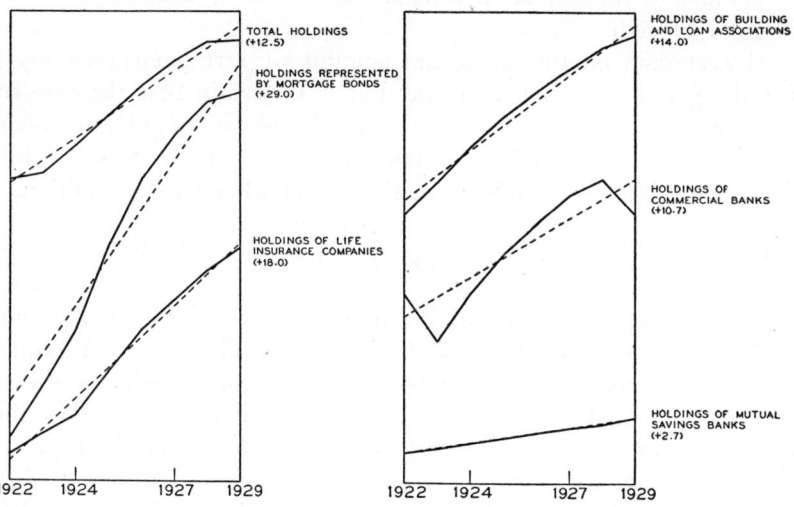

Plotted on ratio scale. The figures in parentheses define average annual rates of change (in percentage form).

ings increased to a figure in excess of 27 billions of dollars in 1929. Some idea of the relative values involved may be had from the fact that the figure for 1922 was equal to about one-third of the total outstanding credit of all banks in the United States in that year, while the figure for 1929 was equal to almost one-half of the total bank credit then outstanding. The average annual rate of increase in urban mortgage holdings between 1922 and 1929 was 12.5 per cent. This rate is far in excess of those relating to aggregate savings, in so far as these may be estimated, and to total volume of commercial credit. Here was one of the points at which a bulge developed in the economic system between 1922 and 1929. The amount of savings and, probably, the amount of credit devoted to urban realty development during this period was excessive, if the average pace of economic growth may be accepted as a criterion.

The rapid development of mortgage bonds as a means of financing real estate operations was a notable feature of this period. The aggregate amount of such bonds increased more than six-fold between 1922 and 1929, the annual rate of increase averaging 29.0 per cent. Next in order, with an average annual rate of increase of 18.0 per cent, were the mortgage holdings of life insurance companies. Holdings of building and loan associations, of commercial banks and of mutual savings banks ranked next, with reference to rates of growth.

Exact data on the aggregate amount of farm mortgage loans for these years are not available, but it is certain that the rate of increase was much lower. Between 1922 and 1929 aggregate farm mortgages probably increased from a figure not far above 8 billions of dollars to something in the neighborhood of 9.5 billions.[1]

### Cost of Capital and Credit

In treating of the availability of capital and of credit, the supplies of these factors are not alone important. Their *cost* is of equal concern to commercial and industrial borrowers. In ordinary times, indeed, the availability of capital and of credit is measured by the business man solely in terms of costs. It is to a consideration of these costs that we now turn.

Various series measuring the cost of capital and of credit to dif-

[1] Cf. Persons, *ibid.*, p. 107.

ferent classes of borrowers between 1922 and 1929 are given in the following table, and are shown graphically in Figure 94.

TABLE 180

BOND AND STOCK YIELDS, REDISCOUNT RATES AND INTEREST RATES, 1922-1929

| (1) Year | (2) Bond yields [a] (per cent) | (3) Stock yields [b] (per cent) | (4) Rediscount rates, Federal reserve banks, 60-90 day commercial paper [a] (per cent) | (5) Rates charged customers on prime commercial paper, 32-36 cities [c] (per cent) | (6) Interest rates, 4-6 months commercial paper [a] (per cent) | (7) Call loan renewal rates [d] (per cent) |
|---|---|---|---|---|---|---|
| 1922 | 4.94 | 6.74 | 4.56 | 6.24 | 4.43 | 4.29 |
| 1923 | 4.98 | 6.92 | 4.48 | 6.10 | 4.98 | 4.85 |
| 1924 | 4.85 | 6.88 | 4.11 | 5.76 | 3.91 | 3.08 |
| 1925 | 4.72 | 5.86 | 3.81 | 5.57 | 4.03 | 4.20 |
| 1926 | 4.60 | 5.77 | 3.99 | 5.61 | 4.24 | 4.50 |
| 1927 | 4.47 | 5.20 | 3.81 | 5.55 | 4.01 | 4.06 |
| 1928 | 4.49 | 4.40 | 4.43 | 5.67 | 4.84 | 6.04 |
| 1929 | 4.70 | 4.17 | 4.99 | 6.08 | 5.78 | 7.61 |
| Average ...... | 4.72 | 5.74 | 4.27 | 5.82 | 4.53 | 4.83 |
| Average annual rate of change (per cent) .. | —1.4 | —7.2 | +0.6 | —0.8 | +2.5 | +8.4 |

[a] The index of bond yields is that of 60 high-grade bonds. The rediscount rates are unweighted averages of the weekly average rates of 12 Federal reserve banks. The 4-6 months interest rates relate to choice, double-name commercial paper. The three series are computed by the Standard Statistics Company, and are published in the *Standard Statistical Bulletin.*
[b] Industrial common stock yields, computed by Leonard P. Ayres of the Cleveland Trust Company.
[c] Simple average of the prevailing rates published in the *Federal Reserve Bulletin.*
[d] Average rate, New York Stock Exchange. *17th Annual Report of the Federal Reserve Board* (1930), p. 80.

The period opens with relatively low official rediscount rates and open-market commercial paper rates. The rate of 4.43 per cent on 4-6 months commercial paper was distinctly below the average of 5.99 for the five years preceding (1917-21), and was also lower than the average rate of 4.85 for the years 1901-13. Bond yields stood at 4.94, below the average of 5.39 for the five years preceding, but above the average of 4.32 for the period 1901-13. Rediscount rates of the twelve Federal reserve banks averaged 4.56 per

## FIGURE 94

### CHANGES IN INTEREST RATES, REDISCOUNT RATES AND BOND AND STOCK YIELDS IN THE UNITED STATES, 1922-1929

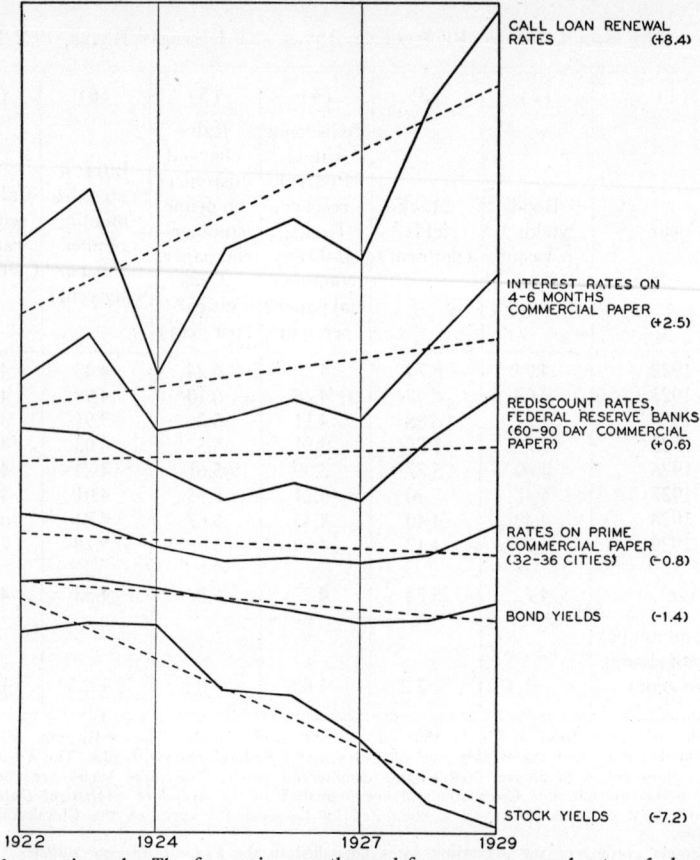

Plotted on ratio scale. The figures in parentheses define average annual rates of change (in percentage form).

cent, materially lower than the figures of 5.96 and 6.13 for the two years preceding. These relatively low rates became lower still during the five years following. The charge to bank customers in the country at large, as determined by averaging rates charged customers on prime commercial paper in 32 cities, stood on a much higher level. This was 6.24 per cent in 1922, as compared with an average of 6.81 for the two years preceding. These rates were not only much higher in absolute terms than were the other series of discount rates cited, but they showed a much smaller decline from the high rates of the preceding two years. Call loan renewal rates on the Stock Exchange in 1922 averaged 4.29 per cent, the lowest of all the rates given. Highest of the rates cited was the average yield on common industrial stocks (Ayres' index). This amounted to 6.74 per cent in 1922.

From 1922 to 1927 the general movement of interest and discount rates was downward. This was an era of cheap money, a cheapness that was stimulated, as we have seen, by heavy increases in the stock of money gold in the country. Certain series reached their lowest points in 1924, but in general the low rates persisted until 1927. In that year the average of the rediscount rates of the Federal reserve banks on 60-90 day commercial paper was 3.81, which was below all market rates. Highest of the rates was the charge to bank customers in various cities, which averaged 5.55 per cent. From 1927 to 1929 all the series listed in Table 180, except stock yields, rose. The advance was sharp in average rediscount rates, in open market rates on commercial paper, and on call loan renewal rates. Stock yields alone continued to decline, a reflection of the continued advance in stock prices.

Because of the shift in direction of movement of interest rates that occurred in most series after 1927, figures defining net average rates of change for the period as a whole must be used with some reservations. Measures of net change for the period are useful in such cases, but their descriptive value is not so great as it is for series with unbroken trends for the period as a whole. Measurements of net annual change are given, with the data to which they relate, in Table 180.

Changes in the cost of capital are perhaps most accurately measured by the trend of high-grade bond yields. Between 1922 and 1929 the yield of 60 high-grade bonds declined at an average rate of 1.4 per cent a year. This decline was quite regular through 1927; there was a very slight advance in 1928 and a sharper rise in 1929. The decline was most rapid in the case of public utility bonds (rate of change —2.2 per cent a year), and least rapid in the case of municipal bonds (rate of change —0.4 per cent a year). Though the direct cost to borrowers must be measured with reference to new issues, this may be taken to indicate that the cost of capital to public utility borrowers declined more rapidly than it did for borrowers in other fields. For railroad bonds the decline was at the rate of 1.6 per cent a year, and for industrial bonds at a rate of 1.0 per cent.[1]

A somewhat different story is told when changes in the cost of capital are measured with reference to the trend of stock yields. One of the most striking features of the post-war investment situation was the great increase of financing through stock issues, accompanied by a relative decline in the amount of financing by bond issues. The yields of stocks at large, as priced in the security markets, do not afford the most accurate index of the cost of new capital to corporate borrowers, but they furnish a general indication of the course which such costs are following. During the period 1922-1929 the yields of common industrial stocks declined at a rate of 7.2 per cent a year. The yields on preferred industrial stocks, on the other hand, declined at an average annual rate of but 2.1 per cent. Preferred stocks stand much closer to bonds, in this respect, than to common stocks. With the yields of these different classes of securities following these courses, it is not strange that corporate borrowers resorted, in greater and greater degree, to common stock issues.[2]

The best single index of the cost of bank credit to borrowers at large is probably the rate charged bank customers on prime commercial loans. The average for the country at large declined during this period at a rate of 0.8 per cent a year. The corresponding series for New York City advanced at an annual rate of 0.8 per cent.

Various other series measuring interest rates are significant for particular purposes. Certain of these are listed above. Between 1922 and 1929 the average rediscount rate on commercial paper at Federal reserve banks advanced at a rate of 0.6 per cent a year. The interest rate on 4 to 6 months commercial paper showed a net ad-

[1] These rates are based upon figures from the *Standard Statistical Bulletin*.

[2] This is particularly true for the years between 1926 and 1929. For the five years 1922-1926 new capital flotations in the form of long-term bonds and notes increased at a rate of 10.8 per cent a year, while those in the form of common stocks increased at a rate of 17.4 per cent. For the three-year period 1927-1929 new capital issues in the form of bonds fell off sharply, in the face of high interest rates, at an annual rate of 30.0 per cent, while new capital issues of common stocks, exclusive of issues of holding companies and investment trusts, increased at the phenomenal rate of 91.8 per cent a year. (In the depression year, 1927, the new issues of bonds were relatively much higher than those in the form of common stocks; the rates cited reflect, in part, the conditions prevailing in that year.)

vance at a rate of 2.5 per cent a year during this period, a rate materially affected by the sharp advance in 1929. The call loan renewal rate increased at an average annual rate of 8.4 per cent.

## Summary: Capital and Credit

This brief survey does not purport to be a comprehensive account of the developments occurring in the markets for capital and credit in this country between 1922 and 1929, nor does it trace the powerful influence of these developments upon the course of economic events at large. We have here attempted merely to define the outlines of these movements, to measure the broader tendencies prevailing in these markets, and to place them against the background of concurrent production and price changes.

These facts have been noted as outstanding: a population increasing at a rate approximating 1.4 per cent a year; an aggregate volume of production and construction growing at a rate slightly above 4 per cent a year; total corporate capital funds being augmented by approximately 6.4 billions of dollars a year, at an average annual rate falling between 3 and 4 per cent. Streams of savings flowing into use through various other channels were increasing in volume at more rapid rates. The effects of the expansion of capital equipment which this swelling volume of funds permitted have only been touched upon; indeed, we lack the knowledge which would permit us to trace them in detail. Technical improvements were facilitated, opportunity for the development of excess capacity presented, the way opened for the release in great volume of loanable funds not subject to control through usual banking channels. Whether the increase in savings (of which corporate capital funds constitute only one embodiment) was such as to disturb economic equilibrium we may not now say. There is every reason to believe, however, that the rapid expansion and subsequent sharp checking of the flow of American capital funds abroad, a phase of the growth of capital touched upon in a later section, played a disturbing part in the working of the world economy.

During this same period primary funds (funds available for use as reserves against bank credit) increased at a rate of 1.6 per cent a year; the aggregate volume of bank credit based upon these reserves increased at a rate of 5.6 per cent a year, a figure well in excess of the growth of production and trade. Here, however, we have a sharp contrast between the movements of the two main streams into which bank credit may be divided. Credit related directly to the market for securities increased by 7.9 per cent a year, while commercial credit (as reflected in 'all other' loans) increased at a rate of but 3.2 per cent a year. To what extent these two streams actually intermingle we do not know, but the external evidence of sharp inflation in the volume of credit based on securities accords with common understanding of the events of this period.

Finally, our statistical record indicates a most spectacular increase in the total volume of urban real estate mortgages during these years, an increase at an average annual rate of 12.5 per cent. In the security markets and in urban realty—here the bulges of excessive activity occurred. Credit expansion in these fields was far out of line with the pace of economic advance in general.

The funds of capital and of credit which were being made available in constantly increasing volume for business and for speculative purposes were to be had at relatively low costs over a large part of the period here studied. The cost of long-term funds (as measured by stock and bond yields) declined steadily, except for a slight advance in bond yields in 1929. The cost of short-term loans for commercial and speculative purposes remained at low levels through 1927, advancing thereafter. In concrete terms, it is noteworthy that stock yields remained below 6.0 per cent between 1924 and 1929 and below 5.0 per cent in 1928 and 1929, that the basic rediscount rates of the Federal reserve banks were below 4.0 per cent in 1925, 1926 and 1927, and that during the four years from 1924 to 1927 call loan renewal rates (annual averages) never exceeded 4.5 per cent.

A variety of causes contributed to the sustained cheapness of both long-term and short-term funds. The great volume of domestic savings, the popularity of common stocks for investment and speculative purposes, the existence of large corporate surpluses in the form of free funds, our large gold holdings, the desire of banking authorities to facilitate restoration of monetary stability abroad—these were instrumental in varying degrees in maintaining cheap money in the United States. The result was that brimming reservoirs of capital and credit could be tapped at will, and at but slight expense, by those in position to borrow in highly organized financial markets. Probably never before in this country had such a volume of funds been available at such low rates for such a long period. Here was one of the major conditioning factors operating in the era of post-war expansion.

## INTERNATIONAL MOVEMENTS OF GOODS AND OF CAPITAL

At the opening of the twentieth century, the date at which the present survey of economic tendencies begins, the United States was entering upon an era of industrial and commercial expansion. The fruits of the Spanish War extended American territories, and the stimulus of new horizons was felt in all our commercial activities. New points of contact with other nations were established, new channels of trade were opened up, and new responsibilities were assumed. The United States was on the way to become a world power. The World War and all the economic and political forces it released completed the process. Thereafter the course of economic events in the United States was to be more closely tied to world developments than ever before. The domestic processes of the last decade may not be studied in isolation. We proceed to a brief review of certain phases of our international economic relations between 1922 and 1929.

### Changes in the Foreign Trade of the United States

Between 1922 and 1929 the aggregate value of imports of merchandise into the United States increased from 3,113 to 4,399 millions of dollars, at an average annual rate of 3.9 per cent; exports (excluding re-exports) increased from 3,765 to 5,157 millions of dollars, at an average rate of 4.0 per cent a year. These value figures indicate approximate equality of the trends of exports and imports. But values reflect the combined influence of volume and price changes. Account must be taken of each of these factors if a true picture of trade movements is to be secured. These series appear in the next table. They are plotted in Figure 95.

The approximate equality of value trends conceals striking divergences of both quantities and prices. The average unit price of exported goods declined during this period at a rate of 2.2 per

## TABLE 181

### EXPORTS AND IMPORTS OF THE UNITED STATES

Index Numbers of Quantity, Unit Price and Aggregate Value, 1922-1929 [a]

| (1) | (2) | (3) | (4) | (5) | (6) | (7) |
|---|---|---|---|---|---|---|
| | Exports | | | Imports | | |
| Year | Quantity | Unit price | Value | Quantity | Unit price | Value |
| 1922 | 100 | 100 | 100 | 100 | 100 | 100 |
| 1923 | 102 | 106 | 110 | 104 | 117 | 122 |
| 1924 | 116 | 104 | 120 | 101 | 114 | 116 |
| 1925 | 123 | 105 | 129 | 107 | 126 | 136 |
| 1926 | 131 | 97 | 125 | 115 | 124 | 142 |
| 1927 | 141 | 91 | 127 | 117 | 114 | 135 |
| 1928 | 148 | 91 | 135 | 118 | 112 | 132 |
| 1929 | 151 | 92 | 137 | 134 | 105 | 142 |
| Average annual rate of change (per cent) .. | +6.5 | −2.2 | +4.0 | +3.9 | 0.0 | +3.9 |
| Index of instability ....... | 1.9 | 3.1 | 2.9 | 2.9 | 5.6 | 5.8 |

[a] Index numbers compiled by the U. S. Department of Commerce. For an explanation of the procedure, see *Commerce Yearbook*, 1930, Vol. 1, p. 85.

cent a year, while there was no appreciable net change in the average price paid for goods imported. (There was an upward movement from 1922 to 1925 in the average price of imported goods, a downward movement thereafter.) Equality of value trends was maintained, under these conditions, by an advance in the quantity of goods exported which was much more rapid than the increase in quantity of goods imported. The rate of increase in the physical volume of exports was 6.5 per cent a year, well above the rate at which domestic production as a whole was expanding. The export trade was an unmistakable positive factor in the economic growth of the United States during this period.

The terms of exchange between imported and exported goods seem to have been changing to our disadvantage over this period. Changes in average export and import prices, and the ratio of export unit prices (i.e., prices received) to import unit prices (prices paid), are shown in Table 182 for the years from 1913 to 1929, excluding 1914-1918.

### FIGURE 95
#### CHANGES IN THE QUANTITIES, VALUES AND AVERAGE PRICES OF IMPORTS AND EXPORTS OF THE UNITED STATES, 1922-1929

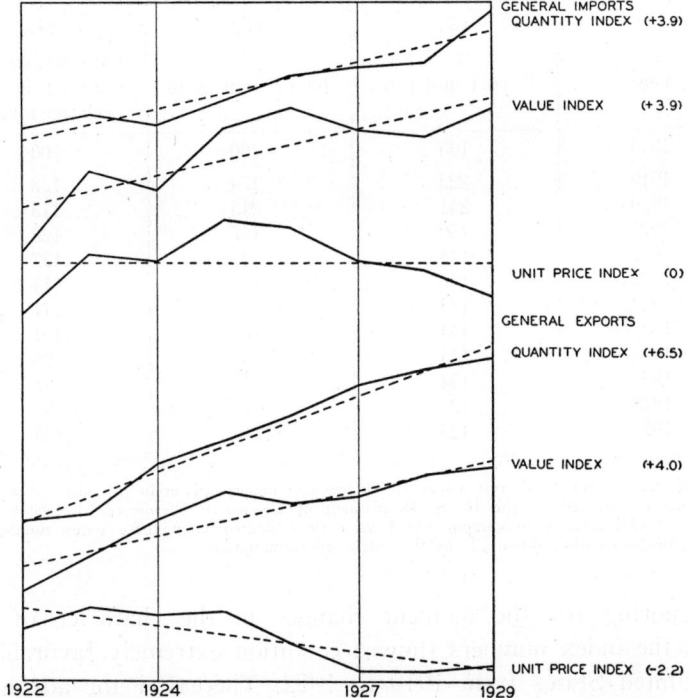

Plotted on ratio scale. The figures in parentheses define average annual rates of change (in percentage form).

The ratios in the last column of Table 182 (expressed for convenience as relatives) may be taken to define changes in the number of units of goods received in exchange for one unit of goods exported.[1] In the present case changes in the ratio may be due to alterations in average exchange values of specific goods, or to changes in the make-up of our foreign trade. These latter changes were so pronounced on the export side during the years covered by the above table that interpretation of the index is clouded.

---

[1] A ratio of this type was first employed by A. L. Bowley in a study of alterations in the terms of exchange between England and her commercial customers. See *The Economic Journal,* Vol. 7, 1897, pp. 274-278, Vol. 13, 1903, p. 628. See also articles by J. M. Keynes in the same journal, Vol. 22, 1912, p. 630, and Vol. 33, 1923, p. 477, for a similar use of the ratio.

## TABLE 182

CHANGES IN EXPORT AND IMPORT PRICES, AND IN THE TERMS OF EXCHANGE BETWEEN IMPORTED AND EXPORTED GOODS, 1913-1929 [a]

| (1) Year | (2) Export unit price | (3) Import unit price | (4) Ratio of export to import price (in relative form) |
|---|---|---|---|
| 1913 | 100 | 100 | 100 |
| 1919 | 223 | 174 | 128 |
| 1920 | 241 | 213 | 113 |
| 1921 | 150 | 117 | 128 |
| 1922 | 138 | 113 | 122 |
| 1923 | 146 | 132 | 111 |
| 1924 | 143 | 129 | 111 |
| 1925 | 144 | 142 | 101 |
| 1926 | 133 | 139 | 96 |
| 1927 | 124 | 130 | 95 |
| 1928 | 125 | 126 | 99 |
| 1929 | 125 | 119 | 105 |

[a] The index numbers of unit prices of exports and imports given in columns (2) and (3) have been constructed by the U. S. Department of Commerce (*Commerce Yearbook*, 1930, Vol. 1, p. 85). Entries in column (4) have been computed from these index numbers by dividing the entries in column (2) by the entries in column (3).

Ignoring for the moment changes in the character of our trade, the index numbers show a condition extremely favorable to the United States from 1919 to 1922. Thereafter the advantage continued, but in lesser degree, until 1925. Not until 1926 was the foreign seller receiving as much in exchange for his goods as he was in 1913.

The wide margin of advantage which import and export price relations yielded to the American exporter during the years prior to 1926 was undoubtedly a factor in domestic business expansion. We have remarked upon the price advantage enjoyed by American manufacturing interests in domestic markets as a result of the price shifts occurring in 1920-21. To some extent the same was true of the American economy as a whole, in its dealing with foreign traders during the troubled years immediately following the war. In physical terms we received more for what we exported than we had during the pre-war years. Our own swelling volume of exports, combined with European industrial recovery, served to lessen this advantage, and by 1926 it had disappeared, so far as we may judge from the present index numbers. The aggregate value of the foreign trade of the United States was maintained in the face of falling export prices through an expansion of the physical volume of exports.[1]

Certain details of the changes in the character of our import trade during this period are shown in the following table. The series are plotted in Figure 96.

TABLE 183

FOREIGN TRADE OF THE UNITED STATES, 1922-1929

Changes in Aggregate Values of Imports, by Major Classes of Commodities

| Commodity group | Absolute value (in millions of dollars) | | Average annual rate of change (per cent) |
|---|---|---|---|
| | 1922 | 1929 | |
| All commodities | 3,113 | 4,399 | +3.9 |
| Crude materials | 1,180 | 1,559 | +3.2 |
| Semi-manufactures | 553 | 885 | +4.8 |
| Finished manufactures | 663 | 994 | +5.1 |
| Crude foodstuffs | 330 | 539 | +7.1 |
| Manufactured foodstuffs | 387 [a] | 424 | −1.6 |

[a] The 1922 figure for imports of manufactured foodstuffs was abnormally low. In 1923 the value of such imports amounted to 530 millions of dollars.

The differences among the rates of change of the several groups shown above are much greater than among the corresponding pre-war rates of change. Imports of crude foodstuffs, and of finished and semi-finished manufactured goods, which were growing most

---

[1] Index numbers of volume and price of domestic exports show an advance of 23 per cent in aggregate volume of exports and a decline of 13 per cent in average per-unit price of exported goods, between 1925 and 1929. This drop may be compared with a decline of less than 8 per cent in domestic wholesale prices during the same period.

It has been suggested above that these price index numbers may be ambiguous because of the changing constitution of our trade. It may be noted, however, that raw materials, raw foodstuffs and manufactured foodstuffs, which dropped most sharply in price between 1925 and 1929, were declining in relative importance among exports, while semi-manufactures and finished manufactures, which showed the smallest price declines among exported goods, were increasing in relative importance. We cannot say, therefore, that the drop in export prices after 1925 was due to the increasing weight given to goods which were falling in price.

### FIGURE 96
### CHANGES IN THE FOREIGN TRADE OF THE UNITED STATES, 1922-1929
#### IMPORTS AND EXPORTS, MAJOR CLASSIFICATIONS

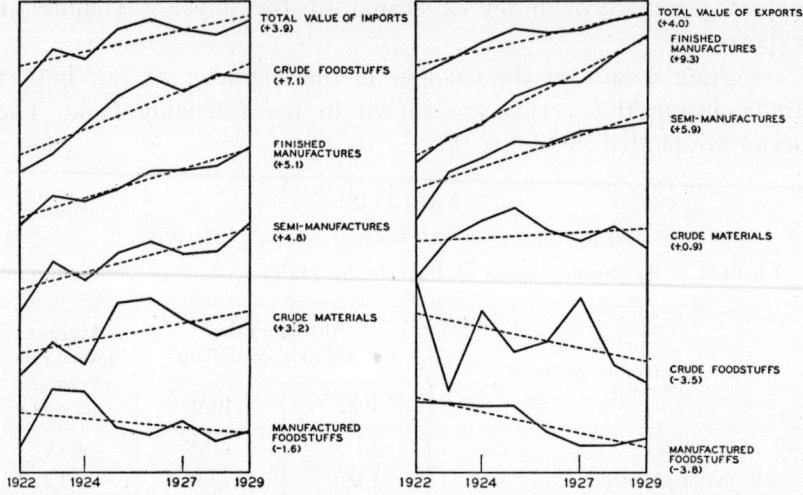

Plotted on ratio scale. The figures in parentheses define average annual rates of change (in percentage form).

rapidly, were increasing in volume at rates more rapid than the corresponding pre-war rates (allowance being made for changes in the purchasing power of the dollar). Imports of crude materials were increasing in value less rapidly than before the war, while imports of manufactured foodstuffs were declining in value in the recent period.[1]

Changes in the values of exports, by major commodity groups, are shown in Table 184, on the following page, and are pictured graphically in Figure 96.

The decline in exports of foodstuffs is due, in considerable part,

[1] Price changes enter, of course, to complicate the picture when values alone are considered. The following rates of change have been derived from volume and value index numbers constructed by W. R. Peabody (*Statistical Bulletin,* American Tariff League, February, 1930).

Annual Rates of Change in Imports, 1922-1929

| Group | Price index | Volume index | Index of aggregate value |
|---|---|---|---|
| Total imports | 0.0 | +3.9 | +3.9 |
| Crude materials | −0.8 | +4.4 | +3.2 |
| Semi-manufactures | +0.7 | +4.1 | +4.8 |
| Finished manufactures | −0.6 | +5.7 | +5.1 |
| Crude foodstuffs | +4.8 | +2.4 | +7.1 |
| Manufactured foodstuffs | −3.0 | +1.4 | −1.6 |

## TABLE 184

### Foreign Trade of the United States, 1922-1929

Changes in Aggregate Values of Exports, by Major Classes of Commodities

| Commodity group | Absolute value (in millions of dollars) | | Average annual rate of change (per cent) |
|---|---|---|---|
| | 1922 | 1929 | |
| All commodities | 3,765 | 5,157 | +4.0 |
| Crude materials | 988 | 1,142 | +0.9 |
| Semi-manufactures | 438 | 729 | +5.9 |
| Finished manufactures | 1,292 | 2,532 | +9.3 |
| Crude foodstuffs | 459 | 270 | —3.5 |
| Manufactured foodstuffs | 588 | 484 | —3.8 |

to a natural falling off from the abnormally large volume of such goods exported to various European countries during the critical period following the war. The recovery of the devastated areas and the general increase in the production of farm products in other areas account for the decline recorded. This decline in the foreign sales of foodstuffs has been a major factor, of course, in the domestic agricultural situation.

The development of American manufacturing and the intensive exploitation of foreign markets in recent years is reflected in the rapid growth of exports of manufactured and semi-manufactured goods, and in the slight advance in our exports of crude materials. In fact, the more rapid increase of exports in recent years, in comparison with the period 1901-13, is attributable entirely to the increased volume of exports of manufactured goods. The decline in exports of foodstuffs was more rapid in the recent than in the earlier period, and the rate of increase in exports of crude materials and semi-finished goods was below the rate of pre-war advance. Exports of finished manufactures, by value, almost doubled between 1922 and 1929.[1]

§ *On the proportion of American manufactured products entering into foreign trade.*—Between 1923 and 1929 exported manufactured

[1] Price and volume index numbers for exports by commodity groups have been constructed by D. J. Cowden for the period 1923-1929 (*Measures of Exports of the United States*, Columbia University Press, New York, 1931). Index numbers

goods constituted a constantly increasing percentage of all manufactured goods produced in the United States. (Data for 1922 on the value of manufactured goods produced are not available.) Figures for census years follow:

| Year | Value of exports of manufactured foods, semi-manufactured goods and finished manufactures (millions of dollars) | Estimated value of manufactured goods produced in United States, excluding duplications [1] (millions of dollars) | Value of exports of manufactured goods as percentage of total value of manufactures |
|---|---|---|---|
| 1923 | 2,625 | 38,200 | 6.9 |
| 1925 | 3,079 | 39,550 | 7.8 |
| 1927 | 3,145 | 40,150 | 7.8 |
| 1929 | 3,745 | 46,250 | 8.1 |

[1] Estimates of the value of manufactured goods are based upon the 'value added' by manufacturing industries and the approximate value of materials used, excluding duplications. The average of maximum and minimum estimates made by the U. S. Department of Commerce (*Commerce Yearbook*, 1931, p. 89) has been used.

of price, volume and value changes for this period will help to explain the value movements noted above:

INDEX NUMBERS OF QUANTITY, AVERAGE PRICE AND AGGREGATE VALUE OF DOMESTIC EXPORTS BY ECONOMIC CLASSES, 1923-1929

(1923-25 = 100)

| Year | Quantity | Average price | Aggregate value | Quantity | Average price | Aggregate value |
|---|---|---|---|---|---|---|
| | Total exports | | | Raw materials | | |
| 1923 | 90 | 101 | 92 | 84 | 109 | 91 |
| 1924 | 102 | 99 | 101 | 100 | 101 | 101 |
| 1925 | 106 | 101 | 108 | 116 | 93 | 108 |
| 1926 | 113 | 93 | 105 | 131 | 73 | 95 |
| 1927 | 121 | 88 | 106 | 126 | 71 | 90 |
| 1928 | 126 | 89 | 113 | 125 | 78 | 98 |
| 1929 | 129 | 88 | 115 | 113 | 76 | 86 |
| | Semi-manufactures | | | Finished manufactures | | |
| 1923 | 89 | 101 | 92 | 91 | 100 | 90 |
| 1924 | 105 | 97 | 100 | 97 | 100 | 97 |
| 1925 | 106 | 102 | 108 | 112 | 100 | 113 |
| 1926 | 105 | 101 | 107 | 119 | 101 | 120 |
| 1927 | 121 | 95 | 114 | 130 | 93 | 121 |
| 1928 | 122 | 94 | 117 | 149 | 92 | 138 |
| 1929 | 116 | 99 | 119 | 166 | 91 | 155 |
| | Raw foodstuffs | | | Manufactured foodstuffs | | |
| 1923 | 94 | 86 | 80 | 105 | 95 | 101 |
| 1924 | 122 | 101 | 122 | 105 | 95 | 99 |
| 1925 | 82 | 117 | 98 | 88 | 113 | 99 |
| 1926 | 103 | 99 | 104 | 81 | 108 | 87 |
| 1927 | 134 | 99 | 130 | 80 | 100 | 80 |
| 1928 | 98 | 94 | 91 | 82 | 97 | 81 |
| 1929 | 93 | 90 | 84 | 85 | 97 | 84 |

The increase in value of manufactured goods exported was substantial, amounting to something more than 40 per cent during this six-year period. In absolute terms the increase amounted to more than one billion dollars. The total value of manufactured goods produced in the United States increased by eight billions of dollars between 1923 and 1929. About one-eighth of this increase was due, therefore, to the increasing value of foreign sales. In comparison with the figure of 46 odd billions of dollars, the total value of manufactured goods, these sums are not great, but as marginal amounts, increments to an existing volume, they were important factors in the developments of this period. In a later section reference is made to the financing of this increased volume of foreign sales.

A clearer picture of the changes in our foreign trade during this period may be secured by considering the alterations occurring among the constituent elements of the total. In the following table the various elements of our import trade are shown as percentages of the total in 1901, 1913, 1922 and 1929.

TABLE 185

Component Elements of the Import Trade of the United States, 1901, 1913, 1922 and 1929

| Commodity group | Percentage of total imports, by value | | | |
|---|---|---|---|---|
| | 1901 | 1913 | 1922 | 1929 |
| Crude materials | 34.2 | 34.3 | 37.9 | 35.4 |
| Semi-manufactures | 16.4 | 16.9 | 17.8 | 20.2 |
| Finished manufactures | 25.6 | 23.7 | 21.3 | 22.6 |
| Crude foodstuffs | 13.3 | 13.1 | 10.6 | 12.2 |
| Manufactured foodstuffs | 10.5 | 12.0 | 12.4 | 9.6 |

The outstanding feature of this table is the constancy of the different elements, as percentages of the total. Semi-finished goods made up a slightly larger fraction of the whole in 1929 than in 1901, and finished goods made up a slightly smaller part, but these changes were relatively slight. With reference to this classification, at least, our import trade has shown remarkable stability.

A similar table relating to exports appears on the next page.

Notable changes in the character of American export trade have occurred within the period of 29 years covered by this table. The decline in exports of foodstuffs, both crude and manufactured, has already been commented upon. This decline, clearly in evidence

TABLE 186

COMPONENT ELEMENTS OF THE EXPORT TRADE OF THE UNITED STATES,
1901, 1913, 1922 AND 1929

| Commodity group | Percentage of total exports, by value | | | |
|---|---|---|---|---|
| | 1901 | 1913 | 1922 | 1929 |
| Crude materials .................... | 28.6 | 34.3 | 26.2 | 22.2 |
| Semi-manufactures ................ | 9.7 | 16.1 | 11.7 | 14.1 |
| Finished manufactures ............. | 23.8 | 31.1 | 34.3 | 49.1 |
| Crude foodstuffs ................... | 13.6 | 5.9 | 12.2 | 5.2 |
| Manufactured foodstuffs ........... | 24.3 | 12.6 | 15.6 | 9.4 |

before the war, was resumed after 1922; in 1929 exports of these classes of foodstuffs were lower, as percentages of the total, than in any of the earlier years for which figures are given. There was some advance in the relative position of semi-finished goods; crude materials have declined in relative importance. Most impressive was the increase in the exports of finished manufactures. These made up less than 24 per cent of the total in 1901 and more than 49 per cent in 1929. This remarkable growth of exports of manufactures, from 322 millions of dollars in 1901 to 2,532 millions of dollars in 1929, represents an eight-fold increase in 28 years. The effects of this increase have been far-reaching. Concurrent and related changes on the financial side are considered in the next section.

## The Balance of International Payments

The international economic relations of the United States during the period 1922-29 cannot be understood if attention be paid to the record of merchandise movements alone. Studies made by the Department of Commerce permit the major movements in the international flow of goods, services, capital and gold to be followed, though it is not possible accurately to measure all the items entering into the balance of international payments. For the purposes of the present survey it is desirable to trace the broader movements only, and this end is served by re-classifying the items given in the balance sheet prepared by the Department of Commerce.[1]

[1] More detailed figures and an explanation of the estimates upon which these are based will be found in *The Balance of International Payments of the United States in 1930,* a publication of the U. S. Department of Commerce.

OTHER ECONOMIC CHANGES, POST-WAR 471

The various items in the international balance sheet may be placed in four general classes. The first group includes items relating to the movements of goods and to services—commodities, services in the transportation of goods and passengers, insurance, advertising, motion picture royalties, cable charges and tourist expenditures. The services rendered foreign tourists in this country are classed with our exports, while services rendered American tourists abroad are classed with our imports. The combination gives a truer picture of the balance of trade, in a broad sense, than is given by merchandise imports and exports alone.

The next class contains items relating to the payment of debts and to charitable and other remittances not arising out of the purchase of goods or services. War debt payments (including both interest and principal), interest on private loans, immigrant remittances, charitable contributions and payments arising out of certain governmental transactions fall in this group. A third class contains all items relating to the movement of capital, long- and short-term,[1] while the fourth group includes gold and currency movements.

The following table gives the estimates of the Department of Commerce, grouped in these four major divisions. Only net figures are given. A final item covers the discrepancies arising from inaccuracies in the estimates.

In following the complex movements of international trade we are not justified in balancing specific items against other specific items, yet it is suggestive to compare the figures in the major classes set up in Table 187. During five of the eight years here covered the balance of trade, in the broad sense implied by lumping together all goods and services, was in our favor; there was a net amount due us for goods sold and services rendered in every year except 1923, 1926 and 1929. In each of the eight years, moreover, a substantial sum was due us as payment of principal on war debts and interest on all debts and investments abroad, after subtracting corresponding amounts owed by us and deducting charitable contri-

---

[1] In accordance with the classification of the Department of Commerce, bond discounts and underwriters' commissions on foreign securities floated in the United States have been placed in this group, and treated as a deduction from the net increase in American long-term investments abroad (par value). For the present purpose underwriters' commissions, as payments for services, should be included with other services, while bond discounts, although legitimately deducted at first, should in succeeding years be amortized and treated as interest. However, these changes would make no significant difference in the figures as given in Table 187.

## TABLE 187
### Balances of International Payments of the United States, 1922-1929 [a]
(In millions of dollars)

| Class of transaction | 1922 | 1923 | 1924 | 1925 | 1926 | 1927 | 1928 | 1929 | Annual average | Total 1922-1929 |
|---|---|---|---|---|---|---|---|---|---|---|
| Goods and services, net | +364 | −100 | +513 | +213 | −149 | +147 | +240 | −31 | +150 | +1197 |
| Payment on debts, net | +193 | +308 | +289 | +300 | +354 | +441 | +418 | +408 | +339 | +2711 |
| Net credits | +557 | +208 | +802 | +513 | +205 | +588 | +658 | +377 | +489 | +3908 |
| Net capital movement | −378 | +33 | −517 | −621 | −181 | −695 | −944 | −306 | −451 | −3609 |
| Net movement of currency and gold (including earmarked gold) | −194 | −245 | −236 | +72 | −72 | +154 | +272 | −120 | −46 | −369 |
| Net debits | −572 | −212 | −753 | −549 | −253 | −541 | −672 | −426 | −497 | −3978 |
| Correction for net discrepancy | +15 | +4 | −49 | +36 | +48 | −47 | +14 | +49 | +8 | +70 |

[a] Explanation: A plus sign on the net item for goods and services means that the United States has exported more in the form of goods and services than it has received.

A plus sign on net debt payments means that the United States has received more in the form of interest payments on private debts abroad, and principal and interest on government debts, than it has paid in the form of immigrant remittances, charitable contributions, payments connected with governmental transactions and payments of interest on foreign debts of the United States.

A minus sign on net capital movement means that the United States has made heavier loans and investments abroad (long- and short-term) than have been made by foreigners in this country.

A minus sign on net movement of gold and currency means that the United States has received more in the form of gold and currency than it has sent away.

butions and immigrant remittances. The net credits, equivalent to the balances due the United States on account of net exports of goods and services and amounts due as war-debt principal and interest on debts abroad, varied from 205 millions of dollars in 1926 to 802 millions of dollars in 1924. The annual average, from 1922 to 1929, was 489 millions of dollars.

The major item on the debit side relates to the net movement of capital. In one year, 1923, the net movement of new capital was toward this country, but in all other years since 1923 the flow was steadily outward. During the eight years covered, the average net investment of new American capital (short- and long-term) was

451 millions of dollars. We have seen, in the preceding paragraph, that when account has been taken of all the goods imported, of all the services rendered, of all the amounts due citizens of other countries on account of investments in this country and of remittances arising out of contributions of various sorts, there remained a net average annual balance due this country of 489 millions of dollars. In large part, this was balanced by new loans and investments abroad made by private American citizens, loans and investments which averaged 451 millions of dollars a year between 1922 and 1929. The difference between these figures (ignoring the discrepancies in the estimates) is accounted for by imports of gold into the United States, and by earmarkings of gold.[1] During five of the eight years studied the net movement of gold was inward. The average amount imported in each of the eight years was about 46 millions of dollars.

We are not here concerned with the mechanism of adjustment of international balances of various sorts, or with the question of causal relations among factors of trade and exchange. For our purpose, accordingly, we may lump the annual items and consider the gross relations prevailing when the eight-year period is treated as a unit. This is done in the last column of Table 187.

During this period a credit balance of 1,197 millions of dollars was accumulated, as a result of the excess of exports of goods and services of various sorts over corresponding imports. In addition, there was due the United States an aggregate net amount of 2,711 millions of dollars in the adjustment of war-debt principal and interest of debts owed the government and citizens of the United States. Total credits amounted to 3,908 millions of dollars. A small portion of this, some 369 millions of dollars, was offset by imports of gold. The major factor in the balancing of accounts, however, was the outward movement of American capital and credits. Between 1922 and 1929 the net outward capital movement amounted to 3,609 millions of dollars, in the aggregate. It was this heavy export of capital which permitted the large export balance of goods and services, and which facilitated the payments made to the government and to citizens of the United States on account of principal and interest of foreign debts and investments.

These capital movements which have played such an important

[1] Certain relatively small movements of American currency are included with the gold figures.

part in international trade relations in recent years merit further attention. We have so far considered only the annual movements, without reference to the aggregate amounts of American investments abroad, and of foreign investments in this country. In the following table are given approximate aggregate amounts of long-term investments of these two classes by years, from 1922 to 1929, together with estimates of net American long-term investments abroad. The series are shown graphically, with lines of trend, in Figure 97.

FIGURE 97

CHANGES IN AMERICAN CAPITAL INVESTMENTS ABROAD
AND IN FOREIGN CAPITAL INVESTMENTS
IN THE UNITED STATES, 1922-1929

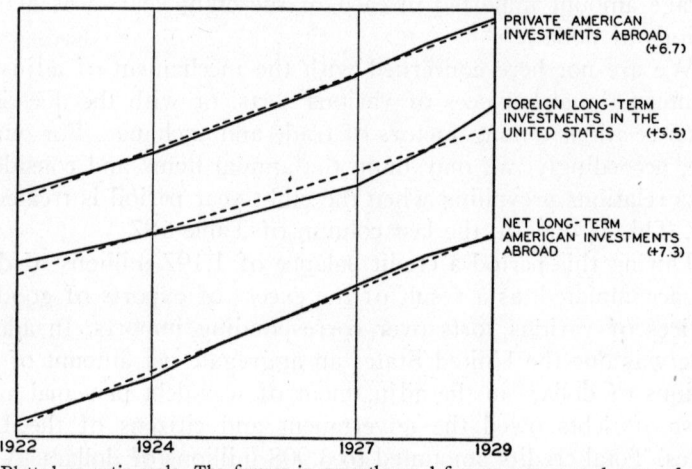

Plotted on ratio scale. The figures in parentheses define average annual rates of change (in percentage form).

The data in Table 188 are subject to a considerable margin of error, as regards absolute magnitudes. Except for convenience in calculation, the last three figures could be omitted, for they suggest an accuracy which the estimates do not possess. However, the rates of change in the series given probably approximate the actual changes with a reasonable degree of accuracy.

From this record it appears that private American investments abroad increased, between 1922 and 1929, from 9,209 millions of dollars to 14,412 millions. The absolute annual increments averaged over 700 millions of dollars, and the average annual rate of increase

## TABLE 188

### FOREIGN INVESTMENTS OF THE UNITED STATES

Estimated Amounts of American Long-term Investments Abroad, of Foreign Long-term Investments in the United States, and of Net Long-term American Investments Abroad, 1922-1929

(In millions of dollars)

| (1) | (2) | (3) | (4) | (5) | (6) |
|---|---|---|---|---|---|
| | Private American investments abroad [a] | | Foreign investments in the United States [b] | | Net long-term American investments abroad |
| Year | at end of year | at middle of year | at end of year | at middle of year | at middle of year [c] |
| 1921 | 8,831 | — | 3,025 | — | — |
| 1922 | 9,587 | 9,209 | 3,028 | 3,026 | 6,183 |
| 1923 | 9,797 | 9,692 | 3,268 | 3,148 | 6,544 |
| 1924 | 10,541 | 10,169 | 3,279 | 3,273 | 6,896 |
| 1925 | 11,294 | 10,918 | 3,472 | 3,376 | 7,542 |
| 1926 | 11,981 | 11,638 | 3,619 | 3,546 | 8,092 |
| 1927 | 12,834 | 12,408 | 3,777 | 3,698 | 8,710 |
| 1928 | 14,029 | 13,432 | 4,254 | 4,016 | 9,416 |
| 1929 | 14,794 | 14,412 | 4,700 | 4,477 | 9,935 |
| Average annual rate of change (per cent) .... | | +6.7 | | +5.5 | +7.3 |
| Index of instability | | 0.9 | | 2.3 | 0.7 |

[a] Excluding war debts to the United States Treasury and short-term loans to foreigners. The entries are based upon estimates of nominal capital, in the case of securities, and upon estimates of original outlay or of present capitalized earning power, in the case of investments in physical property. The end of the year figures as given are derived from the Department of Commerce's estimate as of January 1, 1931; from this have been subtracted, successively, the annual increases in American long-term investments abroad, less discounts and commissions. See *Balance of International Payments of the United States in 1930*, p. 35. The estimate for January 1, 1931, is the mean of the range estimates given by the Department of Commerce.

It should be noted that while the basic January 1, 1931, figure includes securities valued at par, the annual deductions (in working backward) do not relate to increases in par values, but to par values less discounts and commissions. If increases in par values are used as deductions from the base figure, a series is obtained with an average annual rate of change equal to 8.1 per cent instead of 6.7 per cent; the series in column (6) then has a rate of growth of 9.4 per cent instead of 7.3 per cent. It is evident that the figures in the above table do not overstate the rates of growth.

[b] Excluding holdings by alien residents of the United States and all short-term foreign capital kept in this country for dollar-exchange purposes, or invested in acceptances and brokers' loans. The figures are based upon the estimated value of investments, that is, the estimated capitalized value of earnings.

The annual figures given are derived from an estimate as of December 31, 1929, made by Ray Hall (*Balance of International Payments of the United States in 1929*, p. 32); from this have been subtracted, successively, the annual net increases in long-term foreign investments in the United States.

[c] Difference between items in columns (3) and (5).

was 6.7 per cent. During the same period foreign long-term investments in this country increased from 3,026 millions to 4,477 millions, at an average annual rate of 5.5 per cent. Net long-term American investments abroad, derived by taking the difference between the two series already named, increased from 6,183 millions of dollars in 1922 to 9,935 millions in 1929, the average annual rate of increase being 7.3 per cent.

These are large figures. In 1929 aggregate private American investments abroad constituted approximately 6.3 per cent of the total capital funds at the disposal of American corporations. The absolute annual increment in these foreign investments constituted some 10 per cent of the absolute amount by which American corporate capital funds increased annually over the same period.[1] The rate of increase in foreign investments, 6.7 per cent a year, was substantially higher than the rate of increase in American corporate capital funds, which probably approached 4 per cent a year during this period. Net American investments abroad increased at the rate of 7.3 per cent a year. This heavy export of American capital, increasing at rates materially above those characteristic of our domestic economic growth, is, of course, the financial side of the foreign trade picture discussed above. It was this which permitted our favorable balance of trade to continue.

The remarkable stability of growth of American investments abroad is to be noted. From 1922 to 1923 the increase was retarded slightly; from 1927 to 1928 the increase was accelerated. But for the period as a whole the growth was even and regular. The measure of instability indicates an average annual fluctuation of but 0.9 per cent. The increase of foreign investments in this country was less steady. After a rapid increase from 1922 to 1923 the growth was retarded until 1926. Between 1926 and 1929 the increase was rapid, at a rate well above the average figure given for the period as a whole.

## Changes in Distributive Shares

### Wages

The period 1922-29 was marked by a steady advance in both the money earnings and the real earnings of American workers.

[1] A figure of 12 per cent would be derived from the values cited in preceding tables. Since our records of domestic capital issues are incomplete, this figure is undoubtedly too high. Eight or ten per cent is closer to the truth.

Measurements derived from various index numbers of earnings and of wage rates are given in the following tables. The major series are plotted in Figure 98.

TABLE 189

CHANGES IN EARNINGS AND IN WAGE RATES IN THE UNITED STATES, 1922-1929

| Index number or wage series | Average annual rates of change, 1922-1929 | |
|---|---|---|
| | In current dollars (per cent) | In purchasing power [a] (per cent) |
| Composite index of wages (Snyder) [b] | +2.3 | +2.1 |
| Per capita earnings of factory labor [c] | +1.6 | +1.4 |
| Weekly earnings of factory labor [d] | +1.8 | +1.6 |
| Men | +2.1 | +1.9 |
| Skilled | +1.8 | +1.6 |
| Unskilled | +2.6 | +2.4 |
| Women | +0.8 | +0.6 |
| Weekly earnings of factory employees in New York State [e] | +2.2 | +2.0 |
| Hourly earnings of factory labor [d] | +1.9 | +1.7 |
| Wage rates, union [f] | | |
| Per hour | +4.3 | +4.1 |
| Per week | +3.9 | +3.7 |
| U. S. Steel Corporation, wage rates per hour [g] | +4.2 | +4.0 |
| Wages, common labor, road building [h] | +1.8 | +1.6 |
| Farm wages, without board [j] | +1.6 | +1.4 |

[a] Secured by deflating money wages by the U. S. Bureau of Labor Statistics index of cost of living.

[b] Teachers, clerks, factory and unskilled labor. See Carl Snyder, *Business Cycles and Business Measurements*, Macmillan Co., New York, 1927, p. 289. This index combines both wage rates and per capita earnings. Later figures are published in the *Monthly Review* of the Federal Reserve Bank of New York. A revision of this index on the basis of a broader sample was made in July, 1932. The revised index shows rates of increase between 1922 and 1929 of 2.1 per cent a year in money earnings, of 1.9 per cent a year in real earnings.

[c] Derived from aggregate wages paid and average number employed, as given in the Census of Manufactures, with interpolations based on the Federal Reserve Board's indexes of payrolls and factory employment.

[d] These measurements relate to index numbers constructed by the National Industrial Conference Board (*Wages in the United States, 1914-1930*, pp. 54 ff.).

[e] The data for New York State, which include earnings of factory office workers, are collected by the State Department of Labor (*The Industrial Bulletin*, December, 1931, p. 77).

[f] *Monthly Labor Review*, December, 1929, pp. 26-28.

[g] *Survey of Current Business*, 1931 Annual Supplement, p. 180.

[h] U. S. Department of Agriculture, Bureau of Public Roads, *Yearbook of Agriculture*, 1931, p. 1066. The original figures relate to average wage rates per hour.

[j] U. S. Department of Agriculture, Bureau of Agricultural Economics, *Yearbook of Agriculture*, 1931, p. 1023. The original figures relate to average yearly wages.

These index numbers, compiled by various agencies and derived in different ways, tell a story of steadily advancing wages between

### FIGURE 98

CHANGES IN THE EARNINGS AND WAGE RATES
OF EMPLOYED LABOR IN THE UNITED STATES, 1922-1929
(IN CURRENT DOLLARS)

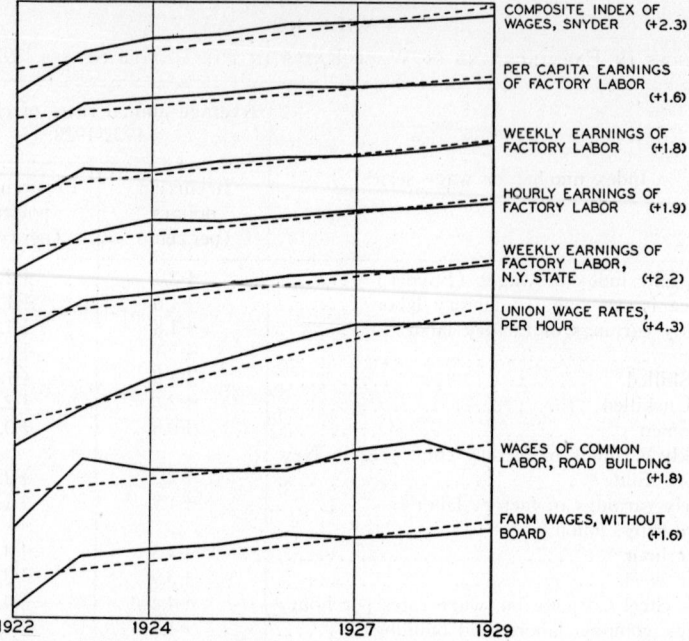

Plotted on ratio scale. The figures in parentheses define average annual rates of change (in percentage form).

1922 and 1929. For labor in manufacturing establishments the annual rate of advance in per capita money earnings averaged 1.6 per cent; as regards real earnings per capita, the rate was 1.4 per cent. The former figure stands very close to the pre-war advance in money wages (the average rate of advance from 1901 to 1913 was 1.7 per cent a year for manufacturing wage-earners), but the change in real wages is in sharp contrast to the decline at the rate of 0.1 per cent a year during the pre-war period. The fact that living costs were advancing between 1922 and 1929 at a rate of but 0.2 per cent a year, as compared with a rate of 1.8 per cent a year for the pre-war period, accounts for the difference in the rates of change in real wages.

Considering the separate classes of factory workers, we find that earnings were advancing more rapidly for men than for women, more rapidly for unskilled male workers than for skilled male workers.

Wage rates show a sharper advance during this period than do earnings, for a steady shortening of the working day was in process between 1922 and 1929. Union wage rates per hour advanced at the rate of 4.3 per cent a year, while union wage rates per full-time week increased at a rate of 3.9 per cent a year.

Other indexes bear out the general evidence of those cited. Real earnings were advancing at rates between 1.4 and 2.0 per cent a year for most classes of employed workers. The group lagging farthest behind in the advance consisted of women factory workers.

§ *Changes in earnings, industrial groups.*—For various groups of manufacturing industries index numbers of changes in aggregate payrolls and in number of employees are available. From these we may derive measurements of per capita earnings of employees in different industrial groups. Rates of change between 1922 and 1929 in money earnings and in real earnings of employees in these industrial divisions are given in the table following.

TABLE 190

Changes in per Capita Earnings of Manufacturing Labor, by Industries, 1922-1929 [a]

| Industry | Average annual rates of change (per cent) | |
|---|---|---|
| | In money earnings | In real earnings [b] |
| Nonferrous metals | +2.7 | +2.5 |
| Paper and printing | +2.3 | +2.1 |
| Iron and steel | +2.2 | +2.0 |
| Machinery | +2.1 | +1.9 |
| Automobiles | +1.7 | +1.5 |
| Lumber products | +1.7 | +1.5 |
| Transportation equipment | +1.5 | +1.3 |
| Food products | +1.3 | +1.1 |
| Textiles | +1.0 | +0.8 |
| Cement, clay and glass | +1.0 | +0.8 |
| Chemicals | +0.9 | +0.7 |
| Leather products | +0.1 | −0.1 |
| Tobacco products | 0.0 | −0.2 |
| All manufacturing industries | +1.8 | +1.6 |

[a] Derived from the Federal Reserve Board's index numbers of factory employment and payrolls. See the *Federal Reserve Bulletin.*
[b] Secured by deflating money earnings by the U. S. Bureau of Labor Statistics index of cost of living.

Employees in but two industrial groups, those manufacturing leather products and tobacco products, suffered declines in their real earnings during this period. In the eleven other industrial groups represented above the real earnings of employed workers advanced at rates varying from 0.7 to 2.5 per cent a year.

The rate of change in per capita earnings, as derived in the present study, depends upon the relation between changes in aggregate payrolls and total employment. For all manufacturing industries, in combination, payrolls increased substantially between 1922 and 1929 (the rate being 2.4 per cent a year), while employment increased only slightly (at a rate of 0.6 per cent a year). In the four industries marked by advances in per capita earnings above the average, employment and payrolls both advanced. Total employment declined in five industrial groups, the tobacco, lumber, leather, textile, and cement, clay and glass industries. Aggregate payrolls remained constant in industries producing lumber products, and declined in the leather and tobacco industries.

The industrial groups covered by the pre-war summary of trends of earnings are not in all respects identical with those shown in the post-war summary. For seven groups comparable figures are obtainable. Rates of change in real earnings in these seven groups during the pre-war and post-war periods are given in the next table.

TABLE 191

CHANGES IN PER CAPITA REAL EARNINGS OF MANUFACTURING LABOR IN SEVEN INDUSTRIAL GROUPS, 1901-1913 AND 1922-1929

| Industrial group | Average annual rates of change in real earnings (per cent) | |
|---|---|---|
| | 1901-1913 | 1922-1929 |
| Land vehicles | +1.5 | +1.4 [a] |
| Textiles | +0.3 [b] | +0.8 |
| Paper and printing | +0.3 | +2.1 |
| Leather products | +0.1 | −0.1 |
| Iron and steel products | −0.1 | +2.0 |
| Tobacco products | −0.8 | −0.2 |
| Lumber products | −1.0 | +1.5 |

[a] An average of the rates pertaining to transportation equipment and to automobiles.
[b] An average of the rates pertaining to clothing and to textiles.

Industries producing land vehicles were the only ones to show a substantial gain in the real earnings of labor between 1901 and 1913. The rate of post-war gain has been slightly below the pre-war advance. Workers in iron and steel and lumber, who suffered declines in real wages before the war, showed steadily rising real earnings during the period just passed. Earnings of workers in tobacco manufacturing plants declined in both periods, the rate of decline being smaller in the post-war period. In only two groups of industries, those producing leather goods and land vehicles were post-war conditions (as regards wage trends) less favorable than pre-war.

This brief statistical record of advancing wage rates and earnings constitutes a mere skeleton outline of a movement of the broadest importance. After two decades during which labor in general did little more than preserve its status, the war brought an improvement in the position of the wage-worker. This gain was consolidated and enhanced during the recession of 1920-21, and in 1922, when the present survey begins, the level of real earnings was probably higher than it had ever been before. The gains recorded in the preceding summary were added to those of the years 1914-21. During the period we are studying the position of the employed industrial laborer was relatively advantageous. His output was high, and was growing, and his standard of living was one which permitted luxuries and comforts probably never before available to wage-workers in general.

Some difficulties there were. Even before the period of expansion was terminated in 1929 a widening margin of unemployed was accumulating. The turn-over of men, the shifting of labor among industries, the enforced displacement of labor—these were becoming more prominent features of industrial progress than they had ever been before.[1] Security of tenure was declining, a condition particularly true as regards men past the prime of life. The rewards for employed men were high, but mechanical improvements and a faster pace were making it harder to hold on. Social instruments of alleviation adequate to the demands of the new technology had not been perfected. These were difficulties already apparent before the check to prosperity occurred. Recession brought them into sharp relief, and precipitated problems which were bound to arise with the persistence of prevailing industrial tendencies.

[1] It is necessary to be cautious in subscribing to the current belief that technological unemployment has greatly increased during recent years, if we disregard special occupational shifts due to war conditions. It is probable that a larger proportion of the working population is technically employed, and that it is less easy on the average for those thrown out of employment by technical changes to revert to farm living, but it is not at all certain that the rate of technical displacement among those employed in technical occupations is appreciably greater than at any time since the Civil War.—Note by M. C. Rorty.

## Profits

The comprehensive statistics of the Bureau of Internal Revenue on corporate incomes, as these are reported in connection with Federal tax returns, are a primary source of information concerning the trend of profits. Changes in net income for the chief corporate divisions are shown in the following table. They appear graphically in Figure 99.

TABLE 192

NET INCOMES[a] OF CORPORATIONS CLASSIFIED BY MAJOR INDUSTRIAL GROUPS, 1922-1929

| (1) | (2) | (3) | (4) | (5) | (6) | (7) | (8) |
|---|---|---|---|---|---|---|---|
| Year | Total[b] | Manufacturing | Construction | Transportation and other public utilities | Public service, professional, amusement, etc. | Trade | Finance[c] |
| Relative numbers | | | | | | | |
| 1922 | 100.0 | 100.0 | 100.0 | 100.0 | 100.0 | 100.0 | 100.0 |
| 1923 | 132.2 | 135.2 | 176.5 | 144.6 | 145.5 | 134.2 | 93.3 |
| 1924 | 112.4 | 104.6 | 231.4 | 139.7 | 152.6 | 115.4 | 109.2 |
| 1925 | 159.8 | 140.1 | 288.5 | 170.4 | 196.2 | 139.1 | 218.0 |
| 1926 | 157.3 | 140.4 | 277.8 | 204.7 | 177.0 | 120.1 | 165.1 |
| 1927 | 136.5 | 116.9 | 284.9 | 177.7 | 143.5 | 114.4 | 195.3 |
| 1928 | 172.5 | 148.1 | 253.8 | 209.5 | 143.6 | 128.2 | 286.7 |
| 1929 | 183.2 | 166.8 | 276.3 | 242.9 | 180.4 | 105.0 | 242.7 |
| Average annual rate of change (per cent)... | +7.3 | +5.3 | +9.4 | +10.8 | +4.0 | −0.2 | +16.2 |
| Index of instability ...... | 9.0 | 9.8 | 17.2 | 8.1 | 13.3 | 9.1 | 13.7 |
| Absolute values (in millions of dollars) | | | | | | | |
| 1922 | 4,770 | 2,641 | 39 | 783 | 89 | 695 | 490 |
| 1929 | 8,740 | 4,406 | 108 | 1,902 | 160 | 730 | 1,189 |

[a] Statutory net income (net profits less tax-exempt interest and dividends received on capital stock of domestic corporations) less deficits of corporations reporting no net income.
[b] The total includes corporations from minor groups not here listed.
[c] Banking, insurance, real estate and holding companies, stock and bond brokers, etc.

Here is a record of rapid but irregular gains in earnings. For all corporate groups the rate of advance averaged 7.3 per cent a year, a figure well in excess of the rate of growth in aggregate value of goods produced, and appreciably higher than the rate of increase

### FIGURE 99
### CHANGES IN CORPORATE NET INCOME IN THE UNITED STATES AS REPORTED TO THE BUREAU OF INTERNAL REVENUE, 1922-1929

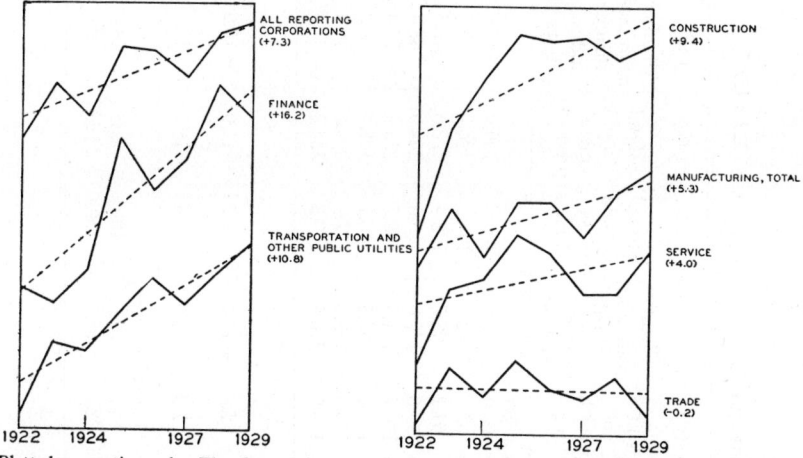

Plotted on ratio scale. The figures in parentheses define average annual rates of change (in percentage form).

in the earnings of labor.[1] The figures suffer from one drawback, the effects of which cannot be approximated with any accuracy. The number of reporting corporations varies from year to year. This variation may serve to swell somewhat the returns reported for later years, but the distortion is probably not serious. Incomes of corporations added to or withdrawn from the total probably constitute but a small percentage of the aggregate figures reported.

Of the constituent corporate groups, enterprises in the fields of finance showed the most striking gains in net income, averaging no less than 16 per cent a year. The net income of construction and public utility corporations (including railroads) increased at rates approximating 10 per cent a year. Here, as phases of the stock market, public utility, and real estate booms, were the spheres of most rapid expansion.

Somewhat more conservative, but impressive enough, is the in-

[1] If to *net income* we add dividends received from other corporations, and interest on tax-exempt bonds, thus approximating *net profits* in customary accounting usage, we secure a series increasing between 1922 and 1929 at a rate of 8.9 per cent a year.

Colonel M. C. Rorty remarks that a great part of the increase of corporation profits during the period 1922-1929 was merely a readjustment of real profits to the post-war level of commodity prices.

TABLE 193

NET INCOMES[a] OF MANUFACTURING CORPORATIONS CLASSIFIED BY INDUSTRIAL GROUPS, 1922-1929

| (1) Year | (2) Food products, beverages and tobacco | (3) Textiles and textile products | (4) Leather and leather products | (5) Rubber and related products | (6) Lumber and wood products | (7) Paper, pulp and products | (8) Printing and publishing | (9) Chemicals, and allied substances | (10) Stone, clay and glass products | (11) Metal and metal products | (12) All other manufacturing industries | (13) Total |
|---|---|---|---|---|---|---|---|---|---|---|---|---|
| | | | | | | Relative numbers | | | | | | |
| 1922 | 100.0 | 100.0 | 100.0 | 100.0 | 100.0 | 100.0 | 100.0 | 100.0 | 100.0 | 100.0 | 100.0 | 100.0 |
| 1923 | 128.7 | 107.6 | 56.9 | 140.3 | 166.9 | 154.2 | 88.0 | 82.3 | 159.0 | 196.7 | 135.4 | 135.2 |
| 1924 | 148.3 | 28.2 | 60.2 | 239.3 | 75.8 | 120.6 | 91.2 | 98.7 | 132.4 | 172.6 | 49.5 | 104.6 |
| 1925 | 148.6 | 65.3 | 73.8 | 627.8 | 92.2 | 160.7 | 99.8 | 137.0 | 150.0 | 244.9 | 48.4 | 140.1 |
| 1926 | 167.1 | 26.2 | 72.7 | 73.3 | 65.0 | 172.2 | 106.7 | 181.3 | 158.7 | 253.7 | 53.0 | 140.4 |
| 1927 | 160.6 | 65.0 | 121.3 | 293.1 | 19.5 | 179.2 | 101.2 | 97.5 | 118.1 | 198.4 | 37.2 | 116.9 |
| 1928 | 188.2 | 42.9 | 77.4 | —[b] | 44.3 | 168.2 | 129.6 | 199.5 | 127.9 | 260.6 | 49.3 | 148.1 |
| 1929 | 195.1 | 35.2 | 63.3 | 98.6 | 42.0 | 169.6 | 138.0 | 216.5 | 119.3 | 334.2 | 37.4 | 166.8 |
| Average annual rate of change (per cent) | +8.2 | −13.6 | +0.4 | — | −18.1 | +6.0 | +5.9 | +13.4 | −0.5 | +11.9 | −15.9 | +5.3 |
| Index of instability | 5.5 | 27.7 | 21.0 | — | 26.5 | 11.3 | 7.0 | 16.6 | 12.4 | 15.7 | 22.8 | 9.8 |
| | | | | | Absolute values (in millions of dollars) | | | | | | | |
| 1922 | 297 | 457 | 64 | 17 | 160 | 62 | 162 | 395 | 109 | 635 | 284 | 2,641 |
| 1929 | 580 | 161 | 40 | 17 | 67 | 104 | 223 | 855 | 130 | 2,122 | 106 | 4,406 |

[a] Statutory net income, less deficits of corporations reporting no net income.
[b] Deficit of 1.3 millions of dollars.

crease of 5.3 per cent a year in the net income of manufacturing corporations, the largest single group in the aggregate. Breaking this group into its component parts we have the figures given on page 484, descriptive of the fortunes of industrial groups.

There is not space here for detailed comment on these figures. The variety of fortunes within the field of manufacturing enterprise is noteworthy. Four industrial groups actually showed declining tendencies in aggregate incomes between 1922 and 1929. The instability of net income is a common characteristic of nearly all the groups.

*The Growth of Profits, Manufacturing Corporations.*—Additional light is thrown on the course of corporate profits between

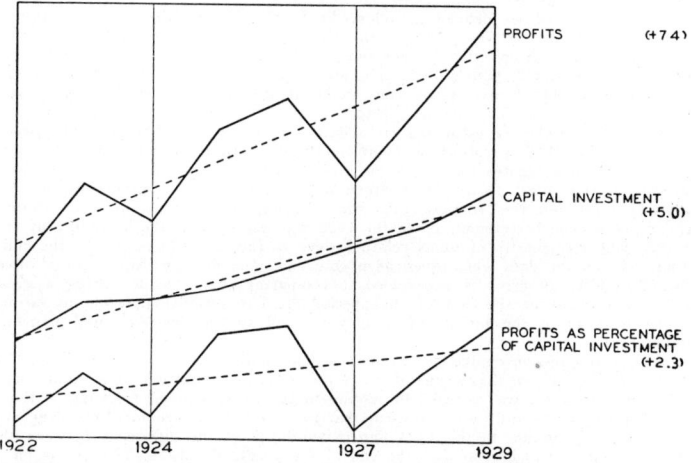

FIGURE 100
CHANGES IN THE PROFITS AND THE CAPITAL INVESTMENT OF 2,046 MANUFACTURING CORPORATIONS, 1922-1929

Plotted on ratio scale. The figures in parentheses define average annual rates of change (in percentage form).

1922 and 1929 by the statistics on profits of manufacturing corporations which were cited in the preceding chapter.[1] The next table contains data relating to the profits and the capital investment of a group of 2,046 manufacturing corporations. The figures are plotted in Figure 100.

[1] These statistics are from *A Source-Book for the Study of Industrial Profits*, R. C. Epstein and F. M. Clark, U. S. Department of Commerce, 1932.

## TABLE 194

Profits, Capital Investment and Profits as Percentage of Capital Investment, 2,046 Manufacturing Corporations, 1922-1929 [a]

| Year | Profits (millions of dollars) | Capital investment [c] (millions of dollars) | Profits as percentage of capital investment |
|---|---|---|---|
| 1922 | 1,784 | 18,305 | 9.7 |
| 1923 | 2,210 | 19,800 | 11.2 |
| 1924 | 2,023 | 20,048 | 10.1 |
| 1925 | 2,564 | 20,641 | 12.4 |
| 1926 | 2,759 | 21,663 | 12.7 |
| 1927 | 2,252 | 22,965 | 9.8 |
| 1928 | 2,736 | 24,319 | 11.3 |
| 1929 [b] | 3,395 | 26,523 [d] | 12.8 [d] |
| Average annual rate of change (per cent) .... | +7.4 | +5.0 | +2.3 |

[a] The terms here used are defined as follows by R. C. Epstein, who made the study for the Department of Commerce: "Net profit is taxable net income, plus non-taxable items where present (i.e., dividends from other corporations and tax-exempt interest), after all charges, but, unless otherwise stated, before Federal taxes. Invested capital, unless otherwise stated, is the total of 'entrepreneurial investment', i.e., common and preferred stock, surplus and undivided profits."

[b] The entries for 1929 are estimated from data relating to 71 manufacturing corporations. The records for the 71 corporations are sufficiently close to those for the larger sample to justify the making of estimates for the larger group for 1929.

[c] The capital investment figures here given differ from those appearing in the report of the Department of Commerce. In that study the sales and profits items were aggregate figures for calendar years. The investment figure for 1922 was given as of the beginning of the year; that for 1923 was a composite of items relating some to the beginning, some to the end of the year; from 1924 on the data were given as of the end of each year. Since capital investment was growing rapidly, an error is introduced in comparing profits made during a given year with capital investment at the end of that period. It has seemed advisable to estimate the capital investment as of the middle of each year, and to set this estimated figure against aggregate profits for the year.

It is these estimates of capital investment which appear above. The figure for 1923, as given in the original source, has been taken as the best approximation to a middle-of-the-year figure. The entry for 1922 was secured by adding to the item as given (relating to the first of the year) one-third of the difference between that item and the figure for 1923. The entry for 1924 was derived by adding to the 1923 figure two-thirds of the difference between that and the given 1924 figure (which related to the end of the year). For 1925 the entry is an average of the original figures relating to the end of 1924 and to the end of 1925. Entries for succeeding years were derived in like manner.

[d] The estimate of profits for 1929 is based upon the relation between profits and investment for a small sample of 71 corporations and for the large sample of 2,046 corporations in 1926 (the year closest to 1929 in the rate of return earned by the corporations in the small group). Capital investment in 1929 for the larger group is estimated from the 1929 investment for the smaller sample, on the basis of the relationship prevailing in 1928.

Among this group of manufacturing corporations aggregate net profits increased at a rate of 7.4 per cent a year between 1922 and 1929. This exceeds by a considerable margin the rate of 5.3 per cent at which the taxable net income of all reporting manufacturing corporations advanced during this period. The coverage of the latter group is greater, of course, but this coverage is not constant, as it is for the group of 2,046 corporations. The difference is doubtless due in part to the fact that net profits, as defined in the Department of Commerce publication, are not identical with net taxable income. Non-taxable items such as dividends from other corporations and tax-exempt interest are included in net profits. Finally, we should note that the completion of mergers, a process of considerable importance during this period, might serve to swell the rate of apparent increase in the profits of a constant number of corporations. As regards manufacturing corporations in general, we shall probably be safe in concluding that the average annual rate of increase in net profits between 1922 and 1929 falls between 5.3 per cent, as a minimum, and 7.4 per cent, as a maximum.[1]

It is a notable fact that aggregate profits increased more rapidly than aggregate capital investment, for this substantial group of manufacturing corporations. The rates of growth between 1922 and 1929 were 7.4 per cent and 5.0 per cent, respectively. The margin between the two represents a definitely rising tendency in profits as a percentage of capital investment. The average rate of advance was 2.3 per cent a year, a noteworthy growth during a period of increasing prosperity. As regards the fortunes of this group there is no evidence that competition and rising costs encroached upon earning power.[2]

[1] Financing through stock issues, with corresponding reduction in bonded indebtedness, would tend to swell net income and profits figures. Such financing, which was a prominent feature of the period under review, doubtless had some effect on data of net earnings, but in the aggregate the effect was not great. Interest payments of manufacturing corporations reporting to the Bureau of Internal Revenue show no evidence of substantial changes in the use made of bonds in corporate financing. The following table gives the percentage of gross receipts paid as interest by manufacturing corporations in the years 1922-29.

| 1922 | 1.39 | 1926 | 1.05 |
| 1923 | 1.09 | 1927 | 1.06 |
| 1924 | 1.13 | 1928 | 1.05 |
| 1925 | 1.02 | 1929 | 0.99 |

[2] The provisional character of the 1929 figures should be noted in this connection. However, there is ample supplementary evidence as to the high profits of 1929. A sample of 722 industrial corporations selected by the Federal Reserve Bank of New York shows aggregate profits in 1929 some 17 per cent greater than in 1928.

Estimates of S. H. Nerlove (*A Decade of Corporate Incomes*, p. 42) relating to all manufacturing corporations in the United States indicate an increase at a rate of 1.6 per cent a year, between 1922 and 1929, in net profits as a percentage of

The actual rates of return on investment are shown in the last column of Table 194. These figures, which define the relation of net corporate profits, before deduction of Federal taxes, to 'entrepreneurial investment' (as represented by common and preferred stock, surplus and undivided profits) range from 9.8 per cent, in 1927, to 12.8 per cent, in 1929. (The figures for 1929 are estimated from returns for a smaller sample.) For the entire period the average rate of return was 11.3 per cent. Between 1922 and 1928, the years covered by the complete record, the rate of return was slightly in excess of 11.0 per cent. Among the corporations here represented, a group which includes the dominant elements among American manufacturing industries, the rate of return on investment was relatively high during these years. Whether it would be equally high if the available statistics covered all manufacturing corporations in the country cannot be definitely determined. The present sample, while comprehensive and well selected, includes a heavy representation of fairly large corporations. But such corporations would still dominate were the sample all-inclusive.[1]

*Dividend Payments.*—The above data relating to profits may be supplemented by figures on dividend payments by all corporations,

---

capital investment. Nerlove's figures, by years, fall somewhat below those secured by Epstein from the Department of Commerce sample. Nerlove's results follow.

| Year | Return on invested capital, manufacturing corporations (per cent) |
|---|---|
| 1922 | 7.5 |
| 1923 | 9.9 |
| 1924 | 7.5 |
| 1925 | 9.6 |
| 1926 | 9.2 |
| 1927 | 7.6 |
| 1928 | 9.2 |
| 1929 | 9.7 |

In comparison with these measurements, the Department of Commerce figures indicate that the group of 2,046 relatively large corporations earned somewhat greater returns, year by year, than did manufacturing corporations at large, and that the rate of advance in these returns between 1922 and 1929 was somewhat greater for the large corporations than for manufacturing corporations in general.

Nerlove's figures for all corporations show an increase, between 1922 and 1929, at a rate of 2.4 per cent a year in net profits as a percentage of capital investment.

[1] The general conclusions of the study summarized above are supported by independent evidence gathered by Joseph H. Forest, in a survey of a group of 141 corporations, primarily, but not exclusively, engaged in manufacturing. (The results appear in an essay entitled *An Analysis of the Rates of Income of Several Industries in the United States, 1930,* which is on file in the Columbia University Library.) In determining rate of return, capital investment was taken to be the

## OTHER ECONOMIC CHANGES, POST-WAR

as reported by the Treasury Department. Total disbursements by all reporting corporations are given in the second column of the table below, for the years 1922-1929. During this same period sub-sum of the common and preferred stock outstanding, plus the profit and loss surplus. Annual income, as used in this study, consisted of net income, after deduction of taxes and interest, as given in published corporation balance sheets.

Treating first the 141 corporations as a group we have the following figures defining the rate of return on capital investment, by years, from 1922 to 1928.

| 1922 | 1923 | 1924 | 1925 | 1926 | 1927 | 1928 | Average, 1922-28 |
|------|------|------|------|------|------|------|------------------|
| 8.7  | 8.9  | 8.9  | 11.8 | 11.7 | 9.1  | 11.0 | 9.6              |

The lowest rate of return, secured in 1922, was 8.7 per cent; the highest, secured in 1925, was 11.8 per cent. The average return for the seven-year period was 9.6 per cent of invested capital, as defined and determined in the manner indicated above. It should be noted that net profits are here taken *after* the payment of all taxes. Net profits in the Department of Commerce study were determined before the deduction of Federal taxes.

Classifying these 141 corporations by industrial groups, Forest secures the following rates of return, as averaged for the period 1922-28:

| Industrial group | Number of corporations | Average rate of return on capital investment, 1922-1928 (per cent) |
|---|---|---|
| Motor parts | 13 | 17.4 |
| Automobiles | 16 | 16.8 |
| Stores | 16 | 16.7 |
| Chemicals | 9 | 16.2 |
| Tobacco | 9 | 12.8 |
| Oil | 18 | 9.5 |
| Rubber | 10 | 7.6 |
| Steel | 20 | 6.7 |
| Copper | 20 | 6.7 |
| Coal | 10 | 2.5 |

These figures relate, of course, to groups of corporations, not to individual companies, yet the average return on investment over this eight-year period varied from 2.5 per cent to 17.4 per cent. If we had figures for individual corporations the rates of return would vary over a much wider range.

Further evidence as to variations of return on investment among manufacturing corporations is furnished by the following figures, based on the data for 2,046 corporations compiled by R. C. Epstein and F. M. Clark. (Net profits are here determined *before* the deduction of Federal income taxes.)

| Industrial group | Number of corporations | Average rate of return on capital investment, 1922-1928 (per cent) |
|---|---|---|
| Printing and publishing | 100 | 21.2 |
| Miscellaneous | 89 | 18.4 |
| Stone, clay and glass products | 114 | 15.0 |
| Leather and leather products | 54 | 12.6 |
| Lumber and wood products | 190 | 11.6 |
| Metal and metal products | 648 | 10.9 |
| Food products, beverages and tobacco | 215 | 10.7 |
| Textiles and textile products | 289 | 9.9 |
| Chemicals and allied substances | 210 | 9.7 |
| Paper, pulp and products | 111 | 8.5 |
| Rubber and related products | 26 | 7.5 |

These figures are based on samples much more comprehensive than those of Forest, and probably represent actual returns more accurately.

stantial amounts were reported as 'dividends received' by these corporations. Subtracting these sums from total dividends paid, we may approximate the amounts actually distributed to individual stockholders. The data, shown below, are portrayed graphically in Figure 101.

TABLE 195

AGGREGATE DIVIDEND PAYMENTS OF ALL CORPORATIONS, 1922-1929

(In millions of dollars)

| Year | Total dividend payments | Dividend payments to individuals |
|---|---|---|
| 1922 | 3,437 | 2,634 |
| 1923 | 4,169 | 3,299 |
| 1924 | 4,339 | 3,424 |
| 1925 | 5,189 | 4,014 |
| 1926 | 5,945 | 4,439 |
| 1927 | 6,423 | 4,766 |
| 1928 | 7,074 | 5,157 |
| 1929 | 8,356 | 5,763 |
| Average annual rate of change (per cent) .............. | +12.8 | +10.8 |
| Index of instability.......... | 2.8 | 3.1 |

Aggregate dividend payments, which include payments on preferred as well as on common stocks, show an increase between 1922 and 1929 at a rate of 12.8 per cent a year. This is substantially higher than the rate of 7.3 per cent which measures the increase in the taxable net income of American corporations during this period, as reported to the Bureau of Internal Revenue.[1] The index of instability in dividend payments is 2.8, much smaller than the corresponding index of 9.0 for net income of all reporting corporations. The passing fluctuations of business which are reflected in corporation earnings do not so immediately affect dividend disbursements. Many of these fluctuations are absorbed by the buffers of surplus and undivided profits.

The distribution of dividends to individuals shows an increase somewhat below that for total dividend disbursements. The average

[1] The difference in rates of change is mainly due to the increase in the percentage of profits disbursed. Total cash dividend payments as a fraction of profits available for distribution ('compiled net profits after deducting tax') increased from about 66 per cent in 1922 to 78 per cent in 1929.

### FIGURE 101
### CHANGES IN AGGREGATE DIVIDEND PAYMENTS OF ALL CORPORATIONS, 1922-1929

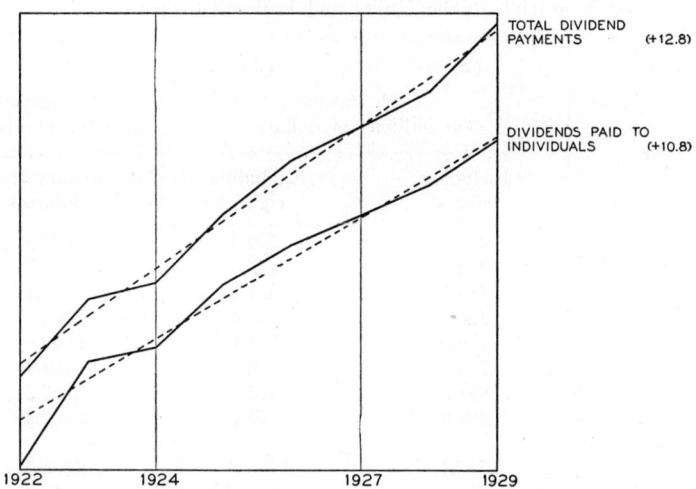

Plotted on ratio scale. The figures in parentheses define average annual rates of change (in percentage form).

annual rate of change for the years 1922-29 was $+ 10.8$ per cent; the index of instability was 3.1.

*Cash Receipts and Capital Gains of Stockholders.*—We secure another view of the fortunes of dividend recipients by tracing the actual dividend disbursements of a selected group of corporations, and measuring, at the same time, changes in the values of rights of various sorts accruing to stockholders, and changes in the market values of the capital sums invested. The sample includes 102 corporations (industrials, public utilities and railroads).[1] Results are summarized in the following tables, and are shown graphically in Figure 102. The changes traced in these tables relate to the total stock outstanding on January 1, 1922. Subsequent issues are disregarded, for the present purpose.

During the year 1922 aggregate dividend payments to stockholders, as of January 1 of that year, amounted to 389.3 millions of

---

[1] The sample included, in 1922, 34.5 per cent of the number of shares listed on the New York Stock Exchange.

## TABLE 196

Cash Income Received from 1922 to 1929, inclusive, by the Holders of All Common Stock Outstanding on January 1, 1922

102 Industrial, Public Utility and Railroad Corporations.[a]

| (1) Year | (2) Cash income (in millions of dollars) Including rights | (3) Cash income (in millions of dollars) Excluding rights | (4) Cash income, including rights, per $10,000 investment on January 1, 1922 (dollars) |
|---|---|---|---|
| 1922 | 416.6 | 389.3 | 640.5 |
| 1923 | 462.3 | 453.6 | 710.7 |
| 1924 | 559.5 | 471.9 | 860.1 |
| 1925 | 522.1 | 512.4 | 802.6 |
| 1926 | 660.0 | 614.1 | 1,014.6 |
| 1927 | 784.1 | 690.4 | 1,205.4 |
| 1928 | 955.7 | 755.4 | 1,469.2 |
| 1929 | 1,191.8 | 857.7 | 1,832.2 |
| Total receipts, eight years ......... | 5,552.1 | 4,744.8 | 8,535.3 |
| Average annual rate of change (per cent) .... | +16.5 | +11.9 | +16.5 |
| Index of instability | 6.5 | 2.2 | 6.5 |

[a] Following are the corporations included in the sample:

                                                                                        Market value of stock as of January 1, 1922 (millions of dollars)

*Railroads (12)*

| | |
|---|---|
| Atlantic Coast Line R.R. Co. | 56.8 |
| Chesapeake and Ohio Ry. Co. | 35.0 |
| Chicago and Northwestern Ry. Co. | 91.6 |
| Chicago, Rock Island and Pacific Ry. Co. | 23.9 |
| New York Central R.R. Co. | 184.1 |
| New York, New Haven and Hartford R.R. Co. | 20.4 |
| Northern Pacific Ry. Co. | 191.6 |
| Pennsylvania Railroad Co. | 335.7 |
| Pere Marquette Ry. Co. | 9.7 |
| Southern Pacific Co. | 257.1 |
| Southern Railway Co. | 22.2 |
| Union Pacific R.R. Co. | 280.4 |
| Total | 1,508.5 |

*Public Utilities (18)*

| | |
|---|---|
| American Telephone and Telegraph Co. | 629.7 |
| Commonwealth Edison Co. | 63.6 |
| Consolidated Gas Co. of New York | 91.0 |
| Consolidated Gas, Electric Light and Power Co. of Baltimore | 13.6 |
| Detroit Edison Co. | 27.9 |
| Edison Electric Illuminating Co. of Boston | 36.8 |
| El Paso Electric Co. | 3.2 |
| Fall River Gas Works Co. | 1.9 |

(*Footnote continued on following page*)

*(Footnote continued from preceding page)*

|  | Market value of stock as of January 1, 1922 (millions of dollars) |
|---|---|
| *Public Utilities (cont.)* |  |
| Lone Star Gas Corp. | 9.2 |
| Massachusetts Gas Cos. | 15.8 |
| Mississippi River Power Co. | 2.1 |
| North American Co. | 15.3 |
| Pacific Gas and Electric Co. | 21.9 |
| Pacific Lighting Corp. | 7.2 |
| Public Service Co. of Northern Illinois | 9.8 |
| Public Service Corp. of New Jersey | 20.6 |
| Twin City Rapid Transit Co. | 7.0 |
| Western Union Telegraph Co. | 90.4 |
| Total | 1,067.0 |
| *Industrial Corporations (72)* |  |
| Allied Chemical and Dye Corp. | 124.7 |
| American Agricultural Chemical Co. | 10.1 |
| American Beet Sugar Co. | 5.2 |
| American Can Co. | 14.3 |
| American Car and Foundry Co. | 43.8 |
| American Cotton Oil Co. (Gold Dust Corp.) | 4.4 |
| American Hide and Leather Co. | 1.5 |
| American International Corp. | 20.3 |
| American Linseed Co. | 5.2 |
| American Locomotive Co. | 27.0 |
| American Radiator Co. | 48.0 |
| American Smelting and Refining Co. | 27.6 |
| American Steel Foundries | 21.0 |
| American Sugar Refining Co. | 25.5 |
| American Tobacco Co. | 114.8 |
| American Woolen Co. | 32.7 |
| Anaconda Copper Mining Co. | 149.6 |
| Baldwin Locomotive Works | 19.6 |
| Bethlehem Steel Corp. | 31.4 |
| Calumet and Arizona Mining Co. | 37.9 |
| Central Leather Co. | 12.4 |
| Chicago Pneumatic Tool Co. | 7.5 |
| Colorado Fuel and Iron Co. | 8.6 |
| Computing-Tabulating-Recording Co. (International Business Machine Co.) | 7.7 |
| Continental Can Co., Inc. | 6.3 |
| Corn Products Refining Co. | 48.3 |
| Cudahy Packing Co. | 8.7 |
| Endicott-Johnson Corp. | 26.4 |
| Famous Players-Lasky Corp. | 16.3 |
| General Electric Co. | 240.2 |
| General Motors Corp. | 205.5 |
| Goodrich (The B. F.) Co. | 21.7 |
| Hart, Schaffner and Marx | 11.0 |
| International Harvester Co. | 78.1 |
| International Nickel Co. | 20.1 |
| Kayser (Julius) and Co. | 5.6 |
| Kelsey Wheel Co., Inc. | 6.0 |
| Kresge (S. S.) Co. | 27.7 |
| Lehigh Coal and Navigation Co. | 39.9 |
| Liggett and Myers Tobacco Co. (Class "B") | 17.9 |
| Loose-Wiles Biscuit Co. | 3.0 |
| Lorillard (P.) Co. | 45.6 |
| Marland Oil Co. | 21.1 |
| Mathieson Alkali Works, Inc. | 2.6 |
| Maxwell Motor Corp. (Class "B"), Chrysler Corp. | 7.4 |
| May Department Stores Co. | 21.6 |

*(Footnote continued on following page)*

494   ECONOMIC TENDENCIES

dollars, and the cash value of rights accruing in that year amounted to 27.3 millions of dollars. Total cash income, on the assumption that rights were turned into cash, was 416.6 millions. This increased, with a slight check in 1925, to 1,191.8 millions of dollars in 1929. The average rate of change was 16.5 per cent per year. The increase in actual dividend disbursements was at the rate of 11.9 per cent a year, but the addition of the cash values of rights brings this up to the rate cited.

This figure relates to aggregate cash income received by all stockholders as of January 1, 1922, but it may also be taken to define the rate of increase in the cash income of a person investing a fixed sum, say $10,000, in the stocks of these corporations on that date, divided precisely as the aggregate amount was divided [see column (4) of preceding table].

To complete the picture we must trace changes in the capital value of the aggregate investment over the same period. This is done in Table 197, following. To facilitate comparison with changes in the cash returns on these stocks the data given in the preceding

*(Footnote continued from preceding page)*

| Industrial Corporations (cont.) | Market value of stock as of January 1, 1922 (millions of dollars) |
|---|---:|
| National Biscuit Co. | 36.9 |
| National Lead Co. | 18.0 |
| New Jersey Zinc Co. | 56.8 |
| Pacific Mills | 33.6 |
| Pan-American Petroleum and Transport Co. (Class "B") | 19.0 |
| Pittsburgh Coal Co. | 20.3 |
| Pressed Steel Car Co. | 8.2 |
| Pullman Co. | 146.1 |
| Railway Steel Spring Co. | 13.4 |
| Republic Iron and Steel Co. | 15.5 |
| Sears, Roebuck and Co. | 64.1 |
| Sloss-Sheffield Steel and Iron Co. | 3.7 |
| Standard Oil Co. of New Jersey | 717.9 |
| Stewart-Warner Speedometer Corp. | 11.8 |
| Studebaker Corp. | 50.0 |
| Texas Co. | 303.4 |
| Union Bag and Paper Corp. | 10.6 |
| U. S. Cast Iron Pipe and Foundry Co. | 2.1 |
| U. S. Industrial Alcohol Co. | 9.6 |
| U. S. Realty and Improvement Co. | 9.9 |
| U. S. Rubber Co. | 44.1 |
| U. S. Steel Corp. | 428.2 |
| Virginia-Carolina Chemical Co. | 8.1 |
| Westinghouse Air Brake Co. | 54.2 |
| Westinghouse Electric and Manufacturing Co. | 71.2 |
| Woolworth (F. W.) Co. | 90.8 |
| Total | 3,929.3 |
| Grand Total | 6,504.8 |

### FIGURE 102
GRAPHIC REPRESENTATION OF INVESTMENT EXPERIENCE OF HOLDERS OF COMMON STOCK IN 102 CORPORATIONS, 1922-1929

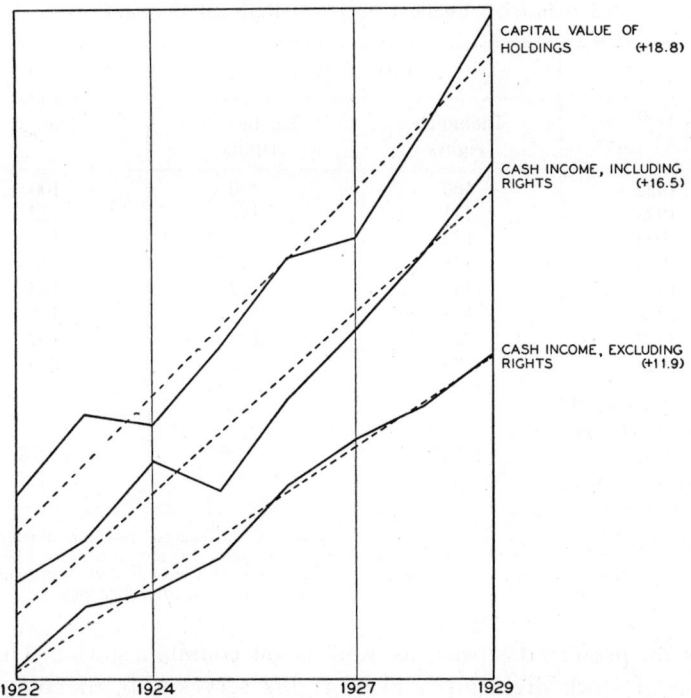

Plotted on ratio scale. The figures in parentheses define average annual rates of change (in percentage form).

table are repeated, in relative form. The series here given are those plotted in Figure 102.

At prevailing market prices the capital value of the aggregate investment increased 235 per cent between January 1, 1922, and January 1, 1929.[1] Over the entire period the average annual rate of increase in the capital value of the investment, as of January 1, was 18.8 per cent.

In explanation of these figures it must be noted that common stock values and dividends on common stocks alone are included. The dividend series derived from Treasury statistics includes pay-

[1] At market prices as of January 1, 1930, the increase in the value of the investment was 189 per cent.

## TABLE 197

RELATIVE NUMBERS DEFINING THE INVESTMENT EXPERIENCE OF HOLDERS OF ALL COMMON STOCK OUTSTANDING ON JANUARY 1, 1922

102 Industrial, Public Utility and Railroad Corporations

| Year | Cash income | | Capital value [a] |
|---|---|---|---|
| | Including rights | Excluding rights | |
| 1922 | 100 | 100 | 100 |
| 1923 | 111 | 117 | 122 |
| 1924 | 134 | 121 | 120 |
| 1925 | 125 | 132 | 145 |
| 1926 | 158 | 158 | 183 |
| 1927 | 188 | 177 | 191 |
| 1928 | 229 | 194 | 252 |
| 1929 | 286 | 220 | 335 |
| Average annual rate of change (per cent) .... | +16.5 | +11.9 | +18.8 |
| Index of instability | 6.5 | 2.2 | 7.3 |

[a] The market price as of January 1 of each year (or the nearest date for which figures were available) has been used to determine the capital value of the investment. For each company this price is multiplied by the number of shares of common stock outstanding on January 1, 1922, plus shares representing stock dividends declared after that date.

ments on preferred stocks, as well as on common stocks. The inclusion of stock dividends and of rights serves also, of course, to swell the returns represented in the above tables. Again, we are here dealing with a group of corporations whose earnings during this period may well have been above the average corporate return. Finally, we stop short of the period of severe liquidation in stock values and of retrenchment in dividend payments which began in 1929. Our figures relate to a prolonged period of prosperity. The comparison of tendencies within this period is our immediate concern.

§ *Returns to stockholders, various corporate groups.*—Changes in dividend disbursements, in the values of rights and in capital values occurring among the constituent groups of the total sample are shown in the several tables following.

Railroads, for which dividend disbursements and value of rights increased at a rate of 8.8 per cent a year, while capital value increased at a rate of 11.5 per cent a year, showed the lowest rates of advance. For

## TABLE 198

MEASUREMENTS DEFINING THE INVESTMENT EXPERIENCE OF THE HOLDERS OF ALL COMMON STOCK OUTSTANDING ON JANUARY 1, 1922

### 72 Industrial Corporations

| (1) | (2) | (3) | (4) | (5) | (6) |
|---|---|---|---|---|---|
| | Cash income [a] | | | | Capital value* in relative numbers |
| Year | Including rights | | Excluding rights | | |
| | In millions of dollars | In relative numbers | In millions of dollars | In relative numbers | |
| 1922 | 200.7 | 100 | 200.2 | 100 | 100 |
| 1923 | 253.0 | 126 | 251.7 | 126 | 125 |
| 1924 | 275.1 | 137 | 260.7 | 130 | 123 |
| 1925 | 307.6 | 153 | 301.3 | 150 | 152 |
| 1926 | 390.9 | 195 | 388.6 | 194 | 197 |
| 1927 | 502.9 | 251 | 456.7 | 228 | 208 |
| 1928 | 585.5 | 292 | 511.7 | 256 | 287 |
| 1929 | 791.6 | 395 | 601.3 | 300 | 402 |
| Total receipts, eight years ......... | 3,307.3 | | 2,972.2 | | |
| Average annual rate of change (per cent) .... | +21.8 | | +17.0 | | +22.4 |
| Index of instability | 5.5 | | 3.4 | | 8.9 |

* As of January 1 of each year.

[a] It is unavoidable that the records of a limited number of large corporations should dominate such aggregates as these. Indeed, these corporations would tend to dominate an all-inclusive sample. If we omit from the above aggregates statistics for four large corporations (General Motors Corp., Standard Oil Co. of N. J., General Electric Co. and the U. S. Steel Corp.), we have the following income record for the remaining companies in the group:

MEASUREMENTS DEFINING THE INVESTMENT EXPERIENCE OF THE HOLDERS OF ALL COMMON STOCK OUTSTANDING ON JANUARY 1, 1922

### 68 Industrial Corporations

| (1) | (2) | (3) | (4) | (5) | (6) |
|---|---|---|---|---|---|
| | Cash income | | | | Capital value* in relative numbers |
| Year | Including rights | | Excluding rights | | |
| | In millions of dollars | In relative numbers | In millions of dollars | In relative numbers | |
| 1922 | 130.8 | 100 | 130.4 | 100 | 100 |
| 1923 | 166.8 | 128 | 165.6 | 127 | 125 |
| 1924 | 179.3 | 137 | 164.9 | 126 | 122 |
| 1925 | 198.9 | 152 | 192.6 | 148 | 156 |
| 1926 | 225.0 | 172 | 222.8 | 171 | 207 |
| 1927 | 242.7 | 186 | 240.8 | 185 | 201 |
| 1928 | 304.1 | 232 | 247.0 | 189 | 265 |
| 1929 | 429.0 | 328 | 297.1 | 228 | 366 |
| Average annual rate of change (per cent) | +16.8 | | +11.2 | | +20.0 |
| Index of instability | 7.1 | | 4.1 | | 8.2 |

* As of January 1 of each year.

## TABLE 199

MEASUREMENTS DEFINING THE INVESTMENT EXPERIENCE OF THE HOLDERS OF ALL COMMON STOCK OUTSTANDING ON JANUARY 1, 1922

### 18 Public Utility Corporations

| (1) | (2) | (3) | (4) | (5) | (6) |
|---|---|---|---|---|---|
| | Cash income [a] | | | | Capital value * in relative numbers |
| Year | Including rights | | Excluding rights | | |
| | In millions of dollars | In relative numbers | In millions of dollars | In relative numbers | |
| 1922 | 110.5 | 100 | 84.1 | 100 | 100 |
| 1923 | 96.3 | 87 | 88.7 | 105 | 116 |
| 1924 | 128.4 | 116 | 87.3 | 104 | 117 |
| 1925 | 91.3 | 83 | 88.0 | 105 | 131 |
| 1926 | 133.7 | 121 | 91.0 | 108 | 155 |
| 1927 | 109.3 | 99 | 91.8 | 109 | 164 |
| 1928 | 183.2 | 166 | 94.2 | 112 | 203 |
| 1929 | 208.4 | 189 | 98.9 | 118 | 255 |
| Total receipts, eight years ......... | 1,061.1 | | 724.0 | | |
| Average annual rate of change (per cent) .... | +10.5 | | +1.9 | | +14.1 |
| Index of instability | 14.9 | | 1.3 | | 5.9 |

\* As of January 1 of each year.

[a] If one large corporation (the American Telephone and Telegraph Co.) be excluded from this group, we have somewhat different results:

MEASUREMENTS DEFINING THE INVESTMENT EXPERIENCE OF THE HOLDERS OF ALL COMMON STOCK OUTSTANDING ON JANUARY 1, 1922

### 17 Public Utility Corporations

| (1) | (2) | (3) | (4) | (5) | (6) |
|---|---|---|---|---|---|
| | Cash income | | | | Capital value * in relative numbers |
| Year | Including rights | | Excluding rights | | |
| | In millions of dollars | In relative numbers | In millions of dollars | In relative numbers | |
| 1922 | 40.0 | 100 | 34.8 | 100 | 100 |
| 1923 | 46.9 | 117 | 39.4 | 113 | 128 |
| 1924 | 55.1 | 138 | 38.0 | 109 | 127 |
| 1925 | 42.0 | 105 | 38.6 | 111 | 157 |
| 1926 | 50.1 | 125 | 41.7 | 120 | 200 |
| 1927 | 60.0 | 150 | 42.5 | 122 | 212 |
| 1928 | 58.5 | 146 | 44.8 | 129 | 271 |
| 1929 | 128.9 | 323 | 49.5 | 142 | 381 |
| Average annual rate of change (per cent) | +15.3 | | +4.3 | | +20.5 |
| Index of instability | 21.4 | | 2.8 | | 7.4 |

\* As of January 1 of each year.

## TABLE 200

MEASUREMENTS DEFINING THE INVESTMENT EXPERIENCE OF THE HOLDERS OF ALL COMMON STOCK OUTSTANDING ON JANUARY 1, 1922

### 12 Railroads

| (1) | (2) | (3) | (4) | (5) | (6) |
|---|---|---|---|---|---|
| | \multicolumn{4}{c}{Cash income} | Capital value * in relative numbers |
| Year | Including rights | | Excluding rights | | |
| | In millions of dollars | In relative numbers | In millions of dollars | In relative numbers | |
| 1922 | 105.4 | 100 | 104.9 | 100 | 100 |
| 1923 | 113.1 | 107 | 113.1 | 108 | 121 |
| 1924 | 156.0 | 148 | 123.8 | 118 | 112 |
| 1925 | 123.2 | 117 | 123.2 | 117 | 138 |
| 1926 | 135.5 | 129 | 134.4 | 128 | 166 |
| 1927 | 171.8 | 163 | 141.8 | 135 | 167 |
| 1928 | 187.0 | 177 | 149.5 | 143 | 194 |
| 1929 | 191.9 | 182 | 157.6 | 150 | 216 |
| Total receipts, eight years ........ | 1,183.9 | | 1,048.3 | | |
| Average annual rate of change (per cent) .... | +8.8 | | +5.8 | | +11.5 |
| Index of instability | 7.6 | | 1.2 | | 3.9 |

* As of January 1 of each year.

stockholders of the group of 72 industrial corporations, cash income advanced at 21.8 per cent a year,[1] while the market value of the invest-

[1] We may secure some check upon this figure, which shows a phenomenally rapid advance in the income received by stockholders of industrial corporations, by constructing an index of dividend payments per share, for industrial corporations. The Standard Statistics Company publishes comparable index numbers of stock prices and of dividend yields on 50 industrial common stocks, which are available weekly from 1926 to date. The price index is the total market value of the stocks in the Standard Statistics sample divided by the number of shares outstanding; the yield index is derived by dividing total dividends paid by the total market value. The product of these two indexes gives the ratio of total dividends to number of shares outstanding, or dividends per share. To secure strict comparability the calculation of this ratio has been carried out on a weekly basis. To the extent that weekly estimates of dividend policy do not correctly reflect actual dividend payments, the annual average may be somewhat in error. It should be noted that the index does not cover the returns to the stockholder in the form of subscription privileges, although correction is made for stock dividends and split-ups. The derived index of dividends per share for 50 industrial corpora-

ment, as of January 1 of each year, increased at a rate of 22.4 per cent a year.[1] Utilities stood between these two limits.

At a later point we shall compare these returns with those received by other economic groups.

## Investment Experience of Bondholders

The returns going to one other group of income recipients, bondholders, are summarized below. The measurements relate to the

TABLE 201

INVESTMENT EXPERIENCE OF A FUND OF $10,000 INVESTED IN BONDS IN JANUARY, 1922, AND REDISTRIBUTED SEMI-ANNUALLY TO MAINTAIN EQUAL DISTRIBUTION, 1922-1929

(These bonds are those included in the Dow-Jones index of bond prices.)

| Year | Interest paid per year | Value of fund[a] |
|---|---|---|
| 1922 | $548 | $10,268 |
| 1923 | 550 | 10,446 |
| 1924 | 554 | 10,573 |
| 1925 | 548 | 10,942 |
| 1926 | 554 | 11,316 |
| 1927 | 552 | 11,605 |
| 1928 | 553 | 11,810 |
| 1929 | 553 | 11,362 |
| Average annual rate of change (per cent) .............. | +0.1 | +1.9 |
| Index of instability........... | 0.3 | 1.5 |

[a] Average of the market values as of January 1 and July 1 of each year.

tions from 1926 to 1929 is given below. Index numbers of aggregate dividends received by those holding stocks in the base year, and of dividends plus rights, derived from the data employed in the present study, are shown in comparison with it.

| Year | Index numbers of dividends per share (derived from Standard Statistics index numbers) | Present sample of 72 industrial corporations | |
|---|---|---|---|
| | | Dividends | Dividends plus rights |
| 1926 | 100.0 | 100.0 | 100.0 |
| 1927 | 121.1 | 117.5 | 128.7 |
| 1928 | 135.4 | 131.7 | 149.8 |
| 1929 | 155.7 | 154.7 | 202.5 |

Over this four-year period the agreement between the index numbers of dividends per share (for 50 industrial corporations), and of aggregate dividends for a constant number of shares (for 72 industrial corporations) is very close.

[1] The Dow-Jones index of prices of industrial stocks, based on average monthly

bonds included in the Dow-Jones index of bond prices.[1]

Actual cash returns to these bondholders increased at an average annual rate of 0.1 per cent, while the value of the investment increased at a rate of 1.9 per cent. The slight increase in return is due to changes in the Dow-Jones sample, and to the shifting of the investment in the averaging process.

### Summary of Changes in Distributive Shares

The fortunes of different classes of income recipients between 1922 and 1929 are indicated by the series brought together for comparison in Table 202, following. These series are not all strictly comparable,[2] but general trends may be traced and compared, with a recognition of the differences among the quantities measured. The data are shown graphically in Figure 103.

Income in current dollars increased for all these classes of recipients, but there were wide differences among the rates of increase of the returns secured by the members of the groups represented. Labor fared well during the eight-year period we are considering, but the holder of common stocks fared even better. Cash receipts alone, without regard to the enhancement of capital values, advanced at rates well above the gains shown for the other classes.[3]

Index numbers relating to the same series, but defining changes

---

high and low prices of 20 stocks (30 since October, 1928), rose at the average annual rate of 19.4 per cent, with an index of instability of 6.3. This index is published in the *Wall Street Journal*.

[1] Use has been made of the compilations of Dwight C. Rose, *Investment Management*, New York, Harpers, 1929, pp. 392-3. The Dow-Jones sample during this period included 40 industrial, public utility and railroad bonds.

[2] The wage figures relate to rates, or to per capita earnings of such workers as are employed; the dividend figures relate to the aggregate returns of those holding all the common stocks of certain corporations at the beginning of the period, or to the returns of one investing a fixed sum, distributed among these stocks. Receipts of bondholders are also of this type.

[3] All these index numbers are, of course, limited in their strict application to the samples actually studied. Generalizing from these samples is particularly hazardous in the field of corporate returns, because of the wide diversity of corporate fortunes during this period. For this reason the study of different samples may yield inconsistent results.

The various figures cited in this chapter, defining changes in corporate net income and in dividend disbursements, come from several different sources, but

## TABLE 202

INDEX NUMBERS OF INCOMES RECEIVED BY WAGE-EARNERS, STOCKHOLDERS AND BONDHOLDERS IN AMERICAN INDUSTRIES, 1922-1929

(In current dollars)

| (1) Year | (2) Composite index of wages [a] | (3) Average earnings of employees, manufacturing [b] | (4) Cash receipts of holders of common stock in 102 corporations [c] | (5) | (6) | (7) | (8) Cash receipts of bondholders [d] |
|---|---|---|---|---|---|---|---|
| | | | All corporations | 72 industrials | 12 railroads | 18 public utilities | |
| 1922 | 100 | 100 | 100 | 100 | 100 | 100 | 100 |
| 1923 | 111 | 110 | 111 | 126 | 107 | 87 | 100 |
| 1924 | 115 | 112 | 134 | 137 | 148 | 116 | 101 |
| 1925 | 116 | 113 | 125 | 153 | 117 | 83 | 100 |
| 1926 | 119 | 115 | 158 | 195 | 129 | 121 | 101 |
| 1927 | 120 | 114 | 188 | 251 | 163 | 99 | 101 |
| 1928 | 121 | 116 | 229 | 292 | 177 | 166 | 101 |
| 1929 | 122 | 117 | 286 | 395 | 182 | 189 | 101 |
| Average annual rate of change (per cent).. | +2.3 | +1.6 | +16.5 | +21.8 | +8.8 | +10.5 | +0.1 |

[a] Snyder's composite index of wages, a combination of the New York State Department of Labor's index of wages of factory workers and index of the wages of clerks in factories, with the Federal Reserve Bank's index of hiring rates for unskilled labor, and the National Education Association's index of average wages for teachers in the United States. See Carl Snyder, *Business Cycles and Business Measurements*, Macmillan Co., New York, 1927, pp. 137 and 289.

[b] Aggregate wages paid, as reported in the Census of Manufactures, divided by the average number of wage-earners. Figures for inter-censal years are based upon the Federal Reserve Board's index numbers of factory payrolls and employment.

[c] Dividends plus cash value of rights. See Tables 197-200.

[d] See Table 201.

reflect with a fair degree of consistency the tendencies of the period. For convenience, they are here summarized:

| Economic element | Average annual rate of increase (per cent) 1922-1929 |
|---|---|
| Net income of all corporations (Bureau of Internal Revenue) | + 7.3 |
| Net income of all manufacturing corporations (Bureau of Internal Revenue) | + 5.3 |
| Net profits of 2,046 manufacturing corporations (Epstein and Clark) | + 7.4 |
| Dividend payments of all corporations (Bureau of Internal Revenue) | + 12.8 |
| Dividend payments to individuals, all corporations (Bureau of Internal Revenue) | + 10.8 |
| Cash income of holders of common stock, including cash value of rights (102 corporations) | + 16.5 |
| Cash income of holders of common stock, not including rights (102 corporations) | + 11.9 |

The difference between the rates of growth of net income and of dividend disbursements is explained, in part, by the fact that an increasing percentage of profits available for distribution was disbursed as dividends, during this period. The percentage was 66 in 1922, 78 in 1929. (These figures are derived from statistics of the Bureau of Internal Revenue.)

## FIGURE 103

### CHANGES IN INCOMES RECEIVED BY WAGE-EARNERS, STOCKHOLDERS AND BONDHOLDERS, IN AMERICAN INDUSTRIES, 1922-1929

(IN CURRENT DOLLARS)

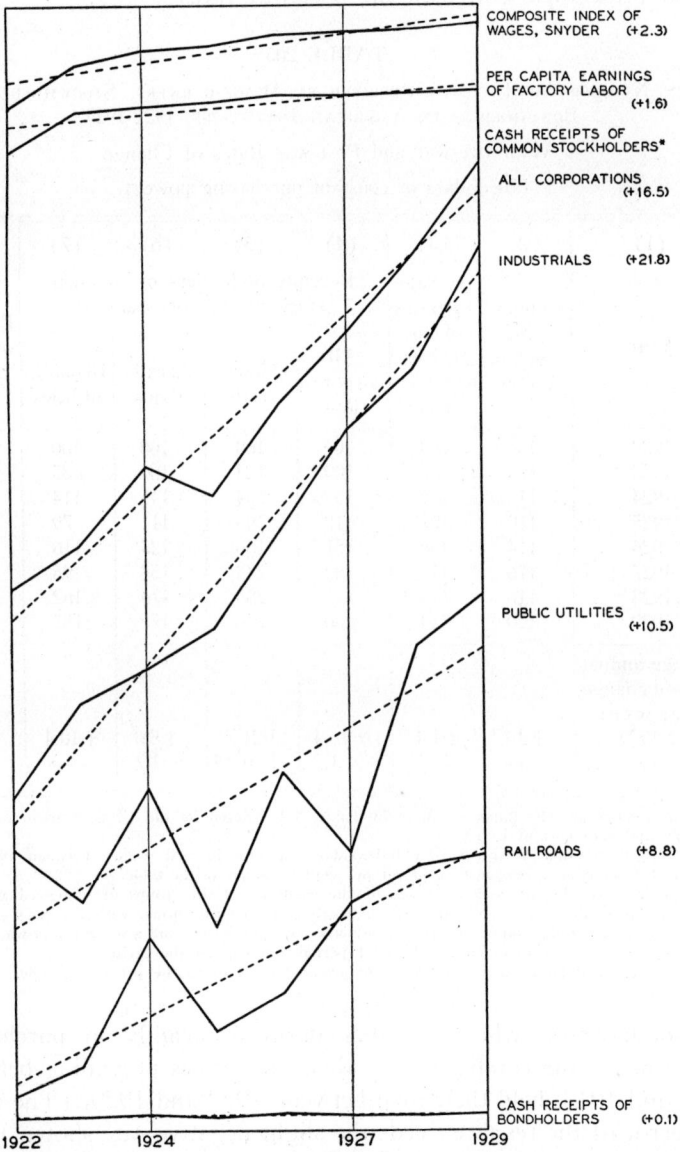

Plotted on ratio scale. The figures in parentheses define average annual rates of change (in percentage form).
* Index numbers derived from sample corporate returns.

in terms of dollars of constant purchasing power, are shown in the next table. Rates of change in corresponding pre-war series are given for comparison with the post-war rates.

TABLE 203

INDEX NUMBERS OF INCOMES RECEIVED BY WAGE-EARNERS, STOCKHOLDERS AND BONDHOLDERS IN AMERICAN INDUSTRIES, 1922-1929 [a]

With Pre-war and Post-war Rates of Change

(In dollars of constant purchasing power)

| (1) | (2) | (3) | (4) | (5) | (6) | (7) | (8) |
|---|---|---|---|---|---|---|---|
| Year | Composite index of wages | Average earnings of employees, manufacturing | Receipts of holders of common stock in 102 corporations | | | | Receipts of bondholders |
| | | | All corporations | 72 industrials | 12 railroads | 18 public utilities | |
| 1922 | 100 | 100 | 100 | 100 | 100 | 100 | 100 |
| 1923 | 109 | 108 | 109 | 123 | 105 | 85 | 98 |
| 1924 | 113 | 109 | 132 | 134 | 145 | 114 | 99 |
| 1925 | 110 | 107 | 119 | 146 | 111 | 79 | 94 |
| 1926 | 114 | 109 | 151 | 186 | 123 | 116 | 97 |
| 1927 | 116 | 111 | 182 | 243 | 158 | 96 | 98 |
| 1928 | 118 | 113 | 225 | 286 | 174 | 162 | 99 |
| 1929 | 120 | 114 | 280 | 386 | 178 | 185 | 99 |
| Average annual rate of change (per cent) | | | | | | | |
| 1922-1929 ... | +2.1 [b] | +1.4 | +16.4 | +21.7 | +8.6 | +10.4 | −0.1 |
| 1901-1913 ... | +0.4 [c] | −0.1 | + 1.2 | + 0.9 [d] | +1.7 | — | −1.2 |

[a] The entries are the index numbers in Table 202 deflated by the U. S. Bureau of Labor Statistics index of cost of living.
[b] A recent revision of the Snyder index shows a gain in real wages, between 1922 and 1929, of 1.9 per cent a year instead of 2.1 per cent as given in the table.
[c] This rate relates to Douglas' index of the earnings of all groups of employed workers, excluding farm labor. Douglas' index is comparable, in general terms, with Snyder's post-war figures. Snyder's index numbers are not strictly comparable for pre-war and post-war years, since factory wages are included for the later period, but not for the earlier.
[d] Industrial and public utility stocks were grouped together in the pre-war sample.

Bondholders, whose incomes declined steadily in purchasing power under the conditions of advancing prices prevailing between 1901 and 1913, held their own between 1922 and 1929. (The probable error of the result exceeds the slight negative rate shown.) The purchasing power of the income of the average wage-earner (as measured by Snyder's index relating to unskilled workers, teachers and clerks and factory workers) advanced between 1922 and 1929, at a much higher rate than did a corresponding index in pre-war years. Industrial wage-earners, whose incomes declined in purchasing power between 1901 and 1913, showed a steady gain in the recent period. Among common stockholders, however, the most phenomenal advances in the purchasing power of cash receipts occurred. Stockholders enjoyed some advantage in pre-war years, but the gains of this group, both absolute and relative, were far more pronounced in the period preceding the recession of 1929. The increase in cash receipts was augmented, moreover, by a great increase in the market value of the capital investment. While the advance lasted (and, of course, the story that carries only through 1929 is an unfinished one) stockholders occupied the position of greatest strategic advantage in the economic system.

The above record applies to the average returns of wage-earners, bondholders and stockholders, as these have been estimated from sample figures. It does not define changes in the aggregate purchasing power of the different economic groups represented. To this problem we now pass.

## Changes in the Aggregate Purchasing Power of Different Economic Classes

In concluding the discussion of the pre-war period an attempt was made to secure a general perspective of the broader changes which had occurred during the thirteen years preceding the war. In that summary three broad streams were distinguished, the stream of population, the stream of physical goods, and the stream of values. Population increased during the pre-war period at a rate of 2.0 per cent a year; the stream of physical goods increased at a rate of about 3.1 per cent a year; while the value stream (the physical volume of goods expressed in monetary terms) increased in volume at a rate approximating 4.9 per cent a year. We may summarize in similar fashion the record of the period 1922-1929.

Between 1922 and 1929 the population of the United States increased at an average annual rate of approximately 1.4 per cent a year. The physical stream of goods (excluding construction) produced by this population increased at an average rate of 3.8 per cent a year. The total stream of values (values, that is, of physical goods alone, not of services) increased at an average annual rate in the neighborhood of 3.3 per cent a year.[1] The rate of increase of population in the recent period was substantially lower than that prevailing in the earlier period, the rate of increase in the physical volume of goods produced was higher, while the rate of increase in values was distinctly lower in the recent period. The post-war rate of change of 3.3 per cent a year in aggregate values contrasts notably with the pre-war rate of 4.9 per cent. The difference is attributable, of course, to post-war price decline, as against pre-war advance.

The effects of these differences in price and value trends have been far-reaching. Certain aspects of these changes may be explored further. Relevant estimates are given in the following table. These are graphically presented in Figure 104.

FIGURE 104

GRAPHIC REPRESENTATION OF POST-WAR TENDENCIES AMONG PRODUCERS OF RAW MATERIALS AND OF MANUFACTURED GOODS*

AVERAGE RATES OF CHANGE IN PURCHASING POWER PER UNIT OF GOODS PRODUCED, IN AGGREGATE PHYSICAL PRODUCTION AND IN AGGREGATE COMMAND OVER GOODS

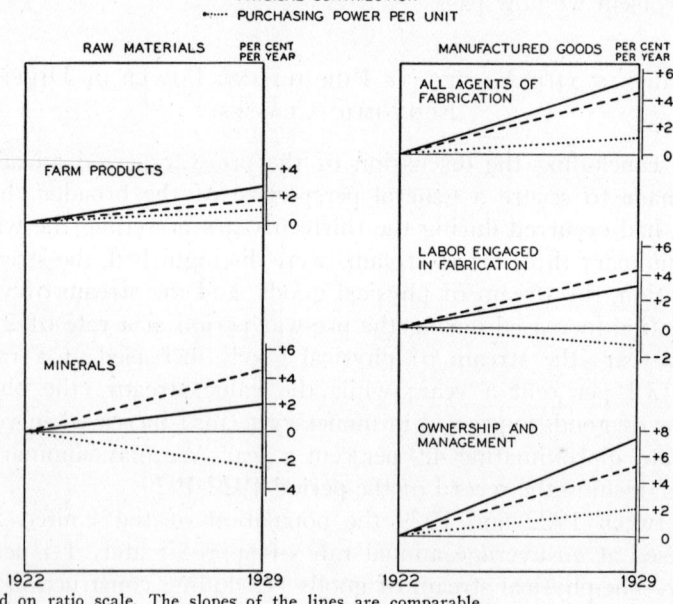

* Plotted on ratio scale. The slopes of the lines are comparable.

[1] Approximations to the total *net* value of production, secured from estimates of the aggregate value of minerals and farm products, value added by manufacture and rail transportation, show a somewhat greater rate of growth, +3.8 per cent.

## TABLE 204

ESTIMATES OF POST-WAR TENDENCIES AMONG PRODUCERS OF ECONOMIC GOODS

Changes in Values of Products and in Command over Goods

(Entries define average annual rates of change, 1922-1929)

| (1) | (2) | (3) | (4) | (5) |
|---|---|---|---|---|
| | | \multicolumn{3}{c}{Change in command over goods and factors in such change} | | |
| Economic group | Change in aggregate value of product (per cent per year) | Change in aggregate command over goods [a] (per cent per year) | \multicolumn{2}{c}{Change in command over goods attributable to alterations in} | |
| | | | purchasing power per unit (per cent per year) | number of physical units (per cent per year) |
| All producers .................... | +3.3 | +3.8 | — | +3.8 |
| Producers of: | | | | |
| Raw farm products............. | +2.2 | +2.7 | +1.0 | +1.7 |
| Raw mineral products.......... | +1.5 | +2.0 | —2.5 | +4.6 |
| Manufactured goods: [b] | | | | |
| All agents of fabrication...... | +5.1 | +5.6 | +1.1 | +4.5 |
| Labor .................... | +2.6 | +3.1 | —1.2 | +4.3 |
| Ownership and management. | +6.8 | +7.3 | +2.0 | +5.2 |

[a] Value figures have been deflated throughout by the Bureau of Labor Statistics index numbers of wholesale prices, which showed an average rate of decline of 0.5 per cent a year between 1922 and 1929. Thus it is command over goods at wholesale, and real prices in wholesale markets, which are measured by entries relating to purchasing power.

The measurements of per-unit purchasing power given in this table differ somewhat from those given in Chapter VII. This is due in part to differences in classifications and in the deflating index numbers employed. The per-unit purchasing power of the commodity groups cited in Chapter VII is measured in terms of the articles included in the 'all commodities' index constructed by the National Bureau of Economic Research, which differs slightly from that of the Bureau of Labor Statistics.

[b] The rates of change relating to manufacturing output have been secured from data compiled in the biennial Censuses of Manufactures, with interpolated figures for inter-censal years. The measurements relate to all manufacturing industries.

In this table we may trace certain elements of the total value stream, and differentiate between the price and quantity factors contributing to the change in each of these elements between 1922 and 1929. Over this period the total value of raw farm products increased at a rate of 2.2 per cent a year, that of raw minerals gained at a rate of 1.5 per cent a year, while the aggregate value added by manufacture increased at a rate of 5.1 per cent. The grand total advanced at an average annual rate of 3.3 per cent. These rates of advance in values represent increases in aggregate purchasing power in wholesale markets at slightly higher rates [see column (3)] because of the declining trend of prices. The aggregate purchasing power of agents of fabrication was advancing at a rate of 5.6 per cent a year, a figure notably higher than that for any other group. The group drawing incomes from manufacturing industries enjoyed a position of exceptional power during this period. In this group the most substantial gain was made by 'ownership and management'—owners and salaried workers, and those receiving rent, interest and taxes from manufacturing industries.[1]

In the last two columns of Table 204 are given rates of change in the two factors contributing to aggregate purchasing power. The growth in physical output and changes in the physical contributions of different fabricating agents, to which the rates of change in column (5) relate, have been discussed in preceding sections.[2] The relatively rapid increase in the output of raw mineral products and of fabricated goods, and the slower growth of production of raw farm products have been noted. Concomitant changes in real worth,

[1] To ensure comparability, purchasing power has been measured for all groups with reference to commodity prices in wholesale markets. For farmers and for industrial workers more precise determination of the actual purchasing power of money incomes is possible, using index numbers of the prices of things farmers buy and, for wage-earners, of the cost of living.

Between 1922 and 1929 prices paid by farmers increased at a rate of 0.3 per cent per year. With aggregate values of raw farm products increasing by 2.2 per cent per year, this means that the aggregate purchasing power of such products increased at a rate of approximately 1.9 per cent per year. During the same period the cost of living for industrial wage-earners increased at a rate of 0.2 per cent a year. The average annual increase of 2.6 per cent in aggregate monetary rewards for this group corresponds, therefore, to an advance of 2.4 per cent a year in aggregate purchasing power.

These rates fall below those cited in column (3) of Table 204. Though not comparable with the figures for the other economic groups there listed, they are probably closer to the truth, for the two groups in question. It should be understood, however, that these rates, with the others presented in the preceding table, are to be taken as indicating the general magnitude of the true values, not as final determinations of these values. Quite apart from the troublesome problem of finding appropriate deflators, independently derived figures of prices, quantities and values are seldom mutually consistent, and the task of reconciling them offers many difficulties.

[2] See footnote, p. 378, for comments on the measurement of the physical contributions of agents of fabrication. Index numbers of fabrication (the Federal Reserve Board's index of manufacturing production) have been used to secure inter-censal estimates of the physical contribution of labor and ownership and management.

per unit, swelled the real exchange value (i.e., aggregate purchasing power) of farm products, substantially lowered the real exchange value of mineral products and reduced somewhat the real exchange value of products of fabrication. Within the latter group there were mixed currents. The real price of the services of labor, per unit of product (labor cost per unit, in dollars of constant purchasing power) was being steadily lowered during this period, while the price paid for the services of ownership and management [1] was advancing. As a result, the rates of advance in the aggregate purchasing power of these groups differed greatly, being 3.1 per cent for labor, 7.3 per cent for the mixed group of owners, creditors and salaried workers.

§ *Comparison of pre-war and post-war tendencies among producers of economic goods.*—These rates gain in significance when compared with similar figures for the pre-war period. Table 67 from Chapter IV is repeated, on page 510, for convenience of reference. Graphic representations of pre-war and post-war movements appear in Figures 34 and 104.

Rates of increase in aggregate values were generally lower in the post-war period, because of the difference in price trends. Exceptions are found in the figures defining the increase in the value of the product of all fabricating agents, and of ownership and management, in manufacturing industries. For the latter group we have 6.8 for the recent period, as against 5.0 for the earlier period.

The more rapid increase in the physical volume of production between 1922 and 1929 is reflected in figures relating to command over goods, which are generally higher for the post-war period. This is notably true for agents of fabrication. These producers gained in aggregate command over goods at a rate of 5.6 per cent a year between 1922 and 1929, as compared with 3.1 per cent between 1901 and 1913. The most conspicuous improvement is found, again, among the group of owners, salaried workers and managers of manufacturing industries. The post-war gain of 7.3 per cent a year is far above the pre-war figure of 3.2 per cent. For manufacturing labor, the rate of increase in aggregate command over goods during the period 1922-29 was only fractionally greater than for the period 1901-13. (It will be recalled that the number of workers was increasing in pre-war years at a rate of 2.7 per cent a year, and advanced during the post-war period at a rate of but 1.0 per cent a year. Real earnings *per capita* increased more rapidly during the recent period.)

With reference to the factors in aggregate purchasing power, it is clear that the more advantageous recent trend for agents of fabrication is due to more favorable price relations and to a more rapid increase of output. For the residual group, here termed 'owners and managers' for

[1] This item includes taxes and other residual elements of cost.

## TABLE 205
### Estimates of Pre-war Tendencies among Producers of Economic Goods
### Changes in Values of Products and in Command over Goods

(Entries define average annual rates of change. For manufacturing industries the figures relate to the period 1899-1914, for other industries to the period 1901-1913.)

| (1) | (2) | (3) | (4) | (5) |
|---|---|---|---|---|
| | | | Change in command over goods and factors in such change | |
| Economic group | Change in aggregate value of product (per cent per year) | Change in aggregate command over goods [a] (per cent per year) | Change in command over goods attributable to alterations in | |
| | | | purchasing power per unit (per cent per year) | number of physical units (per cent per year) |
| All producers .................... | +4.9 | +3.1 | — | +3.1 |
| Producers of: | | | | |
| Raw farm products............ | +4.0 | +2.2 | +0.5 | +1.7 |
| Raw mineral products......... | +5.9 | +4.1 | −1.5 | +5.6 |
| Manufactured goods: [b] | | | | |
| All agents of fabrication .... | +4.9 | +3.1 | −1.3 | +4.5 |
| Labor .................... | +4.8 | +3.0 | −1.1 | +4.1 |
| Ownership and management. | +5.0 | +3.2 | −1.4 | +4.7 |

[a] The index of wholesale prices of the U. S. Bureau of Labor Statistics has been used as a deflator throughout.
[b] These entries relate to all manufacturing industries covered by the Census of Manufactures.

convenience, favorable price developments were most important in improving their relative position in recent years.

In tracing changes in the aggregate purchasing power of different groups of producers, it is desirable to supplement the figures relating to changes occurring between 1922 and 1929 by measurements covering a longer period. The events of 1914-21 may not be ignored in following more recent movements. In the following table are a series of measurements showing the changes which occurred between 1914 and 1929 in various factors named above. (These are, of course, approximations to the true figures, which may not be determined with perfect accuracy.) The relative numbers given define net changes between the terminal years of the period covered.

TABLE 206

SHOWING CHANGES OCCURRING IN THE AGGREGATE VALUES OF GOODS PRODUCED BY CERTAIN ECONOMIC GROUPS, AND CORRESPONDING CHANGES IN COMMAND OVER GOODS, 1914 TO 1929

| (1) | (2) | (3) | (4) | (5) |
|---|---|---|---|---|
| | | Aggregate command over goods and factors affecting aggregate command over goods [a] | | |
| Economic group | Aggregate value of product, 1929 (1914= 100) | Aggregate command over goods, 1929 (1914= 100) | Purchasing power per unit, 1929 (1914= 100) | Number of physical units, 1929 (1914= 100) |
| All producers .................... | 226 | 161 | 100 | 161 |
| Producers of: | | | | |
| Raw farm products............. | 169 | 121 | 97 | 125 |
| Raw mineral products.......... | 290 | 207 | 121 | 171 |
| Manufactured goods: | | | | |
| All agents of fabrication...... | 328 | 234 | 125 | 187 |
| Labor ..................... | 291 | 208 | 115 | 182 |
| Ownership and management. | 353 | 253 | 133 | 191 |

[a] Command over goods relates to purchasing power in wholesale markets.

Between 1914 and 1929 the aggregate value of goods produced in the United States (excluding construction) increased by approximately 126 per cent. Making due allowance for price changes, this represents an increase of 61 per cent in aggregate command over goods.[1] For the three main groups of producers, those engaged in the production of raw farm and raw mineral products and in the

[1] This figure is identical with that measuring the increase in physical volume of production, as given in column (5). This is theoretically proper, since the volume of goods 'commanded' must equal the volume of goods produced. Given complete coverage of all producers and consumers, and given accurate deflating index numbers, the first entry in column (3) would be a weighted average of all the other entries in the column, while the first entry in column (5) would be a weighted average of all the other entries in that column. This is true, by construction, as regards column (5), but, because of the omission of important groups of consumers, it is not true of column (3), nor of the derived column (4).

processes of manufacture, the increases in aggregate value of output between 1914 and 1929 were, respectively, 69, 190 and 228 per cent [see column (2)]. Taking account (roughly, because of deficiencies of data) of the prices at which these money returns were spent, these increases represent corresponding gains in aggregate command over goods of 21 per cent for farmers, of 107 per cent for producers of raw mineral products and of 134 per cent for agents of fabrication [see column (3)]. The relatively weak position of farmers is clear, when this gain of 21 per cent is contrasted with the advance of 61 per cent in the total physical output of the country during this period.

In columns (4) and (5) are measurements defining changes in purchasing power per unit and in output of physical units—factors which, in combination, account for changes in aggregate purchasing power. (Purchasing power has been measured throughout in terms of prices at wholesale. While this is not a thoroughly appropriate standard for any of the productive agents, it has seemed desirable to use the index of wholesale prices as a common deflator.) For farmers, the increase of 21 per cent in aggregate purchasing power was the resultant of a loss of 3 per cent in purchasing power per unit of goods produced, and an increase of 25 per cent in the number of such units. Producers of raw mineral products gained in both respects, per-unit value of products advancing by 21 per cent, number of units produced advancing by 71 per cent. Similarly, agents of fabrication gained 25 per cent in the average value of their contribution, per unit of goods produced, while the volume of fabrication advanced by 87 per cent.

The figures for labor and for 'ownership and management' represent an attempt to appraise the changes in the contributions and in the per-unit value of the contributions of these two classes to the joint product of agents of fabrication. The meaning and the limitations of the measurements have already been discussed. Gains in aggregate value and in aggregate purchasing power were greater for 'ownership and management' (the residual group the return to which includes all of 'value added' except wages). The greater gain in aggregate purchasing power for this group was due, primarily, to a greater increase in the real value, per unit of product, of the contribution of this group. Profits, overhead, all the items that make up the wages of management, represented a considerably larger proportion of the selling price of manufactured goods in 1929 than in 1914.[1]

## Changes in the Aggregate Physical Contributions of Economic Classes in Relation to Changes in their Aggregate Physical Rewards

An index of aggregate purchasing power, of the type employed above, measures changes in what the community is giving, in physical units, for the services of a group of producers. It defines changes in the aggregate physical rewards of given producers. We have previously employed index numbers of the aggregate physical contributions of various producers. The ratio of aggregate physical

[1] It is impossible, using data now available, to secure consistency among index numbers measuring changes in production, prices and values, when these index numbers are independently computed. The figures cited above are not altogether consistent, nor do they agree in all respects with price and value measurements previously presented. A source of error is introduced, too, by measuring the purchasing power of these various producers in terms of wholesale prices. Rough as the measurements are, however, they indicate the general nature of the changes that were taking place over the fifteen-year period that covers the war and the post-war boom. They may serve too, perhaps, to stimulate a more precise determination of the magnitudes involved in these important shifts.

Probably the most serious distortions in the above table result from the use of an index of wholesale prices in determining purchasing power of farmers and of industrial laborers. Correcting these two sets of results, without regard to consistency with the figures for other groups, we have the following measurements. The purchasing power of farmers has been determined with reference to the prices of things farmers buy, the purchasing power of labor with reference to the cost of living of industrial wage-earners.

| Economic group | Aggregate value of product, 1929 (1914 = 100) | Aggregate command over goods and factors affecting aggregate command over goods | | |
|---|---|---|---|---|
| | | Aggregate command over goods, 1929 (1914 = 100) | Purchasing power per unit, 1929 (1914 = 100) | Number of physical units, 1929 (1914 = 100) |
| Producers of raw farm products | 169 | 110 | 88 | 125 |
| Manufacturing labor | 291 | 176 | 97 | 182 |

The increases in aggregate purchasing power, as thus measured, are distinctly less for both groups. For farmers there was a gain of but 10 per cent, for industrial labor a gain of 76 per cent. For each unit of goods produced the farmer received 12 per cent less in 1929, in terms of other goods, than he did in 1914. Industrial workers received in actual purchasing power 3 per cent less in 1929 than in 1914, in return for their contribution to each unit of manufactured goods produced. (Purchasing power per unit means, here, per unit of goods produced, not per worker. As a result of increasing productivity, and other factors, the purchasing power of per capita earnings increased substantially between 1914 and 1929.)

contributions to aggregate physical rewards is a significant index of shifting economic relations. A ratio in excess of unity (or a relative above 100) indicates a larger contribution by a given group, in relation to remuneration received (changes in contributions and rewards being measured with reference to some stated base period), while a value below unity (or a relative below 100) indicates a smaller contribution, with reference to the physical goods commanded in exchange. In the present case we are interested in comparing ratios for 1929 with corresponding ratios for 1923 (or 1922), and for 1914 (or 1913). The materials in the following table, relating to selected manufacturing industries, illustrate the procedure.[1]

TABLE 207

SHOWING ALTERATIONS OCCURRING IN THE TERMS OF EXCHANGE BETWEEN GIVEN GROUPS OF MANUFACTURING PRODUCERS AND ALL PRODUCERS, 1923 TO 1929 AND 1914 TO 1929 [a]

| (1) | (2) | (3) | (4) | (5) |
|---|---|---|---|---|
| | | | Ratio of aggregate production to aggregate purchasing power in 1929 | |
| Producing group | Physical volume of fabrication in 1929 (1923=100) | Aggregate purchasing power of 'value added by manufacture' in 1929 (1923=100) | (1923=100) | (1914=100) |
| All manufacturing industries in sample .......................... | 113.0 | 115.4 | 97.9 | 79.8 |
| Flour and other grain-mill products | 94.5 | 118.7 | 79.6 | 86.4 |
| Slaughtering and meat packing.... | 100.9 | 117.7 | 85.7 | 89.3 |
| Cotton goods ..................... | 104.6 | 86.5 | 121.0 | 74.0 |
| Woolen goods .................... | 83.5 | 79.7 | 104.8 | 60.1 |
| Worsted goods ................... | 75.5 | 71.6 | 105.4 | 56.3 |
| Petroleum refining ............... | 177.1 | 174.2 | 101.6 | 91.7 |
| Iron and steel: blast furnaces..... | 106.7 | 96.9 | 110.1 | 83.4 |
| Iron and steel: steel works and rolling mills .................... | 124.2 | 138.9 | 89.4 | 72.7 |
| Motor vehicles ................... | 123.3 | 144.5 | 85.3 | 151.5 |

[a] These measurements relate to the products of fabrication, not to the total output. It is the contribution of agents of fabrication which is here in question. Purchasing power is measured in terms of commodities in general at wholesale, as these are represented in the index of wholesale prices of the U. S. Bureau of Labor Statistics.

[1] See Chapter IV for a more detailed discussion of ratios of this type.

For the manufacturing industries included in the present sample (62 industries between 1923 and 1927, 60 in 1929) the physical volume of production (fabrication) increased 13.0 per cent between 1923 and 1929. Over the same period the goods commanded in exchange (at wholesale prices) increased in volume by 15.4 per cent. The ratio of aggregate physical contribution to aggregate physical withdrawal decreased from 1.00 to .979 or, in relatives, from 100.0 to 97.9 [see column (4)]. In 1929 the community was receiving somewhat less from manufacturing industries than in

### FIGURE 105
SHOWING ALTERATIONS OCCURRING IN THE TERMS OF EXCHANGE BETWEEN GIVEN GROUPS OF PRODUCERS AND ALL PRODUCERS, 1923 TO 1929 AND 1914 TO 1929

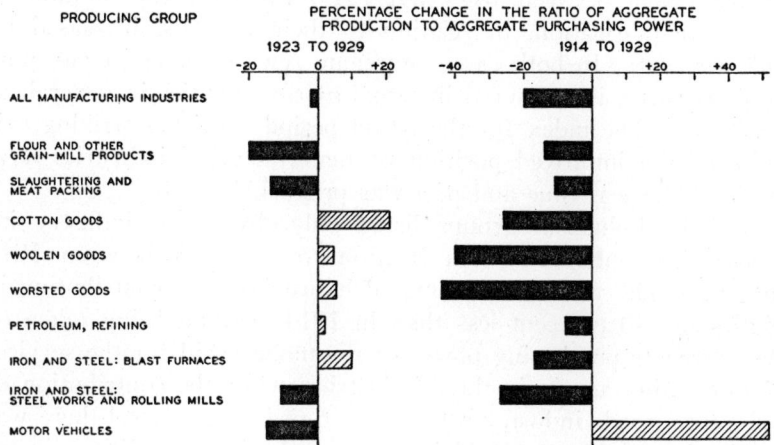

1923, with reference to what the community was paying for manufactured goods. Among the selected industrial groups listed in the table, the contributions of the three textile groups, of the petroleum refining industry and of blast furnaces showed increases, in relation to the goods commanded in exchange, while for milling, slaughtering and meat packing, and the steel and motor industries physical contributions declined, in relation to the rewards received. These movements, expressed as percentage changes in the ratios of aggregate production to aggregate purchasing power, are shown graphically in Figure 105.

But the developments of this six-year period should not be reviewed in isolation. What was the situation prevailing in the base year, 1923, in relation to earlier years? This question has been answered in the concluding pages of Chapter V. We may take account of these earlier changes by expressing the ratio of contribution to reward in 1929 as a relative on the 1914 base for each of the groups named. These relatives appear in column (5) of the above table.

Here we have a completely different picture. For manufacturing industries as a whole the relative for 1929, on the 1914 base, is 79.8. This means that the aggregate physical contribution of agents of fabrication in 1929 was 20.2 per cent less than in 1914, in relation to a constant volume of withdrawals, or of physical rewards. In other words, the contribution of agents of fabrication, per unit of goods commanded in exchange, was 20.2 per cent less in 1929 than in 1914.[1] This change stands in marked contrast to the movement between 1899 and 1914, when the contribution of agents of fabrication, in relation to their rewards, increased by 24.7 per cent. (In both cases aggregate reward, or aggregate purchasing power, is measured in terms of commodities in general, at wholesale.) The index for the recent period furnishes striking evidence of the improved position of manufacturing industries as a result of the war-time and post-war price shifts.

Of the industrial groups listed only the motor industry increased its contribution (in relation to rewards) between 1914 and 1929. The woolen and worsted industries were contributing in 1929 some 40 per cent less than in 1914, account being taken of the aggregate purchasing power of the money paid for the services of fabricating agents in these industries, while the contribution of the cotton goods industry was 26 per cent less. For steel there was a reduction of 27 per cent. Differences in business conditions in the

[1] The index numbers of physical volume and of aggregate purchasing power cited above for all manufacturing industries are based upon data relating to 62 industries. There is no doubt that these index numbers understate the true gain shown by manufacturing industries in the post-war epoch (see Chapter VI). Corrected index numbers for all industries included in the Census of Manufactures (in this case derived on the assumption that fabrication costs per unit of output changed during this period at the same rate among the industries excluded from the sample as among the 62 industries included) are given below, together with ratios based upon them.

|  | Physical volume of fabrication in 1929 (1923 = 100) | Aggregate purchasing power of 'value added by manufacture' in 1929 (1923 = 100) | Ratio of aggregate production to aggregate purchasing power in 1929 (1923 = 100) | Ratio of aggregate production to aggregate purchasing power in 1929 (1914 = 100) |
|---|---|---|---|---|
| All manufacturing industries | 127.3 | 130.1 | 97.9 | 79.8 |

years compared [1] would account in part for these reductions in the ratios of contributions to withdrawals, but not for the extreme changes we have noted. Manufacturing industries were left by the recession of 1920-21 in a position of relative advantage, and preserved a large part of that advantage during the years between 1922 and 1929.[2]

In the next table we summarize a number of ratios of the type just described. Here we compare the situation in 1929 with that prevailing in 1922, and with that of 1913. These movements are shown as percentage changes, in Figure 106.

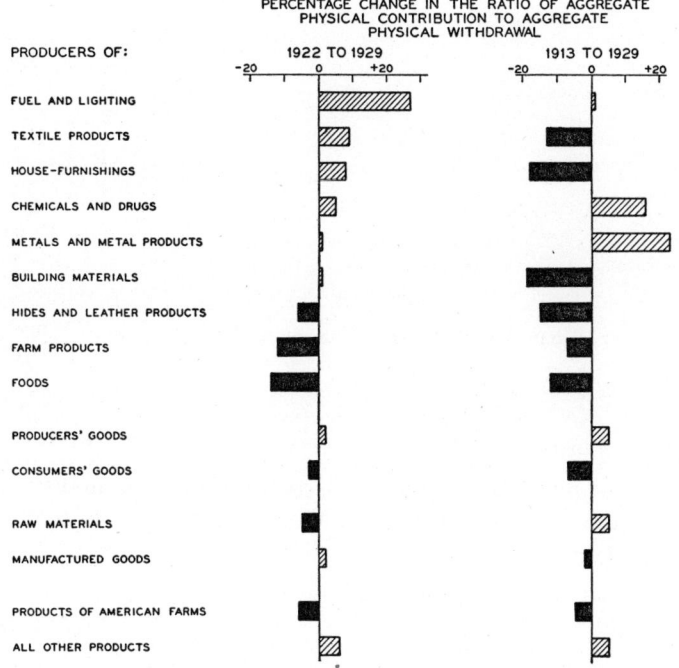

FIGURE 106

SHOWING ALTERATIONS OCCURRING IN THE TERMS OF EXCHANGE BETWEEN GIVEN GROUPS OF PRODUCERS AND ALL PRODUCERS, 1922 TO 1929 AND 1913 TO 1929

[1] The year 1914 was, of course, depressed, while 1929 was prosperous, so far as annual averages go. These conditions would tend to lower the ratios in column (5), particularly for those industries in which profits are materially reduced in years of depression.

[2] It is to be noted that purchasing power is measured in terms of prices at

## TABLE 208

SHOWING ALTERATIONS OCCURRING IN THE TERMS OF EXCHANGE BETWEEN GIVEN GROUPS OF PRODUCERS AND ALL PRODUCERS, 1922 TO 1929 AND 1913 TO 1929

| Economic group | Ratio of aggregate physical contribution to aggregate physical withdrawal, 1929 | |
|---|---|---|
| | (1922=100) | (1913=100) |
| Producers of: | | |
| Fuel and lighting | 127 | 101 |
| Textile products | 109 | 87 |
| House-furnishings | 108 | 82 |
| Chemicals and drugs | 105 | 116 |
| Metals and metal products | 101 | 123 |
| Building materials | 101 | 81 |
| Hides and leather products | 94 | 85 |
| Farm products | 88 | 93 |
| Foods | 86 | 88 |
| | | |
| Producers' goods | 102 | 105 |
| Consumers' goods | 97 | 93 |
| | | |
| All raw materials | 95 | 105 |
| All manufactured goods | 102 | 98 |
| | | |
| Products of American farms | | |
| Raw | 91 | 99 |
| Processed | 95 | 93 |
| Total | 94 | 95 |
| | | |
| Products other than those of American farms | | |
| Raw | 100 | 116 |
| Processed | 108 | 102 |
| Total | 106 | 105 |

The first nine index numbers, relating to commodity groups of the United States Bureau of Labor Statistics, show that during the period between 1922 and 1929 the contributions of producers of

wholesale. This is only an approximation to the truth, justifiable for the present general comparisons because of the impossibility of securing accurate measurements of price changes among all the goods for which the funds represented in 'value added' are expended.

The accuracy of all comparisons is dependent, of course, upon the accuracy of the index of wholesale prices of the U. S. Bureau of Labor Statistics as a measure of changes in the purchasing power of the dollar at wholesale. Here again certain reservations are to be made, but it is not to be doubted that the general drift of prices is reflected in the changes defined by that index.

fuel and lighting, textiles, house-furnishings, chemicals and drugs, metals and metal products, and building materials were increasing, with reference to the physical rewards secured. The other groups made smaller relative contributions than in 1922. More significant in some ways are the figures that contrast the 1929 position with that of 1913. Two groups, producers of chemicals and drugs and of metals and metal products, were making decidedly larger contributions for each unit taken out of the stream of production. The fuel and lighting group made a slightly greater contribution in 1929 than in 1913. Of building materials the contribution in 1929 was 19 per cent less than in 1913 for each unit of goods received in exchange; of house-furnishings, 18 per cent less; of hides and leather products, 15 per cent less; of textiles, 13 per cent less; of foods, 12 per cent less.

A classification of a different type is shown in the second set of figures in the above table. The contribution of makers of producers' goods, relatively to rewards, was in 1929 two per cent greater than in 1922, five per cent greater than in 1913. The relative contribution of makers of consumers' goods was in 1929 three per cent less than in 1922, seven per cent less than in 1913. This decline, reflecting a rise in the real value of consumers' goods, is a movement of considerable importance, which has been commented upon above. Producers of raw materials were constrained to give five per cent more in 1929 than in 1913 for each unit of goods received in return, while producers of manufactured goods contributed two per cent less.[1] Viewing farm and non-farm products as broad groups, it appears that the relative contributions of producers of farm products declined, with reference to the 1913 and 1922 bases, while those of non-farm producers increased. Within each of these groups there is

[1] This is, of course, a quite different index from that cited in Table 207, which showed a decline of 20.2 per cent between 1914 and 1929 in the relative contribution of agents of fabrication. The present index, constructed directly from quoted prices of manufactured goods, relates to selling prices, whereas the index given in Table 207 relates to the cost of *the fabrication process,* per unit of goods, not to the final selling price.

If selling prices of manufactured goods be derived from census data of the type used in securing the measurements in Table 207, the relative for 1929, measuring the ratio of aggregate contribution to aggregate reward, on the 1914 base, is 92.2. This shows a decline of 7.8 per cent in relative contribution, as compared with the decline of 2 per cent shown by an index number derived directly from quoted prices. Differences in procedure and differences in the samples used would account for the discrepancy.

considerable diversity as between the raw and processed divisions. Producers of raw non-farm products contributed no less than 16 per cent more in 1929 than in 1913 with reference to their compensation in terms of physical goods, a situation decidedly weaker than that of producers of farm products in raw state. For this group the contribution in 1929 was one per cent less than in 1913.[1] But the rest of the story may be read from the table.

§ *Contributions and rewards of agents of fabrication.*—By applying this type of analysis to the contributions and rewards of the various

TABLE 209

SHOWING ALTERATIONS OCCURRING IN THE RATIOS OF THE AGGREGATE QUANTITIES PRODUCED BY MANUFACTURING WAGE-EARNERS TO THEIR AGGREGATE PURCHASING POWER, 1923 TO 1929 AND 1914 TO 1929

(Aggregate purchasing power refers to command over items included in the cost of living index of the United States Bureau of Labor Statistics.)

| (1) | (2) | (3) | (4) | (5) |
|---|---|---|---|---|
| Producing group | Physical volume of production in 1929 (1923=100) | Aggregate purchasing power of wages received in 1929 (1923=100) | Ratio of aggregate production to aggregate purchasing power in 1929 | |
| | | | (1923=100) | (1914=100) |
| Wage-earners in: | | | | |
| All manufacturing industries included in the sample .................. | 110.0 | 94.4 | 116.5 | 103.5 |
| Flour and other grain-mill products | 94.5 | 83.2 | 113.7 | 104.4 |
| Slaughtering and meat packing.... | 100.9 | 98.3 | 102.6 | 86.7 |
| Cotton goods ..................... | 104.6 | 81.4 | 128.5 | 100.2 |
| Woolen goods .................... | 83.5 | 73.7 | 113.3 | 82.0 |
| Worsted goods ................... | 75.5 | 70.3 | 107.5 | 73.4 |
| Petroleum, refining .............. | 177.1 | 126.5 | 140.0 | 137.5 |
| Iron and steel: blast furnaces..... | 106.7 | 73.1 | 146.1 | 162.9 |
| Iron and steel: steel works and rolling mills .................... | 124.2 | 107.5 | 115.5 | 105.4 |
| Motor vehicles .................. | 123.3 | 111.3 | 110.8 | 180.5 |

[1] Purchasing power is computed above in terms of general commodity prices at wholesale, a quite faulty instrument in the case of the average agricultural producer. If we utilize an index number of the prices of things farmers buy, together with an index number of the prices received by farmers for their products, we find that farmers as a group contributed 12 per cent more in 1929 than in 1913, 9 per cent less in 1929 than in 1922, in relation to what they received.

agents of production we may better interpret the changes taking place in income distribution. This may be done for labor in manufacturing industries, given statistics of physical output, of aggregate monetary rewards, and the means of converting monetary rewards to physical terms. The index numbers in Table 209 are subject to some margin of error, primarily because of the limitations of all cost of living index numbers, but they probably approximate the truth with reasonable accuracy. As regards volume of production, the terms used must be qualified because there is no means of measuring changes in the specific productivity of any productive agent. Changes in the output of given groups of wage-earners may be due to organizational and mechanical factors, as well as to human factors, and we cannot differentiate these elements.[1]

These movements are shown, as percentage changes, in Figure 107.

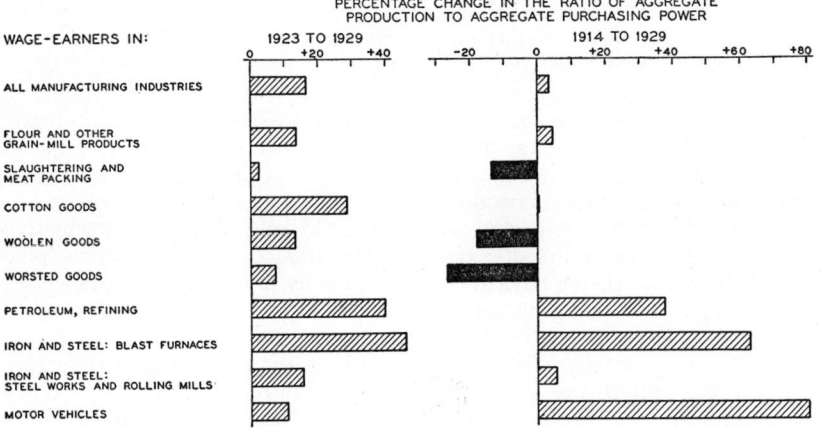

FIGURE 107

SHOWING ALTERATIONS OCCURRING IN THE RATIOS OF AGGREGATE QUANTITIES PRODUCED BY MANUFACTURING WAGE-EARNERS TO THEIR AGGREGATE PURCHASING POWER, 1923 TO 1929 AND 1914 TO 1929

The gain in wages of manufacturing labor has been discussed in preceding pages of this chapter. It is clear from the above record that the contributions of manufacturing labor, in so far as these may be measured in terms of output of manufacturing plants, have more than kept pace with the gain in their rewards. From 1923 to 1929 the increase

[1] At an earlier point, in discussing a procedure similar to the present one, care was taken to point out that in speaking of the ratio of physical contribution to physical reward no ethical judgment was involved. The economic factors involved in any shift in the terms of exchange between economic groups are complex. It is not the purpose of the present study to explore the reasons for these changing ratios.

in the physical contribution of labor in all manufacturing industries, in relation to physical rewards, increased 16.5 per cent. For each unit of goods received (through the expenditure of wages) the contribution of labor was 16.5 per cent greater in 1929 than in 1923. With reference to 1914 as base, the contribution of labor in 1929 was up 3.5 per cent.

Among the constituent groups shown above the 'social contribution' of labor, if we may so term it, increased without exception between 1923 and 1929. For three industries, however, the 1929 ratios were lower than those for 1914.

It is, of course, impossible to measure the separate contribution of each agent of production. Within each industry, it must be assumed, an increase of output is to be credited equally to all the agents of production. When combining production figures for different industries it is possible to take account of the varying importance of different productive agents in assigning weights, and thus, in some measure, to allow for changes in the rôle of the several agents. This has been done in constructing the index numbers of production entering into the ratios given in Table 210, but the limitations of these measurements must be borne in mind. Specific productivity is not measured.

In default of thoroughly satisfactory index numbers of the prices of the goods for which the money incomes of the different agents of production are spent, reduction of such incomes to purchasing power terms has been effected on two different bases in the following table. In deriving the measurements of purchasing power, and corresponding ratios, given in Section A, use has been made of an index of wholesale prices. The measurements in Section B are derived on the assumption that the cost of living index measures changes in the prices of the goods for which the incomes of productive agents are spent.

Over the six-year period between 1923 and 1929 all productive agents except the composite group represented by overhead costs plus profits increased their physical contributions by amounts which exceeded the increases in their physical withdrawals from the stream of production. For sellers of materials the excess increase amounted to 8 per cent, for wage-earners, 10 per cent. (These figures are approximately 14 per cent and 16 per cent, respectively, if purchasing power changes be measured with reference to living costs.) For managers and owners there was a decline of 10 per cent between 1923 and 1929 in the physical contribution per unit of goods received in exchange (or of 5 per cent, with reference to cost of living changes). (For convenience we have designated as 'managers and owners' all those whose remuneration is included in overhead costs plus profits. The terms are not accurate, for salaried employees, creditors and recipients of taxes fall also within this group.) This is a significant movement, the more impressive in that this group has been credited with an addition to physical contribution during this period greater by some four per cent than the addition attributed to either of the other productive agents.

The comparison with the situation in 1914 reveals more striking changes. On the assumption that the index of wholesale prices measures

## TABLE 210

Showing Alterations Occurring in the Aggregate Production of Different Agents, and in the Aggregate Rewards of these Agents, 1923 to 1929 and 1914 to 1929

(Data relating to 62 manufacturing industries in the United States.)

| (1) Economic group | (2) Physical contribution in 1929 (1923=100) | (3) Aggregate purchasing power in 1929 [a] (1923=100) | (4) Ratio of aggregate contribution to aggregate purchasing power in 1929 (1923=100) | (5) Ratio of aggregate contribution to aggregate purchasing power in 1929 (1914=100) |
|---|---|---|---|---|
| **A. Measurements derived when purchasing power is measured with reference to changes in general wholesale prices** | | | | |
| All agents of production | 112.3 | 107.7 | 104.3 | 92.2 |
| Sellers of materials | 111.8 | 103.8 | 107.8 | 98.9 |
| Agents of fabrication | 113.0 | 115.4 | 97.9 | 79.8 |
| Wage-earners | 110.0 | 99.6 | 110.4 | 87.3 |
| Others (represented in overhead plus profits) | 115.5 [b] | 127.8 | 90.4 | 75.5 |
| **B. Measurements derived when purchasing power is measured with reference to changes in cost of living** | | | | |
| All agents of production | 112.3 | 102.1 | 110.0 | 109.2 |
| Sellers of materials | 111.8 | 98.4 | 113.7 | 117.2 |
| Agents of fabrication | 113.0 | 109.4 | 103.2 | 94.5 |
| Wage-earners | 110.0 | 94.4 | 116.5 | 103.5 |
| Others (represented in overhead plus profits) | 115.5 [b] | 121.1 | 95.4 | 89.4 |

[a] Deflated by index numbers computed by the U. S. Bureau of Labor Statistics.

[b] The increasing importance of technical equipment in production is in some degree responsible for the exceptional increase in output attributed to 'others', meaning those agents represented by overhead costs and profits. Increasing profits also affect the results, since weights are based on total overhead costs plus profits. The effects of these two factors are not distinguishable.

changes in the prices of goods for which money incomes were spent, we find that sellers of materials were contributing approximately the same amount in 1929 as in 1914 for each unit of goods withdrawn from the aggregate stream of production. ('Materials' here include semi-processed goods.) Wage-earners were contributing approximately 13 per cent less. The elements represented in the composite of overhead costs plus profits were contributing 24 per cent less, for each unit of goods received in exchange for their services.

This picture is altered if purchasing power changes be measured with reference to cost of living changes. For the cost of living rose much more between 1914 and 1929 than did the level of wholesale prices, and the purchasing power of stated sums of money is correspondingly reduced. On this basis, the ratio of contributions to rewards (in relative terms) increased between 1914 and 1929 from 100 to 117 for sellers of materials, from 100 to 103 for wage-earners, and declined from 100 to 89 for the group represented by overhead costs plus profits. Since the cost of living index comes closer than does the wholesale price index to defining changes in the prices of the goods for which final incomes are spent, these latter measurements are probably the more significant.

The fact that 1914 was a year of depression, while the annual averages for 1929 reflect a high level of prosperity, accounts for some part of the changes noted. This is particularly true of the changes in the ratios relating to overhead costs plus profits. The rewards of this group increased substantially over the fifteen-year period. The increasing importance of mechanical equipment doubtless explains part of this movement, but higher profits contributed to the advance.[1]

---

[1] The limitations of the index numbers of production cited above have been pointed out in earlier sections. They are restricted to standard commodities, for which production statistics are currently compiled, and they fail to take account of the diversification of production and the rapid increase in the production of new and non-standard commodities. Estimates of actual production which are probably closer to the truth than the preceding indexes are shown below, for the several productive agents. The basic ratios are not changed, but the two constituent elements are materially altered. (The index numbers derived from the sample of 62 industries have been corrected on the basis of statistics of aggregate value of product, cost of materials, 'value added', wages, and overhead plus profits for all manufacturing industries covered by the Census of Manufactures.)

ALTERATIONS OCCURRING IN THE AGGREGATE PRODUCTION OF DIFFERENT AGENTS AND IN THE AGGREGATE REWARDS OF THESE AGENTS, MANUFACTURING INDUSTRIES OF THE UNITED STATES

1923 TO 1929 AND 1914 TO 1929

| Economic group | Physical contribution in 1929 (1923 = 100) | Aggregate purchasing power in 1929 (1923 = 100) | Ratio of aggregate contribution to aggregate purchasing power in 1929 | |
|---|---|---|---|---|
| | | | (1923 = 100) | (1914 = 100) |
| A. Measurements derived when purchasing power is measured with reference to changes in general wholesale prices (index of U. S. Bureau of Labor Statistics). | | | | |
| All agents of production | 127.5 | 122.3 | 104.3 | 92.2 |
| Sellers of materials | 125.5 | 116.5 | 107.8 | 98.9 |
| Agents of fabrication | 127.3 | 130.1 | 97.9 | 79.8 |
| Wage-earners | 123.4 | 111.7 | 110.4 | 87.3 |
| Others (represented in overhead plus profits) | 129.9 | 143.7 | 90.4 | 75.5 |
| B. Measurements derived when purchasing power is measured with reference to changes in cost of living (index of U. S. Bureau of Labor Statistics). | | | | |
| All agents of production | 127.5 | 115.9 | 110.0 | 109.2 |
| Sellers of materials | 125.5 | 110.4 | 113.7 | 117.2 |
| Agents of fabrication | 127.3 | 123.3 | 103.2 | 94.5 |
| Wage-earners | 123.4 | 105.9 | 116.5 | 103.5 |
| Others (represented in overhead plus profits) | 129.9 | 136.2 | 95.4 | 89.4 |

## A Comparison of the Fortunes of Different Producing Groups, Pre-war and Post-war

The alterations occurring in the ratios of contributions to rewards between the outbreak of the war and the culmination of postwar prosperity in 1929 differ in certain important respects from the alterations occurring during the years preceding the war. These ratios are shown in the next table. All entries relate to prices at wholesale and to purchasing power in wholesale markets.

TABLE 211

COMPARISON OF ALTERATIONS IN THE TERMS OF EXCHANGE BETWEEN GIVEN GROUPS OF PRODUCERS AND ALL PRODUCERS, 1901 TO 1913 AND 1913 TO 1929 [a]

| Economic group | Ratio of aggregate physical contribution to aggregate physical withdrawal | |
|---|---|---|
| | 1913 (1901=100) | 1929 (1913=100) |
| Producers of: | | |
| Chemicals and drugs | 133 | 116 |
| Metals and metal products | 129 | 123 |
| House-furnishings | 110 | 82 |
| Textile products | 106 | 87 |
| Foods | 99 | 88 |
| Building materials | 99 | 81 |
| Farm products | 93 | 93 |
| Fuel and lighting | 92 | 101 |
| Hides and leather products | 91 | 85 |
| | | |
| Producers' goods | 102 | 105 |
| Consumers' goods | 98 | 93 |
| | | |
| All raw materials | 97 | 105 |
| All processed goods | 101 | 98 |
| | | |
| Products of American farms | | |
| Raw | 96 | 99 |
| Processed | 95 | 93 |
| Total | 95 | 95 |
| | | |
| Products other than those of American farms | | |
| Raw | 97 | 116 |
| Processed | 108 | 102 |
| Total | 105 | 105 |

[a] These measurements are derived from index numbers of prices, at wholesale, constructed by the U. S. Bureau of Labor Statistics and by the National Bureau of Economic Research.

Of the producers represented in the first classification shown above, four were steadily increasing their social contribution, that is, were giving more in physical goods in relation to what they received, during the years preceding the war. Two of these groups, producers of chemicals and drugs and of metal products, continued to increase their relative contributions between 1913 and 1929. For producers of house-furnishings and of textile products there was a complete reversal of tendencies. The social cost of these goods increased appreciably between 1913 and 1929. Of the five groups marked by declining relative contributions prior to the war, all but one (fuel and lighting) continued to move in the same direction in the years that followed.

The other classifications reveal divergent movements. Makers of producers' goods continued to increase their contributions, while makers of consumers' goods contributed less, in relation to the goods received in return. This increasing social cost of consumers' goods has been a notable feature of recent economic tendencies. The slight margin between these two groups which existed in 1913 had been materially widened by 1929.

More striking, because it represents a sharp reversal of earlier tendencies, is the recent movement of raw materials and of processed goods. In 1913 producers of raw materials were contributing less, in proportion to their physical rewards, than in 1901, while fabricating agents were contributing more. But in 1929 producers of raw materials were constrained to give 5 per cent more than in 1913 for each unit of goods received, while fabricating agents gave 2 per cent less. Here is one of the most significant of post-war tendencies. The constantly increasing contribution of fabricating agents and the steadily decreasing cost of their services were outstanding features of pre-war developments. The subsequent change in their relations to producers of raw materials affected the whole structure of economic relations.

The entries in the next category indicate that this shift in the position of raw materials was pronounced for the non-agricultural producer. For a constant amount of physical goods he was forced in 1929 to give 16 per cent more of his products than in 1913.

The pre-war and post-war fortunes of different groups concerned with the production of manufactured goods are contrasted in the following table. The cost of living index, which is not altogether appropriate in all cases, has been used in reducing monetary rewards to physical terms. These movements are graphically portrayed, as percentage changes, in Figure 108.

TABLE 212

Comparison of Alterations in the Ratios of Aggregate Production to Aggregate Rewards, 1899 to 1914 and 1914 to 1929 [a]

Agents of Manufacturing Production

| Economic group | Ratio of aggregate contribution to aggregate purchasing power | |
|---|---|---|
| | 1914 (1899=100) | 1929 (1914=100) |
| Sellers of materials [b]........................ | 103.2 | 117.2 |
| Agents of fabrication........................ | 129.2 | 94.5 |
| Wage-earners ........................... | 122.7 | 103.5 |
| Others (represented in overhead plus profits) | 133.4 | 89.4 |

[a] These measurements are derived from index numbers constructed by the National Bureau of Economic Research. The index numbers are given in Chapter VIII.
[b] 'Materials' include semi-processed goods, fuel, containers, etc., as well as raw materials proper.

FIGURE 108

SHOWING ALTERATIONS OCCURRING IN THE RATIOS OF AGGREGATE PRODUCTION TO AGGREGATE REWARDS, 1899 TO 1914 AND 1914 TO 1929

AGENTS OF MANUFACTURING PRODUCTION

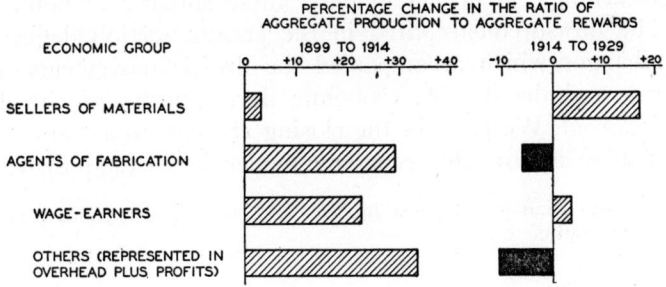

The pre-war story of the relation of agents of fabrication to producers of economic goods in general is one of constantly increasing contribution or, in other terms, of a steadily declining social cost of their services. Agents of fabrication contributed 29 per cent more in 1914 than in 1899, per unit of goods commanded in exchange. Of this group, wage-earners contributed 23 per cent more, while creditors, managers, and owners contributed 33 per cent more.[1] Sellers of materials (this group includes sellers of semi-processed goods, containers, fuel, etc., as well as raw materials) contributed 3 per cent more.

Quite different were the movements following 1914. Wage-earners contributed 3 per cent more in 1929 than in 1914, per unit of goods commanded in exchange, while creditors, owners, salaried workers and managers contributed 11 per cent less. As a group, agents of fabrication contributed some 5 per cent less in 1929 than in 1914, a figure which stands in notable contrast to the increase of 29 per cent in the contribution of fabricating agents between 1899 and 1914. The cheapening of materials is reflected in the increase of 17 per cent in the contribution of sellers of materials, per unit of goods taken in exchange. These figures supplement and reënforce previous evidence concerning the striking change in the economic status of agents of fabrication which has occurred within the last fifteen years.

Economic change is, of course, a story of constant alterations in the relations among economic groups. The depletion of supplies, the improvement of productive facilities, technical changes in production, shifts in consumer demand, the creation of surplus quantities—these and other movements are constantly modifying the terms of exchange among the products and services of different groups. The month-to-month and year-to-year changes in market prices, in wage-earnings, in profits, register these shifting economic relations. The measurements cited in the present section define some of the changes which accompanied the drastic movements of the war years and the notable economic developments of the decade which followed. We pass, in the closing chapter, to a summary account of these and of other economic tendencies of the post-war era.

[1] Profits were high in 1899, low in 1914. This difference explains part of the increase in the ratio.

## CHAPTER X

# A Summary: Some Attributes of the Post-War Decade

THE era of post-war expansion came to an abrupt end with the dramatic stock market collapse of 1929, a collapse which was a phase of a world-wide recession. It is with a perspective set by the depression which followed that we have reviewed the events of this period. The treatment has been restricted to certain limited aspects of a many-sided growth. No attempt has been made to develop a simple theme, or to interpret these complex events in terms of one or two factors alone. We have followed certain threads of change, and have defined as accurately as possible some of the tendencies prevailing during a period which, in retrospect, has already taken on some of the aspects of a golden age. This has been done with the conviction that such definition of tendencies is not only prerequisite to an attack upon the complicated problems raised by the depression itself, but is, as well, essential to a systematic charting of the course of our economic development during the longer future that lies beyond the depression.

There remains the task of preparing a brief résumé of certain of the conditions and tendencies which have been separately treated in the detailed presentation.

*Retardation of Population Growth.* In any general survey of the economic trends of a period, the growth of population furnishes a yard-stick for the appraisal of changes in other economic elements. Changes in the pace of population growth occur slowly and inconspicuously. The forces that bring them about are often obscure, and difficult to define. Yet such changes affect economic processes in innumerable ways. In their wide ramifications they may determine the tone of a whole epoch.

One of the least dramatic and yet one of the most profound of the differences between the pre-war and post-war eras in the United

States is found in the varying rates of population growth. A change from a cumulative growth rate of 2.0 per cent a year to 1.4 per cent a year is a very substantial one indeed, for an element as stable in its behavior as is the population of a country of one hundred million inhabitants. The full effects of this retardation, and of the altered age-group constitution of the population which will result from it, will be felt in the years ahead of us. Yet the change was not without significance for the period just past. The basic standard against which the growth of many other economic elements must be measured was altered, and our interpretation of changes in these other elements must be correspondingly modified.

*Productive Processes.* The distinctive post-war changes in the field of production represented a speeding up of tendencies already in evidence before the war. Certain novel features there were, but in the main the lines of subsequent development are clearly apparent in the earlier period.

Between the depressions which bounded the decade of the 'twenties the rate of increase in the physical volume of production in the United States was clearly in excess of that which prevailed during the period of expansion prior to the World War. This is true in absolute terms. (Pre-war and post-war rates of production growth, excluding construction, were, respectively, 3.1 per cent per year, and 3.8 per cent.) It is more conspicuously true if account be taken of the post-war retardation of population growth. (Per capita of the population, pre-war and post-war rates of advance in production were, respectively, 1.1 per cent and 2.4 per cent per year.) Relatively to the basic needs of the population, the volume of goods of all sorts produced in the United States was being increased between 1922 and 1929 at a rate probably never before maintained for a similar period of time. The technique of physical production had reached a higher development than at any other time in our history.

Evidence to support this statement is found in the record of industrial productivity. During the fifteen years from 1899 to 1914 there was a notable advance in output per wage-earner in manufacturing establishments, a gain of no less than 30 per cent in the decade and a half. Here is the concrete result of the improved equipment, the greater skill, the more efficient organization of American industry which marked the forward movement of the early years of the century. Yet this record was substantially bettered during the decade from 1919 to 1929. Production per wage-earner in manufacturing industries increased by approximately 43 per cent in this single ten-year stretch. Seventy men in 1929 could do the work that required 100 men in 1919. During this decade of remarkable technical accomplishment emphasis was definitely shifted from mere numbers, as a means of accelerating production, to those factors of equipment, skill and organization which enhance the productive powers of the individual worker. It was an unprecedented advance. It appears now to have been an advance to which, under existing conditions of knowledge and with existing instruments of industrial control, our economic system could not be promptly adapted.

Difficulties of adaptation are discernible in several directions, in the records of this decade. An increasing volume of unemployment during an era of economic expansion was, considering its magnitude, a new phenomenon in our history. Equally striking are the related statistics of industrial displacement. The human incidence of industrial change is to be traced in such statistics, which measure the shifting of labor among manufacturing industries. The data of the pre-war period provide a standard of comparison in the interpretation of these figures. Between the terminal years of each of the three five-year census periods falling betwen 1899 and 1914 an average of 21 men out of every 1,000 employed were separated from given manufacturing industries. (The data relate to movements of labor from industry to industry, not to intra-industry shifts.) For the same periods accessions (additions to the number employed) averaged 149 to each 1,000 persons employed. That is, the number employed was expanding, and the number of men forced out of given manufacturing industries was distinctly smaller than the number of new men taken on by other manufacturing industries.

Markedly different is the post-war record. On the average, over each of the three biennial census periods coming between 1923 and 1929, 49 men out of every 1,000 employed were separated from given manufacturing industries. Additions to the number employed averaged 45 to every 1,000 on the payrolls of manufacturing plants. Separations measure the burden placed upon wage-earners by industrial change. That it was a heavy burden during the prosperous period from 1923 to 1929 is indicated by these figures. Not only was the rate of separation much higher than it had been over longer pre-war periods; it was higher than the accession rate, which may be taken as an index of employment opportunities in manufacturing industries. Between 1923 and 1929 men were being turned out of manufacturing industries in greater numbers than in pre-war years, while the numbers of new men taken on were relatively much smaller. High productivity and rapidly expanding production brought instability of employment and uncertainty of income to many, during this era of business prosperity.

Instability and uncertainty were not alone the lot of those workers who were displaced during this period. Although, on the surface, the industrial advance of the 'twenties bore signs of stability, there were certain underlying tendencies toward a basic instability which contained a potential threat to others. Some emphasis has been placed, in preceding pages, on the divergence of growth rates characteristic of different industries and of other elements of the economic system. Such divergence, reflecting changes in productive conditions, changes in technical methods and changes in ultimate demand, is doubtless a necessary feature of a living economy. In some degree, it represents adaptation of certain elements of the economy to changes in other elements. But, inevitable though these differing rates of secular advance may be, it is certain that they involve shifting of labor and capital and a whole host of minor modifications in the structure of the economic system at large. A flexible and adaptable system is necessary, if an organism as complex as that which meets our material needs is constantly to be accommodated to variations in the growth of its constituent parts. Such divergence existed in pre-war years, in fairly pronounced form. If we take account of the numbers engaged and of the magnitudes of the capital sums involved, it is probable that the degree of divergence between 1922 and 1929 exceeded that of the period 1901-1913, and that proportionately heavier strains were placed upon the economic system.

A speeding-up of the rate of industrial displacement, with a corresponding increase in the volume of unemployment, was but one aspect of the problem raised by disparities of growth rates among American industries. Shifts in marketing methods and organizations, obsolescence of equipment, the emergence of new and untried industries with their demands for men, for markets, for capital, for credit and for places in the industrial sun, and the generation of risks which new industries and new methods inevitably bring—these, equally, were manifestations of divergence in rates of economic change. All these served to intensify the demands for flexibility and adaptability in our economic system. These demands were made, moreover, at a time when elements of structural rigidity and inflexibility were apparently growing in strength.

In yet another respect the tendencies of the post-war period served to accentuate certain factors of instability in modern economic life. It is a commonplace, of course, that industrialization has brought a pronounced change in the directions in which our current productive energies are exerted. Under simple conditions, the immediate necessities of life—food, clothing, essential shelter—constitute the chief products of human labor. As the margin between productive power and immediate needs widens, more labor may be devoted to the making of instruments of production and of various goods, durable and non-durable, which satisfy the less imperative needs of man. It is characteristic of such goods (capital equipment, and non-essential consumption goods) that the demand for them is highly elastic, capable of extreme expansion and rapid contraction under the influence of price changes or of changes in the attitudes and expectations of buyers. The same thing is true of certain essential but durable consumers' goods, such as housing. The necessities of existence, on the other hand, particularly those which are non-durable or semi-durable in character, are marked by inelastic demand. Except under extreme conditions the amounts required and currently purchased do not vary greatly. It is difficult to stimulate increased demand for such goods, while contraction of demand is similarly difficult on the side of the user.

These facts have a direct bearing on the stability of processes in a competitive economy. Barring the play of extraneous forces (such as crop failures), less variation is to be expected in production, the larger the proportion of perishable and semi-durable consumption goods in the annual output of an economy. As capital equipment, durable goods in general and non-essential consumers' goods come to occupy a larger place in total output, demand is capable of rapid expansion (under advertising or other stimulus) and of rapid contraction, with corresponding fluctuations in productive activity.[1]

---

[1] As an entry on the credit side of the ledger, we should note that greater productivity of labor and a higher average standard of living may be expected to accompany an increase in the amount of capital equipment employed.

All this is obvious enough. It is important in the present review because tendencies long present in our economic development were speeding the output of goods of elastic demand between 1922 and 1929. As in the period 1901-1913, but in much greater degree, production was becoming diversified in the recent period. The volume of output of those incidental, supplementary, non-standard goods which escape enumeration when account is taken only of the basic staples was expanding at a rapid rate. (The rate of increase in volume of production between 1922 and 1929 is raised from 3.3 per cent a year, for directly measurable physical units, to 3.8 per cent, when these non-standard goods are included. The corresponding pre-war correction was from 2.9 to 3.1 per cent a year.) This diversification of output meant that goods of secondary importance, goods of elastic demand, were occupying a constantly larger place in the budgets of consumers and in the purchases of business buyers. Such diversification brought with it the potentiality of a corresponding contraction, for elasticity may work in two directions.

More direct evidence on this point is furnished by the records of output of durable and non-durable goods. We have seen that the output of durable goods, goods which are relatively unstable in their production, was increasing between 1922 and 1929 at a rate of 5.9 per cent a year, while the production of non-durable commodities advanced at a rate of but 2.8 per cent a year. A margin of the same type prevailed between the turn of the century and the outbreak of the war, and doubtless prevailed during many other periods of industrial expansion. But it is the size of the margin in the post-war decade which is significant. The new productive powers which were generated by improved technique and better equipment during this decade were devoted largely to the output of goods of relatively long life and of correspondingly elastic demand, goods which are characterized by exceptionally high instability of production. In devoting a greater proportion of our productive energies to such durable goods (the proportion so devoted was, roughly, 26 per cent during the pre-war period studied, 34 per cent during the post-war period) we accentuate elements of instability in productive processes.

Finally, we have noted the extremely rapid advance, during the decade of the 'twenties, in the production of that particular class of durable goods which is used in further production. In this period we were ploughing the fruits of industry back into capital equipment at a rate which exceeded even that of the pre-war expansion when the economies of large-scale, capitalistic production were being so earnestly exploited in this country. Our best estimates indicate a pre-war growth of production of capital equipment at a rate of 5.0 per cent a year, a post-war advance at a rate of 6.4 per cent. (These figures relate to annual additions to and replacements of capital equipment, not to the total existing supply.) The standard of living was being maintained, and raised, during the years that fell between the two great post-war depressions, but in even greater degree we were augmenting the instruments of roundabout production. Machines, engines, tools, plants—into the making of these the new productive energies were poured.

Viewing these events in retrospect, a question naturally arises as to whether these new energies were well and wisely expended during this period. When goods are made for immediate sale and direct consumption, errors concerning effective demand are of course possible, but the detection of the error is likely to come fairly promptly. But when we make goods which will eventuate in a finished, consumable product only after the lapse of considerable time and after various intermediate processes have been completed, more serious errors are possible. If we take account of the customary elasticity of demand for capital goods, and of the variability of production which results from business errors, faulty investment, financing with an eye to security markets rather than to markets for goods, we have a highly unstable element indeed in this particular segment of the economic structure. In view of these potential instabilities, the pouring of resources into this field was a particularly significant feature of the expansion of 1922-29.

It is not difficult to point to post-war tendencies in the field of production which, surveyed with the advantages of hind-sight, appear to have contained the seeds of trouble. The truth is that, in large degree, we lack standards based on comprehensive knowledge of economic processes by which we might detect such tendencies before trouble is precipitated. Even after the event we cannot definitely affirm that, with reference to the state of our industrial development and the character of our distributive processes, too large a proportion of our productive resources was being devoted, prior to 1929, to the production of durable goods in general, and of capital equipment in particular. But there is strong indication that this was so.

*Trade Movements and the Balance of International Payments.* Among the factors shaping the economic development of the United States during the present century, those growing out of our international economic relations have increased in relative importance at a rapid rate. The initial stimulus of new world possessions and of wider outlook given by the Spanish War was reënforced by growing economic power and the search for wider markets during the next decade and a half. In the years following 1914 a second and greater stimulus carried us full into the broad stream of international economic activity. The strength of the bonds which tie us to the world economy was increased many-fold. Financially and commercially the economy of the United States became an integral part of the world structure.

During the period 1901-1913 there was a substantial balance of merchandise exports over imports, but imports were growing at a more rapid pace than exports. Crude materials, foodstuffs and semi-manufactured goods were the import groups which were increasing most rapidly. The lag of exports behind imports, in this pre-war advance, was due entirely to declines in the exports of crude and manufactured foodstuffs. Exports of semi-manufactured and finished goods were increasing at notably high rates. Our international economic function was definitely shifting, as the importance of our manufacturing industries increased, and as our food-exporting industries lost place.

After the war-time revolution in our trade and financial relations with the rest of the world, quite different tendencies prevailed. Between 1922 and 1929 the physical volume of exports increased at a rate well above that at which domestic production was advancing (the rate of growth of exports, by volume, was 6.5 per cent a year), while the volume of imports grew at a rate approximating that of domestic production (the rate of growth of imports, by volume, was 3.9 per cent a year). Commodity exports played a more active part, absolutely and relatively, in stimulating domestic production during post-war years than they had done in pre-war years. To a greater extent than before the war semi-manufactured and manufactured goods dominated the post-war advance. Exports of finished manufactures were approximately doubled in aggregate value between 1922 and 1929. (These dominating export groups, it may be noted, consisted largely of goods subject to highly elastic demand—metals, machinery, vehicles, luxuries, durable consumption goods.) A considerable part of the stimulus to this great expansion came from a forced draught of heavy foreign lending, but the effect on the volume and on the character of domestic production was none the less real.

The increase in commodity exports was accompanied by a considerable decline in the average unit price of goods exported, a decline at an average annual rate of 2.2 per cent. The aggregate value of exports did not advance as rapidly as did export volume. This post-war decline in the unit price of exports is associated with a notable aftermath of the war, as regards the international economic relations of the United States. A comparison of export unit prices with import unit prices indicates that, on the average, the goods we exported increased in price between 1913 and 1921 by 28 per cent more than did the goods we imported. That is, the terms of exchange in world markets between the goods we sold and the goods we bought had altered to our material advantage during the interval between 1913 and 1921. This differential advantage persisted, though in lessened degree, during the several years following. Not until 1926 was it reversed. In 1929 the margin again moved to our advantage. (The standard of reference throughout is based on 1913 relations.)

There are some uncertainties attaching to the comparison of export and import prices, but the general situation is clear. After the immediate post-war disturbances had ended, manufacturing nations in general enjoyed an advantage in their price relations with raw-material producing areas. It was a deceptive and temporary advantage in some respects, since it served to reduce the buying power of these raw-material producing areas, but as long as the flow of goods could be maintained the advantage persisted. We kept up the outward flow of goods, and indeed increased it, by means of heavy foreign loans. These loans facilitated foreign sales at favorable prices, to the distinct profit of exporting manufacturers. The steady decline in export prices, relatively to import prices, served to reduce the price advantage toward the end of the post-war period under survey, while at the same time our campaign of foreign lending ran into difficulties of its own. While the advantage persisted, and while sales kept up, the situation was a happy one for the average American exporter. But it did not possess the characteristics of permanence.

As regards the general balance of international payments there are certain points of contrast between pre-war and post-war periods. The following tabular summary reveals these differences.

TABLE 213

BALANCES OF INTERNATIONAL PAYMENTS OF THE UNITED STATES, 1896-1914, 1922-1929

Average Annual Balances of Credits and Debits for Four Major Classes of Transactions [a]

| Class of transaction | Average annual balance, in millions of dollars | | | |
|---|---|---|---|---|
| | 1896-1914 | | 1922-1929 | |
| | Credit | Debit | Credit | Debit |
| Goods and services, net............ | +254 | | +150 | |
| Payment on debts, net............. | | −310 | +339 | |
| Net capital movement............. | + 53 | | | −451 |
| Net movement of currency and gold | | − 9 | | − 46 |
| Correction for net discrepancy...... | + 12 | | + 8 | |

[a] See footnote to Table 187, p. 472, for an explanation of the signs defining the credit and debit character of the items in this table.

There are two major differences between these periods. Payment on debts, a debit item of 310 millions annually in the earlier period, was a credit item of 339 millions in the post-war period. The net capital movement, which was inward at the rate of 53 millions a year between 1896 and 1914, was an outward flow averaging 451 millions a year in the later period. This last item was almost enough in itself to cover the debt payments due us, and to pay for the export balance of goods and services. If it was a forced draught that kept up our expanding volume of exports during this period, this was the form that the draught took.

*The Growth of Capital and Credit.* No generation more than ours has devoted itself to the accumulation of capital funds. The mechanism of investment experienced a mushroom growth in the years following the war, and an elaborate structure, permeating every corner of the country, was developed. The rapid growth of insurance, the increased saving to be expected as a result of greater earnings and expanding profits, the steady impetus to the ploughing back of earnings which derives from the corporate mechanism were supplemented by an influx of funds from individuals who were seeking not so much future incomes as prompt enhancement of capital values. A speculative fervor accentuated the pressure toward increased savings which is a continuing feature of the economic organization and of the social attitudes which now prevail.

Evidence, on the physical side, of the force of this development between 1922 and 1929 has already been discussed. Year by year, a steadily increasing proportion of our current productive power was being devoted to the construction of capital equipment of all sorts. The annual output of such goods increased at the rapid rate of 6.4 per cent a year, a rate materially greater than that for consumption goods. The survey of changes in capital funds substantiates this evidence.

Annual additions to capital funds in the form of proceeds from new capital flotations advanced rapidly. Each year from four to seven and one-half billions of dollars of new funds were received from this source alone. The reduction of the gross debt of the Federal government contributed to this development by adding some billions of dollars to the new funds available for investment between 1922 and 1929.[1] Obligations arising out of the consumptive expenditures of the war years were thus made the vehicle for real, though forced, saving in subsequent years. Forces working toward saving and capital accumulation during these years were reënforced by this debt retirement policy of the central government. From another source, annual corporate savings through additions to surplus, from one to three billions of dollars were annually added to the capital funds available to the business community. Here is the financial side of the rapid increase in the construction of capital equipment already noted.

These additions, and others not specifically mentioned, led to a steady increase in the total supply of invested funds. Aggregate capital funds constitute, of course, a very large sum, much more stable in its changes than are the annual increments. Corporate capital funds alone, we have estimated, increased from approximately 184 billions of dollars in 1922 to 228 billions of dollars in 1929, an increase averaging 3.1 per cent a year. If we recall that the popula-

---

[1] The indebtedness of the Federal government was reduced by about six billions of dollars between 1922 and 1929, but some of the funds thus made available for investment would undoubtedly have been saved had taxes, rather than debt, been reduced.

tion of the country was increasing during this period at a rate of but 1.4 per cent a year, the significance of this advance may be more readily appreciated. As regards both rapidity of growth and magnitude of the sums involved, this expansion of capital funds probably exceeded that recorded during any similar period of our history.

The growth of capital funds had important consequences for the economic system as a whole. It meant a tremendous power of absorption in the securities markets, a buying power which helped to maintain an upward swing in security prices for an exceptionally long period. It facilitated the improvement of the mechanical equipment of American industry, an improvement which went forward at a very rapid rate and which was a major factor in the great increase in the productivity of manufacturing labor during post-war years. In thus facilitating mechanical improvement, the accumulation of new capital was a factor in the problem of technological unemployment. Taken in conjunction with the pronounced rise in popularity of common stocks, as against bonds, the existence of an ample supply of capital funds not only served to provide corporations with the means of improving their mechanical equipment but placed them in relatively stronger financial position by permitting substitution of lower yield obligations for higher, and by facilitating the raising of capital by stock rather than by bond issues. And, not least important, the availability and cheapness of investment funds permitted, if it did not stimulate, a change in the relations between business and banking. There was a tendency, on the part of business, to finance current operations out of investment funds.[1] Commercial credit supplied directly by banks to business played a less important rôle in business operations. One result of this was a decline in the effectiveness of the control which banking interests could exercise over business.

Some of these relationships are, of course, circular. Thus, ample capital enhances the productivity of industry; the productivity of industry conduces to saving, and hence to the accumulation of new supplies of capital. But, considering this as an independent element, the existence of ample supplies of capital explains some of the distinctive characteristics of the post-war economic era in the United States.

[1] The reverse of this, a tendency to utilize short-term funds for investment purposes, affected certain elements of the credit structure.

That mixture of short- and long-term funds which is represented by the loans and investments of banks increased between 1922 and 1929 at a cumulative rate of 5.6 per cent a year, appreciably higher than the rate of increase of capital funds. This expansion, apparently a definitely inflationary movement, exceeded the rate of growth of production and the rate of increase of trade. The grand volume of bank credit was made up, however, of two elements, changing at quite different rates between 1922 and 1929. Credit which had an obvious and direct relation to the market for securities (investments, and loans on securities) increased by 7.9 per cent a year during this period, while 'all other loans', representing, in the main, credit used for commercial purposes, increased in volume by 3.2 per cent a year. Less exact but acceptable data from another source indicate that the aggregate amount of urban realty mortgages increased at an average rate of 12.5 per cent a year between 1922 and 1929.

The story of credit expansion during this period is, then, a record of expansion along sharply delimited lines. Credit was utilized by those to whom it was available in such a way as to enhance values in two major markets—markets for securities and for urban realty. If the excess buying power resulting from the relatively rapid growth of total bank credit affected commodity markets in general, the effect was to maintain rather than to advance prices. There is some indication, as we have seen, that the selling prices of manufactured goods did not decline during this period to a degree commensurate with the fall of production costs. Any inflationary effects felt in commodity markets were of this negative type.

*Movements of Prices and Costs.* The period 1922-1929 followed a fundamental shake-up in economic relations, a shake-up that profoundly modified the terms on which economic agents of all types disposed of their products and their services in the marketplace. These modifications, as well as the tendencies prevailing during the years immediately under review, concern us in this survey.

Far-reaching in its effects was the reversal which the recession of 1920-21 brought in the relations between the prices of raw materials, particularly industrial raw materials, and of the products of manufacture. The story of the years before the war in this country was a story of constantly cheapening manufactured goods. Refinement of technical methods, development of mass production, improvement of management were all tending to lower the prices paid by consumers for the services of fabricating agents. Raw materials as a class, on the other hand, were rising in value, relatively to manufactured goods. The margin of production was being pushed further out, and no widespread improvements of technique at all comparable to those so familiar in manufacturing had been developed. After 1913 a change in conditions occurred. Productive technique improved in the cultivation and extraction of raw products. Rich new territories were exploited, temporary war demands and a rapidly rising price level stimulated rapid expansion in the output of certain of these goods. The termination of the war checked these temporary demands. Perhaps more important, the world-wide deflation of prices found raw material producers unprepared for or unable to adapt themselves to a new order through prompt liquidation, readjustment of costs and adjustment of production to changed demand conditions.

The ending of the war demand and the deflation of prices struck manufacturing interests a sharp blow, just as it did raw material producers. Manufacturing producers, however, were able to liquidate more promptly and to adapt production schedules to marketing possibilities more readily. In some degree, also, manufacturing producers adjusted costs to the new price level. But, as we have seen in Chapter VIII, no thoroughgoing readjustment of costs was made. Labor costs remained at a level materially above that prevailing in 1913-14, and the costs of the services of management and ownership were high, and advancing. The effects of this realignment of economic agents and this reapportionment of purchasing power persisted, to color the economic record of the following decade. The advance in raw material prices between 1921 and 1929 and the relative decline in the prices of manufactured goods diminished the margin between them, but to the end a price advantage persisted for manufacturers. The events of 1929-32 gave another wrench to the price structure more violent, in many respects, than that of 1920-21. But these developments lie beyond our immediate interest.

This cleavage between the prices of industrial raw materials and of manufactured goods has affected economic processes throughout the world. With a limited number of exceptions, raw material producers in all parts of the world were in a position of marked economic weakness during the decade of the 'twenties. This weakness led to numerous ill-starred valorization efforts, impaired the purchasing power of colonial areas, clogged the flow of world trade and placed heavy strains upon the mechanism of international finance. The post-war economic difficulties of industrial areas were intensified by these conditions, though nominal price relations worked to their advantage.[1]

The story of the American farmer is a phase of the tale just told—steady pre-war improvement of status, war-time affluence, abrupt decline in 1920-21, followed by a decade of relatively subnormal purchasing power during which slow recovery failed to restore complete pre-war parity with other classes of producers. Low prices for his products brought depreciation of his capital assets, while the rising value of the monetary unit intensified the burden of his mortgage debt. The record of recovery between 1921 and 1929 must not be under-emphasized, however, for substantial gains were made. A continuation of the tendencies then prevailing would have raised the agricultural producer to his pre-war position in the economic world. But it is now history that these tendencies were rudely checked. The story of 1929-32 is, for the farmer, a repetition of that of 1920-21, except that the recent decline started from no such peak of well-being as had been attained before the earlier fall occurred.

The relations between the purchasing power trends of producers' goods and consumers' goods were identical in the pre-war and post-war periods. Producers' goods were declining slightly in purchasing power, consumers' goods were appreciating slightly. But the developments during the interregnum from 1914 to 1921 are here of particular importance. These developments intensified the effects of preceding trends, substantially cheapening producers' goods, materially enhancing the real values of consumers' goods. So the situation stood in 1922. The succeeding decline in the real per-unit values of producers' goods and the accompanying rise in the real values of consumers' goods tended to widen the margin existing in 1922. The widening was slight; what is significant is the absence of any tendency toward a correction of the breach made in 1920-21.

These measurements indicate that the prices paid by the community for the services of fabricating agents were high after the events of 1920-21, and remained at a high level during the ensuing

[1] See Gustav Cassel, "Disturbances in the World Economy Owing to Relative Changes in Prices", *Skandinaviska Kreditaktiebolaget,* July, 1931, for an effective statement on this subject.

years. There is definite evidence to substantiate this. If we take 1914 as a standard of reference, and if we measure changes in dollars of constant purchasing power, at wholesale, we find that labor costs, per unit of manufactured product, were, in 1921, 38 per cent above the level of the base year (1914), and, in 1923, 27 per cent above that base. These costs declined thereafter, with advancing productivity, but in 1929 remained 15 per cent above the base year level. Similarly measured, overhead charges plus profits, per unit of manufactured product, were, in 1921, 10 per cent greater than in 1914 and, in 1923, 20 per cent greater. By 1929 these charges were 32 per cent above the 1914 level. (The fact that 1914 was a year of depression would serve to increase the value of this index in a subsequent year of prosperity.) The pronounced pre-war tendency toward declining fabrication costs was sharply reversed by the upheaval of 1920-21, and had not definitely reasserted itself, as regards total fabrication costs (including profits), between 1923 and 1929. Over a considerable area of manufacturing activity, indeed, profits per unit of product actually advanced during the period of expansion preceding the 1929 break. These relatively high costs of the services of agents of fabrication mean, of course, that industrial wage-earners, entrepreneurs and others drawing incomes from manufacturing industries were in positions of relative advantage during these years. Urban and financial prosperity was a dominant feature of the period.

The relations among elements of the post-war price structure were in many respects unlike those of pre-war days. In the United States, at least, the post-war economy functioned during the decade of the 'twenties on the basis of a new division of economic elements. On the one side there existed low prices for the materials of fabrication, and relatively low incomes and purchasing power among farmers and raw material producers generally;[1] on the other, a high cost of living, high prices for manufactured goods (notably those intended for consumption), high industrial wages, high profits and industrial prosperity. The high cost of fabrication, the high prices of manufactured goods and the relatively high cost of living were, in some degree, necessary consequences of the general

[1] For most raw materials, such conditions affected producers the world over. We should note, co-existing with these conditions, the continual necessity of borrowing on the part of important raw-material producing areas, a necessity due, in general, to the stage of economic development attained, and not arising directly out of the post-war situation.

acceptance of the principle of high wages and the recognition of the necessity of protecting workers against industrial hazards. This brought desirable social progress in certain directions. The consequences for other economic elements—for the agricultural producer, for the producer of materials in the non-industrialized corners of the world, for lower-grade salaried workers—have not yet been fully explored. It is certain that no permanent adjustment to the new relations among economic elements was secured during the post-war expansion.

In contrast to the apparently favorable price situation on the operating side, for manufacturing industries generally, we have noted the persistence during the period from 1922 to 1929 of relatively high costs of capital equipment. In relation to a pre-war standard, prices of goods intended for use in such equipment remained above the general level. Moreover, construction charges were high. We come to the end of the period in 1929 with a very large volume of new capital equipment of all sorts, much of it constructed under conditions of exceptionally high cost. The full weight of this burden was not felt while activity remained at high levels, but in the years which followed these capitalized costs became a major factor in the problem of readjustment.

Most of the price shifts we have discussed occurred quite sharply during the recession of 1920-21. It is a nice question as to how and why working economic relations were restored and the flow of goods to consumers was resumed so promptly after this recession, with the purchasing power of raw material producers so low and with the prices of consumers' goods at such relatively high levels. The solution of the problem at that time was undoubtedly facilitated by an extraordinary and unprecedented increase in industrial productivity —an advance of 13.6 per cent in output per wage-earner between 1921 and 1923, on top of an increase of 2.9 per cent between 1919 and 1921. The aggregate purchasing power of agricultural producers and of producers of certain other raw materials remained low, but this remarkable gain in industrial productivity, combined with the position of marked price advantage enjoyed by manufacturing producers after 1921, permitted a great advance in the aggregate purchasing power of industrial wage-earners and of other groups drawing their incomes from manufacturing industries. The increased purchasing power of these groups, the stimulus of rapid expansion in the construction industries, and the opening up of new foreign markets more than compensated, at the time, for the low purchasing power of agricultural producers. These conditions permitted the free flow of goods to consumers, even though such goods were relatively high-priced.

The eight years following witnessed some amelioration of the inequalities so conspicuous in 1921. The impact of a new recession in 1929 re-opened many of the old cleavages and raised again many of the problems which the first post-war recession had presented. The nature of the settlement now to be made remains to be determined.

Apart from group changes and structural price shifts, certain more general aspects of the price movements of recent years have been dealt with in the preceding pages. Some significance has been attached to evidences of increasing stability of the individual elements of the price system. There was a persistent decline in the degree of variation of prices, a decline with reference not only to the standards of the disturbed war years, but also as compared with conditions prevailing before the war. There are some reasons for thinking that this decline reflects the growth of control, and indicates a reduction in the sensitivity of prices to changes in market conditions. In the system of prices at large, of course, the flexibility that perfect competitive conditions might give has never existed. It is probable that the degree of flexibility has been declining. The extending sphere of influence of public utilities, with regulated rates; the crystallization of wage rates under collective bargaining; the growing importance of trade associations and of other types of collective agreement among producers (mergers, cartels, export associations); the packaging and trade-marking of goods—all these tend in some degree to change the character of price movements, and to lessen their fluctuations. Whether this tendency toward stability marks the loss of a desirable sensitivity, whether that nice coördination of economic processes which unrestrained competition and price freedom are designed to provide is prevented through price rigidity, we cannot now say. But the available evidence indicates that some such loss of elasticity in the price system may have occurred during the years preceding the current depression.

There is one aspect of this matter which bears upon the course and character of price changes during the recession which began in 1929, in comparison with that of 1920-21. In May, 1920, commodity prices started downward after a sharp eleven-months' advance which had carried the general level up 23 per cent, and after a five-year advance amounting to 142 per cent. The level from which the decline started was not one which bore any of the aspects of permanence. As was noted in an earlier section, the relations among different elements of the price structure which existed in May, 1920, had prevailed for only a short time. They did not represent a consolidated position. Few long-term commitments had been made upon the basis of the 1920 price level. As a result, barriers to liquidation were relatively weak. Within eleven months the index of average prices dropped 44 per cent, at an average rate of 5.1 per cent a month. A violent price recession was concentrated within a period of less than a year.

Sharply different was the creeping, persistent illness which began in July of 1929. During eight years of but slight change in the general price level that consolidation of position which was absent in 1920 had been effected. New price relations had been established during these years, new wage policies had been accepted, enduring commitments had been made, and a sense of the permanence of the existing level of commodity values had been built up. A great volume of debts—mortgages, insurance claims, obligations of all sorts—had been contracted. All these conditions constituted barriers to a downward readjustment of commodity values. These barriers were particularly strong in industries with high overhead costs or with heavy labor charges. The relative slowness of the ensuing decline—1.2 per cent a month to June, 1932, as against 5.1 per cent during the stage of sharp liquidation in 1920-21—reflects in considerable part the continuing presence of obstacles to liquidation which did not exist in comparable degree at the time of the earlier break.

The slow secular inflation which helped to provide the setting for business during the two decades preceding the war was stimulated during the war years, and reached its peak in 1920. During the following decade the net movement was a declining one. We may not now assert that a long period of declining prices lies before us, for a reversal of trend may occur. But until evidence of such a reversal appears we must proceed on the assumption that a tendency toward secular price deflation has played a part in economic processes since 1920.

Long-term price trends are manifest to us in their effects on the cyclical swings of prices. A secular advance, as we have seen, expresses itself in prolonged periods of cyclical price rise, curtailed periods of cyclical decline, while a falling price level is manifest in shortened periods of cyclical rise, extended periods of cyclical decline. Such a secular trend has an important bearing on the recurring problems of readjustment which accompany the uneven cyclical movements of prices, particularly on the problem of readjusting the prices of manufactured goods to a changed general level. In general, whatever the direction of the trend, liquidation during cyclical price recessions is most painful and most tardy among manufactured goods, especially among manufactured consumers' goods. Relatively fixed costs and established prices prevail in the production and sale of these goods. When the trend is a rising one, the persistent, underlying force of the long-term advance in the price level operates to stimulate recovery, after depression, among raw materials, producers' goods and those other groups which are most sensitive to changes in monetary conditions. Some liquidation among fabricated goods there must be at such times, but the upward push of prices, affecting most immediately the commodity groups which suffer most severely in the cyclical drop, shortens and softens the downward revision of values and costs among the tardy elements of the price system. Under these conditions an early restoration of working relations among the laggard groups and the more sensitive commodities is facilitated.

A declining price trend, on the other hand, intensifies all the difficulties of readjustment. Prices of commodities among the groups which are most sensitive to the forces of cyclical recession are further depressed through the persistent push of the long-term factor. Pressure toward liquidation among manufactured goods persists, in aggravated form.

Here, perhaps, is a partial explanation of some of the discrepancies among price groups which persisted throughout the decade of the 'twenties, as well as of the difficulties which ensued. The buoyant stimulus of cheapening money has not been present to speed readjustment and to shorten the period and curtail the degree of liquidation enforced upon manufactured goods. The secular force of changing monetary values has tended to push down the prices of raw materials and of producers' goods, leaving upon manufacturers a weightier burden of readjustment than was theirs in happier times of rising prices. With the heavy investment in capital equipment characteristic of the present age and the great importance of overhead costs in the typical modern industry, the stresses of readjustment necessitated by a protracted period of falling prices might be expected to be more painful and prolonged than in any preceding period of falling prices. Some of these strains we are at present experiencing.

*Changes in the Aggregate Purchasing Power of Producing Groups.* In defining the tendencies of a period, as regards the flow of physical goods, it is not enough to measure changes in the volume of goods produced by various economic groups—by farmers, by producers of raw mineral products, by agents of fabrication. The flow of physical goods to each of these producing groups, in return for its physical contribution, constitutes the other and equally essential half of the story. Unfortunately, we do not have records which permit us to measure directly the number of physical units of goods of all sorts received by farmers, by industrial workers and by other producing groups in exchange for their products. It has been necessary to approach the problem indirectly. From statistics of physical output of goods of a given type, and from records of the change, between stated dates, in the per-unit purchasing power of this output, it is possible to approximate the change in the purchasing power of aggregate output. Variations in this aggregate purchasing power may be taken to measure changes in the volume of physical goods received by a given producing group.

Two points require emphasis. We have sought to measure *changes* in aggregate purchasing power between stated dates, or over a given period. No comparison, in absolute terms, of the aggregate purchasing power of different groups has been attempted. Secondly, a change in the aggregate purchasing power of a given group would accurately define the change in the physical income of that group only if the money income of the group were spent for goods in terms of which per-unit purchasing power is measured. It is not possible to measure changes in per-unit purchasing power with precision for all the groups here studied. The derived measurements define general tendencies, however, and it is with these that we are now concerned.

Between 1922 and 1929 the physical volume of production in the United States (excluding construction) increased at a rate of 3.8 per cent a year. The total flow of goods produced was apportioned among many groups. We deal here with only three.

The stream of goods going to producers of raw farm products and of raw mineral products increased in volume by approximately two per cent a year over this period, while that going to agents of fabrication increased by some five per cent a year. The gain was general, but the advance was far more rapid for manufacturing groups than for the other two. These movements differ somewhat from those of the pre-war era. Out of a stream of goods increasing at a rate of 3.1 per cent a year between 1901 and 1913, the portion going to producers of raw farm products, as a group, increased by slightly more than two per cent a year, that going to producers of raw mineral products increased by about four per cent a year, while that going to agents of fabrication increased by approximately three per cent a year. Manufacturing groups enjoyed no such relative advantage as in the later period.

The rate of change in the aggregate purchasing power of a given group of producers may differ from the rate of change in the physical volume of production of the economic system as a whole because the output of that group is changing at a rate different from that prevailing in the economy as a whole, or because the prices of its products are rising or falling with reference to the prices of the goods bought by the group. The gain in aggregate purchasing power of farmers between 1922 and 1929 reflected favorable price movements as well as increased physical contribution. The same favorable conditions swelled the purchasing power of agents of fabrication. Producers of raw mineral products increased their physical contribution materially, but the declining per-unit purchasing power of their products reduced the rate of gain in command over goods.

We are able to break the group 'agents of fabrication' into two sub-divisions—wage-earners, and a residual group including salaried employees, owners and creditors. There was a marked difference between the rates of gain of these two groups during this period. The aggregate command over goods exercised by manufacturing labor increased at a rate of 3.1 per cent a year between 1922 and 1929; that of 'ownership and management' increased by 7.3 per cent a year. (For both groups, purchasing power is measured in terms of wholesale prices.) The difference here is attributable, primarily, to differing rates of change in the real rewards of the two groups for their respective contributions to each unit of manufactured goods produced. The reward of labor for its contribution to each unit (i.e., labor cost per unit of goods produced, in dollars of constant purchasing power) was declining, while the rewards of 'ownership and management' (i.e., overhead costs plus profits, in dollars of constant purchasing power) were increasing between 1922 and 1929. These differences between post-war tendencies stand in contrast to the pre-war record. Aggregate real rewards increased at about the same rate for these two groups between 1901 and 1913.

These changes should be followed over a longer period, if we are to have a just conception of the relations prevailing in 1929. We may take 1914 as a starting point, and measure, not annual rates of change, but net changes over the fifteen years from 1914 to 1929. In 1929 the aggregate physical volume of production (excluding construction) was approximately 61 per cent greater than in 1914. The volume of goods that could be bought by producers of raw farm products, under the existing price and production conditions, was from 10 to 20 per cent greater in 1929 than in 1914.[1] Though agricultural output was greater in 1929 than in 1914 by about 25 per cent, a loss in per-unit purchasing power prevented an equal increase in the aggregate volume of goods commanded in exchange. For producers of raw mineral products, aggregate command over goods, at wholesale, was approximately doubled between 1914 and 1929, while the physical income of agents of fabrication, similarly measured, increased by about 130 per cent over the same period. Substantial increases in the output of the two latter groups combined with favorable price movements to yield these gains in aggregate purchasing power. There is a wide margin between the 10 to 20 per cent increase in the aggregate physical income of farmers, over this fifteen-year period, and the gains of 100 per cent and more recorded for the other two groups.

Among agents of fabrication the gain was greater for the composite group of salaried workers, owners and creditors than it was for wage-earners. The total physical income of manufacturing labor increased between 1914 and 1929 by from 75 to 100 per cent, while 'ownership and management' gained by from 110 to 150 per cent.[2]

[1] The figure is 10, if purchasing power be measured in terms of the goods farmers buy, 21 if measured in terms of wholesale prices.

[2] The first figure cited, in each case, measures the gain when purchasing power is measured with reference to the cost of living index. The second figure measures the gain when purchasing power is measured in terms of wholesale prices. The latter is not an appropriate standard, but its use is desirable in certain cases when mutually consistent and comparable results for different groups are required.

A more detailed explanation of these figures and a statement concerning their limitations are given in Chapter IX.

No feature of the economic changes of the period which spans the war and the following decade is more striking than these gains of agents of fabrication, notably of the group we have designated 'ownership and management'. Elsewhere we have discussed the price and cost movements which worked to their advantage. Changes in aggregate physical income of the type just defined measure the ultimate gains to which swelling output and favorable price changes both contributed. Together, they served substantially to augment the aggregate real rewards of manufacturing workers and of the owners of manufacturing enterprises.[1]

*Aggregate Contributions in Relation to Aggregate Rewards of Economic Classes.* In appraising economic changes over a period we should set against against the aggregate purchasing power, that is, the *rewards,* of different groups data relating to aggregate output, that is, to the *contributions,* of the same groups. If, between two dates, the output of a given group increases by more than the volume of physical goods commanded in exchange (the physical income) there is, presumably, a social gain. This change might be due to falling production costs, or to price movements unfavorable to the group in question. The statistical record, by itself, furnishes no evidence as to the reasons for the change, nor as to whether the consequences are painful, or the reverse, for the group concerned. But the comparison of changes in physical output with changes in physical income provides a ratio of considerable social significance.

Light is thrown on one striking pre-war tendency by a comparison of these changes, as they affected manufacturing industries. For all agents of fabrication there was an increase of approximately 95 per cent in total production between 1899 and 1914.[2] During the same fifteen-year period the total purchasing power of

[1] These statements are to be interpreted with reference to the several qualifications previously noted. The category 'ownership and management' includes various heterogeneous items which may have been subject to quite unequal changes between 1914 and 1929. Again, the first of these years was marked by business depression, while 1929 was a year of prosperity. These conditions would directly effect volume of output and profits, both of which are important elements in this comparison. Differences due to cyclical variations, however, would not account for the pronounced changes cited. A comparison of 1927 with 1914, both years of business depression, reveals differences of the same general order, for manufacturing labor. For 'ownership and management' the gain in total physical income between 1914 and 1927 lay somewhere between 75 and 110 per cent.

[2] This is the revised figure, corrected to take account of the diversification of manufacturing production during this period.

these producers, measured with reference to changes in the cost of living, increased by about 50 per cent. The 1914 index of 'contributions' (on the 1899 base) exceeded the index of 'rewards' by approximately 29 per cent. For manufacturing labor the corresponding figure was 23 per cent, while for 'ownership and management' in manufacturing industries aggregate 'contributions' in 1914 exceeded aggregate 'rewards' (measured by index numbers on the 1899 base) by 33 per cent. The increases in the physical output of these agents of fabrication, between 1899 and 1914, were materially greater than the increases in the physical goods received in return. There was a social gain (reflected in the lower real per-unit values of manufactured goods) from the services of these producers over this period.

The post-war record shows somewhat different movements. During the expansion from 1923 to 1929 there was an increase of approximately three per cent in the ratio of contributions to rewards, for all agents of fabrication. This conceals divergent tendencies among the two groups of fabricators. For wage-earners in manufacturing industries contributions in excess of withdrawals were piled up during this six-year period. The ratio increased by 16 per cent. But for the mixed group we have called 'ownership and management' the ratio declined by five per cent. The increase in aggregate physical output lagged behind the increase in aggregate physical reward. If we may interpret the ratio of output to rewards as an index of social gain or loss, we may say that there was an incremental social gain from the services of manufacturing wage-earners during this period, an incremental social loss from the services of owners and managers.[1]

But here again a longer view is needed if a true picture of the post-war situation is to be secured. Over the fifteen-year period from 1914 to 1929 the ratio of the aggregate contributions of all agents of fabrication to their aggregate rewards declined by five per cent. The increase in the physical income of this group exceeded the in-

---

[1] These gains and losses were 'incremental', since the data relate only to net additions to contributions and rewards, or net subtractions from them, during the period covered. In interpreting such figures account must be taken of conditions during the base year, which furnishes the standard of reference for all the measurements cited. It should be remembered, too, that figures covering the period 1923 to 1929 relate only to a period of expansion. For all groups, data for 1932 would differ materially from those for 1929.

No ethical judgment is implied in the use of the terms 'gain' and 'loss'.

crease in their physical output. This is in notable contrast to the record of 1899-1914, when an excess contribution of some 29 per cent was piled up by manufacturing producers. Breaking the group into its two components, we find that the ratio of contributions to rewards increased by about three per cent between 1914 and 1929 for manufacturing wage-earners, but declined by approximately 11 per cent for 'ownership and management'. These figures are to be compared, respectively, with advances of 23 and 33 per cent between 1899 and 1914.[1]

Data relating to various other groups of producers have been presented in earlier sections. For raw material producers an excess of rewards over contributions prior to 1913 was succeeded by a growth of contributions exceeding that of rewards, between 1913 and 1929. Sellers of producers' goods increased their contributions by more than the increase of their rewards during both periods. For sellers of consumers' goods, rewards increased more rapidly than contributions during the two periods. Producers of textile products increased their contributions, relatively to their rewards, during the first period, but between 1913 and 1929 the increase of contributions was 13 per cent less than the increase in their rewards.

The story, in detail, need not be repeated here. It is a record, in a word, of fairly substantial changes in the relations between the rewards and contributions of different producing groups, changes which were most pronounced for producers of manufactured goods. Here the persistent pre-war tendency toward an increasing social contribution on the part of this group was followed, after 1914, by a reversal, which increased the aggregate rewards of this group by an amount substantially in excess of the increase in their total physical contribution. For manufacturing labor the excess of rewards was steadily reduced (as a result of declining labor costs) after 1921, and was wiped out by 1929, but for ownership and management an excess of rewards over apparent physical contribution (as measured by index numbers on the 1914 base) persisted through 1929.

These, of course, were but a few of the many threads that interlaced to form the complex pattern of economic change during the years that concern us. Yet it has seemed well, in this summary, to refer to the reverse flow of physical goods, the flow of physical

[1] In defining rewards in this and in the preceding paragraphs of this section, purchasing power has been measured with reference to the cost of living index.

income which balances the flow of physical outgo, and to attempt to trace one or two of the major currents in this stream. In any realistic conception of economic equilibrium the relations between these flows must occupy a central place. Price and cost changes are significant because they define alterations in the balance between these flows. The extreme price changes of the war and immediate post-war eras were charged with tremendous human significance because of their bearing, active or passive, on these basic physical movements. These price changes, and accompanying changes in the balancing flows of physical goods, worked powerfully to shape the course of economic events during the era of post-war expansion.

*Changes in Distributive Shares.* We pass, finally, to the net effects of all these movements on certain distributive shares, to the changes in the ultimate returns to different income recipients. In so far as available data permit, we have followed the fortunes, between the turn of the century and the outbreak of the war, and during the period of post-war prosperity, of three or four major income groups. The earlier period, we have seen, was marked by modest gains in the real earnings, per capita, of all employed workers (a gain of 0.4 per cent a year), by a slight decline in the real earnings of manufacturing wage-earners (—0.1 per cent a year), a considerable decline in the real income of an average bondholder (—1.2 per cent a year), and a substantial though irregular advance (averaging 1.2 per cent a year) in the real income of the average stockholder. These income changes were accompanied by a decline at a rate of 0.8 per cent per year in the capital value of the bondholder's investment, and by an advance at a rate of 2.2 per cent per year in the capital value of the stockholder's investment (capital values being measured in terms of current dollars, in both cases).

Of a different order were the tendencies prevailing between 1922 and 1929. Starting from a relatively high level at the beginning of 1922, the general index of real wages advanced by 2.1 per cent a year during the eight years following. Among employees of manufacturing establishments, real wages per capita advanced by 1.4 per cent a year. Bondholders suffered a slight decline in real income (—0.1 per cent a year), while common stockholders gained in real income at a rate of 16.4 per cent a year. During this period the capital values of invested funds (in current dollars) increased at a rate of 1.9 per cent a year for bondholders, at a rate of 18.8 per cent a year for holders of common stocks.

The story that ends in 1929 is an unfinished one, of course, but the present survey is concerned only with the course of events up to that date. Not all income recipients have been brought into the brief summary of the preceding paragraphs, but those there cited played leading parts in the developments of the decade of the 'twenties. Employed labor improved a position already strong. (As an offsetting factor there was a considerable displacement of labor and a growing volume of unemployment during this period.) Bondholders maintained their positions, with a slight loss of current income and some gain in the capital values of invested funds. Stockholders gained at unprecedented rates, as regards both current income and capital values.

The expansion which dominated the course of economic events during the third decade of the twentieth century started against a background of violent and unbalanced change. The eight years preceding had witnessed the abnormal war-time development (abnormal because the productive and distributive changes and the allocation of investment funds during this period were not such as would be found in a normally functioning economy) and the abrupt reversal of tendencies and relations that took place in 1920 and 1921. On the physical side there existed, at the beginning of the post-war expansion, a definite building shortage and, probably, a deficiency of those types of capital equipment not required by the conditions of war-time demand. Partly because of the effect of the war and of domestic policy on the course of immigration, partly as a result of slowly-acting forces more fundamental in their origin, the factors affecting population growth had been changed. This change was to exert a far-reaching influence in the years succeeding. On the industrial side, the full effects of technical innovations and of a changing attitude toward the problems of production were beginning to be felt. A surge forward in productivity, probably exceeding in its intensity and rivaling in the scope and magnitude of its effects the advance which has given the label of 'industrial revolution' to the events of the late 18th and early 19th centuries in England, was under way. This movement, lowering costs and stimulating production, modifying the returns to producing groups, intensifying the ills of an old evil—unemployment, was to leave a deep impress on the years which followed.

During this period the working of the system of prices was conditioned by two major changes, one reflecting slowly-acting forces, the other an aftermath of the sudden shifts of the first post-war recession. The first of these, an intangible but probably a considerable factor in subsequent developments, was an apparent loss of flexibility in important elements of the price structure. Heavy investment in overhead, price regulation, monopolistic and semi-monopolistic control, trade agreements, changed distributive methods, emphasis on non-price factors in selling, extensive valorization efforts—these and other influences tended to render prices a less sensitive agency for the transmission of economic intelligence, and to make more difficult that prompt adaptation of individual economic elements to changes in other elements which is essential to the working of a competitive economy. What is especially significant about this tendency is that it accompanied changes which tied together even more intimately the individual elements of the general industrial structure. Just when greater complexity of the whole structure and increased interdependence of its component elements were making more imperative a delicate and continuing adjustment of working parts, the agency whose function it is to secure mutual adjustment and prompt adaptation was, it appears, becoming less sensitive to change and less efficient as an instrument of coördination.

The violent movements that accompanied the recession of 1920-21 had brought sharp alterations in the relations among economic elements, alterations of a magnitude that might normally have been expected as a result of years of gradual change. As an earthquake may elevate some areas and submerge others, so certain economic elements were suddenly lifted to positions of new power and influence, while others lost the gains of years. Whether these alterations were such as might later have occurred as a result of slow evolution is not now in question. What is here notable is that these pronounced shifts of economic relations occurred over a very short period, and that no enduring adaptation to them could be promptly effected. In this sense, then, they were unbalanced changes, and in this sense the expansion of 1922-29 started with an unstable foundation.

With such a background the striking advance of 1922-29 was begun. This advance, bounded at the one extreme by a movement which had profoundly modified pre-war relations among the elements of the economic system, ended, in 1929, with still more violent changes impending. The period between constitutes one of the most promising fields of study open to economists. If we are able properly to interpret this complex experience we may hope to determine whether anything approaching true economic equilibrium was achieved within the era bounded by the two great post-war recessions. We may hope, too, to determine more precisely the conditions that conduce to stable economic processes, and to define more accurately than is now possible the limits of tolerance of the existing order, in relation to the stresses and strains to which it is exposed. Both the good and the ill features of this economic experience will repay analysis and appraisal. The economic insecurity, the marked inequalities of distribution, the collapse that crowned the expansion we must learn to avoid. But the period brought also increasing productivity, an expanding volume of production, an advance in the real rewards of the average man—desirable objectives all, under any economic system. A fruitful lesson concerning the attainment of these objectives is to be learned from the experiences of the last decade, if we have the wit to profit by them.

# APPENDICES

# APPENDIX I

## SECTION I

### THE CONSTRUCTION OF INDEX NUMBERS OF PHYSICAL VOLUME OF PRODUCTION, 1901-1913

The index numbers of physical output given in Chapter I are based, in the first instance, upon annual data relating to the production of raw materials and of manufactured goods in the United States. Descriptions of the individual series employed are given in Appendix V. These series, reduced to relatives on the year 1909 as base, have been weighted by value of product, for raw materials, and by 'value added', for manufactured goods, weights being based on 1909 values. (These weights have been modified in a few cases, as is explained below.) Arithmetic means of these weighted relatives provide the unadjusted annual group index numbers. The base of the index numbers has been shifted to 1901 for purposes of presentation.

The commodities included in the major groups are shown in the table on the two following pages.

The weights given to the raw non-ferrous metals (copper, lead, gold, etc.) are not the values of the *refined* products in 1909, but estimates of the value of the ore before smelting and refining. These estimates have been made by subtracting from the values of the refined products the values added in the process of smelting and refining, as given by the Census of Manufactures. A similar estimate has been made for cement. All crops have been weighted by the full value of product. Raw animal products have been weighted by value of product less estimated values of the feed used in their production. This adjustment approximates what may be called 'value added' in the production of animal products, and avoids the duplication involved in counting the feed crops twice.

In general, imputed weights have not been used in combining the series representing processed goods. In a few instances, however, where given series adequately represent further processing operations, weights have been revised to increase the degree of representativeness of the sample. Thus mill consumption of cotton has been taken to represent simple cotton manufactures, and has been weighted by the total 'value added' in these industries. A similar procedure has been followed in securing the weights for the series relating to the production of other textile products and to the output of iron and steel. On the other hand,

## APPENDIX I

### Commodities Used in Construction of Annual Index Numbers of Production, 1901-1913

| Commodity | Products of American farms | Products other than those of American farms | Foods | Non-foods | Articles of human consumption | Articles of capital equipment | Non-durable goods | Semi-durable goods | Durable goods |
|---|---|---|---|---|---|---|---|---|---|
| *Raw Materials* | | | | | | | | | |
| Iron ore ....... | ... | x | ... | x | ... | x | ... | ... | x |
| Zinc ........... | ... | x | ... | x | ... | x | ... | ... | x |
| Lead .......... | ... | x | ... | x | ... | x | ... | ... | x |
| Copper ........ | ... | x | ... | x | ... | x | ... | ... | x |
| Gold .......... | ... | x | ... | x | x | ... | ... | ... | x |
| Silver ......... | ... | x | ... | x | x | ... | ... | ... | x |
| Anthracite coal.. | ... | x | ... | x | x | ... | x | ... | ... |
| Bituminous coal. | ... | x | ... | x | x | x | x | ... | ... |
| Crude petroleum. | ... | x | ... | x | x | ... | x | ... | ... |
| Natural gas .... | ... | x | ... | x | x | x | x | ... | ... |
| Cement, total ... | ... | x | ... | x | ... | x | ... | ... | x |
| Barley ......... | x | ... | x | ... | x | ... | x | ... | ... |
| Oats ........... | x | ... | x | ... | x | ... | x | ... | ... |
| Corn ........... | x | ... | x | ... | x | ... | x | ... | ... |
| Wheat .......... | x | ... | x | ... | x | ... | x | ... | ... |
| Hay ............ | x | ... | x | x | x | ... | x | ... | ... |
| Potatoes ....... | x | ... | x | ... | x | ... | x | ... | ... |
| Cotton ......... | x | ... | ... | x | x | ... | ... | x | ... |
| Tobacco ....... | x | ... | x | ... | x | ... | x | ... | ... |
| Flaxseed ....... | x | ... | ... | x | x | x | ... | x | ... |
| Apples ......... | x | ... | x | ... | x | ... | x | ... | ... |
| Sugar, domestic. | x | ... | x | ... | x | ... | x | ... | ... |
| Cottonseed ..... | x | ... | x | ... | x | ... | x | ... | ... |
| Cattle, total slaughter ..... | x | ... | x | ... | x | ... | x | ... | ... |
| Sheep, total slaughter ..... | x | ... | x | ... | x | ... | x | ... | ... |
| Swine, total slaughter ..... | x | ... | x | ... | x | ... | x | ... | ... |
| Egg receipts ... | x | ... | x | ... | x | ... | x | ... | ... |
| Wool ........... | x | ... | ... | x | x | ... | ... | x | ... |
| *Processed Goods* | | | | | | | | | |
| Flour, wheat ... | x | ... | x | ... | x | ... | x | ... | ... |
| Sugar, total supply ........ | x | x | x | ... | x | ... | x | ... | ... |
| Cattle receipts .. | x | ... | x | ... | x | ... | x | ... | ... |
| Sheep receipts .. | x | ... | x | ... | x | ... | x | ... | ... |
| Hog receipts ... | x | ... | x | ... | x | ... | x | ... | ... |
| Pig iron ....... | ... | x | ... | x | ... | x | ... | ... | x |
| Steel ingots and castings ....... | ... | x | ... | x | ... | x | ... | ... | x |
| Steel rails ..... | ... | x | ... | x | ... | x | ... | ... | x |
| Copper consumption .......... | ... | x | ... | x | ... | x | ... | ... | x |
| Lead consumption | ... | x | ... | x | ... | x | ... | ... | x |

COMMODITIES USED IN CONSTRUCTION OF ANNUAL
INDEX NUMBERS OF PRODUCTION, 1901-1913—*Continued*

| Commodity | Products of American farms | Products other than those of American farms | Foods | Non-foods | Articles of human consumption | Articles of capital equipment | Non-durable goods | Semi-durable goods | Durable goods |
|---|---|---|---|---|---|---|---|---|---|
| *Processed Goods—cont.* | | | | | | | | | |
| Zinc consumption | ... | x | ... | x | ... | x | ... | ... | x |
| Gold used in manufactures and arts | ... | x | ... | x | x | ... | ... | ... | x |
| Silver used in manufactures and arts | ... | x | ... | x | x | ... | ... | ... | x |
| Cotton, mill consumption | x | ... | ... | x | x | ... | ... | x | ... |
| Wool consumption | x | x | ... | x | x | ... | ... | x | ... |
| Silk imports, raw | ... | x | ... | x | x | ... | ... | x | ... |
| Cigars | x | ... | x | ... | x | ... | x | ... | ... |
| Tobacco and snuff | x | ... | x | ... | x | ... | x | ... | ... |
| Cigarettes | x | ... | x | ... | x | ... | x | ... | ... |
| Lime | ... | x | ... | x | x | ... | ... | ... | x |
| Common brick sold | ... | x | ... | x | x | x | ... | ... | x |
| Cement, total | ... | x | ... | x | ... | x | ... | ... | x |
| Cottonseed consumption | x | ... | x | ... | x | ... | x | ... | ... |
| Coke, total | ... | x | ... | x | ... | x | x | ... | ... |
| Zinc and lead pigments | ... | x | ... | x | x | x | ... | x | ... |
| Railroad passenger cars | ... | x | ... | x | ... | x | ... | ... | x |
| Railroad freight cars | ... | x | ... | x | ... | x | ... | ... | x |
| Vessels built | ... | x | ... | x | ... | x | ... | ... | x |
| Motor vehicles | ... | x | ... | x | x | ... | ... | ... | x |
| Fermented liquors | x | ... | x | ... | x | ... | x | ... | ... |
| Distilled spirits | x | ... | x | ... | x | ... | x | ... | ... |

certain series have been reduced in weight because of the exceptionally high coverage of the statistical records (as for series relating to the production of liquors, spirits and tobacco products) or because the industry showed an exceptionally high rate of growth and its inclusion, fully weighted, would have distorted the index (as in the case of automobiles). These series have been given weights based upon the relation of 'value added' in the industries they represent to the 'value added' in all manufacturing industries.

In several cases, series have been included in both groups of a classification. Thus, refined sugar is placed in the group 'products of American farms' with a weight equal to one-fifth of its total weight and in the group 'products other than those of American farms' with a weight of four-fifths, this division corresponding approximately to the amounts of sugar refined from the raw product raised in the United States and from raw sugar imported. Hay fed to work-animals has been considered a non-food, and hay fed to meat and dairy stock has been treated as a food, the same series appearing in both groups with appropriate weights. Since flaxseed is used in the making of paints, it is included in both 'articles for capital equipment' and 'articles for human consumption'. Bituminous coal and natural gas have also been placed in both these groups, because they are used in industries manufacturing capital equipment and consumption goods.

Index numbers for all commodities and for groups, derived by combining the original series, are given below. For raw materials the index numbers cover the years 1901-1914. Indexes for all manufactured groups include entries for the year 1899, to permit later correction by the use of census materials.

Index numbers measuring production changes in the various classifications of raw materials are identical with the indexes given in the text of Chapter I. The above preliminary index numbers for manufactured goods differ from those in Chapter I. Correction is necessary because of the inadequate coverage of the measurements derived from directly available statistics of manufacturing output. The mode of correction is explained below.

In combining the elementary group index numbers to secure measurements for broader groups, additional weighing factors are introduced. Here it is necessary to use 'imputed' weights, i.e., weights based not upon the values of the goods actually included in the enumeration

ANNUAL INDEX NUMBERS OF PRODUCTION (UNCORRECTED)
1901=100

| Year | All raw materials | All processed goods | All commodities |
| --- | --- | --- | --- |
| 1899 |  | 88 |  |
| 1901 | 100 | 100 | 100 |
| 1902 | 119 | 111 | 115 |
| 1903 | 115 | 113 | 114 |
| 1904 | 124 | 106 | 115 |
| 1905 | 127 | 127 | 127 |
| 1906 | 135 | 137 | 136 |
| 1907 | 126 | 140 | 133 |
| 1908 | 130 | 116 | 123 |
| 1909 | 131 | 139 | 135 |
| 1910 | 137 | 146 | 142 |
| 1911 | 134 | 139 | 136 |
| 1912 | 151 | 158 | 155 |
| 1913 | 139 | 167 | 153 |
| 1914 | 149 | 155 | 152 |

ANNUAL INDEX NUMBERS OF PRODUCTION (UNCORRECTED)—*Continued*
1901 = 100

| Year | Products of American farms | | Products other than those of American farms | | All products of American farms | All other products |
|---|---|---|---|---|---|---|
| | Raw | Processed | Raw | Processed | | |
| 1899 | | 92 | | 84 | | |
| 1901 | 100 | 100 | 100 | 100 | 100 | 100 |
| 1902 | 121 | 107 | 104 | 116 | 117 | 114 |
| 1903 | 114 | 111 | 118 | 114 | 113 | 115 |
| 1904 | 125 | 108 | 120 | 104 | 120 | 107 |
| 1905 | 126 | 118 | 137 | 137 | 123 | 137 |
| 1906 | 134 | 122 | 143 | 154 | 130 | 152 |
| 1907 | 121 | 125 | 159 | 157 | 122 | 158 |
| 1908 | 128 | 119 | 146 | 112 | 125 | 118 |
| 1909 | 127 | 126 | 164 | 154 | 126 | 155 |
| 1910 | 131 | 126 | 176 | 168 | 130 | 170 |
| 1911 | 128 | 128 | 174 | 151 | 128 | 154 |
| 1912 | 146 | 134 | 187 | 184 | 142 | 185 |
| 1913 | 130 | 140 | 198 | 196 | 133 | 196 |
| 1914 | 143 | 142 | 186 | 170 | 142 | 173 |

| Year | Foods | | Non-foods | | All foods | All non-foods |
|---|---|---|---|---|---|---|
| | Raw | Processed | Raw | Processed | | |
| 1899 | | 89 | | 88 | | |
| 1901 | 100 | 100 | 100 | 100 | 100 | 100 |
| 1902 | 124 | 104 | 110 | 115 | 119 | 113 |
| 1903 | 116 | 107 | 112 | 116 | 114 | 115 |
| 1904 | 122 | 106 | 128 | 106 | 118 | 113 |
| 1905 | 128 | 112 | 125 | 135 | 125 | 132 |
| 1906 | 134 | 117 | 136 | 148 | 130 | 144 |
| 1907 | 122 | 119 | 135 | 151 | 121 | 146 |
| 1908 | 125 | 119 | 141 | 114 | 124 | 122 |
| 1909 | 131 | 117 | 133 | 151 | 128 | 146 |
| 1910 | 135 | 120 | 142 | 160 | 131 | 155 |
| 1911 | 125 | 130 | 154 | 144 | 126 | 147 |
| 1912 | 148 | 130 | 157 | 173 | 144 | 168 |
| 1913 | 129 | 135 | 160 | 184 | 130 | 177 |
| 1914 | 141 | 135 | 164 | 166 | 139 | 166 |

Annual Index Numbers of Production (Uncorrected)—*Continued*
1901 = 100

| Year | Articles of human consumption | | Articles of capital equipment | | All articles of human consumption | All articles of capital equipment |
|---|---|---|---|---|---|---|
| | Raw | Processed | Raw | Processed | | |
| 1899 | | 92 | | 82 | | |
| 1901 | 100 | 100 | 100 | 100 | 100 | 100 |
| 1902 | 119 | 111 | 115 | 113 | 116 | 113 |
| 1903 | 114 | 114 | 120 | 110 | 114 | 111 |
| 1904 | 124 | 111 | 119 | 97 | 119 | 100 |
| 1905 | 126 | 124 | 141 | 133 | 125 | 134 |
| 1906 | 134 | 126 | 152 | 158 | 130 | 157 |
| 1907 | 124 | 129 | 163 | 160 | 126 | 161 |
| 1908 | 129 | 122 | 143 | 104 | 126 | 110 |
| 1909 | 129 | 137 | 170 | 143 | 133 | 147 |
| 1910 | 134 | 137 | 181 | 163 | 135 | 166 |
| 1911 | 132 | 138 | 173 | 140 | 135 | 145 |
| 1912 | 148 | 148 | 198 | 176 | 148 | 179 |
| 1913 | 135 | 157 | 207 | 184 | 145 | 188 |
| 1914 | 146 | 162 | 182 | 143 | 153 | 149 |

| Year | Non-durable goods | | Semi-durable goods | | Durable goods | | All non-durable goods | All semi-durable goods | All durable goods |
|---|---|---|---|---|---|---|---|---|---|
| | Raw | Processed | Raw | Processed | Raw | Processed | | | |
| 1899 | | 89 | | 96 | | 82 | | | |
| 1901 | 100 | 100 | 100 | 100 | 100 | 100 | 100 | 100 | 100 |
| 1902 | 121 | 105 | 112 | 118 | 110 | 113 | 116 | 115 | 113 |
| 1903 | 117 | 107 | 103 | 123 | 110 | 110 | 114 | 115 | 110 |
| 1904 | 123 | 106 | 137 | 116 | 114 | 99 | 117 | 125 | 100 |
| 1905 | 130 | 113 | 111 | 137 | 134 | 133 | 124 | 126 | 133 |
| 1906 | 134 | 119 | 136 | 135 | 144 | 157 | 129 | 135 | 156 |
| 1907 | 127 | 121 | 115 | 139 | 146 | 159 | 125 | 129 | 158 |
| 1908 | 129 | 119 | 135 | 123 | 134 | 107 | 126 | 128 | 110 |
| 1909 | 135 | 119 | 104 | 156 | 160 | 147 | 130 | 135 | 149 |
| 1910 | 139 | 122 | 118 | 148 | 167 | 168 | 134 | 135 | 168 |
| 1911 | 129 | 131 | 157 | 136 | 158 | 148 | 130 | 145 | 149 |
| 1912 | 152 | 132 | 140 | 152 | 176 | 187 | 146 | 147 | 186 |
| 1913 | 136 | 137 | 142 | 161 | 182 | 199 | 137 | 153 | 198 |
| 1914 | 145 | 135 | 160 | 169 | 166 | 164 | 142 | 166 | 164 |

of commodities of a given type, but upon the aggregate value of production of the entire class of goods of this type. Thus the group 'raw American farm products' was weighted by the value of *all* raw products of American farms, and combined with the group 'processed American farm products', weighted by the value added in the fabrication of all American farm products, to give the group 'products of American farms, raw and processed'. The weights imputed to the various groups are as follows.

(In units of $10,000,000)

| | *Weight* | | *Weight* |
|---|---|---|---|
| Total production | 1617 | Total raw materials | 764 |
| Raw materials | 764 | Farm | 647 |
| Processed goods | 853 | Mineral | 117 |
| Products of American farms | 918 | Products other than those of American farms | 699 |
| Raw | 647 | Raw | 117 |
| Processed | 271 | Processed | 582 |
| Articles of human consumption | 1297 | Articles of capital equipment | 320 |
| Raw | 710 | Raw | 54 |
| Processed | 587 | Processed | 266 |
| Foods | 618 | Non-foods | 999 |
| Raw | 484 | Raw | 280 |
| Processed | 134 | Processed | 719 |
| Non-durable goods | 892 | Semi-durable goods | 297 |
| Raw | 629 | Raw | 94 |
| Processed | 263 | Processed | 203 |
| Durable goods | 428 | | |
| Raw | 41 | | |
| Processed | 387 | | |

Data appearing in the text (p. 40) indicate that the growth of production among manufacturing industries for which statistics of physical volume are not available was more rapid during pre-war years than was the increase in the output of goods for which quantity statistics are published. As regards manufacturing production, index numbers constructed directly from data of quantities produced appear definitely to understate the true rate of growth. Correction is necessary.

The first step in the correction was the modification of group index numbers constructed from census materials, stepping these up in the manner described on pages 39-43 to secure closer approximations to the changes in physical output occurring among all manufacturing industries falling in the given classes. The index numbers thus secured for 1899,

1904, 1909 and 1914 were taken as fixed points. Entries for inter-censal years were secured by arithmetic interpolation based on the annual index numbers of production for the corresponding commodity groups. Because of the greater stability of the corrected index numbers (stability due to wider coverage) the amplitude of the annual fluctuations was reduced somewhat in securing the final interpolated values.[1]

The index numbers thus secured were accepted as final estimates for groups represented by fairly large samples of manufactured goods and showing relatively stable production trends. Such groups included products of American farms, consumption goods, foods, non-durable and semi-durable goods. Index numbers for other groups were secured by subtracting the corrected complementary group index numbers from the corrected all commodities index.[2] For example, index numbers for processed non-foods were secured by subtracting properly weighted

[1] The following table will make the procedure clearer.

ILLUSTRATION OF METHOD OF INTERPOLATION IN DERIVING INDEX NUMBERS OF MANUFACTURING PRODUCTION FOR INTER-CENSAL YEARS

| (1) | (2) | (3) | (4) | (5) | (6) | (7) | |
|---|---|---|---|---|---|---|---|
| Year | Unadjusted annual index 1899=100 | Corrected census index 1899=100 | Adjustment factor (ratio of census index to annual average) | Annual adjustment factor (straight-line interpolation) | Provisional inter-censal estimate (2)×(5) | Final production estimates | |
| | | | | | | 1899=100 | 1901=100 |
| 1899 | 100.0 | 100.0 | 1.0000 | 1.0000 | 100.0 | 100 | — |
| 1901 | 113.3 | | | 1.0342 | 117.2 | 117 | 100 |
| 1902 | 126.2 | | | 1.0514 | 132.7 | 131 | 112 |
| 1903 | 127.6 | | | 1.0685 | 136.3 | 135 | 115 |
| 1904 | 120.3 | 130.6 | 1.0856 | 1.0856 | 130.6 | 131 | 112 |
| 1905 | 144.0 | | | 1.0775 | 155.2 | 153 | 131 |
| 1906 | 155.8 | | | 1.0694 | 166.6 | 163 | 139 |
| 1907 | 158.8 | | | 1.0612 | 168.5 | 166 | 142 |
| 1908 | 131.1 | | | 1.0531 | 138.1 | 144 | 123 |
| 1909 | 157.9 | 165.0 | 1.0450 | 1.0450 | 165.0 | 165 | 141 |
| 1910 | 165.7 | | | 1.0569 | 175.1 | 173 | 148 |
| 1911 | 157.2 | | | 1.0688 | 168.0 | 169 | 144 |
| 1912 | 179.1 | | | 1.0807 | 193.6 | 192 | 164 |
| 1913 | 189.1 | | | 1.0926 | 206.7 | 202 | 173 |
| 1914 | 176.0 | 194.4 | 1.1045 | 1.1045 | 194.4 | 194 | 166 |

The advantage of this method of interpolation lies in the fact that the inter-censal estimates are tied at both ends to the census averages. Unless this is done, discrepancies in the trends of the two series may give rise to an unknown bias in the interpolated values. In some cases the procedure followed has resulted in the inter-censal estimates failing to preserve the direction of the movement shown by the annual index numbers. Wherever this has been true an additional adjustment has been made.

The entries in column (7) are the final estimates after reduction in the amplitude of the swings in the annual averages.

[2] This procedure avoids the direct use of small, inadequate samples in the 'stepping up' process described in the text. The assumptions underlying that method are stronger when applied to all commodities and to the more homogeneous groups. The method employed insures consistent averages throughout.

index numbers for processed foods from the corrected index of aggregate manufacturing production. By similar processes, index numbers of physical production for processed commodities not originating on American farms, for processed articles intended for use in capital equipment, and for processed durable goods were secured. In some cases further minor corrections were made in reconciling these derived index numbers with those secured directly.

DATA RELATING TO DEGREE OF COVERAGE OF INDEX NUMBERS OF PRODUCTION, BY GROUPS [a]

(Actual data in units of $10,000,000)

|  | Total | Products of American farms | Products other than those of American farms | Articles of human consumption | Articles of capital equipment | Foods | Non-foods | Non-durable goods | Semi-durable goods | Durable goods |
|---|---|---|---|---|---|---|---|---|---|---|
| *Manufactured goods* | | | | | | | | | | |
| Total 'value added' reported in Census of Manufactures, 1909 .. | 853 | 271 | 582 | 587 | 266 | 134 | 719 | 263 | 203 | 387 |
| 'Value added' by industries represented in annual index numbers [b].. | 213 | 100 | 113 | 136 | 77 | 62 | 151 | 65 | 63 | 85 |
| Percentage coverage of annual index numbers | 25 | 37 | 19 | 23 | 29 | 46 | 21 | 25 | 31 | 22 |
| 'Value added' by industries represented in index numbers based on census data [c] ........ | 255 | 81 | 174 | 178 | 77 | 43 | 212 | 73 | 74 | 108 |
| Percentage coverage of census index numbers | 30 | 30 | 30 | 30 | 29 | 32 | 29 | 28 | 36 | 28 |
| *Raw materials* | | | | | | | | | | |
| Total value of raw materials, 1909 (farm and mineral products)[d] ... | 764 | 647 | 117 | 710 | 54 | 484 | 280 | 629 | 94 | 41 |
| Value of commodities represented in index numbers ................ | 679 | 566 | 113 | 626 | 53 | 450 | 229 | 563 | 77 | 39 |
| Percentage coverage of index numbers | 89 | 87 | 97 | 88 | 98 | 93 | 82 | 90 | 82 | 95 |

[a] The estimates of the aggregate value of production for the various groups are subject to error, particularly those relating to goods destined for human consumption and for use as capital equipment. The latter grouping includes products utilized in the production of capital equipment, such as bituminous coal (50 per cent of the value of bituminous coal mined in 1909 has been included in the estimate of the aggregate value of raw products destined for capital equipment). For this reason this group may not be considered a sub-classification of all durable goods.

[b] These entries are the weights used in the construction of the annual index numbers. Some degree of imputation is involved. In certain cases this tends to increase the aggregate 'value added', in others to reduce it.

[c] The index numbers given in the text are averages into which three industries (lumber, petroleum and motor vehicles) enter with reduced weights. The full 'value added' of these industries is included in this table.

[d] Value of farm products (less the value of crops fed to livestock) plus value of raw mineral products.

# APPENDIX I

In securing final group index numbers for the major classes covering both raw and processed goods, the indexes for manufactured goods derived by the above procedure were combined with corresponding index numbers of raw material production, weights being imputed on the basis of 1909 values. This final process yields the index numbers given in Chapter I.

No correction of the original index numbers of raw material production was attempted. The degree of coverage of the available annual data was much greater for such materials, about 89 per cent of the value of all raw materials being represented in the series used.

The degree of coverage of the various samples is shown by the entries in the table on page 568.

## SECTION 2

### THE CONSTRUCTION OF INDEX NUMBERS OF PHYSICAL VOLUME OF PRODUCTION, 1922-1929

*General Index Numbers of Physical Output*

The general index numbers of physical output for the post-war period, as given in Chapter VI, have been constructed in a manner similar to that described in the first section of this appendix. However, new annual index numbers of the output of raw agricultural products and of manufactured goods were not computed; instead, the index of the volume of net agricultural production as constructed by the Bureau of Agricultural Economics [1] and the Federal Reserve Board index of manufacturing production [2] were used. In constructing the new index of raw mineral production and in combining the various groups, use was made of arithmetic means of weighted relatives on the average of 1923 and 1925 as base, weights being computed from values for these years.

Descriptions of the series and details as to methods of weighting and averaging used in the index of agricultural production and in the index of manufactures are given in the references cited. A new index of the output of raw minerals was constructed in order to cover this field of production more adequately than is possible with the monthly indexes published.[3] As in the pre-war index, weights are based on the estimated value of the *raw* minerals, before any processing.

The classification of the various series entering into the three an-

[1] *Yearbook of Agriculture, 1931,* p. 974.
[2] *Federal Reserve Bulletin,* February, 1927, pp. 100-103.
[3] The following commodities were used: Iron ore, copper, lead, zinc, gold, silver, bituminous coal, anthracite coal, petroleum, natural gas, sand, crushed stone and cement materials.

nual indexes of the production of agricultural products, minerals, and manufactured goods was similar to that described above for the pre-war indexes, and need not be repeated. The uncorrected annual index numbers of general production, with 1922 as base, follow.

ANNUAL INDEX NUMBERS OF PRODUCTION (UNCORRECTED)

| Year | Volume of net agricultural production (Bureau of Agricultural Economics) | Production of raw minerals (National Bureau of Economic Research) | Production of all raw materials | Production of manufactured goods (Federal Reserve Board) | Total production |
|---|---|---|---|---|---|
| 1922 | 100 | 100 | 100 | 100 | 100 |
| 1923 | 105 | 137 | 112 | 116 | 115 |
| 1924 | 110 | 130 | 115 | 108 | 111 |
| 1925 | 110 | 133 | 115 | 121 | 120 |
| 1926 | 116 | 144 | 122 | 124 | 124 |
| 1927 | 110 | 147 | 119 | 122 | 121 |
| 1928 | 116 | 146 | 122 | 129 | 127 |
| 1929 | 114 | 159 | 124 | 137 | 133 |

The following imputed weights (averages of 1923 and 1925 values) were used in combining the groups:

(In units of $10,000,000)

| | | | | |
|---|---|---|---|---|
| Total production ............ | 4,217 | | Total raw materials.......... | 1,586 |
| Raw materials ............ | 1,586 | | Farm ..................... | 1,165 |
| Processed goods ........... | 2,631 | | Mineral ................... | 421 |
| Products of American farms.. | 1,830 | | Products other than those of American farms ......... | 2,387 |
| Raw ..................... | 1,165 | | Raw ..................... | 421 |
| Processed ................. | 665 | | Processed ................. | 1,966 |

Correction of the annual indexes of manufacturing production by indexes constructed from data in the Census of Manufactures was made in the same fashion as for the pre-war indexes.

## Index Numbers of Physical Output of Finished Products

The various commodities entering into the index numbers of production of finished goods are listed in Chapter VI. As is there explained, the output of certain of these products is represented by the values rather than the quantities produced, adjustment for price changes being made where possible. Because of the general character of price changes during this period the use of value series tends to underestimate, rather than to over-estimate, the rate of growth of the physical volume of production.

The index numbers are weighted arithmetic means of relatives on the averages for the years 1923, 1925 and 1927 as base, with weights determined by the average value of output for these years. (Since only finished goods are included in these index numbers, the full values of the finished products are taken as weights.) In combining averages for the sub-groups imputed weights, based upon estimates of the aggregate values of the output of all goods falling into the particular classification, have been employed. No attempt was made to adjust these index numbers to the revised measurements of physical output of manufactured goods, as was done with the index numbers described in the preceding sections of this appendix.

Because of the inclusion of certain raw products requiring no further fabrication, such as vegetables and fruits, and because of the omission of all semi-finished commodities, such as pig iron, steel, copper, cement and other building materials, the present index numbers of the output of finished goods are not comparable with index numbers of the usual type, measuring the production of manufactured goods.

## APPENDIX II

### CLASSIFICATIONS OF COMMODITIES ENTERING INTO THE INDEX NUMBERS OF WHOLESALE PRICES CONSTRUCTED BY THE NATIONAL BUREAU OF ECONOMIC RESEARCH [a]

(The entries define the numbers of price quotations on the various commodities included in the several classifications for the year 1926. The commodities are those for which wholesale price quotations are currently published by the U. S. Bureau of Labor Statistics.)

| Commodity | Products originating on American farms | Products other than those originating on American farms | Foods | Non-foods | Producers' goods | Consumers' goods | Goods entering into capital equipment | Articles of human consumption | Producers' goods destined for human consumption [b] | Farm crops | Animal products | Forest products | Mineral products |
|---|---|---|---|---|---|---|---|---|---|---|---|---|---|
| All commodities | 235 | 257 | 167 | 325 | 292 | 200 | 160 | 332 | 132 | 124 | 131 | 55 | 171 |
| *Raw materials* | 83 | 59 | 71 | 71 | 108 | 34 | 35 | 107 | 73 | 47 | 47 | 4 | 44 |
| Aluminum | | 1 | | 1 | 1 | | 1 | | | | | | 1 |
| Antimony | | 1 | | 1 | 1 | | 1 | | | | | | 1 |
| Apples, fresh | 3 | | 3 | | | 3 | | 3 | | 3 | | | |
| Bananas | | 1 | 1 | | | 1 | | 1 | | | | | |
| Barley | 1 | | 1 | | 1 | | | 1 | | 1 | | | |
| Beans | 1 | | 1 | | | 1 | | 1 | | 1 | | | |
| Coal: | | | | | | | | | | | | | |
| Anthracite | | 7 | | 7 | | 7 | | 7 | | | | | 7 |
| Bituminous | | 10 | | 10 | 10 | | 10 | | | | | | 10 |
| Cocoa beans | | 1 | 1 | | 1 | | | 1 | 1 | | | | |

# APPENDIX II

| Commodity | | | | | | | | | | |
|---|---|---|---|---|---|---|---|---|---|---|
| Coffee | | 2 | | | 2 | | | 2 | | 1 |
| Copper, ingot | 2 3 | 1 1 1 | 1 2 | | 1 2 3 1 | | 1 2 3 1 7 | 1 2 3 1 | 1 2 3 1 | |
| Copra | | | | | | | | | | |
| Corn | 1 7 | | 1 7 | 3 | 1 3 1 | | | | | |
| Cotton | | | | | 1 | | 1 | 1 | | 1 |
| Cottonseed | | | | | | | | | | |
| Eggs, fresh | | 1 | | 1 | | | 1 | | 1 | |
| Gravel | 3 | | 3 | | 3 1 | | 3 | 3 | 3 | |
| Hay | | | | | 1 | | 1 | | | |
| Hemp | | | | | | | | | | |
| Hides: Domestic | 4 | | | | 4 1 | | 4 1 1 | 4 1 1 | 4 1 1 | |
| Hides: Foreign | | | | | | | | | | |
| Hops | 1 | 1 | | 1 | | | | | 1 | |
| Iron: Ore | | 2 7 1 | | | 2 7 1 | | | | | 2 7 1 |
| Iron: Pig | | | | | | | | | | |
| Lead, pig | | | 1 | | 1 | 1 | 1 | | 1 | |
| Lemons | | | | | | | | | | |
| Livestock: Cattle | 11 | | 11 | | 11 | 3 | 11 | 11 | 11 | |
| Hogs | 2 | | 2 | | 2 | | 2 | 2 | 2 | |
| Sheep | 3 | | 3 | | 3 | | 3 | 3 | 3 | |
| Poultry | 2 | | 2 | | 2 | | 2 | 2 | 2 | |
| | 3 | | 3 | | | | 3 | | 3 | |
| Milk, fresh | 3 | | | | | | | | | |
| Nickel, ingot | | 1 1 | | | 1 1 | | 1 1 | 1 | 1 1 | 1 1 |
| Nitrate of soda | | | | | | | | | | |
| Oats | 1 | | 1 | 1 | 1 | | 1 | | 1 | |
| Onions | 1 | | 1 | 1 | 1 | | 1 | | 1 | |

[a] These classifications do not agree in all respects with those employed in the construction of index numbers of physical production. Adequate representation of particular industrial fields required a somewhat different treatment of commodities in the two cases. 'Goods entering into capital equipment' is the same as the group entitled 'Goods entering into capital equipment'.

[b] The complementary group 'Producers' goods destined for use in capital equipment'.

APPENDIX II—Continued

| Commodity | Products originating on American farms | Products other than those originating on American farms | Foods | Non-foods | Producers' goods | Consumers' goods | Goods entering into capital equipment | Articles of human consumption | Producers' goods destined for human consumption | Farm crops | Animal products | Forest products | Mineral products |
|---|---|---|---|---|---|---|---|---|---|---|---|---|---|
| *Raw materials*—cont. | | | | | | | | | | | | | |
| Oranges | 1 | | 1 | | | 1 | | 1 | | 1 | | | |
| Peanuts | 1 | | 1 | | | 1 | | 1 | | 1 | | | |
| Pepper | | 1 | 1 | | | 1 | | 1 | | 1 | | | |
| Petroleum, crude | | 3 | | 3 | 3 | | | 3 | 3 | | | | 3 |
| Phosphate rock | | 1 | | 1 | 1 | | 1 | | | | | | 1 |
| Potatoes | 5 | | 5 | | | 5 | | 5 | | 5 | | | |
| Quicksilver | | 1 | | 1 | 1 | | 1 | | | | | | 1 |
| Rubber | | 2 | | 2 | 2 | | | 2 | 2 | | | 2 | |
| Rye | 1 | | 1 | | 1 | | | 1 | 1 | 1 | | | |
| Sand | | 1 | | 1 | 1 | | 1 | | | | | | 1 |
| Seeds: | | | | | | | | | | | | | |
| Alfalfa and Timothy | 2 | | 2 | | 2 | | | 2 | 2 | 2 | | | |
| Clover | 1 | | 1 | | 1 | | | 1 | 1 | 1 | | | |
| Flaxseed | 1 | | 1 | | 1 | | | 1 | 1 | 1 | | | |
| Silk, raw | | 3 | | 3 | 3 | | 1 | 3 | 3 | | 3 | | |
| Steel, scrap | | 1 | | 1 | 1 | | 1 | | | | | | 1 |
| Stone, crushed | | 1 | | 1 | 1 | | | | | | | | 1 |
| Sugar, raw | 1 | | 1 | | 1 | | | 1 | 1 | 1 | | | |

# APPENDIX II

| | Col 1 | Col 2 | Col 3 | Col 4 | Col 5 | Col 6 | Col 7 | Col 8 | Col 9 | Col 10 | Col 11 | Col 12 | Col 13 |
|---|---|---|---|---|---|---|---|---|---|---|---|---|---|
| Sulphur | 1 | 1 | | 1 | 1 | | | 1 | 1 | | | | 1 |
| Tankage | | 1 | | 1 | 1 | | | | | | | | 1 |
| Tin, pig | 2 | | 2 | | 1 | | 1 | 2 | 2 | 2 | | | |
| Tobacco leaf | 7 | | 7 | | 2 | | 1 | 7 | 7 | 7 | | | |
| Wheat | | 2 | | 2 | 7 | | | 2 | 2 | | | 2 | |
| Wood pulp | 10 | | | 10 | 2 | | | 10 | 10 | | 10 | | |
| Wool | | 1 | | 1 | 10 | | 1 | | | | 1 | | 1 |
| Zinc, slab | | | | | 1 | | | | | | | | |
| *Manufactured goods* | 152 | 198 | 96 | 254 | 184 | 166 | 125 | 225 | 59 | 77 | 84 | 51 | 127 |
| Acid: |  |  |  |  |  |  |  |  |  |  |  |  |  |
|   Oleic | 1 | | | 1 | 1 | | | 1 | 1 | | 1 | | 1 |
|   Sulphuric | | 1 | | 1 | 1 | | | 1 | 1 | | | | |
| Agricultural implements | | | | | | | 3 | | | | | | 2 |
| Alcohol: |  |  |  |  |  |  |  |  |  |  |  |  |  |
|   Denatured | 1 | 3 | | 3 | 3 | | | 1 | 1 | | | | |
|   Grain | 1 | | 1 | 1 | 1 | | | 1 | 1 | | | | |
| Aluminum sulphate | | 1 | | 1 | 1 | | 1 | 1 | 1 | 1 | | | 1 |
| Ammonia, anhydrous | | 1 | | 1 | 1 | | 1 | 1 | 1 | 1 | | | 1 |
| Asbestos | | 1 | | 1 | 1 | | | | 1 | | | | 1 |
| Asphalt | | 1 | | 1 | 1 | | | | 1 | | | | |
| Automobile tires | | 2 | | 2 | 1 | 2 | | 2 | 1 | 2 | | | 1 |
| Benzene | | 1 | | 1 | 1 | | | 1 | 1 | 1 | | | |
| Binder twine | | 1 | | 1 | 1 | | | 1 | | | | | 1 |
| Bleaching powder | | 1 | | 1 | 1 | | | 1 | | | | | 1 |
| Borax | | 1 | | 1 | 1 | | 1 | 1 | | | | | 1 |
| Brass sheets | | 1 | | 1 | | | | | | | | | |
| Bread | 5 | | 5 | | | 5 | | 5 | | 5 | | | |
| Brick | | 8 | | 8 | 8 | | 8 | | | 1 | | | |
| Burlap | | 1 | | 1 | 1 | | | 1 | | | 9 | | 8 |
| Butter | 9 | | 9 | | | 9 | | 9 | 1 | | | | |

APPENDIX II—Continued

| Commodity | Products originating on American farms | Products other than those originating on American farms | Foods | Non-foods | Producers' goods | Consumers' goods | Goods entering into capital equipment | Articles of human consumption | Producers' goods destined for human consumption | Farm crops | Animal products | Forest products | Mineral products |
|---|---|---|---|---|---|---|---|---|---|---|---|---|---|
| *Manufactured goods—cont.* | | | | | | | | | | | | | |
| Camphor | 3 | | | 1 | | | | 1 | 1 | | | | |
| Carpets | 1 | 1 | 1 | 3 | 1 | 3 | | 3 | | | 3 | | |
| Castor oil | 1 | | | | | 1 | | 1 | | 1 | | | |
| Cattle feed | 4 | | 4 | | 4 | | | 4 | 4 | 4 | | | |
| Cement | | 4 | | 4 | 4 | | 4 | | | | | | 4 |
| Cheese | 2 | | 2 | | | 2 | | 2 | | | 2 | | |
| Coal tar colors | | 4 | | 4 | 4 | | | 4 | 4 | | | | 4 |
| Coke | | 5 | | 5 | 5 | | 5 | | | | | | 5 |
| Copper: | | | | | | | | | | | | | |
| Sheet | | 1 | | 1 | 1 | | 1 | | | | | | 1 |
| Wire | | 1 | | 1 | 1 | | 1 | | | | | | 1 |
| Corn meal | 2 | | 2 | | | 2 | | 2 | | 2 | | | |
| Cotton goods: | | | | | | | | | | | | | |
| Blankets | 1 | | | 1 | | 1 | | 1 | | 1 | | | |
| Denims | 1 | | | 1 | | 1 | | 1 | | 1 | | | |
| Drillings | 1 | | | 1 | | 1 | | 1 | | 1 | | | |
| Duck | 1 | | | 1 | | 1 | | 1 | | 1 | | | |

APPENDIX II

| | | | | | | | | |
|---|---|---|---|---|---|---|---|---|
| | | | | | | 1 | 1 1 | 1 5 |
| | | | | | 1 | | | 3 3 1 3 |
| Flannel | 1 | | 1 | 1 | 1 | | 1 | |
| Gingham | 1 | | 1 | 1 | 1 | | 1 | |
| Hosiery | 2 | | 2 | 2 | 2 | | 2 | |
| Muslin | 1 | | 1 | 1 | 1 | | 1 | |
| Percale | 1 | | 1 | 1 | 1 | | 1 | |
| Print cloth | 1 | | 1 | 1 | 1 | | 1 | |
| Sheeting | 3 | | 3 | 3 | 3 | 3 | 3 | |
| Thread | 1 | | 1 | | 1 | | 1 | |
| Underwear | 2 | | 2 | 2 | 2 | 1 | 2 | |
| Yarns | 4 | | 4 | | 4 | 4 | 4 | |
| Crackers | 1 | | | | 1 | | 1 | |
| Creosote oil | | 1 | | | 1 | | 1 | |
| Cutlery | | | | | | | | 1 |
| Fertilizer materials: | | | | | | | | |
| Acid phosphate | | 1 | | 1 | 1 | 1 | 1 | |
| Muriate of potash | | 1 | | 1 | 1 | 1 | 1 | |
| Sulphate of ammonia | | 1 | | 1 | 1 | | 1 | |
| Mixed fertilizers | | 5 | | 5 | 5 | | 5 | |
| Fish | | 2 | 2 | | | | 2 | |
| Flour: | | | | | | | | |
| Rye | 1 | | 1 | | 1 | | 1 | |
| Wheat | 10 | | 10 | | 10 | | 10 | |
| Fruits: | | | | | | | | |
| Peaches, canned | 1 | | 1 | 1 | 1 | | 1 | |
| Pineapples, canned | | | 1 | | 1 | | 1 | |
| Prunes, dried | 1 | | 1 | | 1 | | 1 | |
| Raisins, dried | 1 | | 1 | | 1 | | 1 | |
| Furniture: | | | | | | | | |
| Bedroom | | 3 | | 3 | 3 | | 3 | 3 |
| Dining room | | 3 | | 3 | 3 | | 3 | 3 |
| Kitchen | | 3 | | 3 | 3 | | 3 | 1 |
| Living room | | 3 | | 3 | 3 | | 3 | 3 |

APPENDIX II—*Continued*

| Commodity | Products originating on American farms | Products other than those originating on American farms | Foods | Non-foods | Producers' goods | Consumers' goods | Goods entering into capital equipment | Articles of human consumption | Producers' goods destined for human consumption | Farm crops | Animal products | Forest products | Mineral products |
|---|---|---|---|---|---|---|---|---|---|---|---|---|---|
| *Manufactured goods—cont.* | | | | | | | | | | | | | |
| Gas, manufactured | | 1 | | 1 | | 1 | | 1 | | | | | 1 |
| Glass | | 4 | | 4 | 4 | | 4 | | | | | | 4 |
| Gloves | 1 | | | 1 | 1 | 1 | | 1 | | | | | |
| Glucose | 1 | | 1 | | 1 | | 1 | 1 | 1 | 1 | | | |
| Glycerine | 1 | | | 1 | 1 | | 1 | 1 | 1 | | 1 | | |
| Harness | 1 | | | 1 | 1 | | 1 | | | | 1 | | 1 |
| Hollow tile | | 1 | | 1 | 1 | | 1 | | | | | | |
| Iron and steel: | | | | | | | | | | | | | |
| Bar iron | | 2 | | 2 | 2 | | 2 | | | | | | 2 |
| Bars | | 1 | | 1 | 1 | | 1 | | | | | | 1 |
| Nails, wire | | 1 | | 1 | 1 | | 1 | | | | | | 1 |
| Pipe | | 2 | | 2 | 2 | | 2 | | | | | | 2 |
| Steel billets | | 1 | | 1 | 1 | | 1 | | | | | | 1 |
| Steel bars | | 1 | | 1 | 1 | | 1 | | | | | | 1 |
| Steel plates | | 1 | | 1 | 1 | | 1 | | | | | | 1 |
| Steel rails | | 2 | | 2 | 2 | | 2 | | | | | | 2 |
| Steel sheets | | 2 | | 2 | 2 | | 2 | | | | | | 2 |

# APPENDIX II

| | | | | | | | | | |
|---|---|---|---|---|---|---|---|---|---|
| Steel skelp | 1 | | | | 1 | | 1 | 1 | | 1 |
| Structural shapes | 2 | | | | 2 | | 2 | 2 | | 2 |
| Tin-plate | 1 | | | | 1 | | 1 | 1 | | 1 |
| Tin-roofing | 1 | | | | 1 | | 1 | 1 | | 1 |
| Tools: | | | | | | | | | | |
|   Augers | 1 | | | | 1 | | 1 | 1 | | 1 |
|   Axes | 1 | | | | 1 | | 1 | 1 | | 1 |
|   Butts | 1 | | | | 1 | | 1 | 1 | | 1 |
|   Chisels | 1 | | | | 1 | | 1 | 1 | | 1 |
|   Door knobs | 1 | | | | 1 | | 1 | 1 | | 1 |
|   Files | 1 | | | | 1 | | 1 | 1 | | 1 |
|   Hammers | 1 | | | | 1 | | 1 | 1 | | 1 |
|   Locks | 1 | | | | 1 | | 1 | 1 | | 1 |
|   Planes | 1 | | | | 1 | | 1 | 1 | | 1 |
|   Plow-bolts | 2 | | | | 2 | | 2 | 2 | | 2 |
|   Saws | 1 | | | | 1 | | 1 | 1 | | 1 |
|   Shovels | 1 | | | | 1 | | 1 | 1 | | 1 |
|   Towels | 2 | | | | 2 | | 2 | 2 | | 2 |
|   Vises | 1 | | | | 1 | | 1 | 1 | | 1 |
|   Woodscrews | 4 | | | | 4 | | 4 | 4 | | 4 |
| Wire, fence | | | | | 1 | 1 | 1 | 1 | | 1 |
| Lard | | 1 | | | | | | | | |
| Lead, pipe | | | | | | | | | | |
| Leather: | | | | | | | | | | |
|   Domestic | | 4 | 4 | 4 | | | 4 | 4 | | |
|   Foreign | | | 1 | 1 | | | 1 | 1 | | |
| Lime | 1 | | | | 2 | | 2 | 2 | 2 | |
| Lime, acetate of | 2 | | | | 1 | | 1 | 1 | 1 | |
| Linseed oil | 1 | | | 1 | 1 | | 1 | 1 | | 1 |
| Litharge | | | | | 1 | | 1 | 1 | | 1 |
| Lithopone | | | | | 1 | | 1 | 1 | | 1 |

APPENDIX II—Continued

| Commodity | Products originating on American farms | Products other than those originating on American farms | Foods | Non-foods | Producers' goods | Consumers' goods | Goods entering into capital equipment | Articles of human consumption | Producers' goods destined for human consumption | Farm crops | Animal products | Forest products | Mineral products |
|---|---|---|---|---|---|---|---|---|---|---|---|---|---|
| *Manufactured goods—cont.* | | | | | | | | | | | | | |
| Lumber: | | | | | | | | | | | | | |
| Cypress | | 1 | | 1 | 1 | | 1 | | | | | 1 | |
| Douglas fir | | 5 | | 5 | 5 | | 5 | | | | | 5 | |
| Gum sap | | 1 | | 1 | 1 | | 1 | | | | | 1 | |
| Hemlock | | 2 | | 2 | 2 | | 2 | | | | | 2 | |
| Maple | | 2 | | 2 | 2 | | 2 | | | | | 2 | |
| Oak | | 2 | | 2 | 2 | | 2 | | | | | 2 | |
| Pine | | 9 | | 9 | 9 | | 9 | | | | | 9 | |
| Poplar | | 1 | | 1 | 1 | | 1 | | | | | 1 | |
| Spruce | | 2 | | 2 | 2 | | 2 | | | | | 2 | |
| Lath | | 2 | | 2 | 2 | | 2 | | | | | 2 | |
| Shingles | | 2 | | 2 | 2 | | 2 | | | | | 2 | |
| Meat: | | | | | | | | | | | | | |
| Beef, cured | 2 | | 2 | | | 2 | | 2 | | | 2 | | |
| Beef, fresh | 9 | | 9 | | | 9 | | 9 | | | 9 | | |
| Lamb | 1 | | 1 | | | 1 | | 1 | | | 1 | | |
| Mutton | 1 | | 1 | | | 1 | | 1 | | | 1 | | |
| Pork, cured | 5 | | 5 | | | 5 | | 5 | | | 5 | | |
| Pork, fresh | 6 | | 6 | | | 6 | | 6 | | | 6 | | |

| | Poultry | Veal | Milk, canned | Molasses | Oatmeal | Oleo oil | Oleomargarine | Paper: Box board | Newsprint | Wrapping | Peroxide of hydrogen | Petroleum products: Fuel oil | Gasoline | Kerosene | Lubricating oil | Rayon | Red lead | Rice | Rosin | Salt | Sewing machines | Shellac | Shoes: Children's | Men's | Women's | Silk goods: Hosiery, pure silk | Hosiery, artificial silk | Spun silk |
|---|---|---|---|---|---|---|---|---|---|---|---|---|---|---|---|---|---|---|---|---|---|---|---|---|---|---|---|---|
|  |  |  |  |  |  |  |  | 1 |  |  |  | 2 | 3 | 2 | 4 | 1 |  |  |  |  | 2 | 2 |  |  |  |  |  |  |
|  |  |  |  |  |  |  |  | 3 | 1 |  |  |  |  |  |  |  |  | 3 |  | 1 |  |  | 1 |  |  |  |  |  |
|  | 2 | 2 | 2 |  | 1 |  |  |  |  |  |  |  |  |  |  |  |  |  |  |  |  |  | 2 | 5 | 4 |  | 2 | 1 |
|  |  |  |  | 1 | 1 |  |  |  |  | 1 |  |  |  |  |  | 2 |  |  |  |  |  |  |  |  |  |  |  |  |
|  |  |  |  |  |  |  |  |  | 1 |  |  | 1 | 1 |  |  | 2 | 1 |  | 4 | 3 |  |  |  |  |  |  |  | 1 |
|  | 2 | 2 | 2 | 1 | 1 | 1 |  |  | 1 | 1 | 1 |  | 2 | 3 | 2 | 4 | 3 | 2 |  | 2 | 2 |  | 2 | 5 | 4 |  | 2 | 1 1 |
|  |  |  |  |  |  |  |  | 3 |  |  |  |  |  |  |  |  | 1 |  |  | 1 |  |  | 1 |  |  |  |  |  |
|  | 2 | 2 | 2 | 1 | 1 |  |  |  |  |  | 1 |  |  | 2 | 2 |  | 2 |  |  | 2 | 2 |  | 2 | 5 | 4 |  | 2 | 1 |
|  |  |  |  |  |  |  | 1 | 3 | 1 | 1 |  |  | 2 | 1 |  | 4 | 3 | 1 |  | 1 |  |  |  |  |  |  |  | 1 |
|  |  |  |  |  |  |  |  | 3 | 1 | 1 | 1 |  | 2 | 3 | 2 | 4 | 3 | 1 |  | 1 | 2 | 1 | 2 | 5 | 4 |  | 2 | 1 1 |
|  | 2 | 2 | 2 | 1 | 1 | 1 | 1 |  |  |  |  |  |  |  |  |  |  |  | 2 |  | 2 |  |  |  |  |  |  |  |
|  |  |  |  |  |  |  |  | 3 | 1 | 1 | 1 |  | 2 | 3 | 2 | 4 | 3 | 1 | 1 | 2 | 2 | 1 |  | 2 |  |  | 1 | 1 |
|  | 2 | 2 | 2 | 1 | 1 | 1 | 1 |  |  |  |  |  |  |  |  |  |  |  | 2 |  |  |  | 2 | 5 | 4 |  |  |  |

APPENDIX II—Continued

| Commodity | Products originating on American farms | Products other than those originating on American farms | Foods | Non-foods | Producers' goods | Consumers' goods | Goods entering into capital equipment | Articles of human consumption | Producers' goods destined for human consumption | Farm crops | Animal products | Forest products | Mineral products |
|---|---|---|---|---|---|---|---|---|---|---|---|---|---|
| *Manufactured goods—cont.* | | | | | | | | | | | | | |
| Silver | | 1 | | 1 | 1 | | 1 | | | | | | 1 |
| Slate | | 1 | | 1 | 1 | | 1 | | | | | | 1 |
| Soap, laundry | 2 | | | 2 | | 2 | | 2 | | | | | |
| Soda: | | | | | | | | | | | | | |
|   Ash | | 1 | | 1 | 1 | | | 1 | 1 | | | | 1 |
|   Bicarbonate | | 1 | | 1 | 1 | | | 1 | 1 | | | | 1 |
|   Caustic | | 1 | | 1 | 1 | | | 1 | 1 | | | | 1 |
|   Silicate | | 1 | | 1 | 1 | | | | | | | | |
| Starch, laundry | 1 | | | 3 | | 3 | | 3 | | 1 | | | |
| Stoves | 1 | 3 | | 1 | 1 | 1 | | 1 | | 1 | | | 3 |
| Sugar | | | 1 | | | | | | | | | | |
| Tableware: | | | | | | | | | | | | | |
|   Dinner sets | | 2 | | 2 | | 2 | | 2 | | | | | 2 |
|   Pitchers, glass | | 1 | | 1 | | 1 | | 1 | 1 | | | | 1 |
| Tallow | 1 | | | 1 | 1 | | | 1 | | | 1 | | |
| Tea | | 1 | 1 | | | 1 | | 1 | | 1 | | | |
| Tobacco | 2 | | 2 | | | 2 | | 2 | | 2 | | | 1 |

APPENDIX II

| | | | | | | | | | | |
|---|---|---|---|---|---|---|---|---|---|---|
| Tubs, iron | | | | 1 | 1 | | | | | 1 |
| Turpentine | | | 1 | 1 | | | | 1 | | | |
| Vegetables, canned: | | | | | | | | | | | |
| Beans | 1 | 1 | 1 | 1 | | 1 | 1 | | 1 | | |
| Corn | 1 | 1 | 1 | 1 | | 1 | 1 | | 1 | | |
| Peas | 1 | 1 | 1 | | | 1 | 1 | | 1 | | |
| Tomatoes | 1 | | | | 1 | 1 | | | 1 | | |
| Vegetable oil: | | | | | | | | | | | |
| Cocoanut | 1 | 1 | | | | | | | | | |
| Corn | 1 | | | | | 1 | | | 1 | | |
| Cottonseed | 1 | 1 | 1 | | | 1 | | | 1 | 1 | |
| Olive | | 1 | 1 | 1 | | 1 | | | 1 | 1 | |
| Palm niger | 1 | | | | | | | | 1 | | |
| Vinegar, cider | | | | | 1 | 1 | | | | | |
| White lead | | 1 | | | 1 | 1 | | | | | 1 |
| Woolen goods: | | | | | | | | | | | |
| Overcoating | 2 | | 2 | | | 2 | | | 2 | | 2 |
| Suiting | 6 | | 6 | | | 6 | | | 6 | | 6 |
| Underwear | 1 | | 1 | | | 1 | | | 1 | | 1 |
| Women's dress goods, all wool | 3 | | 3 | | 3 | 3 | | 3 | 3 | | 3 |
| Cotton warp | 1 | | 1 | | 1 | 1 | | | 1 | | |
| Yarns | 3 | | 3 | | | 3 | | | 3 | | |
| Zinc: | | | | | | | | | | | |
| Oxide | | 1 | 1 | | | 1 | 1 | | 1 | | 1 |
| Sheet | | 1 | 1 | | | 1 | 1 | | 1 | | 1 |

# Appendix III

## Index Numbers[a] of Wholesale Prices by Groups
### 1891-1902, 1902-1913, 1913-1931

| Year | All com-modities | Raw mate-rials | Manu-factured goods | Products originating on American farms | | | Products other than those originating on American farms | | |
|---|---|---|---|---|---|---|---|---|---|
| | | | | Total | Raw | Proc-essed | Total | Raw | Proc-essed |
| 1891 | 100.0 | 100.0 | 100.0 | 100.0 | 100.0 | 100.0 | 100.0 | 100.0 | 100.0 |
| 1892 | 95.0 | 92.6 | 95.7 | 94.7 | 90.0 | 96.0 | 95.3 | 95.1 | 95.3 |
| 1893 | 94.1 | 90.9 | 95.0 | 95.3 | 88.8 | 97.3 | 92.7 | 93.1 | 92.6 |
| 1894 | 85.1 | 80.9 | 86.4 | 85.8 | 78.5 | 87.9 | 84.4 | 83.3 | 84.7 |
| 1895 | 83.5 | 79.3 | 84.7 | 82.5 | 75.3 | 84.6 | 84.5 | 83.4 | 84.9 |
| 1896 | 80.1 | 72.5 | 82.5 | 76.0 | 62.1 | 80.4 | 84.7 | 84.1 | 84.9 |
| 1897 | 79.8 | 76.5 | 80.7 | 77.8 | 70.2 | 80.0 | 81.9 | 83.1 | 81.5 |
| 1898 | 83.1 | 83.1 | 83.1 | 81.7 | 79.8 | 82.2 | 84.6 | 86.3 | 84.1 |
| 1899 | 90.4 | 93.2 | 89.7 | 84.5 | 82.6 | 85.1 | 97.1 | 104.7 | 94.9 |
| 1900 | 98.1 | 99.2 | 97.7 | 91.9 | 88.3 | 92.9 | 105.0 | 110.8 | 103.2 |
| 1901 | 96.3 | 99.0 | 95.5 | 91.7 | 93.4 | 91.3 | 101.3 | 104.6 | 100.3 |
| 1902 | 100.2 | 107.1 | 98.3 | 96.8 | 100.9 | 95.7 | 103.8 | 113.3 | 101.1 |
| 1902 | 100.0 | 100.0 | 100.0 | 100.0 | 100.0 | 100.0 | 100.0 | 100.0 | 100.0 |
| 1903 | 100.6 | 100.3 | 100.7 | 98.5 | 94.8 | 99.5 | 102.8 | 105.7 | 102.0 |
| 1904 | 99.7 | 98.8 | 100.0 | 100.1 | 100.6 | 99.9 | 99.3 | 97.2 | 100.0 |
| 1905 | 102.3 | 100.8 | 102.8 | 101.4 | 98.7 | 102.1 | 103.4 | 102.9 | 103.6 |
| 1906 | 107.8 | 104.1 | 108.8 | 106.5 | 98.0 | 108.7 | 109.2 | 110.3 | 108.9 |
| 1907 | 113.3 | 110.4 | 114.2 | 113.2 | 105.2 | 115.4 | 113.5 | 115.7 | 112.8 |
| 1908 | 105.7 | 101.6 | 106.9 | 109.3 | 104.6 | 110.6 | 101.9 | 98.8 | 102.8 |
| 1909 | 108.2 | 107.8 | 108.3 | 114.3 | 114.8 | 114.2 | 101.9 | 101.5 | 102.0 |
| 1910 | 112.5 | 110.5 | 113.0 | 119.2 | 118.0 | 119.6 | 105.6 | 103.7 | 106.1 |
| 1911 | 108.9 | 111.1 | 108.3 | 115.1 | 117.5 | 114.4 | 102.7 | 105.3 | 101.9 |
| 1912 | 112.6 | 118.7 | 110.9 | 118.6 | 127.2 | 116.5 | 106.4 | 111.1 | 105.1 |
| 1913 | 112.7 | 112.0 | 112.9 | 116.7 | 112.8 | 117.7 | 108.5 | 111.3 | 107.7 |
| 1913 | 100.0 | 100.0 | 100.0 | 100.0 | 100.0 | 100.0 | 100.0 | 100.0 | 100.0 |
| 1914 | 98.2 | 98.7 | 97.8 | 101.2 | 102.4 | 100.5 | 94.8 | 92.7 | 95.5 |
| 1915 | 102.8 | 104.2 | 102.0 | 104.2 | 106.9 | 102.7 | 101.1 | 99.9 | 101.6 |
| 1916 | 129.1 | 127.9 | 129.4 | 123.3 | 125.4 | 122.0 | 135.3 | 132.1 | 136.3 |
| 1917 | 171.2 | 174.4 | 169.4 | 175.8 | 182.0 | 172.2 | 166.4 | 162.9 | 167.1 |
| 1918 | 195.7 | 188.9 | 198.4 | 208.8 | 206.3 | 210.1 | 183.4 | 164.7 | 189.3 |
| 1919 | 203.4 | 196.1 | 206.1 | 223.8 | 221.9 | 224.9 | 184.6 | 161.4 | 192.1 |
| 1920 | 227.9 | 202.2 | 239.5 | 230.7 | 212.5 | 241.9 | 224.8 | 186.6 | 237.5 |
| 1921 | 150.6 | 125.0 | 162.7 | 143.4 | 124.1 | 155.9 | 157.7 | 126.4 | 168.2 |
| 1922 | 148.3 | 133.2 | 154.8 | 145.8 | 136.9 | 151.4 | 150.2 | 127.4 | 157.5 |
| 1923 | 156.4 | 141.5 | 163.0 | 151.9 | 143.5 | 157.0 | 160.6 | 138.6 | 167.9 |
| 1924 | 153.5 | 140.5 | 159.2 | 153.4 | 146.3 | 157.8 | 153.5 | 132.7 | 160.2 |
| 1925 | 159.7 | 152.9 | 162.4 | 165.4 | 159.4 | 169.0 | 154.2 | 143.9 | 157.4 |
| 1926 | 153.4 | 143.7 | 157.5 | 154.3 | 144.1 | 160.5 | 152.2 | 142.9 | 155.0 |
| 1927 | 148.5 | 140.1 | 152.0 | 153.2 | 144.5 | 158.7 | 143.8 | 134.0 | 146.8 |
| 1928 | 150.3 | 144.0 | 153.1 | 160.3 | 155.8 | 163.1 | 141.6 | 128.6 | 145.6 |
| 1929 | 148.3 | 140.7 | 151.5 | 155.9 | 150.4 | 159.2 | 141.4 | 127.7 | 145.7 |
| 1930 | 132.2 | 118.0 | 138.4 | 134.9 | 121.5 | 142.9 | 129.5 | 113.0 | 134.9 |
| 1931 | 109.7 | 92.5 | 117.5 | 105.6 | 89.8 | 115.6 | 113.2 | 96.3 | 118.9 |

*a* See bottom of opposite page.

## Index Numbers of Wholesale Prices

| Year | Producers' goods | | | Consumers' goods | | | Consumers' goods, processed | |
|---|---|---|---|---|---|---|---|---|
| | Total | Raw | Processed | Total | Raw | Processed | Foods | Non-foods |
| 1891 | 100.0 | 100.0 | 100.0 | 100.0 | 100.0 | 100.0 | 100.0 | 100.0 |
| 1892 | 95.0 | 92.7 | 96.2 | 95.0 | 91.9 | 95.3 | 93.4 | 96.7 |
| 1893 | 92.7 | 89.6 | 94.4 | 95.5 | 95.8 | 95.4 | 96.3 | 94.8 |
| 1894 | 83.2 | 79.2 | 85.4 | 87.1 | 87.1 | 87.1 | 86.6 | 87.5 |
| 1895 | 82.6 | 79.1 | 84.6 | 84.4 | 80.1 | 84.9 | 85.0 | 84.8 |
| 1896 | 80.3 | 73.5 | 84.1 | 80.0 | 69.2 | 81.3 | 77.6 | 84.1 |
| 1897 | 79.5 | 76.6 | 81.1 | 80.0 | 76.3 | 80.5 | 79.6 | 81.1 |
| 1898 | 84.0 | 84.3 | 83.8 | 82.3 | 79.2 | 82.6 | 85.8 | 80.5 |
| 1899 | 95.8 | 97.3 | 95.1 | 85.2 | 80.5 | 85.7 | 88.4 | 83.8 |
| 1900 | 103.5 | 103.3 | 103.6 | 92.6 | 85.9 | 93.5 | 94.8 | 92.5 |
| 1901 | 99.7 | 100.4 | 99.3 | 92.8 | 94.3 | 92.7 | 95.5 | 90.7 |
| 1902 | 104.9 | 110.4 | 102.0 | 95.5 | 96.1 | 95.5 | 100.2 | 92.3 |
| 1902 | 100.0 | 100.0 | 100.0 | 100.0 | 100.0 | 100.0 | 100.0 | 100.0 |
| 1903 | 100.4 | 99.4 | 100.9 | 100.7 | 103.4 | 100.4 | 95.3 | 103.8 |
| 1904 | 97.3 | 96.1 | 98.0 | 102.2 | 108.9 | 101.5 | 95.0 | 105.8 |
| 1905 | 101.6 | 100.0 | 102.4 | 103.1 | 103.8 | 103.0 | 98.1 | 106.3 |
| 1906 | 107.6 | 103.8 | 109.5 | 108.0 | 105.1 | 108.3 | 101.1 | 113.0 |
| 1907 | 113.7 | 113.1 | 113.9 | 113.0 | 101.9 | 114.3 | 105.5 | 120.2 |
| 1908 | 102.5 | 100.8 | 103.3 | 109.1 | 104.3 | 109.6 | 105.8 | 112.1 |
| 1909 | 106.0 | 108.2 | 104.9 | 110.5 | 106.5 | 110.9 | 108.2 | 112.6 |
| 1910 | 111.1 | 112.0 | 110.7 | 113.8 | 105.3 | 114.8 | 112.9 | 116.0 |
| 1911 | 106.1 | 109.9 | 104.3 | 111.9 | 115.4 | 111.5 | 110.3 | 112.3 |
| 1912 | 109.5 | 116.0 | 106.5 | 115.8 | 128.4 | 114.5 | 115.1 | 114.1 |
| 1913 | 109.7 | 111.7 | 108.7 | 115.9 | 113.1 | 116.1 | 114.7 | 117.1 |
| 1913 | 100.0 | 100.0 | 100.0 | 100.0 | 100.0 | 100.0 | 100.0 | 100.0 |
| 1914 | 96.3 | 97.8 | 95.4 | 100.8 | 101.8 | 100.5 | 102.0 | 99.0 |
| 1915 | 104.4 | 107.6 | 102.3 | 100.5 | 94.2 | 101.8 | 104.0 | 99.3 |
| 1916 | 138.6 | 128.9 | 144.9 | 116.4 | 115.5 | 116.5 | 116.0 | 117.2 |
| 1917 | 180.1 | 179.5 | 180.2 | 158.6 | 156.9 | 158.8 | 163.7 | 153.1 |
| 1918 | 198.8 | 193.9 | 201.8 | 190.6 | 172.0 | 194.7 | 195.1 | 194.1 |
| 1919 | 200.1 | 195.3 | 203.1 | 207.7 | 197.4 | 209.9 | 206.6 | 213.4 |
| 1920 | 227.2 | 201.1 | 245.0 | 228.3 | 203.9 | 233.5 | 207.4 | 267.4 |
| 1921 | 143.0 | 117.7 | 161.0 | 162.5 | 152.1 | 164.7 | 146.9 | 187.2 |
| 1922 | 143.9 | 127.3 | 154.8 | 154.8 | 153.9 | 154.8 | 140.2 | 173.1 |
| 1923 | 155.4 | 137.2 | 167.6 | 158.1 | 156.9 | 158.2 | 139.0 | 183.4 |
| 1924 | 150.0 | 134.5 | 160.4 | 158.9 | 162.1 | 158.0 | 141.0 | 179.7 |
| 1925 | 152.9 | 144.4 | 158.5 | 169.9 | 184.2 | 167.1 | 157.7 | 178.3 |
| 1926 | 146.2 | 135.0 | 153.6 | 164.5 | 176.1 | 162.1 | 153.4 | 172.4 |
| 1927 | 141.4 | 132.8 | 147.0 | 159.4 | 167.1 | 157.7 | 150.6 | 166.2 |
| 1928 | 143.1 | 136.8 | 147.3 | 161.5 | 169.7 | 159.8 | 152.8 | 168.3 |
| 1929 | 140.8 | 131.4 | 146.9 | 160.2 | 174.8 | 157.2 | 149.8 | 165.9 |
| 1930 | 123.5 | 108.5 | 133.6 | 145.9 | 154.2 | 144.1 | 134.4 | 155.9 |
| 1931 | 102.5 | 84.8 | 114.9 | 121.1 | 122.7 | 120.6 | 107.5 | 136.9 |

*a* Computed by the National Bureau of Economic Research from data collected by the United States Bureau of Labor Statistics. These are geometric averages of relative prices, unweighted, except that prices of important commodities have been represented by more than one series (see Appendix II). See p. 589 for a statement giving the number of price series included in each commodity group.

## Index Numbers of Wholesale Prices

| Year | Goods entering into capital equipment | | | Articles of human consumption | | | Producers' goods destined for human consumption | | |
|---|---|---|---|---|---|---|---|---|---|
| | Total | Raw | Processed | Total | Raw | Processed | Total | Foods | Non-foods |
| 1891 | 100.0 | 100.0 | 100.0 | 100.0 | 100.0 | 100.0 | 100.0 | 100.0 | 100.0 |
| 1892 | 95.4 | 95.1 | 95.4 | 94.8 | 91.7 | 95.8 | 94.5 | 90.4 | 97.6 |
| 1893 | 91.3 | 87.6 | 92.3 | 95.2 | 92.2 | 96.2 | 94.7 | 93.5 | 95.5 |
| 1894 | 82.8 | 77.8 | 84.1 | 86.1 | 82.0 | 87.4 | 83.7 | 83.1 | 84.2 |
| 1895 | 82.8 | 78.2 | 84.0 | 83.8 | 79.7 | 85.1 | 82.5 | 76.0 | 87.6 |
| 1896 | 83.3 | 77.9 | 84.7 | 78.9 | 70.7 | 81.6 | 76.4 | 66.6 | 84.6 |
| 1897 | 79.2 | 76.9 | 79.8 | 80.0 | 76.4 | 81.2 | 80.0 | 71.1 | 87.3 |
| 1898 | 81.8 | 77.9 | 82.8 | 83.7 | 85.0 | 83.3 | 87.0 | 80.0 | 92.5 |
| 1899 | 99.5 | 106.6 | 97.7 | 86.9 | 88.8 | 86.3 | 91.0 | 82.6 | 97.8 |
| 1900 | 107.3 | 113.3 | 105.8 | 94.4 | 94.5 | 94.4 | 98.7 | 89.5 | 106.1 |
| 1901 | 102.1 | 104.2 | 101.5 | 94.0 | 97.1 | 93.0 | 96.5 | 93.7 | 98.7 |
| 1902 | 107.4 | 121.5 | 104.0 | 97.3 | 102.3 | 95.9 | 101.5 | 101.3 | 101.7 |
| 1902 | 100.0 | 100.0 | 100.0 | 100.0 | 100.0 | 100.0 | 100.0 | 100.0 | 100.0 |
| 1903 | 101.6 | 103.0 | 101.3 | 100.1 | 99.3 | 100.4 | 98.7 | 93.0 | 103.4 |
| 1904 | 95.5 | 87.1 | 97.6 | 101.5 | 103.5 | 101.0 | 100.1 | 95.6 | 103.7 |
| 1905 | 102.7 | 95.2 | 104.5 | 102.2 | 102.9 | 102.0 | 100.1 | 95.1 | 104.1 |
| 1906 | 112.2 | 107.7 | 113.3 | 105.9 | 102.8 | 106.9 | 101.4 | 95.3 | 106.4 |
| 1907 | 117.3 | 113.4 | 118.3 | 111.7 | 109.4 | 112.4 | 108.7 | 107.7 | 109.4 |
| 1908 | 101.8 | 91.3 | 104.5 | 107.4 | 105.6 | 107.9 | 103.5 | 104.3 | 102.8 |
| 1909 | 102.6 | 91.3 | 105.5 | 110.6 | 114.5 | 109.5 | 111.0 | 113.1 | 109.4 |
| 1910 | 108.4 | 92.7 | 112.6 | 114.2 | 117.7 | 113.2 | 115.1 | 120.5 | 111.0 |
| 1911 | 103.0 | 94.3 | 105.2 | 111.5 | 117.9 | 109.7 | 110.6 | 118.1 | 105.1 |
| 1912 | 106.0 | 99.6 | 107.6 | 115.5 | 126.5 | 112.4 | 114.7 | 126.4 | 106.3 |
| 1913 | 108.0 | 100.6 | 109.9 | 114.7 | 116.4 | 114.2 | 112.1 | 115.3 | 109.7 |
| 1913 | 100.0 | 100.0 | 100.0 | 100.0 | 100.0 | 100.0 | 100.0 | 100.0 | 100.0 |
| 1914 | 93.2 | 93.1 | 93.2 | 100.2 | 100.2 | 100.2 | 99.6 | 103.3 | 97.0 |
| 1915 | 100.6 | 110.3 | 98.3 | 103.6 | 102.6 | 104.0 | 108.2 | 110.4 | 106.6 |
| 1916 | 135.8 | 144.6 | 133.4 | 126.4 | 123.6 | 127.7 | 141.5 | 124.8 | 154.2 |
| 1917 | 175.9 | 186.1 | 172.1 | 169.3 | 170.7 | 168.3 | 185.2 | 172.2 | 194.7 |
| 1918 | 189.6 | 184.7 | 190.5 | 198.8 | 190.2 | 202.9 | 210.4 | 196.7 | 220.2 |
| 1919 | 190.9 | 161.5 | 199.8 | 209.4 | 207.9 | 209.9 | 211.9 | 218.3 | 207.4 |
| 1920 | 237.2 | 199.6 | 248.7 | 224.1 | 202.6 | 235.3 | 218.6 | 205.1 | 228.1 |
| 1921 | 165.5 | 135.5 | 174.9 | 144.4 | 121.8 | 156.9 | 122.9 | 117.2 | 126.7 |
| 1922 | 158.7 | 137.3 | 165.1 | 143.9 | 131.8 | 150.0 | 130.3 | 122.0 | 136.3 |
| 1923 | 174.3 | 148.5 | 181.9 | 149.0 | 139.1 | 154.0 | 138.2 | 127.9 | 145.7 |
| 1924 | 164.2 | 137.6 | 172.4 | 149.2 | 141.4 | 152.9 | 137.4 | 134.0 | 139.7 |
| 1925 | 163.9 | 142.5 | 170.2 | 158.0 | 156.2 | 158.9 | 143.6 | 144.6 | 142.8 |
| 1926 | 161.8 | 143.1 | 167.2 | 149.9 | 143.7 | 152.9 | 132.1 | 135.5 | 129.7 |
| 1927 | 154.2 | 137.5 | 159.0 | 146.2 | 140.8 | 148.6 | 129.9 | 137.1 | 125.0 |
| 1928 | 152.8 | 133.3 | 158.4 | 149.8 | 147.4 | 150.8 | 135.1 | 146.3 | 127.6 |
| 1929 | 154.0 | 133.9 | 160.0 | 146.0 | 142.7 | 147.7 | 128.8 | 140.8 | 121.1 |
| 1930 | 141.4 | 123.3 | 146.7 | 128.3 | 115.9 | 134.6 | 107.1 | 115.9 | 101.6 |
| 1931 | 125.9 | 110.6 | 130.3 | 102.8 | 87.1 | 111.3 | 81.6 | 86.2 | 78.6 |

# APPENDIX III

### Index Numbers of Wholesale Prices

| Year | Farm crops | | | Animal products | | | Forest products | | |
|---|---|---|---|---|---|---|---|---|---|
| | Total | Raw | Processed | Total | Raw | Processed | Total | Raw | Processed |
| 1891 | 100.0 | 100.0 | 100.0 | 100.0 | 100.0 | 100.0 | 100.0 | | 100.0 |
| 1892 | 91.8 | 85.6 | 93.8 | 99.4 | 99.9 | 99.3 | 96.4 | | 97.1 |
| 1893 | 90.9 | 84.4 | 93.0 | 102.5 | 101.1 | 103.1 | 94.5 | | 94.7 |
| 1894 | 84.2 | 80.0 | 85.5 | 87.8 | 81.0 | 90.6 | 87.9 | | 88.1 |
| 1895 | 80.9 | 72.1 | 83.8 | 85.2 | 83.9 | 85.6 | 88.1 | | 87.9 |
| 1896 | 75.1 | 58.8 | 81.0 | 78.1 | 75.6 | 79.0 | 87.2 | | 86.6 |
| 1897 | 76.0 | 64.8 | 79.8 | 81.8 | 84.0 | 81.0 | 84.9 | | 84.0 |
| 1898 | 79.4 | 75.0 | 80.9 | 87.6 | 91.2 | 86.3 | 85.6 | | 84.3 |
| 1899 | 81.9 | 76.9 | 83.5 | 92.2 | 98.4 | 90.0 | 94.8 | | 93.5 |
| 1900 | 90.4 | 84.3 | 92.4 | 98.7 | 103.0 | 97.1 | 107.0 | | 106.3 |
| 1901 | 90.3 | 91.3 | 90.0 | 96.8 | 98.0 | 96.4 | 100.8 | | 100.6 |
| 1902 | 92.4 | 93.7 | 92.0 | 105.4 | 108.9 | 104.1 | 106.4 | | 107.1 |
| 1902 | 100.0 | 100.0 | 100.0 | 100.0 | 100.0 | 100.0 | 100.0 | | 100.0 |
| 1903 | 99.0 | 98.2 | 99.3 | 97.8 | 94.8 | 98.8 | 106.7 | | 105.9 |
| 1904 | 103.4 | 106.6 | 102.5 | 94.9 | 93.8 | 95.3 | 109.9 | | 108.3 |
| 1905 | 100.9 | 100.5 | 101.0 | 102.2 | 101.6 | 102.4 | 114.0 | | 111.8 |
| 1906 | 104.4 | 98.2 | 106.3 | 109.1 | 105.5 | 110.3 | 123.4 | | 121.6 |
| 1907 | 113.6 | 108.4 | 115.2 | 112.4 | 110.1 | 113.2 | 130.0 | | 129.2 |
| 1908 | 108.1 | 106.3 | 108.7 | 107.3 | 101.5 | 109.4 | 119.0 | | 119.0 |
| 1909 | 109.6 | 112.3 | 108.8 | 115.8 | 112.8 | 116.8 | 122.9 | | 119.9 |
| 1910 | 114.8 | 117.3 | 114.0 | 119.8 | 115.1 | 121.5 | 131.9 | | 127.7 |
| 1911 | 118.1 | 136.3 | 113.2 | 108.4 | 101.4 | 110.8 | 129.6 | | 128.6 |
| 1912 | 119.1 | 143.2 | 112.7 | 117.2 | 113.6 | 118.4 | 129.3 | | 128.6 |
| 1913 | 113.8 | 117.5 | 112.7 | 121.5 | 117.4 | 122.9 | 128.9 | | 129.8 |
| 1913 | 100.0 | 100.0 | 100.0 | 100.0 | 100.0 | 100.0 | 100.0 | 100.0 | 100.0 |
| 1914 | 101.1 | 101.7 | 100.9 | 100.0 | 100.5 | 99.5 | 95.4 | 85.1 | 96.4 |
| 1915 | 103.8 | 105.3 | 103.2 | 102.0 | 104.7 | 100.2 | 92.9 | 78.5 | 94.3 |
| 1916 | 122.9 | 127.2 | 120.6 | 121.2 | 122.1 | 120.5 | 112.3 | 107.8 | 112.8 |
| 1917 | 178.6 | 182.2 | 176.5 | 165.2 | 169.7 | 162.2 | 137.8 | 128.9 | 138.6 |
| 1918 | 211.2 | 197.7 | 220.6 | 197.7 | 199.6 | 196.3 | 156.2 | 102.9 | 163.2 |
| 1919 | 224.2 | 224.0 | 224.3 | 216.6 | 210.5 | 220.1 | 188.8 | 94.4 | 202.3 |
| 1920 | 237.5 | 225.0 | 245.8 | 213.1 | 188.7 | 229.7 | 267.2 | 124.5 | 288.2 |
| 1921 | 140.4 | 128.7 | 148.0 | 138.7 | 113.1 | 157.5 | 154.1 | 59.2 | 168.8 |
| 1922 | 142.1 | 135.5 | 146.4 | 142.9 | 131.3 | 150.5 | 156.2 | 52.8 | 172.9 |
| 1923 | 148.3 | 142.0 | 152.6 | 148.6 | 139.1 | 155.5 | 175.5 | 72.9 | 191.0 |
| 1924 | 154.3 | 152.4 | 155.6 | 145.9 | 135.7 | 153.1 | 156.5 | 60.2 | 171.1 |
| 1925 | 164.9 | 169.9 | 162.0 | 158.9 | 145.9 | 167.9 | 159.7 | 100.6 | 168.0 |
| 1926 | 152.0 | 154.6 | 150.6 | 150.6 | 133.3 | 162.3 | 152.0 | 83.2 | 161.6 |
| 1927 | 147.0 | 149.9 | 145.2 | 151.7 | 135.9 | 162.3 | 142.2 | 70.4 | 152.5 |
| 1928 | 149.5 | 153.9 | 147.1 | 161.0 | 150.5 | 168.2 | 137.8 | 53.4 | 150.6 |
| 1929 | 145.6 | 151.2 | 142.3 | 155.7 | 142.3 | 164.8 | 136.3 | 51.6 | 149.1 |
| 1930 | 126.4 | 125.0 | 127.3 | 132.1 | 110.0 | 147.4 | 120.2 | 39.1 | 133.1 |
| 1931 | 98.6 | 92.9 | 102.4 | 103.2 | 80.3 | 119.8 | 99.8 | 27.2 | 112.3 |

INDEX NUMBERS OF WHOLESALE PRICES

| Year | Mineral products | | | Foods | | | Non-foods | | |
|---|---|---|---|---|---|---|---|---|---|
| | Total | Raw | Processed | Total | Raw | Processed | Total | Raw | Processed |
| 1891 | 100.0 | 100.0 | 100.0 | 100.0 | 100.0 | 100.0 | 100.0 | 100.0 | 100.0 |
| 1892 | 95.3 | 94.8 | 95.4 | 91.4 | 89.1 | 92.7 | 96.6 | 95.7 | 96.7 |
| 1893 | 91.9 | 90.4 | 92.4 | 94.7 | 90.6 | 97.0 | 93.8 | 91.3 | 94.3 |
| 1894 | 83.3 | 81.4 | 84.0 | 85.1 | 81.8 | 86.9 | 85.1 | 80.1 | 86.2 |
| 1895 | 83.3 | 82.6 | 83.5 | 81.3 | 76.3 | 84.1 | 84.4 | 82.0 | 84.9 |
| 1896 | 84.5 | 84.3 | 84.5 | 71.6 | 62.5 | 77.0 | 84.2 | 82.7 | 84.5 |
| 1897 | 80.6 | 82.0 | 80.1 | 75.2 | 69.1 | 78.8 | 81.8 | 83.8 | 81.4 |
| 1898 | 83.1 | 84.0 | 82.8 | 82.2 | 79.3 | 83.8 | 83.5 | 86.6 | 82.9 |
| 1899 | 97.6 | 105.7 | 94.8 | 84.9 | 81.8 | 86.6 | 93.0 | 104.7 | 90.7 |
| 1900 | 103.7 | 111.1 | 101.1 | 91.3 | 87.7 | 93.3 | 101.2 | 110.5 | 99.3 |
| 1901 | 101.4 | 107.1 | 99.3 | 93.9 | 94.1 | 93.8 | 97.3 | 103.5 | 96.1 |
| 1902 | 104.4 | 120.8 | 98.9 | 98.9 | 100.0 | 98.4 | 100.7 | 113.7 | 98.2 |
| | | | | | | | | | |
| 1902 | 100.0 | 100.0 | 100.0 | 100.0 | 100.0 | 100.0 | 100.0 | 100.0 | 100.0 |
| 1903 | 101.9 | 105.2 | 100.7 | 95.1 | 93.8 | 95.7 | 103.0 | 106.4 | 102.3 |
| 1904 | 95.5 | 93.4 | 96.2 | 96.5 | 99.7 | 94.9 | 101.1 | 98.1 | 101.7 |
| 1905 | 99.9 | 97.6 | 100.7 | 97.4 | 97.7 | 97.2 | 104.5 | 103.6 | 104.7 |
| 1906 | 105.6 | 106.1 | 105.5 | 99.4 | 95.9 | 101.3 | 111.5 | 111.9 | 111.4 |
| 1907 | 109.0 | 110.9 | 108.4 | 105.4 | 104.0 | 106.0 | 116.8 | 116.4 | 116.9 |
| 1908 | 97.5 | 96.5 | 97.9 | 104.8 | 102.7 | 106.0 | 106.0 | 100.6 | 107.1 |
| 1909 | 97.3 | 97.0 | 97.5 | 109.3 | 111.7 | 108.1 | 107.7 | 104.5 | 108.3 |
| 1910 | 99.1 | 96.6 | 100.0 | 114.1 | 117.3 | 112.5 | 111.8 | 104.7 | 113.2 |
| 1911 | 93.2 | 96.1 | 92.2 | 113.5 | 122.4 | 109.1 | 107.1 | 101.9 | 108.1 |
| 1912 | 97.4 | 101.5 | 96.0 | 120.6 | 134.4 | 114.0 | 109.3 | 106.4 | 109.9 |
| 1913 | 99.9 | 103.5 | 98.7 | 114.5 | 115.7 | 113.8 | 112.0 | 108.8 | 112.6 |
| | | | | | | | | | |
| 1913 | 100.0 | 100.0 | 100.0 | 100.0 | 100.0 | 100.0 | 100.0 | 100.0 | 100.0 |
| 1914 | 94.8 | 93.7 | 95.1 | 102.4 | 103.1 | 102.0 | 95.8 | 93.9 | 96.2 |
| 1915 | 105.3 | 105.5 | 105.2 | 104.2 | 104.3 | 104.2 | 101.9 | 104.0 | 101.3 |
| 1916 | 148.0 | 139.7 | 150.5 | 119.0 | 122.0 | 116.8 | 135.1 | 135.1 | 135.1 |
| 1917 | 181.7 | 177.0 | 183.0 | 166.5 | 168.3 | 165.4 | 173.7 | 180.8 | 171.3 |
| 1918 | 195.6 | 179.0 | 201.3 | 192.7 | 188.8 | 195.9 | 197.5 | 188.9 | 199.7 |
| 1919 | 184.0 | 165.2 | 190.5 | 209.9 | 210.9 | 209.4 | 199.8 | 180.8 | 205.3 |
| 1920 | 223.0 | 203.7 | 229.5 | 206.4 | 204.7 | 207.9 | 240.6 | 198.7 | 253.5 |
| 1921 | 168.7 | 148.1 | 175.9 | 135.9 | 126.7 | 143.9 | 159.1 | 122.8 | 171.0 |
| 1922 | 155.8 | 146.7 | 158.7 | 134.8 | 129.9 | 138.9 | 156.0 | 136.5 | 161.7 |
| 1923 | 164.3 | 154.5 | 167.5 | 136.3 | 133.0 | 139.0 | 168.4 | 149.9 | 173.7 |
| 1924 | 158.6 | 147.2 | 162.6 | 140.4 | 139.8 | 141.0 | 161.1 | 140.7 | 167.1 |
| 1925 | 156.9 | 151.1 | 158.7 | 156.4 | 157.1 | 156.1 | 161.4 | 148.1 | 165.2 |
| 1926 | 156.7 | 153.1 | 157.7 | 149.5 | 147.5 | 151.3 | 155.5 | 139.3 | 160.3 |
| 1927 | 148.7 | 145.2 | 149.8 | 147.2 | 145.4 | 149.0 | 149.1 | 134.3 | 153.4 |
| 1928 | 147.3 | 141.5 | 149.2 | 152.2 | 153.1 | 151.7 | 149.6 | 134.7 | 153.8 |
| 1929 | 149.1 | 142.4 | 151.1 | 149.8 | 152.7 | 148.0 | 147.7 | 128.8 | 153.4 |
| 1930 | 140.1 | 133.4 | 142.3 | 129.7 | 126.4 | 132.4 | 133.6 | 109.7 | 141.0 |
| 1931 | 126.8 | 121.3 | 128.5 | 100.3 | 94.7 | 105.0 | 114.8 | 90.0 | 122.9 |

# APPENDIX III

There are some variations in the numbers of price series included in the several commodity groups represented in the above table. Disregarding minor changes from year to year, the following summary indicates the size of the sample on which each group index number is based, in each of four major periods:

| Commodity group | Number of price series included | | | |
|---|---|---|---|---|
| | 1891-1902 | 1902-1913 | 1913-1926 | 1926-1931 |
| All commodities .................. | 217 | 227 | 466 | 492 |
| Raw materials .................. | 49 | 49 | 136 | 142 |
| Manufactured goods ............. | 168 | 178 | 330 | 350 |
| Products originating on American farms | | | | |
|    Total ....................... | 111 | 118 | 226 | 235 |
|    Raw ......................... | 24 | 24 | 83 | 83 |
|    Processed ................... | 87 | 94 | 143 | 152 |
| Products other than those originating on American farms | | | | |
|    Total ....................... | 106 | 109 | 240 | 257 |
|    Raw ......................... | 25 | 25 | 53 | 59 |
|    Processed ................... | 81 | 84 | 187 | 198 |
| Producers' goods | | | | |
|    Total ....................... | 111 | 115 | 284 | 292 |
|    Raw ......................... | 38 | 38 | 105 | 108 |
|    Processed ................... | 73 | 77 | 179 | 184 |
| Consumers' goods | | | | |
|    Total ....................... | 106 | 112 | 182 | 200 |
|    Raw ......................... | 11 | 11 | 31 | 34 |
|    Processed ................... | 95 | 101 | 151 | 166 |
|      Foods ................... | 39 | 39 | 80 | 86 |
|      Non-foods ............... | 56 | 62 | 71 | 80 |
| Goods entering into capital equipment | | | | |
|    Total ....................... | 64 | 67 | 152 | 160 |
|    Raw ......................... | 13 | 13 | 32 | 35 |
|    Processed ................... | 51 | 54 | 120 | 125 |
| Articles of human consumption | | | | |
|    Total ....................... | 153 | 160 | 314 | 332 |
|    Raw ......................... | 36 | 36 | 104 | 107 |
|    Processed ................... | 117 | 124 | 210 | 225 |
| Producers' goods destined for human consumption | | | | |
|    Total ....................... | 47 | 48 | 132 | 132 |
|    Foods ....................... | 20 | 21 | 54 | 54 |
|    Non-foods ................... | 27 | 27 | 78 | 78 |

| Commodity group | Number of price series included ||||
|---|---|---|---|---|
| | 1891-1902 | 1902-1913 | 1913-1926 | 1926-1931 |
| Farm crops | | | | |
| Total | 72 | 74 | 124 | 124 |
| Raw | 17 | 17 | 47 | 47 |
| Processed | 55 | 57 | 77 | 77 |
| Animal products | | | | |
| Total | 47 | 52 | 122 | 131 |
| Raw | 13 | 13 | 47 | 47 |
| Processed | 34 | 39 | 75 | 84 |
| Forest products | | | | |
| Total | 22 | 22 | 53 | 55 |
| Raw | — | — | 4 | 4 |
| Processed | 21 | 21 | 49 | 51 |
| Mineral products | | | | |
| Total | 67 | 70 | 158 | 171 |
| Raw | 18 | 18 | 38 | 44 |
| Processed | 49 | 52 | 120 | 127 |
| Foods | | | | |
| Total | 66 | 67 | 161 | 167 |
| Raw | 23 | 23 | 71 | 71 |
| Processed | 43 | 44 | 90 | 96 |
| Non-foods | | | | |
| Total | 151 | 160 | 305 | 325 |
| Raw | 26 | 26 | 65 | 71 |
| Processed | 125 | 134 | 240 | 254 |

# APPENDIX IV

## SECTION I

LIST OF COMMODITIES INCLUDED IN INDEX NUMBERS OF PHYSICAL VOLUME OF MANUFACTURING PRODUCTION, 1899-1914

Based on Census of Manufactures

*Butter, Cheese, and Condensed Milk*
Butter
Cheese [1]
Condensed and evaporated milk
Casein dried from skimmed milk
Cream sold
Skimmed milk sold

*Canning and Preserving: Fruits and Vegetables; Pickles, Preserves and Sauces*
Canned vegetables and soups [2]
Canned fruits [2]
Dried fruits [1]

*Flour-mill and Gristmill Products*
Wheat flour
Rye flour and rye graham
Corn meal and corn flour
Buckwheat flour
Bran and middlings, feed and offal
Hominy and grits
Barley meal

*Ice, Manufactured*
Ice

*Slaughtering and Meat Packing*
Fresh meat:
  Beef
  Veal
  Mutton and lamb
  Pork
  Edible offal and all other fresh meat
Cured meat:
  Beef, pickled and other cured
  Pork, pickled and other cured
Sausage and sausage casings

*Slaughtering and Meat-Packing—cont.*
Lard, oils, and fats:
  Lard, and lard compounds and substitutes [1]
  Oleo oil
  Other oils [3]
Cattle hides and calfskins
Wool
Fertilizers and fertilizer materials [1]

*Rice, Cleaning and Polishing*
Clean rice
Polish
Bran

*Sugar, Beet*
Sugar, beet
Molasses

*Carpets and Rugs, other than Rag*
Axminster and Moquette
Wilton and tapestry velvet
Brussels
Tapestry Brussels
Ingrain carpet
Ingrain art squares
Smyrna rugs
Other rugs [4]

*Cordage and Twine*
Rope and binder twine, exclusive of cotton rope (1899 and 1914 only)
Rope, cable, and cordage:
  Manila hemp (1909 and 1914 only)
  Sisal and Henequen (1909 and 1914 only)
  Cotton (1899, 1909 and 1914 only)

*Cordage and Twine*
  Rope, cable, and cordage—*cont.*
    Jute and all other (1909 and 1914 only)
  Twine, binder:
    All or chiefly manila hemp (1909 and 1914 only)
    All other [1] (1909 and 1914 only)
  Twine, other than binder (1899, 1909 and 1914 only):
    Cotton
    Jute
    Hemp
    Flax
    Other, including mixed [1]

*Cotton Goods*
  Woven goods:
    Unbleached and bleached sheetings, shirtings and muslins
    Ducks
    Ginghams
    Fancy weaves
    Napped fabrics
    Velvets, corduroys, plushes, etc.[4]
    Bags and bagging
    Mosquito netting and similar fabrics [4]
    Tapestries
    Other woven goods [4]
  Yarns manufactured for sale
  Thread
  Twine
  Cotton waste

*Hats, Fur-Felt*
  Finished hats
  Fur-felt hat bodies and hats in the rough

*Hats, Wool-Felt*
  Finished hats
  Wool-felt hat bodies and hats in the rough

*Jute and Linen Goods* (1899, 1909 and 1914 only)
  Yarns for sale
  Linen thread
  Linen fabrics
  Bags and bagging
  Jute carpets and rugs

*Hosiery and Knit Goods*
  Hosiery

*Hosiery and Knit Goods—cont.*
  Shirts and drawers
  Combination suits
  Cardigan jackets, sweaters, etc.[5]
  Shawls
  Hoods, scarfs, etc.[5]
  Gloves and mittens
  Leggings
  Boot and shoe linings
  Jersey cloth and stockinette
  Astrakhan and similar fabrics [4]
  Yarns for sale

*Silk Goods*
  Broad silks
  Velvets
  Plushes
  Upholstery and tapestries [6]
  Machine twist
  Sewing and embroidery, fringe and floss silks [1]
  Organzine, and tram, for sale [1]
  Spun silk, for sale

*Woolen and Worsted Goods*
  All-wool woven goods:
    Wool cloths, woolen overcoatings, dress-goods, etc.[4]
    Worsted coatings, overcoatings, dress-goods, etc.[4]
    Flannels for underwear
    Blankets
    All other [4]
  Union, or cotton mixed, woven goods
    Flannels for underwear
    Unions, tweeds, etc.[4]
    Blankets
    All other [4]
  Cotton warp woven goods
    Wool fillings, overcoatings, dress-goods, etc.[4]
    Worsted fillings, cassimeres, dress-goods, etc.[4]
    Linings, Italian cloths, and lastings [4]
    Horse blankets
    Carriage robes
    All others [4]
  Upholstery goods and sundries—woolens, worsted and mohair [4]
  Yarns for sale:
    Woolen
    Worsted

*Woolen and Worsted Goods*
  Yarns for sale—*cont.*
    Woolen, union or merino
    Worsted, union or merino
    All other [1]
  Worsted tops and slubbing
  Noils
  Waste

*Lumber and Timber Products*
  Lumber, softwoods and hardwoods [7]

*Turpentine and Rosin*
  Turpentine
  Rosin

*Paper and Wood Pulp*
  Newsprint
  Hanging papers
  Book paper
  Cover paper
  Fine paper
  Wrapping paper
  Boards, cardboard, etc.[1]
  Tissue paper
  Blotting paper
  Building papers
  All other paper [1]
  Wood pulp for sale [1]

*Explosives*
  Dynamite
  Nitroglycerin for sale
  Blasting and black gunpowder
  Other explosives [1]

*Fertilizers*
  Fertilizers complete and ammoniated
  Superphosphates, including concentrated phosphates, for sale
  Other fertilizers [1]

*Paint and Varnish*
  Colors (pigments) for sale [1]
  Paints in paste form [1]
  Mixed paints, ready for use [3]
  Water paints and kalsomines, dry or in paste [1]
  Varnishes and Japans [3]
  Fillers:
    Liquid
    Putty

*Salt*
  Salt
  Bromine
  Calcium chloride (1909 and 1914 only)

*Wood Distillation, not including Turpentine and Rosin*
  Wood alcohol:
    Crude, for sale
    Refined, for sale
  Acetate of lime, for sale
  Charcoal
  Turpentine (1904, 1909, and 1914 only)
  Tar, for sale (1909 and 1914 only)

*Coke, not including Gas-House Coke*
  Coke
  Gas
  Tar
  Ammonia and sulphate

*Gas, Manufactured, Illuminating and Heating*
  Gas for sale
  Coke for sale (except 1899)
  Tar for sale (except 1899)
  Ammonia liquors (1909 and 1914 only)

*Petroleum, Refining*
  Naphthas and lighter products (including gasoline)
  Illuminating oils
  Fuel oils
  Lubricating oils
  Residuum or tar, including liquid asphaltic road oils
  Greases
  Paraffin wax

*Boots and Shoes, other than Rubber* (1899, 1904 and 1914 only)
  Boots and shoes [5]
  Slippers
  Other footwear

*Gloves and Mittens, Leather*
  Gloves, mittens and gauntlets [5]

*Iron and Steel: Blast Furnaces*
  Pig iron, including spiegeleisen, ferro-alloys, etc.[1]

*Iron and Steel: Steel Works and Rolling Mills*
  Unrolled steel (for sale or for transfer to other works of same company)
  Ingots
  Direct steel castings

594

*Iron and Steel: Steel Works and Rolling Mills—cont.*
Partly finished rolled products (for sale or for transfer to other works of same company)
  Blooms, billets, slabs, bars, etc.[1]
  Muck and scrap bar
Finished rolled products and forgings
  Rails (open-hearth and Bessemer)
  Structural shapes (not including plates used for making girders)
  Bars, spike and chain rods, bolt and nut rods, horseshoe bars and strips [1]
  Wire rods
  Plates or sheets, not elsewhere specified
  Black plates (or sheets) for tinning
  Skelp, flue, pipes, hoops, bands, and cotton ties
  Nail and tack plate
  Axles, rolled or forged
  Armor plates, gun forgings and ordnance
  Finished products, not elsewhere specified [1]

*Automobiles, including Bodies and Parts*
  Automobiles, all (1899 and 1914 only)
  Touring cars, roadsters, runabouts, closed cars, and all other passenger cars (1904, 1909 and 1914 only)
  Government, municipal, etc., cars (1904, 1909 and 1914 only)
  Business vehicles (merchandise) (1904, 1909 and 1914 only)
    Delivery wagons
    Trucks
    All other

*Motorcycles, Bicycles, and Parts*
  Motorcycles
  Bicycles

*Musical Instruments: Organs*
  Pipe organs
  Reed organs

*Musical Instruments: Pianos*
  Upright pianos
  Grand pianos

[1] Combined on basis of weight.
[2] Combined on basis of number of cases.
[3] Combined on basis of number of gallons.
[4] Combined on basis of area.
[5] Combined on basis of number.
[6] Combined on basis of length.
[7] Combined on basis of length, board measure.

# SECTION 2

### List of Commodities Included in Index Numbers of Physical Volume of Manufacturing Production, 1914-1929

Based on Census of Manufactures

*Butter and Cheese*
  Butter, creamery
  Cheese, all kinds [1]
  Casein, dried (1914-1927 only)
  Whey butter (1927-1929 only)

*Canning and Preserving: Fish, Crabs, Shrimps, Oysters, and Clams*
  Canned fish, oysters, etc.[2]
  Cured fish (smoked, dried, salted and pickled, and boneless)[1]

*Canning and Preserving: Fruits and Vegetables; Pickles, Jellies, Preserves, and Sauces*
Canned vegetables and soups [3]
Canned fruits [3]
Dried fruits [1]

*Chocolate and Cocoa Products (1923-1929 only)*
Chocolate (except coatings):
  Unsweetened
  Sweet
  Milk
Chocolate coatings
Cocoa, powdered:
  In cans of 1 lb. or less
  In cans of more than 1 lb.
  In barrels and drums
Cocoa butter

*Condensed and Evaporated Milk*
Condensed and evaporated milk and buttermilk [1] (1914-1927 only)
Condensed milk (1927-1929 only)
Evaporated milk (1927-1929 only)
Buttermilk, condensed and evaporated (1927-1929 only)
Powdered whole milk, cream, and skim milk; and dried and powdered buttermilk [1] (1914-1927 only)
Powdered milk, cream and skim milk (1927-1929 only)
Dried and powdered buttermilk (1927-1929 only)
Ice-cream mix (1927-1929 only)
Sterilized milk (canned) (1927-1929 only)
Sugar of milk (crude) (1927-1929 only)
Dried casein (1927-1929 only)

*Corn Syrup, Corn Oil, and Starch (1923-1929 only)*
Corn syrup and mixtures of corn syrup and other syrups [1] (1923-1927 only)
Corn syrup, unmixed (1927-1929 only)
Mixtures of corn and other syrups (1927-1929 only)
Corn sugar

*Corn Syrup, Corn Oil, and Starch (1923-1929 only)—cont.*
Corn oil, crude and refined [1] (1923-1927 only)
Corn oil, crude (1927-1929 only)
Corn oil, refined (1927-1929 only)
Starch, total
Corn-oil cake and meal
Stock feed

*Flour and Other Grain-Mill Products*
Wheat flour
Rye flour
Corn meal and corn flour
Buckwheat flour
Bran and middlings, feed and offal (1914-1927 only)
Feed, screenings, etc. (1927-1929 only)
Bran and middlings (1927-1929 only)

*Ice, Manufactured*
Ice

*Slaughtering and Meat Packing, Wholesale*
Fresh meat:
  Beef
  Veal
  Mutton and lamb
  Pork
  Other fresh meat and edible offal
Cured meat (pickled and other cured):
  Beef
  Pork, smoked and not smoked, and cooked hams
Canned meat and canned sausage
Sausage (not canned), meat puddings, headcheese, scrapple, etc., and sausage casings
Lard
Hides, skins and pelts:
  Cattle hides
  Calfskins
  Wool

*Rice Cleaning and Polishing*
Clean rice
Polish
Bran

*Sugar, Beet*
Sugar, beet
Molasses

*Sugar, Cane, not including Products of Refineries*
  Sugar
  Molasses, other than blackstrap
  Syrup

*Sugar Refining, Cane*
  Refined sugar, total (1914-1927 only)
  Refined sugar, hard (1927-1929 only)
  Refined sugar, soft and brown (1927-1929 only)
  Syrup, edible (1927-1929 only)
  Blackstrap and non-edible syrup (1927-1929 only)
  Refiners' syrup and blackstrap (1914-1927 only)

*Asphalted-Felt-Base Floor Coverings (1923-1929 only)*
  Piece goods [4]
  Rugs [4]

*Carpets and Rugs, Wool, other than Rag*
  Carpets
    Axminster
    Wilton
    Brussels
    Tapestry Brussels
    Tapestry velvet
    Ingrain
    Other [4]
  Rugs made of sewed strips
    Axminster
    Wilton
    Other [4]
  Rugs woven whole
    Axminster
    Wilton
    Tapestry velvet
    Tapestry Brussels
    Smyrna
    Chenille
    Wool and paper fiber
    Other [4]

*Cordage and Twine*
  Rope, cable and cordage
    Manila hemp
    Henequen
    Sisal
    Cotton (1919-1927 only)
    Other
  Twine
    Binder

*Cordage and Twine*
  Twine—*cont.*
    Other than binder (1921, 1927 only)
      Cotton (except 1921)
      Flax (except 1921-1925)
      Hemp (except 1921-1925)
      Jute (except 1921-1925)
      All other (except 1921)

*Cotton Goods*
  Sheetings
  Print cloth, voiles, cheese cloth, nainsooks, etc.[4] (1914, 1927 only)
    Print cloth (except 1914)
    Voiles (except 1914 and 1919)
    Tobacco, cheese, butter, bandage cloth (except 1914)
    Lawns, nainsooks, etc. (except 1914)
  Duck, tire, ounce, and numbered (1914, 1927 only)
    Tire cord and other fabrics (except 1914)
    Numbered duck (except 1914)
    Tire duck (except 1914)
    Ounce duck (except 1914)
  Napped fabrics
  Blankets (except 1914)
  Twills and sateens
  Denims and ticks [4] (1914, 1927 only)
    Denims (except 1914)
    Ticks (except 1914)
  Plushes, velvets, corduroys [4] (1914, 1927 only)
    Plushes, velvets, velveteens (except 1914)
    Corduroys (except 1914)
  Drills
  Towels, towelings, washcloths, etc. (except 1914)
  Ginghams
  Bedspreads (except 1914)
  Cottonades, cotton worsted (except 1914)
  Cotton table damask (except 1914)
  Sheet and pillow cases (except 1914)
  Osnaburgs (except 1914 and 1919)
  Pillow tubing
  Mosquito netting and tarlatan
  Cotton tapestries
  Shirtings [4] (1914, 1927 only)
    Entirely cotton (except 1914)

*Cotton Goods*
  Shirtings—*cont.*
    Silk and rayon striped (except 1914 and 1925)
    Silk striped (1925, 1927 only)
    Rayon striped (1925, 1927 only)
  Other woven goods
  Cotton yarns, for sale
  Thread
  Twine
  Cotton waste for sale
  Batting, wadding, and mattress felts (except 1914)
  Cotton card laps, roping, sliver, and rovings (except 1914)

*Felt Goods, Wool or Hair (1923-1927 only)*
  Felt cloths
  Trimming and lining felts, polishing felts, etc.[1]

*Hats, Fur-Felt*
  Finished hats (1914-1927 only)
    Made complete in plant (1927-1929 only)
    Finished from purchased bodies (1927-1929 only)
  Fur-felt hat bodies and hats in the rough (1914-1927 only)
  Hat bodies, for sale as such (1927-1929 only)

*Hats, Wool-Felt*
  Wool-felt hats (1914-1927)
    Finished hats (1927-1929)
  Wool-felt hat bodies and hats in the rough (1914-1927)
  Hat bodies, for sale as such (1927-1929 only)

*Jute and Linen Goods*
  Yarns for sale (principally jute yarns)
  Linen thread
  Linen woven goods
  Jute bagging for baling cotton
  "Other woven goods"

*Knit Goods*
  Hosiery (except infants' and athletic and golf hose) [5]
  Shirts and drawers [6]
  Union suits
  Sweaters, sweater coats, jerseys, etc.

*Knit Goods—cont.*
  Bathing suits
  Scarfs and shawls
  Headwear (except infants')
  Gloves, all types
  Cotton yarns for sale (except 1929)
  Cotton waste for sale (except 1929)

*Lace Goods, Cotton*
  Nottingham lace curtains
  Nottingham lace-curtain nets

*Linoleum and Asphalted-Felt-Base Floor Coverings (1914-1923, 1927 only)*
  Linoleum, total (1914 only)
  Linoleum (1919-1923)
  Floor coverings (1919-1923)

*Linoleum (1923-1929 only)*
  Linoleum piece goods:
    Plain
    Printed
    Inlaid
    Cork carpet
  Linoleum, rugs

*Oilcloth*
  Oilcloth, enameled
  Oilcloth, table, wall, and shelf (1914-1927)
    Table and shelf (1927-1929 only)
    Wall (1927-1929 only)

*Silk Manufactures*
  Broad silks:
    All-silk
    Silk-mixed
  Velvets
  Plushes
  Upholstery goods and tapestries
  Threads and yarns for sale:
    Organzine
    Tram
    Crepe twist (except 1914)
    Spun silk
    Machine twist
    Sewing silk, embroidery, fringe, floss, etc.

*Woolen Goods*
  Woven goods, total (1927-1929 only)
    Suitings
      All wool woolen (1914-1927)
      All wool worsted (1914-1927)

*Woolen Goods*
  Woven Goods
    Suitings—*cont.*
      Wool and cotton mixed (1914-1927)
      All other (1914-1927)
      Domett flannels (1914-1927)
      Blankets cotton-mixed (1914-1927)
      Satinets and linseys (1914-1923, 1927 only)
      Upholstery materials (1923-1927)
      All other woven goods (1914-1927)
    Yarns for sale:
      All wool (1914, 1919, 1927 only)
      All wool woolen (except 1914-1919)
      All wool worsted (except 1914-1919)
      Wool and cotton mixed
      Mohair and similar yarns
      Noils and wool waste

*Wool Shoddy*
  Recovered wool fiber (including carbonized rags)

*Worsted Goods*
  Woven goods (total) (1927-1929 only)
    Suitings
      All wool woolen (1914-1927)
      All wool worsted (1914-1927)
      Wool and cotton mixed (1914-1927)
      All other (1914-1927)
    Upholstery materials (1923-1927 only)
    Other woven goods (1914-1927)
  Yarns for sale
    All wool woolen
    All wool worsted
    Wool and cotton mixed (1914-1927 only)
    All other
  Tops and slubbing
  Noils and wool waste

*Lumber and Timber Products*
  Softwoods
  Hardwoods

*Turpentine and Rosin*
  Turpentine
  Rosin

*Paper and Wood Pulp*
  Newsprint, standard
  Hanging papers
  Poster, novel, news-tablet, lining, etc.[1]
  Book paper (except body stock for coated paper)
  Cover paper
  Writing paper (fine)
  Wrapping paper
  Boards
  Tissue paper
  Absorbent paper
  Building papers
  All other paper [1]
  Wood pulp, for sale (except 1929)

*Bone Black, Carbon Black, and Lampblack (except 1914)*
  Carbon black
  Bone black
  Lampblack

*Explosives*
  Dynamite
  Permissible explosives
  Nitroglycerin (not consumed where produced)
  Blasting powder
  Gunpowder
  Smokeless powder (except 1914 and 1919)
  Fuse powder (except 1914 and 1919)
  All other explosives [1]

*Fertilizers*
  Fertilizers, complete, and ammoniated
  Superphosphates, including concentrated phosphates, for sale
  Fish scrap
  Potash superphosphates, bone meal, and other fertilizers [1] (1914-1927 only)
  Potash superphosphates (1927-1929 only)
  Bone meal (1927-1929 only)
  Other fertilizers (1927-1929 only)
  Sulphuric acid, for sale (except 1929)

*Oil, Cake, and Meal, Cottonseed*
  Oil
  Cake and meal
  Hulls
  Linters

*Oil, Cake, and Meal, Linseed (1923-1929 only)*
Oil
Cake and meal

*Paints and Varnishes*
Pigments (colors), for sale [1]
Paints in paste form
Mixed paints, ready for use
Water paints and kalsomines, dry and in paste form
Varnishes, japans and lacquers (including enamels) [7]
Fillers (except 1927-1929)
  Liquid
  Paste and dry [1]
Varnish stains (1927-1929 only)
Stains, other than varnish stains (1927-1929)
Putty
Bleached shellac

*Salt*
Salt
Bromine
Calcium chloride

*Soap*
Hard soaps, including granulated and powdered soap (1914-1927 only)
Hard soaps (1927-1929 only)
  Toilet
  Foot
  Soap chips
  Laundry white
  Laundry yellow
  Other hard soaps [1]
Granulated and powdered soap (1927-1929 only)
Soap powders (including cleansing and washing powders) (1927-1929 only)
Liquid soap (1927-1929 only)
Soft soap
Paste soap (1927-1929 only)
Special soap articles and soap base, for sale [1] (1927-1929 only)

*Tanning Materials, Natural Dyestuffs, Mordants and Assistants, and Sizes (1923-1929 only)*
Tanning materials (extracts: chestnut, oak, sumac, hemlock, quebracho) [1]

*Tanning Materials, etc.—cont.*
Natural dyestuffs [1]
Mordants [1] (except 1929)
Assistants [1]
Sizes [1]

*Wood Distillation and Charcoal Manufacture*
Methanol, crude, for sale
Methanol, refined
Acetate of lime
Rosin, wood
Charcoal, for sale
Tar, for sale
Turpentine, wood

*Coke, not including Gas-House Coke*
Coke, including screenings for sale [1]
Gas, for sale
Tar, for sale
Ammonia, $NH_3$ equivalent of all forms

*Gas, Manufactured, Illuminating and Heating*
Gas, for sale
Tar, for sale
Ammonium sulphate
Coke, and screenings and breeze, for sale

*Petroleum Refining*
Light products of distillation:
  Gasoline
  Naphtha and other light products of distillation [7]
Illuminating oils
Fuel oils, total
Liquid asphaltic road oils
Residuum or tar
Greases, total
Paraffin wax
Asphalt, other than liquid
Coke, petroleum
Acid oil (1927-1929 only)

*Rubber Products*
Tires and inner tubes:
  Pneumatic
    Automobile: casings
    Automobile: inner tubes
    Motorcycle and bicycle: casings and tubes
  Solid and cushion—motor vehicle (except 1914)

*Rubber Products—cont.*
  Rubberized fabrics (1927-1929)
    Automobile and carriage (1919-1927)
    All other (1919-1927)
  Reclaimed rubber, for sale as such (except 1914)
  Rubber heels, for sale as such (except 1914)
  Rubber soles, including composition or fiber, for sale as such (except 1914)
  Rubber boots (except 1914)
  Rubber shoes (1914, 1927 only)
  Rubber shoes and overshoes (except 1914)
  Canvas rubber-soled shoes (except 1914)

*Cement*
  Portland cement
  Natural and puzzolan cement

*Clay Products (other than pottery) and Nonclay Refractories*
  Common brick
  Vitrified brick or block
  Face brick
  Ornamental, enameled and hollow brick (except 1914)
  Terra cotta (except 1914-1919)
  Hollow building tile (except 1914)
  Roofing tile (except 1914)
  Tile—floor, ceramic mosaic, enameled, glazed ceramic mosaic, faience, and wall (except 1914)
  Draintile (except 1914)
  Sewer pipe (except 1914)
  Brick, fire and high alumina
  Silica brick (except 1914)

*Lime*
  Quicklime
  Hydrated lime

*Sand-Lime Brick*
  Sand-lime brick

*Cast-Iron Pipe*
  Gas and water pipe and fittings (1927-1929 only)
    Bell and spigot (1914-1927)
    Fittings (1914-1927)
    Flanged (1914-1927)
    Culvert (1914-1927)
  Soil and plumbers' pipe and fittings

*Firearms (1923-1929 only)*
  Pistols and revolvers
  Rifles
  Shotguns

*Iron and Steel: Blast Furnaces*
  Pig iron

*Iron and Steel: Steel Works and Rolling Mills*
  Unrolled steel (for sale or for transfer to other works of same company)
  Ingots
  Direct steel castings
  Semi-finished rolled products (for sale or for transfer to other works of same company)
    Blooms, billets and slabs, rolled blooms, charcoal blooms, etc.[1]
    Sheet and tin plate bars
    Muck and scrap bar
  Finished rolled products and forgings
    Rails, including rerolled and renewed
    Rail joints and fastenings, tie-plates, etc.
    Structural shapes (not assembled or fabricated)
    Concrete reinforcing bars (including twisted bars)
    Steel bars
    Iron bars (merchant, etc.)
    Wire rods
    Bolt, nut, spike and chain rods, etc.
    Plates and sheets, total
    Skelp
    Cotton ties, hoops, bands, and strips
    Axles, rolled or forged
    Car and locomotive wheels, rolled or forged (except 1914)
    Armor plate and ordnance
    Finished products, not elsewhere specified
  Scrap iron and steel (not consumed in producing works)

*Wire, Drawn from Purchased Bars and Rods (except 1929)*
  Iron and steel wire, plain and galvanized
  Copper and brass wire
  Wire products; iron and steel:
    Nails and spikes

## APPENDIX IV

**Wire, Drawn from Purchased Bars and Rods** (*except 1929*)
Wire products; iron and steel—*cont.*
  Barbed wire, plain and coated
  Rope, cable and strand
  Woven-wire fence and poultry netting, plain and coated
  Other fabricated iron and steel wire products

**Carriages, Wagons, Sleighs, and Sleds** (*1923-1929 only*)
Wagons
Carriages, buggies and sulkies
Sleighs and sleds (including bobsleds)
Public conveyances and ambulances, and lunch wagons

**Cars, Steam and Electric Railroad, Not Built in Railroad Repair Shops**
Steam railroad cars:
  Passenger day coaches
  Baggage and express (except 1914 and 1919)
  Chair, parlor, dining and buffet, mail and sleeping (except 1914 and 1919)
  All other types of passenger service
  Freight service cars (1914-1927)
    Box (1927-1929 only)
    Caboose (1927-1929 only)
    Flat (1927-1929 only)
    Gondola (1927-1929 only)
    Hopper (1927-1929 only)
    Refrigerator (1927-1929 only)
    Stock (1927-1929 only)
    Tank (1927-1929 only)
    All other (1927-1929 only)
Electric railroad cars:
  Passenger
  Freight (1921-1927 only)
  All other types

**Motor Vehicles, including Bodies and Parts**
Open touring cars, roadsters and runabouts, closed, and all other passenger cars
Public conveyances—busses and taxicabs
Government (federal, state, county and municipal) cars
Light commercial (less than 1 ton)
Trucks (1 ton and over)
Hearses and undertakers' wagons
Passenger chassis, not including bus chassis
Commercial chassis, including bus chassis
Trailers

**Motorcycles, Bicycles, and Parts**
Motorcycles
Bicycles

**Buttons** (*1923-1929 only*)
Buttons, subdivided, in 1929, into:
  Pearl or shell, fresh water, other than shoe
  Pearl or shell, ocean, other than shoe
  Vegetable—ivory
  Metal
  Pyroxylin
  All other

**Musical Instruments: Pianos**
Upright pianos
Upright, player pianos
Grand pianos
Automatic and electric pianos

**Musical Instruments: Organs**
Pipe organs
Reed organs

---

[1] Combined on basis of weight.
[2] Combined on basis of number of 'standard cases'.
[3] Combined on basis of number of cases.
[4] Combined on basis of area.
[5] Combined on basis of number.
[6] Combined on basis of number of pieces.
[7] Combined on basis of volume.

Note: In some cases quantity data for separate products were not available for all census years 1914 to 1929. and aggregate quantities for a group of products were used instead. Thus, 'condensed milk', 'evaporated milk', and 'buttermilk, condensed and evaporated', are listed as separate commodities for 1927 and 1929 only; for the years from 1914 to 1927 only one figure could be used, corresponding to the 'commodity' 'condensed and evaporated milk and buttermilk'.

# APPENDIX V

### Descriptions and Sources of Annual Production Series

(These series are those included in the annual index numbers of production, and those analyzed in the determination of rates of growth and indexes of instability. Descriptions of other series, and their sources, are given in the text where they first appear.)

*Y.-Agr.* = *Yearbook of Agriculture* (annual), published by the U. S. Department of Agriculture.

*F.R.B.* = *Federal Reserve Bulletin* (monthly), published by the Federal Reserve Board.

*M.R.* = *Mineral Resources of the United States* (annual), published by the Bureau of Mines, U. S. Department of Commerce, in two parts (Part I, Metals; Part II, Non-metals).

| Series | Nature of data | Immediate source | Compiling agency or primary source |
|---|---|---|---|
| *Materials* | | | |
| Apples .......... | Total production | *Y.-Agr.* | Bureau of Agr. Economics |
| Barley .......... | Do. | Do. | Do. |
| Cement, total .... | 1901-13: production of total Portland, total Puzzolan and one-half natural cement | *M.R., II* | Bur. of Mines |
| | 1922-29: total production | *F.R.B.* | Do. |
| Coal, anthracite .. | 1901-13: Pennsylvania mine production | *M.R., II* | Do. |
| | 1922-29: mine production | *F.R.B.* | Do. |
| Coal, bituminous . | 1901-13: mine production | *M.R., II* | Do. |
| | 1922-29: mine production | *F.R.B.* | Do. |
| Copper .......... | Mine production | *M.R., I* | Do. |
| Corn ............ | Total production | *Y.-Agr.* | Bur. of Agr. Economics |
| Cotton .......... | Do. | Do. | Do. |

APPENDIX V—Continued

| Series | Nature of data | Immediate source | Compiling agency or primary source |
|---|---|---|---|
| *Materials*—cont. | | | |
| Cottonseed | Estimated from production of lint, by States, adjusting for net weight, and assuming 65 pounds of cottonseed for each 35 net pounds of lint | *Y.-Agr.* | Bur. of Agr. Economics |
| Eggs | Receipts at seven leading markets | *Y.-Agr.* | Do. |
| Flaxseed | Total production | Do. | Do. |
| Gold | Refinery production | *Annual Report of the Director of the Mint* | Director of the Mint |
| Hay | Production of tame hay | *Y.-Agr.* | Bur. of Agr. Economics |
| Lead | Production of crude lead from domestic ores | *M.R., I* | Bur. of Mines |
| Livestock: | | | |
| Cattle and calves | Total slaughter | *Statistics of Meat Production,* 1900-1930 (mimeographed) | Bur. of Animal Industry |
| Cattle | Do. | Do. | Do. |
| Calves | Do. | Do. | Do. |
| Sheep and lambs | Do. | Do. | Do. |
| Swine | Do. | Do. | Do. |
| Milk | Total production | *Y.-Agr.* | Bur. of Agr. Economics |
| Natural gas | Produced and delivered to consumers | 1901-05: estimated by F. G. Tryon 1906-29: *M.R., II* | Bur. of Mines Do. |
| Oats | Total production | *Y.-Agr.* | Bur. of Agr. Economics |
| Oranges | Production in California, Florida, Texas, Arizona, Alabama, Mississippi, Louisiana | Do. | Do. |
| Peaches | Total production | Do. | Do. |
| Petroleum | Total crude production | *M.R., II* | Bur. of Mines |
| Potatoes | Total production | *Y.-Agr.* | Bur. of Agr. Economics |
| Poultry products | Chickens and eggs, estimates of production for sale and for consumption in the farm house | Do. | Do. |

## APPENDIX V—Continued

| Series | Nature of data | Immediate source | Compiling agency or primary source |
|---|---|---|---|
| *Materials*—cont. | | | |
| Rice | Total production, rough | *Y.-Agr.* | Bur. of Agr. Econ. |
| Rye | Total production | Do. | Do. |
| Sand and gravel | Sold or used by producers | *M.R., II* | Bur. of Mines |
| Silver | Refinery production | Annual Report of the Director of the Mint | Director of the Mint |
| Stone | Crushed stone sold or used by producers | *M.R., II* | Bur. of Mines |
| Sugar | Total cane and beet sugar production, continental U. S. | *Y.-Agr.* | Bur. of Agr. Economics |
| Tobacco | Unmanufactured, total production | Do. | Do. |
| Wheat | Total production | Do. | Do. |
| Wool | Total production of fleece and pulled wool | Do. | Do. |
| Zinc | Slab-zinc production from domestic ores | 1901-13: *M.R., I* | Bur. of Mines |
|  |  | 1922-29: *F.R.B.* | American Zinc Institute |
| *Processes of fabrication* | | | |
| Cement, total | 1901-13: production of total Portland, total Puzzolan and one-half natural cement | *M.R., II* | Bur. of Mines |
|  | 1922-29: total production | *F.R.B.* | Do. |
| Cigarettes | Number on which taxes were paid | Annual Report of Commissioner of Internal Revenue | Bur. of Internal Revenue |
| Cigars | Do. | Do. | Do. |
| Coke | Total production | *M.R., II* | Bur. of Mines |
| Common brick | Sold by producers | Do. | Do. |
| Copper | Consumption | *F.R.B.* | American Bur. of Metal Statistics |
|  | 1922-29: blister copper production | Do. | Do. |
| Cotton | Mill consumption of raw cotton | Do. | 1901-03: Latham Alexander Co. 1903-29: Bur. of the Census |
| Cottonseed | Used in manufacture | Review of Econ. Statistics, Nov., 1920 | Bur. of the Census |

APPENDIX V—Continued

| Series | Nature of data | Immediate source | Compiling agency or primary source |
|---|---|---|---|
| *Processes of fabrication*—cont. | | | |
| Distilled spirits .. | Total production, fiscal year | *Statistical Abstract* | Bur. of Internal Revenue |
| Fermented liquors | Do. | Do. | Do. |
| Flour, wheat .... | Total production | 1901-13: *Wheat Studies, Vol. IV*, Food Research Institute | Holbrook Working |
| | | 1922-29: F.R.B. | Russell's *Commercial News* |
| Glass, plate ...... | Do. | *Survey of Current Business* | Plate Glass Mfrs. of America |
| Gold ............ | Used in manufacture | *Statistical Abstract* | Director of the Mint |
| Lead ............ | Available for consumption | Do. | Bur. of Mines |
| | Production of crude lead from domestic ores | F.R.B. | Do. |
| Leather products | | | |
| Boots and shoes | Total production | Do. | Bur. of the Census |
| Leather, sole .. | Do. | Do. | Do. |
| Leather, upper . | Do. | Do. | Do. |
| Lime ............ | Burned and sold | *M.R., II* | Bur. of Mines |
| Lumber ......... | Sum of production of Douglas fir, northern hemlock, redwood, southern pine, North Carolina pine, California white pine and northern pine | *Survey of Current Business* | Reports of lumber associations |
| Flooring ...... | Oak and maple flooring production | F.R.B. | Maple and Oak Flooring Mfrs. Assns. |
| Motor vehicles ... | Production of cars and trucks | 1901-13: *Automobile Facts and Figures* | National Automobile Chamber of Commerce |
| | | 1922-29: F.R.B. | Do. |
| Paper and pulp | | | |
| Book paper .... | Total production | F.R.B. | Federal Trade Commission, Am. Pulp and Paper Mfrs. Assn. |
| Fine paper .... | Do. | Do. | Do. |
| Newsprint .... | Do. | Do. | Do. |
| | Total consumption | Do. | Do. |

## APPENDIX V—Continued

| Series | Nature of data | Immediate source | Compiling agency or primary source |
|---|---|---|---|
| *Processes of fabrication*—cont. | | | |
| Wood pulp .... | Mechanical-pulp production | F.R.B. | Fed. Trade Com. Am. Pulp and Paper Mfrs. Assn. |
| | Chemical-pulp production | Do. | |
| Petroleum products | | | |
| Fuel oil ....... | Total production | F.R.B. | Bur. of Mines |
| Gasoline ...... | Do. | Do. | Do. |
| Kerosene ...... | Do. | Do. | Do. |
| Lubricating oil . | Do. | Do. | Do. |
| Pig iron ........ | Do. | M.R., I | Do. |
| | | F.R.B. | Iron Age |
| Railroad cars | | | |
| Freight cars ... | Total number completed, steam railways | Review of Econ. Statistics, Nov., 1920 | Railway Age |
| Locomotives ... | Total number completed, steam and electric railways | F.R.B. | Bur. of the Census |
| Passenger cars . | Total number completed for steam railways | Review of Econ. Statistics, Nov., 1920 | Railway Age |
| Silk ............ | Raw imports | Statistical Abstract | Bur. of Foreign and Domestic Commerce |
| | Deliveries of raw silk to mills | F.R.B. | Silk Assn. of America |
| | Percentage of looms active | Do. | Do. |
| Slaughtering and meat packing | | | |
| Calves ........ | 1922-29: Federal inspected slaughter | F.R.B. | Bur. of Animal Industry |
| Cattle ........ | Do. | Do. | Do. |
| Cattle and calves | 1901-13: Receipts at nine markets | Y.-Agr. | Bur. of Agr. Economics |
| Hogs ......... | 1901-13: Do. | Do. | Do. |
| | 1922-29: Federal inspected slaughter | F.R.B. | Bur. of Animal Industry |
| Sheep ........ | 1901-13: Receipts at nine markets | Y.-Agr. | Bur. of Agr. Economics |
| | 1922-29: Federal inspected slaughter | F.R.B. | Bur. of Animal Industry |
| Steel ........... | Ingots and castings | M.R., I | Amer. Iron and Steel Institute |
| | Rails | Statistical Abstract | Do. |

APPENDIX V—Continued

| Series | Nature of data | Immediate source | Compiling agency or primary source |
|---|---|---|---|
| *Processes of fabrication*—cont. | | | |
| Sugar .......... | U. S. production plus imports, crop years | Y.-Agr. | Bur. of Agr. Economics and Bur. of Foreign and Domestic Commerce |
| | Meltings of raw cane sugar | F.R.B. | *Willet and Grey's Journal* and *Statistical Sugar Trade Journal* |
| Tin ............ | Deliveries from port warehouses | Do. | N. Y. Metal Exchange |
| Tires | | | |
| Inner tubes .... | Inner-tube production | Do. | Rubber Assn. of America |
| Pneumatic ..... | Pneumatic-tire production | Do. | Do. |
| Tobacco and snuff | Amount on which taxes were paid | *Annual Report of Commissioner of Internal Revenue* | Bur. of Internal Revenue |
| Vessels built .... | Number completed | F.R.B. | Bur. of Navigation |
| Wool .......... | Apparent consumption | 1901-13: *Review of Econ. Statistics,* Nov., 1920 | Natl. Assn. of Wool Mfrs. |
| | Mill consumption of raw wool | 1922-29: F.R.B. | Bur. of the Census |
| | Percentage of loom and spindle hours active | Do. | Do. |
| | Percentage of carpet and rug loom hours active | Do. | Do. |
| Zinc ............ | Apparent consumption | M.R., I | Bur. of Mines |
| | Slab-zinc production | F.R.B. | Amer. Zinc Institute |
| Zinc and lead pigments ......... | Amount sold by domestic manufacturers in the U. S. | M.R., I | Bur. of Mines |

# List of Tables

|   | PAGE |
|---|---|
| 1. Growth of Physical Volume of Production in the United States, 1901-1913 . . . . . . . . . . . . | 2 |
| 2. Raw Materials and Manufactured Goods. Index Numbers of Physical Volume of Production in the United States, 1901-1913 . . . . . . . . . . . . . . | 4 |
| 3. Products of American Farms and All Other Products. Index Numbers of Physical Volume of Production in the United States, 1901-1913 . . . . . . . . . . . . | 14 |
| 4. Products of American Farms and All Other Products, Raw and Processed. Index Numbers of Physical Volume of Production in the United States, 1901-1913 . . . . | 16 |
| 5. Foods and Non-foods. Index Numbers of Physical Volume of Production in the United States, 1901-1913 . . . . | 17 |
| 6. Foods and Non-foods, Raw and Processed. Index Numbers of Physical Volume of Production in the United States, 1901-1913 . . . . . . . . . . . . . . | 19 |
| 7. Articles of Human Consumption and Articles Entering into Capital Equipment. Index Numbers of Physical Volume of Production in the United States, 1901-1913 . . . | 21 |
| 8. Non-durable, Semi-durable and Durable Goods. Index Numbers of Physical Volume of Production in the United States, 1901-1913 . . . . . . . . . . . . | 23 |
| 9. Growth of Manufacturing Production in the United States, 1899-1914. Index Numbers of Physical Volume of Production, Number of Wage-earners and per Capita Output | 26 |
| 10. Changes in Physical Volume of Manufacturing Production in the United States, 1899-1914. Index Numbers for 35 Individual Industries, with Average Annual Rates of Change . . . . . . . . . . . . . . . | 30 |
| 11. Changes in Output per Wage-earner in Manufacturing Industries of the United States, 1899-1914. Index Numbers for 35 Individual Industries, with Average Annual Rates of Change . . . . . . . . . . . . . . | 33 |
| 12. Growth of Manufacturing Production in the United States, 1899-1914. Averages of Aggregate Production and of per | |

## LIST OF TABLES

| | PAGE |
|---|---|
| Capita Output. (Derived from the central items of frequency distributions.) | 35 |
| 13. Growth of Manufacturing Production in the United States, 1899-1914. Index Number of Physical Volume of Production, Number of Establishments and Output per Establishment | 36 |
| 14. Growth of Manufacturing Production in the United States, 1899-1914. Factors Affecting Output per Establishment | 38 |
| 15. Changes in Value Added by Manufacture, 1899-1914 | 40 |
| 16. Illustrating the Derivation of Index Numbers of the Physical Volume of Manufacturing Production, 1899-1914. All Census Industries | 41 |
| 17. Comparison of Index Numbers of Physical Volume of Manufacturing Production in the United States, 1899-1914 | 42 |
| 18. Changes in the Level of Wholesale Prices in the United States, 1901-1913 | 52 |
| 19. Index Numbers of Annual Price Changes and of Price Dispersion in the United States, 1901-1913 | 53 |
| 20. Monthly Variability of Wholesale Prices, 1901-1913 | 54 |
| 21. Index Numbers of Physical Volume, Prices and Aggregate Values of Goods Produced in the United States, 1901-1913 | 56 |
| 22. Raw Materials and Manufactured Goods. Index Numbers of Wholesale Prices in the United States, 1901-1913 | 57 |
| 23. Wholesale Prices of Raw and Manufactured Goods. Summary of Rates of Change and Measurements of Instability, 1901-1913 | 58 |
| 24. Raw Materials and Manufactured Goods. Measurements of Variability of Wholesale Prices, 1898-1913 | 63 |
| 25. Products of American Farms and All Other Products. Index Numbers of Wholesale Prices in the United States, 1901-1913 | 65 |
| 26. Wholesale Prices of American Farm Products and of All Other Products. Summary of Rates of Change and Measurements of Instability, 1901-1913 | 66 |
| 27. Products of American Farms and All Other Products. Measurements of Variability of Wholesale Prices, 1898-1913 | 67 |
| 28. Forest Products, Animal Products, Farm Crops and Mineral Products. Index Numbers of Wholesale Prices in the United States, 1901-1913 | 70 |
| 29. Wholesale Prices of Forest Products, Animal Products, Farm Crops and Mineral Products. Summary of Rates of Change and Measurements of Instability, 1901-1913 | 71 |

## LIST OF TABLES

| | PAGE |
|---|---|
| 30. Forest Products, Animal Products, Farm Crops and Mineral Products. Measurements of Variability of Wholesale Prices, 1898-1913 | 71 |
| 31. Wholesale Prices of Forest Products, Animal Products, Farm Crops and Mineral Products, in Raw and Processed Form. Summary of Rates of Change and Measurements of Instability, Pre-war | 72 |
| 32. Foods and Non-foods. Index Numbers of Wholesale Prices in the United States, 1901-1913 | 75 |
| 33. Wholesale Prices of Foods and of Non-foods. Summary of Rates of Change and Measurements of Instability, Pre-war | 76 |
| 34. Producers' Goods and Consumers' Goods. Index Numbers of Wholesale Prices in the United States, 1901-1913 | 77 |
| 35. Wholesale Prices of Producers' Goods and of Consumers' Goods. Summary of Rates of Change and Measurements of Instability, Pre-war | 78 |
| 36. Producers' Goods Destined for Use in Capital Equipment and for Human Consumption. Index Numbers of Wholesale Prices in the United States, 1901-1913 | 80 |
| 37. Statistics of Selected Manufacturing Industries of the United States, 1899-1914 | 89 |
| 38. Relative Numbers Defining Changes in Important Elements of Manufacturing Production in the United States, 1899-1914 | 92 |
| 39. Index Numbers Measuring Changes in the Apparent Physical Contributions of Different Agents of Manufacturing Production, 1899-1914 | 95 |
| 40. Index Numbers of Aggregate Value, Production and Price, 1899-1914. Manufacturing Industries of the United States | 98 |
| 41. Changes in the Selling Prices of Products of Manufacturing Industries of the United States, 1899-1914. Index Numbers for 35 Individual Industries, with Average Annual Rates of Change | 100 |
| 42. Changes in Selling Price, Cost of Materials and Fabrication Costs, plus Profits, per Unit of Product, 1899-1914. Manufacturing Industries of the United States | 103 |
| 43. Changes in Material Costs, per Unit of Product, Manufacturing Industries of the United States, 1899-1914. Index Numbers for 35 Individual Industries, with Average Annual Rates of Change | 106 |
| 44. Changes in Fabrication Costs, per Unit of Product, Manufacturing Industries of the United States, 1899-1914. | |

## LIST OF TABLES

| | PAGE |
|---|---|
| Index Numbers for 35 Individual Industries, with Average Annual Rates of Change | 107 |
| 45. Changes in Total Fabrication Costs, Labor Costs and Overhead Costs plus Profits, per Unit of Product, 1899-1914. Manufacturing Industries of the United States | 109 |
| 46. Changes in Labor Costs, per Unit of Product, Manufacturing Industries of the United States, 1899-1914. Index Numbers for 35 Individual Industries, with Average Annual Rates of Change | 112 |
| 47. Changes in Overhead Costs plus Profits, per Unit of Product, Manufacturing Industries of the United States, 1899-1914. Index Numbers for 35 Individual Industries, with Average Annual Rates of Change | 114 |
| 48. Movements of Certain Economic Elements in the United States, 1901-1913 | 127 |
| 49. Changes in Money Earnings and Real Earnings of Employed Workers in the United States, 1901-1913 | 135 |
| 50. Measurements of Instability of Growth in the Earnings of Factory Workers in the United States, 1901-1913 | 138 |
| 51. Cash Income Received from 1901 to 1913, inclusive, by the Holders of All Common Stock Outstanding on January 1, 1901. 93 Industrial, Public Utility and Railroad Corporations | 139 |
| 52. Relative Numbers Defining the Investment Experience of Holders of All Common Stock Outstanding on January 1, 1901. 93 Industrial, Public Utility and Railroad Corporations | 143 |
| 53. Cash Income Received from 1901 to 1913, inclusive, by the Holders of All Common Stock Outstanding on January 1, 1901. 66 Industrial and Public Utility Corporations | 144 |
| 54. Relative Numbers Defining the Investment Experience of Holders of All Common Stock Outstanding on January 1, 1901. 66 Industrial and Public Utility Corporations | 145 |
| 55. Estimates of Cash Income from Each of Five Investments of $10,000 Made on January 1, 1901, in Industrial Common Stocks, 1901-1913 | 147 |
| 56. Cash Income Received from 1901 to 1913, inclusive, by the Holders of All Common Stock Outstanding on January 1, 1901. 27 Railroads | 149 |
| 57. Relative Numbers Defining the Investment Experience of Holders of All Common Stock Outstanding on January 1, 1901. 27 Railroads | 150 |
| 58. Estimates of Cash Income from Each of Five Investments | |

LIST OF TABLES 613

PAGE

of $10,000 Made on January 1, 1901, in Railroad Common Stocks, 1901-1913 . . . . . . . . . . . 151
59. Investment Experience of a Fund of $10,000 Invested in Bonds in January, 1901, and Redistributed Semi-annually to Maintain Equal Distribution, 1901-1913 . . . . . 152
60. Index Numbers of Incomes Received by Wage-earners, Stockholders and Bondholders in American Industries, 1901-1913. (In current dollars.) . . . . . . . 154
61. Changes in the Values of Capital Assets of Stockholders and Bondholders, 1901-1914 . . . . . . . . . . 156
62. Index Numbers of Incomes Received by Wage-earners, Stockholders and Bondholders in American Industries, 1901-1913. (In dollars of constant purchasing power.) . 159
63. Foreign Trade of the United States, 1901-1913. Changes in Aggregate Values of Imports, by Major Classes of Commodities . . . . . . . . . . . . . . 162
64. Foreign Trade of the United States, 1901-1913. Changes in Aggregate Values of Exports, by Major Classes of Commodities . . . . . . . . . . . . . . 163
65. Balance of International Payments of the United States, 1896-1914 . . . . . . . . . . . . . . 165
66. Summary of Pre-war Balance of International Payments of the United States . . . . . . . . . . . 166
67. Estimates of Pre-war Tendencies among Producers of Economic Goods. Changes in Values of Products and in Command over Goods . . . . . . . . . . 169
68. Changes in Aggregate Rewards of Agents of Fabrication, and Factors in such Changes, 1899-1914. Manufacturing Industries of the United States . . . . . . . 172
69. Showing Alterations Occurring between 1899 and 1914 in the Terms of Exchange between Given Groups of Manufacturing Producers and All Producers . . . . . . 174
70. Showing Alterations Occurring between 1901 and 1913 in the Terms of Exchange between Given Groups of Producers and All Producers . . . . . . . . . 177
71. Showing Alterations Occurring between 1899 and 1914 in the Terms of Exchange between Manufacturing Labor and All Producers . . . . . . . . . . . 180
72. Showing Alterations Occurring between 1899 and 1914 in the Aggregate Production of Different Agents, and in their Aggregate Rewards . . . . . . . . . . . 181
73. Changes in Physical Volume of Production in the United States, 1913-1922 . . . . . . . . . . . . 188

## LIST OF TABLES

| | PAGE |
|---|---|
| 74. Volume of Construction in the United States, 1913-1922 | 191 |
| 75. Growth of Manufacturing Production in the United States, 1914-1923. Index Numbers of Physical Volume of Production, Number of Wage-earners and per Capita Output | 192 |
| 76. Changes in Physical Volume of Manufacturing Production in the United States, 1914-1923. Index Numbers for 52 Individual Industries | 194 |
| 77. Changes in Output per Wage-earner in Manufacturing Industries of the United States, 1914-1923. Index Numbers for 52 Individual Industries | 195 |
| 78. Growth of Manufacturing Production in the United States, 1914-1923. Index Numbers of Physical Volume of Production, Number of Establishments and Output per Establishment | 197 |
| 79. Growth of Manufacturing Production in the United States, 1914-1923. Factors Affecting Output per Establishment | 198 |
| 80. Changes in Value Added by Manufacture, 1914-1923 | 199 |
| 81. Derived Index Numbers of Physical Volume of Production, 1914-1923. All Manufacturing Industries of the United States | 199 |
| 82. Comparison of Index Numbers of Physical Volume of Manufacturing Production, 1914-1923 | 200 |
| 83. Wholesale Price Movements, 1913-1922 | 201 |
| 84. Index Numbers of Physical Volume, Prices and Aggregate Values of Goods Produced in the United States, 1913-1922 | 203 |
| 85. Raw Materials and Manufactured Goods. Changes in Wholesale Prices and in Purchasing Power, 1913-1922 | 205 |
| 86. Raw Materials and Manufactured Goods. Measurements of Variability of Wholesale Prices, 1898-1913, 1914-1921 | 207 |
| 87. Products of American Farms and All Other Products. Index Numbers of Purchasing Power, in Wholesale Markets, 1913-1922 | 208 |
| 88. Showing Changes in Prices Received by Farmers, in Prices Paid by Farmers and in the Purchasing Power of Farm Products, 1913-1922 | 210 |
| 89. Farm Crops, Animal Products, Mineral Products and Forest Products. Index Numbers of Purchasing Power, in Wholesale Markets, 1913-1922 | 212 |
| 90. Foods and Non-foods. Index Numbers of Purchasing Power, in Wholesale Markets, 1913-1922 | 214 |
| 91. Producers' Goods and Consumers' Goods. Index Numbers of Purchasing Power, in Wholesale Markets, 1913-1922 | 215 |

## LIST OF TABLES

PAGE

92. Producers' Goods Destined for Human Consumption and Processed Consumers' Goods. Index Numbers of Purchasing Power, in Wholesale Markets, 1913-1922 . . . . 217
93. Producers' Goods Destined for Human Consumption and for Use in Capital Equipment. Index Numbers of Purchasing Power, in Wholesale Markets, 1913-1922 . . . . . 219
94. Statistics of Selected Manufacturing Industries in the United States, 1914-1923 . . . . . . . . . . . . 220
95. Relative Numbers Defining Changes in Important Elements of Manufacturing Production in the United States, 1914-1923 . . . . . . . . . . . . . . . . 221
96. Index Numbers Measuring Changes in the Apparent Physical Contributions of Different Agents of Manufacturing Production, 1914-1923 . . . . . . . . . . . 221
97. Index Numbers of Aggregate Value, Production and Price, 1914-1923. Manufacturing Industries of the United States 222
98. Changes in the Selling Prices of Products of Manufacturing Industries of the United States, 1914-1923. Index Numbers for 52 Individual Industries . . . . . . . 223
99. Changes in Selling Price, Cost of Materials and Fabrication Costs, plus Profits, per Unit of Product, 1914-1923. Manufacturing Industries of the United States . . . 225
100. Changes in Material Costs, per Unit of Product, Manufacturing Industries of the United States, 1914-1923. Index Numbers for 52 Individual Industries . . . . . . 227
101. Changes in Fabrication Costs, plus Profits, per Unit of Product, Manufacturing Industries of the United States, 1914-1923. Index Numbers for 52 Individual Industries 229
102. Changes in Total Fabrication Costs, Labor Costs and Overhead Costs plus Profits, per Unit of Product, 1914-1923. Manufacturing Industries of the United States . . . 231
103. Changes in Labor Costs, per Unit of Product, Manufacturing Industries of the United States, 1914-1923. Index Numbers for 52 Individual Industries . . . . . . 234
104. Changes in Overhead Costs plus Profits, per Unit of Product, Manufacturing Industries of the United States, 1914-1923. Index Numbers for 52 Individual Industries . . 236
105. Growth of Physical Volume of Production in the United States, 1922-1929 . . . . . . . . . . . 243
106. Index Numbers of Production and Construction in the United States, 1922-1929 . . . . . . . . . 246
107. Raw Materials and Manufactured Goods. Index Numbers of Physical Volume of Production in the United States, 1922-1929 . . . . . . . . . . . . . . 250

|     |                                                                                                                                                                                 | PAGE |
| --- | ------------------------------------------------------------------------------------------------------------------------------------------------------------------------------- | ---- |
| 108. | Index Numbers of the Physical Output of Movable Goods, 1922-1929. (Based directly upon records of physical production.) | 252 |
| 109. | Products of American Farms and All Other Products. Index Numbers of Physical Volume of Production in the United States, 1922-1929 | 259 |
| 110. | Average Annual Rates of Change in the Production of Identical Commodities, 1901-1913 and 1922-1929 | 262 |
| 111. | Growth of Construction in the United States, 1922-1929. Estimated Values of Total Contracts Awarded | 264 |
| 112. | Growth of Construction in the United States, 1922-1929. Index Numbers of Volume of Construction Secured by Deflating Aggregate Values of Contracts Awarded | 267 |
| 113. | Growth of Construction in the United States, 1922-1929. Index Numbers of Contracts Awarded, by Floor Surface Areas, and of Building Materials Booked and Shipped | 268 |
| 114. | Non-durable Consumption Goods. Index Numbers of Physical Volume of Production of Finished Goods, 1922-1929 | 270 |
| 115. | Semi-durable Consumption Goods. Index Numbers of Physical Volume of Production of Finished Goods, 1922-1929 | 272 |
| 116. | Durable Consumption Goods. Index Numbers of Physical Volume of Production of Finished Goods, 1922-1929 | 274 |
| 117. | Elements of Capital Equipment. Index Numbers of Physical Volume of Production of Finished Goods, 1922-1929 | 278 |
| 118. | Consumption Goods, Capital Equipment and Total Production. Index Numbers of Physical Volume of Production of Finished Goods, 1922-1929 | 280 |
| 119. | Comparison of Production Tendencies, 1922-1929. Durable and Non-durable Goods | 283 |
| 120. | Comparative Values of Durable and Non-durable Goods Produced in the United States, 1899, 1914, 1923 and 1929 | 286 |
| 121. | Comparative Values of Food and Clothing Produced in the United States, 1899, 1914, 1923 and 1929 | 288 |
| 122. | Growth of Manufacturing Production in the United States, 1923-1929. Index Numbers of Physical Volume of Production, Number of Wage-earners and per Capita Output | 290 |
| 123. | Changes in Physical Volume of Manufacturing Production in the United States, 1923-1929. Index Numbers for 62 Individual Industries, with Average Annual Rates of Change | 292 |
| 124. | Changes in Output per Wage-earner in Manufacturing Industries of the United States, 1923-1929. Index Numbers for 62 Individual Industries, with Average Annual Rates of Change | 296 |

LIST OF TABLES 617

PAGE

125. Growth of Manufacturing Production in the United States, 1923-1929. Averages of Aggregate Production and of per Capita Output. (Derived from the central items of frequency distributions.) . . . . . . . . . . . 299
126. Growth of Manufacturing Production in the United States, 1923-1929. Index Numbers of Physical Volume of Production, Number of Establishments and Output per Establishment . . . . . . . . . . . . . . . 299
127. Changes in Output per Establishment in Manufacturing Industries of the United States, 1923-1929. Index Numbers for 62 Individual Industries, with Average Annual Rates of Change . . . . . . . . . . . 302
128. Growth of Manufacturing Production in the United States, 1923-1929. Factors Affecting Output per Establishment 304
129. Changes in Number of Wage-earners per Establishment in Manufacturing Industries of the United States, 1923-1929. Index Numbers for 62 Individual Industries, with Average Annual Rates of Change . . . . . . . . 305
130. Changes in Value Added by Manufacture, 1923-1929 . . 307
131. Illustrating the Derivation of Index Numbers of the Physical Volume of Manufacturing Production, 1923-1929. All Census Industries . . . . . . . . . . . . 308
132. Comparison of Index Numbers of Physical Volume of Manufacturing Production in the United States, 1923-1929 . . . . . . . . . . . . . . . . 309
133. Changes in the Level of Wholesale Prices in the United States, 1922-1929 . . . . . . . . . . . 316
134. Pre-recession Behavior of Wholesale Prices in 29 Countries, 1923-1929 . . . . . . . . . . . . . 318
135. Index Numbers of Physical Volume, Prices and Aggregate Values of Goods Produced in the United States, 1922-1929 322
136. Monthly Variability and Dispersion of Wholesale Prices in the United States, 1890-1929 . . . . . . . . . 325
137. Summary of Valorization Schemes . . . . . . . . 327
138. Index Numbers Measuring Changes in the Prices and Purchasing Power of Raw Materials and of Manufactured Goods, 1922-1929 . . . . . . . . . . . 333
139. Variability of Prices of Raw Materials and of Manufactured Goods under Pre-war, War-time and Post-war Conditions 339
140. Products of American Farms and All Other Products. Index Numbers of Wholesale Prices in the United States, 1922-1929 . . . . . . . . . . . . . . . . 340

## LIST OF TABLES

| | PAGE |
|---|---|
| 141. Products of American Farms and All Other Products. Comparison of Measurements of Monthly Price Variability, 1898-1929 | 346 |
| 142. Index Numbers Measuring Changes in Farm Prices and in the Per-unit Purchasing Power of Farm Products, 1922-1929 | 347 |
| 143. Index Numbers Measuring Changes in Farm Prices and in the Per-unit Purchasing Power of Farm Products, 1913-1929 | 348 |
| 144. Farm Crops and Animal, Forest and Mineral Products. Index Numbers of Wholesale Prices in the United States, 1922-1929 | 350 |
| 145. Farm Crops and Animal, Forest and Mineral Products, Raw and Processed. Index Numbers of Wholesale Prices in the United States, 1922-1929 | 351 |
| 146. Farm Crops and Animal, Forest and Mineral Products. Index Numbers of Purchasing Power in Relation to a Pre-war Base, Selected Years | 352 |
| 147. Foods and Non-foods. Index Numbers of Wholesale Prices in the United States, 1922-1929 | 354 |
| 148. Producers' Goods and Consumers' Goods. Index Numbers of Wholesale Prices in the United States, 1922-1929 | 358 |
| 149. Goods Entering into Capital Equipment and Articles of Human Consumption. Index Numbers of Wholesale Prices in the United States, 1922-1929 | 364 |
| 150. Comparison of Average Annual Rates of Change in Purchasing Power, 1901-1913 and 1922-1929. Commodity Groups of the United States Bureau of Labor Statistics | 371 |
| 151. Statistics of Selected Manufacturing Industries of the United States, 1923-1929 | 376 |
| 152. Relative Numbers Defining Changes in Important Elements of Manufacturing Production in the United States, 1923-1929 | 377 |
| 153. Index Numbers of Aggregate Value, Production and Price, 1923-1929. Manufacturing Industries of the United States | 379 |
| 154. Changes in the Selling Prices of Products of Manufacturing Industries of the United States, 1923-1929. Index Numbers for 62 Individual Industries, with Average Annual Rates of Change | 381 |
| 155. Changes in Selling Price, Cost of Materials and Fabrication Costs, plus Profits, per Unit of Product, 1923-1929. Manufacturing Industries of the United States | 384 |
| 156. Changes in Material Costs, per Unit of Product, Manufacturing Industries of the United States, 1923-1929. Index | |

| | PAGE |
|---|---|
| Numbers for 62 Individual Industries, with Average Annual Rates of Change | 388 |
| 157. Changes in Fabrication Costs, plus Profits, per Unit of Product, Manufacturing Industries of the United States, 1923-1929. Index Numbers for 62 Individual Industries, with Average Annual Rates of Change | 391 |
| 158. Changes in Total Fabrication Costs, Labor Costs and Overhead Costs plus Profits, per Unit of Product, 1923-1929. Manufacturing Industries of the United States | 393 |
| 159. Sales and Profits, 2,046 Manufacturing Corporations, 1922-1929 | 398 |
| 160. Index Numbers of Sales, Prices, Profits and Output, 1922-1929. 2,046 Manufacturing Corporations | 399 |
| 161. Sales, Prices, Profits and Output, 1922-1929. 1,231 Corporations in 45 Manufacturing Industries of the United States | 401 |
| 162. Changes in Labor Costs, per Unit of Product, Manufacturing Industries of the United States, 1923-1929. Index Numbers for 62 Individual Industries, with Average Annual Rates of Change | 405 |
| 163. Changes in Overhead Costs plus Profits, per Unit of Product, Manufacturing Industries of the United States, 1923-1929. Index Numbers for 62 Individual Industries, with Average Annual Rates of Change | 407 |
| 164. Changes in Unit Prices and Unit Costs, Products of Manufacturing Industries of the United States, 1899-1929. (In dollars of constant purchasing power.) | 412 |
| 165. Measurements Relating to the Growth of Population in the United States, 1922-1929, with Corresponding Figures for the Period 1901-1913 | 417 |
| 166. Accessions and Separations of Wage-earners, Manufacturing Industries of the United States, 1899-1929 | 420 |
| 167. Separations of Wage-earners by Industrial Groups, 1899-1914, 1923-1929 | 423 |
| 168. Showing Changes in Certain Elements of the Supply of Capital Funds and in Annual Additions to Capital Funds in the United States, 1922-1929 | 425 |
| 169. New Capital Issues in the United States, and Issues of Investment Trusts, Trading and Holding Companies, 1922-1929 | 427 |
| 170. Estimates of Corporate Savings in the United States. Annual Additions to Surplus and Undivided Profits, 1922-1929 | 429 |
| 171. Estimates of Aggregate Corporate Savings, and of Annual Corporate Savings, 1922-1929 | 432 |

## LIST OF TABLES

| | PAGE |
|---|---|
| 172. Growth of Certain Elements of Capital Funds in the United States, 1922-1929 | 435 |
| 173. Estimated Growth of Corporate Capital Funds in the United States, 1922-1929 | 438 |
| 174. Index Numbers Measuring Changes in the Assets of American Industrial Corporations, 1922-1929 | 440 |
| 175. Changes in Aggregate Primary Funds in the United States and in the Constituent Elements of this Aggregate, 1922-1929 | 443 |
| 176. Uses of Primary Funds in the United States, 1922-1929 | 446 |
| 177. Elements of the Money and Credit Structure, 1922-1929 | 448 |
| 178. Growth of Bank Credit, Reporting Member Banks, 1922-1929 | 450 |
| 179. Elements of Mortgage Indebtedness in the United States, 1922-1929. Estimated Holdings of Urban Real Estate Mortgages | 453 |
| 180. Bond and Stock Yields, Rediscount Rates and Interest Rates, 1922-1929 | 455 |
| 181. Exports and Imports of the United States. Index Numbers of Quantity, Unit Price and Aggregate Value, 1922-1929 | 462 |
| 182. Changes in Export and Import Prices, and in the Terms of Exchange between Imported and Exported Goods, 1913-1929 | 464 |
| 183. Foreign Trade of the United States, 1922-1929. Changes in Aggregate Values of Imports, by Major Classes of Commodities | 465 |
| 184. Foreign Trade of the United States, 1922-1929. Changes in Aggregate Values of Exports, by Major Classes of Commodities | 467 |
| 185. Component Elements of the Import Trade of the United States, 1901, 1913, 1922 and 1929 | 469 |
| 186. Component Elements of the Export Trade of the United States, 1901, 1913, 1922 and 1929 | 470 |
| 187. Balances of International Payments of the United States, 1922-1929 | 472 |
| 188. Foreign Investments of the United States, 1922-1929 | 475 |
| 189. Changes in Earnings and in Wage Rates in the United States, 1922-1929 | 477 |
| 190. Changes in per Capita Earnings of Manufacturing Labor, by Industries, 1922-1929 | 479 |
| 191. Changes in per Capita Real Earnings of Manufacturing Labor in Seven Industrial Groups, 1901-1913 and 1922-1929 | 480 |

PAGE

192. Net Incomes of Corporations Classified by Major Industrial Groups, 1922-1929 . . . . . . . . . . . 482
193. Net Incomes of Manufacturing Corporations Classified by Industrial Groups, 1922-1929 . . . . . . . 484
194. Profits, Capital Investment and Profits as Percentage of Capital Investment, 2,046 Manufacturing Corporations, 1922-1929 . . . . . . . . . . . . . . 486
195. Aggregate Dividend Payments of All Corporations, 1922-1929 . . . . . . . . . . . . . . . 490
196. Cash Income Received from 1922 to 1929, inclusive, by the Holders of All Common Stock Outstanding on January 1, 1922. 102 Industrial, Public Utility and Railroad Corporations . . . . . . . . . . . . . 492
197. Relative Numbers Defining the Investment Experience of Holders of All Common Stock Outstanding on January 1, 1922. 102 Industrial, Public Utility and Railroad Corporations . . . . . . . . . . . . . 496
198. Measurements Defining the Investment Experience of the Holders of All Common Stock Outstanding on January 1, 1922. 72 Industrial Corporations . . . . . . 497
199. Measurements Defining the Investment Experience of the Holders of All Common Stock Outstanding on January 1, 1922. 18 Public Utility Corporations . . . . . 498
200. Measurements Defining the Investment Experience of the Holders of All Common Stock Outstanding on January 1, 1922. 12 Railroads . . . . . . . . . . 499
201. Investment Experience of a Fund of $10,000 Invested in Bonds in January, 1922, and Redistributed Semi-annually to Maintain Equal Distribution, 1922-1929 . . . . . 500
202. Index Numbers of Incomes Received by Wage-earners, Stockholders and Bondholders in American Industries, 1922-1929. (In current dollars.) . . . . . . . . 502
203. Index Numbers of Incomes Received by Wage-earners, Stockholders and Bondholders in American Industries, 1922-1929. With Pre-war and Post-war Rates of Change. (In dollars of constant purchasing power.) . . . . . 504
204. Estimates of Post-war Tendencies among Producers of Economic Goods. Changes in Values of Products and in Command over Goods . . . . . . . . . . . . 507
205. Estimates of Pre-war Tendencies among Producers of Economic Goods. Changes in Values of Products and in Command over Goods . . . . . . . . . . . 510
206. Showing Changes Occurring in the Aggregate Values of Goods Produced by Certain Economic Groups, and Corresponding Changes in Command over Goods, 1914-1929  511

|     |                                                                                                                                                                                                                        | PAGE |
| --- | ---------------------------------------------------------------------------------------------------------------------------------------------------------------------------------------------------------------------- | ---- |
| 207. | Showing Alterations Occurring in the Terms of Exchange between Given Groups of Manufacturing Producers and All Producers, 1923 to 1929 and 1914 to 1929 | 514 |
| 208. | Showing Alterations Occurring in the Terms of Exchange between Given Groups of Producers and All Producers, 1922 to 1929 and 1913 to 1929 | 518 |
| 209. | Showing Alterations Occurring in the Ratios of the Aggregate Quantities Produced by Manufacturing Wage-earners to their Aggregate Purchasing Power, 1923 to 1929 and 1914 to 1929 | 520 |
| 210. | Showing Alterations Occurring in the Aggregate Production of Different Agents, and in the Aggregate Rewards of these Agents, 1923 to 1929 and 1914 to 1929 | 523 |
| 211. | Comparison of Alterations in the Terms of Exchange between Given Groups of Producers and All Producers, 1901 to 1913 and 1913 to 1929 | 525 |
| 212. | Comparison of Alterations in the Ratios of Aggregate Production to Aggregate Rewards, 1899 to 1914 and 1914 to 1929 | 527 |
| 213. | Balances of International Payments of the United States, 1896-1914, 1922-1929 | 538 |

# List of Charts

                                        PAGE

1. Growth of Population and of Physical Volume of Production in the United States, 1901-1913 . . . . . . 3
2. Changes in Physical Volume of Production in the United States, 1901-1913. A. Raw Materials. B. Processed Goods . . . . . . . . . . . . . 6
3. Illustrating the Divergence of Production Trends in the United States, 1901-1913. Raw Materials and Processed Goods . . . . . . . . . . . . 9
4. Growth of Physical Volume of Production in the United States, 1901-1913. Products of American Farms and All Other Products . . . . . . . . . . . . 15
5. Growth of Physical Volume of Production in the United States, 1901-1913. Foods and Non-foods . . . . . 18
6. Growth of Physical Volume of Production in the United States, 1901-1913. Articles of Human Consumption and Articles Entering into Capital Equipment . . . . . 22
7. Growth of Physical Volume of Production in the United States, 1901-1913. Durable, Semi-Durable and Non-durable Goods . . . . . . . . . . . 24
8. Growth of Manufacturing Production in the United States, 1899-1914. Production, Number of Wage-earners and Output per Wage-earner . . . . . . . . . 27
9. Growth of Manufacturing Production in the United States, 1899-1914. Illustrating the Divergence of Production Trends among Manufacturing Industries . . . . . 31
10. Growth of Manufacturing Production in the United States, 1899-1914. Illustrating the Divergence of Trends in Production per Wage-earner in Manufacturing Industries . 34
11. Changes in Volume of Production, Average Price and Aggregate Value of Goods Produced in the United States, 1901-1913 . . . . . . . . . . . . 55
12. Movements of Wholesale Prices in the United States, 1901-1913. Raw Materials and Processed Goods . . . . . 59
13. Movements of Wholesale Prices in the United States, 1901-1913. Price Trends of Twenty Raw Materials and Sixteen Processed Goods . . . . . . . . . . . 60

|   |   | PAGE |
|---|---|---|
| 14. | Movements of Wholesale Prices in the United States, 1901-1913. Raw Materials and Processed Goods . . . . . | 61 |
| 15. | Movements of Wholesale Prices in the United States, 1901-1913. Products of American Farms and All Other Products . . . . . . . . . . . . . . . | 64 |
| 16. | Movements of Wholesale Prices in the United States, 1901-1913. Forest Products, Animal Products, Farm Crops and Mineral Products . . . . . . . . . . . . | 69 |
| 17. | Movements of Wholesale Prices in the United States, 1901-1913. Foods and Non-foods . . . . . . . . | 74 |
| 18. | Movements of Wholesale Prices in the United States, 1901-1913. Producers' Goods and Consumers' Goods . . . | 77 |
| 19. | Changes in Aggregate Value, Volume of Production and Average Price of Products. Manufacturing Industries of the United States, 1899-1914 . . . . . . . . | 98 |
| 20. | Illustrating the Divergence of Price Trends among 32 Manufacturing Industries of the United States, 1899-1914. Average Rates of Change in Selling Price per Unit of Product . . . . . . . . . . . . . . . | 101 |
| 21. | Changes in Average Selling Price, Cost of Materials and Fabrication Costs, plus Profits, per Unit of Product. Manufacturing Industries of the United States, 1899-1914 | 104 |
| 22. | Illustrating the Divergence of Cost Trends among 32 Manufacturing Industries of the United States, 1899-1914. Average Rates of Change in Material Costs per Unit of Product . . . . . . . . . . . . . . . | 105 |
| 23. | Illustrating the Divergence of Cost Trends among 32 Manufacturing Industries of the United States, 1899-1914. Average Rates of Change in Fabrication Costs per Unit of Product . . . . . . . . . . . . . . | 108 |
| 24. | Changes in Average Fabrication Costs, Labor Costs and Overhead Costs plus Profits, per Unit of Product. Manufacturing Industries of the United States, 1899-1914 . . | 110 |
| 25. | Illustrating the Divergence of Cost Trends among 32 Manufacturing Industries of the United States, 1899-1914. Average Rates of Change in Labor Costs per Unit of Product . . . . . . . . . . . . . . . | 113 |
| 26. | Illustrating the Divergence of Cost Trends among 32 Manufacturing Industries of the United States, 1899-1914. Average Rates of Change in Overhead Costs plus Profits per Unit of Product . . . . . . . . . . . | 115 |
| 27. | Movements of Certain Economic Elements in the United States, 1901-1913 . . . . . . . . . . . . | 128 |

LIST OF CHARTS 625

PAGE

28. Changes in Money Earnings of Employed Workers in the United States, 1901-1913. Major Groups . . . . . 136
29. Changes in Money Earnings of Employed Workers in the United States, 1901-1913. Manufacturing Industries . . 137
30. Graphic Representation of Investment Experience of Holders of Common Stock in 93 Corporations, 1901-1913 142
31. Changes in Incomes Received by Wage-earners, Stockholders and Bondholders in American Industries, 1901-1913 . . 155
32. Foreign Trade of the United States, 1901-1913. Changes in Aggregate Values of Imports, by Major Classes of Commodities . . . . . . . . . . . . . 162
33. Foreign Trade of the United States, 1901-1913. Changes in Aggregate Values of Exports, by Major Classes of Commodities . . . . . . . . . . . . . 163
34. Graphic Representation of Pre-war Tendencies among Producers of Raw Materials and Manufactured Goods. Average Rates of Change in Purchasing Power per Unit of Goods Produced, in Aggregate Physical Production and in Aggregate Command over Goods . . . . . . . 170
35. Changes in Physical Volume of Production and Construction in the United States, 1913-1922 . . . . . . . 189
36. Growth of Manufacturing Production in the United States, 1914-1923. Volume of Production, Number of Wage-earners and Output per Wage-earner . . . . . 193
37. Changes in Volume of Production, Average Price and Aggregate Value of Goods Produced in the United States, 1913-1922 . . . . . . . . . . . . . 204
38. Graphic Representation of Changes in the Real Values, per Unit, of Commodities in Selected Groups, 1913-1922 . . 206
39. Graphic Representation of Changes in the Real Values, per Unit, of Commodities in Selected Groups, 1913-1922. Selected Classes of Producers' Goods and Consumers' Goods . . . . . . . . . . . . . . 218
40. Changes in Average Selling Price, Cost of Materials and Fabrication Costs, plus Profits, per Unit of Product. Manufacturing Industries of the United States, 1914-1923 226
41. Changes in Average Fabrication Costs, Labor Costs and Overhead Costs plus Profits, per Unit of Product. Manufacturing Industries of the United States, 1914-1923 . . 232
42. Growth of Population and of Physical Volume of Production in the United States, 1922-1929 . . . . . 244
43. Growth of Physical Volume of Production in the United States, 1922-1929. Raw Materials and Manufactured Goods . . . . . . . . . . . . . . 250

## LIST OF CHARTS

PAGE

44. Changes in Physical Volume of Production of Individual Commodities in the United States, 1922-1929. A. Raw Materials. B. Processed Goods . . . . . . . . . 254
45. Illustrating the Divergence of Production Trends in the United States, 1922-1929 . . . . . . . . . . 257
46. Growth of Physical Volume of Production in the United States, 1922-1929. Products of American Farms and All Other Products . . . . . . . . . . . . 260
47. Growth of Construction in the United States, 1922-1929. Estimated Values of Total Contracts Awarded, 48 States 265
48. Growth of Production of Finished Goods in the United States, 1922-1929. Non-durable Consumption Goods . . 271
49. Growth of Production of Finished Goods in the United States, 1922-1929. Semi-durable Consumption Goods . . 273
50. Growth of Production of Finished Goods in the United States, 1922-1929. Durable Consumption Goods . . . 275
51. Growth of Production of Finished Goods in the United States, 1922-1929. Elements of Capital Equipment . . 277
52. Growth of Production of Finished Goods in the United States, 1922-1929. Total Production, Capital Equipment and Consumption Goods . . . . . . . . . . 281
53. Growth of Production of Finished Goods in the United States, 1922-1929. Total Production, Durable Goods and Non-durable Goods . . . . . . . . . . . 284
54. Growth of Manufacturing Production in the United States, 1923-1929. Volume of Production, Number of Wage-earners and Output per Wage-earner . . . . . . 290
55. Growth of Manufacturing Production in the United States, 1923-1929. Illustrating the Divergence of Production Trends among Manufacturing Industries . . . . . 294
56. Growth of Manufacturing Production in the United States, 1923-1929. Illustrating the Divergence of Trends in Production per Wage-earner in Manufacturing Industries . 298
57. Growth of Manufacturing Production in the United States, 1923-1929. Volume of Production, Number of Establishments and Output per Establishment . . . . . . 300
58. Changes in Volume of Production, Average Price and Aggregate Value of Goods Produced in the United States, 1922-1929 . . . . . . . . . . . . . . 322
59. Movements of Wholesale Prices in the United States, 1922-1929. Raw Materials and Manufactured Goods . . . 333
60. Changes in the Real Values, per Unit, of Raw Materials and of Manufactured Goods, 1913-1929 . . . . . . . 335

## LIST OF CHARTS

PAGE

61. Movements of Wholesale Prices in the United States, 1922-1929. Products of American Farms and All Other Products . . . . . . . . . . . . 341
62. Graphic Representation of Changes in the Real Values, per Unit, of Commodities in Selected Groups, 1913-1929. Products of American Farms and All Other Products . 344
63. Changes in Farm Prices and in the Purchasing Power of Farm Products, 1922-1929 . . . . . . . . . 347
64. Changes in the Average Per-unit Purchasing Power of Farm Products, 1913-1929. Based on Prices Received and Prices Paid by Farmers . . . . . . . . . . 349
65. Movements of Wholesale Prices in the United States, 1922-1929. Animal Products, Farm Crops, Forest Products and Mineral Products . . . . . . . . . . . . 350
66. Movements of Wholesale Prices in the United States, 1922-1929. Foods and Non-foods . . . . . . . . . 355
67. Graphic Representation of Changes in the Real Values, per Unit, of Commodities in Selected Groups, 1913-1929. Foods and Non-foods . . . . . . . . . . 356
68. Movements of Wholesale Prices in the United States, 1922-1929. Producers' Goods and Consumers' Goods . . . 359
69. Graphic Representation of Changes in the Real Values, per Unit, of Commodities in Selected Groups, 1913-1929. Producers' Goods and Consumers' Goods . . . . . 361
70. Movements of Wholesale Prices in the United States, 1922-1929. Articles of Human Consumption and Goods Entering into Capital Equipment . . . . . . . . . 365
71. Graphic Representation of Changes in the Real Values, per Unit, of Commodities in Selected Groups, 1913-1929. Articles of Human Consumption and Goods Entering into Capital Equipment . . . . . . . . . . . 367
72. Graphic Representation of Changes in the Real Values, per Unit, of Commodities in Selected Groups, 1913-1929. Selected Classes of Producers' Goods and Consumers' Goods . . . . . . . . . . . . . . . 368
73. Changes in Aggregate Value, Volume of Production and Average Price of Products. Manufacturing Industries of the United States, 1923-1929 . . . . . . . . 379
74. Illustrating the Divergence of Price Trends among 60 Manufacturing Industries of the United States, 1923-1929. Average Rates of Change in Selling Prices, per Unit of Product . . . . . . . . . . . . . . 383
75. Changes in Average Selling Price, Cost of Materials and Fabrication Costs, plus Profits, Per Unit of Product.

Manufacturing Industries of the United States, 1923-1929. (In dollars of constant purchasing power.) . . . . 385

76. Changes in Average Selling Price, Cost of Materials and Fabrication Costs, plus Profits. Manufacturing Industries of the United States, 1914-1929. (Percentage deviations from 1914 parity, in dollars of constant purchasing power.) . . . . . . . . . . . . . . 387

77. Illustrating the Divergence of Cost Trends among 60 Manufacturing Industries of the United States, 1923-1929. Average Rates of Change in Material Costs and in Fabrication Costs, plus Profits, per Unit of Product . . . . 390

78. Changes in Average Fabrication Costs, Labor Costs and Overhead Costs plus Profits, Per Unit of Product. Manufacturing Industries of the United States, 1923-1929. (In dollars of constant purchasing power.) . . . . 394

79. Changes in Average Fabrication Costs, Labor Costs and Overhead Costs plus Profits. Manufacturing Industries of the United States, 1914-1929. (Percentage deviations from 1914 parity, in dollars of constant purchasing power.) . . . . . . . . . . . . . . 396

80. Changes in Estimated Physical Volume of Sales, in Aggregate Profits and in Profit per Unit of Product. Manufacturing Industries of the United States, 1922-1929 . . 400

81. Changes in Estimated Physical Volume of Sales, in Aggregate Profits and in Profit per Unit of Product. Forty-five Selected Manufacturing Industries, 1922-1929 . . . 402

82. Illustrating the Divergence of Cost Trends among 60 Manufacturing Industries of the United States, 1923-1929. Average Rates of Change in Labor Costs and in Overhead Costs plus Profits, per Unit of Product . . . . . . 404

83. Changes in Average Selling Price, Cost of Materials, Labor Costs and Overhead Costs plus Profits, per Unit of Product. Manufacturing Industries of the United States, 1899-1914 and 1914-1929. (In dollars of constant purchasing power.) . . . . . . . . . . . . 413

84. Changes in the Total Population of the United States, in the Farm Population and in the Number of Wage-earners in Manufacturing Industries, 1922-1929 . . . . . . 417

85. Accession and Separation Rates by Industries. Wage-earners in Manufacturing Industries of the United States . . . 421

86. Changes in Certain Elements of the Supply of Capital Funds in the United States, 1922-1929 . . . . . . . . 424

87. Growth of Certain Elements of Aggregate Capital Funds, 1922-1929 . . . . . . . . . . . . . . 435

## LIST OF CHARTS

PAGE

88. Growth of Assets of Industrial Corporations and of Total Corporate Capital Funds in the United States, 1922-1929 . . . 441
89. Changes in Aggregate Primary Funds and Constituent Elements, 1922-1929 . . . 444
90. Changes in the Uses Made of Aggregate Primary Funds, 1922-1929 . . . 446
91. Changes in Elements of the Money and Credit Structure of the United States, 1922-1929 . . . 449
92. Growth of Bank Credit in the United States, 1922-1929. Reporting Member Banks . . . 451
93. Changes in the Estimated Holdings of Urban Real Estate Mortgages in the United States, 1922-1929 . . . 453
94. Changes in Interest Rates, Rediscount Rates and Bond and Stock Yields in the United States, 1922-1929 . . . 456
95. Changes in the Quantities, Values and Average Prices of Imports and Exports of the United States, 1922-1929 . . . 463
96. Changes in the Foreign Trade of the United States, 1922-1929. Imports and Exports, Major Classifications . . . 466
97. Changes in American Capital Investments Abroad and in Foreign Capital Investments in the United States, 1922-1929 . . . 474
98. Changes in the Earnings and Wage Rates of Employed Labor in the United States, 1922-1929. (In current dollars.) . . . 478
99. Changes in Corporate Net Income in the United States as reported to the Bureau of Internal Revenue, 1922-1929 . . . 483
100. Changes in the Profits and the Capital Investment of 2,046 Manufacturing Corporations, 1922-1929 . . . 485
101. Changes in Aggregate Dividend Payments of All Corporations, 1922-1929 . . . 491
102. Graphic Representation of the Investment Experience of Holders of Common Stock in 102 Corporations, 1922-1929 . . . 495
103. Changes in Incomes Received by Wage-earners, Stockholders and Bondholders, in American Industries, 1922-1929. (In current dollars.) . . . 503
104. Graphic Representation of Post-war Tendencies among Producers of Raw Materials and of Manufactured Goods. Average Rates of Change in Purchasing Power per Unit of Goods Produced, in Aggregate Physical Production and in Aggregate Command over Goods, 1922-1929 . . . 506
105. Showing Alterations Occurring in the Terms of Exchange between Given Groups of Producers and All Producers, 1923 to 1929 and 1914 to 1929 . . . 515

# LIST OF CHARTS

PAGE

106. Showing Alterations Occurring in the Terms of Exchange between Given Groups of Producers and All Producers, 1922 to 1929 and 1913 to 1929 . . . . . . . . . 517
107. Showing Alterations Occurring in the Ratios of Aggregate Quantities Produced by Manufacturing Wage-earners to their Aggregate Purchasing Power, 1923 to 1929 and 1914 to 1929 . . . . . . . . . . . . . . 521
108. Showing Alterations Occurring in the Ratios of Aggregate Production to Aggregate Rewards, Agents of Manufacturing Production, 1899 to 1914 and 1914 to 1929 . . . 527

# Index

Aberthaw Construction Company, 267n, 279n
Accessions in manufacturing industries, 420-2
Activity ratio, 117-121, 411; defined, 117-8
Adequacy ratio, 89, 220, 375-7, 380n; explained, 90, 92-3
Agricultural Economics, Bureau of, 188n, 286n, 341n, 346n
Aluminum, valorization, 329
American Appraisal Company, 267n
American farms, products of (*see* Production; Prices)
American Telephone and Telegraph Co. index of assets of industrial corporations, 440
Andrew, Seymour L., 440n
Animal products (*see* Prices)
Asphalted-felt-base floor coverings, 292, 296, 302, 306, 382, 388, 392, 405, 408, 596 (*see* Linoleum and asphalted-felt-base floor coverings)
Assets of industrial corporations, 440-1
Associated General Contractors, 191n, 268n
Automobiles, including bodies and parts, 30, 33, 100, 106, 107, 112, 114, 194, 195, 224, 228, 230, 236, 237, 293, 297, 302, 305, 381, 388, 391, 405, 407, 514, 520, 594, 601
Ayres, Leonard P., 455n

Balance of international payments, 165-6, 470-6; summary, 536-8
Bank credit (*see* Credit)
Beales, LeVerne, 88n
Bicycles (*see* Motorcycles, bicycles, and parts)
Bondholders, investment experience of, 152-3, 160-1, 500-1; compared with other distributive shares, 153-60, 500-5, 555-6
Bonds, outstanding mortgage, 453-4

Bond yields, 455-7; (*see also* Bondholders)
Bone-black, carbon black and lamp-black, 292, 296, 302, 305, 382, 388, 392, 405, 408, 598
Boots and shoes, other than rubber, 30, 33, 100, 106, 107, 112, 114, 180, 593
Bowley, A. L., 463n
Brick, sand-lime, 194, 196, 223, 227, 229, 235, 237, 292, 296, 303, 306, 381, 389, 391, 405, 407, 600
Brissenden, Paul F., 133, 137, 154
Building (*see* Construction)
Building and loan associations, assets of, 424-6, 431, 435-6; mortgage holdings, 452-4
Bullock, C. J., 165n
Burgess, W. R., 135
Butter and cheese, 194, 196, 224, 228, 229, 235, 237, 293, 296, 302, 306, 381, 388, 391, 405, 407, 594 (*see* Butter, cheese and condensed milk)
Butter, cheese and condensed milk, 30, 33, 100, 106, 107, 112, 114, 591
Buttons, 293, 297, 302, 306, 381, 388, 391, 405, 407, 601

Cahill, W. M., 427n
Call loan renewal rates, 455-8
Camphor, valorization, 328
Canning and preserving: fish, crabs, shrimp, oysters and clams, 195, 197, 223, 227, 229, 235, 237, 292, 296, 302, 305, 382, 388, 392, 406, 408, 594
Canning and preserving: fruits and vegetables; pickles, jellies, preserves, and sauces, 30, 33, 100, 106, 107, 112, 114, 194, 196, 224, 228, 229, 235, 237, 292, 297, 302, 305, 381, 388, 392, 406, 408, 591, 595
Capital
 cost of, 454-8
 international movement of, 165-6, 471-6, 537-8
 summary, 459-61, 538-41

Capital assets of investors (*see* Stockholders; Bondholders)
Capital equipment (*see* Prices; Production): economic characteristics, 281-2; relative value, 20-1
Capital funds
 corporate, 436-41
 Federal reserve banks, 446-8
 supply of: additions, 424-9; aggregate, 129, 424-6, 429-42
Capital investment, manufacturing corporations, 485-8; defined, 486n
Capital issues, new, 424-9, 458n; coverage, 429n
Carpets and rugs, wool, other than rag, 30, 33, 100, 106, 107, 112, 114, 194, 196, 223, 228, 229, 235, 236, 293, 297, 302, 305, 381, 388, 391, 405, 407, 591, 596
Carriages, wagons, sleighs and sleds, 293, 296, 302, 305, 382, 388, 392, 406, 408, 601
Cars, steam and electric railroad, not built in railroad repair shops, 194, 196, 223, 227, 229, 235, 237, 293, 297, 303, 306, 381, 388, 391, 405, 407, 601
Cassel, Gustav, 543n
Cement, 194, 196, 223, 228, 229, 235, 236, 292, 296, 303, 306, 382, 389, 392, 406, 408, 600
Census, Bureau of the (*see* Chapters I, III, V, VI, VIII)
Change, rate of (*see* Rate of change)
Cheese (*see* Butter and cheese)
Chocolate and cocoa products, 292, 296, 303, 306, 381, 388, 391, 406, 408, 595
Clark, F. M., 398, 485-6, 488n
Classifications (*see* Appendix I, II), 1, 4, 5n, 13, 15n, 20n, 23, 51, 70n, 79n, 273n, 333n, 561-3
Clay products (other than pottery) and non-clay refractories, 194, 196, 223, 228, 229, 235, 237, 293, 297, 303, 306, 381, 389, 392, 405, 408, 600
Clearings, bank, 127-132
Clothing, relative value, 287-8
Cocoa products (*see* Chocolate and cocoa products)
Coffee, valorization, 327
Coke, not including gas-house coke, 30, 33, 100, 106, 107, 112, 114, 194, 195, 223, 227, 229, 235, 236, 292, 296, 302, 305, 382, 389, 392, 406, 408, 593, 599

Commerce, Department of, 127n, 309n, 398n, 399n, 462, 464, 468, 470n, 471n, 475, 485n, 486n, 488n
*Commercial and Financial Chronicle*, 424n, 427, 429n, 438
Comptroller of the Currency, 127n
Construction
 contracts awarded, 263-6
 index of costs, 266-7
 shipments of materials, 189, 191, 268
 production and construction (*see* Production and construction)
 volume of, 189, 191-2, 246, 266-9, 274-5, 277-8, 287n
Consumers' goods (*see* Prices; Production); defined, 357-8; relative value, 20-1
Contract work, manufacturing industries, 111n, 232n, 394n
Contributions, apparent physical, of agents of manufacturing production, 94-6, 102n, 221-2, 378n; (*see* Costs)
Contributions relative to rewards, economic classes, 173-84, 513-28; comparison, pre-war and post-war, 525-8; summary, 549-55; (*see also* Purchasing power)
Control of prices: post-war, 327-31; war-time, 186-7
Coombs, Whitney, 135
Coöperative marketing and price stability, 329
Copper, valorization, 328
Cordage and twine, 30, 33, 100, 106, 107, 112, 114, 195, 196, 224, 228, 229, 235, 237, 293, 297, 303, 306, 381, 388, 391, 406, 408, 591, 592, 596
Corn syrup, corn oil and starch, 292, 296, 302, 306, 381, 388, 391, 405, 407, 595
Corporate capital funds (*see* Capital funds, corporate)
Corporate savings (*see* Savings, corporate)
Cost of capital and credit, 454-8
Cost of living index, 127-8, 133, 362n
Costs contrasted, operating and capital, 370-1
Costs in manufacturing industries (*see* Chapters III, V, VIII)
 aggregate: data available, 91, 101-2; in dollars, 89, 220, 376; in relatives, 92, 221, 377
 divergence of trends in, 105, 108, 113, 115, 390, 404

## INDEX

Costs in manufacturing industries (*cont.*)
per unit of product: as factors in price changes, 115-21, 409-12 (*see also* Activity ratio); fabrication, 101-15, 225-37, 384-97, 404-9; labor, 109-15, 230-6, 393-7, 404-6; materials, 101-9, 225-8, 384-90; overhead plus profits, 109-15, 230-7, 393-7, 404-9; summary, 121-3, 239, 412-5
Cotton goods, 30, 33, 100, 106, 107, 112, 114, 174, 180, 194, 196, 223, 227, 229, 235, 236, 293, 297, 303, 306, 382, 389, 392, 406, 408, 514, 520, 592, 596, 597
Cotton, valorization, 327
Cottonseed, oil, cake, and meal, 195, 196, 223, 227, 229, 235, 237, 292, 297, 302, 305, 382, 389, 391, 405, 407, 598
Coverage
decennial censuses, 37n, 420n
production indexes, 568; census indexes, 26n, 90n, 192n, 220, 289n, 377n (*see also* Adequacy ratio)
Cowden, D. J., 467n
Credit
cost of, 454-9
relation to prices and production, 130, 167n, 451-2
summary, 459-61, 538-41
supply of: banks, 126-31, 448-53; book, 442n; commercial, 450-1; investment, 450-1, 453; mortgage, 452-4; primary funds, 442-9; secondary funds, 442-4, 448-52
Currency, Treasury, 443-5
Cyclical fluctuations, 10n, 113, 241, 308n, 403-4, 317-21, 546-7

Day, Edmund E., 46n, 253, 309
Debt, public, 428n
Deflation, process of, (*see* Purchasing power), 58n, 103-4, 133, 168n, 210n, 267, 399, 508n
Dispersion of prices (*see* Prices, dispersion of)
Displacement, industrial, 419-23
Distributive shares, 132-161, 476-505; summary, 153-61, 501-5, 555-6
Divergence of trends (*see* Costs; Prices; Production)
Dividends
cash, 488-91; index of, per share, 499n compared with profits, 501n
received by stockholders (*see* Stockholders)
stock, 139n, 432n, 433

Dodge, F. W., Corporation, 246, 264, 267-8, 274, 279n
Douglas, Paul H., 127n, 132-5, 154, 159, 172n, 173n, 418n, 504n
Dow-Jones indexes, 146-8, 150-3, 156n, 500
Dublin, L. I., 418
Durable consumption goods, production of, 274-5
Durable goods (*see* Prices; Production)
economic characteristics, 24-5, 276, 285-6
relative value, 286-8

Earnings, wage-earners (*see* Wages)
Employment, 127-8, 131-2, 480; (*see* Displacement, industrial; Unemployment)
*Engineering News Record*, 267, 279n, 370n
Epstein, R. C., 398, 485-6, 488n
Establishments in manufacturing industries, 36-39, 197, 299-301; defined, 36n; (*see also* Productivity of manufacturing industries)
Explosives, 30, 33, 100, 106, 107, 112, 114, 194, 196, 224, 228, 230, 235, 237, 293, 296, 302, 306, 381, 389, 391, 405, 407, 593, 598
Exports (*see* Foreign trade)
Export-trade associations and price stability, 330n

Fabrication, agents of (*see* Purchasing power)
Fabrication, changes in degree of, 5, 41n, 95, 307; (*see also* Production, census indexes, revision of)
Fabrication costs, plus profits (*see* Value added by manufacture), 89, 92, 220-1, 376-7; defined, 89n; (*see also* Costs; Profits)
Factor reversal test, 94n
Farm crops (*see* Prices; Production)
Farm population, 417-9
Farm prices (*see* Prices, farm)
Farm products (*see* Prices; Production)
Federal Reserve Board, 188n, 243n, 252n, 274n, 279n, 309n, 443, 446, 450, 455, 479, 502n, 508n, 570
Felt goods, wool or hair, 293, 297, 303, 306, 382, 389, 392, 406, 408, 597

Fertilizers, 30, 33, 100, 106, 107, 112, 114, 195, 196, 224, 228, 230, 235, 237, 292, 296, 303, 306, 381, 388, 392, 406, 408, 593, 598

Finished goods (*see* Production)

Firearms, 292, 297, 302, 305, 381, 388, 391, 405, 408, 600

Fisher, Irving, 26n, 94n

Flexibility in an economic system: need for, 10, 62n, 295; and price stability, 323-33; (*see also* Variation)

Floor coverings (*see* Asphalted-felt-base floor coverings)

Floor space, building contracts (*see* Construction, volume of)

Flour and other grain-mill products, 30, 33, 100, 106, 107, 112, 114, 180, 195, 196, 224, 228, 230, 235, 237, 293, 296, 302, 306, 381, 388, 391, 405, 407, 514, 520, 591, 595

Flux, A. W., 46n

Foods (*see* Prices; Production); relative value, 287-8

Foreign capital issues, 424-5, 427-8

Foreign trade
 exports, 5n, 127-31, 161, 163-4, 251n, 271n, 282n, 461-7, 469-70
 imports, 127-31, 161-2, 164, 271n, 461-7, 469
 influence on domestic production, 5, 251, 271, 282n, 467-9
 summary, 536-8
 terms of exchange, 463-4
 (*see also* Balance of international payments)

Forest, J. H., 488n

Forest products (*see* Prices)

Freight cars, changes in capacity, 294n

Freight, ton miles, 127-8, 131

Frequency of price change (*see* Prices, variability of); defined, 63

Funds, capital (*see* Capital funds)

Gas, manufactured, illuminating and heating, 30, 33, 100, 106, 107, 112, 114, 194, 195, 224, 228, 230, 236, 237, 292, 296, 302, 305, 381, 388, 391, 406, 407, 593, 599

Glover, James W., 47n

Gloves and mittens, leather, 30, 33, 100, 106, 107, 112, 114, 593

Gold standard, post-war restoration of, 319

Gold, stock of, 443-5

Grades, changes in relative importance, as affecting measures of production, 32n

Hall, Ray, 475

Hats, fur-felt, 30, 33, 100, 106, 107, 112, 114, 195, 196, 223, 228, 229, 235, 237, 293, 297, 303, 306, 381, 388, 391, 405, 407, 592, 597

Hats, wool-felt, 30, 33, 100, 106, 107, 112, 114, 195, 197, 223, 227, 229, 234, 236, 292, 296, 302, 305, 382, 389, 392, 405, 408, 592, 597

Hosiery and knit goods, 30, 33, 100, 106, 107, 112, 114, 592; (*see* Knit goods)

Hurlin, R. G., 135

Ice, manufactured, 30, 33, 100, 106, 107, 112, 114, 194, 196, 224, 228, 230, 236, 237, 292, 297, 303, 306, 381, 389, 391, 405, 407, 591, 595

'Ideal' formula, 26n, 34-6, 94n

Immigration, 417-8

Imports (*see* Foreign trade)

Income (*see* Distributive shares; Purchasing power)

Industrial Commission, U. S., 125

Industrial displacement (*see* Displacement, industrial)

Industrial stocks (*see* Stockholders)

Instability of change, index of,
 explained, 3n, 48, 157n
 production: individual series, 12n, 248n; indexes (*see* Producton)
 prices (*see* Prices)
 (*see also* Stability)

Interest paid by manufacturing corporations, 487n

Interest rates, 455-8

Internal revenue, Bureau of, 232n, 394n, 399n, 429, 433, 437n, 442n, 487n, 501n

Investment trusts and holding companies, issues of, 424-7

Iron and steel: blast furnaces, 30, 33, 100, 106, 107, 112, 114, 180, 194, 196, 224, 228, 229, 235, 237, 293, 296, 302, 305, 382, 389, 392, 406, 408, 514, 520, 593, 600

Iron and steel: steel works and rolling mills, 30, 33, 100, 106, 107, 112, 114, 174, 180, 194, 196, 223, 228, 229, 235, 237, 292, 296, 302, 306, 382, 389, 391, 405, 407, 514, 520, 593, 594, 600

Issues, new capital (*see* Capital issues)

# INDEX

Jute and linen goods, 30, 33, 100, 106, 107, 112, 114, 195, 196, 223, 228, 229, 234, 236, 293, 297, 303, 306, 381, 388, 392, 406, 408, 592, 597

Keynes, J. M., 463n
King, W. I., 3n, 127n
Knauth, O. W., 432n
Knit goods, 194, 196, 223, 227, 229, 235, 236, 293, 297, 302, 305, 381, 388, 391, 405, 407, 597; (*see* Hosiery and knit goods)

Labor (*see* Displacement, industrial; Unemployment; Purchasing power; Wage-earners; Wages)
Labor Statistics, Bureau of (*see* Chapters II, IV, V, VII, IX)
Lace goods, cotton, 195, 196, 223, 227, 229, 235, 236, 293, 297, 303, 306, 382, 389, 392, 405, 408, 597
Large-scale production, 45, 125, 300; (*see also* Establishments; Productivity)
Leong, Y. S., 253
Life insurance companies, reserves of, 424-6, 431, 435-6; mortgage holdings, 453-4
Lime, 195, 196, 223, 227, 229, 235, 236, 293, 296, 302, 306, 382, 389, 392, 406, 408, 600
Linen goods (*see* Jute and linen goods)
Linoleum, 293, 297, 303, 306, 381, 388, 391, 405, 407, 597 (*see* Linoleum and asphalted-felt-base floor coverings)
Linoleum and asphalted-felt-base floor coverings, 194, 195, 224, 228, 229, 236, 597
Linseed oil, cake and meal, 292, 296, 302, 305, 382, 389, 391, 405, 407, 599
Loans and investments, bank, 127-132, 450-2 (*see* Credit)
Locomotives, changes in tractive power, 256n
Lotka, A., 418
Lumber and timber products, 30, 33, 100, 106, 107, 112, 114, 195, 197, 223, 227, 229, 235, 236, 293, 296, 302, 306, 382, 389, 392, 405, 408, 593, 598

Machinery, production of, 277-8
Manufactured goods (*see* Prices; Production)

Manufacturing industries (*see* Chapters I, III, V, VI, VIII)
statistics of, 89, 92, 220-1, 376-7
prices and costs, summary, 121-3, 239, 412-5, 541-9
(*see* Costs; Prices; Production; Productivity; Profits)
Margarine, valorization, 329
Margins, price, 87
Materials, cost of, manufacturing industries, 89, 92, 220-1, 376-7; constituent items, 104n; defined, 89n; (*see* Costs)
Measurement of economic movements, 46-49
Meat packing (*see* Slaughtering and meat packing, wholesale)
Mercury, valorization, 328
Milk, condensed and evaporated, 194, 196, 224, 228, 230, 236, 237, 292, 296, 303, 306, 382, 389, 391, 406, 407, 595 (*see* Butter, cheese and condensed milk)
Mill and shop supplies, change in classification, 385n
Mineral products (*see* Prices)
Money (*see* Credit); in circulation, 446-7
Mortgage indebtedness (*see* Credit)
Motorcycles, bicycles, and parts, 30, 33, 100, 106, 107, 112, 114, 195, 196, 224, 228, 230, 235, 237, 293, 297, 302, 305, 381, 390, 391, 405, 407, 594, 601
Motor vehicles, including bodies and parts (*see* Automobiles, including bodies and parts)
Movable goods, output of (*see* Production)
Musical instruments: organs, 30, 33, 100, 106, 107, 112, 114, 195, 196, 223, 228, 229, 235, 236, 293, 297, 303, 305, 381, 388, 391, 405, 407, 594, 601
Musical instruments: pianos, 30, 33, 100, 106, 107, 112, 114, 194, 196, 224, 228, 230, 236, 237, 293, 297, 303, 306, 382, 389, 392, 405, 408, 594, 601

National Industrial Conference Board, 362n, 477n
Nerlove, S. H., 439, 487n
Nitrates, valorization, 328
Non-durable goods (*see* Prices; Production); relative value, 24, 286-8
Non-foods (*see* Prices; Production)

Obsolescence, 21n
Occupations, changes in (*see* **Service industries**)
Oilcloth, 195, 196, 223, 228, 229, 234, 236, 292, 296, 302, 305, 382, 389, 392, 406, 408, 597
Organs (*see* Musical instruments, organs)
Output (*see* Production); per wage-earner (*see* Productivity)
Overhead costs plus profits, manufacturing industries, 89, 92, 220-1, 376-7; constituent items, 111n, 232n, 394n; defined, 89n (*see* Costs; Profits)
'Ownership and management' (*see* Overhead costs plus profits); defined, 95n

Paints and varnishes, 30, 33, 100, 106, 107, 112, 114, 194, 196, 224, 228, 230, 235, 237, 292, 297, 303, 306, 381, 388, 391, 405, 408, 593, 599
Paper and wood pulp, 30, 33, 100, 106, 107, 112, 114, 194, 196, 223, 228, 229, 235, 237, 292, 296, 302, 306, 382, 389, 391, 406, 407, 593, 598
Peabody, W. R., 466n
Perishable goods (*see* Non-durable goods)
Persons, Charles E., 274n, 452-4
Persons, Warren M., 253n, 309n
Petroleum refining, 30, 33, 100, 106, 107, 112, 114, 180, 194, 196, 224, 228, 230, 235, 237, 292, 296, 302, 305, 382, 389, 392, 406, 408, 514, 520, 593, 599
Pianos (*see* Musical instruments, pianos)
Pipe, cast-iron, 194, 197, 223, 228, 229, 235, 236, 293, 297, 303, 306, 382, 389, 392, 405, 408, 600
Population, 2-3, 126-9, 244, 416-9, 529-30; production per capita of (*see* Production)
Potash, valorization, 328
Prices (*see* Chapters II, III, V, VII, VIII)
 classification of commodities, 572-83
 controlled (*see* Control of prices)
 costs and, 121-3, 239, 412-5, 541-9
 credit and (*see* Credit)
 dispersion of, 52-4, 201-2, 324-5; defined, 52n, 325n
 divergence in trends, 60, 62, 86-7, 101, **383**

Prices (*cont.*)
 farm, 209-10, 346-9
 identical commodities in raw and processed state, comparison of, 57-9, 338n
 index numbers of, comparison: National Bureau and Bureau of Labor Statistics, 57n, 333n, 379n; derived from census, derived from price quotations, 99n, 222n, 379n
 index numbers of, wholesale: all commodities, 51-3, 56, 201-4, 316-7, 322; American farm products, all other, 65-9, 206, 208-11, 340-5; capital equipment goods, human consumption goods, 80-1, 363-8; foods, non-foods, 74-6, 206, 213-4, 353-7; forest products, animal products, farm crops, mineral products, 69-74, 211-3, 349-53; other groups, 371-2; producers' goods, consumers' goods, 76-81, 206, 214-9, 357-63; raw materials, manufactured goods, 57-9, 205-8, 332-8, 399; by groups, 1891-1931, Appendix III
 individual commodities, 59-63, 330n, 336n
 influence of rising, 315, 320
 influence on aggregate values, 55-7, 203-4, 321-3
 manufacturing industries, derived from census, 94-101, 103-4, 222-7, 378-87
 measurement of changes in, 96-7
 paid by farmers, 210, 347-9
 post-war decline in, 316-20
 production and, 55-7, 63-4, 66-7, 74, 203-4, 322-3, 370-1
 purchasing power of, wholesale (*see* Prices, index numbers, wholesale)
 retail (*see* Cost of living)
 Snyder's index of general level of, 130n
 tendencies of, summarized, 81-7, 238-40, 372-4, 541-9
 variability of, wholesale: all commodities, 55, 201-3, 325-6; American farm products, all other, 67, 209n, 345-6; foods, non-foods, 76; forest products, animal products, farm crops, mineral products, 71-3, 213n; producers' goods, consumers' goods, 78; raw materials, manufactured goods, 63, 338-9
 variation among, 336n, 348n
 (*see also* Costs)

Primary funds (*see* Credit)
Producers' goods (*see* Prices); defined, 356-7

# INDEX

Production (*see* Chapters I, V, VI)
  annual indexes of: all commodities, 2-4, 55-56, 188-90, 243-6; American farm products, all other, 13-17, 188-90, 258-63; durable goods, non-durable, semi-durable, 23-5, 270-6, 282-8; finished goods, 269-86; foods, non-foods, 17-19, 270-2; capital equipment goods, consumption goods, 20-3, 273-82; raw materials, manufactured goods, 3-13, 188-90, 249-51; unrevised, 251-3, 563-5, 570
  census indexes of manufacturing, 25-31, 95, 192-8, 221-2, 289-95, 378n; commodities included in, 591-601; revision of, 39-43, 198-201, 307-10
  comparison of indexes of manufacturing, 42, 200, 309
  construction and, 246, 273-5, 277-81, 283-4
  construction of annual indexes of, 560-71
  divergence of trends, 5-10, 31, 34, 253-8, 294, 298
  identical commodities, comparison of pre- and post-war tendencies, 260-3
  individual commodities, 5-10, 12n, 248n, 253-6; sources, 602-7
  individual industries, 30-1, 193-5, 292-4
  per capita of population, 2, 21, 129, 244-5
  prices and (*see* Prices)
  tendencies of, summarized, 43-6, 242, 310-4, 530-5
  variation in rates of change, 5-9, 13-14, 32, 34, 46, 58-62, 109, 111
  (*see also* Productivity)

Productivity of manufacturing industries, 25-39, 192-8, 289-304; individual industries, 32-4, 193-7, 296-7, 302-3; output per establishment, 36-39, 197-8, 299-304; output per wage-earner, 25-36, 38, 192-8, 290-9

Products of manufacturing industries, value of, 89, 92, 220-1, 376-7; defined, 89n

Profits,
  compared with dividends, 501n
  corporation, by groups, 482-5
  manufacturing corporations, 397-403, 484-8; aggregate, 398-9, 401, 484; defined, 486n; as percentage of capital investment, 485-8; per unit of product sold, 399-404
  variation in, 409, 488n
  (*see* Overhead costs plus profits)

Public debt (*see* Debt, public)
Public utility stocks (*see* Stockholders)

Pulp, wood (*see* Paper and wood pulp)
Purchasing power (*see* Prices; Costs; Distributive shares)
Purchasing power of economic groups, aggregate, 166-73, 505-13
  factors contributing to changes in, 169-70, 172, 506-7, 510-3
  relative to aggregate contributions, 173-84, 513-28, 552-4
  summary, 549-52

Quality, changes in, 32n, 93-4, 102n, 256n, 294n
Quinine, valorization, 328

Railroad stocks (*see* Stockholders)
Rate of change, average annual,
  accuracy of fit of line measuring, 8n, 47, 71n
  defined, 46
  prices (*see* Prices)
  production: indexes (*see* Production); individual commodities, 5-10, 253-7
Ratio of contributions to rewards (*see* Purchasing power)
Raw materials (*see* Prices; Production)
Rayon, valorization, 329
Real estate mortgages (*see* Credit)
Rediscount rates, 455-9
Rent, manufacturing industries, 111n
Reserves, member banks, 446-9
Revision of index numbers of production, 39-43, 198-201, 307-10
Rice, cleaning and polishing, 30, 33, 100, 106, 107, 112, 114, 194, 196, 224, 228, 230, 236, 237, 293, 296, 302, 305, 381, 388, 391, 405, 407, 591, 595
Rights, subscription (*see* Stockholders)
Robertson, D. H., 426n
Rorty, M. C., 21n, 91n, 133n, 432n, 481n, 483n
Rose, Dwight C., 146, 151-2, 501n
Rowe, J. W. F., 46n
Rubber products, 194, 195, 224, 228, 230, 236, 237, 292, 296, 302, 305, 382, 389, 392, 406, 408, 599, 600
Rubber, valorization, 327
Rugs (*see* Carpets and rugs, wool, other than rag)

638  INDEX

Salaries, manufacturing industries, 91n, 111n, 232n, 394n
Sales, manufacturing corporations, 398-403; relation to profits (*see* Profits)
Salt, 30, 33, 100, 106, 107, 112, 114, 194, 196, 224, 228, 229, 235, 237, 292, 296, 302, 305, 382, 389, 392, 406, 407, 593, 599
Savings banks (*see* Savings deposits); mortgage holdings, 453
Savings, corporate,
annual, 424-6, 428-9
total, 424-6, 431-6
Savings deposits, 127-130, 424-6, 429-31, 435-6
Secondary funds (*see* Credit)
Secondary products, manufacturing industries, 92n
Semi-durable goods (*see* Prices; Production); relative value, 286-7
Sensitivity ratio (*see* Activity ratio)
Separations in manufacturing industries, 420-3
Service industries, 245n, 287n, 419
Shares, distributive (*see* Distributive shares)
Shoes (*see* Boots and shoes, other than rubber)
Silk manufactures, 30, 33, 100, 106, 107, 112, 114, 194, 196, 223, 227, 230, 235, 237, 292, 296, 302, 305, 382, 389, 392, 406, 408, 592, 597
Silk, valorization, 327
Sisal, valorization, 328
Slaughtering and meat packing, wholesale, 30, 33, 100, 106, 107, 112, 114, 174, 180, 194, 196, 224, 228, 230, 235, 237, 293, 297, 303, 306, 381, 388, 391, 405, 407, 514, 520, 591, 595
Smith, E. L., 146-8, 151
Snyder, Carl, 46n, 130n, 133, 135, 477, 502-4
Soap, 194, 196, 224, 228, 229, 235, 237, 293, 296, 303, 306, 381, 388, 391, 406, 407, 599
Sources of annual production series, Appendix V
Stability of economic processes, 1, 3n, 10-13, 17, 19n, 51, 86, 132, 246-8, 285-6, 288, 323-33
Standard deviation, defined, 9n; deficiencies of, 295n

Standard Statistics Company, 455n
Steel (*see* Iron and steel)
Steel, valorization, 329
Stewart, Walter W., 46n, 188n
Stock dividends (*see* Dividends)
Stockholders, receipts and gains of, 138-151, 160-1, 491-500
compared with other distributive shares, 153-60, 500-5, 555-6
compared with profits and dividends paid, 501n
industrial, 144-8, 497
public utility, 144-8, 498
railroad, 148-51, 499
Stock prices (*see* Stockholders); Dow-Jones index, 146n, 500n
Stock yields, 455-8 (*see also* Stockholders)
Sugar, beet, 30, 33, 100, 106, 107, 112, 114, 195, 196, 223, 228, 229, 235, 236, 292, 296, 302, 306, 382, 389, 392, 406, 408, 591, 595
Sugar, cane, not including products of refining, 195, 197, 223, 227, 229, 235, 237, 293, 296, 302, 305, 382, 389, 391, 406, 407, 596
Sugar refining, cane, 194, 196, 223, 228, 230, 235, 237, 293, 296, 303, 306, 382, 389, 391, 406, 407, 596
Sugar, valorization, 327
Sulphur, valorization, 328
Surplus, corporate, 432n, 433

Tanning materials, natural dyestuffs, mordants and assistants, and sizes, 293, 296, 303, 306, 381, 388, 391, 406, 407, 599
Taxes, manufacturing industries, 111n, 232n, 394n
Terms of exchange,
among economic groups (*see* Purchasing power)
between imported and exported goods, 463-4
Textile products, production of, 272-3
Thomas, Woodlief, 46n, 309
Trade,
foreign (*see* Foreign trade)
domestic, 131
Transportation equipment, production of, 277-9
Tucker, R. S., 165n
Turpentine and rosin, 30, 33, 100, 106, 107, 112, 114, 195, 196, 224, 228, 230, 235, 237, 293, 297, 303, 305, 382, 388, 392, 405, 408, 593, 598

# INDEX

Unemployment, 481; technological, 10, 481n (*see* Displacement, industrial)

Valorization schemes, 327-30

Value added by manufacture, changes in, 39-40, 199, 307-8
defined, 89n
(*see also* Costs)

Value of products, manufacturing industries (*see* Products, value of)

Values, changes in aggregate stream of, 56, 167, 203-4, 286-8, 321-3

Variability of prices, monthly (*see* Prices, variability of); defined, 54n, 325n

Velocity of circulation of bank deposits, 130n

Wage-earners in manufacturing industries, 25-29, 192-3, 289-90, 417 (*see also* Productivity of manufacturing industries; Displacement, industrial)

Wages, 127-8, 132-8, 476-81; compared with other distributive shares, 153-60, 500-5, 513, 520-8

Wages paid, manufacturing industries, 89, 92, 220-1, 376-7; defined, 89n; contrasted with salaries, 91n (*see* Costs; Wages)

War, economic changes during the (*see* Chapter V)

War Industries Board, 204n

Water in corporate capital funds, 437

Weights,
census index, 26n, 90-1, 94-5, 377n, 378n
construction and production, index of, 246

Weights (*cont.*)
price dispersion, index of, 53n
prices, indexes of, 333n
production indexes, 560, 566, 570, 571
rates of change, standard deviation of, 8n, 99n, 258n
receipts of stockholders, 140n, 492n

Wheat, valorization, 327

Whelpton, P. K., 416n

Williams, J. H., 165n

Wire, drawn from purchased bars or rods, 194, 196, 224, 228, 229, 235, 237, 293, 297, 303, 306, 382, 389, 392, 406, 408, 600, 601

Wood distillation and charcoal manufactures, 30, 33, 100, 106, 107, 112, 114, 194, 196, 223, 227, 229, 235, 236, 292, 297, 302, 305, 382, 389, 391, 405, 408, 593, 599

Wool shoddy, 195, 196, 224, 228, 229, 235, 237, 293, 296, 303, 306, 381, 388, 392, 405, 408, 598

Woolen and worsted goods, 30, 33, 100, 106, 107, 112, 114, 180, 592, 593

Woolen goods, 194, 196, 223, 228, 229, 235, 236, 293, 297, 303, 306, 381, 388, 392, 405, 408, 514, 520, 597, 598 (*see* Woolen and worsted goods)

Worsted goods, 195, 196, 223, 227, 229, 234, 236, 293, 297, 303, 306, 381, 388, 392, 405, 408, 514, 520, 598 (*see* Woolen and worsted goods)

*Yearbook of Agriculture*, 188n, 210n, 286n, 329n, 346n, 477

Zapoleon, L. B., 330n

Zinc, valorization, 329